GERMANIA

ANZEIGER
DER RÖMISCH - GERMANISCHEN KOMMISSION
DES DEUTSCHEN ARCHÄOLOGISCHEN INSTITUTS

JAHRGANG 99   2021   1.–2. HALBBAND

SCHRIFTLEITUNG FRANKFURT A. M. PALMENGARTENSTRASSE 10–12

MIT 82 TEXTABBILDUNGEN, 3 TABELLEN

Die wissenschaftlichen Beiträge in der Germania unterliegen dem peer-review-Verfahren durch auswärtige Gutachterinnen und Gutachter.
Contributions to "Germania" are subject to peer review by external referees.
Tous les textes présentés à la revue « Germania » sont soumis
à des rapporteurs externes à la RGK.

Der Abonnementpreis beträgt 39,00 € pro Jahrgang. Bestellungen sind direkt an den Verlag zu richten. Mitglieder des Deutschen Archäologischen Instituts und Studierende der Altertumswissenschaften können die Germania zum Vorzugspreis von 19,50 € abonnieren. Studierende werden gebeten, ihre Bestellungen mit einer Studienbescheinigung an die Schriftleitung zu richten. Wir bitten weiterhin, die Beendigung des Studiums und Adressänderungen unverzüglich sowohl dem Verlag (vertrieb@reimer-verlag.de) als auch der Redaktion (redaktion.rgk@dainst.de) mitzuteilen, damit die fristgerechte Lieferung gewährleistet werden kann.

ISBN 978-3-7861-2887-8
ISSN 0016-8874

© 2022 by Römisch-Germanische Kommission des Deutschen Archäologischen Instituts Frankfurt a.M.
Gebr. Mann Verlag · Berlin – www.reimer-mann-verlag.de
Verantwortlicher Redakteur: Alexander Gramsch, Römisch-Germanische Kommission
Graphische Betreuung: Oliver Wagner, Kirstine Ruppel, Römisch-Germanische Kommission
Formalredaktion: Nadine Baumann, Bonn; Susanne Biegert, Bonn; Julia Hahn, Jasmin Köhler,
Tamara Ziemer, Römisch-Germanische Kommission
Satz und Druck LINDEN SOFT Verlag e.K., Aichwald
Printed in Germany

Inhalt

Aufsätze / Articles

Bánffy, Eszter / Egry, Ildikó, Feasting with music? A musical instrument and its context from the later 5th millennium BC Hungary 1

Moore, Daniel W., The Etruscan roots of the Reinheim bracelet 37

Fürst, Sebastian / Schönfelder, Martin / Armbruster, Barbara, Neues zum sogenannten Trinkhornbeschlag von Bad Dürkheim – Zu Goldblecharbeiten der Frühlatènezeit 57

Rubel, Alexander / Varga, Rada, Hercules Magusanus im Lager der *ala I Batavorum milliaria* in Războieni-Cetate (Kreis Alba, Rumänien) 107

Roymans, Nico / Heeren, Stijn, Romano-Frankish interaction in the Lower Rhine frontier zone from the late 3rd to the 5th century – Some key archaeological trends explored 133

Hamerow, Helena / Zerl, Tanja / Stroud, Elizabeth / Bogaard, Amy, The cerealisation of the Rhineland: Extensification, crop rotation and the medieval 'agricultural revolution' in the *longue durée* 157

Diskussionen / Discussions

Päffgen, Bernd, Passau zwischen Spätantike und Mittelalter: Die Ausgrabungsergebnisse in der Klosterkirche Niedernburg 185

Päffgen, Bernd, Frankfurt zur späten Merowingerzeit: Die Aussagen des Grabfunds in der ehemaligen Stiftskirche St. Bartholomäus 203

Korrigenda zu Thomas Meier, Methodenprobleme einer Chronologie der Merowingerzeit in Süddeutschland. Germania 98, 2020 (2021), 237–290. doi: https://doi.org/10.11588/ger.2020.85276 215

Rezensionen / Reviews / Comptes rendus

Grimm, Sonja B., Resilience and Reorganization of Social Systems during the Weichselian Lateglacial in North-West Europe. An Evaluation of the Archaeological, Climatic, and Environmental Record (Shumon T. Hussain) 217

Scharl, Silviane, Innovationstransfer in prähistorischen Gesellschaften. Eine vergleichende Studie zu ausgewählten Fallbeispielen des 6. bis 4. Jahrtausends vor Christus in Mittel- und Südosteuropa unter besonderer Berücksichtigung temporärer Grenzräume (Eszter Bánffy) 221

FRÖHLICH, NICO, Bandkeramische Hofplätze. Artefakte der Keramikchronologie oder Abbild sozialer und wirtschaftlicher Strukturen? (Michael Ilett) 225

JÜRGENS, FRITZ, Der bandkeramische Zentralort von Borgentreich-Großeneder (Kr. Höxter) (Joanna Pyzel) 230

KAUFMANN, DIETER, Die Rössener Kultur in Mitteldeutschland. Die rössenzeitlichen Geräte aus Felsgestein (Eric Biermann) 234

VASIĆ, MILENA, Personal Adornment in the Neolithic Middle East: A Case Study of Çatalhöyük (Oliver Dietrich) 238

DURU, REFIK / UMURTAK, GÜLSÜN, Bademağacı Höyüğü Kazıları I. Neolitik ve Erken Kalkolitik Çağ Yerleşmeleri. Excavations at Bademağacı Höyük I. The Neolithic and Early Chalcolithic Settlements (Christoph Schwall) 243

GUTJAHR, CHRISTOPH / TIEFENGRABER, GEORG (Hrsg.), Beiträge zur Kupferzeit am Rande der Südostalpen. Akten des 4. Wildoner Fachgesprächs am 16. und 17. Juni 2016 in Wildon / Steiermark (Österreich) (Paul Gleirscher) 248

WENTINK, KARSTEN, Stereotype. The Role of Grave Sets in Corded Ware and Bell Beaker Funerary Practices (Martin Bartelheim) 251

CARLIN, NEIL, The Beaker Phenomenon? Understanding the Character and Context of Social Practices in Ireland 2500–2000 BC (Matthias Merkl) 255

FONTIJN, DAVID, Economies of Destruction. How the Systematic Destruction of Valuables Created Value in Bronze Age Europe, c. 2300–500 BC (Ariane Ballmer) 259

KAPURAN, ALEKSANDAR, Velebit, a Tumulus Culture Necropolis in the Southern Carpathian Basin (Vojvodina, Serbia) (Maja Gori) 264

HAUSER, MIRIAM, Der Rest vom Fest. Eine spätbronzezeitliche Grube voller Scherben vom Seckeberg in Frick (Carola Metzner-Nebelsick) 266

LEHNHARDT, ENRICO, Die Anfänge der Eisenverhüttung im Bereich der Przeworsk-Kultur (Paweł Madera) 270

MOORE, TOM, A Biography of Power. Research and Excavations at the Iron Age *oppidum* of Bagendon, Gloucestershire (1979–2017) (Katja Winger) 276

MØBJERG, TINNA / MANNERING, ULLA / ROSTHOLM, HANS / RÆDER KNUDSEN, LISE (Hrsg.), The Hammerum Burial Site. Customs and Clothing in the Roman Iron Age (Karina Grömer) 278

WEIS, FALKO, Der Goldmünzhort und die spätlatènezeitlichen Münzen aus Riegel am Kaiserstuhl (Andrew P. Fitzpatrick) 282

SCHUSSMANN, MARKUS, Die Kelten in Bayern. Archäologie und Geschichte (Peter C. Ramsl) 284

KOKOWSKI, ANDRZEJ, Illerup Ådal 15. Kleinfunde zivilen Charakters (Renata Madyda-Legutko) 288

FURGER, ALEX R., Antike Schmelztiegel. Archäologie und Archäometrie der Funde aus Augusta Raurica / FURGER, ALEX R., Antike Stahlerzeugung. Ein Nachweis der Aufkohlung von Eisen aus Augusta Raurica (Roland Schwab) 292

Lawrence, Andrew, Religion in Vindonissa. Kultorte und Kulte im und um das Legionslager (John Scheid) 297

Istenič, Janka, Roman Military Equipment from the River Ljubljanica. Typology, Chronology and Technology / Rimska Vojaška Oprema iz Reke Ljubljanice. Arheološke in naravoslovne raziskave (Eckhard Deschler-Erb) 300

Monteil, Martial / Van Andringa, William (Hrsg.), Monumentum fecit: Monuments funéraires de Gaule romaine (Thomas Knosala) 305

Márton, András, Les pratiques funéraires en Pannonie de l'époque augustéenne à la fin du 3ᵉ siècle (Stephan Berke) 309

Mohnike, Katharina, Das jüngerkaiser- bis völkerwanderungszeitliche Gräberfeld von Uelzen-Veerßen (Fabian Gall) 312

Kos, Peter, Das spätrömische Kastell Vemania bei Isny III. Auswertung der Fundmünzen und Studien zum Münzumlauf in Raetien im 3. und 4. Jahrhundert (Fleur Kemmers) 316

Hächler, Nikolas / Näf, Beat / Schwarz, Peter-Andrew, Mauern gegen Migration? Spätrömische Strategie, der Hochrhein-Limes und die Fortifikationen der Provinz *Maxima Sequanorum* – eine Auswertung der Quellenzeugnisse (Dominic Moreau) 318

Rundkvist, Martin, At Home at the Castle. Lifestyles at the Medieval Strongholds of Östergötland, AD 1200–1530 (Reinhard Friedrich) 322

Schmid, Christina, Ergrabene Kontexte. Interpretationen archäologischer Fundzusammenhänge auf Burgen (Rainer Atzbach) 326

Cocroft, Wayne D. / Schofield, John, Archaeology of the Teufelsberg. Exploring Western Electronic Intelligence Gathering in Cold War Berlin (Reinhard Bernbeck) 329

Reich, David, Who We Are and How We Got Here. Ancient DNA and the New Science of the Human Past (Jörg Feuchter) 334

Kozatsas, Jannis, The Dialectic of Practice and the Logical Structure of the Tool. Philosophy, Archaeology and the Anthropology of Technology (Matthias Jung) 339

Nakoinz, Oliver, Zentralität: Theorie, Methoden und Fallbeispiele zur Analyse zentraler Orte (Michael Kempf) 343

Furlan, Guido, Dating Urban Classical Deposits. Approaches and Problems in Using Finds to Date Strata (Thomas Lappi) 347

Empfangene Bücher / Books received / Livres reçues 353

Hinweise für Publikationen der Römisch-Germanischen Kommission 355
Guidelines for publications of the Römisch-Germanische Kommission 359
Recommendations pour les publications de la Römisch-Germanische Kommission . . . 363

Die mit den Initialen gekennzeichneten Résumés wurden von Yves Gautier (Y. G.) übersetzt.

Feasting with music?
A musical instrument and its context
from the later 5th millennium BC Hungary

By Eszter Bánffy and Ildikó Egry

Keywords: *Late Lengyel / Ludanice / Balaton-Lasinja cultures / 5th millennium BC / Danube Valley / settlement pit / deposition / musical instrument / feasting*
Schlagwörter: *Späte Lengyel / Ludanice / Balaton-Lasinja Kulturen / 5. Jahrtausend v. Chr. / Donautal / Siedlungsgrube / Deponierung / Musikinstrument / Feasting*
Mots-clés: *cultures de Lengyel tardif / Ludanice / Balaton-Lasinja / cinquième millénaire av. J.-C. / vallée du Danube / fosses d'habitat / dépôt / instrument de musique / festoiement*

Introduction

In this paper we pursue three goals that are interlinked. The primary goal is the publication of a significant find, a clay horn from the second half of the 5th millennium BC along with its full archaeological context, as far as this is still possible three decades after excavation. We regard this goal to be optimally fulfilled with discussing two further points. Our second aim is to summarise the current state of chronological and cultural research. Without clarifying some aspects of the chronological and cultural background, the horn and its two parallel finds deposited together cannot be discussed in sufficient depth to be related. As a consequence of the complicated and disharmonic terminology of the Late Neolithic, Early and Middle Copper Age in Hungary, Eastern Austria, and Slovakia, it also becomes obvious that this unique deposition deserves to be placed in its right chronological context within the late Lengyel, Epilengyel, Balaton-Lasinja and Ludanice cultural circle, highlighting some relations in Transdanubia that have remained less obvious. And last, since not only the clay horn find, but its archaeological context is also meaningful, we try to interpret the assemblage and explore their characteristics, indicating that several of these speak for the remains to be deposited after a shared consumption, presumably as paraphernalia of a communal feast. The circumstances speaking for (and against) this assumption are taken together.

To give some introductory thoughts on the last point mentioned: the power of commensality, acts of shared feasts in a community's life is well attested in the literary sources. Countless ethnographic and socio-psychological studies have demonstrated the importance of feasts in the cohesion of communities, in negotiating and re-affirming personal and group relations or even of the overall hierarchy; broadly speaking, they often negotiate, consolidate, or change the social position and rank of the participants of feasts. Organising and hosting a feast could be the expression of the self-identity and of the cohesion of a smaller group such as a family or community (Hayden 2001, with further literature). It is generally assumed that feasting had been a widespread custom in prehistory. John Robb sees Neolithic cuisine as a generative map for social life (Robb 2007, 156). Feasting is often invoked in the interpretation of special deposits, particularly if there is nothing to indicate the ritual or sacrificial nature of the context. An unusually large amount of animal bones apparently discarded at the same time or shell middens are often regarded as the remains of feasts. All the more so if these represent the remains of large-bodied wild or domestic species and in particular when they are found together with vessels. Yet, assemblages whose every element reflects a deposition after feasting are seldom brought to light from closed contexts, as was the case on a Copper Age site in the Danube Valley in the Carpathian Basin, at Mosonszentmiklós-Pálmajor. We present a horn made of clay here, together with a vessel that can be interpreted as a drum. The assemblage was buried in a meticulous arrangement with whole vessels along with intact cattle bones, remains of the consummation of a large amount of meet. Since the horn gives a strong tone, the chances for dealing with the remains of a feast accompanied with music will also be contemplated on.

In 1993, during their investigation of the Mosonszentmiklós-Pálmajor site, archaeologist András Figler and his colleagues uncovered houses and pits of the late Lengyel and Middle Copper Age Ludanice / Balaton-Lasinja cultures (FIGLER 1996; 1997a; 1997b). A particular pit, described and discussed in this study is one of the contexts, whose function definitely appears to have been non-domestic. Our focus will be on the intact Copper Age clay horn as well as on the overall context and the other finds deposited with it. The clay horn and its context are able to shed significant new light on prehistoric feasts, particularly on the interpretation of the archaeological remains of the less known Neolithic and Copper Age examples in the Carpathian basin and in south eastern Europe.

Background

The northern Transdanubian Danube Valley in the later 5th millennium BC

Mosonszentmiklós-Pálmajor (County Győr-Moson-Sopron, HU) is located on an alluvial plain along the middle Danube section in the north-westerly part of the Carpathian Basin *(Fig. 1)*. From the onset of the Neolithic; this area was occupied by the Central European Linearbandkeramik (LBK, 5350–5000 cal BC), the immediate descendants of the earliest farmers arriving from the Balkans. The LBK and the succeeding Lengyel culture (4900–4400 cal BC) were both distributed over an extensive territory. Two main areas can be distinguished within the immense Lengyel distribution. In the west, the Lengyel complex extended across the greater part of Austria and Moravia, while its eastern variant occupied the vast area from eastern Transdanubia through the mountain region of north-eastern Hungary and eastern Slovakia to south-eastern (Lesser) Poland. One difference between the western Lengyel (or Moravian Painted Ware) and the eastern Lengyel complex is the much greater intensity of occupation on the eastern Lengyel settlements. At Alsónyék, for example, the settlement covered an area of 80 hectares in the 48th–46th centuries BC. It lies in the neighbourhood of similarly large sites such as Zengővárkony and the eponymous site of Lengyel. Large grave groups and cemeteries are known from the eastern Lengyel distribution (over 2300 graves were excavated at Alsónyék alone: BÁNFFY et al. 2016). In contrast, the western Lengyel complex is characterised by smaller, dispersed settlements and we know next to nothing about how the dead were buried. No formal cemeteries have been found and the mortuary record is principally made up of dead who were accorded special treatment (BÁNFFY 1986) such as bodies "dumped" into pits and single, multiple, or partial burials, the latter containing mutilated bodies (BÁNFFY 1985). The Mosonszentmiklós-Pálmajor site can be assigned to the western Lengyel complex both geographically and in terms of its cultural traditions.

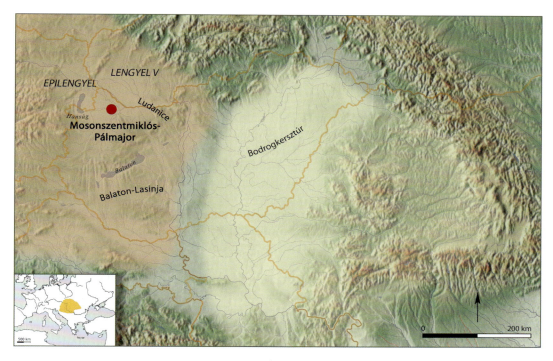

Fig. 1. The central Carpathian Basin in the later 5th millennium BC, with the site of Mosonszentmiklós-Pálmajor indicated.

Given the internal structural changes and the appearance of copper artefacts, the latest phase of the Lengyel sequence can be assigned to the Copper Age. The contemporaneity of this phase with the Early Copper Age of eastern Hungary (c. 4400–4000 cal BC) is also confirmed by radiocarbon dates (BÁNFFY 1996a; RACZKY-SIKLÓSI 2013). In the later 5th millennium BC, during the latest phase of the Lengyel culture, cultural development was moulded by the recurring influx of new population groups and cultural impacts from the Balkans, which precipitated major transformations in southern Transdanubia, in the southwesterly part of the Carpathian Basin. The appearance of early copper and gold metallurgy, of fluted pottery imitating metal vessels of the Balkanic type, and of smaller, more briefly occupied settlements was initially believed to signal a major cultural change and discontinuity (KALICZ 1973; 1980). This led scholars to introduce a new archaeological culture, the Balaton-Lasinja culture.

However, there are persuasive arguments against this initially assumed discontinuity. The settlement excavations and their detailed assessments in the late 20th century indicate that there were no major disruptions in the Lengyel settlement network, nor can any major shifts be observed in the location of the settlements that lay on gently sloping hillsides and on terraces overlooking streams and rivers. Moreover, the onset of the changes assumed to signal the arrival of a new population can be traced to the final, Early Copper Age phase of the Lengyel culture (BÁNFFY 1996a; 1996b). Cultural impacts from the northern Balkans in the wake of the disintegration and restructuring of the late Vinča culture, the southern neighbour of the Lengyel culture, rippled through southern Transdanubia too.

The aforementioned arguments indicate that the late Lengyel development in Transdanubia, in the western part of the Carpathian Basin, was not uniform. Unsurprisingly, the strongest cultural influences from the south can be felt in the western Lengyel complex distributed in the southerly regions bordering on the northern Balkans, as confirmed by the archaeological record from two micro-regions west of Lake Balaton (the Little Balaton micro-region, investigated between 1979–1985, and the Hahót Valley to its west, explored between 1986–1993) (Bánffy 1986; 1996a; 1996b). The settlements and the finds that have been brought to light in these two regions provided clear evidence for the southern impacts during the late Lengyel period. They palpably became more intense during the ensuing Balaton-Lasinja period but did not involve a cultural break or the arrival of a new population. The conventional names for denoting archaeological cultures are still used by researchers despite their obsoleteness, and it should be borne in mind that these are no more than technical categories that have not been discarded solely for the lack of better ones.

The settlement network outlined by more recently analysed and published sites enabled the reconstruction of a trade and cultural communications route leading from the northern Balkans to Central Europe (Bánffy 2001), which undoubtedly survived into the ensuing centuries of the Middle Copper Age.

The southern impacts are attested to differing extents and increasingly weakly in the central and northern regions of Transdanubia. The traits reflecting the continuity of the Lengyel culture and the Balkan impacts could be clearly distinguished on sites in the Budapest area (Virág 1995). Given the sites' northern location and the decreasing intensity of Balkan impacts, the Balaton-Lasinja label was discarded when describing the finds, which were assigned to the Ludanice culture distributed in the northern Carpathian Basin, in northern Hungary and Slovakia. In the Slovakian chronological system established for the 5th millennium BC, the Ludanice culture is often denoted as Lengyel V to highlight the fact that it represents the continuity of the material culture and traditions of the Lengyel culture north of the Danube (Lichardus / Vladár 1964). The label "Epilengyel" used in neighbouring eastern Austria similarly reflects continuity (Ruttkay 1976).

Although Balkan (Balaton-Lasinja) elements can be discerned on the Middle Copper Age sites along the north-western Hungarian section of the Danube, among which Mosonszentmiklós-Pálmajor is no exception, the area is linked by many cultural strands to the Nitra Basin in south-western Slovakia and to the core distribution of the Ludanice culture in the area of the Ludanice (Nyitraludány) site.

Thus, what we see is that the entire vast geographic area with Lengyel antecedents underwent a slow Chalcolithisation, reflected by the series of gradual changes in settlement patterns and lifestyles as well as the adoption of various innovations, rather than cultural gaps in the wake of migrations. The main difference between the Balaton-Lasinja and the Ludanice culture is essentially one of proportion (Bánffy 1994), which in turn reflects the geographic distance from the northern Balkan Vinča and post-Vinča distribution and the long-distance routes, with the cultural impacts diminishing towards the west and northwest.

The slow transformation involved the appearance of smaller settlements which replaced the previous large, permanent settlements. A similar process can be noted not only farther to the east, for example on the Hungarian Plain, where tell settlements were abandoned for smaller, more briefly occupied settlements (Link 2006), but also in south-western Transdanubia, where a smaller Balaton-Lasinja settlement (Bánffy 1993) was identified in the immediate neighbourhood of an extensive later Lengyel period settlement ringed by an enclosure (Barna et al. 2019). An overlap between the two cultures and the Early and Middle Copper Age settlements has been noted on other Transdanubian sites as well (Simon 1990; Bánffy 1996a; 1996b; Éri et al. 1969).

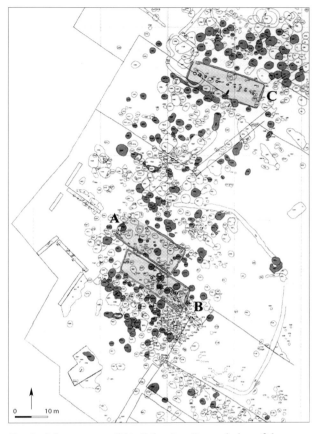

Fig. 2. Mosonszentmiklós-Pálmajor. Ground plan of the western part of the excavation area with the chalcolithic houses and pits indicated.

The Mosonszentmiklós-Pálmajor site

The greater part of the immense volume of finds brought to light during the extensive salvage excavations on the site ahead of large-scale construction projects of the past few decades remains unpublished. The construction of the M1 Motorway between Budapest and Vienna in the early 1990s was preceded by a series of excavations, in the course of which the remains of several Neolithic and Copper Age sites were uncovered in the northwestern Carpathian Basin (in fact, another site was found in the immediate vicinity of the site discussed here, cf. EGRY 2003). The investigation of the Mosonszentmiklós-Pálmajor site involved the excavation of a 9 hectares large area in 1993–1995, representing one of most extensive archaeological operations carried out at the time. Lying on the eastern fringes of the Hanság wetland, the site is located on a roughly 80 hectares large ridge-like hill rising to a height of 3–3.5 m above the surrounding often waterlogged land. The ridge was continuously occupied from the Neolithic onward: population groups of at least ten different periods had established their settlement in this location (FIGLER 1996, 18–19; 1997a; 1997b). Owing to the disturbances from later periods, the Neolithic and Copper Age finds were predominantly found in secondary contexts and only the superposition of the archaeological features and the prehistoric pits yielding finds with a dating value

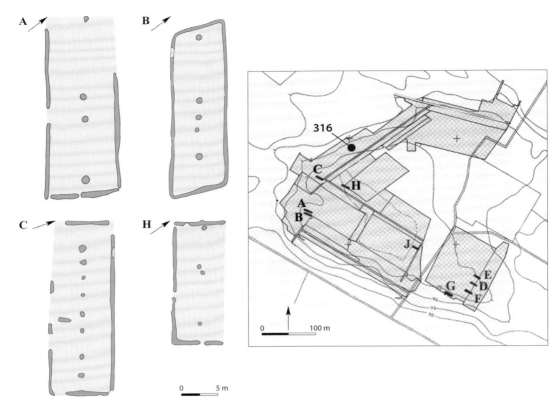

Fig. 3. Mosonszentmiklós-Pálmajor. Details of Houses A, B, C, H and location of Pit 316.

provide some clues for establishing a chronological sequence of the features dating from various periods. The only exceptions are a few undisturbed pits and the remains of buildings, whose bedding trenches and sunken floors were clearly outlined, with the burnt daub debris covering the occupation area with two distinct house groups. The unusual pit discussed here represents one of these exceptions.

The bedding trenches of four houses of the latest Lengyel population that occupied the site between 4500–4400 cal BC came to light in the south-eastern part of the investigated area, where they formed a distinct cluster: the houses had a rectangular groundplan with rounded corners and an inner partition wall dividing the space into two rooms with a ⅓ : ⅔ proportion. The ensuing Ludanice / Balaton-Lasinja community settling in the north-western part of the excavated area had similar rectangular houses, although these buildings had a single room and were of varying sizes. These buildings similarly formed a separate cluster (Houses A, B, C, H and J) (VIRÁG / FIGLER 2007, 355) *(Figs 2–3)*. Six contemporaneous pits could be associated with these houses: in the case of three pits that can be securely assigned to the Balaton-Lasinja / Ludanice period, we may tentatively assume that the vessels recovered from them had been intentionally deposited in these features (Features 78, 438, and 724, yielding six, three, and one intact vessels, respectively). The deposition act seems quite obvious in the case of two other pits as well (Feature 9: nine vessels, and Feature 1159: nine vessels). This study focuses on the sixth pit, Feature 316. All six round pits had an almost identical size and were dug into the open area between the houses by the occupants of the Copper Age settlement. Feature 316, which could equally well be asso-

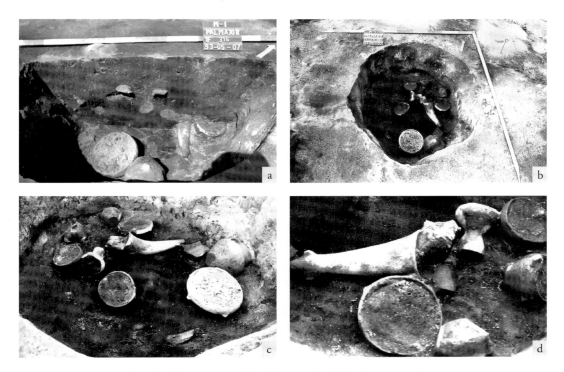

Fig. 4. Mosonszentmiklós-Pálmajor. Pit 316 during excavation.

ciated with House C or H, lay to their north, at some distance from the houses *(Fig. 3)*. Interestingly enough, five of the six pits lay in each other's proximity. Pits 438, 9, and 724 lay closer to the buildings than Pit 316. One good anchor for the site's internal chronology is that Pit 1159 cut the southern wall of House C; however, this detail is not mentioned in the brief site report (Virág / Figler 2007) and its discussion also falls beyond the scope of the present study.

The clay horn and its context

Description of the pit with the clay horn

Pit 316 was a round feature with a flat, even floor, having a diameter of 160 cm and a depth of 46 cm. Although there is no field record of the pit's excavation, the accurate and meticulously made drawings as well as a series of black-and-white photos and a video documenting the pit's excavation have survived. The ensuing description is based on these documents.

The pit's fill was homogenous, made up of loose blackish earth mixed with sand. This black earth was greasy to the touch and the excavator remarked in the field diary that it was probably rich in organic matter. Unfortunately, no samples were taken from this part of the fill. Eight intact vessels lay on the floor of the pit, together with a nearly 40 cm long clay horn which was placed in its centre *(Fig. 4a–d)*. Most of the vessels were found lying in the pit's northern section, while one bowl and two vessel fragments lay in the pit's southern part. An empty space was observed between them, characterised by an especially thick layer of black, greasy, soft soil. Although no samples were taken from this area either, a remark

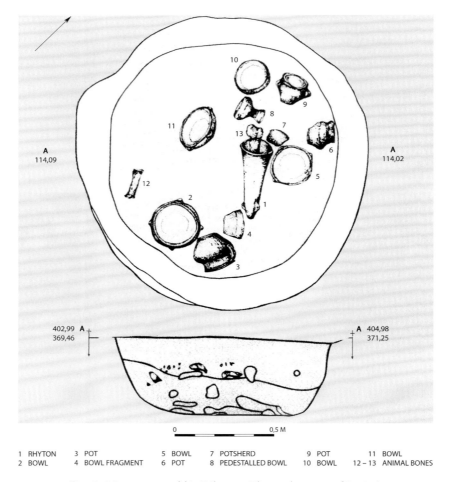

| 1 RHYTON | 3 POT | 5 BOWL | 7 POTSHERD | 9 POT | 11 BOWL |
| 2 BOWL | 4 BOWL FRAGMENT | 6 POT | 8 PEDESTALLED BOWL | 10 BOWL | 12–13 ANIMAL BONES |

Fig. 5. Mosonszentmiklós-Pálmajor. Plan and section of Pit 316.

in the field diary records the impression that a piece of thick fur, leather, or heavy woven textile may perhaps also have been deposited as part of the assemblage.

The clay horn and a pedestalled vessel were both placed on their side close to each other, a jug and a pot, similarly laid on their side, lay a little farther *(Fig. 5)*. Four conical bowls were set around the clay horn, an arrangement that is clearly visible on the photo and the drawings. Three of the vessels recovered from the pit are smaller pots with prominent shoulder *(Fig. 6,1–3)*, three are biconical bowls with lug handles *(Fig. 7,1–3)*, while one is a smaller pedestalled bowl with two pointed knobs on the shoulder *(Fig. 8)*. The clay horn lay immediately beside the latter vessel.

Unfortunately, the vessels themselves have not been found in either of the local museums and their magazines. Our quest resulted in the information that they were sent to a graphic artist to be drawn for a paper by the excavator András Figler and Zsuzsa M. Virág in the early 2000s, but the place where the vessels were stored, perished in flames soon after that. There is only one pedestalled vessel, exhibited in the Mosonmagyaróvár museum, but no permission was given to remove it from there in order to subject it to even slightly destructive examinations. Thus, the only exact hints on the ceramic finds are those that are published by Virág and Figler (2007).

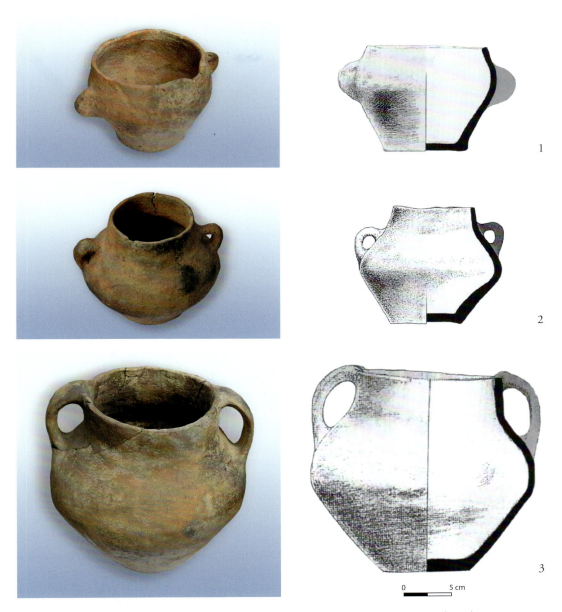

Fig. 6. Mosonszentmiklós-Pálmajor. 1–3 pots from Pit 316. Drawings scale 1 : 4.

Two cattle long bones, an intact femur and a large tibia fragment, were also part of the assemblage. The intact femur was tucked into the wide end of the horn, while the tibia fragment lay near the horn, on the greasy black soil covering the pit's floor, closer to the wall of the pit. Two larger potsherds were also found lying on the floor. We made every effort to find the femur, even corresponding with radiocarbon laboratories thinking that it had perhaps been sent to one for sampling but found no traces of it. It seems likely that the bone had been bagged separately as an "important find" and now lies forgotten somewhere in a museum storeroom. However, we did manage to find the tibia, which could then be

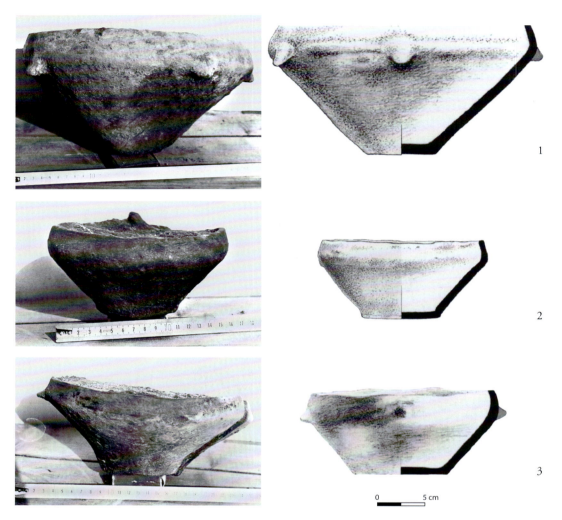

Fig. 7. Mosonszentmiklós-Pálmajor. 1–3 bowls from Pit 316. – Drawings scale 1:4.

Fig. 8. Mosonszentmiklós-Pálmajor. Pedestalled bowl (drum?) from Pit 316. – Drawing scale 1:4.

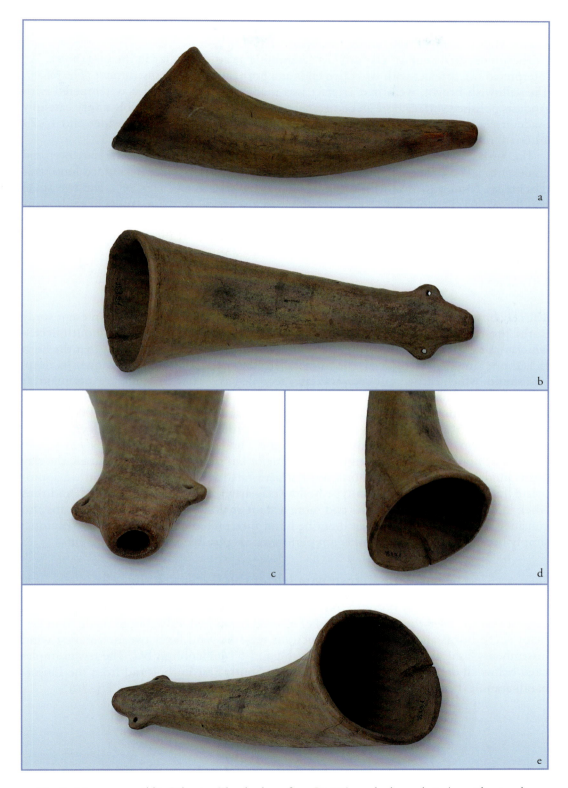

Fig. 9. Mosonszentmiklós-Pálmajor. The clay horn from Pit 316. – a, b, d, e scale 1:4; c without scale.

sampled: the radiocarbon date confirms that the pit is contemporaneous with the settlement's Middle Copper Age houses (see below; *Fig. 13*).[1]

The almost intact curved clay artefact resembling a cattle horn lay in the pit's centre. We interpreted this artefact with two open ends as a horn, as a musical instrument *(Fig. 9a–b)*. The yellowish-brown, well-fired artefact was made of well-levigated clay tempered with sand; its polished surface bore an occasional patch of soot and it was visibly a very carefully made artefact. L. 37.6 cm, Th. 0.6–0.8 cm, diam. of the slightly oval wider end 13.7–14.6 cm, diam. of mouth end 2.5 cm *(Fig. 9c–d)*.

The horn's wider, funnel-like end has a slightly oval opening, while the narrower end grades into a flattened oval opening. Two small, symmetrically placed, rounded loop handles are set 6 cm downward from the horn's narrow mouth end *(Fig. 9e)*. The two small handles with a diameter of 2.5 cm probably had a practical function, most likely for suspending the instrument, possibly from the neck; at the same time, their position on the horn in relation to the entire object recalls the proportions of the human body to some extent.

The musical sound of the horn

The clay horn was blown after its discovery in 1993 by the first author of the present study in the presence of András Figler, the site's excavator. Due to the lack of a mouthpiece – which was either of some organic material and did not survive, or to the fact that the horn lacked one originally – blowing the horn called for a special lipping technique. Its deep, rich sound, which carried quite far, was later recorded as part of an acoustic experiment. It reached a strength of 96.0 dB and a frequency of 215–301 Hz. According to Beate Maria Pomberger's comparative table and description, this sound carried for some 100 m (Pomberger 2016, 55). Due to its overall nature, it was probably an instrument for calling and signalling, being suitable for emitting both deeper and higher notes.

The clay horn from Mosonszentmiklós-Pálmajor has two openings. In contrast, the clay horn's model, the natural cattle horn, was not perforated at its pointed end. With an appropriate lipping technique, ocarina-type hollow clay artefacts can also be sounded, and thus when looking for the horn's closer and more distant analogies, we should by all means also consider artefacts that have been described and interpreted as drinking horns (rhytons) simply because their pointed end is not perforated, as possible musical instruments.

The currently known parallels of the clay horn *(Fig. 10)*

The small number of clay horns in time and space from the onset of the Neolithic onwards suggest that the overwhelming majority of musical horns had indeed been made from cattle or sheep horns and that clay reproductions were few and far between. The first wind instruments fashioned from clay appear in the mid-6th millennium BC. The few examples cited below all date from the Early Neolithic of South-East Europe and from the Linearbandkeramik (LBK), the earliest Neolithic culture of Central Europe (see *Fig. 10*).

---

[1] The radiocarbon measurements were performed at the Curt-Engelhorn-Zentrum Archäometrie GmbH, Mannheim (DE); MAMS 44913.

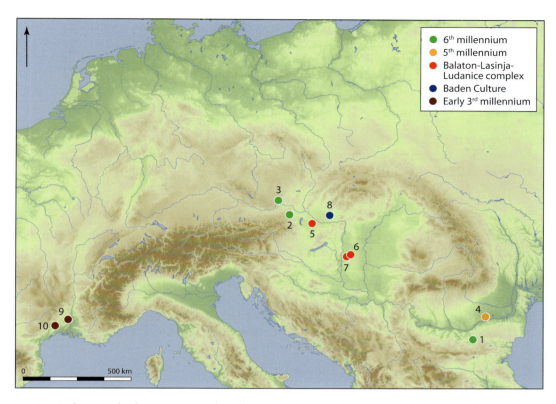

Fig. 10. Prehistoric clay horns mentioned in the text. 1 Ovčarovo-Gorata (BG); 2 Brunn am Gebirge (AT); 3 Breiteneich (AT); 4 Gumelniţa (RO); 5 Mosonszentmiklós-Pálmajor (HU); 6 Császártöltés-Kiscsala (HU); 7 Szihalom-Sóhajtó (HU); 8 Pilismarót-Basaharc (HU); 9 Brugas / Vallabrix, Dép. Gard (FR); 10 Rouet (FR). Green: 6th millennium; yellow: 5th millennium; red: Balaton-Lasinja-Ludanice complex; blue: Baden Culture; brown: early 3rd millennium.

Ovčarovo-Gorata, Bulgaria (c. 5700–5600 cal BC)

According to the current record, the earliest clay horn came to light on this northern Balkanic settlement. The roughly twelve cm long cylindrical object is described as a thin-walled, downward slightly flared object with three perforations near the mouth end on one side and a pair of smaller perforations on the other (Krauss 2014, 166 fig. 100,2). Raiko Krauß cites the artefact from Brunn am Gebirge in support of its interpretation as a clay horn, although he does concede that ocarina-like instruments only became more widespread from the Copper Age onward.

Brunn am Gebirge 2a, Austria (c. 5550 cal BC)

The clay horn from this site is the earliest representative of clay horns visibly imitating natural cattle horns. The settlement itself dates to the earliest, formative phase of the Central European LBK (Stadler 1995; Stadler / Kotova 2010). The clay horn came to light in one of the post-holes of an LBK longhouse and it was therefore interpreted as a foundation deposit. Although the horn was broken and only about 65 % survived, the four perforations on its side could be clearly made out: two near each other near the rim and two farther down on the body. B. M. Pomberger believed that a mouth-piece was needed to play the instrument; she experimented with a reconstructed replica and succeeded in coaxing various sounds from the horn by covering the perforations near the rim. However, no mouth-pieces were discovered on either site (POMBERGER 2016, 38–39 pl. 1,1).

Brunn am Gebirge 2b, Austria (c. 5200 cal BC)

Two fragments interpreted as the remains of a clay horn were brought to light on the extensive LBK settlement near Vienna, dating from the culture's late, Notenkopf period (POMBERGER 2016, 40 pl. 1,2a–b; 1,3a–b).

Breiteneich, Austria (c. 5200 cal BC)

The unstratified find from eastern Austria came to light on a late LBK (Notenkopf) settlement. The 56 mm long fragment comes from the horn's lower, pointed terminal (POMBERGER 2016, pl. 1,4).

The period between the final centuries of the sixth millennium and the later fifth millennium, the horizon from which clay horns are again known, was spanned by the Lengyel culture. Although pedestalled vessels purportedly used as drums can be found in this culture, horns and other wind instruments have not yet been reported from Lengyel contexts.

Gumelniţa, Romania

A clay artefact with curved body and oval end opening described as a rhyton found at Gumelniţa in the Lower Danube region can perhaps also be assigned to the category of clay horns. The artefact is covered with a design of deeply incised triangles combined with white painting in-between (DUMITRESCU 1985, fig. 17).

The next horizon yielding clay horns falls into the Middle Copper Age. The three horns from this period share countless similar traits: the horn discussed here, which can be assigned to the Balaton-Lasinja-Ludanice complex, continuing Lengyel traditions in the Carpathian basin, and the further two clay horns from two distant sites. All three finds are coeval and stand close to each other, although they come from different regions of the Carpathian basin.

Szihalom-Sóhajtó, Hungary *(Fig. 11)*

This clay horn came to light on the outskirts of Szihalom on the northern Hungarian Plain during the salvage excavations preceding the construction of the M3 Motorway. A cemetery section with twenty-seven burials of the Middle Copper Age Bodrogkeresztúr culture was uncovered at the site, alongside a section of the associated settlement. The clay horn was found in the upper part of the fill of Pit 62, in an area lying immediately underneath the humus that was disturbed by later archaeological cultures (SZABÓ 1997, 54–55 fig. 14).

Described as a "ritual vessel" in the exhibition catalogue *Utak a múltba / Paths into the Past*, the Szihalom artefact bears the greatest resemblance to the horn from Mosonszentmiklós-Pálmajor. It is a slightly asymmetrical, cylindrical horn made of clay tempered with sand and fired to a yellowish-brown colour with the occasional grey mottling. The 39 cm long clay horn with two small, rounded loop handles is carefully smoothed: one end has a slightly flaring round opening with straight rim (diam. 9.2 cm), the other end is narrow with a round opening (diam. 1.2 cm). The handles probably served for suspension, simi-

Fig. 11. The clay horn from Szihalom-Sóhajtó. – Scale 1:4.

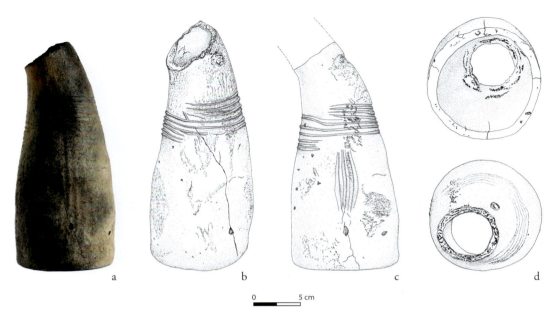

Fig. 12. The clay horn from Császártöltés 10. – Scale 1:4.

larly as in the case of the Mosonszentmiklós horn. However, the anthropomorphic traits, barely perceptible on the latter, are more pronounced on the Szihalom exemplar: the two rounded knobs between the handles can be regarded as the stylised depiction of female breasts.

Császártöltés 10 (Kiscsala, Útőrház I), Hungary *(Fig. 12)*

The unusual clay artefact that can be identified as the fragment of a clay horn was found together with an abundance of good-quality pottery sherds of the Copper Age Bodrogkeresztúr culture on a hill rising above the surrounding land during the field survey conducted on the outskirts of Császártöltés, a settlement lying along Road 54 in the Danube-Tisza interfluve. The slightly curved tubular artefact flares towards one end and narrows towards the other, damaged end. Its body is decorated with a bundle of circumferential lines running parallel to the intact end and a bundle of lines perpendicular to it underneath. L. of fragment 26 cm (reconstructed L. 38–40 cm), diam. of end opening 11 cm (KNIPL 2009a, 145 fig. 1,2–3; 2009b, 98 pls 2–4 fig. 15a–c).

The three roughly contemporaneous clay horns with more or less identical form, size and canonised traits were found on sites in the north-western, north-eastern and central regions of the Carpathian Basin, possibly an indication of the one-time communications network. It also seems likely that the clay imitations were linked by several "original" natural horns *(Fig. 13)*.

From the close of the 4th millennium BC, the Carpathian Basin was occupied by a single cultural complex, the Baden culture. Clay horn fragments came to light from two burials of the cemetery excavated at Pilismarót-Basaharc. Although the artefacts were described as drinking horns, the features shared with clay horns of the preceding two millennia would nevertheless suggest that these were also musical instruments.

Fig. 13. Close parallels in time and space: The three Middle Copper Age clay horns from Hungary (s. *Figs 9–11*). – Scale 1:4.

Pilismarót-Basaharc, Hungary

The two fragments of cattle horn-shaped rhytons are described in detail in the publication of the well-known cemetery of the Baden culture. One was recovered from Grave 359 (TORMA 1973, 494 fig. 5,1; BONDÁR 2015, pl. 12,4), the burial of a roughly 20-year-old adult of indeterminate sex. One end of the curved artefact was broken off (L. 21.5 cm, diam. of mouth 9.5 cm). The perforation can clearly be made out on the photo published in the first excavation report. The artefact is covered with an incised zig-zag pattern, its wide rim with short incisions, while there is "a perforation for suspension" near the pointed base (BONDÁR 2015, 44–45). However, this perforation would rather suggest a function as a musical instrument because two perforations would be needed for suspension and, in any case, a perforation through which a beverage would flow out makes little sense on a drinking horn.

Pilismarót-Basaharc, Hungary

The other fragment interpreted as part of a rhyton comes from Grave 405. The greyish-brown fragment lay on top of the strongly disturbed burial with a stone packing together with a few vessels. It is decorated with an incised zig-zag pattern, similarly to the other piece from the cemetery. The reconstructed length is 22–24 cm (Bondár 2015, 66–67).

Several other possibly analogous finds can be cited from the Late Copper Age of the Carpathian Basin. The Proto-Boleráz culture, appearing in the later fourth millennium, is regarded as the forerunner of the Baden culture, a cultural complex strongly imbued with Lower Danubian cultural elements, and thus the "drinking horn" from Pécsbagota can be seen as a link with the horns of the Baden culture from Mosonszentmiklós-Pálmajor, Császártöltés and Szihalom-Sóhajtó (Kalicz 2001, fig. 4), as can the exemplars from Pilismarót-Basaharc and the fragment of a similar object decorated with a herringbone pattern from Balatonőszöd (Horváth 2014, 191; 203–204 fig. 163,4).

The last period from which several clay wind instruments can be cited is the earlier third millennium. Two finds from France attest to the use of the clay imitations of natural horns.

Brugas / Vallabrix, France (3000–2500 cal BC)

The horn came to light on a site occupied during successive millennia from the Palaeolithic onward, which had been destroyed by modern construction activity (Coularou et al. 1981). The clay horn was found in a small cavity among the settlement features and finds of the Copper Age Fontbuxien site (Coularou et al. 1981, fig. 1). L. 355 mm, diam. of end opening 90 mm, average Th. 7 mm. Its curved form is clearly an imitation of cattle horns. A fluted applied ornament extends from its mid-section to the end. The two perforated lug handles probably had a cord threaded through them for suspension, similarly as on the other clay horns.

Rouet, France (c. 3000–2500 cal BC)

The horn was first published by J. Coularou in 2007. The 3200 mm long horn with an end diameter of 90 mm has a similar curved shape as the piece from Brugas and the Mosonszentmiklós horn. A small knob with two perforations, possibly for suspension, is set on the body roughly halfway down its length. In her study on the experimental reconstruction of prehistoric musical instruments, Tinaig Clodoré-Tissot published a photo of the horn and noted that it took her two hours to make its replica, noting that the greatest difficulty was ensuring that the wall thickness be identical because otherwise it would not produce the desired sound (Clodoré-Tissot 2010, 40–41 fig. 17).

In sum, the clay horns faithfully evoke the form, size and other traits of cattle (or occasionally sheep) horns, not only in early periods but throughout the timespan between the mid-6th and the mid-3rd millennium BC in European regions lying far from each other. These occasional finds strongly suggest that the "prototype" had never disappeared and that natural animal horns were continuously used during the millennia, even if they did not survive in the archaeological record, while their clay replicas were made in exceptional cases only. These finds can, in a sense, be regarded as the tip of the iceberg, as an indication that natural animal horns had been often blown during feasting or had been used for signal calls, a form of communication.

The conjectural drum and its parallels

The pit containing the horn also yielded a 13.7 cm high pedestalled vessel, whose fill had a higher phosphate content than the other ceramics *(Fig. 8)*. The analysis of the geochemical samples taken from the vessels suggests that the vessels had been empty or had contained but a minimal amount of food, at least judging from the occasional higher calcium content and low phosphate values (see below). The somewhat higher phosphate content of the pedestalled vessel is therefore quite puzzling. Perhaps it had been covered with skin, which had seeped into the vessel's interior after its decomposition. The drum skin had perhaps been secured and drawn tight by means of the four, pointed knobs on the carination. If this was indeed the case, the objects deposited in the pit had included not one but two musical instruments.

The use of drums in Neolithic contexts has been posited by several scholars and the cited ethnographic analogies would suggest that the objects in question had been rudimentary goblet drums. Vessels with a tall pedestal and a smaller bowl, known from the late LBK period through the extensive Lengyel distribution to the Early and Middle Copper Age of the Carpathian Basin, i. e. also in the 5th millennium BC (when the Mosonszentmiklós-Pálmajor settlement flourished), were ubiquitous and many could have been used as drums. One good example comes from Großweikersdorf, a site of the Lengyel culture in eastern Austria (POMBERGER 2016, 232 pl. 3,1). With its height of 12.2 cm, it matches the pedestalled vessel from Mosonszentmiklós. Beate Maria Pomberger assigned the vessel to the membranophone category: she made a replica of the ceramic drum, experimented with playing it, and found that it could produce sounds at several different pitches: somewhat deeper sounds could be produced in its centre and higher ones along the edges, depending on the tautness of the skin. The sounds produced by drumming were 76–86 dB and carried as far as 40 m, depending on the outer temperature and the humidity of the air (POMBERGER 2016, 52–53). A strikingly high number of comparable membrane drums have been reported from the Baden period, particularly from the northern sites characterised by a strong Funnel Beaker (TRB) presence (POMBERGER 2016, 233–235 pls 5–7; 10). Many ceramic drums are known from southern Scandinavia, Poland, Moravia and Bohemia from between 3600 and 2400 BC. Most ceramic drums are profusely ornamented: over one-half of the currently known exemplars were recovered from burials or from a location where rituals were performed. Volume 3 of the *Studien zur Musikarchäologie* series lists some 340 drum finds that can be assigned to the TRB culture (LUSTIG 2002).

Analysis of the samples taken from the vessel fills and the animal bones

The animal bones

The pit contained two larger animal bones, as mentioned above, both from cattle. One was an intact femur which was tucked into the opening of the horn so that only its end was visible, as can be clearly seen on the drawings and photos. Regrettably, our efforts to locate this bone proved unsuccessful. In addition to corresponding with several museums in whose storeroom the cattle femur could have been stored, we also contacted the radiocarbon laboratory in Debrecen in the hope that András Figler, the site's excavator, had perhaps sent the bone there for age determination, where it would hopefully be found. Our thrill upon learning that the laboratory's samples included animal bones from the site was short-lived: as it turned out, the bone samples in question originated from the settlement's Bronze Age occupation. We therefore sampled the cattle tibia, which, although broken,

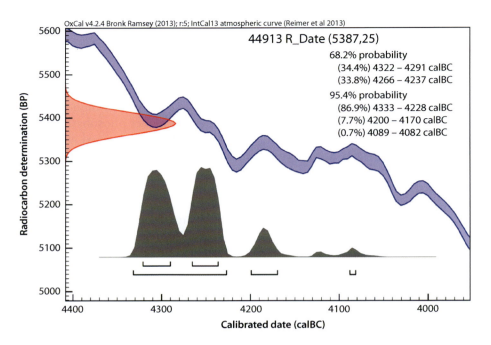

Fig. 14. Mosonszentmiklós-Pálmajor. Radiocarbon dating of Pit 316.

could be found in the storeroom of the Mosonmagyaróvár museum together with the vessels and the soil samples. The bone had been investigated from the zooarchaeological point of view before sampling by Éva Ágnes Nyerges. She could not observe any damages or cutmarks on its surface. The fraction at one end of the tibia could still be a sign for intentional destruction, for accessing the marrow (L. Bartosiewicz, pers. comm.).

Radiocarbon dating

As mentioned in the above, radiocarbon dating was performed on the cattle tibia. Sampling was performed by Balázs Gusztáv Mende, the measurements by Susanne Lindauer and Ronny Friedrich of the Curt-Engelhorn-Zentrum Archäometrie GmbH. Sample MAMS 44913 gave a date of 4333–4228 cal BC (1 σ, 95.4%) and 4322–4291 cal BC (2 σ, 68.2%), respectively *(Fig. 14)*. This corresponds to the Balaton-Lasinja-Ludanice-Lengyel V-Epilengyel horizon (as discussed above) in the western Carpathian Basin and to the coeval Bodrogkeresztúr period, filling the Middle Copper Age in eastern Hungary. This time interval can be equated with the earlier phase of the Balaton-Lasinja and Ludanice horizons (Oross et al. 2011, 398); the detailed assessment of the houses and the finds will no doubt shed additional light on the site's late Lengyel occupation and the possible continuity with the next period, the Balaton-Lasinja-Ludanice phase. However, any speculations in this regard would exceed the scope of this study. The important point is that the result of the radiocarbon dating did not challenge the cultural context of the finds from Pit 316 of the Mosonszentmiklós-Pálmajor site.

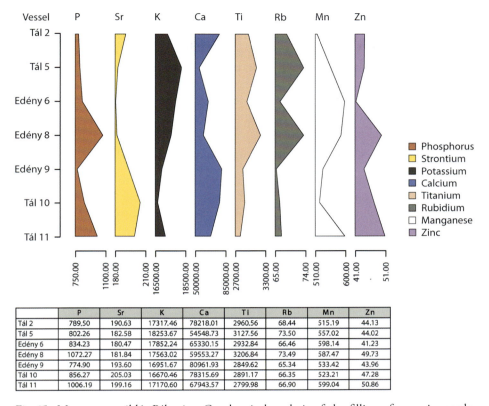

Fig. 15. Mosonszentmiklós-Pálmajor. Geochemical analysis of the filling of ceramic vessels from Pit 316.

The RFA analysis of the soil samples

The fill of each vessel was carefully removed and packaged during the excavation. We used one-half of each fill, putting aside the other half for future analyses. The samples were submitted for geochemical and botanical analyses, which were coordinated by Isabel Hohle: the geochemical analysis was performed by Melani Podgorelec, Romano-Germanic Commission, the botanical analysis by Astrid Stobbe of the J. W. von Goethe University in Frankfurt.

We sampled each vessel for X-ray fluorescence analyses. The pulverised samples were examined with a Portable Thermo Scientific Niton XL3 t analyser. The routine involved four phases of filtering the samples; we used measurement mode environmental samples (minerals with Cu/Zn) for the measurements. A Standard NIST2709a was measured after every tenth measurement in order to eliminate mistakes and to correct standards. For this reason, the metadata were elaborated in several steps. Each sample was measured four times and each sample was given middle range data *(Fig. 15)*.

The phosphorus rates lie between c. 775 to 1070 ppm (parts per million), none of which can be considered to be high. However, calcium contents reached the rate of 81,000 ppm. Besides phosphorus, calcium typically shows elevated values in pits and cooking areas, always indicating a strong anthropogenic impact (Middleton / Price 1996), and therefore in general terms, higher calcium values imply more mussels and shells, while higher phosphorus values are an indicator for decomposed leather and bones (HOLLIDAY 2004, 301–302). Higher calcium values may therefore indicate bone or mussel remains from meals (perhaps some soup) that remained in the vessels after the edible parts had been consumed. Burnt daub or wood ashes, the third component indicating human activity that is primarily characteristic for animal remains, remains in the average ranges, as do the values of strontium, rubidium, manganese, and zinc.

Determination of soil texture, organic matter, and pollen conservation

Samples were taken from the sediment fills of the seven vessels to determine the grain size composition (sieve and pipette method, after SCHLICHTING et al. 1995) as well as the total organic carbon / soil organic matter (TOC/SOM) ratio. In addition, the samples were also examined for possible pollen grains.

The sediments in vessels 316/2, 316/6, and 316/9 consist of loamy sand (silt levels below 40%). Vessels 316/5, 316/8, 316/10, and 316/11 contain silty-loamy sand (silt content over 40%) (AD-HOC-AG BODEN 2005). The high silt content and the fine sand component suggest that the material is of aeolian origin and was subsequently remobilised by the Danube. The organic material contents are remarkably high. Vessel 316/5 has the lowest value at 2.83% (moderately organic). The SOM values of the other vessels are between 4.0 and 5.45% (highly organic). The sediments contain a relatively large proportion of microcharcoal, which is certainly partly responsible for the high organic carbon values. A few heavily corroded pollen grains (especially *Pinus*, Cichorioideae and Poaceae) were found in similar percentages in all vessel fills, probably topsoil material containing high percentages of charred plant remains.

The vessels had probably contained the remains of a stew or a thick broth on their bottom. The consumption of cooked dishes does not exclude that whole joints of meat were also roasted and then carved up, as noted by N. Russel in her discussion of the two main modes of food preparation cooking and roasting and consumption at the Vinča settlement of Opovo (RUSSELL 1999, 162).

We would have liked to submit a sample from the rim of the pedestalled vessel interpreted as a drum for protein analyses, but this would have been impossible without damaging the vessel that is currently displayed in the exhibition of the Mosonmagyaróvár museum. The same holds true for the vessel interiors – it was not possible to conduct any other analyses. While additional data on the composition of the organic material inside the vessels would no doubt have been interesting, the soil samples taken several decades ago did not enable further analyses.

Discussion: a feasting event memorialised in the Mosonszentmiklós-Pálmajor deposit

The context

In the light of the context and the finds of the Copper Age pit uncovered at Mosonszentmiklós-Pálmajor, we may confidently assert that the assemblage can be interpreted as a structured deposition (see e.g. CHAPMAN 2000, with further literature): the intact clay horn and the eight intact vessels around it had been placed into the pit on one specific event. Pit 316 lay in an area that lacked houses, and with the exception of a single pit, the other similar pits were also dug in the open area among buildings. The thick, loose, greasy soil layer overlying the pit's floor would suggest that the floor had been lined with a thick organic material, perhaps an animal hide, a woollen blanket, a thick carpet or some other textile. Placed onto the blanket were food remains, intact vessels and at least one but more likely two musical instruments, since the pedestalled vessel was in all likelihood a membrane drum. The area where the organic cover was the thickest was left empty, with at least no ceramic or bone objects. The bovine long bone tucked into the horn and the other bones lying around the vessels create the impression of having been the remains of food consumed by a group of people, while the vessels did not apparently contain any intentionally deposited food.

The type of meat consumed by the participants also reveals much about the feast itself. The fact that cattle was butchered speaks for an out-of-the-common event: cattle has been up to modern times bred mainly for milk and dairy products and to a lesser extent for meat, so cattle meat consumption was usually not part of the every-day-diet (Marciniak 2005; Gillis et al. 2017). Several archaeological and archaeozoological studies have been devoted to the prominent role of cattle and how they became symbols of wealth and prestige in food-producing societies (Bogucki 2011; Russell 2012; Marciniak / Pollard 2015, 752). There is increasing evidence that milk and milk products were the main staples of the diet in daily life (Ebersbach 1996; Helmer / Vigne 2007; Vaiglova et al. 2018) and that cattle were only slaughtered and consumed on exceptional occasions: "Cows would have been social valuables appreciated and circulated during their lifetimes; when they were eaten, large numbers of people got together for a social occasion" (Robb 2007, 153–154).

Now let us have a closer glimpse at the two bones found in the pit. These bones carry crucial information on the extent of the presumed shared consumption and thus on the interpretation of the whole assemblage as a deposition after feasting. They were identified as cattle femur (intact) and cattle tibia (with a broken end). In order to get an impression of the amount of meat, László Bartosiewicz (pers. comm.) estimates that the weight of one femur and tibia makes 9.1 % within the whole excavated skeleton (some decrease in weight due to fossilisation is to be assumed [see also Reichstein 1994]). Based on modern cattle with an average live weight of 600 kg, this would mean 11.2 % for one hind leg, which might reach the weight of 41.5 kg[2]. Regarding the fact that prehistoric cattle were not stall-fed for their meat, this number could be decreased with 30 % but possibly even with 50 %. Taking all circumstances into account, the most precise estimation of the meat that was consumed before the assemblage with the clay horn became buried with the bones was no less than 20.75–30 kg (Bartosiewicz 1988). There is hard proof for the meat being consumed indeed before the deposition and that solely the bones chewed bare had been deposited (instead, for example, of a complete roasted haunch). This is confirmed by the cattle bone tucked into the horn: the detail photo made during the pit's hand excavation *(Fig. 4d)* clearly reveals that a meaty bone would not have fitted inside the opening and that even the bare cattle bone could hardly be squeezed into the horn's slightly curved body. These circumstances can be taken as clear indication that the consumption of the food had occurred immediately before the act of deposition.

We can also surmise other kinds of food, "side dishes" – vegetables, porridge or similar cereals – were consumed together with this large amount of meat. The vessels accompanying the horn and the food rests might also indicate some soup or pottage (unfortunately, since the vessels are lost, no further investigation for any food remains can be carried out).

---

[2] https://extension.tennessee.edu/publications/Documents/PB1822.pdf.

Consequently, counting with an average amount of meat (flesh with bones) suggested for one person, 250 g, together with side dish, the meat would serve a group of 70–80 people at least. Based on the known number and size of the houses in the settlement, the participants may have involved a considerable part of the whole community, where definitely several families must have come together. According to Michael Dietler (2001, 89), feasts can be defined simply by differences in the sheer quantity of food and drink consumed. This criterion is, presented by the above short analysis, fulfilled in the present case.

The interpretation of this assemblage as the imprint of a single event adds flesh to the bones of the dry facts. The kind and amount of meat consumed, the intact vessels and the musical instruments placed in the described way make a kind of deposition likely that was motivated by a special, festive occasion and realised by a large shared consumption. We interpret the assemblage as a deposition of material remains in the aftermath of a feasting event. Several reasons speak for this.

The first interpretation that usually springs to mind when excavating assemblages of this type is that the pit preserves the remains of a food offering, the remains of a sacrifice of some sort. The analysis of the soil samples from the vessels indicated that they had not contained food (or perhaps only some microscopic food remnants at the bottom, but since the vessels are no longer at our disposal, this question cannot be further investigated). The clean bones, devoid of any meat, placed beside the vessels attest to the consumed dishes.

The arguments for a large shared meal are completed with the above calculations on the amount of meat consumed. Furthermore, the probable selection of vegetables and bread or porridge fulfil the criterion for a communal food consumption event with members of several households: this is one of the points often highlighted by anthropologists when defining feasting (Twiss 2008, 419). Paul Halstead (1996) has pointed out that Neolithic stockbreeding, especially cattle raising, called for close cooperation between households, another important argument for bolstering the conjecture that the feast involving the consumption of cattle meat had been the joint festive occasion of several households.

Beverages were also served to accompany the dishes. Some of the vessels, for example the two jugs, were used for pouring or drinking beverages (as noted above, the vessels could not be sampled). It seems likely that food processing such as salting and smoking meat was practiced from the Early Neolithic in the Carpathian Basin (Bánffy 2015), while the fermentation of milk products was similarly a preservation technique that had been known from the earliest Neolithic period (Helmer / Vigne 2007; Evershed et al. 2008). It has been convincingly demonstrated that the fermentation of cereals was practiced before domestication and the transition to a sedentary lifestyle, as was the production and consumption of fermented alcoholic beverages prepared from fruits and grapes (Dietrich et al. 2012). Alcoholic beverages, as frequent requisites of feasting, are generally attested (Dietler 1990; Dietler / Hayden 2001; Hayden 2014). Alcoholic fermentation might have been discovered long before the domestication of plants and animals during the Neolithic, and the fermentation of cereals enriched this scale of plants used (Guerra-Doce 2017). Alcoholic beverages have a privileged role in feasting, as they amplify the important dramaturgical aspects (Dietler 2001, 73). Fermented beverages could have been produced before the invention of pottery during the Neolithic (Vencl 1994, 307; Sherratt 1995) and there are data about fruit wine, also in the Neolithic of the Carpathian basin (Gyulai 2010). That a part of the Mosonszentmiklós vessels had contained alcoholic beverages, seems thus to have some probability.

Further to eating and drinking, the next argument touches upon the clay horn and the possible drum placed as part of the assemblage. The presence of the horn and the tentatively identified drum strongly suggests that the communal food consumption event was enhanced by music. This might sound a courageous assumption, given the generally scarce archaeological data speaking for feasts, and especially, as oral effects are barely attributed to prehistory. However, the deposit of Mosonszentmiklós, made after a community consumption event, does involve a wind instrument (the horn) and possibly also a drum. The range of sounds that could be produced by blowing the horn (and by beating the membrane drum) is not particularly varied. Yet, the interpretation of these finds as merely signalling instruments would plainly contradict their closed archaeological contexts. The idea to give "performances (singing, dancing, music, oratory, etc.)" comes from a most detailed and widely cited table by Katheryn C. Twiss, on "Common aspects of feasting", which she compiled for interpreting feasting beginning as early as the Pre-Pottery Neolithic (TWISS 2008, 420–422). Thus, the idea of placing musical instruments together with paraphernalia of a community event allows the assumption of 'feasting with music' (hence the title of our study; see also Susan Pollock's view on feasting scenes that involve artefacts used like musical instruments: POLLOCK 2003, 25). We can probably conjecture that songs had been chanted during the feast. Regrettably, we shall never know what these songs were about or whether they had been accompanied with dance movements.

The individual characteristics of the deposition might point in various directions and would allow a number of other interpretations, perhaps. Yet, taking all features together into consideration, the remains seen as one deposition after a communal feasting seems a highly logical inference.

In the following, we shall briefly discuss the role of feasting (and, judging from several similar assemblages recovered from pits, recurring feasting events) in the life of the Copper Age communities of western Transdanubia.

Feasting

"Feast" is an event that is used to describe forms of ritual activity that involve a communal consumption of food and drink, not necessarily implying highly elaborate ceremonies or showing 'sacred' characteristics (DIETLER 2001, 65–67). The tracing of feasts in archaeological remains has been barely investigated so far, the main reason being their extremely difficult visibility in the material culture left behind. At this place, we aim to give background information that underpins our hypothesis on the Mosonszentmiklós-Pálmajor assemblage, admitting that the closer content of this event (i. e. the reasons or occasion for the feasting) cannot be defined.

Following the lead of Claude LÉVI-STRAUSS (1983) as well as of Mary DOUGLAS (1975), it has by now become a commonplace that food and eating does not merely serve the sustenance of life but is an important means of social interaction, of building personal networks, and of negotiating and expressing hierarchy in a particular community and in society as a whole: in this sense, feasts are "central arenas of social action that have had a profound impact on the course of historical transformations" (DIETLER / HAYDEN 2001, 16). Feasts, communal eating and drinking, are generally held on special occasions with a specific purpose such as the evocation of past events or the celebration of an important turning point in an individual's or community's life such as initiation or marriage or other rites of passage (DIETLER / HAYDEN 2001, 28). The events of feasting gained an extraordinary role in societies without hierarchy, or in those, which underwent either transformation or endangered times that both need group identity to be strengthened (BENZ / GRAMSCH 2006, 425–426). In many cases, feasting was both the medium and the arena of achieving peace (SAHLINS 2004, 132–133). John Robb, according to whom "cooking in the Neolithic way meant reproducing Neolithic society", confers an even greater significance to the salient elements of feasting (ROBB 2007, 152–158). The completion of major communal activities such as house building, harvesting and the commemoration of ancestors, or perhaps even establishing some form of contact with them, were all occasions for feasting, during which special dishes were served – either in terms of their amount, variety or quality – even if the vessels and other objects used on these occasions were no different from the ones employed in daily life.

As far as could be inferred from the excavated area, the houses of the Mosonszentmiklós-Pálmajor settlement formed distinct clusters. The six pits that can be associated with feasting were not located immediately beside the houses but in the open area between them, meaning that none could be associated with a specific house or household, the implication being that they held the remnants of a joint feasting event. The report on the settlement does not mention any differences between the orientation, size, internal division, furnishings or finds of the houses, and therefore we have no reason to assume that the family or paterfamilias hosting the feast had enjoyed a more prominent social status.

The deposition as the concluding act of the feast and its location are very telling. The pits lying scattered in the open, shared space would imply that the area was vested with a special significance and that the repeated acts of deposition re-affirmed the framework within which the settlement existed, the boundaries of houses and households, and the open zones between them. The location of the six pits would suggest that there was no designated central area for the feasts and that households took turns in hosting them.

Food sharing – portions of beef enough for 70–80 participants, as discussed above – is in itself a potent act for re-affirming the community's cohesion and for negotiating the finer details of social interaction, and the festive outward trappings no doubt enhanced the event. Finally, the ceremonial deposition of the feast's remnants in a pit specially dug for the purpose ensured that the event would be firmly embedded in the community's cultural memory. The similarity of the pits and their carefully deposited assemblages of intact vessels and other objects attest to the norms regulating acts of deposition. The presence of the pits in the shared space preserved the significance of the outstanding event and it is possible that the pits' location had been marked in some manner. It also seems possible that the allotment of the house plots was permanent and that there was no danger of any construction activity in the empty spaces between them the main point is that no buildings were erected over the pits during the Copper Age.

Together with several other complementary rites, feasting was a shared, festive occasion that was usually accompanied by rhythmic music and other sound effects, joint singing and perhaps instrumental music. "Social eating and drinking are universal social bonding activities that trigger the release of endorphins, and are very likely to have included music in some way early on, as they do today all over the world" (KILLIN 2018, 12). Stephen Mithen described joint singing and recitations accompanied by rhythmic music and perhaps rhythmic movement as a major stimulus to human cognitive and emotional development from the Middle Palaeolithic onward (MITHEN 2007). Later descriptions of feasts from periods with written records often mention that they oft-times involved the theatrical re-enactment of a legend, an ancestor myth or an emotional narrative, often with dancing and joint singing.

On the testimony of the Mosonszentmiklós assemblage, the community's feasts were quite certainly accompanied by music: the horn's deep strong voice can still be sounded today. The vessel beside it, interpreted as a drum, had been the instrument for providing a constant rhythmic background beat. The changing rhythm indicated the transition from one phase to the next during the feast. As Anthony Jackson noted, "a change of rhythm is far more significant than a change of melody" (JACKSON 1968, 296) and has a greater impact on the audience. Feasting thus encapsulated both permanence and rhythmic change and its phases (especially if held as part of rites of passage: cf. Gennep 1960). In contrast to the horn, which emits a single deep basic sound, the dual musical accompaniment expressed the dual nature of feasting.

Conclusion: shared food, shared tunes, shared memories

The context and the finds of Pit 316 uncovered at Mosonszentmiklós-Pálmajor both conform to the material correlates of feasting, which are as follows (Twiss 2008, tab. 1): the consumption of a considerable amount of cattle, a food not generally eaten as part of daily meals in larger quantities; the intact vessel set that included jugs, which had perhaps contained alcoholic beverage(s); the ceramic horn and a possible membrane drum, the material evidence of the musical accompaniment, alongside the remains of food and drink, and finally, the remains of the feast had been carefully deposited beside each other in a pit lined with some thick textile or fur. It must be noted here that the ritual deposition of the food remains, the vessels used during the feast, and the other paraphernalia in pits of the same size and form specifically dug for this purpose indicates that feasts were periodically, possibly regularly held events, rather than a single exceptional occasion. Six pits of this type were uncovered in the investigated area, although there were probably many more on the entire settlement.

Activities performed regularly and in the same manner associated with non-quotidian tasks are more than simple customs because they are embedded in social tradition to the extent that the repeated activity becomes powerful in its own right. Thus, a series of actions performed repeatedly, i.e. ritual activity, is all-important in a community's life (Bourdieu 1977, 166).

Taken together, the Mosonszentmiklós assemblage fulfils the five main criteria for defining a feasting event to the following extent (Dietler 2001, 91):

1. *Spatial distinctions:* the deposition among houses, but at some distance in an open, shared space, speaks for a meal for several households and so might be the venue; yet, the exact place of the shared consumption cannot be exactly said.
2. *Temporal distinctions:* no data regarding e.g. the order of meals, but important data speak for a full synchrony between the archaeological material of the assemblage in the pit and the houses around.
3. *Qualitative distinctions:* we can define the kind of meat and the possible side dish variety, the possible consumption of alcoholic beverages. The are no hints on the customs of consumption, for example, on the order in which the participant (males? females? hierarchy?) are allowed to consume.
4. *Quantitative distinctions:* we do have reliable calculations for a meal serving at least 70 participants.
5. *Behavioural distinctions:* the clay horn and the possible drum speak for actions pointing beyond mere eating and drinking. Further, the reason for or type of the feasting remains mostly unknown. The only exception might be lying in the several similar depositions among houses in the settlements, which speaks for regularity.

Consequently, while the interpretation of the pits, among them of Pit 316, is unambiguous, the custom of deposition following a feast reveals little about the community's social relations. The location of the houses suggests that the shared space was the scene of feasts shared by several households, but it remains unclear whether the feast marked a festive event for the entire community. The remains offer no clues as to whether all occupants of the houses partook in the feast, whether there was an individual or a small group of people, perhaps one or several families with a more prominent role who carved up and distributed the meat, who blew the horn, who recited the legends and myths associated with the ritual, and who performed the act of deposition. The distinct location of the pits conveys the impression that even if each feast did have a master of ceremonies, it might have been a different person or persons on each occasion, perhaps the occupant(s) of the house hosting the feast. As regards the existence of a social hierarchy in the Neolithic of the Carpathian Basin, there is evidence for some stratification from the early 5th millennium onward (Siklósi 2013); however, the deposits from Mosonszentmiklós-Pálmajor offer few clues in this respect. One of the main purposes of the deposition of the paraphernalia of the feast and of the food remains may have been memory-building. The maintenance of community memory was no doubt essential in an age when a human generation was much shorter than today and when it played a much more prominent role in ensuring the community's continuity and survival by reinforcing adherence to social norms and customs.

Finally, it should be recalled that the material correlates of countless similar uncustomary activities concealed in regular pits are known from the western Lengyel complex, including the traditions of the direct Lengyel descendants, from western Hungary, eastern Austria, south-western Slovakia, and southern Moravia. In the overwhelming majority of cases, as for example at Balatonmagyaród-Hídvégpuszta, the excavated features also included human remains, often partial or multiple burials, and these pits were therefore interpreted within the framework of mortuary contexts (Bánffy 1986; 1990/1991, with further literature), even though the practice of deposition in a regular pit can in certain cases have a relevance beyond mortuary archaeology. In other cases, contexts reflecting ritual activity as at Hluboké Masúfky (Altgräfin / Vildomec 1936/1937), where three fragments of the same figurine were deposited in three pits lying far from each other, a clear instance of deliberate fragmentation, became the springboard of other important studies (Chapman / Gaydarska 2007). However, this is perhaps the first time that indubitable indications of a feasting event could be observed in a closed context. It is our hope that the detailed description and discussion of the ceramic horn and the associated finds from Mosonszentmiklós-Pálmajor will contribute to the recognition of similar assemblages and contexts on other sites. Thus, the present study is a contribution to the growing attestations of the prehistoric tradition of feasting.

Acknowledgments

We would like to thank Andrea Vaday for the drawing of the pit during the excavation, Ferenc Karasz for the video documentation and the excavation plans as well as Éva Csapó, who hand-excavated the feature for providing additional information that clarified various details. We are grateful to Gábor Kalla for the stimulating discussions and his insights on prehistoric feasting, to Timothy Darvill and Ricardo Eichmann for sharing their knowledge on music archaeology and their advice. Grateful thanks to László Bartosiewicz for sharing biometrical data on the cattle bones and for estimating the meat consumed, to Tamás Czuppon, Éva Ágnes Nyerges, Balázs Gusztáv Mende and Isabel Hohle for their logistic and other help, to Melani Podgorelec for the geochemical analyses, and to Astrid Stobbe for the soil and botanical analyses. Last but not least, grateful thanks to Alexander Gramsch for his useful comments and suggestions that improved the text.

References

Ad-hoc-AG Boden 2005
  Bundesanstalt für Geowissenschaften und Rohstoffe / Staatliche Geologische Dienste der Bundesrepublik Deutschland (Ad-Hoc-Arbeitsgruppe Boden) (eds), Bodenkundliche Kartieranleitung[5] (Hannover 2005).

Altgräfin / Vildomec 1936/1937
  E. Altgräfin / F. Vildomec, Ein wichtiges neolithisches Idol aus Mähren. Jahrb. Prähist. u. Ethnogr. Kunst 2, 1936/1937, 32–36.

Bánffy 1985
  E. Bánffy, Kultikus rendeltetésű leletegyüttes a Kis-Balaton középső rézkorából [A Middle Copper Age cult assemblage from the Little Balaton Region]. Arch. Ért. 112,2, 1985, 187–192.

Bánffy 1986
  E. Bánffy, Cultic finds from the Middle Copper Age of Hungary – connections to South East Europe. In: A. Bonanno (ed.), Archaeology and Fertility Cult in the Ancient Mediterranean. Papers Presented at the First International Conference on "Archaeology of the Ancient Mediterranean", Malta, 2–5 September 1985 (Amsterdam 1986) 69–77.

Bánffy 1990/1991
  E. Bánffy, Cult and archaeological context in Central and South East Europe in the Neolithic and Chalcolithic. Antaeus 19/20, 1990/1991, 183–250.

Bánffy 1993
  E. Bánffy, A Balaton-Lasinja-kultúra leletei Balatonmagyaród-Homoki-dűlőről [Funde der Balaton-Lasinja-Kultur in Balatonmagyaród-Homoki-dűlő]. Zalai Múz. 5, 1993, 239–250.

Bánffy 1994
  E. Bánffy, Transdanubia and Eastern Hungary in the Early Copper Age. Jósa András Múz. Évk. 36, 1994, 291–296.

Bánffy 1996a
  E. Bánffy, South West Transdanubia as a mediating area. On the cultural history of the Early and Middle Chalcolithic. In: B. M. Szőke (ed.), Archaeology and settlement history in the Hahót Basin South-West Hungary. From the Neolithic to the Roman Age. Antaeus 22, 1996, 157–196.

Bánffy 1996b
  E. Bánffy, Über den Ausklang der Lengyel-Kultur in Transdanubien. In: T. Kovács (ed.), Neuere Daten zur Siedlungsgeschichte und Chronologie der Kupferzeit des Karpatenbeckens. Inv. Praehist. Hungariae 7 (Budapest 1996) 11–28.

Bánffy 2001
  E. Bánffy, Transdanubien: Handelswege und Neolithisierung. In: R. M. Boehmer / J. Maran (eds), Lux Orientis. Archäologie zwischen Asien und Europa. Festschrift für Harald Hauptmann zum 75. Geburtstag. Internat. Arch. Stud. Honoraria 12 (Rahden / Westf. 2001) 21–26.

Bánffy 2015
  E. Bánffy, The beginnings of salt exploitation in the Carpathian Basin (6th–5th Millennium BC). Doc. Praehist. 42, 2015, 1–14.

Bánffy et al. 2016
  E. Bánffy / A. Osztás / K. Oross / I. Zalai-Gaál / T. Marton / É. Á. Nyerges / K. Köhler / A. Bayliss / D. Hamilton / A. Whittle, The Alsónyék story: towards the history of a persistent place. Ber. RGK 94, 1985, 283–318.

Barna et al. 2019
  J. P. Barna / G. Serlegi / Z. Fullár / E. Bánffy, A circular enclosure and settlement from the mid-fifth millennium BC at Balatonmagyaród-Hídvégpuszta. In: E. Bánffy / J. P. Barna (eds), "Trans Lacum Pelsonem". Prähistorische Forschungen in Südwestungarn (5500–500 v. Chr.). Prehistoric Research in South-Western Hungary (5500–500 BC). Castellum Pannonicum Pelsonense 7 (Rahden / Westf. 2019) 117–160.

Bartosiewicz 1988
  L. Bartosiewicz, Biometrics at an early medieval butchering site in Hungary. In: E. A. Slater / J. O. Tate (eds), Science and Archaeology Glasgow 1987. Proceedings of a Conference on the Application of Scientific Techniques to Archaeology, Glasgow, September 1987. BAR Brit. Ser. 196 (Oxford 1988) 361–367.

Benz / Gramsch 2006
    M. Benz / A. Gramsch, Zur sozio-politischen Bedeutung von Festen. Eine Einführung anhand von Beispielen aus dem Alten Orient und Europa. Ethnogr.-Arch. Zeitschr. 47,4, 2006, 417–437.

Bogucki 2011
    P. Bogucki, How wealth happened in Neolithic Central Europe. Journal World Prehist. 4,2/3, 2011, 107–115.

Bondár 2015
    M. Bondár, The Late Copper Age Cemetery at Pilismarót-Basaharc. István Torma's Excavations (1967, 1969–1972) (Budapest 2015).

Bourdieu 1977
    P. Bourdieu, Outline of a Theory of Practice. Cambridge Stud. Social Anthr. 16 (Cambridge 1977).

Chapman 2000
    J. Chapman, Pit-digging and structured deposition in the Neolithic and Copper Age of Central and Eastern Europe. Proc. Prehist. Soc. 61, 2000, 51–67.

Chapman / Gaydarska 2007
    J. Chapman / B. Gaydarska, Parts and Wholes. Fragmentation in Prehistoric Context (Oxford 2007).

Coularou 2007
    J. Coularou, Les instruments de musique en milieu chalcolithique, le cor de la grotte de jarre (Ardèche). Rev. Ardèche Arch. 24, 2007, 19–25.

Coularou et al. 1981
    J. Coularou / J. Vatou / A. Vincent, Une trompe en ceramique dans un niveau chalcolithique (abri no 7 de Brugas, Vallabrix, Gard). Bull. Soc. Préhist. Francaise 78,4, 1981, 106–107.

Clodoré-Tissot 2010
    T. Clodoré-Tissot, Archéo-music. The reconstruction of prehistoric musical instruments: hypothesis and conclusions in experimental music-archaeology. Experimentale Arch. Europa 9, 2010, 31–45.

Dietler 1990
    M. Dietler, Driven by drink. The role of drinking in the political economy and the case of Iron Age France. Journal Anthr. Arch. 9, 1990, 352–406.

Dietler 2001
    M. Dietler, Theorizing the feast. Rituals of consumption, commensal politics, and power in African contexts. In: Dietler / Hayden 2001, 65–114

Dietler / Hayden 2001
    M. Dietler / B. Hayden (eds), Feasts: Archaeological and Ethnographic Perspectives on Food, Politics, and Power (Washington 2001).

Dietrich et al. 2012
    O. Dietrich / M. Heun / J. Notroff / K. Schmidt / M. Zarnkow, The role of cult and feasting in the emergence of Neolithic communities. Antiquity 86, 2012, 679–695. doi: https://doi.org/10.1017/S0003598X00047840.

Douglas 1975
    M. Douglas, Implicit Meanings (London 1975).

Dumitrescu 1985
    V. Dumitrescu, Vorgeschichtliche Kunst Rumäniens. Rumän. Kunst- u. Kulturtrad. (Bucarest 1985).

Ebersbach 1996
    R. Ebersbach, Von Bauern und Rindern. Eine Ökosystemanalyse zur Bedeutung der Rinderhaltung in bäuerlichen Gesellschaften als Grundlage zur Modellbildung im Neolithikum. Basler Beitr. Arch. 15 (Basel 1996).

Egry 2003
    M. I. Egry, Rézkori településrészlet Mosonszentmiklós-Egyéni földek lelőhelyen [Das Detail einer kupferzeitlichen Siedlung auf dem Fundort Mosonszentmiklós-Egyéni földek]. Móra Ferenc Múz. Évk. Stud. Arch. 9, 2003, 95–100.

Éri et al. 1969
    I. Éri / M. Kelemen / P. Németh (eds), Veszprém megye régészeti topográfiája a Veszprémi járás. Magyarország Rég. Topogr. [Arch. Topogr. Hungary] 2 (Budapest 1969).

Evershed et al. 2008
    R. P. Evershed / S. Payne / A. G. Sherratt / M. S. Copley / J. Coolidge / D. Urem-Kotsu / K. Kotsakis / M. Özdoğan / A. E. Özdoğan / O. Nieuwenhuyse / P. M. M. G. Akkermans / D. Bailey / R.-R. Andreescu / S. Campbell / Sh. Farid /

I. Hodder / N. Yalman / M. Özbasaran / E. Biçakci / Y. Garfinkel / Th. Levy / M. M. Burton, Earliest date for milk use in the Near East and southeastern Europe linked to cattle herding. Nature 455, 2008, 528–531. doi: https://doi.org/10.1038/nature07180.

Figler 1996
A. Figler, Mosonszentmiklós-Pálmajor. Az 1993. év régészeti kutatásai. Rég. Füzetek Ser. 1,47, 1996, 18–19.

Figler 1997a
A. Figler, Mosonszentmiklós-Pálmajor. Az 1994. év régészeti kutatásai. Rég. Füzetek Ser. 1,48, 1997, 19–20.

Figler 1997b
A. Figler, Mosonszentmiklós-Pálmajor. Az 1995. év régészeti kutatásai. Rég. Füzetek Ser. 1,49, 1997, 19–20.

Gennep 1960
A. van Gennep, The Rites of Passage (London 1960).

Gillis et al. 2017
R. E. Gillis / L. Kovačiková / St. Bréhard / E. Guthmann / I. Vostrovská / H. Nohálová / R.-M. Arbogast / L. Domboróczki / J. Pechtl / A. Anders / A. Marciniak / A. Tresset / J.-D. Vigne, The evolution of dual meat and cattle husbandry in Linearbandkeramik societies. Proc. Royal Soc. B (Biol. Scien.) 284, 2017, pArt. 0905. doi: https://doi.org/10.1098/rspb.2017.0905.

Guerra-Doce 2015
E. Guerra-Doce, The origins of inebriation: archaeological evidence of the consumption of fermented beverages and drugs in prehistoric Eurasia. Journal Arch. Method and Theory 22, 751–782.

Gyulai 2010
F. Gyulai, Archaeobotany in Hungary. Seed, Fruit, Food and Beverages Remains in the Carpathian Basin: an Archaeobotanical Investigation of Plant Cultivation and Ecology from the Neolithic until the Late Middle Ages. Archaeolingua 21 (Budapest 2010).

Halstead 1996
P. L. J. Halstead, The development of agriculture and pastoralism in Greece: when, how, who and what? In: D. H. Harris (ed.), The Origins and Spread of Agriculture and Pastoralism in Eurasia (London 1996) 296–309.

Hayden 2014
B. Hayden, The Power of Feasts. From Prehistory to the Present (New York 2014).

Helmer / Vigne 2007
D. Helmer / J.-D. Vigne, Was milk a "secondary product" in the Old World Neolithisation process? Its role in the domestication of cattle, sheep and goats. Anthropozoologica 42,2, 2007, 9–40.

Holliday 2004
V. T. Holliday, Soils in Archaeological Research (Oxford 2004).

Horváth 2014
T. Horváth, The Prehistoric settlement at Balatonőszöd-Temetői-dűlő. Varia Arch. Hungarica 29 (Budapest 2014).

Jackson 1968
A. Jackson, Sound and ritual. Man N. S. 3,2, 1968, 293–299.

Kalicz 1973
N. Kalicz, Über die chronologische Stellung der Balaton-Gruppe in Ungarn. In: B. Chropovsky (ed.), Symposium über die Entstehung und Chronologie der Badener Kultur (Bratislava 1973) 131–166.

Kalicz 1980
N. Kalicz, The Balaton-Lasinja culture groups in Western Hungary, Austria and Northwestern Yugoslavia concerning their distribution and origin. Journal Indoeuropean Stud. 8, 1980, 245–271.

Kalicz 2001
N. Kalicz, Die Protoboleráz-Phase an der Grenze von zwei Epochen. In: P. Roman / S. Diamandi (eds), Cernavodă III-Boleráz. Ein vorgeschichtliches Phänomen zwischen dem Oberrhein und der unteren Donau. Symposium Mangalia / Neptun (18.–24. Oktober 1999). Forschungsprogramm "Die Donau – Achse von Zivilisationen". Stud. Danubiana 2 (Bucarest 2001) 385–435.

Killin 2018
A. Killin, The origins of music: Evidence, theory, and prospects. Music & Science 1, 2018, 1–23. doi: https://doi.org/10.1177/2059204317751971.

Knipl 2009a
I. Knipl, Újabb leletek a császártöltési határban. Medinától Etéig. Szentes 2009, 145–147.

Knipl 2009b
I. Knipl, Császártöltés régészeti topográfiája II (Rézkor, Bronzkor). Cumania 24, 2009, 91–133.

Krauss 2014
R. Krauss, Ovčarovo-Gorata. Eine frühneolithische Siedlung in Nordostbulgarien. Arch. Eurasien 29 (Bonn 2014).

Lichardus / Vladár 1964
J. Lichardus / J. Vladár, Zum Problem der Ludanice-Gruppe in der Slowakei. Slovenská Arch. 12, 1964, 69–162.

Lévi-Strauss 1983
C. Lévi-Strauss, The Raw and the Cooked (Chicago 1983).

Link 2006
Th. Link, Das Ende der neolithischen Tellsiedlungen. Ein Kulturgeschichtliches Phänomen des 5. Jahrtausends v. Chr. im Karpatenbecken. Universitätsforsch. Prähist. Arch. 134 (Bonn 2006).

Lustig 2002
M. Lustig, Die neolithischen Tontrommeln im mitteldeutschen und norddeutschen Raum [The Neolithic clay-drums in the area of Middle and Northern Germany]. In: E. Hickmann / A. D. Kilmer / R. Eichmann (eds), The Archaeology of Sound: Origin and Organisation. Stud. Musikarch. 3 (Rahden / Westf. 2002) 171–186.

Marciniak 2005
A. Marciniak, Placing Animals in the Neolithic. Social Zooarchaeology of Prehistoric Farming Communities (London 2005).

Marciniak / Pollard 2015
A. Marciniak / J. Pollard, Animals and social relations. In C. Fowler / J. Harding / D. Hofmann (eds), The Oxford Handbook of Neolithic Europe (Oxford 2015) 745–759. doi: https://doi.org/10.1093/oxfordhb/9780199545841.013.002.

Middleton / Price 1996
W. D. Middleton / T. D. Price, Identification of activity areas by multi-element characterization of sediments from modern and archaeological house floors using inductively coupled plasma-atomic emission spectroscopy. Journal Arch. Scien. 23, 1996, 673–687.

Mithen 2007
St. Mithen, The Singing Neanderthals. The Origins of Music, Language, Mind, and Body (Cambridge 2007).

Oross et al. 2011
K. Oross / T. Marton / A. Whittle / R. E. M. Hedges / L. J. E. Cramp, Siedlung der Balaton-Lasinja-Kultur in Balatonszárszó-Kis-Erdei-dűlő. In: J. Šuteková / P. Pavúk / P. Kalábková / B. Kovár (eds), Panta Rhei. Studies on the Chronology and Cultural Development of South-Eastern and Central Europe in Earlier Prehistory. Presented to Juraj Pavúk on the Occasion of his 75th Birthday. Stud. Arch. et Medievalia 11 (Bratislava 2011) 161–187.

Pollock 2003
S. Pollock, Feasts, funerals, and fast food. In: T. L. Bray (ed.), The Archaeology and Politics of Food and Feasting in Early States and Empires (Boston 2003) 17–38. doi: https://doi.org/10.1007/978-0-306-48246-5_2.

Pomberger 2016
B. M. Pomberger, Wiederentdeckte Klänge. Musikinstrumente und Klangobjekte vom Neolithikum bis zur Römischen Kaiserzeit im mittleren Donauraum. Universitätsforsch. Prähist. Arch. 280 (Bonn 2016).

Raczky / Siklósi 2013
P. Raczky / Zs. Siklósi, Reconsideration of the Copper Age chronology of the eastern Carpathian Basin: a Bayesian approach. Antiquity 87, 2013, 555–573. doi: https://doi.org/10.1017/S0003598X00049127.

Reichstein 1994
H. Reichstein, Die Säugetiere und Vögel aus der frühgeschichtlicher Wurt Elisenhof. Stud. Küstenarch. Schleswig-Holstein A6 (Frankfurt a. M. 1994).

Robb 2007
J. Robb, The Early Mediterranean Village. Agency, Material Culture and Social Change in Neolithic Italy (Cambridge 2007).

Russell 1999
> N. Russell, Yugoslavia. In: J. Robb (ed.), Material Symbols. Culture and Economy in Prehistory. Centre Arch. Investigations Occasional Paper 26 (Carbondale 1999) 153–172.

Russell 2012
> N. Russell, Social Zooarchaeology. Humans and Animals in Prehistory (Cambridge, New York 2012).

Ruttkay 1976
> E. Ruttkay, Beitrag zum Problem des Epi-Lengyel-Horizontes in Österreich. In: H. Mitscha-Märheim / H. Friesinger / H. Kerchler (eds), Festschrift für Richard Pittioni zum siebzigsten Geburtstag. Teil 1. Urgeschichte Arch. Austriaca, Beih. 13 (Vienna 1976) 285–319.

Sahlins 2004
> M. Sahlins, Stone Age Economics (Chicago, New York 2004).

Schlichtling et al. 1995
> E. Schlichting / H.-P. Blume / K. Stahr, Bodenkundliches Praktikum. Eine Einführung in pedologisches Arbeiten für Ökologen, insbesondere Land- und Forstwirte und für Geowissenschaftler² (Berlin, Wien 1995).

Sherratt 1995
> A. Sherratt, Alcohol and its alternatives: symbol and substance in early Old World cultures. In J. Goodman / P. Lovejoy / A. Sherratt (eds), Consuming Habits. Drugs in History and Anthropology (London 1995) 11–46.

Siklósi 2013
> Zs. Siklósi, Traces of Social Inequality during the Late Neolithic in the Eastern Carpathian Basin. Diss. Pannonicae Ser. 4,3 (Budapest 2013).

Simon 1990
> K. H. Simon, Der Stand und die Aufgaben der Neolithikum- und Kupferzeitforschung im Komitat Zala. Zalai Múz. 2, 1990, 47–66.

Stadler 1995
> P. Stadler, Ein Beitrag zur Absolutchronologie des Neolithikums aufgrund der ¹⁴C-Daten in Österreich. In: E. Lenneis / Ch. Neugebauer-Maresch / E. Ruttkay (eds), Jungsteinzeit im Osten Österreichs. Wiss. Schriftenr. Niederösterreich 102/105, Forschber. Ur- u. Frühgesch. 17 (St. Pölten 1995) 210–224.

Stadler / Kotova 2010
> P. Stadler / N. Kotova, Early Neolithic settlement from Brunn-Wolfholz in Lower Austria and the problem of the origin of (western) LBK. In: J. K. Kozłowski / P. Raczky (eds), Neolithisation of the Carpathian Basin. Northernmost Distribution of the Starčevo / Körös Culture (Kraków, Budapest 2010) 325–348.

Szabó 1997
> J. J. Szabó, Szihalom-Sóhajtó. Rézkori temető a Kr. e. IV. évezredből [Copper Age Cemetery from the 4th millennium BC]. In: P. Raczky / T. Kovács / A. Anders (eds), Utak a múltba: az M3-as autópálya régészeti leletmentései [Paths into the Past. Rescue Excavations on the M3 Motorway. Exhibition] (Budapest 1997) 54–55.

Torma 1973
> I. Torma, Die Boleráz-Gruppe in Ungarn. In: B. Chropovsky (ed.), Symposium über die Entstehung und Chronologie der Badener Kultur (Bratislava 1973) 483–512.

Twiss 2008
> K. C. Twiss, Transformations in an early agricultural society: Feasting in the southern Levantine Pre-Pottery Neolithic. Journal Anthr. Arch. 27, 2008, 418–442.

Virág 1995
> M. Zs. Virág, Die Hochkupferzeit in der Umgebung von Budapest und in NO-Transdanubien (Das Ludanice-Problem). Acta Arch. Acad. Scien. Hungaricae 47, 1995, 61–94.

Virág / Figler 2007
> M. Zs. Virág / A. Figler, Data on the settlement history of the Late Lengyel period of Transdanubia on the basis of two sites from the Kisalföld (Small Hungarian Plain). A preliminary evaluation of the sites Győr-Szabadrétdomb and Mosonszentiklós-Pálmajor. In: J. K. Kozlowski / P. Raczky (eds), The Lengyel, Polgár and Related Cultures in the Middle / Late Neolithic in Central Europe [Symposium Krakow, 7th–12th March 2006] (Krakow 2007) 345–364.

VAIGLOVA et al. 2018
P. VAIGLOVA / P. HALSTEAD / M. PAPPA / S. TRANTAPHYLOOU / S. M. VALAMOTI / J. EVANS / R. FRASE / P. KARKANAS / A. KAY / J. LEE-THORP / A. BOGAARD, Of cattle and feasts. Multi-isotope investigation of animal husbandry and communal feasting at Neolithic Makriyalos, northern Greece. Public Library Scien. One 13,6, pArt. e0194474, 2018. doi: https://doi.org/10.1371/journal.pone.0194474.

VENCL 1994
S. VENCL, The archaeology of thirst. Journal European Arch. 2, 1994, 299–326.

Abstract: Feasting with music? A musical instrument and its context from the later 5th millennium BC Hungary

Feasts, occasions of festive commensality, play a prominent role in every human society, and prehistory was no exception. An assemblage suggesting a deposition act performed after feasting came to light from a closed context on a Copper Age site dating from the later 5th millennium BC in the north-westerly region of the Carpathian Basin. One of the pits among the many similar features lying between the houses of the settlement investigated at Mosonszentmiklós-Pálmajor, Hungary, contained a remarkable set of finds: the pit's floor was covered with a greasy, blackish organic layer, onto which were deposited cattle long bones and intact vessels, one interpreted as a drum, alongside an almost intact clay horn, which can still be played as a musical instrument today. The assessment of the musical instrument(s), the other finds and of the overall context was undertaken together with the evaluation of the radiocarbon dates and the botanical analysis of the soil samples taken from the vessels, which strongly indicated that the assemblage can be interpreted as a deposit made after feasting.

Zusammenfassung: Feasting mit Musik? Ein Musikinstrument und sein Kontext aus dem späten 5. Jahrtausend v. Chr. aus Ungarn

Feste, Anlässe festlicher Geselligkeit, spielen in jeder menschlichen Gesellschaft eine prominente Rolle, und auch die Vorgeschichte bildet hier keine Ausnahme. Aus einem geschlossenen Befund einer kupferzeitlichen Fundstelle aus dem späten 5. Jahrtausend v. Chr. im nordwestlichen Karpatenbecken wurde eine Assemblage geborgen, die auf einen Deponierungsakt nach einem Festmahl hindeutet. Eine der vielen Gruben zwischen den Häusern der untersuchten Siedlung in Mosonszentmiklós-Pálmajor, Ungarn, enthielt ein bemerkenswertes Fundensemble: Der Boden der Grube war mit einer schmierigen, schwärzlichen organischen Schicht bedeckt, auf der Langknochen von Rindern und intakte Gefäße deponiert waren, eines davon mit einer möglichen Trommel, daneben ein fast intaktes Tonhorn, das noch heute als Musikinstrument gespielt werden kann. Die Bewertung des Musikinstruments bzw. der Musikinstrumente, der anderen Funde und des Gesamtzusammenhangs erfolgte zusammen mit der Auswertung der Radiokarbondaten und der botanischen Analyse der aus den Gefäßen entnommenen Bodenproben, die deutlich darauf hinweisen, dass die Assemblage als Deponierung nach einem Festmahl interpretiert werden kann.

Résumé : Festoiement en musique ? Un instrument de musique et son contexte à la fin du cinquième millénaire av. J.-C. en Hongrie

Les fêtes, occasions de convivialité festive, jouent un rôle déterminant dans les sociétés et la préhistoire n'échappe pas à la règle. Un contexte clos d'un site chalcolithique de la fin du cinquième millénaire av. J.-C. situé dans le Nord-Ouest du bassin des Carpates a livré un ensemble indiquant le dépôt d'objets à la suite d'un repas festif. L'une des nombreuses fosses identifiées entre les maisons de l'habitat étudié à Mosonszentmiklós-Pálmajor (Hongrie) contenait un étrange ensemble : Le fond de la fosse était recouvert par une couche organique grasse, noirâtre, sur laquelle reposaient des os longs de bovins et des vases intacts, dont un avec un éventuel tambour, à côté une corne en argile presque intacte dont on peut encore jouer aujourd'hui. L'évaluation de l'instrument de musique, respectivement des instruments de musique, des autres objets et du contexte global fut menée parallèlement à l'exploitation des données radiocarbone et de l'analyse botanique des échantillons de terrain extraits des vases. Ces échantillons révèlent clairement que l'ensemble peut être interprété comme un dépôt réalisé à la suite d'un repas festif.

Y. G.

Addresses of authors:

Eszter Bánffy
Römisch-Germanische Kommission
des Deutschen Archäologischen Instituts
Palmengartenstr. 10–12
DE–60325 Frankfurt am Main
eszter.banffy@dainst.de
https://orcid.org/0000-0001-5156-826X

Ildikó Egry
1 Main Street
Newstead
Melrose
GB–Roxburghshire TD6 9DX
egry.ildiko@gmail.com

References of figures:
Figs 1; 14; 15: authors. – *Figs 2–3:* authors and Virág 2007 (permission granted). – *Fig. 4:* photos A. Figler. – *Fig. 5:* graphics A. Vaday. – *Figs 6–8:* photos F. Karasz; graphics Virág 2007 (permissions granted). – *Fig. 9:* photos authors. – *Fig. 10:* authors; K. Ruppel / O. Wagner, RGK. – *Fig. 11:* photos Dobó István Vármúzeum, Eger; G. Szinok. – *Fig. 12:* I. Knipl (permission granted). – *Fig. 13:* authors, Dobó István Vármúzeum, Eger; K. Ruppel / O. Wagner, RGK.

The Etruscan roots of the Reinheim armring

By Daniel W. Moore

Keywords: La Tène period / Reinheim / Potnia Theron / Etruscan / Waldalgesheim
Schlagworte: La-Tène-Zeit / Reinheim / Potnia theron / Etrusker / Waldalgesheim
Mots clés: époque laténienne / Reinheim / Potnia théron / Étrusques / Waldalgesheim

Introduction

The Potnia Theron was a popular motif in the ancient world that depicted a goddess holding onto or surrounded by a variety of animals. It originated in the Near East in the 4th millennium BC and was modelled after the motif of the 'Master of Animals', a male deity depicted subduing wild animals. The motif normally consisted of a female goddess or demon standing between two wild animals, often felines but also birds, deer, or fantastic beasts. The Potnia Theron usually demonstrated mastery over creatures by holding or touching their tails or necks or simply standing between them[1]. This motif was later adopted by both Greek and Etruscan artisans for their own goddesses during the Iron Age[2]. In the late Hallstatt and early La Tène period, Celtic artisans also paired female deities with animals, but the rationale remains obscure. In this paper, I would like to explore the origin of this motif and its possible transmission into central Europe by analysing specific iconographic elements of a gold armring recovered from an early La Tène grave at Reinheim, Germany.

The La Tène period tumulus was discovered in 1954 during rescue excavations in the village of Reinheim (Saarpfalz-Kreis). The burial within the tumulus contained a number of artefacts, including a gold neckring, two gold armrings, two gold finger rings, and two gold and iron fibulae. Two other bronze fibulae, a bronze mirror, and over a hundred glass and amber beads were also found in the tomb chamber. Next to the burial were feasting and drinking vessels: a pair of gold mounts for drinking horns, a pair of bronze basins, and a bronze spouted flagon *(Röhrenkanne)*[3]. The presence of a mirror led the excavators to conclude that this was the grave of a wealthy Celtic female whom they called the 'Princess of Reinheim'[4]. The neckring and the right armring of the deceased *(Fig. 1)* were decorated with figures on both ends that appear to have been inspired by the motif of the Potnia Theron – 'the Mistress of Animals'.

On the Reinheim rings, the beardless, presumably female, figures on the neckring *(Fig. 2)* and armring *(Fig. 3)* have a bird of prey[5] sitting atop their heads. At each end of the ring are 'pommels' or 'balusters', beneath which the faces of owls or lions peer out. These 'pommels' or 'balusters' appear on a number of Celtic rings decorated with human heads or faces and have been interpreted as symbols signaling the depiction of deities or heroes[6].

---

[1] BARCLAY 2001, 373–374.
[2] SPARTZ 1962, 5; ICARD-GIANOLIO 1997, 1026.
[3] KELLER 1965, 13–30.
[4] KELLER 1955, 33.
[5] KELLER (1965, 31) identified it as an eagle but Ross (1967, 273) suggested an owl.
[6] LENERZ-DE WILDE 2006, 343; GUGGISBERG 2010, 208.

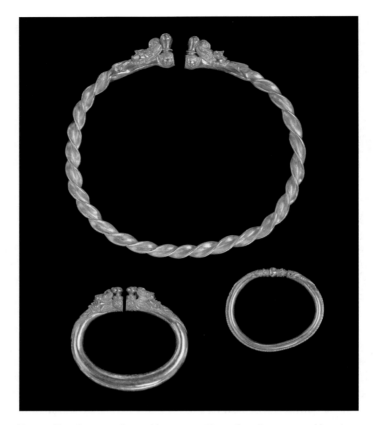

Fig. 1. Reinheim neckring (diameter 172 mm), right armring (diameter 80.5 mm), and left arming (diameter 69 mm).

If these human figures on the Reinheim neckring and armring do indeed belong to the supernatural realm, their depiction with animals suggests an association with the Potnia Theron. That this motif was known in central Europe as early as the 6th century BC is evidenced by its appearance on the handle of the famous Grächwil hydria, a bronze vessel recovered from a Hallstatt grave at Grächwil, Switzerland *(Fig. 4)*.

The hydria was an Italian import, assembled in northern Italy but likely made by Greek craftsmen from the Peloponnese or the Spartan colony of Taranto[7]. Similar to the Reinheim rings, the Potnia Theron on the Grächwil hydria has a raptor bird perched above her head and a coterie of animals on either side, including lions. Although the excavator at Reinheim, Josef Keller, viewed the neckring and the armring as purely Celtic creations, he believed that the Grächwil hydria must have served as a precursor to them[8]. More recently, Rudolf Echt, in his comprehensive study of the Reinheim burial, suggested that Greek artistic influences on the Reinheim rings were more pronounced, citing not only the Grächwil hydria but also the Francois Vase and a gold pendant from Rhodes, which were both 6th century BC artefacts displaying the Greek goddess Artemis as a Potnia Theron[9].

---

[7] For an overview of different opinions on the origin of the hydria, see Frey / Frey 1998, 528.

[8] Keller 1965, 31; see also Guggisberg 2010, 223; Verger 1991, 10; Gran Aymerich 2006, 36.

[9] Echt 2000, 265; Echt 1999, 45.

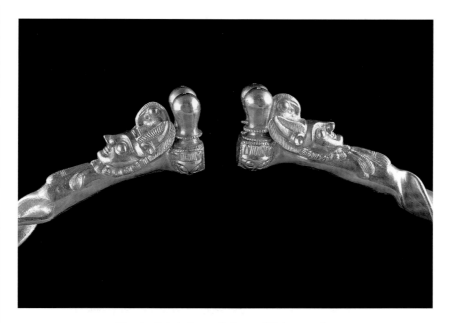

Fig. 2. Reinheim neckring. – Without scale.

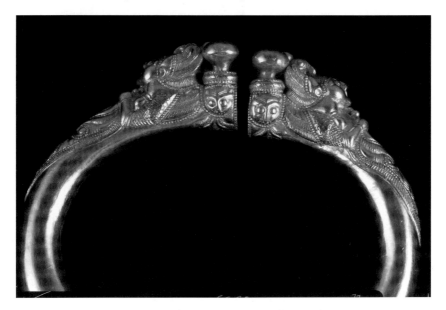

Fig. 3. Reinheim armring. – Without scale.

Echt believed the Celtic artisan combined the imagery of Artemis as a Potnia Theron with the iconography of the Greek Athena / Etruscan Minerva to fashion a unique Celtic Potnia Theron[10]. However, a close examination of three decorative details on the Reinheim armring – (1) the headdress of the goddess, (2) the faces of lions / owls occupying the ends of the armring, and (3) the lower body of the deity – instead suggests that the primary

---

[10] Echt 2000, 264–265; Echt 1999, 50–51.

Fig. 4. Handle of Grächwil hydria (h. 26.4 cm).

influence on the composition of the Reinheim rings was derived from the centuries-old Etruscan Potnia Theron.

The headdress

In Echt's study, he identified depictions of Phrygian helmets on Apulian red-figure vases in southern Italy as the inspiration for the headdress of the Potnia Theron on the Reinheim armring, but there are reasons to be sceptical of this potential link to the art of *Magna Graecia*. The Potnia Therons on the neckring and the armring both wear a type of headdress with a bird perched upon it. The headdress of the Potnia Theron on the armring differs slightly from that on the neckring. Whereas the artisan melds the bird on the headdress with the forehead of the goddess on the neckring, the goddess on the armring appears to wear a helmet with a bird on top of it *(Fig. 5)*[11].

---

[11] ECHT 1999, 49–50; cf. FREY 2004, 37.

Fig. 5. Front view of Reinheim armring. – Without scale.

In Echt's view, the entire ensemble was a Phrygian helmet, a type of helmet distinguished from other types by the forward-leaning apex that was topped sometimes with a bird or a griffin's head. Echt believed that the Celtic artist had based his rendition of the Potnia Theron's helmet on depictions of Athena in Apulian red-figure vase painting, where she is depicted wearing a Phrygian helmet instead of the more common Attic helmet[12]. In particular, he focused on the protective band above the forehead known as the frontlet, which appears on some of the Phrygian helmets that Athena wears in Apulian vase painting and is best represented on a vase in Naples[13]. The frontlet was typical of Attic helmets[14] but does not appear on Phrygian helmets outside of Apulian red-figure vase painting.

When viewed in profile, however, it can be seen that the headdress of the Potnia Theron on the Reinheim armring *(Fig. 6a)* differs significantly from that of Athena in Apulian vase painting *(Fig. 6b)*. First, the triangular 'frontlet' on the Potnia Theron's headdress is banded and appears to be fitted to her head, while the frontlet on the Phrygian helmet has a rounded shape like a diadem and clearly serves as an attachment to the helmet. Second,

[12] ECHT 1999, 49–50.
[13] See LAUBSCHER 1980, 231 and pl. 50,1.
[14] SCHÄFER 1997, 71; HANNAH 1983, 114.

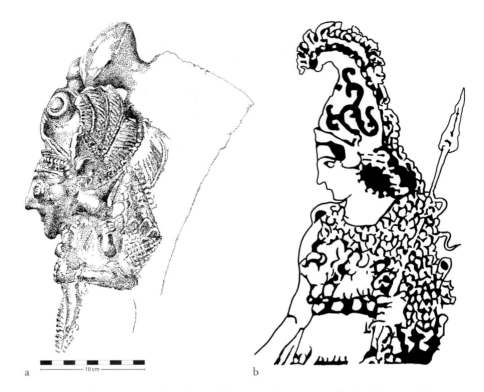

Fig. 6. a Reinheim armring, headdress of the Potnia Theron in profile; b Athena with Phrygian helmet on red-figure Apulian vase.

the bird on the Reinheim armring has two large eyes, a well-defined beak, and fully articulated wings on either side. On the Apulian vase, the bird / griffin's head is purely decorative and depicted only as a protome at the very top of the helmet. No wings are present and a lion's mane appears to crown the top of the mythological creature's head. Placing a fully articulated bird atop the head of a Potnia Theron was not an uncommon motif, having occurred both on the aforementioned Grächwil hydria and in Etruscan art on a 6th century BC Etruscan bronze winged Potnia Theron in the museum of Cortona (IT)[15]. Moreover, the dating of the earliest Apulian vase that depicts Athena with a Phrygian helmet (last decades of the 5th century BC)[16] is essentially contemporaneous with that of the Reinheim armring (400–370 BC)[17]. It would be surprising for Celtic artists in Europe to adopt or innovate a peculiar headdress for Athena around the same time as Apulian vase painters, without a southern Italian trade contact acting as a direct intermediary.

Lions or Owls?

Often the Potnia Theron was depicted with felines, but the two animals that peer out beneath the terminal balusters on the Reinheim neckring and armring appear only as faces and lack any bodies to aid in identification, as can be seen in *Figure 7*.

---

[15] GRAN-AYMERICH 2010–2013, 50 and pl. XIVc.
[16] MUGIONE 2002, 63.
[17] ECHT 1999, 282–283.

Fig. 7. Reinheim armring, detail of lions / owls.

Keller believed the faces of the creatures represented lions but made note of the fact that their faces were lacking a defining characteristic: lower jaws[18]. Nonetheless, he interpreted the dots impressed by the goldsmith at the bottom of the lion's faces as indicative of whiskers, as has Echt more recently[19]. Vincent Megaw, on the other hand, viewed these dots as a possible attempt by the metalworker to delineate the bearded tuft of feathers usually depicted along the bottom of an owl's face[20], and Otto-Herman Frey has drawn attention to the rendition of the noses on the lion / owls on the Reinheim armring. As Frey has noted, for felines in frontal view, Celtic artists usually rendered the nose as broad and rounded at the bottom. On the Reinheim neckring and armring, however, the artist narrowed the nose – presumably to delineate a beak[21].

Part of the difficulty in accepting the possibility that the faces at the ends of the Reinheim neckring and armring could represent owls is the fact that the pairing of the Potnia Theron with owls was uncommon. Yet, the appearance of this goddess with owls decorated the handles of wine-drinking vessels produced in and around the north Etruscan city of Chiusi during the 7th and 6th centuries BC[22]. The motif can be seen on the handle of a 7th century BC *bucchero kyathos* (drinking vessel) from the site of Poggio Civitate, about 50 km west of Chiusi (IT). Recovered from the remains of an elite building complex, the vessel likely had some ritual significance since it was part of a large banqueting service that included nearly 60 drinking vessels and 100 setting or serving vessels[23]. Above the shoulders of a winged Potnia Theron, two owls hover on either side *(Fig. 8)*.

This iconography predates the association of the owl with Athena in Greece[24] and should be understood in its Italic context[25]. In many cultures, the owl has traditionally been viewed

---

[18] KELLER 1965, 31.
[19] ECHT 1999, 35.
[20] MEGAW 1970, 80.
[21] FREY 1992, 54. – For a comprehensive bibliography on the lion / owl debate, see ECHT 2000, 265 no. 26.
[22] See MOORE 2018, 68–69; VALENTINI 1969, 416–418 (nos 1; 2; 18; 24). – The handles of her 'type A' vessels often display the goddess with two birds above her shoulders, described only as 'uccelli' or 'volatili' in Italian. For other examples at Poggio Civitate, see PHILLIPS 1971, 259 figs 8; 13; DONATI / GAMBOGI 1985, 133 cat.-nos 500; 503.
[23] BERKIN 2003, 119–123.
[24] SHAPIRO 1993.
[25] To my knowledge, the only other evidence for this pairing can be seen on 2nd millennium BC Burney relief in the British Museum, which depicts a female deity (perhaps the Near Eastern goddess Astarte – Ištar – Inanna) with taloned feet, standing upon lions and flanked by owls on either side. This clay tablet seems too chronologically and geographically distant to exert any influence on Etruscan or

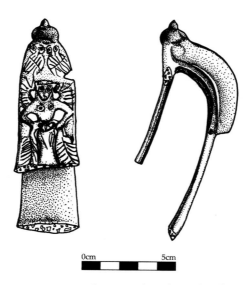

Fig. 8. Potnia Theron with owls on kyathos handle from Poggio Civitate (IT).

as a threat to newborns and infants[26]. The Roman poet Ovid described creatures he called *striges* (from *strix*, 'screech-owl' in Latin) that supposedly attacked newborns at night[27] and it is likely that the Etruscans shared this superstition with their neighbours. Since the Potnia Theron was generally understood to have held power over the creatures she was depicted with[28], the pairing of the Potnia Theron with the owl in Etruscan art may have alluded to the goddess' perceived ability to thwart or control the owl, thereby ensuring the fertility of the mother and protecting the newborn[29]. By choosing to depict this goddess with owls instead of lions, the Celtic artist could have been referring to the iconography of the 7th and 6th century BC Etruscan Potnia Theron, as well as highlighting an aspect of the goddess that set her apart from the Greek goddess Artemis.

The lower body

Lastly, consideration of the lower bodies of the goddesses depicted on the Reinheim armring may lend further credence to the idea that her iconography was based on Etruscan prototypes, and that the Celts associated the goddess depicted on the armring with fertility. On the neckring, only the faces of the goddesses are depicted. On the armring, though, the goddesses possess full torsos and lower bodies (see *Fig. 3; 5*). Their shoulders and arms have decorative scale patterns and wear armrings on their wrists, in similar fashion to the deceased. Spheres sit beneath their chins, three on one side and two on the other. Above their clenched hands, they appear to hold a ring or bracelet in front of their chests[30].

Celtic art. See ALBENDA 2005 and COLLON 2007 for synopses on its origin and interpretation.

[26] ARMSTRONG 1958, 113; GASTER 1942, 45–48; GASTER 1947, 186.
[27] Ov. fast. 6,101–182.
[28] See above, note 1.
[29] See MOORE 2018, 64–67.
[30] KELLER 1965, 32; also LENERZ-DE WILDE 2006, 319; cf. ECHT 1999, 44. – Keller originally suggested that the goddesses appeared to be holding a ring or bracelet in front of their chest, but Echt disagreed with his assessment. He observed that

Fig. 9. Female figure with tree of life design on kyathos handle from Poggio Civitate (IT).

Beneath the rings, the lower bodies become highly abstract. Two tendril-like S-spirals, presumably representative of legs, lead down below the goddess' forearms and are contained in long pointed triangles ornamented with a series of geometric hatchings. Searching for the inspiration for this curious depiction of the lower half of these figures, scholars have cited the tail-like bodies of Graeco-Scythian snake-goddesses[31], but examples of this type are either contemporaneous with, or later than, the Reinheim armring. Although ambivalent about the inspiration behind the lower bodies of these goddesses on the Reinheim armring, Martin Guggisberg drew attention to the appearance of the Potnia Theron with a snake- or tendril-limbed body in early Etruscan art[32]. On Etruscan metalwork, heads or busts sitting atop vegetal motifs[33] and tendril-limbed deities appear as early as the 7th century BC[34]. In ceramics, the handles and struts of 7th and 6th century BC Etruscan bucchero drinking vessels are often combined with a stylised 'tree of life' design, a Near Eastern vegetal motif associated with fertility and regeneration *(Fig. 9)*[35].

Ludwig Curtius, in his seminal work on the development of this motif from ancient times until the present, designated the depiction of a goddess whose lower body was composed of a tendril or vegetal motif as a *Rankenfrau* or *Rankengöttin*[36]. This motif was likely based on the concept of a chthonic earth goddess, which at first developed locally in various

the 'ring' that the goddesses appeared to hold had a furrow down the middle and that rings of this type were not manufactured in the Celtic world during the La Tène period. He offered no certain identification of the object but suggested instead that they were *krotaloi*, musical instruments used by Greek dancers. *Krotaloi*, though, were usually more bell-shaped than ring-shaped (West 1992, 123 and pl. 31) and the significance of their being held by a deity instead of a supplicant is unclear.

[31] Bagley 2013, 72; Kull 1997, 386; cf. Megaw 2005, 42.
[32] Guggisberg 2000, 196–197.
[33] Schauenburg 1957, 218.
[34] Rupp 2007, 213 fig. 2.
[35] Brocato / Regoli 2011, 220–221; Berkin 2003, 101–102; Capecchi / Gunella 1975, 44.
[36] Curtius 1957.

Fig. 10. Potnia Theron on kyathos handle from Chiusi (IT).

places and then later on gained increasing prominence in the Mediterranean when associated with Artemis in Greek art[37]. Maria Ustinova believes the earliest rendition of a goddess of this body-type can be found on 7th or 6th century BC gold plaques from Cerverteri (IT), where two tendrils lead below the chest of a female figure and end in two fan-palmettes bracketed by lion heads[38]. In his global survey of this motif, Walter Veit observed that 7th century BC depictions of a female with a tendril-lower body and palmettes on Etruscan jewellery are more relevant to the development of the *Rankenfrau* or *Rankengöttin* motif in Classical art than that of the Scythian snake-goddess[39]. Particularly relevant to this study is a 7th or 6th century BC bucchero handle housed in the Chiusi museum which displays a motif somewhat similar to that found on the Reinheim armring, wherein the lower body of a Potnia Theron was replaced with a decorative floral motif *(Fig. 10)*[40].

On the Etruscan vessel handle, spiralling volutes take the place of the Potnia Theron's legs while two birds – likely owls – can be seen hovering above the goddess' shoulders. In form, it is very similar to the composition seen on the Reinheim armring. Anthony Tuck has suggested that the Etruscan artist rounded out the lower body of the Potnia Theron on

---

[37] Veit 1990, 24.
[38] Ustinova 2005, 73–74.
[39] Veit (1990, 8) believes the original genesis of this motif can be traced back to Egyptian and Mesopotamian depictions of a Potnia Theron or Magna Mater.
[40] Valentini 1969, 423 no. 24; also Rupp 2007, 213–214 and fig. 3.

Fig. 11. Bronze plate from Waldalgesheim grave. – Scale 2 : 3.

the kyathos handle with a lotus-palmette in order to remind the viewer of the goddess' link to fertility and fecundity[41].

In Celtic art, the use of the *Rankenfrau* or *Rankengöttin* motif for the lower body of a 'Potnia Theron' may not be unique to the Reinheim armring. Claudia Tappert's recent analysis of the goddess depicted on the bronze yoke and wagon fittings recovered from the early La Tène wagon grave at Waldalgesheim (DE) suggests that her iconography was also based on the artistic conventions used for the Etruscan Potnia Theron[42]. On the two bronze plates decorating the yoke of the wagon, the upper bodies of female figures are engraved with a winding tendril-motif on their torsos. When arranged atop the yoke, the plates would have been set back-to-back, giving the female figures a Janus-like configuration, analogous to the figures on the Reinheim rings. Both female figures appear to wear leaf-crowns, suggesting their connection to the supernatural world *(Fig. 11)*[43].

At first glance, the lower bodies of these female figures appear to be missing, but Tappert has suggested that their 'legs' were actually the curved wooden yokes running under the

---

[41] Tuck 2006, 132.
[42] I thank an anonymous reviewer for recommending this article.
[43] Tappert 2017, 176; cf. Bagley 2014, 106.

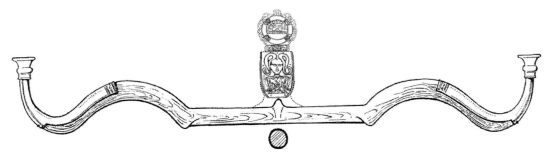

Fig. 12. Bronze plates atop the Waldalgesheim yoke fittings. – Without scale.

bronze plates and sitting on top of the shoulders of the yoked horses, in a fashion similar to a snake goddess or a *Rankenfrau (Fig. 12)*[44].

Tappert points to the Reinheim armring as evidence that this artistic concept had reached the Celtic sphere by the early La Tène period. Set above these bronze plates were bronze openwork yoke mounts that display antithetical birds and tendril motifs. These motifs, Tappert believes, were inspired by depictions of the Potnia Theron on late Iron Age bronze handles from northern Italy, as well as depictions of the Gorgon in Etruscan art. In the latter case, she points to instances where the Gorgon was depicted as giving birth, as on an Etruscan 6th century BC wagon fitting from Perugia and a 4th century BC Etruscan gold bulla, now in the British Museum[45]. In Tappert's analysis, the entire ensemble of the yoke and wagon fittings at Waldalgesheim – a female deity with tendril or snake-limbed legs surrounded by animals – was meant to highlight the fertility of a female goddess associated with animals. Although very different mediums, the iconography of the Reinheim armring and the Waldalgesheim yoke and wagon fittings share the centrality of a 'Potnia Theron' with birds and a tendril-like lower body, linking her to fertility and regeneration. This iconography appears to have its roots in Orientalising Etruria.

Conclusion

Over time, the Potnia Theron motif changed and evolved when adopted by different cultures of the ancient Mediterranean. As the motif travelled from the Near East to Greece, the Potnia Theron became associated with Artemis, the goddess of the hunt[46] and, by extension, nature[47]. In Etruria, the motif of the Potnia Theron was not associated with the Etruscan version of Artemis (Artumes)[48], but rather adopted iconography seemingly based on Phoenician prototypes[49] and associated with fertility[50]. When the motif spread further

---

[44] Tappert (2017, 167–168) prefers the reconstruction of the yoke fittings by Mariën 1961, fig. 4.3, where the bronze plates are attached atop the yoke, versus that of Joachim 1995 fig. 84, where the bronze plates are attached to the yokes themselves.

[45] Tappert 2017, 170–175; a crouching female giving birth is also depicted on a shard from a 6th century BC bucchero vessel from Poggio Colla (IT), see Perkins 2012.

[46] Krauskopf 1998, 174; cf. Icard-Gianolio 1997, 1074.

[47] Christou 1968, 14 and 155.

[48] Krauskopf 1984, 787; cf. Nielsen / Rathje 2009, 268.

[49] Damgaard Andersen 1992–1993, 74–76; Nielsen / Rathje 2009, 267

[50] Maggiani 2012, 400–401; Perkins 2012, 189; Tuck 2006, 132; cf. Damgaard Andersen 1992/1993, 106.

north into Europe, this latter aspect of the Etruscan Potnia Theron may have appealed to some Celtic elites during the late Hallstatt and early La Tène period, even though it had largely fallen out of favour in Etruscan art by the 5th century BC[51].

It was not the motif of the Potnia Theron or Mistress of Animals that prevailed in Celtic art during the La Tène period, however, but that of the Despotes Theron, or 'Master of Animals.' Martin Guggisberg's study on the Master and Mistress of Animals motif in early La Tène art concluded that the Master of Animals motif largely supplanted his feminine counterpart during the 5th century BC. He attributed this shift in focus to the ascendency of a male warrior elite at the beginning of the early La Tène period, who identified more readily with the Master of Animals[52]. In this regard, it is surprising to see the appearance of the Potnia Theron – if that was the intention of the artisans – on objects recovered from the early La Tène sites of Reinheim and Waldalgesheim. It may be more surprising that the iconography of these early La Tène objects appears to be derived from Orientalising Etruria, given the significant temporal and geographic distance separating them. Jennifer Bagley has recently discussed the challenge of interpreting the Mistress or Master of Animals motif in Celtic art. As Bagley observes, early La Tène artisans produced artefacts with sufficient skill and detail that they can be compared to the iconography of the Mistress or Master of Animals in other cultures, but our knowledge of the motif's role in the Near East, Greece, or Etruria can only provide hints of its meaning in the Celtic world. Lacking written sources, Bagley encourages archaeologists to rely on the comparatively robust evidence for the context and usage of early La Tène art to gain a better understanding of the motif's meaning[53].

Taking this approach, consideration of the burial practices associated with early La Tène princely graves can potentially be useful. In her survey of high-status burials during the late Hallstatt and early La Tène period, Carola Metzner-Nebelsick observed that the presence of wagons and precious metal goods in female tombs appeared in a frequency similar to that of males, and that a similar situation could be seen in Orientalising Etruria. She attributed this phenomenon to the emergence of a social structure based on ancestry during the late Hallstatt period, in a manner similar to that theorised by Petra Amann for Orientalising Etruria[54]. In any society relying on familial bonds, the role of women would be elevated because of their key role in ensuring the continuation of the family line. This elevated status was recognised by well-appointed ceremonial graves, with Metzner-Nebelsick suggesting that the contacts established between the two societies during the Hallstatt period provided a paradigm for the female elites of the late Hallstatt and early La Tène period to emulate later on[55]. Thus, similar social dynamics may have undergirded the popularity of the Potnia Theron motif in Etruria and the Celtic world.

The possibility that Celtic elites and artisans of the late Hallstatt and early La Tène period could have been acquainted with Orientalising Etruscan iconography and beliefs should not be discounted. Following Metzner-Nebelsick's analysis, it would have been a logical choice for Celtic artisans to turn to the centuries-old artistic conventions of the

---

[51] Damgaard Andersen 1992/1993, 106–107; see also Guggisberg 2003, 180–181, on this point and its potential implication for the adoption of the Potnia Theron motif during the early La Tène period.
[52] Guggisberg 2010, 231.
[53] Bagley 2019, 199–205.
[54] Amann 2000; see also Tuck 2006; Tuck 2010.
[55] Metzner-Nebelsick 2017, 253–254; cf. Echt (1999, 222) who suggested that the deceased at Reinheim might have been a priestess, but Metzner-Nebelsick (2017, 258) believes that confining a female elite's role in Celtic society to the religious sphere is too narrow a perspective.

Dobesch 1992
G. Dobesch, Die Kelten als Nachbarn der Etrusker in Norditalien. In: L. Aigner-Foresti (ed.), Etrusker nördlich von Etrurien. Etruskische Präsenz in Norditalien und nördlich der Alpen sowie ihre Einflüsse auf die einheimischen Kulturen. Sitzungsber. Phil.-Hist. Kl. 589 (Vienna 1992) 161–178.

Donati / Gambogi 1985
L. Donati / P. Gambogi, Buccheri. In: S. Stopponi (ed.), Case e palazzi d'Etruria (Milan 1985) 131–37.

Echt 1999
R. Echt, Das Fürstinnengrab von Reinheim. Studien zur Kulturgeschichte der Früh-La-Tène-Zeit. Saarbrücker Beitr. Altkde. 69 (Bonn 1999).

Echt 2000
R. Echt, Dionysos et Minerve chez les Celtes. Bijoux et vaisselle de la tombe princière de Reinheim comme sources de la religion celtique ancienne. Cahiers Lorrains 3, 2000, 253–293.

Frey 1992
O.-H. Frey, Keltische Eulen. Zum Bedeutungswandel eines antiken Motivs. In: H. Froning / T. Hölscher / H. Mielsch (eds), Kotinos. Festschrift für Erika Simon (Mainz 1992) 53–55.

Frey 2004
O.-H. Frey, The Celtic concept of the gods: Some preliminary remarks. In: C. Hourihane (ed.), Irish Art. Historical Studies in Honour of Peter Harbison (Dublin 2004) 25–46.

Frey 2011
O.-H. Frey, Betrachtungen über einigen späthallstattzeitliche Fibeln / Osservazioni intorno ad alcune fibule tardo-hallstattiane. In: S. Casini (ed.), Il filo del tempo. Studi di preistoria e protostoria in onore di Raffaele Carlo de Marinis (Bergamo 2011) 375–377.

Frey / Frey 1998
RGA² 12 (1998) 527–529 s. v. Grächwil (L. Frey / O.-H. Frey).

Gaster 1942
T. Gaster, A Canaanite magical text. Orientalia 11, 1942, 41–79.

Gaster 1947
T. Gaster, A magical inscription from Arslan-Tash. Journal Near Eastern Stud. 6, 1947, 186–188.

Gran-Aymerich 2006
J. Gran-Aymerich, Les sources méditerranéennes de l'art celtique, VIe–Ve siècles av. J.-C. In: D. Frère (ed.), De la Méditerranée vers l'Atlantique. Aspects des relations entre la Méditerranée et la Gaule centrale et occidentale (VIIIe–IIe siècle av. J.-C.). Arch. et Culture (Rennes 2006) 19–56.

Gran-Aymerich 2010–2013
J. Gran-Aymerich, La maîtresse des animaux et de la nature dans l'Etrurie orientalisante. Stud. Etruschi 76, 2010–2013, 45–57.

Guggisberg 2000
M. A. Guggisberg, Der Goldschatz von Erstfeld. Ein keltischer Bilderzyklus zwischen Mitteleuropa und der Mittelmeerwelt. Antiqua 32 (Basel 2000).

Guggisberg 2003
M. A. Guggisberg, Sull'imitazione e recezione di modelli iconografici meidterreanei all'interno dell'antica art celtica. In: D. Vitale (ed.), L'immagine tra mondo celtico e mondo etrusco-italico: aspetti della cultura figurativa nell'antichità. Stud. e Scavi (Univ. Bologna) 20 (Bologna 2003) 177–186.

Guggisberg 2010
M. A. Guggisberg. The mistress of animals, the master of animals: Two complementary or oppositional religious concepts in early celtic art? In: D. B. Counts / B. Arnold (eds), The Master of Animals in Old World Iconography. Archaeolingua 24 (Budapest 2010) 223–236.

Hannah 1983
P. A. Hannah, The Representation of Greek Hoplite Body Armour in the Art of the Fifth and Fourth Centuries BC [Diss. Univ. Oxford] (Oxford 1983).

Icard-Gianolio 1997
LIMC 8,1 (1997) 1021–1027 s. v. Potnia (N. Icard-Gianolio).

Jacobsthal 1944
P. Jacobsthal, Early Celtic Art (Oxford 1944).

Joachim 1995
H.-E. Joachim, Waldalgesheim. Das Grab einer keltischen Fürstin. Kat. Rhein. Landesmus. Bonn 3 (Bonn 1995).

Keller 1955
J. Keller, Das Fürstengrab von Reinheim (Kreis St. Ingbert, Saarland). Vorläufiger Bericht. Germania 33, 1955, 33–42. doi: https://doi.org/10.11588/ger.1955.43627.

Keller 1965
J. Keller, Das keltische Fürstengrab von Reinheim (Bonn 1965).

Krauskopf 1984
LIMC 2 (1984) 774–792 s. v. Artemis / Artumes (I. Krauskopf).

Krauskopf 1998
I. Krauskopf, Artemis. In: Etrusca disciplina. I culti stranieri in Etruria. Atti dei convegni IV (Orvieto 1987) e V (Orvieto 1988). Ann. Fondazione Mus. "Claudio Faina" 5 (Orvieto 1998) 171–206.

Kull 1997
B. Kull, Tod und Apotheose. Ikonographie in Grab und Kunst der jüngeren Eisenzeit an der unteren Donau und ihrer Bedeutung für die Interpretation von "Prunkgräbern". Ber. RGK 78, 1997, 197–466.

Laubscher 1980
H. P. Laubscher, Ein Athenakopf im Museo Barracco. In: H. A. Cahn / E. Simon (eds), Tainia, Roland Hampe zum 70. Geburtstag am 2. Dezember 1978 (Mainz 1980) 227–237.

Lenerz-de Wilde 2006
M. Lenerz-de Wilde, Frühlatènezeitliche Ringe mit Maskenzier. Germania 84, 2006, 307–368.

Maggiani 2012
A. Maggiani, La religione. In: G. Bartoloni (ed.), Introduzione all'Etruscologia (Milan 2012) 395–418.

Mariën 1961
M.-E. Mariën, La période de La Tène en Belgique, le Groupe de la Haine. Monogr. Arch. Nat. 2 (Brussels 1961).

Megaw 1970
J. V. S. Megaw, Art of the European Iron Age. A Study of the Elusive Image (New York 1970).

Megaw 2005
J. V. S. Megaw, Early Celtic art without Scythians? A review. In: H. Dobrzanska / J. V. S. Megaw / P. Poleska (eds), Celts on the Margin. Studies in European Cultural Interaction 7th century BC–1st century AD dedicated to Zenon Woźnizk (Kraków 2005) 33–47.

Megaw / Megaw 1994
R. Megaw / J. V. S. Megaw, Through a window on the European Iron Age darkly: fifty years of reading early Celtic art. World Arch. 25, 1994, 287–303.

Metzner-Nebelsick 2009
C. Metzner-Nebelsick, Wagen- und Prunkbestattungen von Frauen der Hallstatt- und frühen Latènezeit in Europa. Ein Beitrag zur Diskussion der sozialen Stellung der Frau in der älteren Eisenzeit. In: J. Bagley / Ch. Eggl / D. Neumann / M. Schefzik (eds), Alpen, Kult und Eisenzeit. Festschrift für Amei Lang zum 65. Geburtstag. Stud. Honoraria 30 (Rahden / Westf. 2009) 237–270.

Moore 2018
D. Moore, The Etruscan goddess Catha. Etruscan Stud. 21, 2018, 58–77. doi: https://doi.org/10.1515/etst-2017-0030.

Mugione 2002
E. Mugione, Le immagini di Atena con elmo frigio nella ceramica italiota. In: L. Cerchiai (ed.), L'iconografia di Atena con elmo frigio in Italia meridionale. Atti della giornata di studi, Fisciano, 12 giugno 1998. Quad. Ostraka 5 (Naples 2002) 63–80.

Müller 2009
F. Müller, Kunst der Kelten: 700 v. Chr.–700 n. Chr. (Stuttgart 2009).

Nielsen / Rathje 2009
M. Nielsen / A. Rathje, Artumes in Etruria: the borrowed goddess. In: T. Fischer-Hansen / B. Poulsen (eds), From Artemis to Diana: The Goddess of Man and Beast. Acta Hyperborea 12 (Copenhagen 2009) 261–301.

Perkins 2012
P. Perkins, The Bucchero childbirth stamp on a late Orientalizing Period shard from Poggio Colla. Etruscan Stud. 15, 2012, 146–201. doi: https://doi.org/10.1515/etst-2012-0014.

Phillips 1971
K. M. Phillips, Bryn Mawr College excavations in Tuscany, 1970. Am. Journal

Arch. 75, 1971, 257–261. doi: https://doi.org/10.2307/503960.

Ross 1967

A. Ross, Pagan Celtic Britain. Studies in Iconography and Tradition (London, New York 1967).

Rupp 2007

W. L. Rupp, The vegetal goddess in the Tomb of the Typhon. Etruscan Stud. 10, 2007, 211–219. doi: https://doi.org/10.1515/etst.2004.10.1.211.

Schäfer 1997

T. Schäfer, Andres Agathoi. Studien zum Realitätsgehalt der Bewaffnung attischer Krieger auf Denkmälern klassischer Zeit. Quellen u. Forsch. Ant. Welt 27 (Munich 1997).

Schauenburg 1957

K. Schauenburg, Zur Symbolik unteritalischer Rankenmotive. Mitt. DAI Rom 64, 1957, 198–221.

Shapiro 1993

H. A. Shapiro, From Athena's owl to the owl of Athens. In: R. Rosen / J. Farrell (eds), Nomodeiktes. Greek Studies in Honor of Martin Ostwald (Ann Arbor 1993) 213–224.

Spartz 1962

E. Spartz, Das Wappenbild des Herrn und der Herrin der Tiere in der minoisch-mykenischen und frühgriechischen Kunst (Munich 1962).

Tappert 2017

C. Tappert, Unbeholfen oder genial? Zur ikonographischen Deutung der Rankenornamentik auf den Jochbeschlägen im keltischen Prunkgrab von Waldalgesheim. In: D. Brandherm (ed.), Memento dierum antiquorum … Festschrift für Majolie Lenerz-de Wilde zum 70. Geburtstag. Arch. Atlantica Monogr. 1 (Hagen / Westf. 2017) 161–182.

Tuck 2006

A. Tuck, The social and political context of the 7th century architectural terracottas and Poggio Civitate. In: I. Edlund-Berry (ed.), Deliciae Fictiles 3. Architectural Terracottas in Ancient Italy. New Discoveries and Interpretations. Proceedings of the International Conference held at the American Academy in Rome, November 7–8, 2002 (Oxford 2006) 130–35.

Tuck 2010

A. Tuck, The mistress of animals, the master of animals: Two complementary or oppositional religious concepts in early Celtic art? In: D. B. Counts / B. Arnold (eds), The Master of Animals in Old World Iconography. Archaeolingua 24 (Budapest 2010) 211–221.

Ustinova 2005

Y. Ustinova, Snake-limbed and tendril-limbed goddesses in the art and mythology of the Mediterranean and Black Sea. In: D. Braund (ed.), Scythians and Greeks. Cultural Interactions in Scythia Athens and the Early Roman Empire (sixth century BC–first century AD) (Exeter 2005) 64–79.

Valentini 1969

A. Valentini, Il motivo della Potnia Theron sui vasi di bucchero. Stud. Etruschi 37, 1969, 414–442.

Veit 1990

W. Veit, Die Rankengöttin. Bruckmanns Pantheon 48, 1990, 14–27.

Verger 1991

S. Verger, L'utilisation du répertoire figuratif dans l'art celtique ancien. Hist. Art 16, 1991, 3–17.

Washburn 2001

D. Washburn, Remembering things seen: Experimental approaches to the process of information transmittal. Journal Arch. Method and Theory 8, 2001, 67–99.

Wendling 2018

H. Wendling, Frühkeltische Kunst: Vergangene Bildwelten – Vergessene Mythen. In: R. Kastler / F. Lang / H. Wendling (eds), Faber Salisburgi. Festschrift für Wilfried K. Kovacsovics zum 65. Geburtstag. ArchaeoPlus 10 (Salzburg 2018) 359–375.

West 1992

M. L. West, Ancient Greek Music (Oxford 1992).

Abstract: The Etruscan roots of the Reinheim armring

The figural decoration on the armring recovered from the early La Tène grave at Reinheim displays a goddess with a bird perched on her head and animals behind her shoulders. While reminiscent of the Mediterranean Potnia Theron (Mistress of Animals), the iconography of this deity remains obscure, though influences from Hallstatt, Greek, Scythian, and north Italian art have been identified. This study argues that three particular aspects of the armring's decoration – the headdress of the goddess, the animals she was depicted with, and the stylisation of her lower torso – place the primary influence for this artistic composition in Orientalising Etruria.

Zusammenfassung: Die etruskischen Wurzeln des Reinheimer Armreifs

Die figürliche Darstellung auf dem Armreif aus dem frühlatènezeitlichen Grab von Reinheim zeigt eine Göttin mit einem Vogel, der sich auf ihrem Kopf niedergelassen hat, und Tieren hinter ihren Schultern. Sie erinnert an die mediterrane Potnia theron (Herrin der Tiere), doch bleibt die Ikonographie dieser Gottheit unklar, wenn auch Einflüsse aus der Hallstatt-, der griechischen, skythischen und norditalischen Kunst festgestellt werden konnten. In dieser Studie wird argumentiert, dass drei spezifische Aspekte der Darstellung auf dem Armring – der Kopfschmuck der Göttin, die Tiere, mit denen sie dargestellt wurde, und die Stilisierung ihres unteren Körperteils – den Haupteinfluss für diese künstlerische Komposition im orientalisierenden Etrurien verorten.

Résumé : Les racines étrusques du bracelet de Reinheim

La représentation figurée sur le bracelet provenant de la tombe laténienne ancienne de Reinheim montre une déesse avec un oiseau posé sur sa tête et des animaux derrière ses épaules. Elle évoque ainsi la Potnia thérôn méditerranéenne (maîtresse des animaux), mais son iconographie reste floue, bien que l'on puisse constater des influences artistiques hallstattiennes, grecques, scythes et nord-italiennes. Cette étude réunit des arguments soutenant que trois aspects spécifiques de cette représentation – le couvre-chef de la déesse, les animaux qui l'accompagnent, ainsi que la stylisation de la partie inférieure de son corps – permettent d'attribuer à l'Étrurie orientalisante l'influence principale contribuant à cette composition artistique.

Y.G.

Address of author:

Daniel W. Moore
Department of Languages, Literatures, and Linguistics
Indiana State University
Root Hall A-145
424 North 7th Street
US–Terre Haute, IN 47809-1928
Daniel.Moore@indstate.edu

References of figures:

Figs 1–3; 5: Museum für Vor- und Frühgeschichte Saarbrücken. – *Fig. 4:* Bern, Bernisches Historisches Museum. – *Fig. 6:* Drawing by Stephanie Gleit after Echt 1999, pl. 13,1; drawing by St. Gleit after Cambitoglou / Trendall 1961, pl. 4,15. – *Fig. 7:* Echt 1999, pl. 12,3; photograph M. Zorn. – *Fig. 8:* Berkin 2003, fig. 15,30; drawing St. Gleit. – *Fig. 9:* Berkin 2003, fig. 17,36; drawing St. Gleit. – *Fig. 10:* Drawing by St. Gleit after Valentini 1969, pl. 107b. – *Fig 11:* Tappert 2017, fig. 1,5, based on the reconstruction of Müller 2009, fig. 10. – *Fig 12:* Tappert 2017, fig. 4, based on the reconstruction of Mariën 1971, fig. 66,1.

Neues zum sogenannten Trinkhornbeschlag von Bad Dürkheim – Zu Goldblecharbeiten der Frühlatènezeit

Von Sebastian Fürst, Martin Schönfelder und Barbara Armbruster

Schlagwörter: Gold / Trinkhorn / Frühlatènezeit / Elitengrab / Kunsthandwerk
Keywords: Gold / drinking horn / Early La Tène period / elite tomb / arts and crafts
Mots-clés: Or / corne à boire / La Tène ancienne / tombeau d'élite / artisanat

Einleitung

Neben dem Halsring und dem maskenverzierten Knotenring zählen sicherlich die Fragmente eines mutmaßlichen Trinkhornbeschlags zu den bekanntesten Goldobjekten des in die zweite Hälfte des 5. Jahrhunderts v. Chr. datierenden Elitengrabs von Bad Dürkheim. Da der Grabinhalt im Zuge der Bauarbeiten für die Bahnstrecke Bad Dürkheim-Ludwigshafen-Oggersheim im Jahre 1864 undokumentiert geborgen wurde, fehlen nicht nur genauere Kenntnisse zum Befund; auch kann davon ausgegangen werden, dass das bekanntgewordene Beigabenensemble nicht vollständig ist[1]. Zudem sind einige der geborgenen Stücke teils stark beschädigt. Neben dem in vier Stücke zerbrochenen Goldhalsring existieren auch von dem sogenannten Trinkhornbeschlag nur noch sechs zum Teil sehr kleine Fragmente.

Gerade einmal sechs Jahre nach der Entdeckung erfolgte eine erste Rekonstruktion der durchbrochen gearbeiteten Goldblechfragmente durch Ludwig Lindenschmit d. Ä., in seinem 1870 publizierten zweiten Band der „Alterthümer unserer heidnischen Vorzeit" *(Abb. 1a)*[2]. Eine leicht abgewandelte Rekonstruktion veröffentlichte Paul Jacobsthal 1944 in seinem mittlerweile zu den Klassikern der Latèneforschung zählenden *opus magnum* „Early Celtic Art" *(Abb. 1b)*[3]. Aufgrund der großen Popularität dieser beiden Werke sind beide Rekonstruktionen recht bekannt geworden. Die frühe Rekonstruktion der Bleche wurde daher nicht mehr infrage gestellt.

Vincent Megaw sah in den beiden erhaltenen Masken der Bleche eine vexierbildhafte Kippfigur, die, je nachdem von welcher Seite aus man sie betrachtet, entweder eine junge

---

[1] Es handelte sich wahrscheinlich um das Körpergrab einer Frau, die in einer Grabkammer unter einem Tumulus bestattet wurde; Bardelli 2017a, XIII. – Das Grab enthielt neben den bereits erwähnten Goldobjekten noch einen weiteren Armring, der jedoch nur aus einfachem Golddraht gefertigt wurde, sowie einen Goldblechstreifen und ein kleines Goldscheibchen (dieses ist jedoch verschollen). Ein mutmaßlicher Spiegel, einige Gewebereste, zwei Radreifen und zwei Bernsteinperlen gelten ebenfalls als verschollen. Darüber hinaus konnten Wagenteile, eine Schnabelkanne, ein etruskischer Dreifuß mit Löwenfüßen sowie ein Stamnos aus Vulci (IT) geborgen werden. – Für eine vollständige Auflistung der Beigaben siehe jüngst Bardelli 2017a, XIV–XV; 2017b; vgl. auch Lindenschmit d. Ä. 1870, Taf. 1–2; Sprater 1928, 111–115 Abb. 122–124; Joachim 2012, 95–103.

[2] Lindenschmit d. Ä. 1870, Taf. 2.

[3] Jacobsthal 1944, Nr. 28 Taf. 25,28.

 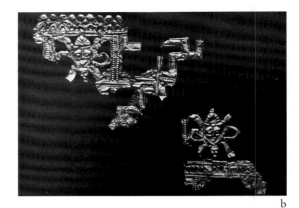

Abb. 1. Bad Dürkheim, Elitengrab. a Erste publizierte Rekonstruktion der Goldfragmente und Ansprache als Trinkhornbeschlag durch Ludwig Lindenschmit d. Ä.; b leicht veränderte Rekonstruktion durch Paul Jacobsthal.

Person mit Diadem oder einen alten Mann mit langem Vollbart darstellt[4]. Dieses Beispiel wurde infolgedessen häufig aufgegriffen und untermauerte die Popularität des Stücks.

Seit September 2017 widmet sich das von ANR und DFG geförderte Forschungsprojekt „CELTIC GOLD – Fine metal work in the Western La Tène culture" der archäologischen und archäometrischen Erforschung latènezeitlicher Goldobjekte mit Fokus auf das Gebiet der westlichen Latènekultur[5]. In diesem Zusammenhang wurden auch die goldenen Relikte aus dem besagten Elitengrab von Bad Dürkheim ausführlich untersucht[6]. Es bot sich daher die günstige Gelegenheit, sich des „Desiderats" einer Überprüfung der Rekonstruktion von L. Lindenschmit anzunehmen[7]. Aufgrund mehrerer Unstimmigkeiten in den Motiven der zusammengesetzten Teile der bisherigen Rekonstruktion wurde erneut eine systematische Anpassung der Fragmente vorgenommen, deren Ergebnisse im Folgenden vorgestellt werden sollen. Weiter soll die Herstellungstechnik dieses Stückes im Kontext zeitgleicher Parallelen geklärt werden. Abschließend soll auch die Ansprache als Trinkhornbeschlag hinsichtlich ihrer Pro- und Contra-Argumente kritisch abgewogen werden, da doch die Größe des erhaltenen Fragments auch andere Interpretationen zulassen würde.

Beschreibung

Um die Neurekonstruktion besser nachvollziehen zu können, ist zunächst eine Beschreibung aller Bestandteile, ihrer Konstruktionsweise sowie des verwendeten Verzierungskanons erforderlich. Bei den einzelnen Fragmenten handelt es sich um sechs unterschiedlich große Stücke aus einem rund 0,03 mm dünnen Goldblech *(Abb. 2)*. Bereits auf den ersten

---

[4] MEGAW 1969. – Kritisch hierzu: NORTMANN 2017, 50.

[5] DFG-Projektnummer 322994757, ANR-Projektnummer 16-FRAL-0001.

[6] Neben der optischen und mikroskopischen Dokumentation erfolgten auch REM-, RFA- und LA-ICPMS-Analysen zur Ermittlung der Elementzusammensetzungen sowie Herstellungs- bzw. Fügetechniken durch Roland Schwab und Nicole Lockhoff. – Für die freundliche Unterstützung bedanken wir uns bei Lars Börner und Lucius Alsen vom Historischen Museum der Pfalz in Speyer. – Für anregende Diskussionen und hilfreiche Hinweise danken wir allen Projekt-Partnern, insbesondere Laurent Olivier vom Musée d'Archéologie Nationale in Saint-Germain-en-Laye.

[7] NORTMANN 2017, 48.

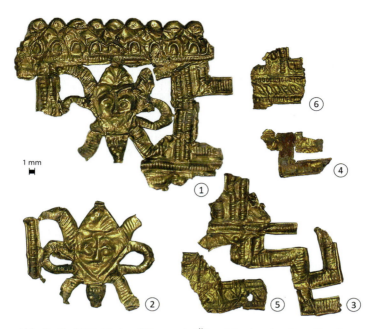

Abb. 2. Bad Dürkheim, Elitengrab. Übersicht der einzelnen Bruchstücke.

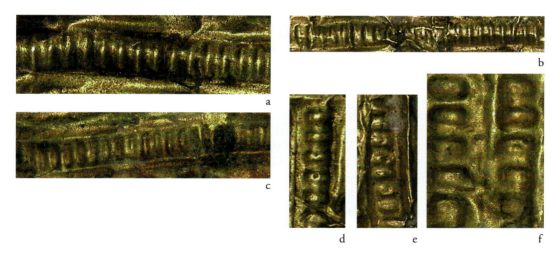

Abb. 3. Bad Dürkheim, Elitengrab. a Waagrechte Perlleiste von Stück 1 auf Seite des Kinns; b waagrechte Perlleiste von Stück 1, Stirnseite; c Rückseite der waagrechten Perlleiste von Stück 1, Kinnseite; d senkrechte Perlleiste von Stück 1 neben der linken Gesichtshälfte; e senkrechte Perlleiste von Stück 1 neben der rechten Gesichtshälfte; f Rückseite von Stück 3.

Blick wird deutlich, dass es sich um eine Durchbrucharbeit mit mindestens zwei erhaltenen Masken handelt, die, wie das besterhaltene Stück 1 suggeriert, wohl in Form von annähernd quadratischen Metopen aufgebaut war. Dabei gehen wir von einem oberen und einem unteren Register aus. Das nicht-figürliche Zierrepertoire umfasst eine sogenannte Schuppenleiste, eine Torsionsborte, breite geschwungene oder gewinkelte Leiterbänder sowie verschiedene Perlleisten. Es lassen sich eng gerippte *(Abb. 3a–c)* und breit geperlte *(Abb. 3d–f)* Leisten unterscheiden. Besonders viele Perlleisten sind noch auf Bruchstück 1 sichtbar. Dort bilden sie den quadratischen Rahmen der Maske. Hier zeigt sich, dass die breit geperlte Variante ausschließlich bei den vertikalen und die enggerippte nur bei den horizontalen Leisten vorkommt.

Technologische Aspekte

Der reich verzierte und durchbrochene Beschlag ist nur in Fragmenten erhalten. Daher kann nicht präzisiert werden, ob der Beschlag eine geschlossene, zylindrische Ausgangsform hatte oder aus einem planen rechteckigen Blech entwickelt wurde, das schließlich – sofern es sich tatsächlich um einen Trinkhornbeschlag handelt – zu einem leicht konischen Zylinder gebogen wurde.

Alle erhaltenen Teile weisen darauf hin, dass das Ensemble ehemals aus zwei sich überlagernden Blechen, einem bronzenen und einem goldenen, gefertigt war. Trotz fortgeschrittener Korrosion sind noch Reste des Bronzeblechs, vor allem unter den umgeschlagenen Rändern des Goldblechs, erhalten *(Abb. 4)*. Damit bestätigt sich die bereits von P. Jacobsthal nur implizit erwähnte und von Dirk Krausse konkret geäußerte Konstruktionsweise, die teilweise von anderen Autoren hingegen verworfen wurde[8].

Die friesartige, teils figürliche Verzierung des Blechbeschlages ist durch die Pressblechtechnik erzeugt. Dazu wurde zunächst ein geschmiedetes Blech aus einer Kupferlegierung (Zinn-Bronze?) durch Ziselieren und Punzieren mit einem Relief verziert. Die Konturen der ajourierten Bereiche wurden sodann mit Hilfe eines Meißels mit geschärfter Schneide herausgetrennt. Erst nach dem Trennvorgang wurde das dünne Goldblech über das Bronzeblech – wie über einen Pressmodel – gedrückt. Dabei zeichnen sich auch die Konturen der Durchbruchsarbeit ab. Anschließend löste man das Goldblech vom Bronzeblech wieder, um es ebenfalls mit Durchbrüchen zu versehen. Um die Ränder des Goldblechs um das Bronzeblech bördeln zu können, haben die Aussparungen des Goldblechs etwas kleinere Abmessungen. Die beiden gleich verzierten Teile wurden anschließend wieder, dem Relief entsprechend, passend übereinandergelegt und sodann durch Umschlagen bzw. Bördeln der verschiedenen Ränder des Goldblechs (zwei parallele, begrenzende Ränder des breiten Blechstreifens, und zahlreiche Ränder der Durchbruchsarbeiten) um die Bronzeblechränder zusammengefügt. Abschließend wurde der fertige bi-metallische Zierbeschlag über den Träger geschoben.

Im Unterschied zur herkömmlichen Pressblechtechnik, bei der die Motive von einem massiven Pressmodel direkt auf das Goldblech übertragen werden, liegt hier eine seltenere Variante vor, bei der das Bronzeblech als Motivträger (und somit als Pressmodel) fungiert und mit dem dünnen Goldblech mechanisch fest verbunden bleibt.

---

[8] P. Jacobsthal (1944, Nr. 28) und in der Folge auch Megaw (1969, 85) erwähnen eine grüne Patina. – D. Krausse (1996, 196) spricht unter Berufung auf eine Mitteilung von Lothar Sperber konkret von erhaltenen Bronzeblech- und Harzresten (bei letzteren handelt es sich sehr wahrscheinlich um die von Lindenschmit vorgenommene Stabilisierung der Bleche durch eine Art Wachs; vgl. hierzu die Ausführungen zu Stück 6 weiter unten); in seiner Liste 9 Nr. 3 auf S. 407 erwähnt D. Krausse jedoch weder Bördelung noch Reste von Bronzeblech. – Kritisch bezüglich einer Bördelung und Blechhinterfütterung äußern sich explizit Hans Nortmann (2017, 48) und implizit Hans-Eckart Joachim (2012, 98). – Auf das Problem, dass mangelnde Informationen zu etwaigen Bronzeblechhinterfütterungen eine typologische Aufbereitung des Fundstoffs erschweren, wird im letzten Abschnitt näher eingegangen. P. Jacobsthal (1944, Nr. 28) und in der Folge auch V. Megaw (1969, 85) erwähnen eine grüne Patina.

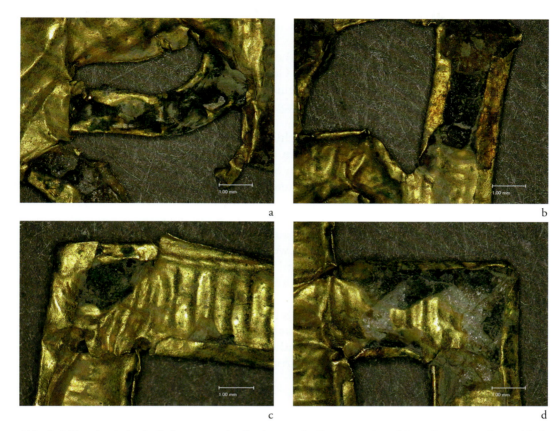

Abb. 4. Mikroskopische Aufnahmen von den Rückseiten der Fragmente 2 und 3 mit Resten von Bronzeblech unter der Umbördelung. a Rückseite des Fragments 2 im Bereich der seitlichen Schlaufe mit senkrechter Perlleiste; b oberer Bereich der senkrechten Perlleiste desselben Fragments; c–d Details der Rückseite des Fragments 3 im Bereich des Swastika-Motivs.

Im Gegensatz zur herkömmlichen Pressblechtechnik können nicht nur dünnere Goldbleche verwendet werden, sie sind sogar unerlässlich, um die Motive des Bronzeblechs besser hervortreten zu lassen. Die Verwendung eines Bronzeblechs als stabilisierende Unterlage und Motivträger ermöglicht also einen ökonomischen Umgang mit dem Edelmetall. Vielleicht sollte das Ensemble aus zwei Metallen auch vortäuschen, es handele sich um ein massives Goldblech. Da die bronzene Unterlage vollständig mit Goldblech überzogen ist, war das Bronzeblech beim Gebrauch des Beschlages auf einem Trinkhorn oder einem anderen Gegenstand nicht sichtbar und hatte daher keinen farblichen Effekt. Allerdings war das künstlerische Anliegen des Gesamtobjektes zweifarbig, indem der ajourierte Beschlag im Zusammenspiel mit dem andersfarbigen Material des Untergrundes kontrastierte.

Die Verwendung dieser speziellen Verbundstoff-Technik ist nicht auf dieses Stück beschränkt. Aus der Latènezeit sind weitere Goldschmiedearbeiten mit Bronzeblechunterlage bekannt. Darunter finden sich etwa die Scheiben des Typs Weiskirchen. Diese sind oft aus drei Materialien, Gold, Kupferlegierung und Eisen, zusammengesetzt[9].

---

[9] Auch bei einigen Scheibenfibeln findet sich die Pressblechtechnik aus einer Bronzeunterlage und dünnem, angedrücktem Goldblech, allerdings sind diese nicht durchbrochen gearbeitet. Gut zu sehen ist dies bei dem Scheibenfibelfragment von Hoppstädten (Lkr. Birkenfeld, DE), Hügel 2 (HAFFNER

Fragmente 1 und 2 mit Masken und Tierköpfen

Fragment 1 ist das größte (29 mm × 36 mm) erhaltene Bruchstück dieser Durchbrucharbeit (vgl. *Abb. 2,1*). Im Zentrum steht das Gesicht einer bartlosen Person mit einer Palmette über dem Kopf, bei der es sich um eine Art Diadem („Palmettenkrone") handeln könnte – auch wenn sich archäologische Belege für einen solchen Gegenstand bisher nicht fassen lassen[10].

Bei Fragment 2 handelt es sich hauptsächlich um eine weitere Maske (vgl. *Abb. 2,2*). Interessant sind die kleinen Unterschiede in den Details beider Figuren[11]. Im Vergleich zur Maske von Stück 1 wirkt diejenige von Stück 2 stärker rautenförmig. Die „Palmettenkrone" ist dreieckiger und die Wangen- und Kinnpartie wirken geradliniger und etwas schematischer als bei der Maske von Stück 1. Auch die Gestaltung der Augenbrauen und der Stirn unterscheiden sich. Es ist unklar, ob sie mithilfe derselben Model hergestellt wurden oder inwieweit diese Unterschiede auf eine Deformierung im Grab bzw. bei der Bergung oder Restaurierung zurückgeführt werden können. Zumindest die Maße (Breite auf Höhe der Augen ca. 7 mm, Höhe 17 mm) sind bei beiden im jetzigen Zustand in etwa identisch, was hinsichtlich der Gesamtrekonstruktion nicht unproblematisch ist, wie weiter unten noch gezeigt wird.

Von den Randeinfassungen hat sich an Stück 2 nur eine Stelle an der Seite erhalten. Vor dem Hintergrund der Gesamtrekonstruktion handelt es sich hierbei jedoch um eine wichtige Stelle, denn im Gegensatz zur Maske von Fragment 1 liegt hier keine doppelte Perlleiste vor[12]. Aufgrund des fehlenden Bartwuchses lässt sich das Geschlecht der dargestellten Person nicht sicher bestimmen[13].

J. V. S. Megaw sah in den Masken eine Kippfigur: In der Ausrichtung, wie sie in den Rekonstruktionen von Lindenschmit und Jacobsthal vorliegt, wurden die Masken als Gesicht eines Jünglings mit Palmettenkrone interpretiert. Sobald man sie allerdings um 180° dreht, erscheint seiner Meinung nach das Gesicht eines alten Mannes, wobei die ursprüngliche Kopfbedeckung einen langen Vollbart bildet.

Bei der mikroskopischen Untersuchung der beiden Fragmente fiel auf, dass unterhalb der Masken in der „Jünglingsansicht" jeweils ein kleiner Tierkopf dargestellt wurde *(Abb. 5)*. Diese Köpfe fanden unserer Kenntnis nach bisher keine Erwähnung[14]. Vielmehr wurden sie zumeist als ein „Dreipass aus Punktbuckeln" angesprochen, was in Anbetracht der wenig detaillierten Fotografie Jacobsthals und insbesondere aufgrund der bekannten Zeichnung Lindenschmits in den „Alterthümern" völlig verständlich ist, denn auch dort wurden sie als Dreipass, wie er in der Frühlatènekunst oft zu finden ist, abgebildet[15]. Interessant ist jedoch, dass die Zeichnung in seinem unpublizierten Handskizzenbuch allerdings eindeutig zwei Tierköpfe wiedergibt[16].

1976, Taf. 137,3), das ebenfalls im Rahmen des CELTIC GOLD-Projektes untersucht werden konnte.

[10] Vgl. das Motiv der Blattkrone, das sich im Fürstengrab 1 vom Glauberg (DE) auch anscheinend dinglich manifestiert hat (FRÖLICH 2006).

[11] Den Hinweis verdanken wir Michael Ober, RGZM.

[12] Dass es sich auch nicht um einen Riss handeln kann, der einen doppelten Perldraht teilte, wird durch die Rückseite bestätigt, wo man deutlich die beidseitige Bördelung erkennen kann.

[13] MEGAW 1969. – Auf diese Interpretation wird weiter unten näher eingegangen.

[14] NORTMANN 2017, 50.

[15] Gleiches gilt für die späteren Zeichnungen von Elfie Eschmann (Speyer) und Franz-Josef Dewald (Rheinisches Landesmuseum Trier), vgl. BARDELLI 2017a, 49 Abb. 8–10.

[16] BARDELLI 2017a, Taf. 5 und besonders gut auf dem Buchtitel zu erkennen.

Abb. 5. Detail der beiden Tierköpfe unterhalb der beiden Masken. a Tierkopf von Fragment 1; b Tierkopf von Fragment 2.

Aufgrund der geringen Größe sind die beiden Tierköpfe an den Fragmenten 1 und 2 sehr abstrakt gehalten. Es lässt sich daher nicht genau sagen, welches Tier dargestellt wird. Zumindest ein Karnivor – etwa ein Hund / Wolf oder Bär – erscheint recht wahrscheinlich. Da die beiden Bleche unterschiedlich stark deformiert sind, unterscheiden sich beide Darstellungen ein wenig. Ob dies beabsichtigt war und zwei verschiedene Kreaturen dargestellt werden sollten, ist zwar eher unwahrscheinlich, aber auch nicht ganz auszuschließen. Der Tierkopf von Fragment 1 wirkt zumindest heute schmaler und langgezogener und ähnelt damit eher einem Caniden.

Durch den Tierkopf unterhalb der Maske wird gewissermaßen ein motivisch-ästhetisches Gegengewicht zur kegelförmig zulaufenden Palmette gebildet. So entsteht eine doppelkonische Gesamtkomposition.

Unter Berücksichtigung des Tierkopfes unterhalb des „Jünglingsgesichtes" lassen sich die beiden oberen und unteren Leiterbänder auch als die Gliedmaßen eines ausgestreckt liegenden, erlegten Tieres interpretieren[17]. Vielleicht symbolisieren die beiden Bögen an den Flanken der Maske den Körper des Tieres und er wurde nur als Umriss dargestellt, um die Silhouette der Maske[18] und den Gesamtcharakter der Durchbruchsarbeit nicht zu plump wirken zu lassen.

Metopenfeld

Da Fragment 1 zumindest noch Reste von allen vier begrenzenden Perlleisten aufweist, lässt sich die Größe und Form des Zierfeldes gut abschätzen (vgl. *Abb. 2,1*): Es handelte sich anscheinend um ein annähernd quadratisches Rechteck mit einer Breite von rund 2,3 cm und einer Höhe von rund 1,8 cm[19]. Die senkrechte Abtrennung des Feldes erfolgte über eine gedoppelte, breite Perlleiste, während der untere Abschluss lediglich durch eine einfache, eng gerippte Perlleiste erfolgte.

---

[17] Bisher wurde meist „eine ausgeschnittene Version des Lotusknospen-Motivs" (MEGAW 1969, 85) oder eine „stilisierte Blüte" (ECHT 1999, 130) angenommen; NORTMANN (2017, 48) spricht von „einem kurvolinearen Netz" und von einem „Stegnetz", das man als „rudimentäres Lotus- und Palmettenarrangement" auffassen kann.

[18] Man bedenke den bereits erwähnten doppelkonischen Aufbau dieser Maskendarstellung und die Parallelen mit Basse-Yutz (FR) und Reinheim (DE).

[19] Eine exakte Angabe ist aufgrund des stark verbogenen Erhaltungszustands nicht möglich.

Abb. 6. Detail der Schuppenborte von Stück 1.

Schuppenborte

Über der oberen horizontalen, eng gerippten Perlleiste schließt eine sogenannte Schuppenborte an (*Abb. 6*; vgl. *Abb. 2,1*)[20]. Sie setzt sich aus insgesamt drei übereinander angeordneten Reihen jeweils unterschiedlicher Einzelmotive zusammen: Die untere Reihe besteht aus einem eingeprägten Bogenmotiv. Darüber schließt eine weitere, allerdings um einen halben Bogen versetze und anders gestaltete Reihe an. Da diese bis in die Zwickel der darunter liegenden Bögen zieht, entsteht ein Art Peltamotiv. Eine besondere Plastizität erhalten diese Pelten durch ihre leichte Wölbung. Den oberen Abschluss der Borte bilden ähnlich gewölbte, etwas breitere peltaförmige Motive. Auf der Rückseite sind sie mit recht breitem Rand umgebördelt. Da die leicht versetzten bzw. überlappenden Bögen der oberen beiden Reihen zudem plastisch gewölbt sind, erinnert das Motiv bei näherer Betrachtung nicht nur an Fischschuppen, sondern auch an einen geschlossenen Kiefernzapfen.

Schuppenborten sind gerade bei Trinkhornbeschlägen sehr häufig anzutreffen, worauf weiter unten noch näher eingegangen wird. Da die Schuppenborte in all diesen Fällen den oberen Abschluss bildet, erscheint dies auch für das Bad Dürkheimer Stück wahrscheinlich. Hieraus ergeben sich wichtige Konsequenzen für die Gesamtausrichtung des Stücks, denn von jener Schuppenborte, die wiederum von einer einfachen, enggerippten Perlleiste begleitet wird, gehen im rechten Winkel nur doppelte Perlleisten ab. Diese ist an der rechten Seite des Zierfeldes von Stück 1 noch vollständig erhalten (vgl. *Abb. 2,1*) und wird schließlich von einer einfachen, eng gerippten Leiste rechtwinklig gekreuzt. Darunter

---

[20] Der Begriff wird von Nortmann (2017, 48) als auch in ähnlicher Weise bereits von Megaw (1969) verwendet.

lassen sich in der Flucht der linken Doppelleiste sogar noch die ersten beiden Perlbuckel der darunter anschließenden Leiste erkennen. Die nächste wichtige Erkenntnis bezüglich der Gesamtrekonstruktion ist also, dass im unteren Register eher mit einer einfachen senkrechten Perlleiste zu rechnen ist. So lassen sich alle Fragmente bereits grob orientieren: Doppelte Perlleisten müssen senkrecht ausgerichtet werden und zur oberen Reihe gehören; enger gerippte, einfache Perlleisten sind waagrecht orientiert, flauere, einfache Perlleisten wiederum senkrecht ausgerichtet, aber eher der unteren Reihe zuzuordnen.

Die geometrischen Fragmente 3 und 4

Für die Rekonstruktion der Gesamtgestaltung des Bleches ist das Fragment 3 (vgl. *Abb. 2,3*) sehr aufschlussreich, denn es zeigt neben einem rechtwinklig mäandrierenden Motiv aus Leiterbändern auch den Schnittpunkt von vier Feldern. Eine doppelte und eine einfache Perlleiste werden von einer längeren, eher gerippt wirkenden Leiste rechtwinklig geschnitten. Dabei liegen die rechte Perlleiste der doppelten Ausführung und die einfache Perlleiste in einer Flucht.

Aus den vorherigen Überlegungen zur Position der Perlleisten im Gesamtgefüge lässt sich bereits die Orientierung des Stücks festlegen: Die doppelte Perlleiste gehört zur oberen Reihe, die lange, eher gerippte Leiste kennzeichnet eine horizontale Begrenzung. Dadurch ist wiederum klar, dass das mäandrierende geometrische Muster von Fragment 3 rechts unten zu einer Metope der unteren Reihe gehören muss. Das geometrische Motiv wird durch rund 2 mm breite Stege in Form eines Leiterbandes, bestehend aus je einer glatten Randleiste und dazwischen befindlichen Querrippen, erzeugt. In den Ecken scheinen die Rippen der rechtwinklig aufeinandertreffenden Leiterbänder im 45°-Winkel aufeinander zuzulaufen, wie an einer Stelle von Fragment 3 deutlich wird. In den übrigen Fällen ist der Übergang zwischen den Leiterbändern nicht mehr zu erkennen.

Zwar sind die vier Ecken der angrenzenden Zierfelder am Schnittpunkt der Perlleisten nur wenig erhalten, dennoch lassen sie sich anhand einiger kleiner Details recht gut zuordnen. Denn die rechte obere Ecke ist dreieckig gefüllt und stimmt hinsichtlich der Gestaltung mit der rechten unteren Ecke des Maskenfeldes überein[21].

Betrachtet man nun die linke untere Ecke am vorliegenden Stück 3, fällt zunächst ein großer Perlbuckel und ein bogenförmig zugeschnittener Ansatz mit Leiterbandzier auf. Auch diese Stelle lässt sich auf Fragment 1 identifizieren: Sie entspricht dort den oberen Ecken des Zierfeldes.

Kurz zusammengefasst bedeutet dies also für das Fragment 3 und somit auch für die Gesamtrekonstruktion, dass die rechte obere und die linke untere Metope wieder mit einer Maske verziert waren und somit ein diagonal alternierendes Muster an Zierelementen anzunehmen ist.

Tatsächlich passt Fragment 3 aufgrund der Fehlstellen genau an den linken unteren Bereich von Stück 1. Dass es sich nicht nur um eine motivisch passende Position handelt, sondern beide tatsächlich einst ein Stück bildeten, wird durch die mikroskopische Untersuchung der Bruchkanten erhärtet. Hier zeigen die Bruchstellen an den Stücken 1 und 2 recht große Ähnlichkeiten wie auch die Bruchstellen von Stück 1 und von Stück 3.

---

[21] Erleichtert wird die Zuordnung durch den Umstand, dass die Maskenmetope annähernd senkrecht achsensymmetrisch aufgebaut zu sein scheint. Zwar fehlt, wie erwähnt, die linke untere Ecke bei Fragment 1, doch wird anhand der übrigen Teile deutlich, dass linke und rechte, nicht aber obere und untere Hälfte gespiegelt werden können.

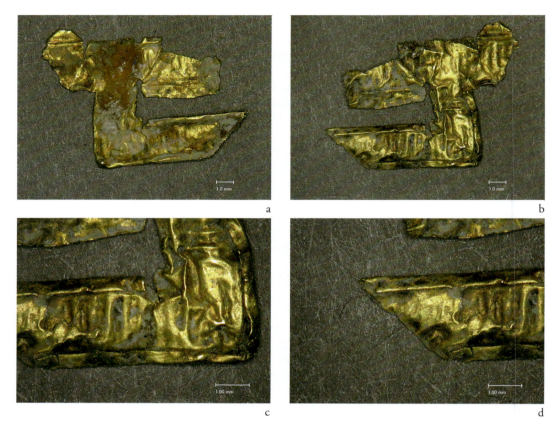

Abb. 7. Stück 4. a Versehentlich mit Wachs oder einem Harz stabilisierte Vorderseite des Goldblechs; b Übersicht der eigentlichen Rückseite; c–d Details der tatsächlichen Rückseite mit den umgeschlagenen Rändern.

Bei Fragment 4, dem kleinsten Teil des Ensembles (8 × 10 mm), handelt es sich um ein weiteres Stück eines geometrischen Motivs (*Abb. 7*; vgl. *Abb. 2,4*). Wie schon bei Stück 3 ist auch hier ein Leiterband diagonal abgebrochen. Aufgrund fehlender weiterer Verzierungselemente lässt sich das Fragment nicht weiter im Gesamtgefüge der Durchbrucharbeit verorten. Auch direkte Anpassungen finden sich an diesem Stück nicht. Bei der von P. Jacobsthal verwendeten Fotografie hatte das Stück noch einen heute fehlenden Fortsatz (vgl. *Abb. 1,2*). Bei der mikroskopischen Analyse wurde deutlich, dass L. Lindenschmit im Zuge seiner Restaurierungsmaßnahmen anscheinend die Vorder- und Rückseite verwechselte und daher versehentlich die eigentliche Vorderseite mit einer Art Wachs stabilisierte *(Abb. 7a)*, wie man an den umgebördelten Rändern auf der vermeintlichen Vorderseite klar erkennt *(Abb. 7b–d)*.

Die Fragmente 5–6 mit Torsionsborte

Das kleine Fragment 5 (19 × 12 mm; *Abb. 2,5*) besteht zum größten Teil aus einer rund 3 mm breiten, von je einer einfachen gerippten Perlleiste eingefassten Borte mit einem Torsionsmotiv, das sich aus aneinandergereihten leicht S-förmig gebogenen, sich an den Enden verjüngenden Einzelelementen zusammensetzt. Hierbei handelt es sich allem Anschein nach um den unteren Abschluss des Gesamtensembles, da es auf der unteren Seite trotz der verhältnismäßig langen erhaltenen Fläche keine erkennbaren Bruchkanten gibt, die auf ein fehlendes Zierelement deuten, sondern der komplette Bereich ursprünglich gebördelt war (dies ist besonders gut auf der Rückseite zu erkennen)[22]. Ein stellenweise kreisrundes Loch in der Mitte der Torsionsborte deutet darauf hin, dass die Durchbruchsarbeit inklusive der Bronzeunterlage mithilfe eines Nietstifts an einer Unterlage fixiert worden war. Eine rechtwinklig auf die Torsionsborte von Stück 5 treffende Perlleiste markiert die Grenze zweier Metopen. Auf der linken Seite verweisen die rechtwinkligen Leiterbänder, wie sie auch von den Fragmenten 1 und 3 bekannt sind, auf ein geometrisches Zierfeld. Die dreieckige Blechfüllung und der Rest eines tropfenförmigen Buckels sind bereits von den Fragmenten 1 und 3 bekannt und daher als unterer Abschluss der „Vorderläufe" unter einer Maske identifizierbar. Auch an dieser Stelle bestätigt sich also ein Wechsel von geometrischer und figürlicher Metope.

Die parallel verlaufenden Kanten der Bruchstellen von Stück 5 und Stück 2 sowie ein Abdruck in der Perlleiste von Stück 5, der von Position und Breite her gut zu dem kleinen Tierkopf von Stück 2 passen könnte, machen es sehr wahrscheinlich, dass diese beiden Teile einst zusammengehörten. Aufgrund der unter dem Mikroskop passenden Bruchstellen lässt sich die fragmentarische Ecke des linken geometrischen Feldes von Stück 5 mit dem Winkelornament von Stück 3 verbinden.

Das Fragment 6 (10 × 10 mm; vgl. *Abb. 2,6*) zeigt einen ähnlichen Ausschnitt wie Fragment 5. Allerdings ist die Torsionsborte deutlich kürzer und die Überreste der beiden Metopen sind spiegelverkehrt angeordnet. Links von der Perlleiste befand sich also einst ein Maskenfeld und rechts signalisiert ein parallel zur Torsionsborte ausgerichtetes Leiterband eine angrenzende geometrische Metope. Zwar passen die Bruchstelle von Fragment 6 und die rechte untere Bruchstelle von Maske 2 aufgrund der starken Beschädigung nicht so gut aneinander wie dies in anderen Fällen glückte, doch ergeben beide Teile – auch in Kombination mit Fragment 5 – genau die Größe einer Metope.

Gesamt(re)konstruktion

Zusammengefasst ergibt sich aus den einzelnen Erkenntnissen zu Formparallelen und aus den Bruchkantenanpassungen der in *Abbildung 8* dargestellte Vorschlag einer Rekonstruktion[23]. Einzig das kleine Fragment Nr. 4 lässt sich aufgrund fehlender (oder nicht erkannter) Anpassungen keiner Stelle exakt zuordnen.

Für die Rekonstruktion sind insbesondere die Enden der geschwungenen Leiterbänder in den Ecken der Metopenfelder mit Maskenzier wichtig, denn die oberen Enden unterscheiden sich in einigen Details von den unteren. So zeigt sich anhand des besonders gut erhaltenen linken oberen Leiterbandes von Fragment 1 (*Abb. 8*, orangefarbene Markierung), dass sie in einer runden Punze direkt in den Ecken der Metopen enden. Die unteren Leiterbänder, die jeweils von der Kinnpartie der Maske ausgehen, sind leicht S-förmig gestaltet, weshalb der Winkel, in dem sie auf die Ränder der Metopen treffen, leicht von demjenigen der oberen Leiterbänder abweicht. Besonders auffällig ist jedoch, dass die unte-

---

[22] Man beachte in diesem Zusammenhang die Rekonstruktion Jacobsthals *(Abb. 1,2)*, der das Stück umgekehrt anpasste und daher von mindestens drei Registern ausgehen musste.

[23] Hierbei wurde eine Collage aus den einzelnen Blechfragmenten erstellt. Die farbigen Markierungen kennzeichnen gleiche Motive oder Anpassungen mit weitgehend parallel verlaufenden Kanten.

Abb. 8. Gesamtrekonstruktion mit Markierungen. Kreise kennzeichnen Formparallelen (Stellen, die ein Pendant innerhalb des Gesamtwerks besitzen und sei es die gegenüberliegende, spiegelverkehrte Seite). – Gelbe Rechtecke: Stellen mit verhältnismäßig parallel verlaufenden Kanten, die für eine direkte Anpassung zweier Stücke sprechen. – Rot: Ecken mit ausgefüllten Zwickeln im Bereich der „Vorderläufe" der Maskenmetope. – Orange: entsprechen den Stellen der „Hinterläufe". – Grün: Ansatzpunkte der geometrischen Felder. – Blau: Torsionsborte und Perllleisten. Die verschiedenen Typen von Perllleisten wurden in unterschiedlichen Blautönen gehalten.

ren Leiterbänder in flache, dreieckige Blechabschnitte münden, welche die gesamte untere Ecke ausfüllen (*Abb. 8*, rote Markierung). Im oberen Bereich dieser dreieckigen Zwickel befindet sich jeweils eine tropfenförmige Punze. Diese Stelle besitzt einen hohen Wiedererkennungswert und ließ sich auch an den Stücken 5 und 6 nachweisen. Weitere wichtige Indizien bei der Rekonstruktion waren die doppelt ausgeführten vertikalen Perllleisten im Gegensatz zu den einfachen unteren sowie die engere, stärker gerippte Form der waagrechten Leisten im Vergleich zu den flauer wirkenden vertikalen.

Abbildung 9a zeigt eine Darstellung des Rekonstruktionsvorschlags ohne die Markierungen, aber vor dem Hintergrund einer zeichnerischen Gesamtrekonstruktion, um einen besseren Eindruck von der Gesamtwirkung der Durchbruchsarbeit zu erhalten. Diesem Rekonstruktionsvorschlag zufolge handelt es sich also um eine Durchbruchsarbeit aus zwei übereinander angeordneten Metopenreihen, die von zwei unterschiedlichen Borten, einer tordierten unten und einer Schuppenborte oben, eingefasst wurden. Innerhalb der Zierfelder oder Metopen wechseln sich allem Anschein nach nur zwei Motive ab. Zudem ist die Motivfolge in den beiden Reihen um jeweils ein Feld verschoben, sodass sich eine schachbrettartige Anordnung ergibt.

Neues zum sogenannten Trinkhornbeschlag von Bad Dürkheim

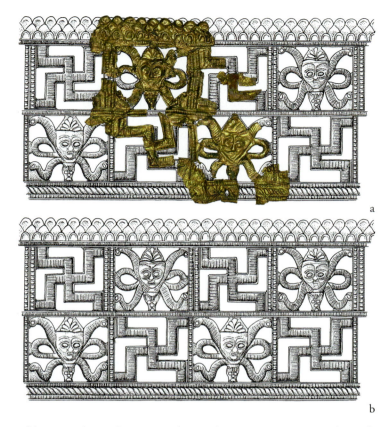

Abb. 9. Zeichnerische Gesamtrekonstruktion. a mit Anpassung der noch vorhandenen Stücke; b Reinzeichnung.

Problematisch erscheint allerdings die Klärung einer einstigen bogenförmigen Gesamtgestaltung des Blechs, um der konischen Hornform zu entsprechen. Die erhalten gebliebenen Teile sind zu gering und zu kleinteilig zerbrochen. Zudem sind sie teils deutlich verbogen und es ist unklar, wie ihr Zustand bei der Auffindung war und wie stark sie geradegebogen wurden, was mit Goldblechen damals öfter gemacht wurde, wie später gezeigt wird. Dies führt – auch hinsichtlich der Rekonstruktion – zu einem widersprüchlichen Befund: Einerseits wirken die Leiste und die Reste der Metope gerade, andererseits besteht die obere Metopenzeile aus einer doppelten und die untere nur aus einer senkrechten Perlleiste. Anhand der Stücke 1 und 3 sieht man, dass die untere Leiste einmal bündig mit der linken (Stück 1) und einmal mit der rechten (Stück 3) darüber befindlichen Doppelperlleiste endet. Anhand der Überreste der daneben befindlichen Metopen lässt sich eine Regelhaftigkeit erkennen: Das Maskenfeld ist in beiden Fällen das mutmaßlich vergrößerte Feld. Dies führt jedoch zu einem Problem, denn die beiden Masken, die aufgrund der noch verbundenen Randleisten jeweils der oberen und der unteren Reihe angehören, sind annähernd gleich breit. Wenn das Blech gerade ausgerichtet auf einem zylindrischen oder planen Untergrund befestigt worden wäre, entstünde eine Lücke, die irgendwie gefüllt werden müsste. Man könnte annehmen, dass dieses Detail eingebaut wurde, um die Breite des unteren Feldes dezent verringern zu können, ohne dass es zu auffälligen Fehlstellen gekommen wäre – schließlich hätte es auf ein konisches Horn befestigt werden müssen.

Doch die Breite einer zusätzlichen Perlleiste im oberen Register beträgt lediglich 1–2 mm. Wie weiter unten noch gezeigt wird, würde diese geringe Verbreiterung selbst bei einer Länge von acht Feldern wohl nicht ausreichen, um einen passenden Bogen für das konische Horn zu erzeugen.

Diese Fragen und Unsicherheiten stellten sich auch bei der Anfertigung der zeichnerischen Rekonstruktion *(Abb. 9b)*. Aufgrund der in der heutigen Form sichtbaren geraden Ausrichtung des Blechs haben wir uns für eine gerade Rekonstruktion entschieden. Gestützt wurde diese Entscheidung dadurch, dass es ein wenig so wirkt, als sei eine Art Pufferblech an den seitlichen Schlaufen der Maske von Stück 2 vorhanden, wodurch das Feld insgesamt breiter gestaltet werden könnte. Eine bogenförmige Gestaltung des Beschlags wäre allerdings ebenfalls denkbar.

Rekonstruktion der ursprünglichen Größe

Anhand der Höhe des Metopenfeldes von Stück 1 von ca. 1,8 cm (die auch für die untere Metopenreihe hypothetisch angenommen wird) sowie 0,7 cm für die Schuppenborte und weiteren 0,5 cm für die Torsionsborte liegt die rekonstruierte Höhe des Blechs bei rund 5,0 cm. Vergleicht man das Stück aus Bad Dürkheim mit den übrigen Beschlägen dieser Art, liegt das Maß im oberen Bereich zwischen dem Exemplar aus Dörth (4,0 cm; Rhein-Hunsrück-Kreis, DE) und dem größten bekannten Zierblech aus Eigenbilzen (5,7 cm; Prov. Limburg, BE)[24].

Die seitlichen Grenzen des Motivs sind allem Anschein nach nicht zu fassen. Da sowohl am linken als auch am rechten Rand noch Ansätze für weitere Metopen vorhanden sind, war das Blech also mindestens vier Felder breit. Eine Krümmung, wie z.B. beim Goldblech von Eigenbilzen, die für ein gebogenes Horn als Grundlage sprechen würde, ist allerdings nicht feststellbar. Die Breite kann nur an Stück 1 ermittelt werden, da hier noch zwei gegenüberliegende senkrechte Doppelreihen vorhanden sind. Eingedenk der Tatsache, dass die Metope deutlich verbogen ist, lässt sich ein Breite des Metopenfeldes (jeweils von der Mitte der doppelten Perlleiste aus gemessen) von rund 2,3 cm ermitteln. Bei vier Feldern läge die Mindestlänge bei ca. 9,2 cm. Mit der Formel $U = 2 \pi r$ erhält man einen Mindestdurchmesser von rund 2,9 cm, was so gering ist, dass eigentlich nur drei Erklärungen wahrscheinlich sind: 1) Entweder es fehlt noch der größte Teil des Beschlags oder 2) er wurde nicht im Bereich der Mündung, sondern eher im unteren Bereich des Trinkhorns angebracht[25] oder 3) die Durchbruchsarbeit war auf einem gänzlich anderen Objekt (etwa einer Zierscheibe oder einem Gürtelhaken) befestigt (wobei sich die Erklärungen 1 und 3 nicht ausschließen). In Anbetracht der komplexen Motivik erscheint die Erklärung 2 eher unwahrscheinlich, denn sowohl das Swastika-Motiv als auch die Gesichter würden bei einer derart starken Krümmung, wie sie bei einem Mindestdurchmesser von

---

[24] Das Stück aus Bescheid (DE), Hügel 6, ist mit 2,4 cm am kleinsten, das Blech aus Weiskirchen, Hügel 2 (Lkr. Merzig-Wadern, DE), kommt auf 2,8–3 cm; Reinheim liegt mit 3,38 u. 3,25 cm im Mittelfeld. – Allerdings handelt es sich sowohl bei Bescheid als auch bei Weiskirchen nicht um durchbrochen gearbeitete Stücke. – Vergleicht man alle Maße der acht Zierbänder, so zeigt sich, dass die beiden aus Reinheim und das Stück aus Weiskirchen mit einer Oberfläche von rund 45–50 cm² eine Gruppe eher zierlicher Bleche bilden, während die beiden Stücke aus Dörth und der Beschlag von Bescheid, Hügel 6, zwischen ca. 82 und 90 cm² besitzen und jenes aus Eigenbilzen mit 123 cm² noch einmal deutlich größer ist.

[25] Nur in Pellingen „Dreikopf" Hügel 1 (DE) und Schwarzenbach „Fürstengrab" 1 (DE) scheint ein echter Randbeschlag vorhanden gewesen zu sein; vgl. *Anhang*.

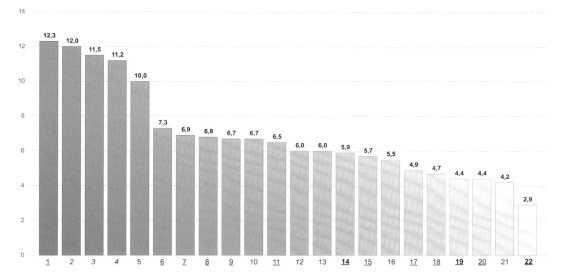

Abb. 10. Verteilung der unterschiedlichen Durchmesserrekonstruktionen. – 1 Bescheid (Lkr. Trier-Saarburg, DE), Hügel 6, Blechband; 2 Schwarzenbach (Lkr. Hof, DE), Grab 1, Randbeschlag der Schale; 3 Dürrnberg (AT), Grab 59, Randbeschlag (Dm. außen 12,6 cm, Innendm. geschätzt); 4 Pellingen (Lkr. Trier-Saarburg, DE), Randbeschlag; 5 Auvers-sur-Oise (Dép. Val-d'Oise, FR), Deckel; 6 Kleinaspergle (Lkr. Ludwigsburg, DE), längliches Blechband 1; 7 Dörth (Rhein-Hunsrück-Kreis, DE), Blechband 1; 8 Eigenbilzen (Prov. Limburg, BE), Blechband; 9 Kleinaspergle, längliches Blechband 2; 10 Schwarzenbach, Grab 1, Deckel 1; 11 Dörth, Blechband 2; 12 Mülheim-Kärlich (Lkr. Mayen-Koblenz, DE), Grab 4, Randbeschlag; 13 Schwarzenbach, Grab 1, Deckel 2; 14 Bad Dürkheim (8 Register); 15 Somme-Bionne (Dép. Marne, FR), Blechband; 16 Groß-Rohrheim (Lkr. Bergstraße, DE), Manschette 1; 17 Weiskirchen (Lkr. Merzig-Wadern, DE), Hügel 2, Blechband; 18 Reinheim (Saarpfalz-Kreis, DE), Blechband 1; 19 Bad Dürkheim (sechs Register); 20 Reinheim, Blechband 2; 21 Groß-Rohrheim, Manschette 2; 22 Bad Dürkheim (vier Register). – Kursiv: Randbeschläge; fett: Varianten des Bad Dürkheimer Beschlags; unterstrichen: Blechbänder.

2,9 cm entstünde, nicht richtig erfasst werden können[26]. Da die Anzahl der Metopenfelder immer eine gerade sein muss, weil sich sonst an den Fügestellen Motivdopplungen ergeben würden, kann die nächstgrößere Variante nur aus sechs Feldern bestanden haben. Die sich hieraus ergebende Länge von 13,8 cm und der Durchmesser von 4,4 cm entsprächen dem einen Beschlag von Reinheim (Saarpfalz-Kreis, DE; vgl. *Anhang*). Auch hier handelt es sich nicht um einen Mündungsbeschlag, sondern eher um eine Verzierung im mittleren Bereich. Eine Variante mit acht Registern ergäbe eine Länge von 18,4 cm und einen entsprechenden Durchmesser von 5,9 cm. Eine Auflistung der noch rekonstruierbaren Durchmesser verschiedener Beschläge *(Abb. 10)* zeigt, dass diese Variante zwischen dem Beschlag von Somme-Bionne (Dép. Marne, FR) und Mülheim-Kärlich, Hügel 4 (Lkr. Mayen-Koblenz, DE), läge. Generell zeigt die Verteilung der rekonstruierbaren Durchmesser einen kontinuierlichen Verlauf, den man bei Verzierungen eines natürlichen Produktes wie einem Horn auch erwarten darf[27]. Auffällig ist die deutliche Zweiteilung hinsichtlich

---

[26] Die Blechfragmente wurden womöglich nach ihrer Entdeckung plattgedrückt, doch wirken sie nicht allzu stark gekrümmt.

[27] Bei dieser Aufstellung wurden alle Beschläge verwendet, die einen Aufschluss über einen Durchmesser erlauben – also Randbeschläge, Manschetten und natürlich auch die bandförmigen Blechbeschläge. Daher muss bedacht werden, dass sie sich je nach Beschlagart auch an unterschiedlichen Stellen des Horns befanden.

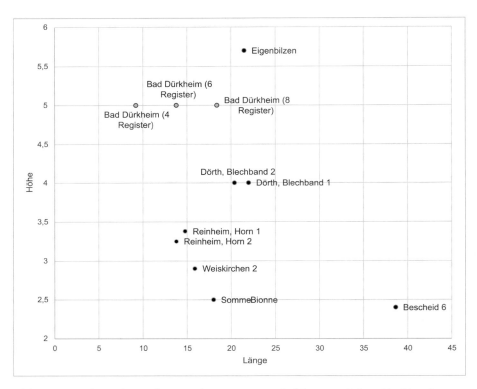

Abb. 11. Verteilung der Höhen- und Längenwerte frühlatènezeitlicher Blechbänder von Trinkhörnern.

des Durchmessers. Die Beschläge aus Bescheid (Lkr. Trier-Saarburg, DE), Hügel 6, aus Schwarzenbach (Lkr. St. Wendel, DE), Grab 1[28], sowie der bronzene Beschlag aus Pellingen (Lkr. Trier-Saarburg, DE), Hügel 1, setzten sich deutlichen von den anderen Stücken ab. Dies liegt vermutlich daran, dass es sich bei diesen Stücken wahrscheinlich um Beschläge von Auerochsenhörnern handelt[29]. Die Verteilung der Höhen- und Längenwerte der bandförmigen Blechbeschläge allein *(Abb. 11)* zeigt, dass alle vollständigen Beschläge bis auf das bereits erwähnte aus Bescheid, Hügel 6, hinsichtlich ihrer Länge in einem Korridor zwischen 13,8 (Reinheim) und 22 cm (Dörth) liegen. Hier wäre die idealisierte Rekonstruktion des Bad Dürkheimer Stücks mit insg. sechs Registern dem unteren Bereich zuzuordnen, aber bereits im Rahmen des Bekannten. Die hypothetische Variante mit acht Registern läge indes in etwa im Mittelfeld der bekannten Funde. Die Höhe der Bleche variiert in ähnlicher Weise[30]. Die recht gesicherte Höhe von rund 5,0 cm ordnet das Bad Dürkheimer Blech im oberen Bereich ein.

[28] Hier könnte es sich tatsächlich um eine Schale handeln, wenngleich auch die Wandung anscheinend falsch rekonstruiert wurde und das scheibenförmige Blech am Boden der „Schale" nicht zugehörig ist oder auch hier die Form falsch rekonstruiert wurde; vgl. die ausführliche Diskussion bei KRAUSSE 1996, 199–217.

[29] Vgl. KRAUSSE 1996, 187; 217, der dies auch für Bescheid und Schwarzenbach in Erwägung zieht.

[30] Die Darstellung mag eine stärkere Varianz suggerieren, doch die geringste Höhe, die ausgerechnet das längst Blech von Bescheid, Hügel 6, besitzt, beträgt gerade einmal 2,4 cm, während Eigenbilzen mit 5,7 cm mehr als doppelt so hoch ist. Die relativen Größenunterschiede sind also hinsichtlich Höhe und Breite in etwa vergleichbar.

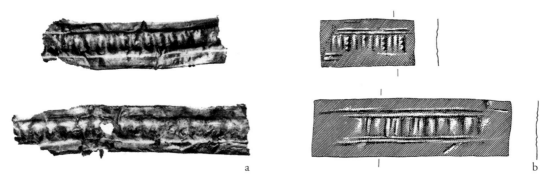

Abb. 12. Schmale Stege aus dünnem Goldblech mit Perlleistenverzierung. a Bescheid (Lkr. Trier-Saarburg), Hügel 4; b Murten-Löwenberg (Kt. Freiburg, CH), Hügel 1, Grab 3.

Diese recht ausführlichen Berechnungen verschiedener hypothetischer Längen waren wichtig, um zu zeigen, dass dem Blech aller Wahrscheinlichkeit nach entweder ein über fünfzigprozentiger Verlust widerfuhr oder dass es sich nicht um einen großen bandförmigen Beschlag handelte. Ein derart kurzer bandförmiger Beschlag ist nicht nur bisher unbekannt und wirkt daher hinsichtlich der Länge isoliert, sondern auch bezüglich der Motivik würde ein derart kurzer Beschlag kaum die mit den menschlichen Masken intendierte Wirkung erzielen, da die Gesichter, aber auch das Mäandermotiv stark verzerrt werden würden. Eine eindeutige Bestimmung der Länge ist aufgrund dieser hypothetischen Überlegungen nicht möglich.

Einordnung der Motive

Nachdem nun die Gesamtkomposition und die ungefähre Größe eingehend geschildert wurden, soll im Folgenden eine Einordnung der Motive in Bezug auf andere in etwa zeitgleiche Arbeiten erfolgen, um die kulturellen Verbindungen und Einflüsse besser einordnen zu können.

Parallelen zu den schmalen Stegen mit Perlleistenverzierung wie bei der Bad Dürkheimer Arbeit liegen aus zwei Gräbern vor: Zum einen handelt es sich um zwei kleine Fragmente aus dem Hügel 4 von Bescheid, deren Zierkontext jedoch unklar ist[31], und zum anderen um zwei ähnlich gestaltete Goldblechstreifen aus Murten-Löwenberg (Kt. Freiburg, CH), Hügel 1, Grab 3, die zusammen mit einigen Bronzeresten im Bereich der Hüfte gefunden und als Reste eines Gürtels angesprochen wurden *(Abb. 12a–b)*[32].

---

[31] HAFFNER / LAGE 2008/2009, 47 Nr. 6. – Die beiden Fragmente sind nur noch 1,2 bzw. 1,5 cm lang und 0,2 cm breit. Sie lagen zusammen mit zwei weiteren sehr kleinen und unverzierten Goldblechresten (Nr. 4–5; erh. L. 0,98 bzw. 1,1 cm) verstreut im Bereich eines Holzverfärbungsstreifens. D. Krausse sah in den beiden Goldblechstreifen formale und technische Übereinstimmungen mit den Manschetten aus Groß-Rohrheim (Lkr. Bergstraße, DE), weshalb er sie „mit einiger Wahrscheinlichkeit als Trinkhornbeschläge" deutete (KRAUSSE 1996, 195). Allerdings handelt es sich bei den Manschetten aus Groß-Rohrheim nicht um einfache schmale Stege mit Perlleistenzier mit beidseitiger Umbörtelung. Sie sind vielmehr deutlich komplexer aufgebaut (JORNS 1966, 224 Abb. 1). Eine Ansprache der drei Goldblechfragmente aus Bescheid, Hügel 4, als Bestandteile eines Trinkhornbeschlags erscheint aufgrund der mangelnden Fundlage und der nur vagen stilistischen Parallelen fraglich.

[32] SCHWAB 1984, 72; 76 Abb. 7e. – Die Fragmente besitzen eine Breite von 2 cm und eine Länge von 8 bzw. 4 cm. Hanni Schwab datiert das Grab in die Stufe Ha D2, aber sowohl der Ringschmuck als auch die beiden Doppelpaukenfibeln mit langer Armbrustkonstruktion und (nicht mehr erhaltener)

Masken

Hier seien zunächst die beiden Masken als besonders individuelle Zierelemente des Blechs zu nennen. Jennifer Bagley rechnet sie ihrer dritten Gruppe der anthropomorphen Kopfdarstellungen zu, die eine Zwitterstellung zwischen naturalistischen und sehr schematischen Darstellungen einnehmen: „Sie sind deutlich plastischer ausgestaltet, die einzelnen Elemente sind gegeneinander abgesetzt"[33]. Diese Gruppe besitzt einen Verbreitungsschwerpunkt „zwischen Mittelrhein, Mosel und Main, mit Ausläufern nach Frankreich, in die Schweiz und an die Donau bis nach Niederösterreich"[34]. Dass diese Gruppe so weit streut, liegt allerdings auch an der recht weit gefassten Gruppierung, die bei ihr z. B. auch die abstrakt wirkenden Darstellungen an der Unterseite der Ausgüsse der Kannen aus Basse-Yutz (Dép. Moselle, FR) oder die Darstellungen auf dem Helm von Agris (Dép. Charente, FR) auf der einen sowie Gesichtsdarstellungen auf einigen Fußpaukenfibeln der Variante Speikern auf der anderen Seite umfasst[35]. Diese weit gefasste Gruppe erscheint stilistisch zu uneinheitlich, was sich letztlich auch in ihrem Verbreitungsbild widerspiegelt. Den Masken aus Bad Dürkheim scheinen unseres Erachtens vier Darstellungen besonders nahezustehen, da sie ebenfalls eine „Palmettenkrone" besitzen und in Verbindung mit unterhalb des Kinns befindlichen Zierden eine grob rautenförmige Grundstruktur in der Komposition aufweisen. Hierbei handelt es sich insbesondere um die beiden Masken am oberen und unteren Ende des Henkels der Röhrenkanne aus Reinheim *(Abb. 13a–b)*, die eine fast identische Palmettenkrone sowie einen Vollbart als stilistisches Gegengewicht zur Erzeugung der doppelkonischen Form aufweisen. Aber auch die Attaschen der beiden Schnabelkannen aus Basse-Yutz besitzen einen ähnlichen dreieckigen Kopfschmuck, wobei das untere stilistische Gegengewicht durch die seitlichen Locken und ein mittiges Kreiselement erzeugt wird *(Abb. 13c)*[36]. Eine dritte Parallele, die den Basse-Yutz-Masken sehr nahesteht, stammt vom Attaschenbeschlag der Röhrenkanne vom Glauberg (Wetteraukreis, DE), Hügel 1, Grab 2 *(Abb. 13d)*. Diese Fundorte sind in etwa zeitgleich und nicht allzu weit voneinander entfernt. Alle vier Darstellungen besitzen einen Bart – im Falle von Reinheim sogar einen Vollbart – weshalb auch in Bad Dürkheim eine männliche Person wahrscheinlicher ist[37]. Alle Vergleiche stammen von Bestandteilen des Trinkservices – von zwei Röhrenkannen und zwei Schnabelkannen. Aus Goldblech gefertigte Masken, die ebenfalls als Trinkhornbeschläge interpretiert werden, stammen aus Schwarzenbach, Grab 1, und aus Ferschweiler (Lkr. Bitburg-Prüm, DE). Letztere ähnelt aufgrund der seitlich am Kopf verlaufenden und sich unter dem Kinn treffenden schraffiert dargestellten Zöpfe sowie dem Oberlippenbart zumindest den beiden Attaschenfiguren aus Basse-Yutz und vom Glauberg *(Abb. 13e)*.

Wie eingangs erwähnt, sah J. V. S. Megaw in den Masken eine Kippfigur[38]. Die anhand der Zeichnung vorgelegte Interpretation wirkt in der Tat glaubhaft und auch geradezu

---

Ziersehne (SCHWAB 1984, 76 Abb. 7a–b) sprechen für eine Datierung nach Ha D3 (vgl. HANSEN 2010, Liste 1 Nr. 205; KAENEL 1990, 216 Tab. 12).

[33] BAGLEY 2014, 113.
[34] BAGLEY 2014, 113.
[35] BAGLEY 2014, Taf. 48–56.
[36] MEGAW / MEGAW 1990. – Vgl. jüngst FREY 2014.
[37] Als weitere Vergleichsstücke für die „Palmettenkrone" nennt H. NORTMANN (2017, 50) zudem die Steinplastiken aus Pfalzfeld (DE), Heidelberg (DE) und vom Glauberg, die Goldscheibe von Weiskirchen und den Goldfingerring aus Rodenbach (DE). Diese Beispiele erscheinen uns jedoch als zu weit entfernt. Denn bei allen drei Steinskulpturen handelt es sich um spitzovale Motive als Bestandteil einer Blattkronenkappe. Und auch die beiden Palmetten auf den Köpfen von Weiskirchen und Rodenbach sind anders gestaltet und erzeugen eine andere Silhouette.

[38] MEGAW 1969.

Abb. 13. a–b Masken mit „Palmettenkrone" am Henkel der Röhrenkanne von Reinheim (Saarpfalz-Kreis); c Maske mit abgewandelter „Palmettenkrone" von der Attasche einer Schnabelkanne aus Basse-Yutz (Dép. Moselle, FR); d Masken von der Attasche der Röhrenkanne aus Hügel 1, Grab 2, vom Glauberg (Wetteraukreis, DE); e Ferschweiler (Lkr. Bitburg-Prüm, DE).

typisch für die Kunst der Frühlatènezeit, die bereits im Early Style mit kognitiven Phänomenen wie der multistabilen Wahrnehmung oder dem *Hidden Faces*-Effekt, der auch als Vexierbild bekannt ist, spielte[39]. Allerdings spiegeln die Zeichnungen nur einen gewissen

[39] Bei der multistabilen Wahrnehmung „kippt" die Betrachtungsweise eines Gegenstandes, wie etwa bei der bekannten Zeichnung „Meine Frau und meine Schwiegermutter" von William Ely Hill oder

Aspekt der Wahrnehmung dieser Masken wider. Der einstige, makellose Zustand mit einer sauber definierten Palmettenkrone und klaren Gesichtszügen mag diese Deutung vielleicht erschwert oder gar nicht intendiert haben. Andererseits ist es interessant, dass die nächste Parallele zu den Masken, die beiden Gesichter an den Reinheimer Attaschen, oben eine Palmettenkrone und unten einen Vollbart besitzen. Megaws Interpretation zufolge wären in Bad Dürkheim also beide Attribute in einer Darstellung vereint. Zudem erfährt die Doppeldeutigkeit nun durch die Tierdarstellung eine weitere Verstärkung der Symbolkraft. Denn es wandelt sich nicht nur ein Jüngling zu einem bärtigen Greis mit großen Tränensäcken, sobald das Horn gestürzt wird, weil es zur Neige geht. Das Tierwesen steht in dieser Perspektive über dem Alten und strebt empor.

Hunde- oder wolfsartige Wesen, wie sie unterhalb der Masken dargestellt sind, wären auf der Kanne von Basse-Yutz vertreten *(Abb. 14a)*. Damit zeigt sich neben den Masken mit Palmettenkrone eine weitere stilistische Verbindung zwischen den beiden Fundorten. Der Tierkopf von Fragment 2 wirkt indes etwas breiter und gedrungener, wodurch er eher an den Tierkopf der Gürtelschnalle aus dem „Fürstengrab" 1 aus Hügel 1 vom Glauberg erinnert *(Abb. 14b)*[40]. Selbst die ungewöhnlichen Haare zwischen den Ohren haben beide Darstellungen gemein. Eine ähnlich schlichte Haardarstellung in Form von parallel angeordneten kurzen Strichen zeigt sich auch auf einem anderen Stück des Bad Dürkheimer Grabes, nämlich bei den beiden Wesen an den Enden des länglichen Goldblechstreifens *(Abb. 14c)* – auch wenn die dort dargestellten Tiere aufgrund des breiten Kopfes und der behaarten Wangen eher an katzenartige Wesen erinnern. Weiter entfernt sind die aus einer Bleilegierung gefertigten Tierköpfe aus dem Ha D3-zeitlichen Reitergrab 13, Hügel 2, von Magdalenska gora in Slowenien *(Abb. 14d)*[41]. Wie bei den Bad Dürkheimer Tierköpfen besitzen auch diese insgesamt 14 Köpfe eine recht schematische Darstellung, bei der insbesondere die durch parallele Rillen angedeuteten Haare zwischen den Ohren[42] und die großen runden Augen auffallen.

---

bei der sogenannten „Rubinschen Vase", benannt nach dem Psychologen Edgar John Rubin. Im Early Style der Stufe Lt A finden sich solche Darstellungen meist in den Ornamentkompositionen aus Blüten, Palmetten und Ranken, bei denen Einzelelemente mehreren unterschiedlichen Objekten zugerechnet werden können. Ähnlich, aber nicht identisch ist der *Hidden Faces*-Effekt, dem das kognitive Phänomen der Pareidolie zugrunde liegt, bei der man in abstrakten Mustern und Formen Wesen oder Gegenstände zu erkennen glaubt. Ein Beispiel aus der Frühlatènezeit, bei dem gleich beide Wahrnehmungsformen zum Tragen zu kommen scheinen, stammt sogar von anderen Trinkhornbeschlägen: Rudolf Echt sah in den Reinheimer Beschlägen einen ähnlichen Effekt, da man dort bei der Haltung eines gefüllten Hornes zunächst ein Blütenmotiv erkennen kann, während seiner Meinung nach eine Greifendarstellung dominiert, sobald das Horn geleert und damit umgedreht wird (vgl. ECHT 1999, 127). Folgt man der Interpretation Echts, käme hierbei also zunächst eine Kippfigur zum Tragen, aber auch ein *Hidden Faces*-Effekt, da der Greif nicht figürlich konkret dargestellt, sondern im Gehirn aus abstrakteren Formen konstruiert wird.

[40] BAITINGER / PINSKER 2002, 253 Abb. 247 Kat.-Nr. 1.13.1.

[41] TECCO HVALA u. a. 2004, Taf. 27,38.

[42] Die slowenischen Stücke werden als Rinderköpfe interpretiert und dementsprechend die Ohren als Hörner. Allerdings liegen die Augen von Rindern wie bei vielen potenziellen Beutetieren eigentlich an den Seiten des Schädels, um einen besseren Rundumblick zu ermöglichen, während die Augen von Beutegreifern wie in den vorliegenden Abbildungen nach vorne gerichtet sind und näher beieinander liegen, um die für die Jagd erforderliche räumliche Wahrnehmung zu gewährleisten.

Abb. 14. a Hundeartiges Wesen von einer der beiden Schnabelkannen aus Basse-Yutz; b Raubtierkopf am Gürtelbeschlag aus Hügel 1, Grab 1, vom Glauberg; c Tierkopfdarstellung auf dem länglichen Goldblech aus dem Elitengrab von Bad Dürkheim; d Tierkopf aus Magdalenska gora (SI), Hügel 2, Reitergrab 13.

Swastika

Im Gegensatz zu den bereits eingehender behandelten Masken mit dem kleinen Tierkopf wurde das geometrische Feld aufgrund der starken Fragmentierung noch nicht in seiner Gesamtheit beschrieben. Anhand des Rekonstruktionsvorschlags wird deutlich, dass die Metopenfelder mit zwei sich kreuzenden Treppenmäandern gefüllt sind. Man könnte dieses Motiv auch als eine erweiterte Swastika bezeichnen, bei der die vier Arme, von der Mitte aus gesehen, zunächst gegen den Uhrzeigersinn abgewinkelt sind und anschließend ein weiteres Mal rechtwinklig abknicken – dieses Mal jedoch in die entgegengesetzte Richtung. Das Motiv setzt sich also aus vier S-förmigen Winkelbändern zusammen. Dadurch verläuft in den Ecken der Metope ein kleines Stück immer zunächst parallel zur Perlleistenbegrenzung.

Swastiken sind vereinzelt bereits in der Hallstattzeit auf Blecharbeiten bekannt[43]. Bei dem Gürtelblech aus Hügel 1, Nachbestattung 1, der Gießübel-Talhau-Nekropole (Lkr. Sigmaringen, DE) kommt noch hinzu, dass es wie eine Durchbruchsarbeit wirkt, wenngleich es gegossen und nicht aus getriebenem Blech besteht *(Abb. 15a)*[44]. In der Frühlatènezeit kommt das Swastika-Motiv nur vereinzelt und eher in der abgewandelten, geschwungenen Form des Viererwirbels vor[45]. Mit seinem winkeligen, starrgeometrischen Erscheinungsbild passt es nicht mehr so recht in die pflanzlich-organische, von S-Ranken, Palmetten, Lotusblüten und anderen Wirbeln dominierte Ästhetik des Early Style oder gar des Waldalgesheim-Stils. Eine Ausnahme bilden die zahlreichen Bronzearbeiten in der Aisne-Marne-Kultur, bei denen es sich einerseits um Durchbruchsarbeiten im Bereich der Pferde- und Wagenbeschläge und andererseits um Ziselierungen auf Waffen handelt[46].

Bereits Jacobsthal wies auf die Ähnlichkeit des Bad Dürkheimer Goldblechbeschlags mit mehreren goldenen Blechen aus der Nekropole von Trebeniště in Nordmazedonien hin[47]. Sie wurden gleich in mehreren Gräbern entdeckt und unterscheiden sich nur in kleineren Details[48]. Die Stücke sind nicht nur durchbrochen gearbeitet, sondern besitzen auch ein

---

[43] Vgl. z. B. auf dem Wagenbeschlag aus der Býčí skála-Höhle (Okr. Blansko, CZ; BARTH 1987, 107 Abb. 2) oder auf einer Fibel aus Böotien (GR; JACOBSTHAL 1944, Taf. 242a). Es handelt sich dort zwar um einfache Swastiken, aber auch diese werden in Form von Leiterbändern dargestellt und befinden sich in Metopen, die teils durch Perlleisten begrenzt sind. – Im osteuropäischen Raum wurden viele sogenannte thrako-skythische Pferdescheiben des 5. Jahrhunderts v. Chr. in Form von Viererwirbeln / Swastiken gestaltetet z. B. aus Olbia (Obl. Mykolajiw, UA; HODDINOTT 1981, 99 Abb. 92 oben links); mit unbekanntem Fundort aus Bulgarien (SALMONY 1937, 97 Abb. 6); Dolenjske Toplice V/33, Lt A (SI; TERŽAN 1976, Taf. 38,2–3); Magdalenska gora, Hügel 2, Grab 38, Ha D3 (TECCO HVALA u. a. 2004, Taf. 35,15); Magdalenska gora (KROMER 1986, 59 Abb. 54,5); Stična, Hügel 48, Grab 99, Ha D3 (SI; JOVANOVIĆ 1976, 27 Abb. 5). – Zur Datierung der Funde und den östlichen Einflüssen auf die frühkeltische Kunst im Allgemeinen siehe PARE 2012, bes. 157 f.

[44] KURZ / SCHIEK 2002, Taf. 11,117.

[45] Vgl. z. B. die drei Schmuckplatten aus dem Jochgraben des Wagengrabs von Somme-Bionne (MOREL 1875, 113), die Tonflasche Hidegség (Kom. Győr-Moson-Sopron, HU; STEAD / HUGHES 1997, Taf. 39). Vgl. auch JACOBSTHAL 1944, Taf. 270; 280–283 mit weiteren Beispielen.

[46] Vgl. z. B. die Zierscheibe von Bourcq „la Banière" (Dép. Ardennes, FR) und den Wagenbeschlag von Prunay (Dép. Marne, FR; LAMBOT 2014, 690; 695 Abb. 10) oder den Helm von Somme-Tourbe „La Gorge-Meillet" (Dép. Marne, FR; SCHÖNFELDER 2004, 208 Abb. 2; 210 Abb. 4). Ferner finden sich Swastiken auf den Schwertscheiden von Vert-la-Gravelle (Dép. Marne, FR; JACOBSTHAL 1944, Nr. 90 Taf. 56), Ciel (Dép. Saône-et-Loire, FR; GINOUX 1994, Taf. 6,3) und Rezi-Reziczeri (Kom. Zala, HU; STEAD / HUGHES 1997, Taf. 68,1) sowie auf einem Fries des Pergamon-Altars als Teil einer keltischen Tracht (JACOBSTHAL 1944, Nr. 132 Taf. 73). Ein erweitertes gekreuztes Mäandermotiv ist in einer Metope auf einem Ring des Wagens von Waldalgesheim (DE) abgebildet (JACOBSTHAL 1944, Nr. 156 Taf. 99 f.).

[47] JACOBSTHAL 1944, 82 Taf. 240d. – Zur Nekropole allgemein siehe auch STIBBE (2003, 55), der alle reichen Gräber an das Ende des 6. Jahrhunderts v. Chr. datiert.

[48] Bruchstücke stammen aus den Gräbern II, VI und VII (FILOW 1927, 10; 12–13; 20–22 Abb. 18; ARDJANLIEV u. a. 2018, 238 Kat.Nr. 22; 255 Kat.Nr. 61; 264 Kat.Nr. 81–82). – Neben den durchbrochen gearbeiteten Blechen enthielten die meisten auch Stabdreifüße; ganz so wie das Bad Dürkheimer Grab – auch das Grab VII.

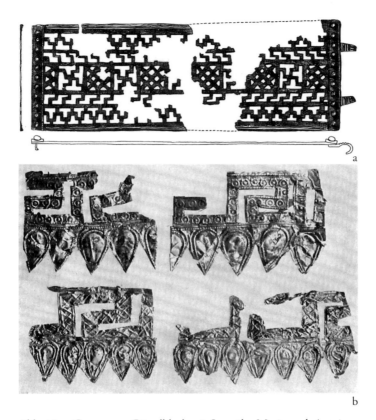

Abb. 15. a Gegossenes Gürtelblech mit Swastika-Motiv nach Art einer Durchbruchsarbeit aus Herbertingen-Hundersingen (Lkr. Sigmaringen, DE) „Gießübel" Hügel 1, Grab 1; b durchbrochen gearbeitete Goldbleche mit Mäandermotiv aus Trebenište (MK), Grab VII.

Mäandermotiv *(Abb. 15b)*. Der Rand besteht aus tropfenförmigen Spitzblättern, die der Schuppenborte aus Bad Dürkheim stilistisch ebenfalls nahestehen. Teilweise sind Zierelemente auch durch Perlleisten abgegrenzt. P. Jacobsthal geht hier von einer thrakischen Arbeit aus, sieht aber in dem Mäandermotiv einen deutlichen „Hallstatt look"[49]. Hierin erkannte er jedoch eine ausgesprochene Ausnahme östlicher Durchbruchsarbeiten, die sonst üblicherweise eine Tierornamentik aufweisen. Geometrische Durchbruchsarbeiten sieht er insbesondere im nordalpinen Hallstattraum und in Italien.

In allen drei Gräbern von Trebenište (Gräber II, VI und VII), in denen die durchbrochenen Goldbleche vorkommen, lagen sie in der Nähe des Helmes[50]; selbst in Grab VI, bei dem der Helm nicht, wie sonst üblich, im Bereich des Kopfes lag, sondern auf dem rechten Unterschenkel. In diesem Grab lagen die Goldbleche zwischen den Knien. In zwei Fällen (Gräber VI und VII) lagen Bernstein- bzw. Glasperlen in der Nähe. In allen Gräbern waren zudem weitere Goldblechbeschläge anderer Form im direkten Umfeld gefunden worden. Es scheint sich also mit hoher Wahrscheinlichkeit nicht um einen Trinkhornbeschlag

[49] Jacobsthal 1944, 82.

[50] Filow 1927, 5 Abb. 4,13.16; 9 Abb. 8,18; 10 Abb. 9,11.17.

gehandelt zu haben, sondern vermutlich um den Besatz eines Kleidungsstückes. Diese Hypothese wird dadurch untermauert, dass in Trebenište die Gefäßbeigaben regelhaft im Fußbereich platziert wurden. Bei den beiden reich ausgestatteten Elitengräbern I und VIII, die beide unter anderem auch eine Goldblechmaske[51] enthielten, gehörte zum umfangreichen Trinkservice jeweils auch ein silbernes Trinkhorn[52]. Diese lagen in beiden Fällen bei den übrigen Gefäßen unterhalb des Fußbereichs[53]. Noch weiter östlich, nämlich von der südrussischen Halbinsel Taman, liegt ein weiterer Beschlag aus Goldblech vor, bei dem es sich sogar um einen Trinkhornbeschlag handeln könnte[54]. Er stammt aus dem Bol'shaia Bliznitsa-Sippengrabhügel und besitzt einen Mäanderfries als unteren Abschluss, der auch als Swastika gelesen werden kann. Allerdings datieren die Gräber des Hügels bereits in die zweite Hälfte des 4. Jahrhunderts v. Chr.[55].

Torsions- und Schuppenborten: Motivvergleich

Wie bereits erwähnt, ergibt sich die Orientierung des Blechs zum einen aus der Darstellung der menschlichen Köpfe; zum anderen existieren einige stilistische Parallelen mit anderen Objekten hinsichtlich der Position von Torsions- und Schuppenborten. Insbesondere letztere sind an mehreren Trinkhörnern gut belegt. Dabei kommen sie in unterschiedlich komplexen Varianten vor. In Bescheid, Hügel 6, bildet eine einfache Bogenleiste den oberen Abschluss des Blechs *(Abb. 16a)*[56]. Aufgrund der Hufeisenform ähnelt sie der unteren Reihe der Bad Dürkheimer Schuppenborte. Auch die Bogenreihe auf der Goldblechrosette von Ferschweiler, die ebenfalls zum Kreis der mutmaßlichen Trinkhornbeschläge zählt, weist eine solche Zier auf *(Abb. 16b)*[57]. Eine einfache Reihe aus Perllleistenbögen besitzt das leider nur noch fragmentarisch erhaltene runde Stück mit großem Korallencabochon aus Groß-Rohrheim (Lkr. Bergstraße, DE; *Abb. 16c)*[58]. Doch auf dem Bescheider Blech findet sich noch eine weitere, etwas komplexere Variante zur dortigen Bogenreihe: In Reihe 3 wurde jeder zweite Zwickel einer ganz ähnlichen hufeisenförmigen Bogenreihe mit einem tropfenförmigen Element verziert. Da es sich bei dem Stück aus Bescheid, Hügel 6, um einen gut dokumentierten Fund handelt, ist die Orientierung der über eine große Breite erhaltenen Bogenborte eindeutig[59]. Die zweireihige Variante wie in Bescheid findet sich in leichter Abwandlung auch an zwei Stellen von Horn 2 aus dem Kleinaspergle (Lkr.

---

[51] Solche Goldblechmasken erinnern ebenfalls an die Miniaturmasken von Bad Dürkheim, Ferschweiler oder Schwarzenbach.

[52] ARDJANLIEV u. a. 2018, 232 Kat.Nr. 12; 288 Kat. Nr. 131; vgl. FILOW 1927, 30 Nr. 35 Taf. VI,1 (Grab 1). – KRSTIĆ 2018, 46 Abb. 5 (Grab VIII).

[53] FILOW 1927, 4 Abb. 3,27; KRSTIĆ 2018, 43, Abb. 1,28.

[54] MEGAW 1975, 30 Taf. IV,5. – Die Schreibweise dieses Fundorts variiert in der Literatur; so findet sich z. B. auch Bol'shaia Blitznitza, Bolshaia Bliznitza, Bliznitsa Bol'shaia oder in der englischsprachigen Literatur bisweilen Great Blitznitza oder lediglich Taman.

[55] BERNHARD / SZTETYŁŁO 1976.

[56] HAFFNER / LAGE 2008–2009, 72.

[57] JACOBSTHAL 1944, Nr. 30 Taf. 25; HAFFNER 1976, Taf. 1,9; 131,2.

[58] JORNS 1966, 224 Abb. 1. – Die heutige Rekonstruktion, bei der das Goldblech oben auf das große Korallencabochon geklebt wurde, ist mit hoher Wahrscheinlichkeit falsch. In allen bisher bekannten Fällen wurde stets ein verziertes Bronzeblech als Basis für ein sehr dünnes Goldblech verwendet, wobei man das Gold aus Gründen der Materialersparnis im Bereich unterhalb des Cabochons aus Koralle oder Bernstein stets ausspare.

[59] Der stilistisch ähnlichere Beschlag aus Dörth wurde bedauerlicherweise nach der Auffindung zunächst flach gepresst und gerade ausgerichtet, sodass nicht mit letzter Sicherheit von einer Ober- und Unterseite gesprochen werden kann. Der Beschlag von Bescheid wurde hingegen *in situ* gefunden.

Abb. 16. Schuppenborten auf Trinkhornbeschlägen. a Bandförmiger Blechbeschlag aus Bescheid, Hügel 6 (Lkr. Trier-Saarburg); b Goldblechrosette aus Ferschweiler (Lkr. Bitburg-Prüm); c Scheibenförmiger Abschluss (?) aus Groß-Rohrheim (Lkr. Bergstraße); d tüllenförmiger Endbeschlag aus Asperg, Kleinaspergle (Lkr. Ludwigsburg), Horn 2; e tüllenförmiger Endbeschlag aus Asperg, Kleinaspergle, Horn 1; f bandförmiger Blechbeschlag aus Trebenište (MK), Grab VIII.

Ludwigsburg, DE; *Abb. 16d)*[60]. Eine richtige Schuppenborte im Sinne zweier Reihen aus leicht versetzten Bögen findet sich schließlich auf Horn 1 des Kleinaspergle *(Abb. 16e)*[61]. Darüber hinaus finden sich in einigen Schuppenborten auch noch Miniaturvarianten der tropfenförmigen gewölbten Zierelemente, wie sie bereits auf Horn 2 und in Bescheid begegneten. Im Gegensatz zu den glatten hufeisenförmigen Bögen jener Schuppenborten sind sie auf Horn 1 nur durch eine Perlleiste oder durch eine Kombination aus glattem und Perlleistenbogen gestaltet.

Auch die silbernen Trinkhörner aus Trebenište, Grab I und Grab VIII, besitzen im mittleren Bereich eine Schuppenborte, bestehend aus zwei, um eine halbe Bogenbreite versetzte Bogenreihen *(Abb. 16f)*[62]. Auf den mediterranen, noch hallstattzeitlichen Einfluss dieses Motivs ging bereits Hans Nortmann kurz ein, der die nicht weit entfernt gelegenen Gräber aus Wallerfangen (Lkr. Saarlouis, DE) und Kobern-Gondorf (Lkr. Mayen-Koblenz, DE) als frühe Beispiele aus der Region anführte[63].

In Wallerfangen findet sich das Bogenmotiv auf zwei Goldblecharmringen[64]. Im Wagengrab 2 von Kobern-Gondorf auf einer Scheibenfibel[65], die wiederum große Ähnlichkeit mit einer weiteren Scheibenfibel vom Züricher Üetliberg (CH) aufweist[66]. Ein prominentes Ha D3-zeitliches Beispiel für solche hufeisenförmigen Reihen ist der Halsring von Vix (FR) *(Abb. 17)*[67].

Es zeigt sich, dass die Schuppenborte an vielen goldenen Trinkhornbeschlägen in unterschiedlich komplexer bzw. rudimentärer Form vorhanden ist. Hierbei werden die einzelnen Elemente – Bogen, Peltamotiv und Tropfen – teilweise leicht abgewandelt und wie in einem Baukastensystem unterschiedlich kombiniert. Dabei offenbart sich eine deutliche Ähnlichkeit hinsichtlich der Einzelkomponenten.

Schuppenborten und die simplere Variante der Bogenreihen waren populäre Zierelemente der Latènekultur und es ließen sich noch zahlreiche weitere Objekte aus verschiedenen Materialien nennen, die eine solche Verzierung in ebenso vielen technischen

---

[60] KIMMIG 1988, Taf. 37. – Der Unterschied besteht darin, dass das gewölbte umgekehrt-tropfenförmige Motiv von Horn 2 zwischen jedem Bogen platziert ist, während es in Bescheid nur nach jedem zweiten Bogen platziert wurde.

[61] KIMMIG 1988, Taf. 36. Vgl. auch die angeführten Beispiele S. 242 Abb. 137, unter denen auch das Bad Dürkheimer Stück angeführt wird (Abb. 137,6). – Bereits P. JACOBSTHAL (1944, 166 f. Nr. 16–17) bezeichnete die beiden Trinkhornbeschläge aufgrund ihrer unterschiedlichen Verzierung als „scale-horn" (Jacobsthals Nr. 16 / Kimmigs Horn 2) und „guilloche-horn" (Jacobsthals Nr. 17 / Kimmigs Horn 1).

[62] ARDJANLIEV u. a. 2018, 288.

[63] NORTMANN 2017, 52. – Eine späthallstattzeitliche Tradition, wie H. Nortmann dies anführt, kann höchstens in der Spiralkonstruktion gesehen werden, die allerdings bei einigen Lt A-zeitlichen Fibeln vorkommt. Scheibenfibeln im Allgemeinen können als Leitform der Stufe Lt A angesehen werden.

[64] HAFFNER 1976, Taf. 13,2–3; ECHT / THIELE 1994, 30–33 Abb. 5.

[65] WEGNER 2006, 41 Abb. 19,1.

[66] MÜLLER 2009, 82 Abb. 78. – Hier ließe sich noch die Goldscheibe von Hochscheid „Fuckerichsheide" (Lkr. Bernkastel-Wittlich, DE) Hügel 1 anführen, die ebenfalls einen geperlten Bogenkranz besitzt. – Schlichte Schuppenleisten, die nur aus versetzten Bogenreihen bestehen, finden sich z. B. auf der Schnabelkanne von Weiskirchen, Hügel 1 (HAFFNER 1976, Taf. 13), auf einem durchbrochen gearbeiteten Blech aus Mülheim-Kärlich, Grab 4, (JOACHIM 1979, 527 Abb. 17,2) und am silbernen Siebtrichter aus Lavau (Dép. Aube, FR; DUBUIS 2016). – In diesem Zusammenhang sollte auch auf den aus heimischer Produktion stammenden Deckel aus Bad Dürkheim hingewiesen werden, auf dem mehrere Reihen von Bogenleisten vorhanden sind (BARDELLI 2017a, Taf. 24).

[67] Vgl. auch die bereits deutlich latènoiden Bogenornamente auf dem Geweihschieber von der Heuneburg (DE) und der Lanzenspitze aus dem Zentralgrab von Hügel 1 der Gießübel-Talhau-Nekropole (KRAUSSE u. a. 2015, 102 Abb. 102; 103 Abb. 103).

Abb. 17. Vix (Dép. Côte d'Or, FR). Detail des Halsrings aus dem Fürstinnengrab.

Umsetzungen aufzeigen[68]. Gleiches gilt auch für die Torsionsborte. Auch sie kommt in mannigfachen Variationen auf latènezeitlichen Objekten vor[69], weshalb wir uns hier auf die Parallelen auf Goldbeschlägen beschränken möchten.

Eine ähnliche Torsionsborte wie auf dem mutmaßlichen Trinkhornbeschlag von Bad Dürkheim findet sich gleich im selben Grab, nämlich an den Längsseiten des länglichen Goldbeschlags, der möglicherweise auch Teil des Trinkhorns war *(Abb. 18)*. Die schmalen, horizontal verlaufenden Stege am durchbrochenen Blech von Eigenbilzen ähneln der Bad Dürkheimer Borte ebenfalls, sind jedoch schmaler *(Abb. 19a)*. Ein weiteres Fragment aus Eigenbilzen, das nicht zum durchbrochen gearbeiteten Beschlag gehört, besitzt eine größere Nähe zum Bad Dürkheimer Stück *(Abb. 19b)*. Auch auf dem sogenannten Horn 2 (von Jacobsthal aufgrund der Verzierung auch als „guilloche-horn" bezeichnet[70]) aus dem Kleinaspergle findet sich eine entferntere Parallele zur Torsionsborte. Zwar sind dort die einzelnen Torsionselemente nur an einer Seite verjüngt, doch dies könnte damit zusammenhängen, dass möglicherweise gleichzeitig die Anmutung von Widderhörnern erzielt werden sollte, was zudem durch ihre Querkerbung betont wird[71]. Keine Torsionsborte im

---

[68] Z. B. der Gürtelbeschlag von Rascheid, Hügel D I (DE; Haffner 1976, Taf. 7); Besseringen „Am Müllenberg" (DE; Haffner 2014, 82 Abb. 1).

[69] Weitere Torsionsborten finden sich z. B. an den Pressblechen zwischen den Zapfen des Halsrings vom Glauberg (dort auch auf der bronzenen Schwertscheide), auf dem bronzenen Metallbeschlag von Weitbruch (Dép. Bas-Rhin, FR), der recht ähnlich gestalteten Rückseite des Gürtelhakens von Weiskirchen, Hügel 1, oder der Scheide von Vraux (Dép. Marne, FR), Grab 24. – Vgl. zudem Jacobsthal 1944, Taf. 262,28. – Dass die Torsionsborte insbesondere im griechisch-mediterranen Raum sehr beliebt war, kann auch an den zahlreichen Beispielen aus der bereits erwähnten Nekropole von Trebenište nachvollzogen werden: Ardjanliev u. a. 2018.

[70] Jacobsthal 1944.

[71] Damit wäre zugleich eine stilistische Verbindung zu den Widderköpfen an den Trinkhornenden gegeben.

Abb. 18. Längliches Goldblech aus dem Elitengrab von Bad Dürkheim.

engeren Sinn, aber zumindest eine tordierte Form weist auch der mutmaßliche Randbeschlag eines Trinkhorns aus dem Grab 4 von Mülheim-Kärlich auf[72].

Zusammenfassend zeigte die Suche nach Parallelen zur Motivik des Bad Dürkheimer Beschlags ein heterogenes Bild: Masken sind zwar bekannt, doch in Ferschweiler ist eine Ansprache als Trinkhornbeschlag mangels weiterer Indizien unsicher. Bei der Maske vom Dürrnberg (AT) ist die Zugehörigkeit zu einer Röhrenkanne gesichert. Rein technisch handelt es sich jedoch um ein sehr ähnliches Stück, denn die Basis der Bad Dürkheimer Masken bestand aus ähnlich gestalteten Bronzeblechen, wenngleich diese dünner waren. Es wurde ferner deutlich, dass die Torsionsborte auf den latènezeitlichen Trinkhornbeschlägen deutlich seltener vertreten ist als die Schuppenborte.

Die übrigen Goldblechbeschläge

Nachdem die Konstruktionsweise des mutmaßlichen Trinkhornbeschlags eingehend behandelt wurde, bedarf es noch einer Beschäftigung mit den beiden weiteren Goldblechbeschlägen aus dem Grab. Hierbei handelt es sich um den bereits erwähnten länglichen, mittlerweile in zwei Teile zerbrochenen Goldblechstreifen *(Abb. 18)*[73] und ein kleines, verschollenes Goldblechscheibchen[74].

Der 11,5 cm lange goldene Pressblechstreifen besitzt je eine mit Perlleistenkranz verzierte Rundel an den Enden, mit ca. 1 cm Durchmesser. In beiden Fällen befindet sich im mittleren Bereich im Innern des Perlkranzes eine rundliche Öffnung. Nach Aussage der Zeichnung von E. Eschmann[75] scheint das verschollene Scheibchen genau in diesen Perlkranz zu passen, wodurch eine Funktion als goldener Beschlag eines Nietkopfes wahrscheinlich ist, wie sie während der gesamten Frühlatènezeit in verschiedenen Größen häufig vorkommen[76]. Daran schließt sich jeweils ein breiter Satyrkopf mit Backenbehaarung,

---

[72] Günther 1934, Taf. 1,13–15.
[73] Joachim 2012.
[74] Bardelli 2017a, XIV–XV Nr. 5; 18; Nortmann 2017, 50 f.
[75] Nortmann 2017, 51 Abb. 11.
[76] Z. B. auf den Scheibenfibeln von Reinheim oder auf den Halsringen von Leimersheim (DE) oder Mondelange (FR) sowie auf den beiden Münsinger-

Abb. 19. Blechbeschläge aus Eigenbilzen (Prov. Limburg, BE). a Detail der schmalen Torsionsborte des durchbrochen gearbeiteten Blechs; b Torsionsborte auf einem weiteren Blechfragment.

menschlicher Nase, tropfenförmigen Augen und S-förmig geschwungenen Brauen an. Zwischen den spitzen Ohren sind die Haare in ähnlicher Weise gestaltet, wie bei den kleinen Tierköpfen unter den Masken der Fragmente 1 und 2.

In der Mitte des Bandes befindet sich ein Punzmotiv, das aus einer Kombination aus Punkt und Tropfenform besteht und wie ein Ausrufezeichen angeordnet ist. Durch diese Verzierung wirkt es so, als sei die intendierte „Leserichtung" des Motivs eine horizontale.

Fibeln des letzteren Fundorts, die wiederum einer Fibel aus Worms „Rädergewann" (DE; Stümpel 1991, 50 Abb. 8,A3) sehr nahestehen, die ebenfalls eine solche Verzierung des Nietkopfes aufweist.

Dies spräche in der Konsequenz eher für einen weiteren Beschlag direkt am Trinkhorn, statt eines Beschlags für einen Lederriemen, an dem das Horn aufgehängt werden konnte. Andererseits sind die bisher gesicherten, vollständig erhaltenen Trinkhornbeschläge so gearbeitet, dass sie bündig überlappen. Zwei Rundeln an den Enden als Abschluss würden bei einem Trinkhorn kaum Sinn ergeben[77]. Letztlich kann hierzu nur spekuliert werden. Eine solche Darstellung begegnet in der eisenzeitlichen Motivwelt recht häufig. Einerseits im mediterranen Raum, aber auch auf vielen Gegenständen der Stufe Lt A, wie z. B. auf den beiden Trinkhornbeschlägen von Reinheim[78] oder auf einigen Blechen aus Grab 1 von Schwarzenbach[79]. Auch der obere Abschluss des Eigenbilzener Blechs steht diesem Motiv näher als der typischen Bogenreihe oder Schuppenborte. Als potenzieller Trinkhornbeschlag wurde auch ein Goldblechfragment vom Kemmelberg im belgischen Heuvelland (Gem. Kemmel; Prov. Westflandern) interpretiert[80].

Bestandteile von Trinkhörnern

Überblickt man die bisher gefundenen Teile, die in der Frühlatènezeit als Trinkhornbeschläge interpretiert wurden (vgl. *Anhang*), lassen sich zehn unterschiedliche Gruppen von Zierelementen unterscheiden:

1. Deckel: D. Krausse bemerkte bereits, dass Trinkhörner mit Deckel in der Eisenzeit zwar ungewöhnlich sind, doch führt er ein etruskisches Beispiel aus *Satricum* (Le Ferriere, Prov. Latina, IT) an und sieht auch in den beiden Goldblechscheiben Nr. 4 und 5 aus Schwarzenbach, Grab 1, „ohne jeden Zweifel" Deckel[81]. Weitere Deckel sind in ihrer Ansprache jedoch deutlich unsicherer. Im Gegensatz zu dem zylindrisch gearbeiteten etruskischen Stück sind die bisher bekannten latènezeitlichen Objekte flach oder leicht konisch gewölbt. Dabei muss der Durchmesser eines solchen Gold- und / oder Bronzebeschlags nicht zwingend mit dem Trinkhorndurchmesser korrelieren, da diese vermutlich auf hölzernen oder bronzenen Unterlagen befestigt waren, die wiederum einen größeren Durchmesser besaßen[82]. Eine solche Konstruktion ist auch deshalb nachvollziehbar, da gerade ein Trinkhorndeckel einer gewissen Stabilität bedarf und deshalb eine Art von Ring an der Innen- oder Außenseite der Mündung oder eine ringförmige Nut benötigt.
2. Randbeschläge: Sie umfassen den Rand des Horns, sind ringförmig und besitzen einen Schlitz an ihrer Unterseite, in die das Horn eingepasst wird, z. B. bei den Stücken von Schwarzenbach „Fürstengrab" 1; Mülheim-Kärlich, Wagengrab 4, oder, diesmal in

---

[77] Man könnte argumentieren, dass sich die beiden Rundeln überlappten, was gleichzeitig den einzelnen mutmaßlichen Nietkopfbeschlag erklären würde, doch dann wäre wiederum die Frage offen, weshalb beide Rundeln gleichartig verziert wurden. Latènezeitliche Goldblecharbeiten zeigen hier in vergleichbaren Fällen einen gewissen Pragmatismus; man denke nur an die vielen ausgesparten Stellen auf Scheibenfibeln oder Scheiben vom Typ Weiskirchen, die einst von einer Korallenzier verdeckt waren.
[78] ECHT 1999, Taf. 9,6–7.
[79] JACOBSTHAL 1944, Taf. 29,38–40.45; HAFFNER 1976, Taf. 143 p. r.
[80] WARMENBOL 2018, 389 Abb. 5. – Da jenes Stück jedoch aus einer Siedlung stammt, erscheint es wenig wahrscheinlich, dass es sich um einen Trinkhornbeschlag handelt.
[81] KRAUSSE 1996, 144 f. *(Satricum)*; 215 f.
[82] Diese Möglichkeit erwägt D. Krausse auch in Zusammenhang mit der dritten Scheibe aus Schwarzenbach, deren Befestigung an der Schalenrekonstruktion von ihm bezweifelt wird (KRAUSSE 1996, 216).

Eisen, aus Grab 59 vom Dürrnberg. Auch die bronzenen Fragmente aus dem „Dreikopf" bei Pellingen zierten einst vermutlich den Rand eines Gefäßes. Ob es sich immer um Trinkhörner gehandelt hat, kann jedoch nicht sicher geklärt werden.

3. Große bandförmige Blechbeschläge: Hierzu zählen das Stück aus Bad Dürkheim sowie die bereits erwähnten Vergleiche; sie besitzen sehr unterschiedliche Durchmesser von 4,7 bis 12,3 cm; ihre Breite variiert von 2,4–5,7 cm. Sie lassen sich grob in zwei Typen unterscheiden, je nachdem, ob sie durchbrochen gearbeitet wurden oder nicht. Wie das Beispiel des eisernen Trinkhorns aus Hochdorf (DE) gut zeigt, können solche Bleche auch ganz am Rand des Trinkhorns gesessen und die Position eines Randbeschlags (bei anderer Konstruktionsweise) übernommen haben[83].

4. Manschettenringe: Sie sind ringförmig aufgebaut und besitzen einen massiven Bronze- oder Eisenkern, wodurch sie eine Rippe bilden; zudem existiert bei den drei bekannten Stücken aus Groß-Rohrheim, Eigenbilzen und dem Kleinaspergle eine Rille in der Mitte zur Aufnahme einer Korallenzier. Auch hier liegen gesicherte Belege durch das eiserne Trinkhorn von Hochdorf vor[84].

5. Einzelbeschläge (inkl. länglicher Bänder): In einigen Fällen liegen mehrere Einzelbeschläge vor, wie etwa aus Schwarzenbach, Grab 1. Hierbei handelt es sich um Masken sowie gerade und gebogene Bänder, die sich teilweise verjüngen. Ebenfalls häufig vertreten sind verschiedene Palmettenmotive. Eine Ansprache als Bestandteil eines Trinkhorns ist in vielen Fällen daher sehr unsicher. In einigen Fällen gelang der einwandfreie Nachweis eines Trinkhorns anhand von Hornfibrillen wie in Grab 1 von Schwarzenbach[85], andererseits zeigen die bereits erwähnten Beispiele aus Lavau (FR) und dem Kleinaspergle sowie die funktional wie optisch nahestehenden Kannenbeschläge, auf die noch näher eingegangen wird, dass stets mit ungewöhnlichen Applikationen gerechnet werden muss. Eine Überschneidung der Goldbleche dieser Gruppe von Zierelementen besteht insbesondere mit den Deckelbestandteilen (Gruppe 1) sowie mit den scheibenförmigen Abschlüssen (Gruppe 7).

6. Tüllenförmige Endbeschläge: Diese Materialgruppe ist ähnlich klar mit den Trinkhörnern assoziiert wie die Manschettenringe (Gruppe 4) und ein Teil der bandförmigen Blechbeschläge (Gruppe 3). Hier sind zuvorderst die bereits mehrfach angesprochenen Beschläge vom Kleinaspergle zu nennen. Ein weiteres, jedoch deutlich kleineres und schlichteres Stück aus Bourges (Dép. Cher, FR) „Route de Dun" besteht aus Bronze und ist in Form eines Tierkopfes (Widder?, Rind?) gestaltet[86]. In der Schnauze des Tieres an der Tüllenspitze befindet sich ein kleiner Bronzering und nahe der Tüllenmündung jeweils ein Schäftungsloch pro Seite.

7. Scheibenförmige Abschlüsse: Sie bilden ebenfalls eine schwierige Gruppe, wenn es um die Sicherheit bei der Ansprache als Trinkhornbeschlag geht. Auch die Abgrenzung zu den Deckelbeschlägen ist in vielen Fällen nicht möglich. So nahm etwa Alfred Haffner bei einigen Beschlägen aus Grab 1 von Schwarzenbach eine solche Funktion als scheibenförmiger Abschluss an und legte entsprechende Rekonstruktionen vor[87]. D. Krausse wiederum sah von einer solchen Zuordnung unter Berufung auf den großen Durchmesser von 4,6 cm allerdings ab[88]. Ähnlich problematisch erscheint die Ansprache der Goldblechrosette und des profilierten Korallenknopfs aus Groß-Rohrheim als

---

[83] Krausse 1996, Taf. 11.
[84] Krausse 1996.
[85] Krausse 1996, 212 f. Abb. 166.
[86] Déchelette 1927, 813 Abb. 568,5; Kimmig 1988, 210 Nr. 4; Lenerz-de Wilde 1988, 232 Abb. 141,1; Krausse 1996, 407 Nr. 6.
[87] Haffner 1991, 162.
[88] Krausse 1996, 215 f. Abb. 168.

Abschluss des Trinkhorns, wie dies von Werner Jorns vorgeschlagen wurde[89]. Auch die scheibenförmigen Abschlüsse fußen auf hallstattzeitlicher Tradition, wie auch in diesem Fall das eiserne Trinkhorn von Hochdorf gut belegt[90]. Dem Blech aus Groß-Rohrheim ähneln gleich mehrere Stücke aus Ungarn. Insbesondere die drei Goldblechringe aus Mezőtúr-Újváros (Gem. Szolnok, Kom. Jász-Nagykun-Szolnok) besitzen einen Rand aus Kreisaugen, der an die Kontur der Schuppenborte des südhessischen Stücks erinnert[91]. Sie datieren in das zweite Viertel oder die Mitte des 5. Jahrhunderts v. Chr. Die drei Goldscheibchen aus Szentes-Vekerzug (Kom. Csongrád), Grab 27, in Südostungarn sind zwar nicht durchlocht, doch ähneln sie den südhessischen und ostungarischen Stücken ebenfalls[92]. Bei den ungarischen Funden wird eine Funktion als Kleiderbesatz vermutet.

8. Ketten: Aus der Latènezeit sind bisher nur die Ketten aus dem Kleinaspergle aus einem unmittelbaren Zusammenhang mit Trinkhörnern bekannt[93]. Doch auch hier kann wieder auf die Hallstattzeit, nämlich auf das reiche Kettengehänge von Kappel-Grafenhausen (Ortenaukreis, DE), Hügel 3, Grab 1, verwiesen werden[94].

9. Ziergehänge: Eng mit den Ketten verbunden sind verschieden geformte Ziergehänge, wie sie auch an den Enden der Ketten von Kappel, Hügel 3, befestigt sind. Dort sind sie zwar aus Bronzeblech, doch wie bereits erwähnt, muss für so gut wie jede Bronzeblecharbeit prinzipiell mit einer edleren Umsetzung mit einem aufplattierten Goldblech gerechnet werden. Im Elitengrab von Hochdorf gelang zudem der Nachweis von recht komplexen Ziergehängen aus Knochenperlen[95]. Eine Abgrenzung zu Einzelbeschlägen (Gruppe 5) ist aufgrund der schlechten Befundlage bei latènezeitlichen Trinkhörnern bisher nicht zweifelsfrei möglich.

10. Goldscheibchen: Die meist nur 1–2 cm kleinen runden Goldblechscheibchen sind relativ häufig in latènezeitlichen Gräbern anzutreffen, so etwa in Reinheim, Wadern-Gehweiler (DE), Hoppstädten (DE), Hügel 2, Remmesweiler (DE) „Batterie", Dörth und einigen weiteren. D. Krausse widmete ihnen bereits einen ausführlichen Exkurs, weshalb hier nicht näher auf die Stücke eingegangen werden muss[96]. Er stellt den multifunktionalen Charakter dieser Scheibchen heraus und betont, dass sie zwar auch, aber nicht ausschließlich für Trinkhornbeschläge wie z. B. Lederriemen verwendet wurden. In einigen Fällen könnte es sich um Kleidungs- oder Gürtelbeschläge gehandelt haben, in anderen sind auch Reste von Fibeln oder anderen Objekten denkbar. In Wagengrab 3 von Mülheim-Kärlich waren die beiden 1,2 bzw. 1,3 cm kleinen Scheibchen aus dünnem Goldblech zu beiden Seiten eines Knopfs aus Knochen mit vierkantigem

---

[89] JORNS 1966, 224 Abb. 1c–d; 2. – Insbesondere die Rekonstruktion des Blechs erscheint nicht schlüssig, denn sie liegt als eine Scheibe vor, die höchstens eine leicht konische Oberfläche, vermutlich aber eher eine völlig plane geziert haben könnte. Für eine Zier, wie sie in Abb. 2 jedoch vorgeschlagen wurde, bedürfte es einer konischen bis zylindrischen Röhre. Die knopfförmige Gestaltung des Korallenstücks (Abb. 1d) spricht eher für einen Deckel, das mittlerweile leider verschollene Goldscheibchen (Abb. 1e) eher für einen scheibenförmigen Abschluss.

[90] KRAUSSE 1996, Taf. 11.

[91] KISFALUDI 1983, 70 Abb. 1.

[92] FOULON / KEMENCZEI 2001, 126 Nr. 64.

[93] KIMMIG 1988, Taf. 40 f.

[94] DEHN u. a. 2005, 84; 195.

[95] KRAUSSE 1996, 74 f. Abb. 55.

[96] KRAUSSE 1996, 197–199 Liste 10. – Krausse fasst den Begriff der Goldscheibchen allerdings deutlich weiter als die hier im Fokus stehenden kleinen, sehr ähnlich aussehenden dünnen Blechscheibchen der Stufe Lt A und führt daher z. B. auch die wesentlich größeren Goldblechbuckel aus Kappel, Hügel 1 (KIMMIG / REST 1954, Taf. 10,2–4), oder die Nietköpfe aus dem Grafenbühl (DE; ZÜRN 1970, Taf. 20,8–14) an.

Mittelstück befestigt[97]. D. Krausse sieht eine gewisse Ähnlichkeit zwischen den latènezeitlichen Blechen und einigen Stücken aus dem italisch-etruskischen bzw. hallstattzeitlichen Raum und erwägt einen kulturellen Zusammenhang im Sinne einer „Homologie", darüber hinaus zählt er einige Funde aus dem oberitalisch-venetischen Gebiet auf[98]. In diesem Zusammenhang sollten auch noch auf einige Goldbleche aus Ungarn eingegangen werden, die noch nach Ha D3 datieren, aber eine sehr große Übereinstimmung mit den latènezeitlichen Scheibchen aufweisen; so etwa die 19 Scheibchen aus Ártánd (Kom. Hajdú-Bihar) in Ostungarn[99]. Wie auch bei den Blechen aus Groß-Rohrheim führt also erneut eine Fährte zu stilistisch wie chronologisch nahestehenden Parallelen ins östliche Ungarn.

Funktion und kulturhistorische Einordnung

Nachdem nun die Blechfragmente neu rekonstruiert und die Motive stilistisch eingeordnet wurden, stellt sich die Frage, ob die Ansprache als Trinkhornbeschlag tatsächlich so „unumstritten" ist, wie jüngst von H. Nortmann attestiert[100]. Wolfgang Kimmig konnte in seinem knappen, aber informativen Abriss der Forschungsgeschichte zu den Goldblechbeschlägen bereits zeigen, dass die Ansprache vieler Stücke als Trinkhörner erst spät einsetzte[101]. Eine räumlich wie zeitlich äußerst umfangreiche Studie zur „Idee der Trinkhornsitte" legte D. Krausse im Rahmen seiner Arbeit zum Trink- und Speiseservice von Hochdorf vor[102]. Auch über 20 Jahre später ist ihr kaum etwas hinzuzufügen.

Problematische Identifikation

Organische Gefäße: Trinkhorn oder Kanne

Die meisten mutmaßlichen Trinkhornbeschläge stammen aus Altgrabungen oder aus gestörten Gräbern und wurden oftmals nach heutigen Maßstäben unsachgemäß restauriert und teilweise wohl auch falsch rekonstruiert[103]. Nur in wenigen Fällen lässt sich ein Trinkhorn derart gut nachweisen, wie es in Hochdorf oder im Kleinaspergle möglich war. Im Bad Dürkheimer Fall wie auch bei fast allen weiteren eisenzeitlichen Trinkhörnern fehlen die organischen Reste des eigentlichen Horns. Zu den wenigen Ausnahmen gehören die Spuren von Hornfibrillen an einem der länglichen Goldbleche aus Schwarzenbach, Grab 1[104]. Bei den organischen Resten vom Beschlag aus dem Elitengrab von Pellingen handelt es sich laut Krausse „mit Sicherheit nicht um Holz, sondern sehr wahrscheinlich um Horn"[105].

Die Ansprache als Trinkhornbeschlag erfolgte in vielen Fällen aufgrund von Analogieschlüssen, die von den wenigen sicheren Funden abgeleitet wurden. Ein Rückschluss von

---

[97] Joachim 1979, 517 f. Abb. 9.
[98] Krausse 1996, 198.
[99] Foulon / Kemenczei 2001, 97 Abb. 56.
[100] Nortmann 2017, 48. – J. V. S. Megaw ging in seinem Aufsatz von 1969 noch nicht explizit von Trinkhornbeschlägen aus, sondern ließ die Frage offen. Lediglich bei der Befestigungsweise ging er von einer Fixierung „auf Holz oder Leder" aus (Megaw 1969, 85).
[101] Kimmig 1988, 196–211. – Ein entscheidender Durchbruch in der Identifikation von Trinkhornbeschlägen erfolgte erst 1962 mit der Publikation von M. É. Mariën zu dem Goldblechbeschlag aus Eigenbilzen in Belgien (Mariën 1962).
[102] Krausse 1996, 95–230.
[103] Krausse 1996, 186 f.
[104] Krausse 1996, 212 f. Nr. 21 Abb. 166.
[105] Krausse 1996, 217.

der gleichartigen Herstellungsweise und technischen Übereinstimmung auf eine ähnliche Verwendung ist allerdings problematisch, denn wenn man sich z. B. die runden, mit Goldfolie plattierten Bronzeblechscheiben anschaut, so sind diese auf ganz unterschiedlichen Gegenständen zu finden[106]. Zudem stellt sich die Frage, inwiefern auch Vergleiche mit Bronzeblechen ohne Goldplattierung in Betracht gezogen wurden. Denn gerade im östlichen Bereich der Hallstatt- und Latènekulturen geben diese Funde immer wieder Hinweise auf verschiedene, überwiegend aus organischem Material bestehende Objekte. Und die Aufwertung eines Objektes durch die Anbringung einer Goldfolie läge gerade bei solchen Gegenständen nahe.

Prunkgräber wie Hochdorf oder das Kleinaspergle zeigen, wie breitgefächert die Verwendung von Gold und Silber zur Dekoration von Gegenständen in Elitengräbern war. Auch die spektakulären Beigaben aus dem jüngst entdeckten Elitengrab von Lavau, allen voran die schwarzfigurige Oinochoe mit silber- und goldblechbeschlagenem Standfuß, goldenem Gefäßrand und Verzierungen aus Silber und Gold auf Henkel nebst Attasche, stellen einmal mehr die Bandbreite an Goldverzierungen eindrucksvoll unter Beweis[107]. Betrachtet man die Geschichte der Elitengräber, so zeigen sich immer wieder neue Entdeckungen von ungewöhnlichen Objekten oder zumindest ungewöhnlichen Verzierungen, die überraschten und viele bis dato vielleicht nicht für möglich hielten. Sie mahnen dazu, mit unvoreingenommenem Blick alle Möglichkeiten in Betracht zu ziehen, statt sich von vornherein durch eine Gleichsetzung von „bandförmigem Beschlag" mit „Trinkhorn" einzuschränken.

Es wird deutlich, dass die vergleichsweise hohe Zahl mutmaßlicher frühlatènezeitlicher Trinkhörner auf einer recht unsicheren Datenbasis beruht. Dies ist auch für Bad Dürkheim der Fall. Da an dieser Stelle keine umfassende kritische Bewertung aller bekannten Goldblechbeschläge mutmaßlicher Trinkhörner erfolgen kann, soll lediglich für die Bad Dürkheimer Bleche geprüft werden, welche Alternativen infrage kommen könnten.

Im Vergleich zu allen übrigen mutmaßlichen Trinkhornbeschlägen besitzt das Bad Dürkheimer Stück eine außergewöhnliche Verzierung mit einem Mäandermotiv und einer Aufteilung in annähernd quadratische Metopen. Im Gegensatz zu den sonst meist vorherrschenden floralen Ornamenten eignet sich diese stark geometrische Grundkomposition mit vielen rechten Winkeln kaum für die konische Oberfläche eines Rinder- oder Auerochsenhornes. Rechtwinklige Strukturen wirken nur bei geringem Neigungswinkel, da ansonsten zu starke Verzerrungen auftreten. Es sind zwar auch trapezoide Metopenfelder auf einigen Gefäßen bekannt, doch zeigen die Fragmente des Bad Dürkheimer Beschlags durchweg rechte Winkel.

Dieser Neigungseffekt verstärkt sich noch, je höher ein Blech ist. Und im Vergleich zu den anderen Blechen ist das Bad Dürkheimer Stück eines der höchsten; nur das Stück aus Eigenbilzen ist höher. Versuche, das „Blech"[108] in Originalgröße an einem rund 45 cm langen Stierhorn zu befestigen, erbrachten bei der längeren Variante mit acht Metopen im oberen Bereich eine Lücke von 1,8 cm. Bei der kürzeren Variante, bestehend aus sechs Metopenfeldern, die entsprechend weiter unten an der Spitze des Horns befestigt werden musste, waren es sogar 2,8 cm.

---

[106] Insbesondere im 2012 entdeckten dritten Elitengrab von Worms-Herrnsheim (DE) zeigen sich ganz ähnlich gestaltete Goldbleche sowohl als Teil der Schuhknöpfe wie auch als Zierde auf der Schwertscheide (freundl. Hinweis Günter Brücken).

[107] Darüber hinaus gehörten zum Trinkservice u. a. auch noch ein weiterer goldverzierter Standfuß, der offenbar Teil eines organischen Gefäßes gewesen war, sowie ein silbervergoldetes Sieb und ein Sieblöffel aus Silber; Dubuis u. a. 2015, 1199 f. Abb. 9; Dubuis / Millet 2017, 10 f. Abb. 9.

[108] In Form eines Papierausdrucks.

D. Krausse schilderte die wechselvolle Interpretationsgeschichte der sogenannten „Schale" aus Hügel 1 von Schwarzenbach, die im Laufe der Zeit als Goldkrone, Stirnschmuck und auch als Helm gedeutet wurde, bevor sie als „Prachtschale" rekonstruiert wurde, was von A. Haffner wiederum angezweifelt wurde, der dann eine Umdeutung als Trinkhornbeschlag vornahm[109]. Krausse selbst blieb bei seiner Interpretation noch sehr vorsichtig und ließ offen, ob es sich bei dem durchbrochen gearbeiteten Blech und dem Randstück um eine Schale oder ein Trinkhorn handelte; lediglich bei der „Bodenscheibe" war er sich sicher, dass sie nicht in dieser Form zum Gefäß gehörte[110]. Zahlreiche Goldschalen sind bereits aus der Hallstattzeit bekannt[111].

Geometrische Mäanderverzierungen und Metopenfelder sind neben Gürtelbeschlägen auch häufig als Zierelement von Keramikgefäßen, insbesondere in der Aisne-Marne-Region, zu finden, wo in einigen Fällen sogar zwei Register mit Metopenfeldern und diagonal alternierenden Mustern vorkommen[112]. Metopen und Mäander auf Keramikgefäßen finden sich in vielen weiteren Regionen während der Frühlatènezeit, wie zum Beispiel vom Kemmelberg (Prov. Westflandern) in Belgien, wo sogar eine Scherbe mit swastikaartigem Mäandermotiv vorliegt[113].

Unter den Holzgefäßen, die mit Bronzebeschlägen verziert wurden, lässt sich die Röhrenkanne aufgrund ihrer charakteristischen Tülle besonders gut nachweisen[114]. Dies muss jedoch nicht bedeuten, dass nicht auch andere Gefäße in ähnlicher Weise verziert wurden.

Neben anderen Status- bzw. Prestigeobjekten enthielt das Elitengrab 44/2 von Dürrnberg „Moserstein" (Land Salzburg, AT) auch die zerfallenen Reste einer hölzernen Kanne mit elf Bronzebeschlägen[115]. Unter anderem findet sich auch hier eine menschliche Maske. Die ebenfalls aus dem Grab stammenden Goldblechbeschläge wurden zu beiden Seiten des Kopfes gefunden und gehören daher weder zu einem Trinkhorn noch zu einem Gefäß.

---

[109] Krausse 1996, 199–204.
[110] Krausse 1996, 217–218.
[111] Vgl. z. B. Wehringen (DE), Hügel 8; Hochdorf; Stuttgart-Bad Cannstatt (DE), Grab 1; Apremont (Dép. Haute-Saône, FR), Grab 1; Vix. – Die Literatur zu diesen Stücken ist vielfältig: vgl. z. B. Kimmig 1999; Kimmig 1991; Krausse 1996, 90–95; Krausse 2003.
[112] Siehe z. B. Desenne 2003; Demoule 1999, 159–160; 350; 360; 363; 364; 367; 372; 374; 378; 380; 384; 395.
[113] van Doorselaer 1975, 83 Taf. I,1.6.8; 84 Taf. II,2.5.
[114] Eine erste Auflistung der keltischen Röhrenkannen (auch der tönernen und bronzenen) erfolgte durch W. Dehn (1969) weitere (bronzene) Stücke wurden später durch R. Echt (1999, 117–122) ergänzt. – Die Stücke aus Grab 46/2 „Moserstein" (Penninger 1972, 81–83 Taf. 50–52) und aus Grab 102 vom Dürrnberg (Moosleitner u. a. 1974, 68–69 Taf. 167) sowie die beiden nordwestböhmischen Exemplare aus Hostomice nad Bílinou (Dehn 1969, 130 Abb. 4,4) und Čižkovice (Filip 1956, 47 Abb. 13,1.2.12; 336 Taf. 20,1–3) (beide Ústecký kraj, CZ) ebenso die Kanne aus Brno-Maloměřice (Filip 1956, 400–401 Abb. 14 Taf. 77; 78; Müller 2009, 214 f. Abb. 282–284) (Jihomoravský kraj, CZ) und das 2009 entdeckte Exemplar aus Roseldorf in Niederösterreich (Holzer 2014) sind, bis auf Grab 102, allerdings jünger als das Bad Dürkheimer Grab. Die beiden letztgenannten Stücke datieren bereits an das Ende von Lt B2 bzw. in ein frühes Lt C1 (Holzer 2014, 88). – W. Dehn (1969, 130) sah die drei Bronzebeschläge aus Grab 9 vom Dürrnberg (Penninger 1972, 48 f. Taf. 7,12–14) als Teile einer hölzernen Kanne an, allerdings war er unsicher, ob es sich auch um eine Röhrenkanne handelte. Die Fundlage an der rechten Hüfte und vor allem die Form der Beschläge lassen aber auch an einen Gürtel denken – zumal bei Penninger keine Holz- sondern lediglich in einem Fall „auf der Rückseite leichte Rostspuren" (Penninger 1972, 49) erwähnt werden.
[115] Penninger 1972, 76–80 Taf. 48. – Das Grab enthielt unter anderem einen zweirädrigen Wagen, einen goldenen Armring, drei Goldblechbeschläge auf Bronzeblech, eine griechische Tonschale sowie eine umfangreiche Waffenausstattung.

Aus dem rund 85 km südlich von Bad Dürkheim gelegenen und ebenfalls in die Stufe Lt A datierenden Kriegergrab 1 des Hügels 1 von Weitbruch (Dép. Bas-Rhin, FR) kam ein ungewöhnlicher Bronzebeschlag zum Vorschein, der laut Wolfgang Dehn „durchaus den röhrenförmigen Ausguss einer Holzkanne umschlossen haben" kann[116]. Wie bei dem Bad Dürkheimer Blech ist auch bei jenem Stück der untere Abschluss in Form einer Torsionsborte gestaltet und die darüber befindlichen Verzierungen sind in mehrere Felder untergliedert.

Die hölzerne Röhrenkanne aus Grab 71 von Arbedo-Molinazzo[117] (Kt. Tessin, CH) ist fast vollständig mit Bronzeblechen verziert, die einige durchaus erwähnenswerte Parallelen mit den Goldblechbeschlägen aus Bad Dürkheim besitzen. Es erscheint einer Überlegung wert, ob nicht eine regionalisierte Variante eines ähnlichen Holzgefäßes auch in Bad Dürkheim ursprünglich einmal mit dem Goldblech verziert war. So fällt zunächst auf, dass die Beschläge des Kannenkörpers ebenfalls in Metopen gegliedert sind[118]. Diese bestehen zwar ausschließlich aus einem Schachbrettmuster aus Holz und Bronzestücken, die in den Holzkörper gehämmert wurden, aber zumindest wurde auch bei dem Bad Dürkheimer Stück eine geometrische Komponente für eine Metopenvariante beibehalten. Als Metopengrenzen fungieren bei dem Tessiner Stück große und weit auseinander liegende Kreisaugenpunzen, die in Bad Dürkheim in die im Latènegebiet populäre Perlleiste umgewandelt wurden.

Ein ähnliches Schachbrettmuster, bestehend aus sich abwechselnden Bronze- und Eisenplättchen, findet sich auch als Verzierung der beiden Räder auf dem Wagen in Mülheim-Kärlich, Grab 4[119]. Die Bruchstücke eines umgebördelten schnurartig verzierten Reifens aus dünnem Goldblech und vier kleine mit Kreisen verzierte und zusammengelegte, mit Nietlöchern versehene Beschläge aus dünnem Goldblech sind in ihrer Ansprache unsicher. Während Adam Günther von Trinkhornbeschlägen ausging, vermutete Gustav Behrens einen Randbeschlag und kleine Wandungsbeschläge eines Holzbechers[120]. Die Lage im unteren Körperbereich in der Nähe der Schnabelkanne macht die Anbringung an einem wie auch immer gearteten Trinkgefäß wahrscheinlich, wenngleich die Anmerkung Günthers irritiert, wonach es sich um „zusammengelegte" Goldbleche handelt. Dies erinnert an das längliche Blech aus Lonnig-Kobern (DE)[121], das mittig gefaltet aufgefunden wurde und daher kaum als ein Trinkhornbeschlag anzusprechen ist. Vielmehr könnte es sich um den Beschlag einer Aufhängung handeln. Aber auch jeglicher andere Beschlag an einem schmalen, beidseitig sichtbaren Objekt muss in Betracht gezogen werden. Ein weiterer Umstand, der bei den Goldbeschlägen von Mülheim-Kärlich, Grab 4, etwas irritiert, ist die Lage der tordierten Schauseite, denn diese ist vor allem im Innenbereich verziert, während sie nur wenig auf die Außenseite reicht. Bei einem Trinkhornrandbeschlag wäre jedoch

---

[116] DEHN 1969, 130; JACOBSTHAL 1944, Taf. 270,284; SCHAEFFER 1930, 96 f. Abb. 88 f. – Für einige Bronzeteile aus dem zerstörten Elitengrab von Laumersheim (Lkr. Bad Dürkheim, DE), das nur rund 12 km von Bad Dürkheim entfernt liegt, schlug W. Kimmig ebenfalls eine Röhrenkanne vor (KIMMIG 1944–1950), doch wurden verschiedentlich bereits Bedenken gegenüber dieser Ansprache und der vorgelegten Rekonstruktion geäußert (vgl. z. B. DEHN 1969, 126; ECHT 1999, 117), die jüngst von Regina Molitor anhand einer neuen Rekonstruktion bestätigt werden konnten.

[117] ULRICH 1914, 260 Taf. 35,4; EBERT 1924, 143; 271 Taf. 98B; 198–199; DÉCHELETTE 1927, 654,4; JACOBSTHAL 1944, 203 Nr. 395 Taf. 198 f.

[118] Auch auf der Röhrenkanne aus Ton von Poix (Dép. Marne, FR) wurde eine Metopenzier angebracht, von der Dehn eine lokale Inspiration aus der Marnekeramik annahm, aber aufgrund der Verzierung unter dem Henkelansatz gleichsam betonte, dass hier eine Bronzeattasche imitiert werden sollte (JACOBSTHAL 1944, Taf. 209,407; DEHN 1969, 127 f. 132 Abb. 2).

[119] GÜNTHER 1934, 10 f. Taf. 1,1–5.

[120] GÜNTHER 1934, 9 f. Taf. 1,13–18.

[121] WEGNER 2006, 43 Abb. 21.

zu erwarten, dass beide Seiten – und tendenziell sogar eher die Außenseite – verziert sein müssten. Die Verzierung würde besser zu einem Standfuß oder einer Art Teller passen.

Gürtel

Neben der Möglichkeit einer Verwendung als Beschlag eines Gefäßes aus Holz soll letztlich auch noch eine weitere potenzielle Verwendung in die Überlegungen miteinbezogen werden: So ist nicht *per se* ausgeschlossen, dass es sich bei dem Blech einst um die Verzierung eines Gürtels gehandelt haben könnte. Beschläge aus dünnem Goldblech auf Gürteln waren während der Hallstattzeit durchaus bekannt[122]. Insbesondere die beiden bereits erwähnten Goldblechstreifen mit Perllleistenverzierung aus Grab 3 von Murten-Löwenberg (vgl. *Abb. 12b*) weisen eine besondere Ähnlichkeit mit den Perllleistenstegen von Bad Dürkheim auf. Da die Fragmente zusammen mit Bronzeresten im Bereich der Hüfte zwischen den Armringen gefunden wurden und sich die übrigen Beigaben alle in der üblichen Trachtlage befanden, ist eine Ansprache als Teil eines Gürtels plausibel[123]. Quadratische bis rechteckige Felder, die oft auch Swastika-Motive enthalten, finden sich häufig auf späthallstattzeitlichen Gürtelblechen[124]. Besonders das bereits erwähnte durchbrochen gearbeitete Stück aus Hügel 1, Nachbestattung 1 der Gießübel-Talhau-Nekropole nahe der Heuneburg bei Herbertingen-Hundersingen (DE) (vgl. *Abb. 15a*)[125] ähnelt auch aufgrund der Gestaltung des sich kreuzenden Treppenmäanders dem Bad Dürkheimer Goldblechbeschlag. Das Feld neben dem Treppenmäander beinhaltet ein streng geometrisches Motiv aus zwei langen, X-förmigen Geraden, die diagonal durch das quadratische Feld laufen, sowie einem kleinen Quadrat, das um 45° gekippt ist, sodass die Ecken dieser Raute die Kanten des Metopenfeldes mittig treffen. Insgesamt entstehen so acht Berührungspunkte mit dem Metopenfeld. Legt man das Maskenmotiv des Bad Dürkheimer Beschlags über dieses Muster, so zeigt sich eine Ähnlichkeit in Bezug auf das Kompositionsschema *(Abb. 20)*[126]. Nach oben und nach unten werden die quadratischen „Metopenfelder" in der Mitte zudem durch ein Mäanderband abgetrennt, das wie eine rechtwinklige, noch ganz im Stil der Hallstattzeit verwurzelte Variante einer Torsionsborte wirkt. Auf dem bronzenen kästchenförmigen Gürtelbeschlag aus dem Lt A-zeitlichen Grab von Bofflens „Bois de Tranchecuisse" (Kt. Waadt, CH) ist ebenfalls eine metopenartige Aufteilung in quadratische Felder zu sehen. Das Motiv des zentralen Feldes wird von Walter Drack und Gilbert Kaenel ebenfalls als gekreuzter Treppenmäander rekonstruiert[127].

---

[122] Vgl. Hansen 2010, 280 Liste 6: Hochdorf (Lkr. Ludwigsburg), Zentralgrab des „Grafenbühl" bei Asperg (Lkr. Ludwigsburg; Zürn 1970, 23 f. Taf. 20,3), Grab 1 des Hohmichele nahe Altheim-Heiligkreuztal (Lkr. Sigmaringen, DE); Grab 505 von Hallstatt (Bez. Gmunden, AT; Eluère 1987, 89 Abb. 57); unsicher sind bei Hansen Grabhügel 1 von Düdingen „Birchwald" (Kt. Freiburg, CH) sowie Hügel 1, Grab 3 von Murten „Löwenberg (Kt. Freiburg, CH). – Möglicherweise gehören auch die goldenen Nietköpfe aus Apremont „La Motte aux Fées", Grab 1 (Eluère 1987, Abb. 72) zu einem Gürtelbeschlag.

[123] Schwab 1984, 72. – Das von L. Hansen (2010, 109) erwähnte Gürtelblech vom Typ Cannstatt stammt nicht aus demselben Grab, sondern aus Grab 1B (Schwab 1984, 71; 76 Abb. 6), weshalb auch seine Unsicherheit in Bezug auf die Zusammengehörigkeit der Goldblechfragmente zum Gürtelblech aufgrund der unterschiedlichen Maße hinfällig ist.

[124] Vgl. z. B. Haguenau-Kurzgeländ Hügel 2, Grab II (FR) (Schaeffer 1930, 53 Abb. 47).

[125] Kurz / Schiek 2002, Taf. 11,117.

[126] Vgl. hier auch das Gürtelblech aus Hettingen-Inneringen (Lkr. Sigmaringen, DE): Zürn 1987, Taf. 348.

[127] Drack 1964, Taf. E,3; Kaenel 1990, Taf. 1,5. – Dass sich das Motiv der Swastika auf Gürteln möglicherweise noch weit länger erhielt, deutet ein Detail auf dem Siegesrelief des Pergamonaltars an (Jacobsthal 1944, Taf. 73,132).

Abb. 20. Kompositionsschema der Maskenfelder von Bad Dürkheim; vgl. dazu das Kompositionsschema am durchbrochen gearbeiteten Gürtelblech aus Hügel 1, Nachbestattung 1, der Gießübel-Talhau-Nekropole (vgl. *Abb. 15a*).

Goldene Verzierungen auf Kleidungsstücken sind aus der Hallstattzeit in verschiedenen Gräbern zum Vorschein gekommen. So etwa die mindestens 150 Goldzwecken unterschiedlicher Größe, die aus dem Zentralgrab von Hügel 1 der Gießübel-Talhau-Nekropole stammen[128]. Ein U-förmiger Krampen, wie er auch im Zentralgrab vorkommt, fand sich auch in der zentralen Kammer des Hohmichele (DE). Dort sind auch einige dünne Goldblechfäden vorhanden, die eine exakte Parallele im Grafenbühl (DE) besitzen und daher auf eine Herstellung in einer Werkstatt hindeuten[129], obwohl das Grab rund 100 Jahre jünger ist. Nochmals jünger sind die Silberblechfäden aus dem neu entdeckten Elitengrab von Lavau. Dank der modernen Untersuchungsmethoden lässt sich dort einwandfrei nachweisen, dass sie einen Ledergürtel schmückten und in Form von S-Leiern mit darüber und darunter verlaufendem Band aus Zickzack- oder Wellenlinien angeordnet waren[130]. Diese drei Fundorte verdeutlichen das Traditionsverständnis bei solch einer Zierde, das sich über mehr als ein Jahrhundert erstreckt. Erst in jüngeren Grabungen konnte geklärt werden, welche Gegenstände verziert waren und wie schwierig der Nachweis darüber ist[131].

[128] KURZ / SCHIEK 2002, 97 Nr. 103–105 Taf. 9,103–105.
[129] SCHORER u. a. 2018, 216 f.
[130] DUBUIS 2016.
[131] Die Verwendung von Bronzezwecken auf Ledergürteln ist kein seltenes Phänomen, wie z. B. die beiden gut dokumentierten Ledergürtel aus Hügel 1 vom Glauberg belegen (FLÜGEN 2002; BOSINSKI 2002). Ein Gürtel mit einem flächigen Besatz aus Bronze, der aus Grab 4 von Hügel 17 der Speckhau-Nekropole bei Altheim-Heiligkreuztal (Lkr. Biberach, DE) stammt, konnte dank moderner Methoden ebenfalls als solcher identifiziert werden (ARNOLD / MURRAY 2015, 115 Abb. 2). – Auch die bronzenen Rundkopfzwecken aus Hügel 5 des Grabhügelfeldes vom Burrenhof bei Grabenstetten (Lkr. Reutlingen, DE), die einigen goldenen Formen in der Zentralkammer des Hügel 1 der Gießübel-Talhau-Nekropole ähneln, steckten teilweise noch in Leder (vgl. RAUB 2002, 143 f.), was für einen Gürtelbesatz sprechen könnte.

Ein weiterer Punkt, der für eine Deutung als Gürtelbeschlag spräche: Die Motivik ist überwiegend für eine Blickrichtung ausgelegt. Die Maße passen in das Spektrum frühlatènezeitlicher Gürtel. Zudem ist es nicht unwahrscheinlich, dass das Blech wie bereits erwähnt auch gerade und nicht gebogen konstruiert wurde. Darüber hinaus sind insbesondere bei den hallstattzeitlichen Gürtelblechen Metopen ebenso beliebt wie das Swastika-Motiv. Im nahegelegenen Worms-Herrnsheim (DE) wurden Gürtelbleche noch in Ha D3 getragen, wie das Grab 2 aus Kreisgraben 1 in der Flur Langgewann I belegt[132]. Figürliche Gürtelbleche sind aus der Situlenkunst des Südostalpenraums nicht selten, wie die Beispiele aus Vače oder Stična in Slowenien zeigen[133].

Mit den übrigen Trinkhörnern lässt sich das Motiv aus Bad Dürkheim indes kaum stilistisch vergleichen, wenn man von unspezifischen Details wie der Torsionsborte absieht, die nämlich auch auf zahlreichen anderen Objekten vorkommt. Viele der übrigen Trinkhörner sind sich untereinander deutlich ähnlicher.

Als Gegenargument spricht der Umstand, dass bisher sonst keine weitere durchbrochene Gürtelzier existiert und dass die erwähnten Gürtelbleche nicht in die Frühlatènezeit reichen. In diesem Zusammenhang sollte jedoch bedacht werden, dass sich die Elitengräber jener Zeit zwar einerseits durch einen hohen Individualismus und eine gewisse Experimentierfreude hinsichtlich der Beigaben[134] auszeichnen, aber andererseits auch durch einen gewissen Hang zu Traditionsobjekten[135]. Gerade im Beigabenensemble von Bad Dürkheim finden sich zahlreiche ältere Objekte. So ergaben neuere Forschungen durch Giacomo Bardelli ein deutlich älteres Datum des Herstellungszeitraums, nämlich das letzte Viertel des 6. Jahrhunderts v. Chr.; weshalb es sich bei dem Dreifuß um das älteste Importobjekt im Grab handelt, das vermutlich lange tesauriert wurde[136]. Aber auch Stamnos und Schnabelkanne datieren noch in die Späthallstattzeit[137].

Neben einer Verwendung als Zierelement auf einem Gefäß oder als Gürtelbeschlag ließen sich natürlich auch andere Objekte in Betracht ziehen, die aufgrund ihrer Größe und Form prinzipiell geeignet gewesen wären, mit einem Beschlag verziert worden zu sein. Auch hier sollte wieder auf den Einfallsreichtum eisenzeitlicher Goldschmiede bzw. Feinhandwerker hingewiesen werden.

Abschließende Bemerkungen

Die Datierung des Grabes von Bad Dürkheim wurde häufig diskutiert und eine grobe Datierung in die zweite Hälfte des 5. Jahrhunderts v. Chr. und somit in die Stufe Lt A ist unstrittig[138]. Feinchronologisch wurde es zumeist in eine mittlere, klassische Phase datiert,

---

[132] ZYLMANN 2006, 68.
[133] Vgl. z. B. GLEIRSCHER 2002, 53; 57 oder MEGAW 1975, 29 Taf. 3,3.
[134] Man denke an die Goldblechbeschläge an den beiden Kylices aus dem Kleinaspergle oder an den goldverzierten Rand und Standfuß der Kanne aus Lavau.
[135] Hier ließen sich z. B. die schwerpunktmäßig in die Stufe Ha D3 datierenden Stangengliederketten in Reinheim und Worms-Herrnsheim oder die deutlich ältere Röhrenkanne aus dem Grab von Waldalgesheim anführen.
[136] BARDELLI 2019, 306 f. 326; 332 Abb. 336. –

J. V. S. Megaw ging noch von einer Datierung des Dreifußes um 420 v. Chr. – also gut 100 Jahre jünger – aus, weshalb er, nach Abzug der Transportdauer und Benutzungszeit, von einer Niederlegung in den ersten Jahrzehnten des 4. Jahrhunderts v. Chr. ausging (MEGAW 1969, 85).
[137] Der Stamnos wurde von Brian B. SHEFTON (1995, 11) ins erste Viertel des 5. Jahrhunderts datiert; die leider nur noch in Fragmenten erhaltene Schnabelkanne von Dirk VORLAUF (1997, 167–169) grob in das zweite oder dritte Viertel des 5. Jahrhunderts v. Chr.
[138] Vgl. JOACHIM 2012, 113–115.

wie etwa die Stufe Lt A2 bei R. Echt oder in die Gruppe der „klassischen" Lt A-Gräber nach D. Krausse[139]. Die hier vorgestellte Rekonstruktion des Goldbleches mit seiner hallstattzeitlichen Anmutung aufgrund der Metopenfelder und der Mäanderzier sowie das völlige Fehlen von Rankenornamenten spricht für eine frühe Stellung des Stückes innerhalb der klassischen Lt A-Phase. Dies steht in Einklang mit den nüchtern wirkenden Bogenreihen auf dem Stamnosdeckel und dem hohen Alter der etruskischen Importe und damit dem ganzen Grab.

Die hier vorgelegte Rekonstruktion des Bad Dürkheimer Beschlags und die anschließende Diskussion der einzelnen Zierelemente machten die isolierte Stellung innerhalb der Gruppe mutmaßlicher Trinkhornbeschläge im Hinblick auf die Stilistik deutlich. Mit dem Mäandermotiv, der Metopengestaltung und dem alternierenden Motivwechsel steht das Stück einerseits in der Tradition hallstattzeitlicher Gürtelbleche oder südosteuropäischer Kleidungsbeschläge. Andererseits zeigen sich zeitgleiche Parallelen in der westlichen Keramik der Aisne-Marne-Kultur. Hallstattzeitliche goldene Gefäße auf der einen und latènezeitliche Bronzebeschläge auf organischen Gefäßen auf der anderen Seite verweisen auf einen großen Variantenreichtum in Bezug auf die metallische Verzierung von ganz unterschiedlichen Gefäßtypen. Die (teilweise falsch rekonstruierte) Schale aus Schwarzenbach, Grab 1, und die beiden Kylices aus dem Kleinaspergle verdeutlichen, dass auch Goldblechbeschläge auf verschiedenen Gefäßformen angebracht wurden. Die bis dahin völlig singulären Gold- und Silberapplikationen an der schwarzfigurigen Oinochoe sowie einem organischen Gefäß aus dem neu entdeckten Elitengrab von Lavau unterstreichen diese Beobachtung.

Das Ziel dieser Ausführungen war es nicht, eine Ansprache als Trinkhornbeschlag zu widerlegen. Vielmehr sollte dafür plädiert werden, dass eine Verwendung in anderen Zusammenhängen denkbar ist und Argumente hierfür abgewogen werden müssen, bevor durch eine vorschnelle Ansprache als Teil eines Trinkhornbeschlags der Blick für weitere, individuellere Gegenstände verstellt wird. Nach Sichtung aller metallenen Trinkhornbeschläge dieses Zeitabschnitts und zahlreicher möglicher metallener Bestandteile von Trinkhörnern (vgl. *Anhang*) gibt es für das Stück aus Bad Dürkheim keine typologische Verbindung zu nachweislichen Elementen solcher Trinkgefäße, nur der Dekor der Schuppenborte lässt stilistische Bezüge erkennen. Die rechteckige Grundform erschwert zudem die Verwendung an einem gebogenen und gewölbten Körper. Zusammenfassend muss aufgrund der mangelnden Befunddokumentation und der weitgreifenden Parallelen die Funktion des Bleches offenbleiben. Eine pauschale Ansprache als Trinkhornbeschlag kann somit nicht aufrechterhalten werden.

Die bisherigen Untersuchungen im Projekt CELTIC GOLD konnten aufzeigen, dass frühlatènezeitliche Goldblecharbeiten regelhaft auf gepunzten und getriebenen Bronzeblechen beruhen. Sie waren der eigentliche Formgeber und Motivträger, auf die das dünne Goldblech aufplattiert und an den Rändern um das Bronzeblech gebördelt wurde. Solche Verzierungen finden sich auf den unterschiedlichsten Objekten wie Scheibenfibeln, Zierscheiben vom Typ Weiskirchen oder Ziernieten – und eben auch Trinkhornbeschlägen. Man kann davon ausgehen, dass es keinerlei „Denkverbote" unter den latènezeitlichen Kunsthandwerkern bzw. ihren Auftraggebern gab, welche Objekte nicht mit Goldblech verziert sein durften. Diese sollten wir uns bei der Interpretation der Goldbleche auch nicht auferlegen.

---

[139] Echt 1999, 267; 270 Abb. 73; Krausse 2006, 94 Abb. 35.

Literaturverzeichnis

ARDJANLIEV u. a. 2018
P. Ardjanliev / K. Chukalev / T. Cvjeticanin / M. Damyanov / V. Krstić / A. Papazovska (Hrsg.), 100 years of Trebenishte [Ausstellungskat.] (Sofia 2018).

ARNOLD / MURRAY 2015
B. Arnold / M. L. Murray, Zwei hallstattzeitliche Grabhügel der Hohmichele-Gruppe im „Speckhau". In: D. Krausse / I. Kretschmer / L. Hansen / M. Fernández-Götz (Hrsg.), Die Heuneburg – keltischer Fürstensitz an der oberen Donau. Führer Arch. Denkmäler Baden-Württemberg 28 (Darmstadt 2015) 114–116.

BAGLEY 2014
J. M. Bagley, Zwischen Kommunikation und Distinktion. Ansätze zur Rekonstruktion frühlatènezeitlicher Bildpraxis. Vorgesch. Forsch. 25 (Rahden / Westf. 2014).

BAITINGER / PINSKER 2002
H. Baitinger / B. Pinsker (Hrsg.), Das Rätsel der Kelten vom Glauberg. Glaube – Mythos – Wirklichkeit. Eine Ausstellung des Landes Hessen in der Schirn Kunsthalle Frankfurt, 24. Mai bis 1. September 2002 (Stuttgart 2002).

BARDELLI 2017a
G. Bardelli (Hrsg.), Das Prunkgrab von Bad Dürkheim 150 Jahre nach der Entdeckung. Monogr. RGZM 137 (Mainz 2017).

BARDELLI 2017b
G. Bardelli, Die wahre italische Faszination. Die Funde aus dem keltischen Grab von Bad Dürkheim und ihre Geschichten. Mosaiksteine 14 (Mainz 2017).

BARDELLI 2019
G. Bardelli, I tripodi a verghette in Etruria e in Italia centrale. Origini, tipologia e caratteristiche. Monogr. RGZM 149 (Mainz 2019).

BARTH 1987
F. E. Barth, Die Wagen aus der Býčí skála-Höhle, Gem. Habruvka, Bez. Blanska, CSSR. In: F. E. Barth (Hrsg.), Vierrädrige Wagen der Hallstattzeit. Untersuchungen zu Geschichte und Technik. Monogr. RGZM 12 (Mainz 1987) 103–119.

BERNHARD / SZTETYŁŁO 1976
M. L. Bernhard / Z. Sztetyłło, Phanagoria. In: R. Stillwell / W. L. MacDonald / M. H. McAlister (Hrsg.), The Princeton Encyclopedia of Classical Sites (Princeton 1976).

BOSINSKI 2002
M. Bosinski, Gürtel aus Grab 2. In: Baitinger / Pinsker 2002, 153–154.

DECHELETTE 1927
J. Déchelette, Manuel d'archéologie préhistorique celtique et gallo-romaine 4. Second âge du Fer ou époque de la Tène² (Paris 1927).

DEHN 1969
W. Dehn, Keltische Röhrenkannen der älteren Latènezeit. Pam. Arch. 60, 1969, 125–133.

DEHN u. a. 2005
R. Dehn / M. Egg / R. Lehnert, Das Hallstattzeitliche Fürstengrab im Hügel 3 von Kappel am Rhein in Baden. Monogr. RGZM 63 (Mainz 2005).

DEMOULE 1999
J.-P. Demoule, La culture de l'Aisne-Marne: périodisation et comparaisons. In: J.-P. Demoule (Hrsg.), Chronologie et société dans les nécropoles celtiques de la culture Aisne-Marne du VIe au IIIe siècle avant notre ère. Rev. Arch. Picardie. Num. spécial 15 (Senlis 1999) 143–168.

DESENNE 2003
S. Desenne, Décryptage d'un mode d'expression de la culture Aisne-Marne: elaboration d'une grille de lecture du décor céramique. In: O. Buchsenschutz (Hrsg.), Décors, images et signes de l'âge du Fer européen. Actes du XXVIe colloque international de l'A.F.E.A.F. (Paris et Saint-Denis, 9–12 mai 2002) (Tours 2003) 63–76.

VAN DOORSELAER 1975
A. van Doorselaer, Der Kemmelberg, ein keltischer Herrensitz? Alba Regia 14, 1975, 79–84.

DRACK 1964
W. Drack, Ältere Eisenzeit der Schweiz. Kanton Bern 4. Materialh. Ur- u. Frühgesch. Schweiz 4 (Basel 1964).

Drda / Rybova 1995
P. Drda / A. Rybová, Les Celtes de Bohême. Collect. Hesperides (Paris 1995).

Dubuis 2016
B. Dubuis (Hrsg.), Grand Est, Aube, Lavau, « Zac du Moutot ». Un complexe funéraire monumental II. Catalogue du mobilier de la tombe princière. Rapport de fouille archéologique (Metz 2016).

Dubuis / Millet 2017
B. Dubuis / É. Millet, Chronique d'une découverte exceptionnelle. La nécropole et la tombe « princière » de Lavau. Vie Champagne 89, 2017, 2–23.

Dubuis u. a. 2015
B. Dubuis / D. Garcia / É. Millet, Les contacts entre la Méditerranée archaïque et le monde celtique: le cas de la tombe de Lavau (Aube). Comptes Rendus Séances Année 2015, 1185–1212.

Ebert 1924
M. Ebert (Hrsg.), Reallexikon der Vorgeschichte (1924).

Echt 1999
R. Echt, Das Fürstinnengrab von Reinheim. Studien zur Kulturgeschichte der Früh-La-Tenè-Zeit. Saarbrücker Beitr. Altkde. 69 = Blesa 2 (Bonn 1999).

Echt / Thiele 1994
R. Echt / W.-R. Thiele (Hrsg.), Von Wallerfangen bis Waldalgesheim. Ein Beitrag zu späthallstatt- und frühlatènezeitlichen Goldschmiedearbeiten. Saarbrücker Stud. u. Mat. Altkde. 3 (Bonn 1994).

Eluère 1987
C. Eluère, Das Gold der Kelten (München 1987).

van Endert 1987
D. van Endert, Die Wagenbestattungen der späten Hallstattzeit und der Latènezeit im Gebiet westlich des Rheins. BAR Internat. Ser. 355 (Oxford 1987).

Filip 1956
J. Filip, Keltové ve stredni Evrope. Mon. Arch. 5 (Prag 1956).

Filow 1927
B. D. Filow, Die archaische Nekropole von Trebenischte am Ochrida-See (Berlin, Leipzig 1927).

Flügen 2002
Th. Flügen, Gürtel aus Grab 1. In: Baitinger / Pinsker 2002, 151–153.

Foulon / Kemenczei 2001
B. Foulon / T. Kemenczei (Hrsg.), Trésors préhistoriques de Hongrie. Collection du Musée National Hongrois. [Exposition] Musée des Antiquités Nationales Saint-Germain-en-Laye, 10 octobre 2001–7 janvier 2002 (Paris 2001).

Frey 2014
O.-H. Frey, Zur Attaschenzier der Schnabelkannen von Basse-Yutz. In: C. Gosden / S. Crawford / K. Ulmschneider (Hrsg.), Celtic Art in Europe. Making Connections. Essays in Honour of Vincent Megaw on his 80th Birthday (Oxford 2014) 101–104.

Frölich 2006
R. Frölich, Experiment Glauberg – zur Blattkrone des Keltenfürsten. Denkmalpfl. u. Kulturgesch. 3, 2006, 34–36.

Ginoux 1994
N. Ginoux, Les fourreaux ornés de France du Ve au IIe siècle avant J.-C. Études Celtiques 30, 1994, 7–86. doi: https://doi.org/10.3406/ecelt.1994.2031.

Gleirscher 2002
P. Gleirscher, Das hallstattzeitliche Gräberfeld von Frög bei Rosegg. Texte und Bilder aus dem Urgeschichtszentrum Frög-Rosegg. Rudolfinum – Jahrb. Landesmus. Kärnten 2002, 35–64.

Greifenhagen 1970
A. Greifenhagen, Schmuckarbeiten in Edelmetall 1. Fundgruppen (Berlin 1970).

Günther 1934
A. Günther, Gallische Wagengräber im Gebiet des Neuwieder Beckens. Germania 18, 1934, 8–14. doi: https://doi.org/10.11588/ger.1934.35062.

Haffner 1976
A. Haffner, Die westliche Hunsrück-Eifel-Kultur. Röm.-Germ. Forsch. 36 (Berlin 1976).

Haffner 1991
A. Haffner, The princley tombs of the celts in the Middle Rhineland. In: Moscati u. a. 1991, 155–162.

Haffner 2014

A. Haffner, Das frühkeltische Prunkgrab „Am Müllenberg" von Besseringen-Merzig im nördlichen Saarland. Arch. Mosellana 9, 2014, 81–112.

Haffner / Lage 2008–2009

A. Haffner / M. Lage, Die frühkeltische Fürstengrabnekropole von Bescheid, „Bei den Hübeln", Kreis Trier-Saarburg. Trierer Zeitschr. 71/72, 2008–2009, 27–142.

Hansen 2010

L. Hansen, Hochdorf VIII. Die Goldfunde und Trachtbeigaben des späthallstattzeitlichen Fürstengrabes von Eberdingen-Hochdorf (Kr. Ludwigsburg). Forsch. u. Ber. Vor- u. Frühgesch. Baden-Württemberg 118 (Stuttgart 2010).

Hartmann 1978

A. Hartmann, Ergebnisse spektralanalytischer Untersuchung späthallstatt- und latènezeitlicher Goldfunde vom Dürrnberg, aus Südwestdeutschland, Frankreich und der Schweiz. In: L. Pauli (Hrsg.), Der Dürrnberg bei Hallein III. Auswertung der Grabfunde. Münchener Beitr. Vor- u. Frühgesch. 18 (München 1978) 601–617.

Hoddinott 1981

R. F. Hoddinott, The Thracians (London 1981).

Holzer 2014

V. Holzer, Ein Holzurnengrab mit bronzenen Zierbeschlägen aus Roseldorf, Niederösterreich, Objekt 39. Germania 90, 2012 (2014) 69–96.

Jacobsthal 1944

P. Jacobsthal, Early Celtic Art (Oxford 1944).

Joachim 1979

H.-E. Joachim, Die frühlatènezeitlichen Wagengräber von Mülheim-Kärlich, Kr. Mayen-Koblenz. In: Beiträge zur Urgeschichte des Rheinlandes 3. Rhein. Ausgr. 19 (Köln, Bonn 1979) 518–556.

Joachim 1998

H.-E. Joachim, Das frühlatènezeitliche Fürstengrab von Dörth, „Wald Gallscheid", Rhein-Hunsrück-Kreis. In: A. Müller-Karpe / H. Brandt / H. Jöns / D. Krausse / A. Wigg (Hrsg.), Studien zur Archäologie der Kelten, Römer und Germanen in Mittel- und Westeuropa. Alfred Haffner zum 60. Geburtstag gewidmet. Internat. Arch. Stud. Honoraria 4 (Rahden / Westf. 1998) 245–275.

Joachim 2012

H.-E. Joachim, Die frühlatènezeitlichen Prunkgräber von Bad Dürkheim und Rodenbach, Pfalz. Zum derzeitigen Forschungsstand. In: U. Recker / B. Steinbring / B. Wiegel (Hrsg.), Jäger – Bergleute – Adelige. Archäologische Schlaglichter aus vier Jahrtausenden. Festschrift für Claus Dobiat zum 65. Geburtstag. Internat. Arch. Stud. Honoraria 33 (Rahden / Westf. 2012) 91–120.

Jorns 1964

W. Jorns, Groß-Rohrheim. Trinkhornbeschlag. Fundber. Hessen 4, 1964, 187–189.

Jorns 1966

W. Jorns, Ein Frühlatènezeitlicher Trinkhornbeschlag von Groß Rohrheim, Kr. Bergstraße. Jahresschr. Mitteldt. Vorgesch. 50, 1966, 223–226.

Jovanović 1976

B. Jovanović, Примерци животињског стила скитског и трачкогвозденог доба у Југославији. Les exemples du style animalier de l'âge du Fer scythe et thrace en Yougoslavie. Starinar N. S. 27, 1976, 19–31. http://viminacium.org.rs/wp-content/uploads/files/starinar/Starinar_27_1976.pdf (letzter Zugriff: 20.4.2022).

Kaenel 1990

G. Kaenel, Recherches sur la période de La Tène en Suisse occidentale. Analyse des sépultures. Cahiers Arch. Romande 50 (Lausanne 1990).

Kimmig 1944–1950

W. Kimmig, Ein Wagengrab der frühen Latènezeit von Laumersheim (Rheinpfalz). Germania 28, 1944–1950, 38–50. doi: https://doi.org/10.11588/ger.1944.45944.

Kimmig 1988

W. Kimmig, Das Kleinaspergle. Studien zu einem Fürstengrabhügel der frühen Latènezeit bei Stuttgart. Forsch. u. Ber. Vor- u. Frühgesch. Baden-Württemberg 30 (Stuttgart 1988).

Kimmig 1991

W. Kimmig, Edelmetallschalen der späten Hallstatt- und frühen Latènezeit. Arch. Korrbl. 21, 1991, 241–253.

Kimmig 1999

W. Kimmig, Coupes en métal précieux du Hallstatt final et du début de la Tène. In: B. Chaume / J.-P. Mohen / P. Périn (Hrsg.), Archéologie des Celtes. Mélanges à la mémoire de René Joffroy. Protohist. Européenne 3 (Montagnac 1999) 195–206.

Kimmig / Rest 1954

W. Kimmig / W. Rest, Ein Fürstengrab der späten Hallstattzeit von Kappel am Rhein. Jahrb. RGZM 1, 1954, 179–216. doi: https://doi.org/10.11588/jrgzm.1954.0.31060.

Kisfaludi 1983

J. Kisfaludi, Szkítakori sír Mezőtúrról. Arch. Ért. 110, 1983, 69–73. https://adt.arcanum.com/hu/view/ARCHERT_1983_110/?query=s%C3%ADr&pg=70&layout=s (letzter Zugriff: 20.4.2022).

Krausse 1995

D. Krausse, Der Mündungsbeschlag. In: H. Nortmann / S. K. Ehlers, Die frühlatènezeitlichen Grabhügel auf dem „Dreikopf" bei Pellingen, Kreis Trier-Saarburg. Trierer Zeitschr. 58, 1995, 69–142, hier 113–117.

Krausse 1996

D. Krausse, Hochdorf III. Das Trink- und Speiseservice aus dem späthallstattzeitlichen Fürstengrab von Eberdingen-Hochdorf (Kr. Ludwigsburg). Forsch. u. Ber. Vor- u. Frühgesch. Baden-Württemberg 64 (Stuttgart 1996).

Krausse 2003

D. Krausse, La phiale. In: C. Rolley (Hrsg.), La tombe princière de Vix (Paris 2003) 217–231.

Krausse 2006

D. Krausse, Eisenzeitlicher Kulturwandel und Romanisierung im Mosel-Eifel-Raum. Die keltisch-römische Siedlung von Wallendorf und ihr archäologisches Umfeld. Röm.-Germ. Forsch. 63 (Mainz 2006).

Krausse u. a. 2015

D. Krausse / I. Kretschmer / L. Hansen / M. Fernández-Götz (Hrsg.), Die Heuneburg – keltischer Fürstensitz an der oberen Donau. Führer Arch. Denkmäler Baden-Württemberg 28 (Darmstadt 2015).

Kromer 1986

K. Kromer, Das östliche Mitteleuropa in der frühen Eisenzeit (7.–5. Jh. v. Chr.). Seine Beziehungen zu den Steppenvölkern und antiken Hochkulturen. Jahrb. RGZM 33, 1986, 3–93.

Krstić 2018

V. Krstić, Grave VIII. The Tomb of Beautiful Antiquities. In: P. Ardjanliev / K. Chukalev / T. Cvjeticanin / M. Damyanov / V. Krstić / A. Papazovska (Hrsg.), 100 years of Trebenishte [Ausstellungskat.] (Sofia 2018) 43–48.

Kurz / Schiek 2002

S. Kurz / S. Schiek, Bestattungsplätze im Umfeld der Heuneburg. Forsch. u. Ber. Vor- u. Frühgesch. Baden-Württemberg 87 (Stuttgart 2002).

Lambot 2005

B. Lambot, La Tombe à chars d'Évergnicourt (Aisne), "Le Tournant du Chêne". In: G. Auxiette / F. Malrain (Hrsg.), Hommages à Claudine Pommepuy. Rev. Arch. Picardie, Numéro spécial 22 (Amiens 2005) 327–354. doi: https://doi.org/10.3406/pica.2005.2737.

Lambot 2014

B. Lambot, Le char de Prunay (Marne, France), véhicule d'un "aristocrate" du début du second âge du fer en Champagne. In: P. Barral / J.-P. Guillaumet / M.-J. Roulière-Lambert / M. Saracino / D. Vitali (Hrsg.), Les Celtes et le Nord de l'Italie (Premier et Second Âges du fer). Actes du XXXVIe colloque international de l'A.F.E.A.F. (Vérone, 17–20 mai 2012). Rev. Arch. Est 36 (Dijon 2014) 683–703.

Lenerz-de Wilde 1988

M. Lenerz-de Wilde, Ornamentstudien. In: W. Kimmig, Das Kleinaspergle. Studien zu einem Fürstengrabhügel der frühen Latènezeit bei Stuttgart. Forsch. u. Ber. Vor- u. Frühgesch. Baden-Württemberg 30 (Stuttgart 1988).

Lindenschmit d. Ä. 1870

L. Lindenschmit d. Ä. (Hrsg.), Die Alterthümer unserer heidnischen Vorzeit 2 (Mainz 1870). https://mdz-nbn-resolving.de/urn:nbn:de:bvb:12-bsb10985425-5.

Mariën 1962

M. É. Mariën, Eigenbilzen et Hallein. In:

M. Renard (Hrsg.), Hommages à Albert Grenier 3. Collect. Latomus 58,3 (Bruxelles 1962) 1113–1116.

Mariën 1987
M. É. Mariën, Het vorstengraf van Eigenbilzen. Publ. Mus. Tongeren 37 (Beringen 1987).

Megaw 1969
J. V. S. Megaw, Doppelsinnigkeit in der keltischen Kunst, dargestellt an einem. Beispiel aus dem Fürstengrab von Bad Dürkheim. Pfälzer Heimat 20, 1969, 85–86.

Megaw 1975
J. V. S. Megaw, The orientalizing theme in Early Celtic Art: east or west? Alba Regia 14, 1975, 15–33.

Megaw / Megaw 1990
J. V. S. Megaw / M. R. Megaw (Hrsg.), The Basse-Yutz find: Masterpieces of Celtic art. The 1927 discovery in the British Museum. Reports Research Comm. Soc. Antiqu. London 46 (London 1990).

Michálek 1977
J. Michálek, Knižecí mohyly z časné doby laténské u Hradiště, okr. Písek. Příspěvek k historii nálezu z r. 1858. Arch. Rozhledy 29, 1977, 634–645.

Miltner 1863
J. B. Miltner, Zpráva o některých, v letech 1858–1860 v okoli Piseckém nalezených starožitnostech. Pam. Arch. 5, 1863, 43–44.

Moosleitner u. a. 1974
F. Moosleitner / L. Pauli / E. Penninger, Der Dürrnberg bei Hallein II. Münchner Beitr. Vor- u. Frühgesch. 17 (München 1974).

Morel 1875
L. Morel, Découvertes de Somme-Bionne (Marne). In: Congrès Archélogique de France, XLIIe session (1875) 86–131.

Morel 1898
L. Morel, La Champagne souterraine. Matériaux et documents ou résultats de 35 années de fouilles archéologiques dans la Marne (Reims 1898).

Moscati u. a. 1991
S. Moscati / O.-H. Frey / V. Kruta / B. Raftery / M. Szabó (Hrsg.), The Celts [Austellungskat. Venedig 1991] (London 1991).

Müller 2009
F. Müller (Hrsg.), Kunst der Kelten. 700 v. Chr.–700 n. Chr. [Ausstellungskat.] (Bern, Stuttgart 2009).

Nortmann 2017
H. Nortmann, Die Goldfunde. In: Bardelli 2017a, 41–52.

Nortmann / Ehlers 1995
H. Nortmann / S. K. Ehlers, Die frühlatènezeitlichen Grabhügel auf dem „Dreikopf" bei Pellingen, Kreis Trier-Saarburg. Trierer Zeitschr. 58, 1995, 69–142.

Pare 2012
C. F. E. Pare, Eastern Relations of Early Celtic Art. In: C. F. E. Pare (Hrsg.), Kunst und Kommunikation. Zentralisierungsprozesse in Gesellschaften des europäischen Barbarikums im 1. Jahrtausend v. Chr. [Teilkolloquium SPP 1171 April 2008 Mainz]. RGZM-Tagungen 15 (Mainz 2012) 153–178.

Penninger 1972
E. Penninger, Der Dürrnberg bei Hallein I. Katalog der Grabfunde aus der Hallstatt- und Latènezeit. Münchner Beitr. Vor- u. Frühgesch. 16 (München 1972).

Raub 2002
C. J. Raub, Untersuchung dekorativer hallstattzeitlicher Gold-, Silber- und Bronzekrampen. In: S. Kurz / S. Schiek, Bestattungsplätze im Umfeld der Heuneburg. Forsch. u. Ber. Vor- u. Frühgesch. Baden-Württemberg 87 (Stuttgart 2002) 143–155.

Reinhard 2003
W. Reinhard, Studien zur Hallstatt- und Frühlatènezeit im südöstlichen Saarland. Blesa 4 (Metz 2003).

Reinhard 2017
W. Reinhard, Die Kelten im Saarland. Denkmalpfl. Saarland 8 (Saarbrücken 2017).

Salmony 1937
A. Salmony, Lead Plates in Odessa. Eurasia Septentrionalis Ant. 11, 1937, 91–102.

Schaeffer 1930
C. F.-A. Schaeffer, Les tertres funéraires préhistoriques dans la forêt de Haguenau II. Les tumulus de l'âge du Fer (Haguenau 1930).

Schneider 2012
F. N. Schneider, Neue Studien zur Hunsrück-Eifel-Kultur. Münchner Arch. Forsch. 2 (Rahden / Westf. 2012).

Schönfelder 2004
M. Schönfelder, Le casque de la tombe à char de Somme-Tourbe « La Gorge-Meillet » (Marne). Ant. Nat. 36, 2004, 207–214.

Schorer u. a. 2018
B. Schorer / V. Leusch / R. Schwab, New insights into Hallstatt gold from southwest Germany. Technological aspects and material analyses. In: R. Schwab / P.-Y. Milcent / B. Armbruster / E. Pernicka (Hrsg.), Early Iron Age Gold in Celtic Europe. Society, Technology and Archaeometry. Proceedings of the International Congress held in Toulouse, France, 11–14 March 2015. Forsch. Archäometrie u. Altwiss. 6,1 (Rahden / Westf. 2018) 181–229.

Schwab 1984
H. Schwab, Ein späthallstatt- bis frühlatènezeitlicher Bestattungsplatz in Murten-Löwenberg (Kt. Freiburg). Arch. Korrbl. 14, 1984, 71–79.

Shefton 1995
B. B. Shefton, Leaven in the dough: Greek and Etruscan imports north of the Alps – The classical period. In: J. Swaddling / S. Walker / P. Roberts (Hrsg.), Italy in Europe: Economic relations 700 BC – AD 50. British Mus. Occasional Papers 97 (London 1995).

Sprater 1928
F. Sprater, Die Urgeschichte der Pfalz. Zugleich Führer durch die vorgeschichtliche Abteilung des Historischen Museums der Pfalz[2]. Veröff. Pfälz. Ges. Förd. Wiss. Speyer 5 (Speyer 1928).

Stead / Hughes 1997
I. M. Stead / K. Hughes, Early Celtic Designs. British Mus. Pattern Books (London 1997).

Stibbe 2003
C. M. Stibbe, Trebenishte: the Fortunes of an Unusual Excavation. Stud. Arch. 121 (Roma 2003).

Stümpel 1991
B. Stümpel, Latènezeitliche Funde aus Worms. In: B. Stümpel (Hrsg.), Beiträge zur Latènezeit im Mainzer Becken und Umgebung. Mainzer Zeitschr. Beih. 1 (Mainz 1991) 43–66.

Tecco Hvala u. a. 2004
S. Tecco Hvala / J. Dular / E. Kocuvan, Železnodobne gomile na Magdalenski gori. Narodni Muz. Slovenije Kat. in Monogr. 36 (Ljubljana 2004).

Teržan 1976
B. Teržan, Certoška fibula. Arh. Vestnik 27, 1976, 317–536. http://av.zrc-sazu.si/pdf/Terzan_AV_27_1976.pdf (letzter Zugriff: 20.4.2022).

Ulrich 1914
R. Ulrich, Die Gräberfelder in der Umgebung von Bellinzona Kt. Tessin (Zürich 1914).

Vorlauf 1997
D. Vorlauf, Die etruskischen Bronzeschnabelkannen. Eine Untersuchung anhand der technologisch-typologischen Methode. Internat. Arch. 11 (Espelkamp 1997).

Warmenbol 2018
E. Warmenbol, Iron Age gold in Belgium and the southern Netherlands. In: R. Schwab / P.-Y. Milcent / B. Armbruster / E. Pernicka (Hrsg.), Early Iron Age Gold in Celtic Europe. Society, Technology and Archaeometry. Proceedings of the International Congress held in Toulouse, France, 11–14 March 2015. Forsch. Archäometrie u. Altwiss. 6,1 (Rahden / Westf. 2018) 385–405.

Wegner 2006
H.-H. Wegner, Die Wagengräber von Lonnig und Kobern, Kreis Mayen-Koblenz. Ber. Arch. Mittelrhein u. Mosel 11, 2006, 21–45.

Zürn 1970
H. Zürn, Hallstattforschungen in Nordwürttemberg. Die Grabhügel von Asperg (Kr. Ludwigsburg), Hirschlanden (Kr. Ludwigsburg) und Mühlacker (Kr. Vaihingen). Veröff. Staatl. Amt Denkmalpfl. Stuttgart A16 (Stuttgart 1970).

Zürn 1987
H. Zürn, Hallstattzeitliche Grabfunde in Württemberg und Hohenzollern. Forsch. u. Ber. Vor- u. Frühgesch. Baden-Württemberg 25 (Stuttgart 1987).

Zylmann 2006
D. Zylmann, Die frühen Kelten in Worms-Herrnsheim (Worms 2006).

Zusammenfassung: Neues zum sogenannten Trinkhornbeschlag von Bad Dürkheim – Zu Goldblecharbeiten der Frühlatènezeit

Im Rahmen einer neuerlichen Untersuchung der Goldbeigaben des frühlatènezeitlichen Elitengrabes von Bad Dürkheim konnte eine neue Rekonstruktion der sechs erhaltenen Goldblechfragmente vorgenommen werden, die bislang weitgehend unhinterfragt als Bestandteile eines Trinkhornbeschlags angesprochen wurden. Die stilistische und technologische Einordnung dieses Stücks bildet den Ausgangspunkt zu einer Binnentypologie. Für den vorliegenden Beschlag sollen die Verwendungsmöglichkeiten offen ausgelotet werden. Aufgrund der stilistischen Parallelen zu anderen Beschlägen der Späthallstatt- und Frühlatènezeit kann eine eindeutige Ansprache als Trinkhornbeschlag nicht aufrechterhalten, aber auch nicht verworfen werden. Die Beobachtungen im Rahmen des CELTIC GOLD-Projektes ergaben weiter, dass frühlatènezeitliche Arbeiten aus dünnem Goldblech regelhaft auf einer bronzenen Unterlage befestigt waren.

Summary: News on the so-called drinking horn fitting from Bad Dürkheim – On sheet gold work of the Early Latène Period

Within the framework of a new investigation of the gold grave goods of the Early Latène elite grave of Bad Dürkheim, a new reconstruction of the six preserved gold sheet fragments could be carried out, which until now had been addressed largely unquestioned as components of a drinking horn fitting. The stylistic and technological classification of this piece forms the starting point for an internal typology. For the present fitting, the possible uses are to be openly explored. Due to the stylistic parallels to other fittings of the Late Hallstatt and Early Latène periods, it is not possible to maintain an unambiguous classification as a drinking horn fitting, but neither can it be rejected. Observations within the framework of the CELTIC GOLD project further revealed that early Latène work made of thin gold sheet was regularly fixed to a bronze base.

Résumé : Du nouveau sur les cornes à boire de Bad Dürkheim – Objets en feuilles d'or du Second Âge du Fer

Dans le cadre d'une nouvelle étude des objets funéraires en or de la tombe d'élite de Bad Dürkheim, datant de la période LT A, une nouvelle reconstruction des six fragments de tôle d'or conservés a pu être effectuée, lesquels étaient jusqu'à présent considérés sans ambiguïté comme des éléments d'une applique de corne à boire. La comparaison stylistique et technologique de cette pièce constitue le point de départ d'une typologie interne. Pour cette applique, les utilisations possibles doivent être explorées de manière ouverte. En raison des parallèles stylistiques avec d'autres pièces de la période du Hallstatt final et La Tène ancienne, une référence sans ambiguïté à des pièces de corne à boire ne peut pas être maintenue, mais elle ne peut pas non plus être rejetée. Les observations effectuées dans le cadre du projet CELTIC GOLD ont en outre révélé que les premières œuvres de la periode La Tène ancienne réalisées en fine tôle d'or étaient régulièrement fixées sur une base en bronze.

Anschriften der Verfasser*innen:

Sebastian Fürst
Universität des Saarlandes
Altertumswissenschaften / Vor- und Frühgeschichte
Gebäude B3.1
DE–66123 Saarbrücken
sebastian.fuerst@uni-saarland.de
Curt-Engelhorn-Zentrum Archäometrie gGmbH
D6,3
DE–68159 Mannheim
sebastian.fuerst@ceza.de
https://orcid.org/0000-0002-5977-7389

Martin Schönfelder
Römisch-Germanisches Zentralmuseum
Leibniz-Forschungsinstitut für Archäologie
Ernst-Ludwig-Platz 2
DE–55116 Mainz
schoenfelder@rgzm.de
https://orcid.org/0000-0002-2595-7904

Barbara Armbruster
Laboratoire d'Archéologie TRACES – UMR 5608 du CNRS
Maison de la Recherche
Université de Toulouse 2 Jean Jaurès
5, allées Antonio-Machado
FR–31058 Toulouse Cedex
barbara.armbruster@univ-tlse2.fr

Abbildungsnachweis:
Abb. 1a: Lindenschmit 1870, Taf. 1,5. – *Abb. 1b:* Jacobsthal 1944, Taf. 25,28. – *Abb. 2–8; 16a–c; 20:* S. Fürst – *Abb. 9:* Zeichnung: M. Ober; Fotos: S. Fürst. – *Abb. 12a:* Haffner / Lage 2008/2009, 47 Nr. 6. – *Abb. 12b:* Schwab 1984, 76 Abb. 7e. – *Abb. 13a–b:* Keller 1965, Taf. 20; 23. – *Abb. 13c:* British Museum, Bildnr. 1929,0511.1, AN1240556001. – *Abb. 13d:* Müller 2009, 98 Abb. 102. – *Abb. 13e; 14c; 17–19:* B. Armbruster. – *Abb. 14a:* British Museum, Bildnr. 1929,0511.1, AN593534001. – *Abb. 14b:* Baitinger / Pinsker 2002, 253 Abb. 247, Kat.-Nr. 1.13.1. – *Abb. 14d:* Tecco Hvala u. a. 2004, Taf. 27,38. – *Abb. 15a:* Kurz / Schiek 2002, Taf. 11,117. – *Abb. 15b:* Filow 1927, 20 Abb. 18. – *Abb. 16d:* Kimmig 1988, Taf. 37. – *Abb. 16e:* Kimmig 1988, Taf. 36. – *Abb. 16f:* Ardjanliev u. a. 2018, 288. – *Anhang*: Verf., Gestaltung O. Wagner (RGK).

Anhang

Zusammenstellung der (potenziellen) frühlatènezeitlichen Trinkhornbeschläge mit Goldbeschlägen (fett hervorgehoben); andere Materialien werden gesondert genannt. Alle Maße in cm, sofern nicht anders angegeben. Fragezeichen kennzeichnen Objekte, deren Zuordnung zum Trinkhorn nicht gesichert ist. – Die Tabelle basiert bis auf wenige Änderungen auf der Liste 9 bei Krausse 1996.

Fundort	Anzahl	Goldbeschläge vom Trinkhorn	Nachweis
Asperg, „Kleinaspergle", Nebenkammer (Lkr. Ludwigsburg), männl.	2	**2 schmale Goldblechbänder** (L. 23 u. 21, Br. 0,7–0,8); 2 Kettchen aus Silber (L. 13,5 u. 13,3); **2 ringförmige Goldbleche** (Deckel?) (Dm. 3,2 u. 3), 1 rundes knopfartiges Objekt aus Koralle(?), **12 kl. runde Goldscheibchen** (Dm. 0,8); 14 Einzelbeschläge unbekannter Funktion, evtl. von Gehänge; **2 tüllenförmige Endbeschläge** aus Goldblech mit Widderköpfen (L. 14,5 u. 16,5)	Krausse 1996, 407 Liste 9,1–2
Auvers-sur-Oise (Dép. Val-d'Oise, FR)	1	**1 Deckel**: Koralleneinlagen und dünnes aufplattiertes Goldblech auf profilierter Bronzescheibe, die auf einer dickeren konischen Bronzescheibe sitzt; Goldblech am Rand mit kleinen Nietstiften fixiert und um Bronzeblech gebördelt (Dm. 10)	Jacobsthal 1944, 167 Nr. 19 Taf. 19–20,19; Eluère 1987, 137; Moscati u. a. 1991, 198; Echt 1999, 325 Nr. 8
Bad Dürkheim	1?	**1 bandförmiger Blechbeschlag** (L. mind. ca. 9,2); 1 längliches Einzelblech unbekannter Funktion; **2 Goldscheibchen** (vermutl. Nietkopfbeschläge des länglichen Bleches)	
Bescheid „Bei den Hübeln", Hügel. 4 (Lkr. Trier-Saarburg), Körpergrab, männl.	1?	**1 bandförmiger Blechbeschlag oder Einzelbeschläge**: 2 kurze Abschnitte eines schmalen Goldbandes (L. 1,5 u. 1,2, Br. 0,32); 2 dünne, unverzierte Goldfolien ohne erkennbare Originalkanten (1,3 × 0,55; 1,1 × 0,7)	Krausse 1996, 407 Liste 9,5; Haffner / Lage 2008–2009
Bescheid „Bei den Hübeln", Hügel 6 (Lkr. Trier-Saarburg), Körpergrab, männl.	1	**1 bandförmiger Blechbeschlag**: stark fragmentierter verzierter Beschlag aus Goldfolie (L. Oberkante 37,4; Br. 2,4, max. Mündungsdm. 12,3; Materialstärke 0,01–0,02 mm)	Krausse 1996, 407 Liste 9,4; Haffner / Lage 2008–2009
Dörth „Waldgallscheid" (Rhein-Hunsrück-Kr.)	2	**2 bandförmige Blechbeschläge**, durchbrochen gearbeitete Zierbänder aus Goldblech (Dm. 6,9 bzw. 6,5; L. 20,4 u. 22; Br. 4); nach Auffindung flachgehämmert; evtl. zugehörig: **4 Goldblechscheibchen** (Dm. 1,4)	Jacobsthal 1944, 168 Nr. 26 Taf. 24,26; Greifenhagen 1970, 86 Taf. 65; Haffner 1976, 46 f. Taf. 179,4; Krausse 1996, 196; 407 f. Liste 9,8–9; Joachim 1998, 253 Abb. 6
Eigenbilzen, „Cannesberg" (Prov. Limburg, BE)	1	**1 bandförmiger Blechbeschlag**, durchbrochen gearbeitet (errechneter Mindest-Dm. 6,8; L. 21,5; Br. 5,7; Materialstärke: 0,1 mm); nach Auffindung flachgehämmert; 1 Manschettenring, fragmentiert, goldplattiert, m. Koralle (äußerer Dm. 3,9); 2 Einzelbeschläge, fragmentiert; **2 Goldscheibchen**	Mariën 1962; Mariën 1987, 31–34 Abb. 13–15; Krausse 1996, 408 Nr. 10
Évergnicourt, „Le Tournant du Chêne" (Dép. Aisne, FR) Wagengrab, männl.	1–2?	**1 bandförmiger Blechbeschlag(?) / 2 Einzelbeschläge(?)**: 2 kl. Fragmente eines Silberblechs, eines 50 cm von Schädel entfernt, das andere aus Abraum; 2 scheibenförmige Abschlüsse(?) aus Silber (Dm. 2,2)	Lambot 2005, 339 Abb. 12; 341
Ferschweiler (Lkr. Bitburg-Prüm)	1?	**3 Einzelbeschläge**: 1 Maske aus Goldblech (H. 4,2; Br. 3,9); 1 Goldscheibchen (Dm. 2,3); 1 Goldblechrosette mit Mittelloch (Dm. 5,2)	Haffner 1976, 49; 174; 406 Nr. 10 Taf. 1,8–10; 130,1–3; Eluère 1987, 96 Abb. 112; Krausse 1996, 408 Liste 9,11
Groß-Rohrheim (Lkr. Bergstraße)	1–2	**2 Manschettenringe** aus Bronze m. aufplattiertem	Jorns 1964; Jorns 1966;

Fundort	Anzahl	Goldbeschläge vom Trinkhorn	Nachweis
		Goldblech u. Koralleneinlage (innerer Dm. 4,2 u. 5,5); **1 scheibenförmiger Abschluss(?)** (Dm. 1,9); **1 Deckel(?):** Goldblechrosette (äußerer Dm. 2,3; innerer Dm. 1,1), zugehörig: Knopf aus Koralle (Dm. 1,55, H. 1,25)	Krausse 1996, 408 Liste 9,12
Hradiště (Okr. Písek, CZ), undokumentierte Funde aus verschiedenen Gräbern, evtl. sogar versch. Hügeln	1?	**1 Deckel(?):** ringförmige Goldblechrosette mit ausgespartem Zentrum (Dm. 3,2; Dm. Aussparung 1,3); vermutl. zugehörig: kleines Goldblechscheibchen (Dm. 0,6), vermutl. Beschlag eines Nietkopfes	Miltner 1863; Michálek 1977; Drda / Rybova 1995, 40–43; Krausse 1996, 408 Liste 9,13
Mülheim-Kärlich (Lkr. Mayen-Koblenz), Wagengrab 4	1	**1 Randbeschlag** (verschollen): geschlitztes Goldblech mit schnurartiger Verzierung (Dm. 6); **4 Einzelbeschläge:** 3 dreieckige und 1 länglicher Goldblechbeschlag (L. 1,2–16)	Günther 1934, 8 f. Taf. 1, 13–18; Haffner 1976, 47; Joachim 1979, 524; 527 Abb. 17,1; Krausse 1996, 408 Liste 9,14; Hansen 2010, 266 Liste 2,33
Reinheim (Saarpfalz-Kr.), „Katzenbuckel", Grab A, weibl.	2	**2 bandförmige Blechbeschläge:** leicht konisch, (max. Dm. 4,7 u. 4,4; Br. 3,38 u. 3,25; Gew. 4,1 bzw. 3,4 g), durchbrochen gearbeitet, in Treib- u. Presstechnik verziert, angeblich ohne Bronzeblech; **Mittelbleche u. sonst. Teile:** 3 Rosetten aus Goldblech (Dm. 1,0–1,03), ebenfalls weiße Masse an Rückseite	Keller 1965, 35 f. Nr. 7–9 Taf. 12,6–8; 14; 15 unten; Echt 1999, 126–131 Taf. 9,3–7
Schwarzenbach (Lkr. St. Wendel), „Fürstengrab 1", evtl. männl.	≥2	**1 Randbeschlag** evtl. von Trinkhorn oder aber von Gefäß wie das durchbrochen gearbeitete Band (max. Dm. 12,0); **2–3 Deckel** (Dm. 7,0); **ca. 50 Einzelbeschläge**, u. a. Masken, schmale Bänder, gebogene Segmente; alle Beschläge einst gebördelt und mit Bronzeblechunterlage	Haffner 1976, 47; 200–204 Nr. 15 Taf. 140–144; Hartmann 1978, 612 f. Nr. Au 4671–4672; Krausse 1996, 199–218; 409 Liste 9,17–18; Hansen 2010, 267 Liste 2,41
Somme-Bionne (Dép. Marne, FR), „L'Homme Mort" bzw. „La Tommelle", männl.	1	**1 bandförmiger Blechbeschlag:** Fragm. Goldband, mit drei Reihen von getrieben Buckeln verziert, an Längskante gezahnt, keine Durchbruchsarbeit (L. noch 18; Br. 2,5)	Morel 1898, Taf. 8,1–2; Jacobsthal 1944, 168 Nr. 25; Van Endert 1987, 144–146 Taf. 88; Krausse 1996, 409 Liste 9,19
Wadern-Gehweiler (Lkr. Merzig-Wadern) „Preußenkopf", Grab 1/1	1	**4 Goldscheibchen:** Zugehörigkeit zu einem Trinkhorn eher unwahrscheinlich; 2 ungeloch mit eingedelltem Mittelbuckel und eingepunztem Leiterband entlang des Randes auf abgesetzter konzentrischer Rippe; Rand umgeschlagen (Dm. 1,1); auf quadratisches (0,7 × 0,65) organisches Material geklebt, an dem sich Profilierung der Goldscheibchen erhalten hatte; 2 zentr. gelochte Scheibchen mit radialem Strichband (Dm. 0,85)	Reinhard 2003, 186 Taf. 98,4; Schneider 2012, 267 Nr. P-25,8; Reinhard 2017, 161 Abb. 142,1.5; 164 Nr. 5; 165 Abb. 146
Weiskirchen (Lkr. St. Wendel), „Schanzenknöppchen", Hügel 2, männl.	1	**1 bandförmiger Blechbeschlag:** leicht konisch, vermutl. einst Bronzeblechhinterfütterung (max. Dm. 4,9; Br. 2,8–3,0; Materialstärke 0,03 mm)	Haffner 1976, 47 f. 219 f. Taf. 15,1; 163,4; 164; Krausse 1996, 409 Liste 9,20; Reinhard 2003, 201 Nr. 51 Taf. 100,4; Hansen 2010, 268 Liste 2,52
Sonstige Trinkhörner			
Pellingen (Lkr. Trier-Saarburg) „Dreikopf" Hügel 1, männl.	1	**1 Randbeschlag:** Fragment eines Randbeschlags aus Bronze mit gefelderter Zierborte mit Andreaskreuzen (rekonstr. Dm. oben 11,2; unten 9,4)	Nortmann / Ehlers 1995, 86 f. Nr. c Abb. 12; s. bes. Krausse 1995; Krausse 1996, 408 Liste 9,14a
Bourges (Dép. Cher, FR) „Route de Dun"	1?	**1 tüllenförmiger Endbeschlag** aus Bronze mit Ring an Tierkopf (Widder?, Rind?), nahe Tüllenmündung je ein Schäftungsloch pro Seite (L. ca. 2,75; Mündungsdm. ca. 1,25)	Déchelette 1927, 813 Abb. 568,5; Kimmig 1988, 210 Nr. 4; Lenerz-De Wilde 1988, 232; 246 Abb. 141,1; Krausse 1996, 407 Nr. 6

Hercules Magusanus im Lager der *ala I Batavorum milliaria* in Războieni-Cetate (Kreis Alba, Rumänien)

Von Alexander Rubel und Rada Varga*

Schlagwörter: Bataver / Dakien / Dacia superior / provinzialrömische Epigraphik / Onomastik / Militärreligion / Rekrutierung
Keywords: Batavians / Dacia / Dacia superior / provincial epigraphy / onomastics / army religion / recruitment
Mots clés: Bataves / Dacie / Dacie supérieure / épigraphie provinciale / onomastique / religion militaire / recrutement

Einleitung

Zwischen den beiden Legionslagern *Potaissa* (heute Turda, RO) und *Apulum* (heute Alba Iulia, RO) im Limeshinterland befindet sich das erst seit kurzem systematisch untersuchte Lager der *ala I Batavorum milliaria* in Războieni-Cetate (Kreis Alba) *(Abb. 1)*[1]. In unmittelbarer Nähe (etwa 3 km) befindet sich die wichtige Salzlagerstätte Ocna Mureș (identifiziert als das antike *Salinae*[2]), deren Schutz wohl ausschlaggebend für die Standortwahl war (ein Blick auf die Karte zeigt die Position des Lagers genau zwischen den beiden Legionsstandorten in Dakien, jedoch wurde die *legio V Macedonica* erst im Jahr 168 n. Chr. nach *Potaissa* verlegt, als das Lager der Bataver bereits seit mindestens 30 Jahren existierte[3]). Die Einheit war hier schon in hadrianischer Zeit stationiert. Sie kam aus *Pannonia superior* nach Dakien[4]. Das älteste bekannte Diplom der Einheit in *Dacia superior* datiert auf 136–138 n. Chr. und stammt aus *Drobeta*[5]. Sie verblieb bis zur Aufgabe der Provinz *Dacia* unter Aurelian (ca. 274 n. Chr.) am gleichen Ort (dokumentiert durch zwei Inschriften, je nach Lesart auf 260–268 oder 253 n. Chr. datiert[6]), ihr Lager wurde durch Ziegelstempel bereits früh im siebenbürgischen Ort Războieni-Cetate lokalisiert[7]. Auch die Größe der rund 5,2 ha umfassenden Anlage, die bei den jüngsten geomagnetischen Untersuchungen rekonstruiert wurde, bestätigt diese Zuordnung, ebenso wie die nur für eine *ala milliaria* sinnvolle Barackengröße und -anzahl. An das Lager schließt sich im Westen und Norden eine ausgedehnte Zivilsiedlung (Militärvicus) mit vielen Steinbauten an, wobei das südlich

---

* Diese Arbeit wurde ermöglicht durch eine Projektförderung der rumänischen Forschungsförderungsbehörde im Erziehungs- und Wissenschaftsministerium UEFISCDI, Projektnummer PN-III-P4-ID-PCE-2020-0383.
[1] Ausführlich zu allen Aspekten mit weiterer Literatur Mischka et al. 2018. Für wertvolle Hinweise danken die Autoren Florian Matei-Popescu und Ioan Piso.
[2] Mihailescu-Bîrliba 2018.
[3] RE XII,2 (Stuttgart 1925) 1572–1575 s. v. *Legio* (E. Ritterling); Piso 2005, 119.
[4] AE 1997, 1782; RE Suppl. IX (München 1962) 618 s. v. *Pannonia*, Auxiliartruppen (A. Mócsy).
[5] Piso / Benea 1984, 278; Petolescu 2002, 64. – Allgemein: Wagner 1938, 16.
[6] Bărbulescu 2012, 55; Piso 2014, 125–146.
[7] Die Ziegelstempel wurden jüngst publiziert: Piso / Varga 2018.

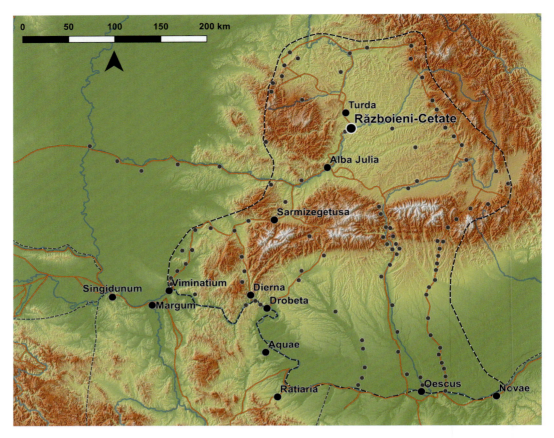

Abb. 1. Karte der Provinz *Dacia* mit dem Fundort sowie den Legionsstandorten der *legio V Macedonica* (*Potaissa* / Turda) und der *XIII Gemina* (*Apulum* / Alba Iulia).

und östlich gelegene Areal nicht untersucht werden konnte *(Abb. 2)*. Die hier zu besprechende Inschrift kann als weiterer Hinweis für die Stationierung der Bataver an diesem Standort angesehen werden.

Vorstellung der Inschrift

Die hier ausführlich vorzustellende Weihinschrift für Hercules Magusanus wurde bereits 1979 von Schulkindern im südlichen Lagerbereich im Garten eines Anrainers entdeckt und bislang nur in „grauer" Literatur erwähnt *(Abb. 2)*[8]. Der Fundort kann sicherlich nicht der ursprüngliche Standort der Inschrift gewesen sein. Über diesen lässt sich nur spekulieren. Der Stein könnte etwa bei spätkaiserzeitlichen Reparaturarbeiten eine sekundäre Verwendung gefunden haben, wobei offenbleiben muss, ob er ursprünglich im Lager selbst

[8] Mit abwegiger Lesung bei MOGA 1996, 183–185. Siehe weiter mit Abbildung POPOVICI / VARGA 2010. Zuletzt erwähnen auch DERKS / TEITLER 2018, 71 kurz die Inschrift und den Band von POPOVICI und VARGA (2010). Rada Varga hatte die Autoren persönlich über die Inschrift informiert. Nach Abschluss unseres Manuskripts wurde Rada Vargas ursprüngliche (und unzutreffende) Lesung der Inschrift auch in der Epigraphik Datenbank Clauss / Slaby, EDCS (https://db.edcs.eu/epigr/epi_de.php), eingestellt (nach Auskunft des Betreibers am 19.05.2020).

Abb. 2. Războieni-Cetate. Umzeichnung und Interpretation des Magnetikbefunds mit Fundort der Inschrift (roter Punkt: Fundstelle der Inschrift; rote Linien: aus dem Magnetogramm erschließbare Steinmauern; blau: Graben und Wallanlage des Lagers; lila: Straßen innerhalb und außerhalb des Lagers; grüne Punkte: starke Dipole, als Öfen interpretiert; gelb: moderne Störungen wie Gasleitung und ehemaliges LPG Areal).

aufgestellt war. Heute ist der Inschriftenstein Teil der historischen Sammlung der örtlichen Mittelschule. Das Monument befindet sich in einem schlechten Erhaltungszustand, was einerseits den Witterungsbedingungen und der seit seiner Auffindung ungeeigneten Lagerung geschuldet ist, andererseits aber auch dem Material selbst. Es handelt sich dabei um einen sehr porösen und brüchigen Kalkstein aus der Region. Wie viele andere Funde aus Războieni-Cetate sowie auch aus der Umgebung stammt dieser Stein aus dem etwa 23 km entfernten Steinbruch von Podeni (nahe *Potaissa* / Turda).

Die Weihinschrift wurde in nachlässiger und ungleichmäßiger Weise ausgeführt. Sie verfügt über eine unverzierte Basis und eine bescheidene, mit geometrischen Dreiecksmotiven verzierte Bekrönung, die einer reduzierten Darstellung eines Giebels entspricht. Die Art der Dekoration des oberen Teils mit einem Fronton ist keine Seltenheit in Dakien, die Ausführung dieses Stücks ist indes ausgesprochen einfach, fast schon primitiv. Der obere Teil des Monuments verfügt über keinen *foculus*. Die unbehauene, rohe Rückseite des Steins suggeriert eine ursprünglich wandnahe Aufstellung des Monuments.

Maße: Höhe 54 cm (Basis 19 cm, Bekrönung 12 cm, Inschrift 23 cm), Breite 20 cm, etwa in der Mitte ist der Stein in zwei Teile gebrochen *(Abb. 3–4)*.

Abb. 3. Războieni-Cetate. Foto des Inschriftensteins.   Abb. 4. Războieni-Cetate. Zeichnung der Inschrift.

HERCV
LI MAC
VSAN
O FLAV
ADRIAN

Die Buchstaben sind äußerst ungleichmäßig. Erste Zeile: H, E, R, C, V – 3 cm; die Buchstaben der zweiten Zeile – 4 cm; dritte Zeile: alle Buchstaben 4 cm, außer S – 5 cm; vierte Zeile: O und F sehr schlecht erhalten, ca. 4,5 cm, L – 4,5 cm, V – 3,9 cm; fünfte Zeile: bei A, I, A ist nicht der gesamte Buchstabe erhalten, D – 2 cm, R – 3 cm, N – höchstens 2 cm.

Die Weihung ist überaus einfach gehalten. Der Text enthält nur den Götternamen im Dativ sowie den Namen des Dedikanten. Aufgrund des kaiserlichen Cognomens (natürlich nicht im Sinne einer direkten Verbindung zum Kaiser, etwa durch Bürgerrechtsverleihung) kann der Name Flav(ius) Hadrianus[9] als durchaus selten gelten, wenngleich nicht als

[9] In einer ersten Lesung wurde der Name des Dedikanten noch als L. M. Hadrianus angegeben (POPOVICI / VARGA 2010, 101). Diese Lesung erscheint uns unwahrscheinlich, besonders hinsichtlich der sonst

einzigartig[10]. Die Verwendung der *duo nomina* anstatt der *tria nomina* ist ein typisches Kennzeichen des 3. Jahrhunderts, welches sich nach der *Constitutio Antoniniana* (212) zunehmend durchsetzt und zur Regel wird[11].

Dieser Sachverhalt sowie die paläographische Analyse der Form und Ausführung der Buchstaben[12], aber auch der Name des Dedikanten, lässt uns die Inschrift recht spät datieren, in die erste Hälfte bis zur Mitte des 3. Jahrhunderts n. Chr. In Ermangelung einschlägiger und aussagekräftiger paläographischer Studien zur Provinz *Dacia* fällt eine exaktere Datierung durchaus schwer. Dennoch würden wir aus unserer Erfahrung im Umgang mit den Inschriften aus dieser Donauprovinz behaupten, dass die Ausführung der Schrift im vorliegenden Fall nachlässig erfolgte, mit unregelmäßigen Buchstaben in der gleichen Zeile, mit unterschiedlichen Ausführungen des gleichen Buchstabens, in fast kursiver Form notiert[13]. Dies deutet nach unserer Einschätzung deutlicher auf das 3. Jahrhundert n. Chr. hin, in welchem diese Phänomene zunehmend zu beobachten sind[14]. Der Dedikant ist somit als römischer Bürger anzusprechen, ob aktiver Soldat, Veteran oder gar Zivilist mit anderem Status, lässt sich nicht entscheiden. Die Tatsache, dass die Inschrift auf dem Lagergelände aufgefunden wurde (wenngleich durch landwirtschaftliche Eingriffe sicher nicht *in situ*) spricht aber – wie auch weitere Gründe, die wir im Folgenden darlegen – für eine direkte Verbindung der Inschrift für den batavischen Gott mit der Einheit.

Diskussion und Kontext

Die Geschichte der *ala* und Überlegungen zur Rekrutierung

Die Frage lokaler Rekrutierungen in den Auxiliareinheiten der römischen Armee ist seit langem Gegenstand ausführlicher Diskussionen[15]. Im Falle batavischer Einheiten wird die Rekrutierungsfrage aufgrund der Entwicklungen im Gefolge des Aufstandes von 69 n. Chr. besonders intensiv diskutiert[16]. Trotz neuer Erkenntnisse aus der Epigraphik (bes. Militärdiplome) gilt für die umstrittene Rekrutierungsfrage immer noch die treffliche Einschätzung Yann Le Bohecs über die sich aus Krafts bahnbrechender Arbeit zur Rekrutierung an Rhein und Donau ergebenden Regeln: „Die erste Regel lautet, dass es keine Regel gibt"[17]. Dennoch lassen sich einige Argumente anführen, weshalb bei Spezialeinheiten, deren Angehörige über besondere, v. a. in ihren Herkunftsgebieten vermittelte Qualifikationen verfügten, auch in späterer Zeit noch aus der ursprünglichen Aushebungsregion rekrutiert wurde; ein Sachverhalt der auch auf batavische Einheiten, besonders auf Reitertruppen,

---

schwer erklärbaren großen Lücke in Zeile vier. Für unsere neue Lesung spricht auch die Tatsache, dass die letzten Buchstaben der vierten Zeile (LAV) recht gut lesbar sind und die beiden horizontalen Hasten des vorigen Buchstabens, den wir als F lesen wollen, noch erkennbar sind.

[10] Das Cognomen Hadrianus begegnet uns noch (allerdings als nichtkaiserliches) in Italien, *Hispania* und *Moesia inferior* (SCHULTZE 1904, 187; LÖRINCZ 1999, 173).

[11] GILLIAM 1965; SALWAY 1994, 141; VARGA 2012, 205.

[12] Hierzu allgemein THOMPSON 1906; vgl. besonders GRAHAM 1992, 169–224 und KEPPIE 2001, 28. – Wenngleich für die dakischen Inschriften nicht sehr viele einschlägige Studien vorliegen, lassen sich wichtige paläographische Datierungselemente klar bestimmen, hierzu GUDEA / COSMA 1992, 204–205.

[13] Auffällig ist die fast kursive Umsetzung des S, besonders am Ende des Götternamens, vgl. hierzu VOLOȘCIUC 2017, 66.

[14] LASSÈRE 2007, 35 f.

[15] Grundlegend KRAFT 1951. – Siehe aus der Vielfalt neuerer Literatur z. B. LE BOHEC 1993, 101–110; GALLET / LE BOHEC 2007; ECK 2003; 2016; DANA / ROSSIGNOL 2017.

[16] RAEPSAET-CHARLIER 1978; ROXAN 1997; ROYMANS 2004; DERKS / ROYMANS 2006.

[17] LE BOHEC 1993, 102.

zutreffen könnte. Wegen des Aufstands des Iulius Civilis kam es zu einer ganzen Reihe von Dislokationen von Einheiten und die Revolte war möglicherweise auch der Grund für mutmaßliches Unbehagen der römischen Führung, batavische Einheiten ethnisch-kompakt bestehen zu lassen und diese auch noch heimatnah zu stationieren[18]. Entsprechend ging die Forschung recht einhellig davon aus, dass in der Folge weniger Bataver in diese ursprünglich exklusiv batavischen Einheiten rekrutiert wurden[19]. Neue Diplome und die *Vindolanda*-Täfelchen liefern jedoch die Grundlage für eine Neuevaluierung des Sachverhalts.

Dieser scheint bei genauerem Hinsehen nun um einiges komplexer zu sein. Wir wissen zwar, dass die *ala*, die bei Ausbruch des Aufstands am Niederrhein stationiert war, zu den Rebellen überlief[20]. Dabei nutze Civilis die Nachfolgestreitigkeiten der Römer im Bürgerkrieg und wählte die Seite Vespasians. Tacitus behauptet jedoch, dass es sich bei der Unterstützung Vespasians gegen die Truppen des Vitellius durch einige batavische Einheiten lediglich um eine Schutzbehauptung der Aufständischen gehandelt habe, jedoch könnte auch ein wahrer Kern in dieser Information enthalten sein. Civilis betont, dass seine rebellierenden Bataver bei wechselhaftem Kriegsglück darauf verweisen könnten, dass sie die Vitellius treuen Truppen im Auftrag Vespasians attackiert hätten[21]. Entsprechend kann der Bataveraufstand mit gewissem Recht auch als Teil des römischen Bürgerkriegs betrachtet werden, wobei bestimmte Einheiten die Partei des Vitellius, andere die Vespasians wählten[22]. Auf diese Weise würde sich erklären, weshalb die *ala I Batavorum milliara* nach Ausweis eines Militärdiploms aus Elst im Jahr 98 n. Chr. noch immer am Niederrhein stationiert war[23]. Denn obwohl in den Aufstand involviert, wurde die Einheit nicht unmittelbar verlegt, wie etwa die batavischen Kohorten[24]. Die Einheit wurde erst nach der Jahrhundertwende nach Pannonien verlegt, wo sie erstmals 112 n. Chr. über ein

---

[18] VAN ROSSUM 2004.

[19] Géza ALFÖLDY (1968) und Willem J. H. WILLEMS (1984) gehen von weitgehender Neubesetzung der Einheiten aus. Gegen diese Auffassung haben zuletzt Sébastien GALLET und Yann LE BOHEC (2007) sowie David B. CUFF (2010) argumentiert und die anhaltende ethnisch homogene Rekrutierung (nicht nur bei Batavern) auch im 2. Jahrhundert n. Chr. betont. Ihnen widerspricht Ian HAYNES (2013, passim, bes. 135–143).

[20] Tac. hist. 4,18,4; 4,56,3. – Es wird bisweilen vermutet, dass die Einheit nach dem Bataveraufstand aufgelöst wurde und die in Pannonien und Dakien auftauchende *ala I Batavorum milliaria* eine Neugründung sei. Mit Verweis auf neue Militärdiplome und die Weiterverwendung der Kohorten in Britannien ist jedoch eine Kontinuität wahrscheinlicher, vgl. HAALEBOS 2000, 42.

[21] Tac. hist. 4,14: *„Ne Romanis quidem ingratum id bellum, cuius ambiguam fortunam Vespasiano imputaturos: victoriae rationem non reddi"*. Vgl. Tac. hist. 4,21.

[22] URBAN 1985. – Dies schließt natürlich nicht aus, dass die aufständischen Bataver auch eine eigene Agenda verfolgten.

[23] HAALEBOS 2000, 31–72.

[24] Allerdings gilt es auch zu bedenken, dass die Verlegung der Einheiten nach Britannien nicht unbedingt als Strafversetzung gesehen werden muss oder als Wunsch der römischen Führung, die Bataver als Vorsichtsmaßnahmen nicht heimatnah zu stationieren. Sie wurden nur wieder dorthin zurückgeschickt, wo sie bereits vorher gedient hatten. Über die Reorganisation der batavischen Kohorten siehe ALFÖLDY 1968, 47–48. Die Kohorten I und II sind erstmals außerhalb Britanniens für Pannonien in einem Diplom von 98 n. Chr. belegt (CIL XVI 42). Von dort wird die erste Kohorte nach Dakien verlegt (WEISS 2002), die zweite nach *Noricum* (CIL XVI 174). Mit den „*Vindolanda*-Tablets" sind die Kohorten III und IX noch ungefähr bis 90 n. Chr. für die Insel belegt. Die *cohors III* taucht in Raetien in einem Diplom von 107 n. Chr. auf (CIL XVI 55), nach 135 n. Chr. wird sie jedoch nach *Pannonia inferior* transferiert und in Raetien durch die *cohors IX* ersetzt (LÖRINCZ 2001, Nr. 305). Um 130 n. Chr. herum befinden sich die vier batavischen Kohorten also in verschiedenen Provinzen, wobei *Dacia* die einzige Provinz ist, in welcher zwei batavische Einheiten stationiert waren (eine Kohorte und eine *ala*).

Militärdiplom belegt ist[25]. Als Grund für die Verlegung wird man die Dakerkriege annehmen dürfen, an welchen die Einheit teilnehmen oder als Reserveeinheit in der Nähe des Kriegsschauplatzes stationiert werden sollte.

Der Aufstand des Iulius Civilis hat möglicherweise die Aufmerksamkeit der römischen Militärführung auf die möglichen Gefahren ethnisch homogener Hilfstruppen gelenkt, welche als Stammesverbände unter lokalen Anführern ins römische Militär rekrutiert worden waren. Gleichwohl wurde weiterhin auch lokal rekrutiert, lediglich – so vermutet man – wurde der Anteil gebürtiger Bataver in den Einheiten reduziert[26]. Van Rossum betont entsprechend, dass sich auch in späterer Zeit der Kern der batavischen Einheiten aus Angehörigen germanischer Stämme zusammensetzte[27]. Erst für die Zeit um das Ende des 1. Jahrhunderts n. Chr. spricht er von einer möglichen „Denationalisierung" der batavischen Einheiten durch deren Transfer in entferntere Regionen des Reiches, insbesondere an die Donau, wohin auch unsere *ala I Batavorum milliara* zunächst entsandt wurde[28]. Auch für andere Einheiten, die als Elitetruppen galten oder für deren operativen Einsatz Spezialkenntnisse erforderlich waren (etwa palmyrenische Bogenschützen), lässt sich Rekrutierung aus der Herkunftsregion über lange Zeiträume hinweg belegen, etwa bei den *Palmyreni sagittarii*, ebenfalls in Dakien stationiert, die über Generationen ihre orientalischen Götter in den Karpaten verehrten[29]. Besonders auffällig hinsichtlich der Rekrutierung von Soldaten aus der Herkunftsregion über viele Generationen hinweg ist der Fall der *cohors I Hemesenorum milliaria Antonina Aurelia sagittariorum equitata civum Romanorum*, die ursprünglich im syrischen *Emesa* ausgehoben worden war und nach 180 bis mindestens 252 n. Chr. an der Donau in *Intercisa* (heute Dunaújváros, Kreis Fejér, HU) stationiert war. Dort wurde seit 1906 das Gräberfeld des *vicus* mit rund 2500 Gräbern und bedeutenden Steindenkmälern ausgegraben. Der epigraphische Befund zeigt sowohl auffällig viele Individuen, die nach Aussage ihrer Namen aus Syrien stammten, als auch die durch die Inschriften belegte intensive Verehrung ‚orientalischer' Götter[30]. Bei ausgewiesenen Elitetruppen, wie den berittenen Batavern, die berühmt für ihre Flussüberquerungen zu Pferde in voller Montur waren[31] und entsprechend spezielles Training von Jugend an absolvieren mussten, kann man analog vermuten, dass zumindest teilweise weiterhin Spezialisten aus dem Herkunftsgebiet rekrutiert wurden[32]. Zumindest für andere Batavereinheiten lässt sich ein solcher Sonderstatus bis ins 2. Jahrhundert n. Chr. belegen.

---

[25] LÖRINCZ 2001, Nr. 306 Kat. 510.

[26] VAN ROSSUM 2004, 116–117.

[27] VAN ROSSUM 2004, 128. – Ob Auxiliareinheiten allgemein seit flavischer Zeit üblicherweise eher lokal an den Standorten (so etwa HAYNES 1999; HAYNES 2013; ECK 2016) oder überregional und ‚international' (etwa aus den Ursprungsregionen) rekrutierten, ist umstritten. LE BOHEC (1993, 107 f.) betont, dass auch in späterer Zeit etwa hälftig auch weiterhin aus entfernten Regionen rekrutiert wurde. Ähnlich mit weiteren Argumenten CUFF 2010.

[28] VAN ROSSUM 2004, 120–123. – Vgl. dagegen STROBEL 1987, der betont, dass auch im 2. und 3. Jahrhundert noch batavische Anführer die Truppen befehligt hätten.

[29] IDR III/1 Nr. 135–136; 142–143, ausführlich SANIE 1981, vgl. ȚENTEA 2012. – Grundlegend DOMASZEWSKI 1895, 52. – Allgemein zu den Rekrutierungen LE BOHEC 1993, 102–109; GALLET / LE BOHEC 2007. – Zu anderen Spezialeinheiten und ihren spezifischen Göttern siehe weiter auch FITZ 1972; BIRLEY 1978; CUFF 2010.

[30] FITZ 1972. Die Inschriften sind im von Fitz 1991 herausgegebenen 5. Band der RIU gesammelt. Siehe ausführlich die Diskussion bei CUFF 2010, 12–16.

[31] Cass. Dio 60,20; 69,9; Tac. hist. 4,12,3; vgl. CIL III 3676.

[32] Zu den besonderen Fähigkeiten und dem guten Ruf der batavischen Reiter als Hilfstruppen ROSELAER 2016, 151 mit weiteren Belegstellen. – FISCHER 2001, 107 verweist darauf, dass auch die batavischen Reiter als Spezialeinheit ihre Angehörigen aus der Ursprungsregion nachrekrutierten. In diesem Sinne auch CUFF 2010, passim. SCHOLZ 2009, 143,

Weil es sich bei der batavischen *ala* und den *cohortes milliariae* um ausgesprochene Eliteeinheiten handelte, war man auch darum bemüht, diesen Charakter beizubehalten. Deshalb und da sie offenbar mit Civilis auf der Seite der Flavier gestanden haben, blieb wohl der Sonderstatus der Batever- und Tungrerkohorten innerhalb der römischen Armee auch nach 70 n. Chr. erhalten, und bis in die spätseverische Zeit wurden diese *cohortes milliariae* von Präfekten und nicht von Tribunen befehligt. Diese entstammten – so Karl Strobel in seiner Untersuchung zu den *cohortes* – bis in die zweite Hälfte des 2. Jahrhunderts vor allem dem batavischen Adel[33]. Batavische Einheiten wurden unmittelbar nach dem Aufstand wieder in Britannien eingesetzt, wo sie bereits zuvor gedient hatten. Vier *cohortes* waren entscheidend in der Schlacht gegen die Caledonier am *Mons Graupius* gewesen[34]. Aus Britannien kommt auch ein interessanter Fall, der ein Licht auf das Alltagsleben im Lager wirft und wichtige Informationen über die Angehörigen der Einheit bietet: Ein *decurio* mit Namen Masclus schreibt dem Präfekten Flavius Cerialis und bittet ihn untertänigst um die Sendung von Bier für die Mannschaft. Die Vorliebe für dieses Getränk macht den Angehörigen dieser batavischen Einheit bereits trotz seines lateinischen Namens in den Augen moderner Kommentatoren zu einem „waschechten" Germanen[35]. Dass er seinen Vorgesetzten Cerialis als *rex* anspricht, zeigt aber recht eindeutig, dass hier ‚indigene' Traditionen in einen römischen Militärkontext überführt wurden. Zurecht wird man deshalb hinter dem *rex* Cerialis eben einen der *nobilissimi* vermuten, welche traditionellerweise (*vetere instituto*) nach Tacitus die batavischen Einheiten anführten[36], eventuell sogar einen Spross der *stirps regia*[37]. Die *Vindolanda*-Täfelchen haben nach ihrer Publikation unter den Historikern für einiges Aufsehen gesorgt, zeigen sie doch an, dass die batavischen und tungrischen Einheiten noch über eine Generation nach ihrer Verlegung nach Britannien ihre Neuzugänge aus der „Heimat" am Niederrhein rekrutierten[38]. Dies mag mit dem Elitestatus der Einheiten, wie auch mit dem militärisch-elitären Selbstverständnis der Batever allgemein zusammenhängen, die sich gerade über ihre Sonderrolle in der römischen Armee definierten und, wie Roymans mehrfach betont hat, ihre Identität und ihren ethnischen Zusammenhalt dieser Sonderstellung und ihrem Militärethos verdanken[39].

Die prosopographischen und onomastischen Daten zur *ala I Batavorum milliaria* lassen leider keine genaueren Angaben zur Herkunft des Führungspersonals zu, welche uns zu ähnlichen Rückschlüssen führen würden, wie sie mit guten Argumenten für die *cohortes* geltend gemacht wurden. Auch hinsichtlich der Mannschaftsdienstgrade lassen sich nur wenige klare Aussagen treffen (s. u.), jedoch spricht einiges dafür, dass der batavische Elitestatus auch bei der *ala* bis in spätere Zeit gewahrt wurde. Gerade die Kohorten hatten sich auch in der Folge, besonders in den Dakerkriegen, bleibende Meriten erworben und wurden vielfach durch den Kaiser geehrt[40]. Vor diesem Hintergrund lassen sich weitere Fragen formulieren: Kann noch in späterer Zeit von einem ethnisch-batavischen Charakter

---

kommt anhand der onomastischen Studien zu den Soldatennamen in Heidenheim (DE) (*ala II Flavia milliaria*) zu einem interessanten Schluss: Die ‚internationale' Herkunft der Reiter dieser Elitetruppe (etwa aus *Africa, Hispania* und Gallien) sei eben gerade dem Elitestatus der Einheit zuzuschreiben, da nicht genügend qualifizierte Rekruten in der Region verpflichtet werden konnten.

[33] STROBEL 1987, 291; vgl. Tac. hist. 4,12,3: „*cohortibus, quas vetere instituto nobilissimi popularium regebant*".

[34] Tac. Agr. 36,1.

[35] NELSON 2005, 65 und MCLAUGHLIN 2018 zur Bedeutung des Bieres in diesem Kontext.

[36] Tac. hist. 4,12,3.

[37] Tac. hist. 4,13,1. – CUFF 2011; BIRLEY 2001; 2008; ECK 2005, 666–667; BOWMAN 2006, 87; DICKEY 2002, 106–107.

[38] BIRLEY 2001 kommt auf 164 batavische Namen aus *Vindolanda*.

[39] ROYMANS 2001, 96–98; ROYMANS 2004, 227–234.

[40] Etwa bekamen die *cohortes I* und *II* das kollektive Bürgerrecht durch Trajan verliehen: LÖRINCZ 2001, 145 Nr. 22.

der Angehörigen der Einheit gesprochen werden und könnte die dem Hercules Magusanus gewidmete Inschrift dafürsprechen? Oder lässt sich die Setzung einer Inschrift für diese Gottheit im 3. Jahrhundert als ein Reflex einer Regimentstradition dieser Eliteeinheit verstehen? Im Folgenden diskutieren wir beide Möglichkeiten unter Berücksichtigung der komplexen Thematik von ethnischer Zugehörigkeit und „Germanentum". Ihrem Charakter nach ist die Weihung natürlich „privat", dass sie allerdings nur zufällig dem wichtigsten Gott der Bataver gelten sollte, schließen wir im gegebenen Kontext aus. Eine Verbindung zum batavischen Charakter der Einheit bzw. zu ihrer Tradition drängt sich auf, zumal drei weitere Inschriften aus Dakien den Batavergott nennen (s. u.). Entsprechend könnten entweder die Herkunft des Dedikanten oder sein „Corpsgeist" als Angehöriger dieser traditionsreichen Eliteeinheit entscheidend für die Wahl des Adressaten der Weihinschrift gewesen sein.

Hercules Magusanus und die Bataver

Der Gott Hercules Magusanus gilt als wichtigste Gottheit der niedergermanischen Bataver[41]. Aus rund 20 in der Mehrzahl in Niedergermanien gefundenen Inschriften ist dieser Gott bekannt[42]. Aber auch Angehörige der *equites singulares Augusti* in Rom weihten ihm zur Zeit Elagabals (218–222 n. Chr.) einen Votivaltar, wobei diese in der Inschrift genannten Bataver in Niedergermanien rekrutiert worden sind[43]. Dass die Gottheit germanischen Ursprungs gewesen sein könnte, zumindest aber in das eng begrenzte niedergermanische Kerngebiet gehört, bezeugen etwa die Weihenden, die sich in vielen Fällen durch sprachwissenschaftliche Analyse dem Namen nach oder aufgrund der Stammesbezeichnung (nach *natione* oder *domo*) in den Texten eindeutig als „Germanen" oder konkreter als Bataver identifizieren lassen. Diese unspezifischen ethnischen Zuschreibungen, die durchaus dem militärischen Umfeld entstammen dürften, sind allerdings nur bedingt aussagekräftig (zum Germanenbegriff siehe weiter unten Abschnitt „Batavische Identitäten und ‚Germanentum'"). Die räumliche Verteilung der Weihungen an Hercules (siehe Verbreitungskarte *Abb. 5*) hat einen Schwerpunkt in den heutigen Niederlanden, dem Gebiet, in dem in der Antike der Stamm der Bataver siedelte[44]. Aber auch in Orten in Deutschland, wie Xanten[45], Köln[46] und Bonn[47] auf dem Gebiet der Ubier, fanden sich Inschriften für Hercules Magusanus, ebenso in Britannien, in Mumrills, wo eine Einheit der niedergermanischen Tungerer stationiert war *(ala I Tungrorum)*[48]. Darüber hinaus taucht Hercules Magusanus auch neben Hercules Deusoniensis auf Münzemissionen des Postumus (260–269 n. Chr.) auf, der sich bekanntlich auf seine angeblichen batavischen Wurzeln berief[49], was die min-

---

[41] ROYMANS 2004, 235–250. – Die folgende Darstellung nach RUBEL 2016, 92–94.

[42] Hierbei sind auch die nicht ganz eindeutigen Inschriften mitgerechnet, in denen der Göttername unvollständig erscheint. Alle Inschriften mit weiteren Angaben in der EDCS. Eine ältere Übersicht bietet GUTENBRUNNER 1936, 220 f.; siehe auch STOLTE 1986, 626–629.

[43] CIL VI 31162; siehe auch SPEIDEL 1994a, Nr. 62. – Die jüngste Diskussion hierzu bei DERKS / TEITLER 2018, 62 f. mit weiterer Literatur.

[44] AE 1994, 1282; AE 1994, 1284; AE 2009, 925–928; CIL XIII 8705.

[45] AE 1977, 570; CIL XIII 8610.

[46] CIL XIII 8492; CIL XIII 10027.

[47] AE 1971, 282; CIL XIII 8010.

[48] RIB 2140. Eine Weihung eines *duplicarius* dieser *ala*. Eine weitere ist aus der *Gallia Belgica* bekannt: ILB 139bis.

[49] STOLTE 1986, 629. – Postumus stammte aus *Germania inferior*, ob nun wirklich von batavischer Herkunft, wie bereits antike Quellen suggerieren, ist nicht mit Sicherheit zu bestimmen. Jedoch wollte er zumindest den Anschein einer solchen Herkunft erwecken. ELMER 1941, Kat. 558–559; KÖNIG 1981, 132–136; WIGHTMAN 1985, 194; DRINKWATER 1987, 78–80; 163.

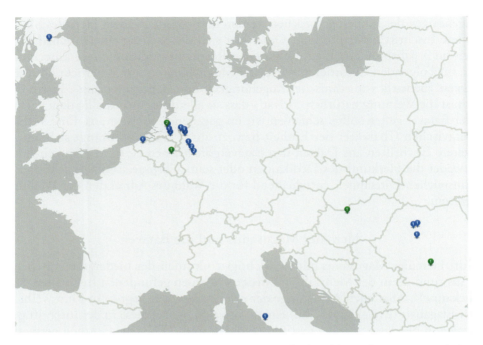

Abb. 5. Verbreitungskarte der Hercules-Magusanus-Inschriften (blau: sicher; grün: unsicher).

destens regionale Bedeutung des niedergermanischen Gottes auch für diese relativ späte Phase unterstreicht, wenngleich die hier präsentierte Inschrift durchaus eher in die erste Hälfte des 3. Jahrhunderts gehören könnte. Den auf Niedergermanien konzentrierten Inschriftenbefund haben zuletzt Petermandel und Spickermann als mögliches Anzeichen dafür gedeutet, „dass alle nicht niedergermanischen Zeugnisse von Soldaten aus der *Germania inferior* sozusagen exportiert worden waren"[50]. Die hier präsentierte Inschrift bestätigt diese Einschätzung.

Hercules Magusanus gilt als der wichtigste Stammesgott der Bataver, dem die bedeutendsten Heiligtümer der Region, wie etwa der Tempel von Empel (NL), geweiht waren[51]. Aufgrund der geographischen Zuordnung ins Batavergebiet und der oft als Germanen identifizierbaren Dedikanten gilt der germanische, genauer batavische Ursprung dieses *interpretatione Germanica* mit Hercules identifiziertem Gottes als erwiesen[52]. Die älteste Inschrift, die aus der Mitte des 1. Jahrhunderts n. Chr. stammt, zeigt darüber hinaus an, dass wir es offenbar wirklich mit einem ursprünglichen Gott Magusanus zu tun haben, der dann von den germanischen Verehrern dem Hercules zugeordnet wurde, denn die Inschrift ist *Magusano Herculi* geweiht (in dieser Wortfolge), der Name wird also nicht

---

[50] PETERMANDEL / SPICKERMANN 2022, 87. Man vergleiche aber unsere Verteilungskarte mit derjenigen von PETERMANDEL / SPICKERMANN 2022, 86, welche mehrere Inschriften als sicher ausweisen, die aus unserer Sicht eindeutig unsicher bleiben müssen.

[51] ROYMANS 2004, 6; 14 bes. 235–250. Ähnlich ROYMANS / DERKS 1990, 219–238; DERKS 1998, 98. – Zum Tempel in Empel siehe ROYMANS / DERKS 1990, 443–451. – Kritische Diskussion bei PETERMANDEL / SPICKERMANN 2022, 87.

[52] WAGNER 1977, 418; vgl. DE VRIES 1970, 109. Umfassend ROYMANS 2004, 235–250. – Zur Problematik der *interpretatio* in der Religionsgeschichte CHIAI et al. 2012 mit methodischen Fragestellungen.

adjektivisch gebraucht[53]. Diese älteste Inschrift stammt zudem aus dem Kerngebiet der Bataver am Niederrhein, nämlich aus dem 10 km von Empel entfernten Ort Ruimel (NL) im Nijmegener Gebiet. Diese Überlegungen zur rheinländischen Herkunft werden auch von der Linguistik bestätigt. Wenngleich hier im Gegensatz zu anderen, eindeutigeren Namensgebungen bei römisch-germanischen Gottheiten keine letztendliche Gewissheit erzielt werden kann, führt Norbert Wagner überzeugende Argumente an, dass die Bildung Magusanus von *Maguz/s-naz abzuleiten sei (zu germ. *mag „können"), worunter „der zur Kraft, Stärke Gehörige", bzw. „deren Herr" zu verstehen sei[54]. Möglicherweise ist aber auch eine keltische Wurzel anzunehmen, die jedoch „eine fortschreitende Germanisierung" zeige[55]. Die Bedeutung des ursprünglichen *mogi-sénos ‚mächtig und alt', weist bedeutungsmäßig in die gleiche Richtung. Petermandel und Spickermann haben allerdings zurecht darauf hingewiesen, dass der im Dunkeln liegende Ursprung von Magusanus (sie vermuten keltischen Einfluss) keine Rolle spielt, da wir es mit einem rein römischen Kult romanisierter Bataver im militärischen Umfeld zu tun haben; „Personen, die sich als römisch verstehen"[56]. Daraus leiten sie zur Frage über mögliche „nichtrömische" Elemente im Kult des Hercules Magusanus folgende Überlegung ab: „Es lässt sich daher festhalten, dass in den erhaltenen Quellen Hercules Magusanus als eine sehr römische Gottheit sichtbar wird. Das spräche dafür, Magusanus nur als erklärenden keltischen Beinamen zu verstehen, der einen ganz normalen römischen Hercules als ‚mächtigen Alten' beschreibt und ihm einen lokalen Aspekt im Sinne von ‚unser Hercules' verleiht"[57].

Aus den dakischen Provinzen sind drei weitere Inschriften für diese Gottheit bekannt[58]. Eine Inschrift aus Ciumăfaia (RO) wurde von einer unter denjenigen, die sich mit dem römischen Dakien beschäftigen, sehr bekannten Persönlichkeit in Dakien geweiht, die wichtige Funktionen innerhalb der Verwaltung des nördlichen Teils der Provinz inne hatte[59]. Es handelt sich um Publius Aelius Maximus, *eques Romanus* und *a militiis,* ehemals *duumvir quinquennalis* und *flamen* in Napoca (RO), später *[sacerdos] arae Augusti n(ostri), coronatus Daciarum III* und *decurio* in *Apulum* oder Napoca[60]. Bei dieser Inschrift handelt es sich um ein interessantes Beispiel für regionalen Synkretismus, taucht der Gott vom Niederrhein hier doch als „Deus Invictus Hercules Magusanus" auf[61]. Besonders interessant für unseren Zusammenhang ist ein Weihaltar aus Gherla (RO), der von einem der Soldaten namens Aurelius Tato gestiftet wurde (*stator* in der *ala II Pannoniorum*)[62]. Der

---

[53] CIL XIII 8771: *Magusa/no Hercul(i) / sacru(m) Flav(u)s / Vihirmatis fil(ius) / [s]ummus magistra(tus) / [c]ivitatis Batavor(um) / v(otum) s(olvit) l(ibens) m(erito).* Vgl. STOLTE 1986, 629; ausführlich BOGAERS 1960, 263–317. – Zum Problem des Synkretismus sowie der Bildung von Identifikationspaaren (Göttergleichung) siehe die grundlegenden Überlegungen von HAINZMANN 2016 zum keltischen Apollo-Grannos als Beispiel für die Verschmelzung zweier selbstständiger Gottheiten aus dem griechisch-römischen und dem ‚indigenen' Pantheon.

[54] WAGNER 1977, 421 f.

[55] DE BERNARDO STEMPEL 2014, 28 f.; ausführlich TOORIANS 2003.

[56] PETERMANDEL / SPICKERMANN 2022, 89–91 Zitat 91.

[57] PETERMANDEL / SPICKERMANN 2022, 92.

[58] AE 1977, 702; 704; AE 1995, 1280.

[59] AE 1977, 702.

[60] ILD 554 = CERom-19/20, 861 = AE 1969/70, 548 = AE 1971, 395 = AE 1999, 1279. Über die Verbindung dieses hochrangigen Beamten zu Hercules Magusanus lässt sich nur spekulieren. Es muss offenbleiben, ob er etwa durch Dienst im Rheinland oder Kontakt zu batavischen Einheiten anderswo in Berührung mit dieser Gottheit gekommen ist.

[61] Eine Diskussion findet sich bei NEMETI 2005, 138–139. Bei der Weihung eines *optio* Aurelius Marius an einen *Deus Mag[...]* ist umstritten, ob hier Magusanus ergänzt werden sollte (AE 1995, 1290).

[62] AE 1977, 704.

[63] MAYER 1957, 330; LÖRINCZ / REDŐ 2002, 109.

Beiname Tato[63] ist nicht sehr häufig und kommt auch am Niederrhein vor (wenngleich er nicht germanischen Ursprungs ist), weshalb man den Unteroffizier in Verbindung mit der Nennung des Hercules Magusanus herkunftsmäßig dieser Region zuordnen will[64]. Die Verbindung zu den batavischen Einheiten (neben der *ala* war auch die *cohors I Batavorum milliaria* in Dakien stationiert – in *Certinae* / Romita, Kreis Sălaj, RO) muss deshalb aus unserer Sicht das entscheidende und zumindest ursprüngliche Element für die Verehrung des Gottes in dieser Region gewesen sein[65].

Die Weihungen an Hercules Magusanus in den dakischen Provinzen verweisen zumindest teilweise auf Soldaten von wahrscheinlich batavischer Herkunft, die – wie auch die batavischen Reiter aus Rom[66] – ihrem heimatlichen Gott danken. Gerade der Fall der *equites singulares* aus Rom beleuchtet die Problematik onomastischer Zuweisungen. Unter diesen Elitereitern war ein beträchtlicher Anteil aus batavischen Einheiten rekrutiert worden[67]. Sie dominierten die Truppe dermaßen, dass die Einheit auch schlicht als „die Bataver" bekannt war[68]. Nach Ausweis ihrer Grabmonumente lässt sich ihre batavische Herkunft nur anhand der Zusatzangaben mit *domus* oder *natione* erschließen, da die Namen weitgehend lateinischen Ursprungs sind[69]. Hier zeigt sich, dass die Zuordnung nach vermeintlich „germanischen" Namen an ihre Grenzen stößt, wenngleich der batavische ‚Charakter' der Truppe als gesichert gilt.

Batavische Identitäten und „Germanentum"

Dies wirft das allgemeine Problem ethnischer Zuordnungen und Fragestellungen auf, welche in der von der Nationalgeschichtsschreibung der Gründerzeit geprägten Forschung lange Zeit eine herausragende Rolle gespielt haben. Erst seit den um ethnologische Methoden erweiterten Ansätzen der 1960er Jahren, wobei besonders die bahnbrechende Arbeit „Stammesbildung und Verfassung" von Reinhard Wenskus[70], aber auch die Wiener Schule um Herwig Wolfram[71] zu nennen wären, hat sich herauskristallisiert, dass auch ethnische Gruppen der Antike und der Völkerwanderungszeit in erster Linie als „imagined communities" (so B. Anderson über die modernen Nationen[72]) betrachtet werden müssen. Neben einzelnen kleineren, aus der antiken Ethnographie und Geschichtsschreibung bekannten Stammesgruppen (etwa unsere Bataver) sind besonders die als historiographische Leitbilder der deutschen Nationalgeschichtsschreibung so bedeutenden „Germanen" als das erkannt worden, was sie nach gegenwärtig herrschender Meinung heute sind: Zunächst einmal ein übergeordnetes Konstrukt der römischen Politik und Geschichtsschreibung, dann, als Ideal einer nach Ursprüngen und Gründungsmythen dürstenden modernen Nationalgeschichtsschreibung, auch ein symbolisch aufgeladener Schubladenbegriff der Forschung[73].

---

[64] Nach WEISGERBER 1968, 180 ist der Name für die *Germania inferior* typisch; vgl. HORN 1970; WAGNER 1977, 417.

[65] Vgl. auch WOLLMANN 1972, 247–251.

[66] CIL VI 31162.

[67] SPEIDEL 1994b, 38–55 Nr. 4; VAN ROSSUM 2004, 128. – Eine umfängliche Liste bei DERKS / TEITLER 2018, 62.

[68] Cass. Dio 55,24; 69,9; IK 56 Nr. 1,63A. B. Vgl. AE 1978, 802; SPEIDEL 1994b, 39–40; VAN ROSSUM 2004; VAN DRIEL-MURRAY 2003, 204. – Für die ebenfalls auch als „Batavi" bekannten *Germani corporis custodes* gilt das gleiche, etwa Suet. Cal. 43. Siehe dazu die Diskussion bei DERKS / TEITLER 2018, 59–61 mit weiterer Literatur.

[69] SPEIDEL 1994b, 81–87; VAN DRIEL-MURRAY 2003, 204–205.

[70] WENSKUS 1961.

[71] Z. B. WOLFRAM 1990; POHL 2016; 2019; 2021.

[72] ANDERSON 1983.

[73] Dazu zuletzt etwa die ausführlichen Diskussionen in FRIEDRICH / HARLAND 2021 und BRATHER et al. 2021.

Es waren in der Tat die Römer, die „aus den Völkern östlich des Rheins und nördlich der Donau die Germanen machten"[74]. Das von den Römern mit Caesar und Tacitus begründete Germanenkonzept konnte sich nach der hohen Kaiserzeit als Kategorie nicht durchsetzen (als germanisch geltende Kriegerverbände des 3. Jahrhunderts und der Spätantike wie etwa die Goten und andere ostgermanische Völker werden in vielen Quellen zusammenfassend als Skythen oder mit Eigennamen angesprochen, nur die mit dem eigentlichen, rechtsrheinischen Germanien in unmittelbarer Nähe zu den germanischen Provinzen verbundenen Gruppen wie Franken und Alamannen galten als Germanen). Die deutschen Humanisten waren es dann, die die Germanen als Konzept wiederentdeckten. Ihnen folgte die Geschichtsschreibung des 19. Jahrhunderts, welche alle Gruppen, die germanische Idiome sprachen, nach Fundmaterial und mit sprachwissenschaftlichen Argumenten in bestimmte Kategorien unterteilte (Ost- und Westgermanen usw.). Die Gesamtheit der „Germanen" wurde zu den Vorfahren der modernen Deutschen deklariert und ihre Erforschung zu einer „hervorragend nationalen Wissenschaft" erhoben (Gustaf Kossinna). Der künstliche Oberbegriff „Germanen" beschreibt also sowohl in den antiken Texten, wie auch besonders in modernen Darstellungen eben keine ethnographischen Realitäten, sondern reifiziert nur die vermeintliche Zusammengehörigkeit diverser Gruppen, die bestenfalls bestimmte sprachliche und religiöse Gemeinsamkeiten aufwiesen. Gleichwohl haben die Römer durchaus auch die Bataver in diesem Sinne „erschaffen", als eine Abteilung der Chatten sich nach Caesars gallischen Kriegen mit Erlaubnis von Rom im Rheindelta ansiedelte und so unter den Auspizien der Römer mit Gruppen von Einheimischen (etwa Eburonen) die Bataver bildete[75]. Die Ethnogenese der Bataver und ihr auf ein spezifisches Militärethos gegründetes Zusammengehörigkeitsgefühl sind ohne Rom nicht denkbar.

Obwohl Ethnizität seit der zweiten Hälfte des letzten Jahrhunderts mit anderen Maßstäben gemessen wird und etwa ethnische Deutungen von Fundmaterial seit der Jahrtausendwende einer rigorosen Kritik unterzogen wurden[76], bilden bis heute die Probleme der Herkunft der „Germanen" und ihrer „Ethnizität" Kernfragen der Germanenforschung. Dabei hat sich immer deutlicher herauskristallisiert, dass dieser Ansatz eher die modernen Wahrnehmungen als die antiken Realitäten widerspiegelt. Innerhalb der komplexen Konstruktion individueller Identitäten spielte die ethnische in der Antike möglicherweise eine weit geringere Rolle als heute. Kulturelle, soziale, situations- sowie umgebungsbedingte Identitäten waren aus heutiger Sicht in den kaiserzeitlichen Provinzen und im Barbaricum wesentlich wichtigere Kategorien[77]. Jedoch hat zuletzt Steuer aus archäologischer Perspektive eine Reihe von Argumenten angeführt „die für vielfältige Gemeinsamkeiten der Bevölkerungsgruppen in Germanien sprechen könnten, für einen ‚germanischsprachigen' Kommunikationsraum"[78]. In der hier präsentierten Diskussion dient der knappe Hinweis auf das Problemfeld von Ethnizität und Germanenbegriff nur als ein *caveat* bezüglich des

---

[74] WOLFRAM 1990, 24. Siehe ausführlich LUND 1995. – Der aktuelle Stand der Diskussion um den Germanenbegriff und seine wissenschaftliche Verwendbarkeit bei FRIEDRICH / HARLAND 2021; vgl. POHL 2021.

[75] Tac. Germ. 29; ROYMANS 2001; 2004, 195–250; VAN ROSSUM 2004, 114.

[76] Beispielsweise POHL 2019; POHL / MEHHOFER 2010; BRATHER 2004; 2008.

[77] Aus dem umfangreichen Schrifttum nur z. B. BARTH 1969 (grundlegend), weiter JONES 1997; BRATHER 2008; REVELL 2008; MATTINGLY 2011; GARDNER et al. 2013; MCINERNY 2014.

[78] STEUER 2022, 25–30 Anm. 25. Steuer verweist dabei besonders auf Runenschrift, Bestattungssitten und auf überregionale Netzwerke, die sich durch verbreitete Keramik- und Schmuckformen, Verwendung des Tierstils u. ä. konstituieren (später auch durch Goldgubber und Brakteaten). Daraus sei allerdings, so Steuer einschränkend, kein „Gemeinschaftsbewusstsein der Bewohner Germaniens" abzuleiten (STEUER 2022, 6).

Umgangs mit eindeutigen Zuschreibungen zum „Germanischen". Wenngleich gerade in der Onomastik die Sprachwissenschaft wichtige Erkenntnisse zur Herkunft von Eigennamen im römischen Militär und bei Götternamen beitragen konnte, bleiben doch viele Unsicherheiten, und vor allem wird wenig berücksichtigt, dass Träger lateinischer Namen keineswegs nicht auch „barbarischer" Herkunft sein konnten. Besonders gängige lateinische „Allerweltsnamen" verdunkeln den regionalen, sprachlichen und ethnischen Hintergrund ihrer Träger, zumal Auxiliarsoldaten oft erst bei ihrer Rekrutierung anstelle ihrer einheimischen Namen für ihre Vorgesetzten leichter auszusprechende lateinische erhielten[79].

Interpretation und Schlussfolgerungen

Vor diesem Hintergrund lassen sich für das noch weitgehend unerforschte Römerlager in Războieni-Cetate verschiedene Aspekte genauer beleuchten. Zum einen kann die neue Inschrift aus Războieni-Cetate als ein weiterer Hinweis für die durch Ziegelstempel und den geophysikalischen Survey bereits gesicherte Identifikation des Fundplatzes mit dem Standort der batavischen *ala milliaria* gelten. Die niedergermanische Gottheit wurde von den Auxiliartruppen nach Dakien exportiert und hier nach Ausweis der Inschrift auch im 3. Jahrhundert n. Chr. verehrt. Bleibt zu fragen, ob diese Verehrung auf einen auch zu späteren Zeiten klar identifizierbaren ethnisch batavischen Kern der Einheit zurückzuführen sein könnte, oder ob der Hercules Magusanus von Războieni-Cetate eher als Teil einer Regimentstradition gesehen werden muss und gewissermaßen als Schutzpatron der Einheit gelten kann, obwohl bei dauerhafter Stationierung in Dakien auch lokale und regionale Rekrutierungen für das 3. Jahrhundert anzunehmen sind[80]. Hinsichtlich der Zusammensetzung der Einheit wird man annehmen dürfen, dass sie zumindest zu Beginn ihrer Stationierung in *Dacia superior* noch einen batavischen Kern gehabt haben wird[81]. Bei den Angehörigen der Einheit, deren Namen aus Inschriften bekannt sind, lässt sich mit sprachwissenschaftlichen Überlegungen wenig gewinnen. Ethnische Zuordnungen sind schwierig und verweisen in den wenigsten Fällen auf Bataver oder germanische Onomastik. Gleichwohl hat Wollmann versucht, die germanischen Hilfstruppen Dakiens anhand der Inschriften auch onomastisch zu erfassen. „Die ethnische Zusammensetzung und die Herkunft der Truppen ist mit Hilfe der [...] angeführten Inschriften leicht zu identifizieren. Danach handelt es sich vorwiegend um Germanen und Kelten aus dem Rheingebiet"[82]. Mit diesem sicheren Brustton der Überzeugung würde man das heute vielleicht nicht mehr formulieren. Ein sicherer Fall ist in unserem Zusammenhang allenfalls Aurelius Batavus aus *Apulum*[83]. Ein weiterer interessanter Fall wäre der offenbar aus dem Umfeld des Lagers in Războieni stammende Ael(ius) Verecundinus. Er ist nach Auskunft einer Inschrift aus *Apamea natus in Dacia ad Vatabos*[84]. Ansonsten gehören die von Wollmann aufgelisteten Soldaten und Veteranen zu anderen Einheiten oder sie lassen sich keinen bestimmten

---

[79] Scholz 2009, 142.
[80] Petolescu 2002, 43–46. Ausführlich Cuff 2010. Allgemein Eck 2016, 111–126. – In leichter Abwandlung der Deutung von Petermandel / Spickermann 2022, 92, wäre Hercules Magusanus für die batavische Eliteeinheit „unser Hercules". Siehe auch die Diskussion oben Anm. 19.
[81] van Rossum 2004, 113–133.
[82] Wollmann 1975, 168.
[83] IDR III/5, 352–353 Nr. 451. Dazu Wollmann 1972. Die Zugehörigkeit zur *ala* lässt sich indes (trotz der Nähe zu *Apulum*) nicht sicher feststellen, auch die *cohors I Batavorum milliaria* kommt in Frage.
[84] AE 1993, 1577; IDRE II 411. – Hier handelt es sich sicher um eine ebenso typische wie häufige Verwechslung der Konsonanten b und v. Der Name könnte keltischen Ursprungs sein, ist jedenfalls häufig im westlichen Teil des Reichs belegt: Băluță 1990, 83–85.

Truppen zuordnen und eine Zuordnung zur *ala* wäre Spekulation. Dasas Scenobarbi, der in einer Grabinschrift für das 2. Jahrhundert n. Chr. belegte Soldat der *ala Batavorum*, war seinem Namen nach kein Bataver, sondern Illyrer[85]. Die übrigen sicher belegten Namen von Angehörigen der Einheit sind ebenfalls nicht germanischen Ursprungs[86]. Gleichwohl lassen sich für andere Batavereinheiten eine ganze Reihe von Beispielen finden, auch von Kommandanten von Kohorten, die sogar für das 3. Jahrhundert n. Chr. eine Herkunft vom Niederrhein nahe legen[87]. Auch van Rossum zweifelt nicht daran, dass der Kern batavischer Einheiten auch zu späteren Zeiten aus Rekruten vom Niederrhein bestand[88].

Hier ließe sich noch ein weiterer Befund ergänzen. Bei der Analyse der Onomastik der batavisch dominierten kaiserlichen Leibgarden fällt auf, dass viele Angehörige der ersten Generationen von Rekruten griechische Namen aufweisen. Bei diesen handelte es sich offenbar um (ungefähre) Übersetzungen batavischer Namen, die von den Vorgesetzten und romanisierten Kameraden nur sehr schwer auszusprechen waren. Diese griechischen Namen wurden dann in den Soldatenfamilien weiterverwendet und tauchen beispielsweise auch in *Vindolanda* im 2. Jahrhundert n. Chr. auf[89]: „Presumably names such as Corinthus, Elpis and Paris originally mask (to the Romans) unpronounceable Batavian names, but it is significant that they ultimately become native, military names, implying family pride in a long tradition of military careers"[90]. Auf einem Keramikfragment, das bei den von Alexander Rubel 2018 durchgeführten Ausgrabungen eines *contuberniums* in Războieni-Cetate entdeckt wurde, findet sich, neben anderen, das gut entzifferbare Besitzergraffito eines Dionysius (*post coctarum* eingeritzt). Das Fundstück gehört in die Mitte des 2. Jahrhunderts n. Chr[91]. Auch wenn eine Schwalbe noch längst keinen Frühling macht, kann dieser Befund mit aller Vorsicht in die Reihe der Argumente aufgenommen werden, welche auf eine noch über längere Zeit zu verfolgende batavische Basis der *ala* verweisen. Allerdings lassen sich noch weitere Beobachtungen für die *ala I Batavorum milliaria* ergänzen. Der immer mit Vorsicht zu bewertende prosopographische Befund ist hierbei vom archäologischen zu scheiden. Die archäologischen Funde verweisen auf eine enge Verbindung zum Niederrhein, ausgewiesen vor allem durch Importe und eine ganze Reihe lokaler Imitationen[92]. Unter diesen stechen Terra sigillata-Fragmente heraus, die im Bereich der Zivilsiedlung des Lagers gefunden wurden, sowie insbesondere zwei Gefäße mit plastischem Gesichtsdekor, die aus dem Rheinland stammen[93].

---

[85] CIL III 7800 ; IDR III/5, 398 Nr. 522. Vgl. Petolescu 2002, 65; Alföldy 1969, 185.

[86] T. Attius Tutor (CIL III 5331 = IDRE 248), T. Vibius Pius (AE 1933, 270), C. Iulius Corinthianus (CIL III 1193 = IDR III/5, 542), Dasas Scenobarbi (CIL III 7800 = IDR III/5, 522), Atilius Celsianus (CIL III 933 = IDR III/4, 72), Aelius Dubitatus (IDR III/5, 475), Aurelius Occon Quetianus (AE 1991, 1348), Aelius Verecundinus (AE 1993, 1577). – Hierzu mit weiterer Diskussion Popovici / Varga 2010, 64–67. – Zum *praefectus* Rhesus siehe den Verweis auf die Publikation und Diskussion bei Bărbulescu 2012 respektive Piso 2014. – Zu drei neuen Namen in Graffiti siehe Varga et al. in Druck.

[87] Strobel 1987, 271–292 mit weiteren Beispielen, vgl. dagegen van Rossum 2004, 123–125.

[88] van Rossum 2004, 128.

[89] Birley 2001; van Driel-Murray 2003, 201; Derks 2009, 243.

[90] van Driel-Murray 2003, 210.

[91] Varga et al. in Druck.

[92] Varga / Crizbăşan 2019, 149–150. Hierbei müssen die besonderen Gegebenheiten am Fundort in Betracht gezogen werden, insbesondere die Tatsache, dass die oberen Schichten durch landwirtschaftliche Nutzung zerstört wurden und die bisher durch Ausgrabungen belegten Kulturschichten nur bis ins spätere 2. Jahrhundert datieren, allenfalls ausnahmsweise ins frühe 3. Jahrhundert.

[93] Rusu-Bolindeț / Onofrei 2010, 401–447; Bounegru / Varga 2020, 221–232. – Zur Lokalisierung und Datierung dieser „Gesichtsurnen" siehe Braithwaite 1984; 2007. – Zur Verbindung der rheinländischen Typen zum militärischen Umfeld außerhalb Germaniens (es handelt sich um von

Abb. 6. Gefäß mit Gesichtsdekor aus Războieni-Cetate. Herkunft: Niederrhein.

Terra sigillata gilt gemeinhin als Anzeichen von Wohlstand und verweist auf ökonomische Netzwerke, Handelsverbindungen, Märkte etc. Hinsichtlich der Terra sigillata-Importe in Dakien kann man allgemein zwei Provenienzen und Perioden unterscheiden: Zunächst stammte der Großteil der Importe in den ersten drei Vierteln des 2. Jahrhunderts n. Chr. weitgehend aus Lezoux in Zentralgallien (FR) (ca. 66 %). Zur Zeit der Severer fiel der Anteil der Ware aus Lezoux auf 9 % zurück, wobei Sigillaten aus Rheinzabern nun den Großteil der Importe ausmachten[94]. Bei Sigillaten aus Războieni-Cetate handelt es sich nur zu einem geringen Teil um Importe, der Großteil ist lokaler Produktion zuzurechnen. Die Importe lassen sich den Phasen 135–160 und 160–190 n. Chr. zuordnen und stammen aus Lezoux. Sie können eindeutig der ersten „Welle" der Bataver zugeordnet werden, die in hadrianischer Zeit nach Războieni-Cetate kamen. Später entstanden in eigener Produktionsstätte am Ort lokale Imitationen[95]. Zu den spektakulärsten Keramikfunden an diesem Fundplatz gehören aber die zwei genannten Gefäße mit Gesichtsdekor[96]. Von einem ist nur der rechte Augenbereich erhalten, das zweite ist jedoch zu einem beträchtlichen Teil intakt geblieben und lässt sich gut rekonstruieren *(Abb. 6a–b)*. Die Vase wird von zwei Phallusdarstellungen bestimmt, eine auf der Rückseite des Gefäßes, die zweite im linken Wangenbereich des dargestellten grotesken Gesichts mit geschlossenen Augen. Die frühesten bekannten Vergleichstücke stammen aus dem Rheinland und von der Grenze zu Rätien[97]. Sie gehören klar zum Repertoire der rheinländischen Legionen der ersten Hälfte des 1. Jahrhunderts n. Chr. Ihre Verbreitung lässt sich auch an der oberen Donau und in die Niederlande verfolgen, der Heimat der Bataver[98]. Die meisten Exemplare dieses Gefäßtyps stammen aus Köln, Colchester (GB) und Nijmegen (NL)[99]. Sie wurden während der Kaiserzeit im Kontext von Begräbnisritualen genutzt[100], fanden später aber auch und vor allem Gebrauch im Alltagsleben, etwa im Hausschrein beim täglichen Opfern[101]. Die Exemplare aus Războieni-Cetate weisen keine Brandspuren auf, sind also mit großer Wahrscheinlichkeit nicht im Rahmen von Begräbnisritualen genutzt worden. Diesen Artefakten kommt bei der Beurteilung des kulturellen Kontexts hohe Bedeutung zu. Die

den Truppen mitgeführte kultische Objekte, die bisweilen auch als Urnen Verwendung fanden) siehe DARLING 2015.
[94] RUSU-BOLINDEȚ 2016, 381–382.
[95] VARGA / CRIZBĂȘAN 2019, 143–144.
[96] BOUNEGRU / VARGA 2020.
[97] BRAITHWAITE 1984, 100.
[98] BRAITHWAITE 2007, 397.
[99] BRAITHWAITE 1984, 100.
[100] BRAITHWAITE 1984, 31; DARLING 2015, 640.
[101] BRAITHWAITE 2007, 396.

besonderen Importe weisen auf nachhaltige Verbindungen, Handels- und Tauschkontakte ins Rheinland hin.

Will man die Ergebnisse zusammenfassen, so wird man anhand des Vergleichs zu anderen Spezialeinheiten und mit dem Fundmaterial zumindest für das 2. Jahrhundert n. Chr. noch einen batavischen Kern der Eliteeinheit bzw. enge Kontakte ins Herkunftsgebiet vermuten können, ergänzt freilich durch lokale Rekrutierungen[102]. Ob dieser Kern noch im 3. Jahrhundert n. Chr. durch Nachrekrutierung von Spezialisten vom Niederrhein weiter bestand, oder ob die Verehrung des Hercules Magusanus durch die Soldaten der *ala I Batavorum milliaria* in Războieni-Cetate eine ererbte Regimentstradition war, lässt sich nicht entscheiden. Derartige kultische Traditionen sind durchaus bekannt, nicht nur im Falle ausgemachter Elite- und Spezialtruppen[103]. Angesichts des Elitestatus dieser Reitereinheit und der Parallelen sowohl zu batavischen Einheiten in Britannien als auch zu syrischen Spezialeinheiten von Bogenschützen (nur z. B. *Palmyreni sagittarii, cohors Hamiorum sagittaria*[104]) scheint es keineswegs ausgeschlossen, dass die Inschrift für Hercules tatsächlich ein Soldat vom Niederrhein gestiftet hat. Wir halten jedoch die traditionelle Verbindung der Mitglieder der Einheit zur Hauptgottheit der niederrheinischen Bataver im Sinne einer identitätsstiftenden, ererbten Regimentstradition für das wahrscheinlichere Motiv der Weihung in der ersten Hälfte des 3. Jahrhunderts n. Chr. Die ursprüngliche batavische Herkunft der Soldaten der Einheit, die vielleicht noch lange mit Rekruten aus Niedergermanien versorgt wurde, und die daraus möglicherweise entstandene Regimentstradition führten dazu, dass auch noch im 3. Jahrhundert Hercules Magusanus seinen Weg vom Rhein bis ins ferne Dakien fand. Die mehrfach belegte Verehrung des Hercules Magusanus in Dakien kann, zumindest was den Ursprung des Kultes angeht, nur durch die Verbindung zu den batavischen Einheiten in dieser Provinz erklärt werden, von denen die bis zur Aufgabe der Provinz in Războieni-Cetate stationierte *ala* die bedeutendste war.

Războieni-Cetate wird für die Zukunft ein sehr wichtiger Fundplatz bleiben. Es handelt sich um den einzigen Ort im ehemaligen Imperium Romanum, an dem ein Lager einer *ala milliaria* und die ausgedehnte Zivilsiedlung fast völlig frei zugänglich und zu mehr als 70 % nicht modern überbaut sind[105]. Weitere Ausgrabungen (die von staatlicher rumänischer Förderung abhängig sind) werden sich zunächst auf die spektakulären Steinbauten im nördlichen Teil des *vicus* konzentrieren. Allerdings verspricht auch der Lagerbereich weiteres Potential. Bei einer kleinflächigen Grabung konnte in einem einzigen *contubernium* eine ganze Reihe von Gefäßfragmenten mit Besitzergraffiti geborgen werden[106].

Literaturverzeichnis

Zitierwerke und Sigel

AE	L'Année Épigraphic	EDCS	Epigraphik Datenbank Clauss / Staby. https://db.edcs.eu/epigr/epi_de.php
CERom	C. C. Petolescu, Cronica epigrafica a României (CERom-19/20 = C. C. Petolescu, Cronica epigrafica a României. SCIVA 52/53, 2001/2002, 267–300.)	IDR	Inscriptiones Daciae Romanae (Bukarest 1975 ff.)

---

[102] Siehe oben Anm. 15; 19; vgl. Eck 2003, 220–228.
[103] Stoll 2009.
[104] Spaul 2000, 408–409; siehe auch oben Anm. 29.
[105] Die übrigen bekannten Standorte in Deutschland und Großbritannien, Aalen, Heidenheim (beide Baden-Württemberg, DE) und Stanwix (district Carlisle, GB) sind weitgehend modern überbaut.
[106] Varga et al. in Druck.

IDRE C. C. Petolescu, Inscriptiones Daciae Romanae. Inscriptiones extra fines Daciae repertae (Bukarest 1996 ff.)

IK Inschriften griechischer Städte in Kleinasien (IK 56 = M. H. Sayar [Hrsg.], Die Inschriften von Anazarbos und Umgebung 1. Inschriften aus dem Stadtgebiet und der nächsten Umgebung der Stadt. Inschr. griech. Städte Kleinasien 56 [Bonn 2000].)

ILB A. Deman / M.-T. Raepsaet-Charlier, Les inscriptions latines de Belgique (Brüssel 1985/²2002)

ILD C. C. Petolescu, Inscriptii latine din Dacia (ILD) / Inscriptiones latinae Daciae (Bukarest 2005)

RIU Die römische Inschriften Ungarns (Budapest 1972 ff.)

Literatur

Alföldy 1968
G. Alföldy, Die Hilfstruppen der römischen Provinz Germania inferior. Epigr. Stud. 6 (Düsseldorf 1968).

Alföldy 1969
G. Alföldy, Die Personennamen in der römischen Provinz Dalmatia. Beitr. Namenforsch. N. F. Beih. 4 (Heidelberg 1969).

Anderson 1983
B. Anderson, Imagined Communities: Reflections on the Origin and Spread of Nationalism (London 1983).

Băluţă 1990
C. L. Băluţă, Relief votiv dedicat Eponei descoperit la Războieni-Cetate. Stud. şi Cerc. Istor. V 41, 1990, 83–86.

Bărbulescu 2012
M. Bărbulescu, Inscripţiile din castrul legionar de la Potaissa. The Inscriptions of the Legionary Fortress of Potaissa (Bukarest 2012).

Barth 1969
F. Barth (Hrsg.), Ethnic Groups and Boundaries. The Social Organization of Difference (Bergen, Oslo 1969).

de Bernardo Stempel 2014
P. de Bernardo Stempel, Keltische Äquivalente klassischer Epitheta und andere sprachliche und nicht-sprachliche Phänomene im Rahmen der sogenannten ‚interpretatio Romana'. Zeitschr. Celt. Philol. 61, 2014, 7–48. doi: https://doi.org/10.1515/zcph.2014.003.

Birley 1978
E. Birley, The religion of the Roman army: 1895–1977. In: W. Haase (Hrsg.), Aufstieg und Niedergang der römischen Welt (ANWR). Rise and Decline of the Roman World. Band 16,2. Teilband: Religion (Heidentum: Römische Religion, Allgemeines [Forts.]). Aufstieg u. Niedergang Röm. Welt 2,16,2 (Berlin, New York 1978) 1506–1541. doi: https://doi.org/10.1515/9783110851335-014.

Birley 2001
A. R. Birley, The names of the Batavians and Tungrians in the Tabulae Vindolandenses. In: Th. Grünewald (Hrsg.), Germania inferior. Besiedlung, Gesellschaft und Wirtschaft an der Grenze der römisch-germanischen Welt. RGA Ergbd. 28 (Berlin, New York 2001) 241–260. doi: https://doi.org/10.1515/9783110823554.241.

Bogaers 1960
J. E. Bogaers, Civitas en stad van de Bataven en Canninefaten. Ber. ROB 10, 1960, 263–317. https://hdl.handle.net/2066/26343.

Le Bohec 1993
Y. Le Bohec, Die römische Armee. Von Augustus zu Konstantin d. Gr. (Stuttgart 1993).

Bounegru / Varga 2020
G. Bounegru / R. Varga, Two face pots from the vicus of Războieni-Cetate (Alba County). In: S. Nemeti / E. Beu-Dachinm / I. Nemeti / D. Dana (Hrsg.), The Roman Provinces. Mechanisms of Integration (Cluj-Napoca 2020) 221–232.

Bowman 2006
A. Bowman, Outposts of empire: Vindolanda, Egypt and the empire of Rome. Journal Roman Arch. 19, 2006, 75–93. doi: https://doi.org/10.1017/S1047759400006279.

BRAITHWAITE 1984
G. BRAITHWAITE, Romano-British face pots and head pots. Britannia 15, 1984, 99–131. doi: https://doi.org/10.2307/526586.

BRAITHWAITE 2007
G. BRAITHWAITE, Faces from the Past: A Study of Roman Face Pots from Italy and the Western Provinces of the Roman Empire. BAR Internat. Ser. 1651 (Oxford 2007). doi: https://doi.org/10.30861/9781407300856.

BRATHER 2004
S. BRATHER, Ethnische Interpretationen in der frühgeschichtlichen Archäologie. Geschichte, Grundlagen und Alternativen. RGA Ergbd. 42 (Berlin, New York 2004). doi: https://doi.org/10.1515/9783110922240.

BRATHER 2008
S. BRATHER, Archaeology and Identity. Central and East Central Europe in the Earlier Middle Ages. Florilegium Magistrorum Historiae Archaeologiaeque Antiquitatis et Medii Aevi 2 (Bukarest 2008).

BRATHER et al. 2021
S. BRATHER / W. HEIZMANN / ST. PATZOLD (Hrsg.), Germanische Altertumskunde im Wandel 1. Archäologische, philologische und geschichtswissenschaftliche Beiträge aus 150 Jahren. RGA Ergbd. 100,1 (Berlin, Boston 2021) doi: https://doi.org/10.1515/9783110563061.

CHIAI et al. 2012
G. F. CHIAI / R. HÄUSLER / CH. KUNST, Einleitung. Interpretatio: Religiöse Kommunikation zwischen Globalisierung und Partikolarisierung. In: G. F. Chiai / R. Häusler / Ch. Kunst (Hrsg.), Interpretatio romana / graeca / indigena. Religiöse Kommunikation zwischen Partikularisierung und Globalisierung. Mediterraneo Ant. 15 (Pisa 2012) 13–30.

CUFF 2010
D. B. CUFF, The auxilia in Roman Britain and the Two Germanies from Augustus to Caracalla. Family, Religion and 'Romanization' [Diss. Univ. Toronto] (Toronto 2010). https://tspace.library.utoronto.ca/bitstream/1807/24732/1/Cuff_David_B_201006_PhD_thesis.pdf (letzter Zugriff: 10.5.2022).

CUFF 2011
D. B. CUFF, The king of the Batavians: Remarks on Tab. Vindol. III, 628. Britannia 42, 2011, 145–156. doi: https://doi.org/10.1017/S0068113X11000092.

DANA / ROSSIGNOL 2017
D. DANA / B. ROSSIGNOL (Hrsg.), Entrer dans l'armée romaine: bassins de recrutement des unités auxiliaires (I^e–IIe siècles après J.-C.). Rev. Internat. Hist. Militaire Ancienne 6 (Paris 2017).

DARLING 2015
M. DARLING, Face pots and the Roman army. [Rez. zu]: G. Braithwaite, Faces from the Past: A Study of Roman Face Pots from Italy and the Western Provinces of the Roman Empire. BAR Internat. Ser. 1651 (Oxford 2007). Journal Roman Arch. 23, 2015, 643–650. doi: https://doi.org/10.1017/S1047759400002865.

DERKS 1998
T. DERKS, Gods, Temples and Ritual Practices. The Transformation of Religious Ideas and Values in Roman Gaul. Amsterdam Arch. Stud. 2 (Amsterdam 1998).

DERKS 2009
T. DERKS, Ethnic identity in the Roman frontier. The epigraphy of Batavi and other Lower Rhine tribes. In: T. Derks / N. Roymans (Hrsg.), Ethnic Constructs in Antiquity. The Role of Power and Tradition Amsterdam Arch. Stud. 13 (Amsterdam 2009) 239–282.

DERKS / ROYMANS 2006
T. DERKS / N. ROYMANS, Returning auxiliary veterans in the Roman Empire: some methodological considerations. Journal Roman Arch. 19, 2006, 121–135. doi: https://doi.org/10.1017/s1047759400006292.

DERKS / TEITLER 2018
T. DERKS / H. TEITLER, Batavi in the Roman Army of the Principate. An inventory of the sources. Bonner Jahrb. 218, 2018, 53–80. doi: https://doi.org/10.11588/bjb.2018.1.79812.

DICKEY 2002
E. DICKEY, Latin forms of Address: from Plautus to Apuleius (Oxford 2002).

VON DOMASZEWSKI 1895
A. VON DOMASZEWSKI, Die Religion des

römischen Heeres. Westdt. Zeitschr. Gesch. u. Kunst 14 Sonderabdruck (Trier 1895). https://resources.warburg.sas.ac.uk/pdf/bkg225b2415416.pdf (letzter Zugriff: 12.5.2022).

van Driel-Murray 2003
C. van Driel-Murray, Ethnic soldiers. The experience of the Lower Rhine tribes. In: Th. Grünewald / S. Seibel (Hrsg.), Kontinuität und Diskontinuität. Germania inferior am Beginn und am Ende der römischen Herrschaft. RGA Ergbd. 35 (Berlin 2003) 200–217. doi: https://doi.org/10.1515/9783110900903.200.

Drinkwater 1987
J. F. Drinkwater, The Gallic Empire. Separatism and Continuity in the North-Western Provinces of the Roman Empire, A. D. 260–274. Historia 52 (Wiesbaden 1987).

Eck 2003
W. Eck, Eine Bürgerrechtskonstitution Vespasians aus dem Jahr 71 n. Chr. und die Aushebung von brittonischen Auxiliareinheiten. Zeitschr. Papyr. u. Epigr. 143, 2003, 220–228.

Eck 2005
W. Eck, Militärisches und ziviles Alltagsleben am Hadrianswall. [Rez. zu]: A. K. Bowman / J. D. Thomas, The Vindolanda Writing-Tablets. Tabulae Vindolandenses 3 (London 2003). Journal Roman Arch. 18, 2005, 663–668. doi: https://doi.org/10.1017/S104775940000787X.

Eck 2016
W. Eck, Die Entwicklung der Auxiliareinheiten als Teil des römischen Heeres in der frühen und hohen Kaiserzeit. Eine Teilsynthese. In: C. Wolff / P. Faure (Hrsg.), Les auxiliaires de l'armée romaine: des alliés aux fédérés. Actes du sixième congrès de Lyon (23-25 octobre 2014). Collect. Études et Rech. Occident Romaine 51 (Paris, Lyon 2016) 111–126.

Elmer 1941
G. Elmer, Die Münzprägung der gallischen Kaiser von Postumus bis Tetricus in Köln, Trier und Mailand. Bonner Jahrb. 146, 1941, 1–106. doi: https://doi.org/10.11588/bjb.1941.0.73981.

Fischer 2001
Th. Fischer (Hrsg.), Die römischen Provinzen. Eine Einführung in ihre Archäologie (Stuttgart 2001).

Fitz 1972
J. Fitz, Les Syriens à Intercisa. Collect. Latomus 122 (Brüssel 1972).

Friedrich / Harland 2021
M. Friedrich / J. M. Harland (Hrsg.), Interrogating the 'Germanic'. A Category and its Use in Late Antiquity and the Early Middle Ages. RGA Ergbd. 123 (Berlin, Boston 2021). doi: https://doi.org/10.1515/9783110701623.

Gallet / Le Bohec 2007
S. Gallet / Y. Le Bohec, Le recrutement des auxiliaires d'après les diplômes militaires et les autres inscriptions. In: M. A. Speidel / H. Lieb (Hrsg.), Militärdiplome. Die Forschungsbeiträge der Berner Gespräche von 2004. Mavors Roman Army Researches 15 (Stuttgart 2007) 267–292.

Gardner et al. 2013
A. Gardner / E. Harris / K. Lomas (Hrsg.), Creating Ethnicities and Identities in the Roman World. Bull. Inst. Class. Stud., Suppl. 120 (London 2013). doi: https://doi.org/10.14296/917.9781905670796.

Graham 1992
D. G. Graham, Textual Scholarship (London, New York 1992).

Gilliam 1965
J. F. Gilliam, Dura Rosters and the Constitutio Antoniniana. Historia 14, 1965, 74–92.

Gudea / Cosma 1992
N. Gudea / C. Cosma, Contribuții la paleografia latină romană din Dacia. Acta Mus. Porolissensis 16 (Cluj-Napoca 1992) 201–247.

Gutenbrunner 1936
S. Gutenbrunner, Die germanischen Götternamen der antiken Inschriften. Rhein. Beitr. u. Hülfsbücher germ. Philol. u. Volkskde. 24 (Halle 1936).

Haalebos 2000
J. K. Haalebos, Traian und die Hilfstruppen am Niederrhein. Ein Militärdiplom des Jahres 98 n. Chr. aus Elst in der Over-Betuwe (Niederlande). Saalburg Jahrb. 50, 2000, 31–72.

HAINZMANN 2016
M. Hainzmann, Apollini Granno: Explikatorisches Beinamenformular oder Göttergleichung? Ein „Modellfall". In: K. Matijević (Hrsg.), Kelto-Römische Gottheiten und ihre Verehrer. Akten des 14. F. E.R. C.AN.-Workshops Trier, 12.–14. Oktober 2015. Pharos 39 (Rahden / Westf. 2016) 230–256.

HAYNES 1999
I. Haynes, Military service and cultural identity in the auxilia. In: A. Goldsworthy / I. Haynes (Hrsg.), The Roman Army as a Community. Journal Roman Arch., Suppl. 34 (Portsmouth 1999) 165–174.

HAYNES 2013
I. Haynes, Blood of the Provinces. The Roman Auxilia and the Making of Provincial Society from Augustus to the Severans (Oxford 2013).

HORN 1970
H. G. Horn, Eine Weihung für Hercules Magusanus aus Bonn. Bonner Jahrb. 170, 1970, 233–250. https://journals.ub.uni-heidelberg.de/index.php/bjb/article/download/80496/74542 (letzter Zugriff: 12.5.2022).

JONES 1997
S. Jones, The Archaeology of Ethnicity: Constructing Identities in the Past and Present (London, New York 1997).

KEPPIE 2001
L. Keppie, Understanding Roman Inscriptions (Baltimore 2001).

KÖNIG 1981
I. König, Die gallischen Usurpatoren von Postumus bis Tetricus. Vestigia 31 (München 1981).

KRAFT 1951
K. Kraft, Zur Rekrutierung der Alen und Kohorten an Rhein und Donau. Diss. Bernenses 3 (Bern 1951).

LASSÈRE 2007
J.-M. Lassère, Manuel d'Épigrahie Romaine[2] (Paris 2007).

LÖRINCZ 1999
B. Lörincz (Hrsg.), Onomasticon Provinciarum Europae Latinarum (OPEL) 2. Cabalicius–Ixus (Wien 1999).

LÖRINCZ 2001
B. Lörincz, Die römischen Hilfstruppen in Pannonien während der Prinzipatszeit 1. Die Inschriften. Wiener Arch. Stud. 3 (Wien 2001).

LÖRINCZ / REDÖ 2002
B. Lörincz / F. Redö (Hrsg.), Onomasticon Provinciarum Europae Latinarum (OPEL) 4. Quadratia–Zures (Wien 2002).

LUND 1995
A. A. Lund, Die Erfindung der Germanen. Der altsprachliche Unterricht 38, 1995, 4–20.

MAYER 1957
A. Mayer, Die Sprache der alten Illyrier 1. Schr. Balkankomm., Linguist. Abt. 15/16 (Wien 1957).

MATTINGLY 2011
D. J. Mattingly, Imperialism, Power, and Identity. Experiencing the Roman Empire (Princeton 2011).

MCINERNY 2014
J. McInerny (Hrsg.), A Companion the Ethnicity in the Ancient Mediterranean (Chichester 2014).

MCLAUGHLIN 2018
J. J. McLaughlin, King of beers: alcohol, authority, and identity among Batavian soldiers in the Roman *auxilia* at Vindolanda. Ancient Soc. 48, 2018, 169–198. doi: https://doi.org/10.2143/AS.48.0.3285201.

MIHAILESCU-BÎRLIBA 2018
L. Mihailescu-Bîrliba, The importance of salt exploitation in Roman Dacia. The case of Ocna Mureș (Salinae). Journal Ancient Hist. and Arch. 5,4, 2018, 32–36. doi: https://doi.org/10.14795/j.v5i4.347.

MISCHKA et al. 2018
C. Mischka / A. Rubel / R. Varga, Das Lager der *ala I Batavorum milliaria* und sein *vicus* in Războieni-Cetate (Jud. Alba / RO). Geophysikalische Untersuchungen und historische Einordnungen. Arch. Korrbl. 48, 2018, 377–405. doi: https://doi.org/10.11588/ak.2018.3.75234.

MOGA 1996
V. Moga, Inscriptions inédits a Apulum. In: M. Porumb (Hrsg.), Omaggio a Dinu Adamesteanu (Cluj-Napoca 1996) 183–185.

NELSON 2005
> M. NELSON, The Barbarian's Beverage: A History of Beer in Ancient Europe (London, New York 2005).

NEMETI 2005
> S. NEMETI, Sincretismul religios în Dacia romană (Cluj-Napoca 2005) [französ. Übersetzung: Le syncrétisme religieux en Dacie Romaine (Cluj-Napoca 2019)].

PETERMANDEL / SPICKERMAN 2022
> W. PETERMANDEL / W. SPICKERMANN, Hercules Magusanus. In: K. Matijević / R. Wiegels (Hrsg.), Kultureller Transfer und religiöse Landschaften. Zur Begegnung zwischen Imperium und Barbaricum in der römischen Kaiserzeit. Abhandl. Akad. Wiss. Göttingen N. F. 52 (Berlin, Boston 2022) 81–96.

PETOLESCU 2002
> C. C. PETOLESCU, Auxilia Daciae. Contribuție la istoria militară a Daciei romane (Bukarest 2002).

PISO 2005
> I. PISO, An der Nordgrenze des Römischen Reiches. Ausgewählte Studien 1972–2003. Heidelberger Althist. Beitr. u. Epigr. Stud. 41 (Stuttgart 2005).

PISO 2014
> I. PISO, Zur Reform des Gallienus anläßlich zweier neuer Inschriften aus den Lagerthermen von Potaissa. Tyche 29, 2014, 125–146.

PISO / BENEA 1984
> I. PISO / D. BENEA, Das Militärdiplom von Drobeta. Zeitschr. Papyr. u. Epigr. 56, 1984, 263–295.

PISO / VARGA 2018
> I. PISO / R. VARGA, Les éstampilles militaires de Razboieni-Cetate. Acta Mus. Porolissensis 41, 2018, 263–290. http://muzeuzalau.ro/wp-content/uploads/2019/01/LES-ESTAMPILLES-MILITAIRES-DE-RAZBOIENI-CETATE.pdf (letzter Zugriff: 12.5.2022).

POHL 2016
> W. POHL, Die Völkerwanderung. Eroberung und Integration³ (Stuttgart 2016).

POHL 2019
> W. POHL, Historiography and Identity – Methodological Perspectives. In: W. Pohl / V. Wieser (Hrsg.), Historiography and Identity 1. Ancient and Early Christian Narratives of Community. Cultural Encounters in Late Antiquity and the Middle Ages 24 (Turnhout 2019) 7–50.

POHL 2021
> W. POHL, Vom Nutzen des Germanenbegriffes zwischen Antike und Mittelalter: eine forschungsgeschichtliche Perspektive. In: S. Brather / W. Heizmann / St. Patzold (Hrsg.), Germanische Altertumskunde im Wandel 1. Archäologische, philologische und geschichtswissenschaftliche Beiträge aus 150 Jahren. RGA Ergbd. 100,1 (Berlin, Boston 2021) 287–306. doi: https://doi.org/10.1515/9783110563061-011.

POHL / MEHOFER 2010
> W. POHL / M. MEHOFER (Hrsg.), Archaeology of Identity – Archäologie der Identität. Forschungen zur Geschichte des Mittelalters 17. Denkschr. Phil.-Hist. Kl. 406 (Wien 2010).

POPOVICI / VARGA 2010
> P. POPOVICI / R. VARGA, Ad Vatabos: monografie arheologică a localității Războieni-Cetat (Cluj-Napoca 2010).

RAEPSAET-CHARLIER 1978
> M.-T. RAEPSAET-CHARLIER, Le lieu d'installation des vétérans auxiliaires romains d'après les diplômes militaires. Ant. Class. 47, 1978, 557–565. doi: https://doi.org/10.3406/antiq.1978.1918.

REVELL 2008
> L. REVELL, Roman Imperialism and Local Identities (Cambridge 2008). doi: https://doi.org/10.1017/CBO9780511499692.

ROSELAER 2016
> S. T. ROSELAER, State organised mobility in the Roman Empire: legionaries and auxiliaries. In: L. de Light (Hrsg.), Migration and Mobility in the Early Roman Empire. Stud. Global Social Hist. 23 (Leiden 2016) 138–157. doi: https://doi.org/10.1163/9789004307377_008.

VAN ROSSUM 2004
> J. A. VAN ROSSUM, The end of the Batavian Auxiliaries as "national" units. In: L. de Light (Hrsg.), Roman Rule and Civic Life: Local and Regional Perspectives. Proceedings of the Fourth Workshop of the International Net-

work "Impact of Empire (Roman Empire, c. 200 B. C.–A. D. 476)", Leiden, June 25–28, 2003. Impact of Empire (Roman Empire, 27 B. C.–A. D. 406) 4 (Amsterdam 2004) 113–133. doi: https://doi.org/10.1163/9789004401655_008.

Roymans 2001
N. Roymans, The Lower Rhine triquetrum coinages and the ethnogenesis of the Batavi. In: Th. Grünewald (Hrsg.), Germania inferior. Besiedlung, Gesellschaft und Wirtschaft an der Grenze der römisch-germanischen Welt. RGA Ergbd. 28 (Berlin, New York 2001) 93–145. doi: https://doi.org/10.1515/9783110823554.93.

Roymans 2004
N. Roymans, Ethnic Identity and Imperial Power. The Batavians in the Early Roman Empire. Amsterdam Arch. Stud. 10 (Amsterdam 2004).

Roymans 2009
N. Roymans, Hercules and the construction of a Batavian identity in the context of the Roman Empire. In: T. Derks / N. Roymans (Hrsg.), Ethnic Constructs in Antiquity. The Role of Power and Tradition. Amsterdam Arch. Stud. 13 (Amsterdam 2009) 219–238.

Roymans / Derks 1990
N. Roymans / T. Derks, Ein keltisch-römischer Kultbezirk bei Empel (Niederlande). Arch. Korrbl. 20, 1990, 443–451. https://research.vu.nl/ws/portalfiles/portal/35383962/1990_AK_20_Empel.pdf (letzter Zugriff: 11.5.2022).

Roxan 1997
M. M. Roxan, Settlement of veterans of the auxilia – a preliminary study. In: W. Groenman-van Waateringe / B. L. van Beek / W. J. H. Willems / S. L. Wynia (Hrsg.), Roman Frontier Studies 1995. Proceedings of the XVIth International Congress of Roman Frontier Studies. Oxbow Monogr. 91 (Oxford 1997) 483–491.

Rubel 2016
A. Rubel, Religion und Kult der Germanen (Stuttgart 2016).

Rusu-Bolindeţ 2016
V. Rusu-Bolindeţ, Supply and consumption of terra sigillata in Roman Dacia during the Severan dynasty. In: A. Panaite / R. Cîrjan / C. Căpiţă (Hrsg.), Moesica et Christiana. Studies in Honour of Professor Alexandru Barnea (Brăila 2016) 379–409.

Rusu-Bolindeţ / Onofrei 2010
V. Rusu-Bolindeţ / C. Onofrei, Date noi privind activitatea militară şi cultura materială a alei I Batavorum de la Războieni-Cetate. In: V. Rusu-Bolindeţ / T. Sălăgean / R. Varga (Hrsg.), Studia archaeologica et historica in honorem magistri Dorin Alicu (Cluj-Napoca 2010) 401–447.

Salway 1994
B. Salway, What's in a name? A Survey of Roman Onomastic Practice from c. 700 BC to AD 700. Journal Roman Stud. 84, 1994, 124–145. doi: https://doi.org/10.2307/300873.

Sanie 1981
S. Sanie, Cultele orientale în Dacia Romana (Bukarest 1981).

Scholz 2009
M. Scholz, Das Reiterkastell Aquileia / Heidenheim. Die Ergebnisse der Ausgrabungen 2000–2004. Forsch. u. Ber. Vor- u. Frühgesch. Baden-Württemberg 110 (Stuttgart 2009).

Schultze 1904
W. Schultze, Zur Geschichte lateinischer Eigennamen (Berlin 1904).

Spaul 2000
J. Spaul, Cohors 2. The Evidence for and a Short History of the Auxiliary Infantry Units of the Imperial Roman Army. BAR Internat. Ser. 841 (Oxford 2000). doi: https://doi.org/10.30861/9781841710464.

Speidel 1994a
M. P. Speidel, Die Denkmäler der Kaiserreiter – Equites singulares Augusti. Beih. Bonner Jahrb. 50 (Bonn 1994).

Speidel 1994b
M. P. Speidel, Riding for Caesar. The Roman Emperors' Horse Guards (London 1994).

Steuer 2022
H. Steuer, „Germanen" aus der Sicht der Archäologie – was allein die Ausgrabungsergebnisse sagen. In: K. Matijević / R. Wiegels (Hrsg.), Kultureller Transfer und religiöse Landschaften. Zur Begegnung zwischen

Imperium und Barbaricum in der römischen Kaiserzeit. Abhandl. Akad. Wiss. Göttingen N. F. 52 (Berlin, Boston 2022) 5–33. doi: https://doi.org/10.1515/9783110716580-002.

Stoll 2009
O. Stoll, Integration und doppelte Identität. Römisches Militär und die Kulte der Soldaten und Veteranen in Ägypten von Augustus bis Diokletian. In: R. Gundlach / C. Vogel (Hrsg.), Militärgeschichte des pharaonischen Ägypten. Altägypten und seine Nachbarkulturen im Spiegel der aktuellen Forschung. Krieg Gesch. 34 (Paderborn 2009) 419–458.

Stolte 1986
B. H. Stolte, Die religiösen Verhältnisse in Niedergermanien. In: W. Haase (Hrsg.), Aufstieg und Niedergang der römischen Welt (ANWR). Rise and Decline of the Roman World. Band 18,1. Teilband: Religion (Heidentum: Die religiösen Verhältnisse in den Provinzen). Aufstieg u. Niedergang Röm. Welt 2,18,1 (Berlin, New York 1986) 592–671. doi: https://doi.org/10.1515/9783110861464-012.

Strobel 1987
K. Strobel, Anmerkungen zur Geschichte der Bataverkohorten in der hohen Kaiserzeit. Zeitschr. Papyr. u. Epigr. 70, 1987, 271–292.

Țentea 2012
O. Țentea, Ex oriente ad Danubium. The Syrian Units on the Danube Frontier of the Roman Empire. Centre Roman Military Stud. 6 (Cluj-Napoca 2012). doi: https://doi.org/10.13140/RG.2.1.4246.1604.

Thompson 1906
E. M. Thompson, Handbook of Greek and Latin Palaeography (London 1906).

Toorians 2003
L. Toorians, Magusanos and the "Old Lad": a case of germanicised celtic. North-Western European Language Evolution 42, 2003, 13–28.

Urban 1985
R. Urban, Der 'Bataveraufstand' und die Erhebung des Iulius Classicus. Trierer Hist. Forsch. 8 (Trier 1985).

Varga 2012
R. Varga, *Constitutio Antoniniana*. Law and individual in a time of change. In: V. V. Dementyeva (Hrsg.), Ancient Civilisation: Political Institutions and Legal Regulation. Proceedings of the International Web Conference (Yaroslavl 2012) 199–209.

Varga / Crizbăşan 2019
R. Varga / C. Crizbăşan, The impact of the Batavian auxiliaries on the community at Războieni-Cetate (Alba County). Case study: the ceramic artefacts. In: L. Mihailescu-Bîrliba / W. Spickermann (Hrsg.), Roman Army and Local Society in the Limes Provinces of the Roman Empire. Papers of an International Conference, Iași, June 4–6, 2018. Pharos 42 (Rahden / Westf. 2019) 139–162.

Varga et al. in Druck
R. Varga / A. Rubel / G. Bounegru, Pottery vessels with *graffiti* discovered in the fort of *ala I Batavorum* in Dacia. Electrumvarga 2023, in Druck.

Voloşciuc 2007
A. Voloşciuc, Scrierea cursivă în Dacia romană. Analele Banatului N. S. 15, 2007, 57–68. doi: https://doi.org/10.55201/DSWS4009.

de Vries 1970
J. de Vries, Altgermanische Religionsgeschichte² (Berlin, New York 1956–1957, unveränderter Nachdruck 1970).

Wagner 1938
W. Wagner, Die Dislokation der römischen Auxiliarformationen in den Provinzen Noricum, Moesien, und Dakien, von Augustus bis Gallienus. Neue Dt. Gesch., Abt. Alte Gesch. 5 (Berlin 1938).

Wagner 1977
N. Wagner, Hercules Magusanus. Bonner Jahrb. 177, 1977, 417–422. doi: https://doi.org/10.11588/bjb.1977.1.78948.

Wenskus 1961
R. Wenskus, Stammesbildung und Verfassung. Das Werden der frühmittelalterlichen gentes² (Köln, Wien 1977).

Weisgerber 1968
L. Weisgerber, Die Namen der Ubier. Wiss. Abhandl. Arbeitsgemeinschaft Forsch. Land Nordrhein-Westfalen 34 (Köln 1968).

Weiss 2002
P. Weiss, Neue Diplome für Soldaten der Exercitus Dacicus. Zeitschr. Papyr. u. Epigr. 141, 2002, 241–251.

Wightman 1985
E. M. Wightman, Gallia Belgica (Berkeley, Los Angeles 1985).

Willems 1984
W. J. H. Willems, Romans and Batavians: a regional study in the Dutch eastern river area. Ber. ROB 32, 1984, 206–213. https://hdl.handle.net/1887/11881.

Wolfram 1990
H. Wolfram, Das Reich und die Germanen. Zwischen Antike und Mittelalter[2] (Berlin 1990).

Wollmann 1972
V. Wollmann, Ein Bataver im römischen Heer in Dakien. Germania 50, 1972, 247–251.

Wollmann 1975
V. Wollmann, Germanische Volks- und Kulturelemente im römischen Dakien. Germania 53, 1975, 166–174.

Zusammenfassung: Hercules Magusanus im Lager der *ala I Batavorum milliaria* in Războieni-Cetate (Kreis Alba, Rumänien)

Dieser Aufsatz präsentiert und diskutiert eine neue Hercules-Magusanus-Inschrift, die in Războieni-Cetate, dem Standort der *ala I Batavorum milliaria*, entdeckt wurde und die in unmittelbarem Zusammenhang mit der dort zwischen ca. 130 und 271 n. Chr. stationierten Reitereinheit gesehen werden muss. Neben Keramikfunden, die ebenfalls auf das Rheinland verweisen, zeugt die in die erste Hälfte des 3. Jahrhunderts n. Chr. zu datierende Inschrift von einer mit den Batavern des Ursprungsgebiets der Einheit in Verbindung stehende Regimentstradition, die möglicherweise auch noch in einer Zeit wirksam war, als wahrscheinlich nicht mehr oder in geringerem Ausmaße aus der Herkunftsregion rekrutiert wurde.

Abstract: Hercules Magusanus in the legionary fort of the *ala I Batavorum milliaria* in Războieni-Cetate (distr. Alba, Romania)

The current article focuses of an inscription dedicated to Hercules Magusanus. The epigraph was discovered at Războieni-Cetate (Alba County, RO), the site where the *ala I Batavorum milliaria* was stationed in *Dacia* between (approx.) 130–271 AD. The monument most probably dates from the first half of the 3rd century. Along with the ceramic imports coming from the Rhine area discovered on site, the presence of this deity indicates a Batavian cultural substratum of the settlement, preserved over time, even when the recruits of the *ala* were not generally coming from that given region anymore.

Résumé : Hercules Magusanus dans le camp militaire de l'*ala I Batavorim milliaria* en Războieni-Cetate (distr. Alba, Roumanie)

L'article se concentre sur une inscription dédiée à Hercule Magusanus. L'épigraphe a été découvert à Războieni-Cetate (Alba, RO), le site où l'*ala I Batavorum milliaria* a été stationné en *Dacia* entre (environ) 130–271 après J.-C. Le monument date très probablement de la première moitié du 3e siècle. Parallèlement à la découverte sur place des imports de céramiques en provenance du Rhin, la présence de cette divinité indique un substrat culturel batave du village, préservé au fil du temps, même lorsque la plupart des recrues de l'*ala* ne venaient plus de cette région.

Anschriften der Verfasser:

Alexander Rubel
Institutul de Arheologie
al Academiei Române, Filiala Iași
Strada Codrescu 6
RO–700479 Iași
rubel@arheo.ro

Rada Varga
Institutul de Studii Avansate StarUBB
Universitatea Babeș-Bolyai
Moților 11
RO–400001 Cluj-Napoca
rada.varga@ubbcluj.ro

Abbildungsnachweis:
Abb. 1: Carsten Mischka (Erlangen). – *Abb. 2:* Carsten Mischka (Erlangen). – *Abb. 3:* Rada Varga (Klausenburg / Cluj). – *Abb. 4:* Romeo Ionescu (Archäologisches Institut Iași). – *Abb. 5:* Rada Varga (Klausenburg / Cluj). – *Abb. 6:* Rada Varga (Klausenburg / Cluj).

Romano-Frankish interaction in the Lower Rhine frontier zone from the late 3rd to the 5th century – Some key archaeological trends explored

By Nico Roymans and Stijn Heeren

Keywords: Lower Rhine / frontier / depopulation / Franks / migration / gold / foederati
Schlagworte: Niederrhein / Grenze / Entvölkerung / Franken / Migration / Gold / foederati
Résumé: Rhin inférieur / frontière / dépeuplement / Francs / migration / or / foederati

Introduction[1]

The fall of the Western Roman Empire and its causes are among the most heavily debated topics in European history and archaeology. The negative view of decline and fall, inspired by the title of Edward Gibbon's seminal work "Decline and Fall of the Roman Empire" (1776–1788), prevailed during the 19th and 20th centuries, but by the end of the 20th century more nuanced interpretations of the Late Roman period began to appear. Many scholars employing the term Late Antiquity see the period from the late 2nd to the 7th century in Western Europe as one of transformation from the Roman to the Carolingian empire and describe the various changes in neutral terms rather than the pejorative vocabulary of decline[2].

Probably the most important of all aspects of the end of the Western Roman Empire is the role played by 'barbarians', meaning non-Romans from outside the empire. In general, there are currently two prevailing views on this issue: firstly, one that stresses a great degree of relatively peaceful accommodation of barbarian groups by Rome, following initial violent interventions[3]; and a second view which stresses a more destructive role and settlement by conquest, ratified by western imperial authorities after the territories had already been invaded and de facto lost. Scholars like Peter Heather, Bryan Ward-Perkins, and Jean-Michel Carrié consider external barbarian violence as the prime force behind the fall of the Roman West and they criticise the theory that the empire "was quietly 'transformed' by the peaceful 'accommodation' into it of some Germanic barbarians"[4].

---

[1] This publication was prepared in the framework of the "Portable Antiquities of the Netherlands" (PAN) project, and finished during the research project "Constructing the Limes. Employing citizen science to understand borders and border systems from the Roman period until today", which are both funded by the Netherlands Organisation for Scientific Research (NWO) and carried out by the Archaeological Department of *Vrije Universiteit Amsterdam*, with other partners; C-LIMES is led by the University of Utrecht. We thank Mrs Annette Visser (New Zealand) for correcting the English of this paper. We are also grateful to two anonymous reviewers and Alexander Gramsch (RGK Frankfurt) for their comments on an earlier draft of this paper. It goes without saying that responsibility for the contents remains with us.

[2] For a historiographic overview, see HALSALL 2007, 19–22, and more recently CARRIÉ 2014.

[3] GOFFART 1980; HALSALL 2014.

[4] WARD-PERKINS / HEATHER 2005 (blog) cited by CARRIÉ 2014, 195; WARD-PERKINS 2005; HEATHER 2005.

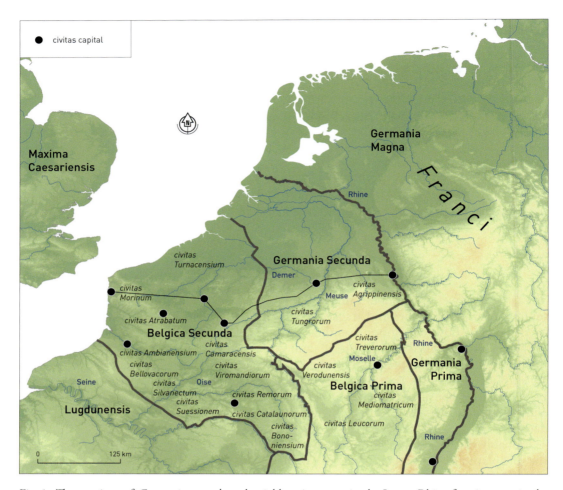

Fig. 1. The province of *Germania secunda* and neighbouring areas in the Lower Rhine frontier zone in the 4th century.

Northern Gaul and the Lower Rhine frontier area provide evidence to advance these discussions. The region has a solid tradition of archaeological research and has yielded a considerable amount of well-excavated and published fieldwork. While the degree of archaeological visibility and preservation differs according to region, the quality ranges from adequate to excellent. Because the region experienced widespread depopulation in the 3rd century, we are able to conduct a very effective study of immigration in the late 4th / early 5th century. In addition, collaboration between professional archaeologists and private metal detector hobbyists has resulted in the discovery, investigation and publication of significant Late Roman gold hoards and other items of interest[5]. The Lower Rhine frontier zone is therefore an interesting 'laboratory region' that can sharpen our picture of the complex Romano-barbarian interaction.

[5] ROYMANS / HEEREN 2015; 2017. See also below. – Metal detection has been legal in the Netherlands under certain conditions since 2016. Detectorists are obliged to ask permission from the landowner and to report their finds. They are allowed to keep the objects in private possession, but in case of hoards they have to share the financial value with the landowner. Metal finds by private individuals are published online: https://www.portable-antiquities.nl.

The aim of this paper is to present a regional case study in which we focus on some key aspects of this discussion and explore the potential of new evidence and methodologies. Our study area *(Fig. 1)* roughly corresponds to the northern half of the province of *Germania inferior*, later called *Germania secunda*, and the adjacent areas east and north of the Lower Rhine. We will discuss four interrelated topics: 1. the substantial depopulation of the countryside in the northern half of *Germania secunda* in the later 3rd century, 2. the nature of the Lower Rhine *limes* in the later 3rd and 4th centuries, 3. the influx of new immigrant groups after the late 4th century, and 4. the draining of Roman gold to the Lower Rhine frontier in the late 4th and early 5th centuries. We will discuss the available archaeological evidence and interpret it against the background of the historical information. We will end with some concluding remarks and prospects for further research. Most of the primary data for this study were gathered in a joint research programme (2012–2016) carried out by *Vrije Universiteit Amsterdam* and Ghent University[6].

The Late Roman frontier dynamics in the Lower Rhine region are closely linked to the appearance of the Franks. 'Franks' is a Roman collective label for a series of smaller tribes in the areas east and north of the Lower Rhine who had long maintained relations with the Roman Empire. However, it wasn't until the early 3rd century that they were given this name by the Roman authorities. The ethnicon 'Franks' was subject to change in the course of time, with the 3rd-century meaning differing considerably from that of the 5th century[7]. We will argue below that Frankish groups underwent a serious social transformation during the Late Roman period and that this was closely tied to increasing interaction – both friendly and hostile – with the Roman Empire. Viewed from this perspective, the Franks can be regarded as a 'product' of the complex dynamics in the Late Roman frontier[8].

Depopulation in the northern half of Germania inferior (later 3rd century)

From the late 1st to the 3rd centuries, the area south and west of the Lower Rhine belonged to the Roman province of Germania inferior. The province most likely had six civitates: the Agrippinensis around Cologne, the Traianensis with its capital of Xanten, the Tungri with Tongres as its centre, the Batavi around Nijmegen, the Cananefates with a capital at Voorburg near modern-day The Hague, and the Frisiavones in the coastal area of Zeeland[9]. Apart from official towns and secondary centres, the settlements in the countryside of this Roman province are especially well researched. Villas, usually comprising several stone buildings, form the majority of rural settlements in the fertile loess areas in the south of the province, while non-villa settlements with native-style wooden byre-houses are the norm in the northern zone, which consists mainly of sandy soils and riverine clay soils[10]. In this northern zone many of the rural settlements have a common occupation history involving foundation around the start of the 1st century AD, a peak in the late 1st or early 2nd century, and gradual decline in the late 2nd and 3rd century *(Fig. 2)*[11]. Evidence of occupation in the subsequent early and middle part of the 4th century is very scarce, although some sites were reoccupied in the very late 4th or early 5th century (see below section "The influx of new immigrant groups"). This sequence, which was similar for many settlements, is based primarily on dendrochronological dates for well constructions, and secondly on

---

[6] See HEEREN 2016 and the various contributions to ROYMANS et al. 2017.
[7] DE BOONE 1954; ZÖLLNER 1970; TAAYKE 2003.
[8] On the study of Roman frontiers, see WHITTAKER 1994 and BREEZE 2018.
[9] BOGAERS 1972; RAEPSAET-CHARLIER 2002/2003.
[10] ROYMANS 1996; VOS 2009; HEEREN 2009; HABERMEHL 2013; ROYMANS et al. 2015.
[11] HEEREN 2009, 49–74; 2015, 281–287; VOS 2009, 89–99; DE BRUIN 2019, 213–219.

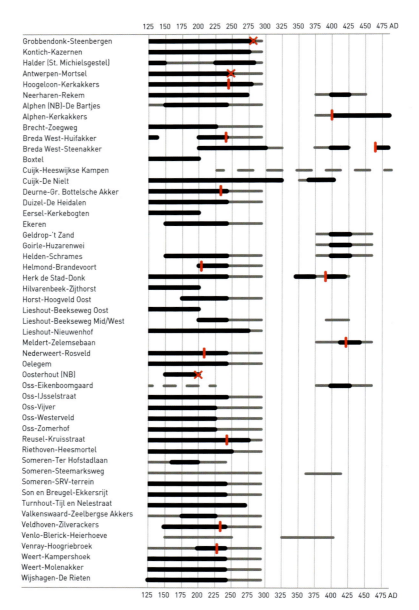

Fig. 2. Diagram of habitation trajectories of excavated rural settlements in the Meuse-Demer-Scheldt region in the later Roman period, showing an almost complete depopulation in the later 3rd century and partial resettlement in the late 4th / early 5th century. – Thick horizontal line: habitation period with good evidence; thin horizontal line: dating evidence uncertain; red cross: supposed fire catastrophe; vertical red line: dendrochronological date of well.

mobile finds (e. g. coins, brooches, and pottery) from the settlements and their cemeteries. Radiocarbon dates are rare and are generally not sufficiently precise. The dendrochronological dates available for the area show building activity into the AD 240s and perhaps the 250s, followed, as noted, by new foundations in around 400[12].

[12] Heeren 2015; additions in Heeren 2017, tab. 1.

Archaeologists usually argue that *absence of evidence* is not the same as *evidence of absence*. There are, however, additional arguments to support the view that in the Dutch river area and the Dutch-Belgian Meuse-Demer-Scheldt area, rural habitation had largely disappeared in the 4th century. As well as a lack of dendrochronological dates or *mobilia* for the early and middle part of the 4th century, built structures are also absent from that period, whereas later ones are present. House plans dated to c. AD 400 can be traced in several settlements (see below section "The influx of new immigrant groups"), but these lack obvious features belonging to the intermediate period[13]. This contrasts with sites north of the Rhine, where dendrochronology has identified early and mid-4th-century activity and where plentiful house plans and *mobilia* have been found[14].

The large-scale rural depopulation as described for the Dutch river and Meuse-Demer-Scheldt areas, which were essentially non-villa landscapes, is less complete for the villa landscapes in the Cologne hinterland and the Belgian Hesbaye region. Several survey studies of the number of active sites in the Cologne hinterland are available, yielding data that are to some extent quantifiable. Of older date but still useful is the study by Gechter and Kunow[15], who used pottery from fieldwalking campaigns and excavations as an approximation of the habitation history of several subregions. Thus the Kevelaerer Donkenland and Kempener Lehmplatte, located north of the road from Tongres to Cologne, show declining site numbers from the 2nd to the 3rd century and a complete absence of sites in the 4th century. Regions south of the road, such as the Cologne-Bonner Niederterrasse, Rheinbacher Lössplatte, and Hürtgener Hochfläche, show survival rates (the number of 4th-century villas compared to early 3rd-century ones) of 71%, 52%, and 30% respectively. For the Aldenhovener Platte, Lenz argues that the decline had already begun about the middle of the 3rd century, but this was followed by a gradual rise in the number of sites in the late 3rd, early 4th, and later 4th centuries[16]. The number of early 4th-century villas (21) is for 56% of that of early 3rd-century sites.

Concluding our discussion of the countryside, we see large-scale depopulation in the north of the province. There are regional differences: in the Cananefatian area and the north of the Tungrian area (between the rivers Meuse, Demer, and Scheldt; *Figs 1–2*), depopulation seems to have been near complete. In the Batavian and Traianensian area, this is less certain. Built structures dating to the early and middle part of the 4th century have not been documented so far, but the presence there of 4th-century coins and crossbow brooches does indicate some activity. It is important to note that the depopulation thesis is based on a large number of excavated settlements, which provide the best quality information. The uncertainties come from the less well studied areas.

We should be aware that the depopulation of the countryside was paralleled by a serious urban decline or even collapse in our study region. The *civitas* centres of Voorburg *(Forum Hadriani)* and Nijmegen-Waterkwartier *(Ulpia Noviomagus)* were abandoned more or less completely in the late 3rd century. A new military fortification was erected at Nijmegen-Valkhof[17], a site recently identified as *Castra Herculis*, one of the forts said to have been restored by Julian II in 358[18]. At Xanten and Tongres new defensive circuits were set around a much reduced core[19]. Since Xanten was probably now called *Tricensimae*, a

---

[13] Berkvens / Taayke 2004; Heeren 2017, 155–159.
[14] Large settlements, for instance Van Es 1967; Taayke et al. 2012. – Dendrochronology: Erdrich 1998 cites several examples.
[15] Gechter / Kunow 1986.
[16] Lenz 1999.
[17] De Jonge et al. 2006; Van Enckevort / Thijssen 2002; Willems et al. 2009.
[18] Verhagen / Heeren 2016.
[19] Otten / Ristow 2008; Vanderhoeven 2017.

or even the collapse of the *limes*[34]. As a rule, a reduction in the military occupation of the *limes* led directly to incursions and pillaging by Frankish war bands, while periods of recovery were linked to successful campaigns against Frankish groups by Postumus (c. 260), Probus (c. 275), Constantius (c. 290), Constantine I (c. 310), and Julian II (c. 358)[35]. These campaigns sought not only to ensure the security of the Gallic hinterland, but also to keep the strategic Rhine corridor open to allow grain shipments from Britannia (see below).

We may conclude with certainty that there was no definitive *Limesfall* in the Lower Rhine area in the late 3rd century. The notion of the *limes* as a series of forts along the Rhine was alive and well throughout the 4th century[36]. However, archaeology shows that the former Rhine *limes* was never fully restored and we should assume brief periods of collapse. Barbarian pressure on the *limes* has proved to be a phenomenon of all periods, and is linked to the martial ideology and practices of Frankish groups for whom taking part in raids was considered a normal stage in the cosmologically embedded life-cycle of male individuals[37].

How this picture of a fitful functioning of the *limes* in the 4th century exactly relates to the described dramatic population decline and collapse of the civil infrastructure in the northern half of *Germania secunda*, still remains unclear. It is evident, however, that the large-scale abandonment of productive agricultural land must have made the Roman military along the Rhine highly dependent on grain imports from other provinces for its food supply. In this context we should probably understand the historical reports of British grain shipments to the Rhine area in the Late Roman period[38].

The influx of new immigrant groups (late 4th / early 5th century)

Returning to the dendrochronological dates of well constructions in the southern Netherlands (note 12 and *Fig. 2*), we will now focus on the new wells that appeared more than a century after the cessation of well construction in the 3rd century. There are some *post quem* dates of AD 383 and 393; the first reliable *ad quem* dates are 401–403 (Alphen-Kerkakkers) and 402 (Gennep-Stamelberg).

For the Meuse-Demer-Scheldt region, attempts have been made to connect new immigration with a passage in Ammian Marcellinus in which emperor Julian II negotiated with the *Salii* about access to the area (AD 358). However, both the outcome of the talks (Julian II defeated the Salians and sent them away) and the date argue against such an early immigration[39]. In fact, the archaeological dates between 401 and 402 tie in perfectly with another passage in the written sources, where Claudianus states that *magister militum* Stilicho withdrew all the Rhine troops to northern Italy in the winter of 401/402 to defend Honorius, who was besieged by Goths in Milan and Ravenna[40]. It is quite possible that Stilicho regulated the access of allied groups to the area rather than allow uncontrolled immigration by whoever came after the Roman withdrawal.

---

[34] For an overview of the military history of the Lower Rhine region in the Late Roman period, see the excellent thesis of De Boone 1954. Cf. also Van Es 1981, 47–54 (largely relying on De Boone 1954); Zöllner 1970, 1–43; Fischer 2020, 218–219; 262–273.

[35] De Boone 1954; Lendering / Hunink 2018, 32–33; 60; Zöllner 1970; Fischer 2020, 262–273. – Constantine III (c. 408) is the last Roman general who is credited with restoring the Rhine border. Zos. hist. 6,3,3 reports that Constantine 'let rule a total security along the Rhine, which has been neglected since the age of Julian'.

[36] Paneg. 6,11.

[37] Bazelmans 1999, 3–9.

[38] Heeren 2018.

[39] Amm. 17,8. – Cf. Theuws 2008 for comments on the unfounded connection of immigrant settlements to this historical event.

[40] Claud. Goth. 419–429.

Archaeologists usually argue that *absence of evidence* is not the same as *evidence of absence*. There are, however, additional arguments to support the view that in the Dutch river area and the Dutch-Belgian Meuse-Demer-Scheldt area, rural habitation had largely disappeared in the 4th century. As well as a lack of dendrochronological dates or *mobilia* for the early and middle part of the 4th century, built structures are also absent from that period, whereas later ones are present. House plans dated to c. AD 400 can be traced in several settlements (see below section "The influx of new immigrant groups"), but these lack obvious features belonging to the intermediate period[13]. This contrasts with sites north of the Rhine, where dendrochronology has identified early and mid-4th-century activity and where plentiful house plans and *mobilia* have been found[14].

The large-scale rural depopulation as described for the Dutch river and Meuse-Demer-Scheldt areas, which were essentially non-villa landscapes, is less complete for the villa landscapes in the Cologne hinterland and the Belgian Hesbaye region. Several survey studies of the number of active sites in the Cologne hinterland are available, yielding data that are to some extent quantifiable. Of older date but still useful is the study by Gechter and Kunow[15], who used pottery from fieldwalking campaigns and excavations as an approximation of the habitation history of several subregions. Thus the Kevelaerer Donkenland and Kempener Lehmplatte, located north of the road from Tongres to Cologne, show declining site numbers from the 2nd to the 3rd century and a complete absence of sites in the 4th century. Regions south of the road, such as the Cologne-Bonner Niederterrasse, Rheinbacher Lössplatte, and Hürtgener Hochfläche, show survival rates (the number of 4th-century villas compared to early 3rd-century ones) of 71%, 52%, and 30% respectively. For the Aldenhovener Platte, Lenz argues that the decline had already begun about the middle of the 3rd century, but this was followed by a gradual rise in the number of sites in the late 3rd, early 4th, and later 4th centuries[16]. The number of early 4th-century villas (21) is for 56% of that of early 3rd-century sites.

Concluding our discussion of the countryside, we see large-scale depopulation in the north of the province. There are regional differences: in the Cananefatian area and the north of the Tungrian area (between the rivers Meuse, Demer, and Scheldt; *Figs 1–2*), depopulation seems to have been near complete. In the Batavian and Traianensian area, this is less certain. Built structures dating to the early and middle part of the 4th century have not been documented so far, but the presence there of 4th-century coins and crossbow brooches does indicate some activity. It is important to note that the depopulation thesis is based on a large number of excavated settlements, which provide the best quality information. The uncertainties come from the less well studied areas.

We should be aware that the depopulation of the countryside was paralleled by a serious urban decline or even collapse in our study region. The *civitas* centres of Voorburg *(Forum Hadriani)* and Nijmegen-Waterkwartier *(Ulpia Noviomagus)* were abandoned more or less completely in the late 3rd century. A new military fortification was erected at Nijmegen-Valkhof[17], a site recently identified as *Castra Herculis*, one of the forts said to have been restored by Julian II in 358[18]. At Xanten and Tongres new defensive circuits were set around a much reduced core[19]. Since Xanten was probably now called *Tricensimae*, a

---

[13] Berkvens / Taayke 2004; Heeren 2017, 155–159.
[14] Large settlements, for instance Van Es 1967; Taayke et al. 2012. – Dendrochronology: Erdrich 1998 cites several examples.
[15] Gechter / Kunow 1986.
[16] Lenz 1999.
[17] De Jonge et al. 2006; Van Enckevort / Thijssen 2002; Willems et al. 2009.
[18] Verhagen / Heeren 2016.
[19] Otten / Ristow 2008; Vanderhoeven 2017.

reference to the 30th legion, and the surrounding countryside appears to have been empty, it seems likely that Xanten had lost its function as a *civitas* capital and now served as a military base[20].

The causes of the depopulations are unclear. Warfare, barbarian incursions, and the Plague of Cyprian are mentioned in the written sources for this period (see the section below), while modern authors have proposed soil degradation[21]. However, these factors could never account for the swift and near total depopulation of large regions. While they may have caused population decline and partial depopulation, forced abandonment would explain the sheer scale of the phenomenon in some areas and it better fits the evidence. An interesting hypothesis is that we are dealing here with the forced deportation of groups to interior Gaul by the Roman authorities[22]. Late Roman panegyrics mention two cases of deportations of Frankish groups from the northern *civitates* in the late 3rd century by respectively Maximian Augustus and Constantius Chlorus[23]. These Franks had settled shortly before in Batavia, where they were commanded by a leader from that area, possibly Postumus[24]. Interestingly, there is another source in which secessionist emperor Postumus and his successor Victorinus are said to have commanded 'Celts and Franks' as auxiliary troops[25]. Local indigenous groups (Batavians?) may have made common cause with the Frankish newcomers and consequently received the same punishment from the Roman authorities after the defeat of the secessionist 'Gallic' empire, namely deportation as *laeti* to interior Gaul. Their destination may well have been the Picardie in Northern France, since *Praefecti laetorum Batavorum*, interpreted as recruiting officers of Batavian *laeti* are attested at Arras and Noyon[26].

No Limesfall on the Lower Rhine in the later 3rd century?

Among German archaeologists in particular, the end of Roman military installations along the borders of the northern provinces in the third quarter of the 3rd century is regarded as one of the pillars of archaeological chronology[27]. The theory of *Limesfall* was first established for the Obergermanisch-Raetische *limes* and was based on three key elements:

1. the *limes* forts were attacked and overrun by Germanic peoples;
2. the events were dated to the years AD 259/260 because of the lack of coins struck after that period; and
3. the forts and hinterland were deserted for ever after. In addition to coins, the main evidence came from destruction layers at the intensively researched fort of Niederbieber. Published in the 19th century, this theory is still widely accepted[28].

---

[20] Otten / Ristow 2008.
[21] Groenman-Van Waateringe 1980.
[22] Heeren 2015, 290–294.
[23] Paneg. 8,21 (Constantio Caesari); Paneg. 6,5,3 (Constantino Augusto). – Cf. De Boone 1954, 57–58.
[24] Paneg. 6,5,3 (Constantino Augusto). – Lendering / Hunink 2018, 60. – The Franks were led by a former native of the place (Latin: *quondam alumnus*), probably of Roman provincial origin. Nixon / Rodgers [= Paneg.] suggest that reference is made here to Carausius the Menapian, however both W. J. De Boone (1954, 36; 42; 58) and Willem Willems (1986, 249) strongly argue that he should be identified as Postumus. Identified as Menapian, Carausius cannot easily be named an *alumnus* of the Franks.
[25] Hist. Aug. 6,2: *tyranni triginta*.
[26] Not. dign. occ. XLII, 217.
[27] Schallmayer 1987.
[28] Hoffmann 1823; Ritterling 1901; cf. Heeren 2016.

A similar *Limesfall*, with a slightly different chronology, was postulated from the 1980s onwards for the Lower Rhine area[29]. Coin series in this area usually break off around AD 270 or 275. However, destruction layers like the one at Niederbieber on the Obergermanisch-Raetische *limes* are absent along the Lower Rhine. Past published evidence of destruction cannot withstand a critical re-evaluation: destruction is often *assumed* in the case of the presence of a coin hoard, interpreted as a *Versteckhort*, or as ending coin lists.

Coin dates are a recurring element in these interpretations. All too often the end of a coin list was simply interpreted as the end of habitation at a site. Yet the supply of fresh coin was unstable: the 'soldier-emperors' of the mid-3rd century, for instance, reigned only very briefly or were mainly in the field, and therefore struck limited quantities of coin. Although the last soldier-emperors and Tetrarchs did strike larger numbers of coins in the late 3rd century, these were distributed in the East and barely reached the north-west provinces; in fact, older coins continued to circulate in these frontier zones during this period. Thus an absence of certain coins doesn't automatically mean the cessation of coin circulation and therefore doesn't need to imply site abandonment[30].

Added to that, many ceramic and brooch types were previously dated with reference to the assumed *Limesfall*. The literature on the dating of material culture is littered with the end date of AD 260 or 270/275, all because of the coin-based assumption that sites terminated around this time. If we abandon the basic assumption of stable coin supply and combine the lack of burnt layers with the knowledge that old coinage would have filled the gap left by an interrupted, failed or minimal supply, we can conclude that the theory of *Limesfall* is less well-substantiated, at least for the Lower Rhine *limes*. The material culture of the so-called Niederbieber horizon needs to be re-dated to include the late 3rd century[31].

Coins were again struck in large numbers by the government of Constantine I and distributed widely. Coin issues of his reign are very numerous at sites showing ample activity in the early 4th century, such as Tongres[32] and the Nijmegen-Valkhof area[33]; also numerous are issues from the subsequent Valentinianic period. In this period of ubiquitous coinage, the absence of coins at a site is indeed significant, and discontinuous use must be considered a serious option.

However, rejection of the *Limesfall* theory doesn't mean that the Lower Rhine *limes*, with its line of forts, continued to function unchanged. There is surprisingly little evidence dating to the early and middle part of the 4th century. Based on coins and crossbow brooches, there was some activity at a small number of forts in the present-day Netherlands. In Germany, starting at Xanten and moving south, we see a rise in the number of castella with proven 4th-century activity. For the early 5th century, the number of archaeological finds at *limes* sites increases once again along all parts of the Lower Rhine, with brooches, hairpins, and belt components from the period around AD 400 being relatively common. The nature of this later activity is unclear. The castella may have been manned by proper garrisons, but it is also possible that local groups used the former military forts in different ways.

But how does this archaeological picture of the Lower Rhine *limes* relate to the information we have from historical sources? The military history of the late 3rd and 4th centuries can best be characterised as a fitful period in which times of strength, when Roman military influence was restored in the Lower Rhine region, alternated with times of weakness

---

[29] See various contributions in Horn 1987 and Bechert / Willems 1995.
[30] Stribrny 1989; Kropff / Van der Vin 2003.
[31] Heeren 2016, 197–203.
[32] Vanderhoeven 2017.
[33] Steures 2012.

or even the collapse of the *limes*[34]. As a rule, a reduction in the military occupation of the *limes* led directly to incursions and pillaging by Frankish war bands, while periods of recovery were linked to successful campaigns against Frankish groups by Postumus (c. 260), Probus (c. 275), Constantius (c. 290), Constantine I (c. 310), and Julian II (c. 358)[35]. These campaigns sought not only to ensure the security of the Gallic hinterland, but also to keep the strategic Rhine corridor open to allow grain shipments from Britannia (see below).

We may conclude with certainty that there was no definitive *Limesfall* in the Lower Rhine area in the late 3rd century. The notion of the *limes* as a series of forts along the Rhine was alive and well throughout the 4th century[36]. However, archaeology shows that the former Rhine *limes* was never fully restored and we should assume brief periods of collapse. Barbarian pressure on the *limes* has proved to be a phenomenon of all periods, and is linked to the martial ideology and practices of Frankish groups for whom taking part in raids was considered a normal stage in the cosmologically embedded life-cycle of male individuals[37].

How this picture of a fitful functioning of the *limes* in the 4th century exactly relates to the described dramatic population decline and collapse of the civil infrastructure in the northern half of *Germania secunda*, still remains unclear. It is evident, however, that the large-scale abandonment of productive agricultural land must have made the Roman military along the Rhine highly dependent on grain imports from other provinces for its food supply. In this context we should probably understand the historical reports of British grain shipments to the Rhine area in the Late Roman period[38].

The influx of new immigrant groups (late 4th / early 5th century)

Returning to the dendrochronological dates of well constructions in the southern Netherlands (note 12 and *Fig. 2*), we will now focus on the new wells that appeared more than a century after the cessation of well construction in the 3rd century. There are some *post quem* dates of AD 383 and 393; the first reliable *ad quem* dates are 401–403 (Alphen-Kerkakkers) and 402 (Gennep-Stamelberg).

For the Meuse-Demer-Scheldt region, attempts have been made to connect new immigration with a passage in Ammian Marcellinus in which emperor Julian II negotiated with the *Salii* about access to the area (AD 358). However, both the outcome of the talks (Julian II defeated the Salians and sent them away) and the date argue against such an early immigration[39]. In fact, the archaeological dates between 401 and 402 tie in perfectly with another passage in the written sources, where Claudianus states that *magister militum* Stilicho withdrew all the Rhine troops to northern Italy in the winter of 401/402 to defend Honorius, who was besieged by Goths in Milan and Ravenna[40]. It is quite possible that Stilicho regulated the access of allied groups to the area rather than allow uncontrolled immigration by whoever came after the Roman withdrawal.

---

[34] For an overview of the military history of the Lower Rhine region in the Late Roman period, see the excellent thesis of De Boone 1954. Cf. also Van Es 1981, 47–54 (largely relying on De Boone 1954); Zöllner 1970, 1–43; Fischer 2020, 218–219; 262–273.

[35] De Boone 1954; Lendering / Hunink 2018, 32–33; 60; Zöllner 1970; Fischer 2020, 262–273. – Constantine III (c. 408) is the last Roman general who is credited with restoring the Rhine border. Zos. hist. 6,3,3 reports that Constantine 'let rule a total security along the Rhine, which has been neglected since the age of Julian'.

[36] Paneg. 6,11.

[37] Bazelmans 1999, 3–9.

[38] Heeren 2018.

[39] Amm. 17,8. – Cf. Theuws 2008 for comments on the unfounded connection of immigrant settlements to this historical event.

[40] Claud. Goth. 419–429.

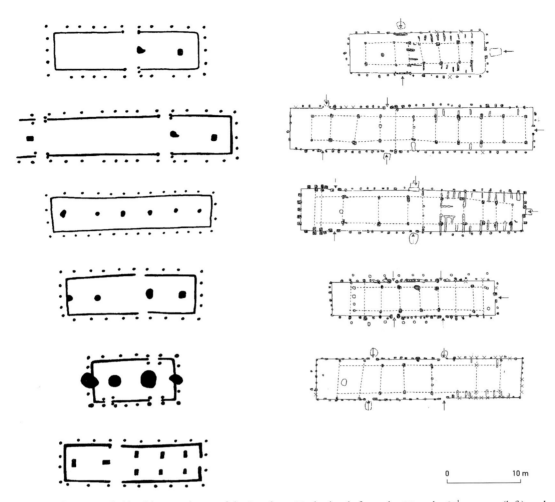

Fig. 3. The two-aisled building tradition of the Southern Netherlands from the 1st to the 3rd century (left) and the three-aisled building tradition of the Northern Netherlands from the 2nd to the 5th century (right).

Where did the immigrants come from? And can this question even be answered? In the German tradition of *ethnische Deutung*, certain weapons (*francisca* – Frankish axe) and metal dress accessories (such as tutulus brooches) would point to Germanic (Frankish or Saxon) settlers from the east bank of the Rhine[41]. However, several theory-oriented archaeologists, mainly in Anglophone literature, have argued that style change doesn't automatically mean a shift of peoples. Trade and even imitation could account for the presence of foreign objects or styles, with no true migration being involved. Furthermore, several of the objects deemed 'Germanic' were actually produced in the frontier zone as a result of close interaction, rather than imported from distant parts[42]. This process – in which new forms and practices arise through interaction – produces what has been called a 'mixed civilisation'[43].

---

[41] For instance WERNER 1958; BÖHME 1974; BÖHME 1999.

[42] HALSALL 2000.

[43] WHITTAKER 1994, 222–237.

Fig. 4. The settlement of Breda-Steenakker with two-aisled farmsteads dated to the 2nd and 3rd centuries to the west and a three-aisled farmhouse with several sunken huts to the northeast. Handmade pottery dates these features to the Late Roman period.

It is archaeologically impossible to make an ethnic distinction between 'barbarians' and 'Romans' on the basis of military dress and weapons alone. "The armies confronting one another in the 5th century, whether they fought for or against Rome, increasingly resembled one another as regards their varied composition and weaponry, which had become standardized through mutual borrowing"[44].

While the above doubts are in themselves justified, we find more clues to the northern origin of the new settlers in the former Roman province. Apart from the *mobilia* (both the jewellery and pottery are of Rhine-Weser-Germanic style), clues are provided by the house plans and diet of the new settlers. As stated earlier, rural settlements both within and outside the Roman province consisted of wooden longhouses with a living area for people

[44] Carrié 2014, 185.

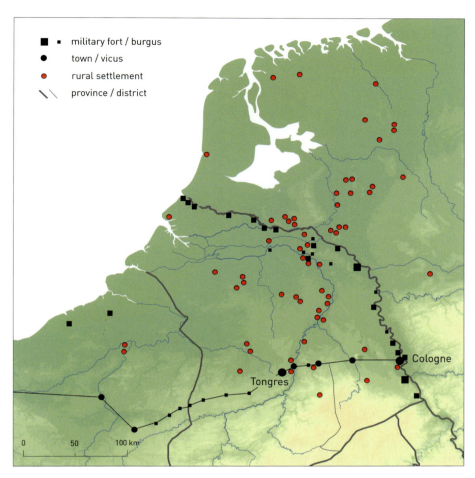

Fig. 5. Distribution of excavated Germanic-type settlements (red dots) with three-aisled farmhouses and sunken huts from the late 4th and early 5th centuries in *Germania Secunda*.

and a byre-section for animals. North of the Rhine, these farmhouses had a three-aisled structure (*Fig. 3*, right)[45]. This was the case from prehistory throughout the Roman period until well into the Middle Ages. Sunken-featured outbuildings, wooden constructions with a lowered floor, were the norm here in the Roman and medieval periods. In the area south of the Meuse, the dominant building style from the 1st to the 3rd centuries was a two-aisled structure, involving a single row of interior posts, for both farmhouses and outbuildings (*Fig. 3*, left)[46]. The same building style predominated in the Dutch Eastern river area, but some farmhouses also show a combination of a two-aisled part in the living quarters and a three-aisled part in the byre-section. In the newly emerging settlements south of the Rhine in around AD 400, three-aisled main buildings and sunken huts are well in evidence (*Figs 4–5*).

The well-known maxim 'you are what you eat' shows the close connection between foodways and identity. Rye has been found in considerable quantities in the immigrant settlements of the late 4th and 5th centuries. Before that time it was unknown as a culti-

---

[45] Waterbolk 1999; 2009.   [46] Schinkel 1994.

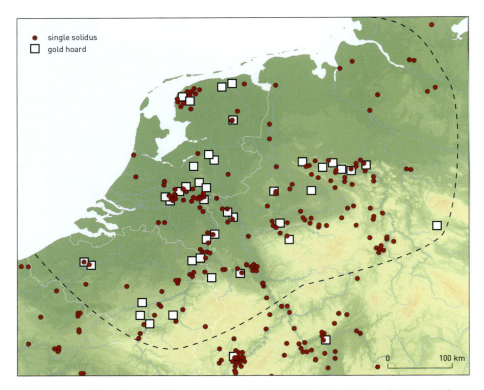

Fig. 6. General distribution of Late Roman gold finds (AD 364–460) in the Lower Rhine frontier zone between the Scheldt and Elbe.

vated plant in the area south of the Rhine. From the 1st century onwards, however, rye was an important part of the diet in the communities inhabiting the sandy soils north of the Rhine. This is an important clue to the northern origin of the settlers south of the Rhine[47].

Helena Hamerow and Stefan Burmeister have warned against using house types as indicators of migration, since the house forms chosen as the main residence in immigration areas may change rapidly as a result of social interaction with other groups, as happened for instance in Anglo-Saxon England and early-modern America[48]. House types were easily copied and are therefore not necessarily indicative of the original provenance of the inhabitants. The same holds true for pottery styles and decoration. However, pottery production techniques, the interior division of houses and the style of outbuildings are less directed by outward appearance and more by habitus[49]. Such 'internal' cultural practices belonged to the 'private' domain and remained relatively stable for a long period and are therefore more suitable for studying migration.

However, Hamerow and Burmeister's examples concerned immigration in areas that were already inhabited. In our case study, the immigration area was severely depopulated in the 3rd century, probably in the third quarter of that century, which means that the area had been almost completely uninhabited for over a century when the new immigration began in around AD 400. An obvious first point to make is that a new population in an almost entirely depopulated area was by definition made up of immigrants. A second point

---

[47] HIDDINK 1999, 157–162; HEEREN 2017, 163 (including table and references).

[48] HAMEROW 1999; BURMEISTER 2000.

[49] HAMEROW 1999; BURMEISTER 2000.

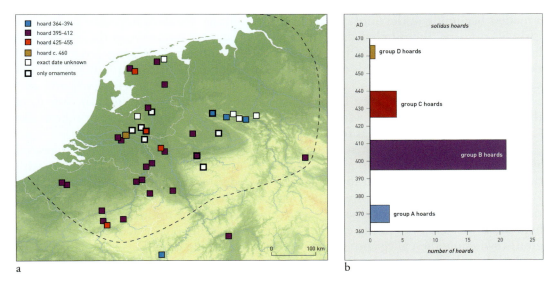

Fig. 7. Distribution of Late Roman gold hoards (a) and their chronology in the Lower Rhine frontier region and surroundings (b).

is that social interaction with autochthonous groups was minimal, which explains why the house types didn't change, as was the case in the examples mentioned above. Given the clues from mobile finds, house architecture and diet, it is highly likely that the immigrants came from the area north of the Rhine, probably from the Elbe-Weser triangle or the region of modern Drenthe and the Veluwe, where we find the best examples of the house plans of the immigrant settlements[50].

Further support for the settlers' origins is provided by the political context of Roman payments to external allies, as shown by studying gold hoards in combination with the written sources. This is the subject of the next section.

Gold flows to the Lower Rhine frontier and the payment of foederati (late 4th/5th century)

The Lower Rhine frontier zone of the late 4th and early 5th centuries has yielded evidence of an exceptional influx of Roman gold in the form of solidi and ornaments that were probably made from melted-down solidi. This gold flow is a key dataset for analysing the nature and chronology of the Romano-Frankish interaction in the context of the Late Roman frontier, and it also allows us to make interesting comparisons with the historical evidence.

Of significance is firstly the general distribution pattern of the Roman gold finds *(Fig. 6)*. This reveals an entirely open Rhine frontier, with dense concentrations of find spots on both the western and eastern sides of the Lower Rhine. Assuming that the total weight of the documented gold finds represents less than 1% of the original gold influx, we can make a rough estimate of the total volume of gold flow to the Lower Rhine frontier: this must have been several thousand kilos at least[51].

The temporal patterning of the gold influx also prompts some interesting observations. Four phases can be distinguished, based on the dating of the hoard finds *(Fig. 7)*. We see

[50] Van Es 1967; Hiddink 1999; Waterbolk 2009; Taayke et al. 2012   [51] Roymans 2017, 57.

a modest beginning in the third quarter of the 4th century, followed by a clear peak in the early 5th century. The number then falls again in the second quarter of the 5th century, before disappearing after a final hoard in c. 460 AD. Another interesting development is the spatial distribution of hoards over time. The earliest hoards are concentrated in the area east of the Rhine. In the early 5th century they went on to cover the area both east and west of the Lower Rhine. Of interest is the entirely rural distribution pattern of the hoards in the province of *Germania secunda*; they are absent from contemporary urban centres like Cologne and Tongres, as well as from Roman military sites.

How should we interpret these patterns in social and historical terms? There is general agreement that gold circulation in Late Roman frontier regions was closely bound up with the military sphere as payment to soldiers and to leaders of federate war bands[52]. The Late Roman gold influx into the Lower Rhine region reflects payments by the Roman authorities or usurpers to Frankish allies *(foederati)* in exchange for military support. It is our hypothesis that the peak in the early 5th-century gold influx relates above all to Frankish groups switching their allegiance to the usurper Constantine III (407–411) in 407[53]. This marked the collapse of effective Roman state authority in the Lower Rhine region. There is indeed some historical evidence that Constantine III's power relied heavily on his alliances with Germanic groups, in particular the Franks[54].

The study of changing gold flows can tell us about shifts in the power balance between the Western Roman Empire and Frankish groups. The practice of Roman authorities making substantial gold payments from the late 4th century onwards points to the free, federate status of Frankish groups. They make regular appearances in the historical sources as military allies and troop providers, and they succeeded in exploiting to maximum advantage the civil wars between the emperor and usurpers like Constantine III. The gold payments began in about 370 to groups who at that time were still living east of the Lower Rhine. In the early 5th century they also inhabited areas west of the Rhine, probably as a consequence of formal land allotments by Roman authorities during this phase.

This system of regular gold payments sparked a process of increasing complexity and social hierarchy within the Frankish groups. Frankish warlords became more powerful as their traditional tribal power base began to rely increasingly on external gold payments from the Romans, enabling them to reward their followers. Historical sources tell us that Frankish groups were already supplying troops to the Roman army in the late 3rd and early 4th centuries. This happened following their defeat by the Romans, when they had become subordinate peoples, or *laeti*. The power differences were still highly asymmetrical during this phase, as also evidenced in historical reports about the forced deportation of defeated Frankish groups to depopulated regions in interior Gaul[55]. The Roman authorities do not appear to have made gold payments to Frankish groups in this early phase. As mentioned above, payments seem to have only started in the third quarter of the 4th century. The weakening power of the Roman state meant the relative strengthening of that of Frankish groups, whose status in this phase shifted from subordinates or *laeti* into federates[56].

A final question is how to explain the exceptional concentration of Late Roman gold in the Lower Rhine frontier zone compared with the relative rarity of gold finds in the southern provinces of Roman Gaul. Factors such as the impact of specific hoarding practices

---

[52] Martin 2009; Roymans 2017; Fischer / Lind 2017; Guest 2008.
[53] Roymans 2017.
[54] Zos. hist. 6,2,4; Greg. Tur. Franc. 2,9. – Cf. Hoffmann 1995, 560; Roymans 2017, 68.
[55] See above note 23.
[56] De Boone 1954, 129.

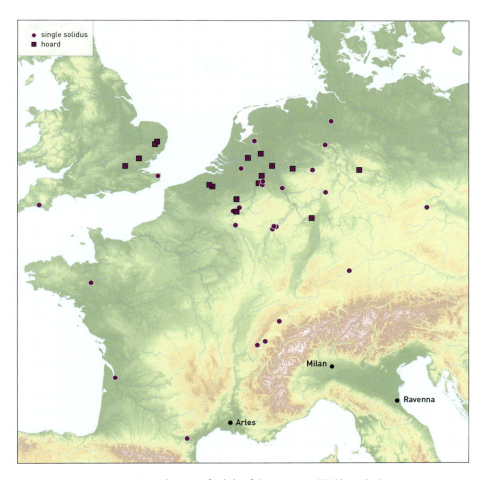

Fig. 8. Distribution of solidi of Constantine III (407–411).

among Germanic groups may have played a role here. The most attractive explanation, however, relates to another aspect of the federate status of Frankish groups: their exemption from paying taxes. We find almost no gold hoards in southern Gallo-Roman regions, despite the fact that there too the solidus was the standard currency in all manner of transactions in the public and private spheres. One example is the distribution of *solidi* of Constantine III *(Fig. 8)*; almost no gold coins of him are known outside the Lower Rhine frontier zone. There is a remarkable absence of hoards around Arles, where Constantine III had his residence for three years. This brings us to a methodological issue: the distribution map of solidus hoards and isolated solidi doesn't show a representative picture of the true circulation of these coins. In the Roman provinces the government was able to maintain its revenue by constantly creaming off the gold circulation through taxation. The exceptional density of gold finds in the Lower Rhine frontier zone indicates that, as *foederati*, the Frankish groups living there fell outside the Roman taxation cycle. Here the gold flowed in one direction only, and in principle was forever lost to the Roman treasury[57].

---

[57] ROYMANS 2017, 75.

It is interesting to compare this flow of Roman gold to Germanic groups in the Lower Rhine frontier with precious metal flows to groups in other parts of "barbarian" Europe. Fraser Hunter and Kenneth Painter point to the different situation in northern Britain and Ireland where Roman *Hacksilber* dominates the picture[58]. It is difficult to explain this macro-regional patterning in precious metal flows to Late Roman frontiers. Hunter and Painter suggest that it may have been a matter of deliberate local choice; British groups may have preferred payment in silver above gold. More plausible, however, seems a link with the much more threatening power position of Frankish groups which enabled them to negotiate a special federate status with the Roman authorities in return for substantial gold payments and permission to settle on Roman land in *Germania secunda*[59].

Conclusion

While the different themes discussed above each generate interesting interpretations, it is only when viewed in conjunction that they produce a novel picture of the nature and dynamics of Romano-Frankish interaction. We can identify two stages in the process of decline and collapse of Roman state power and infrastructure in *Germania secunda*. The first clearly relates to the '3rd-century crisis'. The archaeological evidence shows that the depopulation of the countryside in the later 3rd century went hand in hand with urban decline, or even urban collapse, in the northern half of *Germania secunda*. This rural and urban collapse, rather than attacks by barbarian groups, may have been the reason for the military authorities to leave the Lower Rhine unguarded, for at least some decades. Although the situation stabilised in the early 4th century, the central government lacked the power and finances to fully restore the Rhine *limes*, and the countryside was not repopulated, nor was there a move towards local urban reform. The *civitates* of the *Batavi*, *Cananefates*, and *Frisiavones* were dispensed with once and for all as tax-paying administrative units, and the same is true of the northern half of the *civitas Tungrorum*.

The second stage covers the early 5th century, which saw the definitive collapse of the Roman administrative system in this area. The influx of Roman gold into the Lower Rhine region was clearly linked to the archaeologically documented settlement of Frankish immigrant groups. The gold payments to Frankish groups symbolise the weakened power of the Roman state, which had definitely lost its imperial monopoly on military violence at the frontier; they paid external groups to uphold the frontier. This case study also shows that the settlement of Frankish immigrant groups in the frontier zone was substantial and should not be underestimated.

In the coming years, new research will be able to corroborate and further hone the picture outlined above, primarily with regard to proof (rather than an assumption) of migration. A first pilot project started in 2018, based on material from some recently excavated Late Roman sites and burials in the Dutch river delta[60]. The focus – from an anthropological perspective – will be on investigating the farmsteads, burials, and material culture of first-generation Germanic settlers. A wide range of science-based methods is used, including strontium isotope studies of human remains. We expect inhumed individuals to show isotope values consistent with both the Holocene Dutch river delta and other landscape types, while the style of house plans and the provenance of the mobile material culture provide additional clues to their origins.

---

[58] Hunter / Painter 2013; Hunter / Painter 2017, 91–94.

[59] Roymans 2017, 74–76.

[60] Heeren, NWO-funded research 342-60-004.

Above all, this case study shows how interaction between the 'Franks' and the western Empire from the 3rd to 5th centuries changed the 'Franks' and their roles and status, and in turn changed provincial Roman society. We argue for a model of an increasing power position of Frankish warlords, who used Roman gold and booty to consolidate and expand their war bands, thereby cutting across traditional tribal boundaries. In the 5th century, successful Frankish warlords had settled in former Roman territory, where they sought to legitimise their renewed power position by assuming Roman offices. This finally resulted in them claiming both a barbarian and Roman identity, a phenomenon that is so strikingly expressed in the famous Childeric burial at Tournai. Even in the 5th century, however, the Franks did not yet form a tribal state or well-defined ethnic group, but should rather be seen as an external collective name for a number of Germanic groups in the Lower Rhine frontier zone[61].

The view that the collapse of the Roman state in the northern frontier province was caused by the destructive power of Frankish invaders is too simplistic and therefore unsatisfactory. Other factors were also important, in particular civil war between the imperial government and the long series of usurpers in Gaul, who used external barbarian forces as their instrument of power. This latter practice implied a weakening of the Roman position in two ways: the independent agency of barbarian groups could lead to unexpected outcomes, and – since these forces required gold payments that subsequently remained outside the Roman taxation cycle – this imposed a heavy burden on the imperial treasury. The long-term history of the Franks shows that they were allies of Rome just as often as they were its opponents, and we know of several examples of Frankish leaders acting as Roman military commanders. A shortage of manpower and financial resources as a result of a long period – decades or even centuries – of endemic warfare led to the slow suffocation of the imperial system. Although there is now general agreement that many elements of the 'ancient world' survived the 5th century in the 'successor states', there is no doubt that the Western Empire definitively collapsed as a state system in 476, and that military pressure from Germanic groups was one of the key variables in that process. Thus both 'decline and fall' and 'transformation of the ancient world' are interesting perspectives in the debate and can be considered two sides of the same coin[62]. The Lower Rhine case study shows that archaeology can contribute to this debate by providing powerful regional bodies of evidence. In this respect, our optimism that we can make progress in a centuries-old debate is justified.

Finally, this case study shows that we have to address the issue of 'barbarian' movement and settlement of groups from *Germania magna* into the Empire in a nuanced way, allowing for both the more peaceful as well as the more destructive paradigms, depending on the groups involved. On the one hand we have the highly destructive mode of movement. Examples are the Rhine crossing of Vandals, Alans, and Sueves in 405–406 and their wanderings towards Brittany, Iberia, and Africa[63]. On the other hand there is the agreed movement and settlement of barbarian groups in alliance with official or usurper consent[64]. This 'agreed relatively peaceful settlement as federates' view would fit best with the short-distance move and settlement of Frankish groups to *Germania secunda* in the early 5th century, where they were probably paid by Constantine III to help defend the Rhine frontier. However, in the 3rd century we saw the usurper-supported immigration, followed

---

[61] Theuws 2008, 766–767; Esmonde Cleary 2013, 376–386.
[62] Roymans / Heeren 2017; Heeren 2017.
[63] Kulikowski 2000.
[64] Goffart 1980.

by official rejection and deportation – presented as a reaction against violent incursion in the written sources. Therefore, the Lower Rhine area presents case studies of various ways and receptions of immigration in different periods[65].

References

Primary sources

Amm.
> J. C. Rolfe, Ammianus Marcellinus. Rerum gestarum, Libri qui supersunt. Loeb Classical Library 300/315/331 (Cambridge, London 1950/1940/1939).

Claud. Goth.
> M. Plattnauer, Claudianus. Bello Gothico. Loeb Classical Library 135/136 (Cambridge, London 1956). doi: https://www.doi.org/10.4159/DLCL.claudian_claudianus-gothic_war.1922.

Greg. Tur. Franc.
> L. Thorpe, The history of the Franks by Gregory of Tours. Penguin Classics L295 (Harmondsworth 1974).

Hist. Aug.
> J. P. Callu / O. Desbordes / St. Ratti / R. Turcan / F. Paschoud, Histoire Auguste. Collect. Univ. France, Sér. Latine 305/311/335/359/365 (Paris 1992).

Not. dign.
> O. Seeck, Notitia dignitatum accedunt Notitia Urbis Constantinopolitanae et Laterculum Prouinciarum (Berlin 1876, reprint Frankfurt 1962).

Paneg.
> C. E. V. Nixon / B. S. Rodgers, In Praise of Later Roman Emperors: The Panegyrici Latini. Introduction, Translation and Historical Commentary with the Latin Text of R. A. B. Mynors. Transformation Class. Heritage 21 (Berkeley 1994). doi: https://doi.org/10.1525/9780520342828.

Zos.
> F. Paschoud, Zosimus, Historia Nova / Histoire nouvelle. Collect. Univ. France (Paris 1971).

Modern works

Bazelmans 1999
> J. Bazelmans, By Weapons made Worthy. Lords, Retainers and their Relationship in Beowulf. Amsterdam Arch. Stud. 5 (Amsterdam 1999).

Bechert / Willems 1995
> T. Bechert / W. J. H. Willems (eds), De Romeinse rijksgrens tussen Moezel en Noordzeekust (Utrecht 1995).

Berkvens / Taayke 2004
> R. Berkvens / E. Taayke, Germanische Besiedlung der späten Kaiserzeit in Breda-West (NL). In: M. Lodewijckx (ed.), Bruc Ealles Well. Archaeological Essays Concerning the Peoples of North-West Europe in the First Millennium AD. Acta Arch. Lovaniensia Monogr. 15 (Leuven 2004) 37–46.

Bogaers 1972
> J. E. Bogaers, *Civitates* und *Civitas*-Hauptorte in der nördlichen *Germania inferior*. Bonner Jahrb. 172, 1972, 310–333. doi: https://doi.org/10.11588/bjb.1972.1.83560.

Böhme 1974
> H. W. Böhme, Germanische Grabfunde des 4. und 5. Jahrhunderts zwischen unterer Elbe und Loire. Studien zur Chronologie und Bevölkerungsgeschichte. Münchner Beitr. Vor- u. Frühgesch. 19 (Munich 1974).

Böhme 1999
> H. W. Böhme, Sächsische Söldner im römischen Heer. Das Land zwischen Ems und Niederelbe während des 4. und 5. Jahrhunderts. In: F. Both / H. Aouni (eds), Über allen Fronten. Nordwestdeutschland

---

[65] We owe thanks to one of the anonymous reviewers for highlighting this issue.

zwischen Augustus und Karl dem Grossen. Sonderausstellung Staatliches Museum für Naturkunde und Vorgeschichte Oldenburg vom 3. Oktober bis 21. November 1999. Arch. Mitt. Nordwestdeutschland Beih. 26 (Oldenburg 1999) 49–73.

De Boone 1954
W. J. De Boone, De Franken van hun eerste optreden tot de dood van Childerik (Groningen 1954).

Breeze 2018
D. Breeze, The value of studying Roman frontiers. Theoretical Roman Arch. Journal 1,1, p. 1, 2018, 1–17. doi: https://doi.org/10.16995/traj.212.

De Bruin 2019
J. De Bruin, Border Communities at the Edge of the Roman Empire: Processes of Change in the *Civitas Cananefatium*. Amsterdam Arch. Stud. 28 (Amsterdam 2019).

Burmeister 2000
St. Burmeister, Archaeology and migration. Approaches to an archaeological proof of migration. Current Anthr. 41, 2000, 539–567. doi: https://doi.org/10.1086/317383.

Callu / Loriot 1990
J.-P. Callu / X. Loriot, La dispersion des aurei en Gaule romaine sous l'Empire, II: L'or monnayé. Cahiers Ernest Babelon 3 (Juan-les-Pins 1990).

Carrié 2014
J.-M. Carrié, The historical path of "Late Antiquity". From transformation to rupture. In: R. Lizzi Testa (ed.), Late Antiquity in Contemporary Debate (Newcastle upon Tyne 2014) 174–214.

Van Enckevort / Thijssen 2002
H. Van Enckevort / J. R. A. M. Thijssen, Cuijk. Een regionaal centrum in de Romeinse tijd (Utrecht 2002).

Van Enckevort et al. 2017
H. Van Enckevort / J. Hendriks / M. Nicasie, Nieuw licht op donkere eeuwen. De overgang van de laat-Romeinse tijd naar de vroege middeleeuwen in Zuid-Nederland. Nederlandse Arch. Rapporten 58 (Amersfoort 2017). https://www.cultureelerfgoed.nl/binaries/cultureelerfgoed/documenten/publicaties/2017/01/01/nieuw-licht-op-donkere-eeuwen/NAR058_Nieuw_licht_in_donkere_eeuwen_web.pdf (last access: 5 May 2022).

Erdrich 1998
M. Erdrich, Terra Nigra-Fußschalen wie Chenet 342 oder Gellep 273: eine salisch-fränkische Keramikgattung. Germania 76, 1998, 875–884.

Van Es 1967
W. A. Van Es, Wijster. A Native Village Beyond the Imperial Frontier, AD 150–425 (Groningen 1967).

Van Es 1981
W. A. van Es, De Romeinen in Nederland³ (Bussum 1981).

Esmonde Cleary 2013
S. Esmonde Cleary, The Roman West, AD 200–500. An Archaeological Study (Cambridge 2013). doi: https://doi.org/10.1017/CBO9781139043199.

Fischer / Lind 2017
S. Fischer / L. Lind, Late Roman Gaul. Survival amidst collapse? In: T. Cunningham / J. Driessen (eds), Crisis to Collapse. The Archaeology of Social Breakdown. Aegis 11 (Louvain 2017) 99–130.

Fischer 2020
Th. Fischer, Gladius. Roms Legionen in Germanien. Eine Geschichte von Caesar bis Chlodwig (Munich 2020).

Gechter / Kunow 1986
M. Gechter / J. Kunow, Zur ländlichen Besiedlung des Rheinlandes in römischer Zeit. Bonner Jahrb. 186, 1986, 377–396. doi: https://doi.org/10.11588/bjb.1986.0.63853.

Goffart 1980
W. Goffart, Barbarians and Romans, AD 418–584: the Techniques of Accommodation (Princeton 1980).

Groenman-Van Waateringe 1980
W. Groenman-van Waateringe, The disastrous effect of the Roman occupation. In: R. Brandt / J. Slofstra (eds), Roman and Native in the Low Countries. Spheres of Interaction. BAR Internat. Ser. 184 (Oxford 1983) 147–157.

Guest 2008
P. Guest, Roman gold and Hun kings. The use and hoarding of solidi in the late fourth and fifth centuries. In: A. Bursche /

R. Ciołek / R. Wolters (eds), Roman Coins Outside the Empire. Ways and Phases, Contexts and Functions. Proceedings of the ESF / SCH Exploratory Workshop, Radziwiłł Palace, Nieborów (Poland), 3–6 September 2005. Collect. Moneta 82 (Wetteren 2008) 295–307.

Habermehl 2013
D. S. Habermehl, Settling in a Changing World. Villa Development in the Northern Provinces of the Roman Empire. Amsterdam Arch. Stud. 19 (Amsterdam 2013). doi: https://doi.org/10.1515/9789048518227.

Halsall 2000
G. Halsall, Archaeology and the late Roman frontier in northern Gaul. The so-called "Föderatengräber" reconsidered. In: W. Pohl / H. Reimitz (eds), Grenze und Differenz im frühen Mittelalter. Phil.-Hist. Kl. Sitzungsber. 287 = Forsch. Gesch. Mittelalter 1 (Vienna 2000) 167–180.

Halsall 2007
G. Halsall, Barbarian Migrations and the Roman West 376–568[2] (Cambridge 2007).

Halsall 2014
G. Halsall, Two worlds become one. A "counter-intuitive" view of the Roman Empire and "Germanic" migration. German Hist. 32,4, 2014, 515–532. doi: https://doi.org/10.1093/gerhis/ghu107.

Hamerow 1999
H. Hamerow, Anglo-Saxon timber buildings: the continental connection. In: H. Sarfatij / W. J. H. Verwers / P. J. Woltering (eds), In Discussion with the Past: Archaeological Studies presented to W. A. van Es (Amersfoort 1999) 119–128.

Heather 2005
P. Heather, The Fall of the Roman Empire. A New History (Basingstoke 2005).

Heeren 2009
St. Heeren, Romanisering van rurale gemeenschappen in de civitas Batavorum. De casus Tiel-Passewaaij. Nederlandse Arch. Rapporten 36 (Amersfoort 2009). https://research.vu.nl/en/publications/romanisering-van-rurale-gemeenschappen-in-de-civitas-batavorum-de (last access: 5 May 2022).

Heeren 2015
St. Heeren, The depopulation of the Lower Rhine region in the 3rd century. An archaeological perspective. In: N. Roymans / T. Derks / H. A. Hiddink (eds), The Roman Villa of Hoogeloon and the Archaeology of the Periphery. Amsterdam Arch. Stud. 22 (Amsterdam 2015) 271–294.

Heeren 2016
St. Heeren, The theory of 'Limesfall' and the material culture of the late 3rd century. Germania 94, 2016, 185–209. doi: https://doi.org/10.11588/ger.2016.39072.

Heeren 2017
St. Heeren, From Germania Inferior to Germania Secunda and beyond. A case study of migration, transformation and decline. In: Roymans et al. 2017, 149–178.

Heeren 2018
St. Heeren, Military might for a depopulated region? Interpreting the archaeology of the Lower Rhine area in the Late Roman period. In: P. Diarte-Blasco / N. Christie (eds), Interpreting Transformations of People and Landscapes in Late Antiquity and the Early Middle Ages: Archaeological Approaches and Issues (Oxford 2018) 137–147.

Hiddink 1999
H. A. Hiddink, Germaanse samenlevingen tussen Rijn en Weser. 1ste eeuw voor–4de eeuw na Chr. (Amsterdam 1999).

Hoffmann 1823
C. F. Hoffmann, Ueber die Zerstörung der Römerstädte an dem Rheine zwischen Lahn und Wied (Neuwied 1823). https://www.digitale-sammlungen.de/view/bsb10047758?page=1 (last access: 5 May 2022).

Hoffmann 1995
D. Hoffmann, Edowech und Decimius Rusticus. In: F. E. Koenig / S. Rebetez (eds), Arculiana. Ioanni Boegli anno sexagesimo quinto feliciter peracto amici discipuli collegae socii dona dederunt A. D. XIIII kalendas decembris MDCCCCLXXXXV [Festschrift zum 65. Geburtstag von Hans Bögli] (Avenches 1995) 559–568.

Horn 1987
H. G. Horn (ed.), Die Römer in Nordrhein-Westfalen (Stuttgart 1987).

Hunter / Painter 2013
F. Hunter / K. Painter (eds), Late Roman Silver. The Traprain Treasure in Context (Edinburgh 2013).

Hunter / Painter 2017
F. Hunter / K. Painter, *Hacksilber* in the Late Roman and Early Medieval world. Economics, frontier politics and imperial legacies. In: Roymans et al. 2017, 81–96.

De Jonge et al. 2006
W. De Jonge / J. Bazelmans / D. de Jager (eds), Forum Hadriani. Van Romeinse stad tot monument (Utrecht 2006).

Kropff / van der Vin 2003
A. Kropff / J. van der Vin, Coins and continuity in the Dutch river area at the end of the third century AD. European Journal Arch. 6, 2003, 55–87. doi: https://doi.org/10.1179/eja.2003.6.1.55.

Kulikowski 2000
M. Kulikowski, Barbarians in Gaul, usurpers in Britain. Britannia 31, 2000, 325–345. doi: https://doi.org/10.2307/526925.

Lendering / Hunink 2018
J. Lendering / V. Hunink, Het visioen van Constantijn. Een gebeurtenis die de wereld veranderde (Utrecht 2018).

Lenz 1999
K.-H. Lenz, Siedlungen der römischen Kaiserzeit auf den Aldenhovener Platte. Rhein. Ausgr. 45 (Cologne, Bonn 1999).

Martin 2009
M. Martin, Edelmetallhorte und -münzen des 5. Jahrhunderts in Nordgallien und beiderseits des Niederrheins als Zeugnisse der frühfränkischen Geschichte. In: M. Müller / S. Ristow (eds), Grabung, Forschung, Präsentation. Xantener Ber. 15 (Mainz 2009) 1–50. https://apx.lvr.de/media/apx/lvr_archaeologischer_park_/forschung/publikationen/Xantener_Berichte_Band_15.pdf (last access: 9 May 2022).

Otten / Ristow 2008
T. Otten / S. Ristow, Xanten in der Spätantike. In: M. Müller / H.-J. Schalles / N. Zieling (eds), Colonia Ulpia Traiana. Xanten und sein Umland in römischer Zeit. Xantener Ber., Sonderbd. 1 (Mainz 2008) 549–582.

Raepsaet-Charlier 2002/2003
M.-Th. Raepsaet-Charlier, Vielfalt und kultureller Reichtum in den *civitates* Niedergermaniens. Bonner Jahrb. 202/203, 2002/2003, 35–56. doi: https://doi.org/10.11588/bjb.2002.0.42249.

Ritterling 1901
E. Ritterling, Zwei Münzfunde aus Niederbieber. Bonner Jahrb. 107, 1901, 95–131. doi: https://doi.org/10.11588/bjb.1901.0.36774.

Roymans 1996
N. Roymans, The sword or the plough. Regional dynamics in the romanisation of Belgic Gaul and the Rhineland area. In: N. Roymans (ed.), From the Sword to the Plough. Three Studies on the Earliest Romanisation of Northern Gaul. Amsterdam Arch. Stud. 1 (Amsterdam 1996) 9–126.

Roymans 2017
N. Roymans, Gold, Germanic *foederati* and the end of imperial power in the Late Roman North. In: Roymans et al. 2017, 57–80.

Roymans / Heeren 2015
N. Roymans / St. Heeren, A Late Roman solidus hoard with Hacksilber from Echt (the Netherlands). Arch. Korrbl. 45, 2015, 549–562.

Roymans / Heeren 2017
N. Roymans / St. Heeren, The Late Roman solidus hoard from Lienden (prov. Gelderland/NL). A window on Romano-Frankish contacts in the mid-5th-century Lower Rhine region. Arch. Korrbl. 47, 2017, 397–412.

Roymans et al. 2015
N. Roymans / T. Derks / H. Hiddink (eds), The Roman Villa of Hoogeloon and the Archaeology of the Periphery. Amsterdam Arch. Stud. 22 (Amsterdam 2015).

Roymans et al. 2017
N. Roymans / St. Heeren / W. De Clerq (eds), Social Dynamics in the Northwest Frontiers of the Late Roman Empire. Beyond Decline or Transformation. Amsterdam Arch. Stud. 26 (Amsterdam 2017).

Schallmayer 1987
E. Schallmayer, Zur Chronologie in der

römischen Archäologie. Arch. Korrbl. 17, 483–497.

SCHINKEL 1994
C. SCHINKEL, Zwervende erven. Bewoningssporen in Oss-Ussen uit bronstijd, ijzertijd en Romeinse tijd. Opgravingen 1976–1986 [PhD thesis Univ. Leiden] (Leiden 1994).

STEURES 2012
D. C. STEURES, The Late Roman Cemeteries of Nijmegen. Stray Finds and Excavations 1947–1983. Nederlandse Oudheden 17 (Amersfoort, Nijmegen 2012). https://www.cultureelerfgoed.nl/binaries/cultureelerfgoed/documenten/publicaties/2013/01/01/the-late-roman-cemeteries-of-nijmegen/NO17_The_Late_Roman_Cemeteries_of_Nijmegen_part_1_Text_webA.pdf; https://www.cultureelerfgoed.nl/binaries/cultureelerfgoed/documenten/publicaties/2013/01/01/the-late-roman-cemeteries-of-nijmegen/NO17_The_Late_Roman_Cemeteries_of_Nijmegen_part_2_Figures_webA.pdf (last access: 9 May 2022).

STRIBRNY 1989
K. STRIBRNY, Römer rechts des Rheins nach 260 n. Chr. Kartierung, Strukturanalyse und Synopse spätrömischer Münzreihen zwischen Koblenz und Regensburg. Ber. RGK 70, 1989, 351–505.

TAAYKE 2003
E. TAAYKE, Wir nennen sie Franken und sie lebten nördlich des Rheins, 2.–5. Jh. In: E. Taayke / J. H. Looijenga / O. H. Harsema / H. R. Reinders (eds), Essays on the Early Franks. Groningen Arch. Stud. 1 (Groningen 2003) 1–23.

TAAYKE et al. 2012
E. TAAYKE / CH. PEEN / M. VAN DER HARST-VAN DOMBURG / W. K. VOS, Ede vol erven. Germaanse bewoning op de rand van een wereldrijk (500 voor Chr. tot 500 na Chr.) (Leiden 2012).

THEUWS 2008
F. THEUWS, ‚terra non est'. Zentralsiedlungen der Völkerwanderungszeit im Maas-Rhein-Gebiet. In: H. Steuer / V. Bierbrauer (eds), Höhensiedlungen zwischen Antike und Mittelalter von den Ardennen bis zur Adria. RGA Ergbd. 58 (Berlin, New York 2008) 765–793. doi: https://doi.org/10.1515/9783110211856.765.

VANDERHOEVEN 2017
A. VANDERHOEVEN, The Late Roman town of Tongeren. In: ROYMANS et al. 2017, 127–148.

VERHAGEN / HEEREN 2016
J. VERHAGEN / ST. HEEREN, 'Castra Herculis: de naam van de Romeinse militaire versterking in Nijmegen herontdekt'. Westerheem 65, 2016, 239–49.

VOS 2009
W. K. VOS, Bataafs platteland. Het Romeinse nederzettingslandschap in het Nederlandse Kromme-Rijngebied. Nederlandse Arch. Rapporten 35 (Amersfoort 2009). https://research.vu.nl/en/publications/bataafs-platteland-het-romeinse-nederzettingslandschap-in-het-ned (last access: 9 May 2022).

WARD-PERKINS 2005
B. WARD-PERKINS, The Fall of Rome and the End of Civilization (Oxford 2005).

WARD-PERKINS / HEATHER 2005
B. WARD-PERKINS / P. HEATHER, The Fall of Rome. An Author Dialogue. OUPblog. December 22, 2005. https://blog.oup.com/2005/12/the_fall_of_rom_2/ (last access: 20 May 2022).

WATERBOLK 1999
H. T. WATERBOLK, From Wijster to Dorestad and beyond. In: H. Sarfatij / W. J. H. Verwers / P. J. Woltering (eds), In Discussion with the Past. Archaeological Studies presented to WA van Es (Zwolle 1999) 107–117.

WATERBOLK 2009
H. T. WATERBOLK, Getimmerd verleden. Sporen van voor- en vroeghistorische houtbouw op de zand- en kleigronden tussen Eems en IJssel (Groningen 2008).

WERNER 1958
J. WERNER, Kriegergräber der ersten Hälfte des 5. Jahrhunderts zwischen Schelde und Weser. Bonner Jahrb. 158, 1958, 372–413. doi: https://doi.org/10.11588/bjb.1958.1.81180.

WHITTAKER 1994
D. R. WHITTAKER, Frontiers of the Roman Empire. A Social and Economic Study (London 1994).

WILLEMS 1986
W. J. H. WILLEMS, Romans and Batavians: A Regional Study in the Dutch Eastern River Area (Amersfoort 1986).

WILLEMS et al. 2009
W. J. H. WILLEMS / H. VAN ENCKEVORT / J. R. A. M. THIJSSEN, Romans and Franks: changes in late antiquity. In: W. J. H. Willems / H. van Enckevort (eds), VLPIA NOVIOMAGVS Roman Nijmegen. The Batavian capital at the imperial frontier. Journal Roman Arch., Suppl. 73 (Portsmouth 2009) 95–105.

ZÖLLNER 1970
E. ZÖLLNER, Geschichte der Franken bis zur Mitte des sechsten Jahrhunderts (Munich 1970).

Abstract: Romano-Frankish interaction in the Lower Rhine frontier zone from the late 3rd to the 5th century – Some key archaeological trends explored

This paper presents a case study on the development of the Lower Rhine region from the late 3rd to the 5th century AD. The focus is on the province of *Germania secunda* and the adjacent areas east and north of the Rhine with a special attention for the Romano-Frankish interaction. Four interrelated themes are discussed: 1. the widespread depopulation of the countryside in the northern half of *Germania secunda* in the late 3rd century; 2. the question of the *Limesfall* in the same period; 3. the influx of new Frankish immigrant groups in the late 4th and early 5th century, and 4. the draining of Roman gold to the Lower Rhine frontier in the same phase. On the basis of these developments we gain a better picture of the rise and transformation of Frankish groups. These groups underwent a process of increasing hierarchisation and militarisation during the Late Roman period and this process was closely tied to intense interaction – both friendly and hostile – with the Roman Empire. From this perspective, the Franks can be regarded as a 'product' of the Late Roman frontier.

Zusammenfassung: Römisch-fränkische Interaktion im niederrheinischen Grenzgebiet vom späten 3. bis zum 5. Jahrhundert – Die Untersuchung einiger wichtiger archäologischer Trends

Dieser Beitrag stellt eine Fallstudie zur Entwicklung des Niederrheingebiets vom späten 3. bis zum 5. Jahrhundert n. Chr. vor. Der Schwerpunkt liegt dabei auf der Provinz *Germania secunda* und den angrenzenden Gebieten östlich und nördlich des Rheins mit besonderem Augenmerk auf der römisch-fränkischen Interaktion. Es werden vier miteinander verknüpfte Themen behandelt: 1. die weitgehende Entvölkerung der Landschaft in der nördlichen Hälfte der *Germania secunda* im späten 3. Jahrhundert, 2. die Frage des Limesfalls im selben Zeitraum, 3. der Zustrom neuer fränkischer Einwanderergruppen im späten 4. und frühen 5. Jahrhundert und 4. die Abwanderung des römischen Goldes an die Niederrhein-Grenze in derselben Phase. Auf Grundlage dieser Entwicklungen gewinnen wir ein besseres Bild vom Aufstieg und Wandel der fränkischen Gruppen. Diese Gruppen durchliefen in der spätrömischen Zeit einen Prozess zunehmender Hierarchisierung und Militarisierung, der eng mit einer intensiven – sowohl freundlichen als auch feindlichen – Interaktion mit dem Römischen Reich verbunden war. Aus dieser Perspektive können die Franken als ein „Produkt" der spätrömischen Grenze betrachtet werden.

Résumé : Interactions entre Romains et Francs aux confins du Rhin inférieur de la fin du 3ᵉ au 5ᵉ siècle – Étude de quelques tendances archéologiques importantes

Cette contribution présente une étude de cas portant sur l'évolution territoriale du Rhin inférieur de la fin du 3ᵉ au 5ᵉ siècle ap. J.-C. Elle met l'accent sur la province de *Germania secunda* et les territoires limitrophes à l'est et au nord du Rhin avec une attention particulière portée sur les interactions entre Romains et Francs. On traite ici quatre thèmes étroitement liés : 1. le dépeuplement avancé de la moitié nord de la *Germania secunda* à la fin du 3ᵉ siècle ; 2. la question de la chute du limes à la même époque ; 3. la pénétration d'immigrants francs à la fin du 4ᵉ et au début du 5ᵉ siècle ; 4. la fuite de l'or romain aux frontières du Rhin à la même époque. Ces différentes évolutions permettent d'obtenir une meilleure vue d'ensemble sur l'essor et la transformation des groupes francs. Ces groupes subissent au Bas-Empire un processus de hiérarchisation et de militarisation lié étroitement à d'intenses interactions – tant amicales qu'hostiles – avec l'Empire romain. Vu sous cet angle, on peut considérer que les Francs sont un « produit » de la frontière du Bas-Empire.

Y. G.

Adresses of authors:

Nico Roymans
Vrije Universiteit Amsterdam
Faculteit Geesteswetenschappen
Department of Archaeology, Classics and Near Eastern Studies
De Boelelaan 1105
NL–1081 HV Amsterdam
n.g.a.m.roymans@vu.nl

Stijn Heeren
Portable Antiquities of the Netherlands
Vrije Universiteit Amsterdam
Faculteit Geesteswetenschappen
Department of Archaeology, Classics and Near Eastern Studies
De Boelelaan 1105
NL–1081 HV Amsterdam
s.heeren@vu.nl
https://orcid.org/0000-0001-9265-3882

References of figures:
Fig. 1: after Heeren 2017, fig. 3. – *Fig. 2:* after Heeren 2015, tab. 5, with additions. – *Fig. 3:* after Schinkel 1994, appendix *(left)*; after Waterbolk 1999, 108 fig. 1 *(right)*. – *Fig. 4:* after Berkvens / Taayke 2004, fig. 1. – *Fig. 5:* references for the settlements are available in Heeren 2015; 2017; Van Enckevort et al. 2017. – *Fig. 6:* after Roymans 2017, fig. 1, with additions. – *Fig. 7:* after Roymans 2017, fig. 2, with some additions. – *Fig. 8:* based on data in Callu / Loriot 1990, with additions by the authors.

The cerealisation of the Rhineland: Extensification, crop rotation and the medieval 'agricultural revolution' in the *longue durée*

By Helena Hamerow, Tanja Zerl, Elizabeth Stroud, and Amy Bogaard

Keywords: Early medieval farming / crop rotation / agricultural revolution / crop stable isotopes / functional weed ecology / Lower Rhine basin

Schlagwörter: Frühmittelalterliche Landwirtschaft / Fruchtfolge / Agrarrevolution / stabile Isotope der Kulturpflanzen / funktionale Unkraut-Ökologie / Niederrheinische Bucht

Mots-clés: Début de l'agriculture médiévale / rotation des cultures / révolution agricole / isotopes stables des systèmes agricoles anciens / écologie fonctionnelle des adventices / bassin du Rhin inférieur

Introduction

This paper presents results from a research project (*'Feeding Anglo-Saxon England. The Bioarchaeology of an Agricultural Revolution'* hereafter FeedSax), that aims to generate direct evidence for the cultivation regimes that sustained, between c. AD 800–1200, an exceptionally rapid growth of populations, towns, and markets and enabled landowners to amass considerable wealth. Three key innovations made this increase in overall grain yields possible: two- and three-field crop rotation, which enabled a larger proportion of arable land to be brought under cultivation and winter and summer crops to be grown in the same year; increased use of the mouldboard plough, which allowed farmers to cultivate heavier, more fertile soils; and 'low input' cultivation regimes which maintained the fertility of fields by means of regular, short fallow periods (during which sheep grazed on the stubble and weeds in the fallow field) rather than by intensive manuring and tilling. This allowed farmers greatly to extend the area of land under cultivation by decreasing the amount of input – manure and human labour – per land unit, a process referred to here as 'extensification'. The result was substantially greater overall yields despite a decline in yield per unit of land area. In many parts of northern Europe, these innovations eventually culminated in a variety of forms of open field farming.

While the origins and spread of open fields have been debated for well over a century, existing approaches have had to rely primarily on indirect evidence such as later medieval or post-medieval documents and maps, scatters of pottery sherds associated with manuring, and a small number of early medieval sources such as documents recording grants of land (Renes 2010; Banham / Faith 2014; Hall 2014; Dyer et al. 2018). FeedSax seeks to advance this debate by generating direct evidence for the conditions in which crops were grown using a range of scientific methods. Functional ecological analysis of the weed flora that grew in amongst the crops and was harvested with them was undertaken to assess growing conditions in terms of soil fertility, soil working (disturbance), and the seasonality of crop growth. This approach reveals the net impact of practices such as manuring, tillage, and weeding as well as crop sowing times. Stable isotope ratios in preserved (charred) cereal grains – barley (*Hordeum vulgare* L.), oat (*Avena sativa* L.), and rye (*Secale cereale* L.) – were also measured in order to investigate the degree to which productivity was boosted by manuring, as reflected in soil nitrogen values. This approach can also help establish whether different cereal crops were grown in the same soil conditions, and thus potentially were grown in rotation in the same fields. Faunal remains from excavated medieval settlements and pollen data have also been examined, although these analyses lie outside the scope of the present paper.

FeedSax focuses primarily on evidence from medieval England; however, a collaboration with the *Labor für Archäobotanik* of the University of Cologne has provided an opportunity to analyse hundreds of archaeobotanical samples from the Lower Rhine Basin within the framework of the project. The archaeobotanical samples analysed derive from settlements excavated over many years, mostly in advance of open cast lignite mining to the west of Cologne *(Fig. 1; Tab. 1)*. This is a region where the adoption of the mouldboard plough and three-course rotation are traditionally dated on the basis of written sources – above all Carolingian polyptychs, inventories of the resources owned by royal and monastic estates – to the later 8th and 9th centuries, although fully developed open field farming involving communal management of arable at the village level is generally not thought to have emerged until sometime between the 10th and 13th centuries (HILDEBRANDT 1988; RÖSENER 1992; HENNING 1994; VERHULST 2002, 65; DEVROEY 2003).

This exceptional archive of closely dated crop remains and associated weed assemblages provides a long-term sequence of agricultural change over several millennia against which the medieval data can be assessed. To this end, a functional ecological analysis of the weed flora associated with crops from the Neolithic to the Middle Ages was conducted. The results of these analyses enable us to situate the expansion of cereal cultivation in the heartland of the Carolingian Empire within a much longer chronological framework than is currently possible in England, namely from the introduction of farming in the region in the later 6th millennium BC, through the Iron Age and Roman periods, to the central Middle Ages. In addition, a crop stable isotope analysis of medieval samples was undertaken to investigate crop rotation. This proved to be possible, however, only for the 5th to 8th centuries, as later samples proved to consist largely of single cereals, primarily rye.

The present paper focuses on the results of these analyses and considers where medieval farming fits within a broad trend towards lower input growing conditions that began in later prehistory. In particular, it examines the impact on farming practices of the end of the Roman system of supplying grain to towns and the military, and whether post-Roman farming reverted, as traditionally assumed, to smaller-scale, more intensive cultivation practices (DUBY 1954; WHITE 1962). The origins of systematic crop rotation are also considered, as it is one of several innovations thought to have arisen between the Seine and the Rhine during the 8th and 9th centuries, which ultimately enabled substantial cereal surpluses to be produced. The mobilisation of these surpluses has traditionally been regarded as a major factor in the development of the bipartite manor and the shift of agriculturally based wealth from southern to northern Europe (cf. DUBY 1954; WHITE 1962; see also MITTERAUER 2010). FeedSax provides new, direct evidence against which this chronological sequence can be tested.

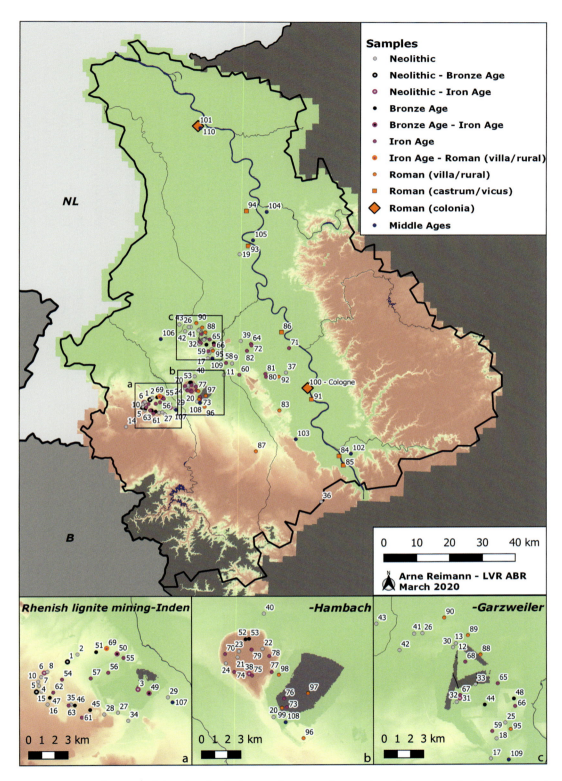

Fig. 1. Topographic map of the Rhineland, showing location of excavations that produced archaeobotanical samples. Coloured gradation from green to brown according to elevation: 0, 85, 170, and 255 m above sea level.

No.	Location	Site (abbrev.)	Phase 1	Phase 2
1	Aldenhoven	AL 1/Ald 1	Neolithic	Bronze Age
2	Aldenhoven 3	Ald 3	Neolithic	
3	Aldenhoven-Langweiler	LW 1	Neolithic	Iron Age
4	Aldenhoven-Langweiler	LW 2	Neolithic	
5	Aldenhoven-Langweiler	LW 3 & 6	Neolithic	Bronze Age
6	Aldenhoven-Langweiler	LW 8	Neolithic	Iron Age
7	Aldenhoven-Langweiler	LW 9	Neolithic	
8	Aldenhoven-Niedermerz	NM 1A	Neolithic	
9	Bedburg-Garsdorf	Gars	Neolithic	
10	Aldenhoven-Langweiler	LW 16	Neolithic	
11	Bergheim-Glesch	Glesch	Neolithic	
12	Borschemich 1 and 6	Borsch 1 & 6	Neolithic	
13	Borschemich 5	Borsch 5	Neolithic	
14	Würselen-Broichweiden	BW 1	Neolithic	
15	Eschweiler-Laurenzberg	LB 7	Neolithic	
16	Eschweiler-Laurenzberg	LB 8	Neolithic	
17	Frimmersdorf 2	FR 2	Neolithic	
18	Frimmersdorf 43	FR 43	Neolithic	
19	Gellep-Stratum, Ossumer Feld Oss		Neolithic	
20	Hambach 11	HA 11	Neolithic	
21	Hambach 260	HA 260	Neolithic	
22	Hambach 32	HA 32	Neolithic	
23	Hambach 502	HA 502	Neolithic	
24	Hambach 8	HA 8	Neolithic	
25	Morken-Harff	Harff	Neolithic	
26	Hochneukirch 33	Hoch 33 & 28	Neolithic	
27	Inden 1	IN 1	Neolithic	
28	Inden 3	IN 3	Neolithic	
29	Inden-Pier, Güldenberg	WW 134	Neolithic	
30	Jüchen 65 B1	Jüc	Neolithic	

No.	Location	Site (abbrev.)	Phase 1	Phase 2
31	Jüchen-Garzweiler	FR 137	Neolithic	Iron Age
32	Jüchen-Garzweiler	FR 98/251	Neolithic	
33	Jüchen-Garzweiler	FR 2001/103	Neolithic	
34	Inden-Lamerdsorf	LAM	Neolithic	
35	Eschweiler-Lohn	LN 3	Neolithic	
36	Meckenheim	Meck	Neolithic	
37	Köln-Mengenich	Meng	Neolithic	
38	Niederzier-Hambach	HA 382	Neolithic	Iron Age
39	Oekoven	Oek	Neolithic	
40	Rödingen	Röd	Neolithic	
41	Wanlo	Wanlo	Neolithic	
42	Wanlo 55	Wanlo 55	Neolithic	
43	Jülich-Wickrath 118	Wick 118	Neolithic	
44	Bedburg-Königshoven	FR 48	Bronze Age	
45	Eschweiler-Lohn	WW 14	Bronze Age	
46	Eschweiler-Lohn	WW 36	Bronze Age	
47	Eschweiler-Lohn	WW 73/09	Bronze Age	
48	Grevenbroich-Gustorf	FR 52	Bronze Age	
49	Inden-Altdorf	WW 127	Bronze Age	Iron Age
50	Jülich-Bourheim	WW 111	Bronze Age	Iron Age
51	Jülich-Bourheim	WW 93/53	Bronze Age	
52	Jülich-Güsten	HA 82/457	Bronze Age	
53	Titz-Rödingen	HA 514	Bronze Age	
54	Aldenhoven-Niedermerz	NM 16	Iron Age	
55	Aldenhoven-Pattern	WW 94/169	Iron Age	
56	Aldenhoven-Pattern	WW 94/7	Iron Age	
57	Aldenhoven-Pattern	WW 88/131	Iron Age	
58	Bedburg-Königshoven	FR 3	Iron Age	
59	Bedburg-Königshoven	FR 51	Iron Age	
60	Bergheim	FR 74	Iron Age	

No.	Location	Site (abbrev.)	Phase 1	Phase 2
61	Eschweiler-Dürwiss	WW 41	Iron Age	
62	Eschweiler-Laurenzberg	WW 51	Iron Age	
63	Eschweiler-Lohn	WW 33 & 34	Iron Age	
64	Frixheim-Anstel	Frix	Iron Age	
65	Grevenbroich-Gustorf	Gust	Iron Age	
66	Jüchen-Garzweiler	FR 84/88	Iron Age	
67	Jüchen-Garzweiler	FR 2000/89	Iron Age	
68	Jüchen-Garzweiler	FR 2007/2	Iron Age	
69	Jülich-Bourheim	WW 94/376	Iron Age	Roman (*villa* / rural)
70	Jülich-Welldorf	HA 503	Iron Age	
71	Köln-Worringen Blumenberg	Blum	Iron Age	
72	Nettesheim-Butzheim	Nett	Iron Age	
73	Niederzier	HA 510	Iron Age	
74	Niederzier-Hambach	HA 490	Iron Age	
75	Niederzier-Hambach	HA 511	Iron Age	
76	Niederzier-Hambach	HA 512	Iron Age	
77	Niederzier-Steinstraß	HA 59	Iron Age	
78	Niederzier-Steinstraß	HA 407	Iron Age	
79	Niederzier-Steinstraß	HA 513	Iron Age	
80	Pulheim-Brauweiler	PR 2005/5000	Iron Age	
81	Pulheim-Sinthern	PR 2003/5002	Iron Age	
82	Rommerskirchen	Rom	Iron Age	
83	Aachen-Süsterfeldstraße	Aac	Roman (*villa* / rural)	
84	Bonn, *Legionslager*	Bo	Roman (*castrum* / *vicus*)	
85	Bonn, *vicus* IKBB	PR 2006/5000	Roman (*castrum* / *vicus*)	
86	Dormagen-Römerstraße	Do	Roman (*castrum* / *vicus*)	
87	Erftstadt-Friesheim	Fries	Roman (*villa* / rural)	
88	Jüchen-Belmen	FR 129	Roman (*villa* / rural)	
89	Jüchen-Kamphausen	Jü	Roman (*villa* / rural)	

No.	Location	Site (abbrev.)	Phase 1	Phase 2
90	Jüchen-Neuotzenrath	PR 1999/113	Roman (*villa* / rural)	
91	Köln-Alteburg	FB 1998.001	Roman (*castrum* / *vicus*)	
92	Köln-Widdersdorf	FB 1999.009	Roman (*villa* / rural)	
93	Krefeld-Gellep	Gell	Roman (*castrum* / *vicus*)	
94	Moers-Asberg	NI 2010/1044	Roman (*castrum* / *vicus*)	
95	Morken-Harff, Am Messweg	Ha/Haf	Roman (*villa* / rural)	
96	Niederzier-Hambach	HA 86	Roman (*villa* / rural)	
97	Niederzier-Hambach	HA 132	Roman (*villa* / rural)	
98	Niederzier-Hambach	HA 412	Roman (*villa* / rural)	
99	Niederzier-Steinstraß, München Busch	HA 69	Roman (*villa* / rural)	
100	*Colonia Claudia Ara Agrippinensium* (CCAA)	CCAA	Roman (*colonia*)	
101	*Colonia Ulpia Traiana* (CUT)	CUT	Roman (*colonia*)	
102	Bonn-Bechlinghoven	OV 2007/108; OV 2010/137; OV 2006/173; OV 2007/100; OV 2008/103; OV 2009/138	Middle Ages	
103	Bornheim-Walberberg	OV 2010/142; OV 2011/23	Middle Ages	
104	Duisburg Alter Markt	DUI 6017	Middle Ages	
105	Duisburg-Serm	PR 2015/5000	Middle Ages	
106	Erkelenz-Tenholter Str.	NW 2008/1084	Middle Ages	
107	Inden-Pier	WW 2011/90; WW 2011/91; WW 2014/53	Middle Ages	
108	Niederzier, Wüstweiler	HA 500	Middle Ages	
109	Kaster	Ks/Ksf	Middle Ages	
110	Xanten, Markt	NI 2009/1052	Middle Ages	

Tab. 1. Key to *Figure 1*.

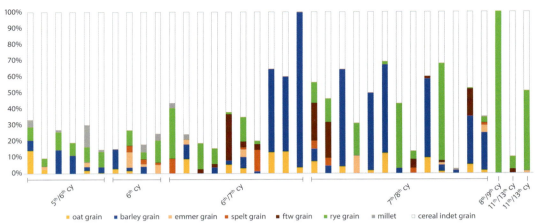

Fig. 2. Bonn-Bechlinghoven: Summary of the cereal grain composition of samples (where n ≥ 30 items) in chronological sequence.

Materials and Methods

Prehistoric samples of grains and associated arable weed seeds (n = 389) came from 35 Iron Age sites, eleven Bronze Age sites, and 42 Neolithic sites. The Roman samples (n = 97) came from 20 sites: twelve *villae* or farms, two *coloniae*, Xanten *(Colonia Ulpia Traiana)* and Cologne *(Colonia Claudia Ara Agrippinensium)*, and six *castra* or related *vici*. Most of the samples represent the fills of pits or postholes and include some grain-rich deposits likely to represent redeposited storage material. One set of samples, from Krefeld-Gellep, derived from a *horreum*.

The medieval samples (n = 131) came from seven settlements: one urban site, Duisburg, and six rural sites, Bornheim-Walberberg, Inden-Pier, Erkelenz-Tenholter Straße, Kaster, Niederzier, Wüstweiler, and Bonn-Bechlinghoven. Only two of these, Bonn-Bechlinghoven and Erkelenz-Tenholter Straße, produced sufficient quantities of well-preserved grains suitable for stable isotope analysis. Therefore it was possible to investigate crop rotation only for these two settlements and only in relation to their pre 10th century phases, as later samples were heavily dominated by a single cereal, primarily rye. This may reflect the fact that by the 10th century, high value bread cereals had come to predominate in the Rhineland (HILDEBRANDT 1988, 277; see also ZERL / MEURERS-BALKE 2012). We illustrate the diachronic increase in rye at Bonn-Bechlinghoven, the largest crop assemblage, in *Figure 2*. From the 10th century onwards, barley and oats too are regularly documented in larger quantities in settlements of this region (cf. KNÖRZER / GERLACH 1999, 109; ZERL 2019a).

The excavations at Bonn-Bechlinghoven *(Fig. 1,102)*, between 2007 and 2011, uncovered evidence for 21 farmsteads, including 47 ground-level buildings and 36 *Grubenhäuser*, dating to between the later 5th century and the end of the 9th century *(Fig. 3*; WEILER-RAHNFELD in prep.; preliminary reports i. a. WEILER-RAHNFELD 2009; WEILER-RAHNFELD 2010). A high medieval phase was also identified, although evidence from the beginning of the 10th to the beginning of the 11th century was lacking. Most of the charred plant remains derive from *Grubenhäuser*, although the most grain-rich samples came from three storage pits. None of the samples analysed appears to represent stored cereals charred *in situ*, but sample composition suggests that some if not most were comprised of redeposited stored grain, probably representing the harvests of several productive units.

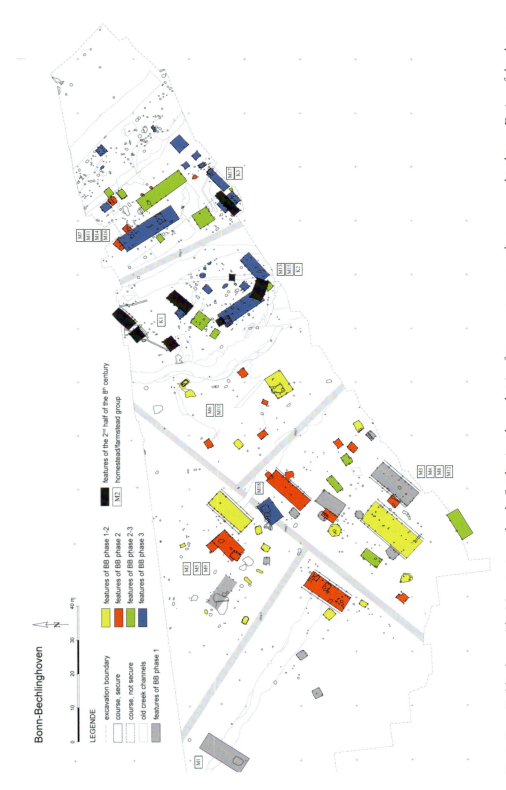

Fig. 3. Bonn-Bechlinghoven: The Merovingian and early Carolingian phases showing former watercourses and reconstructed pathways. Dating of the phases: 1 = AD 460/480–530/550; 2 = AD 530/550–640/660; 3 = AD 640/660–730/740 (after Weiler-Rahnfeld in prep. with some modifications).

The multi-period settlement at Erkelenz-Tenholter Straße *(Fig. 1,106)*, excavated in 2008, produced Iron Age, Roman and medieval settlement remains, including one of the few Carolingian rural settlements known from this part of the Rhineland (AEISSEN 2009; AEISSEN / SCHAMUHN 2011). A house, two granaries, a barn, a smithy and numerous pits were identified. Although features of 9th to 10th century date were identified, archaeobotanical remains were only recovered from 8th to 9th century features. Most samples came from postholes associated with two earth-fast timber buildings; none is from a storage context, although it is again likely that most of the samples analysed represent redeposited stored material[1].

The sites at both Erkelenz-Tenholter Straße and Bonn-Bechlinghoven are believed to represent ordinary villages, although their precise status must remain uncertain in the absence of associated written evidence. What excavated farmsteads at settlements such as these represent in terms of holdings is also unclear. There is general agreement that, apart from the great royal and monastic estates, most holdings during the 8th and 9th centuries were highly fragmented and spread across several settlements (INNES 2000, 77). The holdings of numerous different landowners might thus lie "side by side, often … all in the same village" (ZELLER et al. 2020, 76).

Functional weed ecology

Two earlier studies provided the foundation for the analyses conducted here. First, a functional ecological study of weed flora developed under traditional agricultural regimes in Asturias, Spain, and Haute Provence, France, successfully differentiated between high- and low-input farming methods (BOGAARD et al. 2016). The study used discriminant analysis to develop a model for differentiating fields managed with high inputs per unit area (intensive manuring and weeding) from those, like medieval open fields, receiving low inputs (low / no manuring and weeding). This was achieved on the basis of five functional traits that predict the response of weed species to soil fertility and / or disturbance due to tillage and weeding: specific leaf area (leaf area / leaf dry weight), canopy height and diameter, the ratio of leaf area per node to fresh leaf thickness, and flowering duration *(Fig. 4)*. As this model is based on functional traits rather than weed species *per se*, which may have restricted biogeographical distributions, it can be applied successfully to different climatic zones, as shown by BOGAARD et al. (2016). This model is also suitable for archaeobotanical studies since it is based on the presence or absence of weed species in different farming regimes, rather than their ubiquity within individual fields.

In the second study, of modern weed flora in Germany in autumn- and spring-sown crops, functional traits relating to the timing and duration of flowering were found to predict autumn versus spring germination and hence association with different sowing seasons (BOGAARD et al. 2001). In particular, weed species with early and short flowering periods are associated with autumn germination and autumn-sown crops, whereas weed species with late and / or long flowering periods are associated with spring germination and spring-sown crops. In conjunction with correspondence analysis, these relationships were used to explore crop and weed associations in medieval archaeobotanical assemblages as evidence of systematic autumn versus spring sowing of particular cereal species, as expected in rotation of autumn- and spring-sown crops.

---

[1] The dating of the archaeobotanical samples is based on the associated ceramic assemblages.

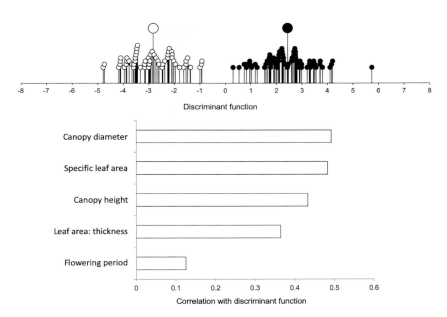

fig. 4. Upper diagram shows the relationship of Haute Provence fields (open circles) and Asturias fields (filled circles) to the discriminant function extracted to distinguish these two groups (larger symbols indicate group centroids); the bar chart below shows correlations between the functional attribute scores used as discriminating variables and the discriminant function.

Archaeobotanical samples from the University of Cologne archive, containing at least ten seeds of potential weed taxa identified to species level, were entered into the classification phase of the discriminant analysis as unknown cases, in order to assess their similarity to the modern high- versus low-input regimes. Edible fruits and nuts that were probably collected, and other woody perennials unlikely to set seed in arable conditions, were excluded as potential arable weeds. The threshold of ten potential weed seeds is both minimal and arbitrary; higher thresholds and additional criteria for distinguishing potential weeds from other sources of wild taxa support the approach taken here (Bogaard 2004; Zerl 2019b). *Figure 1* shows the distribution of these samples across the region and chronological periods (see *Appendix, Table 3*, for details of sites and samples).

Stable isotope analysis

Stable carbon and nitrogen isotope analyses were conducted on 51 cereal grain samples from Bonn-Bechlinghoven (40 samples) and Erkelenz (eleven samples). Samples were selected based on the external and internal morphology which indicated that the seeds were charred at between 230 °C and 300 °C (Stroud et al. submitted). Each sample consisted of five to ten cereal grains, homogenised into a bulk sample (see *online Suppl. Mat.* doi: https://doi.org/10.11588/data/XAHRIG). The samples were pre-screened for contaminants following Vaiglova et al. (2014) using Fourier transform infrared spectroscopy with attenuated total reflectance (Agilent Technologies Cary 640 FTIR instrument with a GladiATR™ accessory from PIKE technologies). No contaminants were detected, and so the samples were run without pre-treatment on a Sercon 20-22 EA-GSL isotope mass spectrometer operating in continuous flow mode at the School of Archaeology's Research Laboratory for Archaeology and the History of Art, University of Oxford. Carbon and nitrogen stable isotopic values were measured separately due to the low percentage of nitrogen in the samples. Samples were drift corrected using an internal alanine standard, while they were normalised to the AIR scale for nitrogen using IAEA-N1 and IAEA-N2; for carbon they were normalised to the VPDB scale using IAEA-CH7 and CH6. A check standard of EMA-P2 was added to all runs to aid the calculation of errors, while every tenth sample was duplicated. Following Szpak et al. (2017), the precision was calculated as ±0.08‰, the accuracy ±0.13‰, and standard uncertainty ±0.15‰ for carbon. For nitrogen, precision was ±0.26‰, accuracy was ±0.5‰, and standard uncertainty was ±0.56‰ (see *Appendix, Tables 4–7*, and *online Suppl. Mat.* for full analytical conditions).

Results: Trends in extensification based on a functional ecological study of weed flora

The question of whether a trend towards extensification could be established, from relatively 'high-input' and small scale, to 'low-input' and larger scale, was addressed by comparing the discriminant scores of samples from the different chronological periods, as presented in *Figures 5–8*.

Neolithic to Iron Age

The discriminant scores of samples dating to the Neolithic and Bronze Age are shown in *Figure 5*, entered into the classification phase of the discriminant analysis *(Fig. 4)* as unknown cases. A clear contrast is apparent between the Neolithic and the Late Bronze Age samples. The Neolithic samples are concentrated between the modern 'high-input' and 'low-input' groups but include a significant proportion overlapping with the 'high-input' group; in contrast, the Late Bronze Age samples nearly all resemble 'low-input' fields. The few Early Bronze Age samples span the 'high-' to 'low-input' range. The discriminant scores of samples dating to the Early, Middle, and Late Iron Age are shown in *Figure 6*. Samples from these periods exhibit an overall trend towards increasingly 'low-input' growing conditions. A trend towards lower soil fertility and disturbance is therefore apparent all the way from the Neolithic to the Late Bronze Age and continuing through the Iron Age.

Roman to Medieval

This part of the Rhineland lay in the hinterland of the Roman *limes*. It contained not only large numbers of troops needing to be fed but also two sizeable urban populations at the *coloniae* of Xanten and Cologne (Brüggler et al. 2017; Reddé 2018). *Figure 7* shows the discriminant scores for three groups of Roman sites: *castra* and *vici*; the *coloniae*; and farms and *villae*. The samples from *castra* and *vici* continue the late prehistoric trend towards 'low-input' conditions, suggesting distinctively extensive cereal production. It thus appears likely that these communities were provisioned with cereals grown on *villae* geared to surplus production, some potentially arriving via long distance networks specifically responsible for supplying the military. In contrast, the samples from the *coloniae* (Xanten and Cologne) have much more variable scores, including new extremes at both the 'low-' and 'high-input' ends of the spectrum. The very low scores observed in a small group of samples from the *coloniae* appear to derive from a cereal production regime with markedly lower soil fertility / disturbance than even that which provisioned the *castra* and *vici*. The wide spread of scores for samples from farms and *villae* plausibly reflect a range of inten-

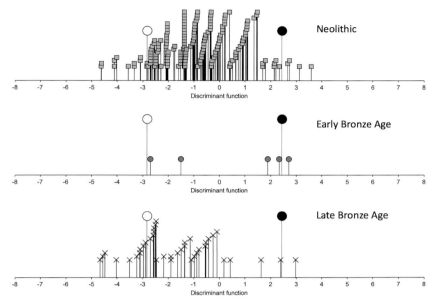

Fig. 5. Discriminant scores of Neolithic and Bronze Age weed assemblages.

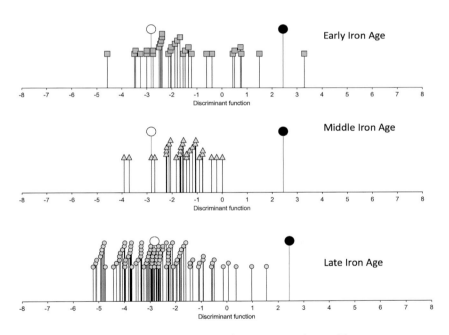

Fig. 6. Discriminant scores of Iron Age weed assemblages.

sive / infield production, perhaps signalling some cultivation of smaller holdings, as well as extensive / outfield production (cf. REDDÉ 2018).

Figure 8 shows the discriminant scores for the two largest medieval weed assemblages – from Bonn-Bechlinghoven and Bornheim-Walberberg – as well as for the remaining medieval sites. All three groups show a clear emphasis on 'low-input' growing conditions, thus

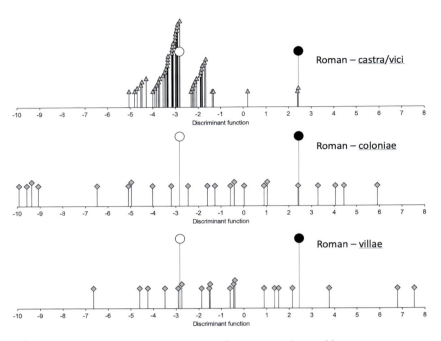

Fig. 7. Discriminant scores of Roman weed assemblages.

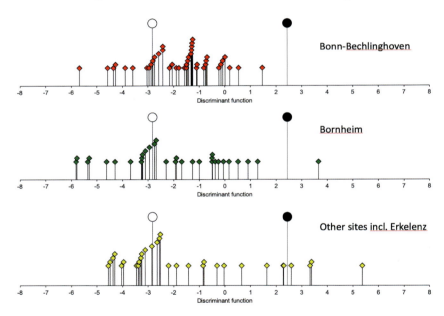

Fig. 8. Discriminant scores of medieval weed assemblages.

maintaining the general chronological trend. They broadly resemble the profile of the Late Iron Age, and without the extreme low-input focus of the Roman *castra / vici*. There is, however, a small 'tail' of samples straying into 'high-input' growing conditions that is reminiscent of the Roman farms and *villae*.

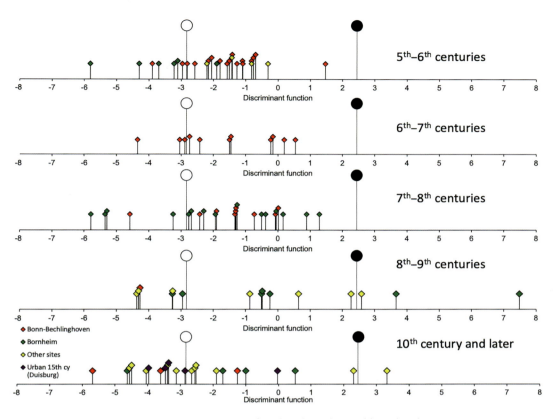

Fig. 9. Discriminant scores of medieval weed assemblages by phase.

The medieval results are broken down by phase in *Figure 9*. Adjacent phases are chronologically overlapping; perhaps for this reason, but also because of small sample numbers, it is difficult to distinguish a clear trend through the 6th to 9th centuries. Certainly, no reversion to 'prehistoric' cultivation conditions is evident in the post-Roman centuries. Comparison of the 5th/6th century samples with the 10th century and later samples does, however, reveal that the 'centre of gravity' within the predominant 'low-input' focus has shifted from relatively high scores in the 5th/6th century to lower scores in the 10th century and later samples. Thus, it is apparent that within the medieval period there was a further, subtle shift towards increasingly 'low-input' growing conditions.

To sum up, there is a broad trend towards lower input growing conditions and management throughout later prehistory, reaching an extreme in some production sectors of the Roman period, with a more subtle continuation or reiteration of this trend within the medieval period itself. In light of regional palynological data (Becker 2005; Kalis / Meurers-Balke 2007; Cheyette 2008; Brüggler et al. 2017), it is clear that the overall trend towards 'low-input' cereal growing is in fact one of spatial expansion in arable production at the expense of woodland: in other words, true extensification. The medieval two- and three-field regimes should therefore be seen as fitting within a broader, long-term trend of extensification. Other complementary approaches are needed to investigate medieval developments further, however, in particular the emergence of systematic rotation of autumn- and spring-sown crops, the topic to which we now turn.

Results: Crop Rotation

Three-field crop rotation is considered by some 'to be the most important innovation of medieval agriculture', but whether it was already practiced in the early medieval period has been much debated (Rösener 1992, 55–56; Henning 1994, 110–112; Devroey 2003, 108–111; Henning 2014, 332). To advance this debate, the crop and weed data for the settlement of Bonn-Bechlinghoven were subjected to correspondence analysis (CA) to assess crop sowing season using weed flowering time / duration categories that predict germination season; this provides information relating to crop rotation complementary to that indicated by the stable isotope data. The correspondence analysis of samples *(Fig. 10)* from all phases of occupation (5th/6th century to 11th–13th centuries) reveals a close association of spring-germinating weeds (late- and long-flowering) with oat and barley, and an association of autumn-germinating weeds (early / short-flowering) with rye and, somewhat more loosely, with wheats (glume and free-threshing), suggesting two distinct sowing times[2]. Further analyses (not shown) of subsets of samples from early and later phases (i.e. 5th/6th to 7th centuries, and 7th/8th century and later) confirmed that these associations of spring sowing indicators with oat and barley on the one hand, and of autumn sowing indicators with wheats and rye on the other, are apparent throughout the site's occupation. It therefore appears that sowing certain cereals in autumn and others in spring was routinely practised before a systematic rotation of autumn and spring cereals was introduced in the 7th/8th century, as indicated by the stable isotope data, discussed below. A correspondence analysis of crop and weed data from Bornheim-Walberberg (not shown) was inconclusive as regards crop sowing times since the distributions of taxa and samples predominantly reflect crop processing differences rather than the growing conditions of different crops. The Erkelenz assemblage was too small to permit correspondence analysis.

The results of the carbon isotopic analysis of material from Bonn-Bechlinghoven and Erkelenz show both similarities and differences. At Bonn-Bechlinghoven, rye (-23.5 ± 0.6‰), oats (-25.2 ± 0.2‰), and barley (-25.1 ± 0.3‰) have $\delta^{13}C$ values which show a separation between rye and the two other species; this was expected due to the known physiological differences between these crops (Hamerow et al. 2020). This physiological difference is also seen when the samples are plotted by phase, with barley and oat having similar values, while rye always has more positive values *(Fig. 11)*. The similar values of barley and oat are interesting as research on modern barley and oat indicates that these two species should be offset when cultivated in the same soil conditions (Hamerow et al. 2020). The Bonn-Bechlinghoven results therefore indicate that barley and oats were not cultivated in the same soil conditions during the 6th/7th century phase; it is, however, difficult to demonstrate this solely based on an analysis of carbon. Nitrogen must also be considered.

The stable nitrogen isotope values for Bonn-Bechlinghoven are moderate to high at 5.7 ± 1.2‰ (rye), 6.6 ± 0.3‰ (oat) and 7.1 ± 1.6‰ (barley). The higher barley $\delta^{15}N$ mean value is due to a phase-related phenomenon, with the higher values occurring in

---

[2] Broomcorn millet is a very minor presence in the assemblage and so no conclusions can be drawn about either its status as a crop or its sowing time. Interestingly, in chapter 62 of the *Capitulare de villis vel curtis imperrii*, an estate ordinance from around AD 800 generally attributed to Charlemagne (Mischke 2013, 34–37; http://capitularia.uni-koeln.de/capit/pre814/bk-nr-032/ [last access: 28 February 2021]), millet is not mentioned among the cereals (annona) but among the root crops and garden plants (e.g. legumes [legumines]). Therefore, it can perhaps be assumed that millet was not cultivated in the cereal fields.

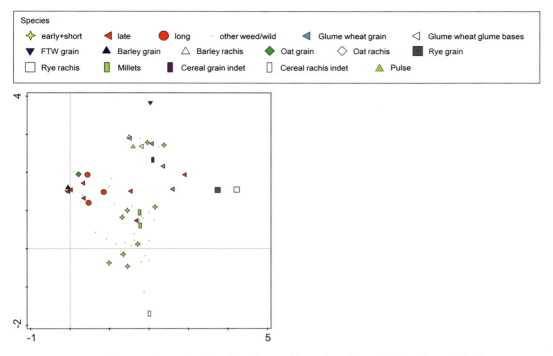

Fig. 10. Correspondence analysis of medieval weed assemblages from Bonn-Bechlinghoven. The first two axes are shown: axis 1 (horizontal) and axis 2 (vertical). Axis 1, which separates autumn- and spring-germinating weeds, accounts for 21 % of all variation in the dataset.

the 6th/7th century phase. *Figure 11*, showing the samples by phase, shows the changes in δ15N values over time, with the samples from the 6th/7th century phase showing clear species-specific δ15N soil enrichment. Oat, rye and barley were cultivated on soils which had different stable nitrogen isotopic ratios, with barley (7.7 ± 0.4 ‰) on more enriched soils and rye (5.1 ± 1.3 ‰) on more depleted soils. An analysis of variance indicates that rye is significantly different from barley *(Tab. 2)*. There is, furthermore, a marked shift in the following phase (7th/8th century): barley and rye now had similar values (6 ± 2.4 ‰ and 4.8 ± 0.6 ‰ respectively), a similarity which is even more marked if the single outlying barley sample is removed (4.9 ± 0.4 ‰) (*Tab. 2*, t-test insignificant). The results show a shift from species-specific cultivation conditions for rye, barley and oats – either due to naturally occurring soil differences, or through the preferential addition of manure to barley – to the cultivation of barley and rye on soils with similar 15N enrichment. The explanation proposed here is the introduction of crop rotation in the 7th/8th century phase, so that barley and rye were now grown in rotation in the same fields.

Another temporal change shown in the data from Bonn-Bechlinghoven is the enrichment of rye from the moderate levels seen in the 7th/8th century phase to higher levels in the 8th/9th and 11th–13th centuries. The change seen in rye's δ15N from the 7th/8th century to the 8th/9th century phases is statistically significant (t-test p < 0.05; *Tab. 2*) and suggests either an increase in the manuring of rye – which is unlikely given that the functional weed data clearly indicate a low-input regime – or an expansion of cultivation in this period onto soils enriched in 15N. A 15N enrichment over time has also been noted by the authors at the early medieval town of Stafford, in England, where, again thanks to functional weed data, it has been linked to the expansion of arable cultivation onto heavier, more fertile soils

Site	Phase	Species	Isotope	Test	DF	Chi, T or F value	P-value	Post hoc test		P-value
Bonn-Bechlinghoven	6–7th	All	Carbon	Kruskal-Wallis	2	Chi-squared = 14.58	**0.001**	Dunn	Oat-barley Rye-barley Rye-oat	0.098 **<0.001** **<0.001**
Bonn-Bechlinghoven	6–7th	All	Nitrogen	Kruskal-Wallis	2	Chi-squared = 22.78	**<0.001**	Dunn	Oat-barley Rye-barley Rye-oat	**<0.001** **<0.001** 0.3
Bonn-Bechlinghoven	7–8th	All	Nitrogen	T.test	4.86	T =1.05	0.343			
Bonn-Bechlinghoven	7–8th and 8–9th	Rye	Nitrogen	T.test	3.57	T = -3.1	**0.043**			
Erkelenz-Tenholter Straße	All	All	Carbon	ANOVA	2(8)	F = 11.4	**0.005**	Tukey	Rye-oat Oat-barley Barley-rye	**0.005** **0.013** 0.948
Erkelenz-Tenholter Straße	8–9th	Oat, Rye	Nitrogen	T.test	4.11	T = -1.785	0.147			
Erkelenz-Tenholter Straße	All	All	Nitrogen	ANOVA	2(8)	F = 1.416	0.298			
Erkelenz-Tenholter Straße	8–9th	All	Nitrogen	ANOVA	2(6)	F = 2.245	0.187			

Tab. 2. The results of statistical tests on the Bonn-Bechlinghoven and Erkelenz-Tenholter Straße isotopic data. Significant p-values are shown in bold.

which were potentially seasonally waterlogged (HAMEROW et al. 2020). It is not possible to compare the rye samples from Bonn-Bechlinghoven with any other species during the period examined and therefore to establish whether or not such enrichment is species-specific. The weed data do, nevertheless, suggest a general trend towards extensification when samples from the 7th/8th century phase are compared with those from later phases *(Fig. 9)*. Thus, the enrichment in ^{15}N is unlikely to be linked to manuring and could instead be linked to the expansion of rye cultivation onto heavier, naturally ^{15}N-enriched soils by the 8th/9th century phase.

The site of Erkelenz-Tenholter Straße produced samples predominantly from the 8th–9th centuries, with two samples broadly dated to between the 8th and 11th centuries. The three species isotopically examined (barley, rye, and oat) have δ^{13}C values which are slightly different to those of Bonn-Bechlinghoven, mainly due to the more positive δ^{13}C value of the barley, which is statistically significantly different from oat (p < 0.05) but not from rye *(Tab. 2)*. Caution needs to be applied with respect to the barley value, however, due to the low number of samples (n = 3), one of which is only broadly dated. The offset between rye and oat is expected because of the difference found between modern rye and oat cultivated in the same conditions; the similar value of the barley and the rye does not, however, conform to current understanding of barley's physiological offset.

The nitrogen values also present a different picture to those of Bonn-Bechlinghoven *(Fig. 12)*. The δ^{15}N is low to moderate at Erkelenz, ranging between 3.6‰ and 5.9‰. Unlike at Bonn-Bechlinghoven, the Erkelenz δ^{15}N mean values and ranges for barley (4.9 ±0.9‰) and rye (4.8 ±0.8‰) are very similar, while oat is slightly lower and less variable (3.4 ±0.35‰). Thus, there is no statistically significant difference between the

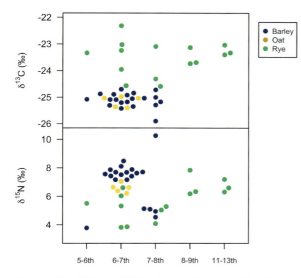 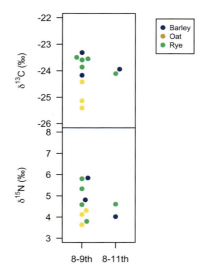

Fig. 11. The $\delta^{13}C$ and $\delta^{15}N$ values for Bonn-Bechlinghoven cereal samples by chronological phase.

Fig. 12. The $\delta^{13}C$ and $\delta^{15}N$ values for Erkelenz cereal samples by chronological phase.

three species, regardless of whether the two broadly dated samples are included or not (*Tab. 2*). This indicates that the crops at Erkelenz were cultivated in soils which had similar but low ^{15}N enrichment, results which are consistent with crop rotation in the 8th–9th centuries.

Discussion

The fate of Roman fieldscapes in northern Gaul in the 5th and 6th centuries has been the subject of considerable debate. Some have argued for economic catastrophe and the abandonment of arable, while others emphasise broad continuities in the rural economy (Ouzoulias 1997; 2001). The faunal record is somewhat less ambiguous and appears to reflect at least some return to less specialised, more self-sufficient animal husbandry regimes after the main markets for meat declined (Hamerow 2002, 146–147; Pigière / Goffette 2019). A study of land use in the Elsbach valley, between Elfgen and Belmen (Rhein-Kreis Neuss), also in the lignite mining zone west of Cologne, suggests that "farming activities strongly decreased" in the 4th century, while the 5th and 6th centuries saw woodland regeneration and only small-scale farming (Becker 2005, 234). The 7th and 8th centuries saw some woodland clearance and expansion of cereal cultivation with settlements and their fields returning to the valley in the 9th and 10th centuries when, "due to Carolingian clearing activities and the 3-field-system, the area of arable land expanded" (Becker 2005, 235). It should be noted, however, that the Elsbachtal study is largely based on pollen data and waterlogged macrofossils, and so reflects the local, natural vegetation from one river valley, whereas the FeedSax results present a regional picture seen through the lens of crops and their associated weeds. These results preclude any significant reversion to high-input cultivation regimes as would be expected had there been a substantial reduction in the scale of arable farming in the post-Roman centuries. Instead, the weed flora from the early medieval settlements included in our study reflect a broad continuation of the primarily low-input regimes of the region's Roman farms and *villae*.

With regard to seasonal sowing, the historian Lynn White Jr. observed that there is in the written sources "no indication of … spring planting as a regular custom before documents of 765 and 771; thereafter it is frequently mentioned" (WHITE 1940, 152 no. 1; cf. HILDEBRANDT 1988, 276). The documents he referred to relate to practices on large monastic and royal estates and cannot be assumed to have been widespread. The results of our analyses of weed flora indicate, however, that consistent sowing of certain cereals in spring and others in autumn was in fact already a well-established practice in this part of the Rhineland by the middle of the 8th century and was not restricted to royal and monastic lands (cf. DEVROEY 2003). Spring- and autumn-sowing was already practiced at Bonn-Bechlinghoven in the 5th/6th century phase of occupation and continued thereafter, with oat and barley being closely associated with late-flowering, and hence predominantly spring-germinating, weeds (such as *Fallopia convolvulus* [L.] Á. Löve, *Persicaria lapathifolia* [L.] Delarbre, and *Persicaria maculosa* Gray) and rye being associated with early-flowering and hence mostly autumn-germinating weeds (such as *Rumex acetosella* L., *Valerianella dentata* [L.] Pollich, and *Veronica hederifolia* L.); wheat occurs mostly with autumn sowing indicators but also some spring sowing indicators. That wheat should be sown in both autumn and spring is unsurprising given the frequent references to both 'winter wheat' and 'summer wheat' in Carolingian polyptychs. The polyptych relating to Saint-Maur-des-Fossés (FR), c. 869–878 AD, for example, refers explicitly to summer and winter wheat: "Each [holding] does three ploughing services for the winter-wheat, three for the second ploughing, and three for the summer-wheat" (HÄGERMAN / HEDWIG 1990, 95)[3].

As for systematic crop rotation, the polyptychs indicate that in northern Francia, two- and three-course rotation was already practiced by the 9th century (VERHULST 2002, 61–64). Verhulst regarded true, regulated three-field rotation – where most or all of the arable belonging to a village was divided into three (or more) roughly equal parts – as exceptional in this early period, however, and argued that communally managed rotation at the village level and use of the mouldboard plough did not become widespread until the 11th century at the earliest (VERHULST 1990, 22–23; see also DEVROEY 2003, 110). The isotopic analysis of samples from Bonn-Bechlinghoven has demonstrated that while barley, oat and rye were not grown in systematic rotation during the 6th/7th century phase, by the 7th/8th century phase, barley and rye probably were. Although the evidence from Erkelenz-Tenholter Straße was restricted to the 8th/9th century phase, the results suggest that there too, barley, oat, and rye were grown in systematic rotation. While we cannot tell whether the arable of these communities, or of individual farmers, was divided into two, three, or more parts for the purpose of rotation, our results indicate that systematic rotation was practiced in this region by the 8th century.

It is unclear from written sources whether three-course rotation originated on demesne land and whether peasants used it on their own lands (VERHULST 2002, 62–63). The archaeobotanical remains from Bonn-Bechlinghoven and Erkelenz provide direct evidence for the early practice of systematic crop rotation by farmers in what appear to be ordinary villages. The methods used here cannot, of course, tell us how the fields in which these crops were grown were laid out. The archaeobotanical evidence does, however, demonstrate that early medieval agriculture in this region did not revert to small-scale, intensive farming as imagined by Lynn White Jr. when he described peasant practices as "amazingly

---

[3] It is likely that the 'second ploughing' refers to the preparation of the fallow for winter sowing. The authors are indebted to Nicolas Schroeder for his help in translating this passage, as well as to the University of Leicester website, 'Carolingian Polyptyques' (https://www.le.ac.uk/hi/polyptyques/index.html).

primitive – almost Neolithic" (White 1967, 89). Instead, early medieval farming in this region represented not stagnation or decline, but rather the continuation of a long-term trend towards large-scale, low-input cereal cultivation. The results presented here further indicate that by the 8th century systematic crop rotation was practiced in at least some ordinary villages, and that it pre-dated by at least two centuries the kind of highly extensive, low-input cereal farming associated with open fields.

Supplementary Material

Supplementary Material on the stable carbon and nitrogen isotope analyses conducted on the cereal grain samples can be found online at https://doi.org/10.11588/data/XAHRIG.

Acknowledgements

The FeedSax project is supported by the European Research Council (ERC) under the European Union's Horizon 2020 research and innovation programme under grant agreement No. 741751. The authors would like to thank the peer reviewers and the following for their advice and assistance: Lisa Lodwick, Mark McKerracher, Samantha Neil, Nicolas Schroeder, Steve Bödecker, and Arne Reimann. We are also grateful to Sarah Mallet for undertaking the French translation.

Bibliography

Primary Sources

'Carolingian Polyptyques'
See homepage of University of Leicester website: https://www.le.ac.uk/hi/polyptyques/index.html (last access: 14 October 2022).

Hägerman / Hedwig 1990
D. Hägerman / A. Hedwig (eds), Das Polyptychon und die Notitia de Areis von Saint-Maur-des-Fossés. Analyse und Edition. Francia Beih. 23 (Sigmaringen 1990).

Secondary Sources

Aeissen 2009
M. Aeissen, Erkelenz, Bebauungsplan GO2.2/2, "Tenholter Straße". Schlussbericht. ArchaeoNet [unpubl. report] (Bonn 2009).

Aeissen / Schamuhn 2011
M. Aeissen / S. Schamuhn, Kelten – Römer – Karolinger. Ergebnisse einer Ausgrabung an der Tenholter Straße in Erkelenz. Heimatkalender des Kreises Heinsberg 2011, 38–57.

Banham / Faith 2014
D. Banham / R. Faith, Anglo-Saxon Farms and Farming (Oxford 2014).

Becker 2005
W.-D. Becker, Das Elsbachtal. Die Landschaftsgeschichte vom Endneolithikum bis ins Hochmittelalter. Rhein. Ausgr. 56 (Mainz 2005).

Bogaard 2004
A. Bogaard, Neolithic Farming in Central Europe: an Archaeobotanical Study of Crop Husbandry Practices (London, New York 2004).

Bogaard et al. 2001
A. Bogaard / G. Jones / M. Charles / J. G. Hodgson, On the archaeobotanical inference of crop sowing time using the FIBS method. Journal Arch. Scien. 28, 2001, 1171–1183. doi: https://doi.org/10.1006/jasc.2000.0621.

Bogaard et al. 2016
A. Bogaard / J. Hodgson / E. Nitsch / G. Jones / A. Styring / C. Diffey / J. Pouncett / C. Herbig / M. Charles / F. Ertuğ / O. Tugay / D. Filipovic / R. Fraser, Combining functional weed ecology and crop stable isotope ratios to identify cultivation intensity: a comparison of cereal production regimes in Haute Provence, France and Asturias, Spain. Veget. Hist. Archaeobot. 25, 2016, 57–73. doi: https://doi.org/10.1007/s00334-015-0524-0.

Brüggler et al. 2017
M. Brüggler / K. Jeneson / R. Gerlach / J. Meurers-Balke / T. Zerl / M. Herchenbach, The Roman Rhineland. Farming and consumption in different landscapes. In: M. Reddé (ed.), Gallia Rvstica 1. Les campagnes du nord-est de la Gaule, de la fin de l'âge du Fer à l'Antiquité tardive. Ausonius Mém. 49 (Bordeaux 2017) 19–95.

Cheyette 2008
F. L. Cheyette, The disappearance of the ancient landscape and the climatic anomaly of the Early Middle Ages: a question to be pursued. Early Medieval Europe 16, 2008, 127–165. doi: https://doi.org/10.1111/j.1468-0254.2008.00225.x.

Devroey 2003
J.-.P Devroey, Économie rurale et société dans l'Europe franque (VIe–IXe siècles). Tome 1. Fondements matériels, échanges et lien social. Belin Sup Hist. (Paris 2003).

Duby 1954
G. Duby, La révolution agricole médiévale. Rev. Géogr. Lyon 2, 1954, 361–366. doi: https://doi.org/10.3406/geoca.1954.2010.

Dyer et al. 2018
Ch. Dyer / E. Thoen / T. Williamson, The rationale of open field systems. A collection of essays. In: Ch. Dyer / E. Thoen / T. Williamson (eds), Peasants and their Fields. The Rationale of Open Field Agriculture, c. 700–1800 (Turnhout 2018) 1–4.

Hall 2014
D. Hall, The Open Fields of England (Oxford 2014).

Hamerow 2002
H. Hamerow, Early Medieval Settlements. The Archaeology of Rural Communities in North-West Europe 400–900 (Oxford 2002).

Hamerow et al. 2020
H. Hamerow / A. Bogaard / M. Charles / E. Forster / M. Holmes / M. McKerracher / S. Neil / Ch. Bronk Ramsey / E. Stroud / R. Thomas, An integrated bioarchaeological approach to the 'Medieval Agricultural Revolution': A case study from Stafford, England, c. AD 800–1200. European Journal Arch. 23, 2020, 585–609. doi: https://doi.org/10.1017/eaa.2020.6.

Henning 1994
F.-W. Henning, Deutsche Agrargeschichte des Mittelalters: 9. bis 15. Jahrhundert (Stuttgart 1994).

Henning 2014
J. Henning, Did the agricultural revolution go east with the Carolingian conquest? Some reflections on early medieval rural economics of the *Baiuvarii* and *Thuringi*. In: J. Fries-Knoblach / H. Steuer / J. Hines (eds), The Baiuvarii and Thuringi: An Ethnographic Perspective. Stud. Hist. Archaeoethn. 9 (Woodbridge 2014) 331–359.

Hildebrandt 1988
H. Hildebrandt, Systems of agriculture in Central Europe up to the tenth and eleventh centuries. In: D. Hooke (ed.), Anglo-Saxon Settlements (Oxford 1988) 275–290.

Innes 2000
M. Innes, State and Society in the Early Middle Ages. The Middle Rhine Valley 400–1000 (Cambridge 2000).

Kalis / Meurers-Balke 2007
A. J. Kalis / J. Meurers-Balke, Landnutzung im Niederrheingebiet zwischen Krieg und Frieden. In: G. Uelsberg (ed.), Krieg und Frieden. Kelten – Römer – Germanen [Begleitbuch zur gleichnamigen Ausstellung im Rheinischen LandesMuseum Bonn, 21.6.2007–6.1.2008] (Darmstadt 2007) 144–153.

Knörzer / Gerlach 1999
K.-H. Knörzer / R. Gerlach, Geschichte der Nahrungs- und Nutzpflanzen im Rheinland. In: K.-H. Knörzer / R. Gerlach / J. Meurers-Balke / A. J. Kalis / U. Tegtmeier / W.-D. Becker / A. Jürgens, Pflanzen-

spuren. Archäobotanik im Rheinland: Agrarlandschaft und Nutzpflanzen im Wandel der Zeit. Mat. Bodendenkmalpfl. Rheinland 10 (Cologne 1999) 67–127.

Mischke 2013

B. Mischke, Kapitularienrecht und Urkundenpraxis unter Kaiser Ludwig dem Frommen (814–840) [PhD thesis Univ. Bonn] (Bonn 2013). https://nbn-resolving.org/urn:nbn:de:hbz:5-31571.

Mitterauer 2010

M. Mitterauer, Why Europe? The Medieval Origins of Its Special Path (Chicago 2010).

Ouzoulias 1997

P. Ouzoulias, Le Déprise Agricole du Bas-Empire: Un mythe historiographique? In: P. Ouzoulias / P. van Ossel (eds), Les Campagnes de l'Île-de-France de Constantin à Clovis (Paris 1997) 10–20.

Ouzoulias 2001

P. Ouzoulias (ed.), Les Campagnes de la Gaule à la fin de l'Antiquité. Actes du colloque, Montpellier, 11–14 mars 1998 (Antibes 2001).

Pigière / Goffette 2019

F. Pigière / Q. Goffette, Continuity and change in animal exploitation and the transition from antiquity to the early medieval period in the Belgian and Dutch loess region. Quaternary Internat. 499, 2019, 101–111. doi: https://doi.org/10.1016/j.quaint.2017.10.025.

Reddé 2018

M. Reddé, The impact of the German frontier on the economic development of the countryside of Roman Gaul. Journal Roman Arch. 31, 2018, 131–160. doi: https://doi.org/10.1017/S1047759418001265.

Renes 2010

H. Renes, Grainlands. The landscape of open fields in a European perspective. Landscape Hist. 31, 2010, 37–70. doi: https://doi.org/10.1080/01433768.2010.10594621.

Rösener 1992

W. Rösener, Agrarwirtschaft, Agrarverfassung und ländliche Gesellschaft im Mittelalter. Enzyklopädie Dt. Gesch. 13 (Oldenburg 1992).

Ruas / Zech Matterne 2012

M.-P. Ruas / V. Zech-Matterne, Les avoines dans les productions agro-pastorales du Nord-Ouest de la France. Données carpologiques et indications textuelles. In: V. Carpentier / C. Marcigny (eds), Des hommes aux champs. Pour une archéologie des espaces ruraux du Neolithique au Moyen Age (Rennes 2012) 327–365.

Stroud et al. submitted

E. Stroud / A. Bogaard / M. Charles / H. Hamerow, Turning up the heat: assessing the impact of charring regime on the morphology and stable isotopic values of cereal grains. Journal Arch. Scien., submitted.

Szpak et al. 2017

P. Szpak / J. Z. Metcalfe / R. A. Macdonald, Best practices for calibrating and reporting stable isotopes measurements in archaeology. Journal Arch. Scien. Reports 13, 2017, 609–616. doi: https://doi.org/10.1016/j.jasrep.2017.05.007.

Vaiglova et al. 2014

P. Vaiglova / Ch. Snoeck / E. Nitsch / A. Bogaard / J. Lee-Thorp, Impact of contamination and pre-treatment on stable carbon and nitrogen isotopic composition of charred plant remains. Rapid Commun. Mass Spectrometry 28, 2014, 2497–2510. doi: https://doi.org/10.1002/rcm.7044.

Verhulst 1990

A. Verhulst, The agricultural revolution of the Middle Ages reconsidered. In: B. S. Bachrach / D. Nicholas (eds), Law, Custom and the Social Fabric in Medieval Europe (Kalamazoo 1990) 17–28.

Verhulst 2002

A. Verhulst, The Carolingian Economy (Cambridge 2002).

Weiler-Rahnfeld 2009

I. Weiler-Rahnfeld, Eine fränkische Siedlung des 6.–7. Jahrhunderts in Bonn-Bechlinghoven. Arch. Rheinland 2009, 131–133.

Weiler-Rahnfeld 2010

I. Weiler-Rahnfeld, Der frühmittelalterliche Siedlungsplatz von Bonn-Bechlinghoven. Arch. Rheinland 2010, 140–142.

WEILER-RAHNFELD in prep.
I. WEILER-RAHNFELD, Die merowingerzeitliche Siedlung von Bonn-Bechlinghoven. Rhein. Ausgr. 82 (in preparation).

WHITE 1940
L. WHITE Jr., Technology and invention in the Middle Ages. Speculum 15, 1940, 141–159. doi: https://doi.org/10.2307/2849046.

WHITE 1962
L. WHITE Jr., Medieval Technology and Social Change (London 1962).

WHITE 1967
L. WHITE Jr., The life of the silent majority. In: R. S. Hoyt (ed.), Life and Thought in the Early Middle Ages (Minneapolis 1967) 85–100.

ZELLER et. al. 2020
B. ZELLER / C. WEST / F. TINTI / M. STOFFELLA / N. SCHROEDER / C. VAN RHIJN / S. PATZOLD / T. KOHL / W. DAVIES / M. CZOCK, Neighbours and Strangers. Local Societies in Early Medieval Europe (Manchester 2020).

ZERL 2019a
T. ZERL, Archäobotanische Untersuchung in der hochmittelalterlichen Siedlung Inden-Pier. In: T. Rünger, Gesellschaft und Gewerbe im ländlichen Raum des 12. Jahrhunderts. Bonner Beitr. Vor- u. Frühgesch. Arch. 21 (Bonn 2019) 203–214.

ZERL 2019b
T. ZERL, Archäobotanische Untersuchungen zur Landwirtschaft und Ernährung während der Bronze- und Eisenzeit in der Niederrheinischen Bucht. Rhein. Ausgr. 77 (Darmstadt 2019).

ZERL / MEURERS-BALKE 2012
T. ZERL / J. MEURERS-BALKE, Die Geschichte des Roggens im Rheinland. Arch. Rheinland 2012, 37–39.

Abstract: The cerealisation of the Rhineland: Extensification, crop rotation and the medieval 'agricultural revolution' in the *longue durée*

This paper presents selected results of a research project designed to generate direct evidence for the spread of low-input cereal farming and crop rotation, key elements of the so-called 'Medieval agricultural revolution'. This type of farming greatly increased overall crop production, enriching landowners and fuelling population growth. The results presented here situate these developments within the *longue durée* of farming in the lower Rhine basin, from the Neolithic to the central Middle Ages. They also have important implications for our understanding of agricultural production during the Roman to post-Roman transition.

Zusammenfassung: Die Zerealisierung des Rheinlands: Extensifikation, Fruchtfolge und die mittelalterliche „Agrarrevolution" in der *longue durée*

In diesem Beitrag werden ausgewählte Ergebnisse eines Forschungsprojektes präsentiert, das direkte Belege für die Verbreitung des Low-Input-Getreideanbaus und der Fruchtfolge im frühmittelalterlichen Europa, Schlüsselelemente der so genannten „Agrarrevolution", liefern soll. Diese Art der Landwirtschaft führte zu einer erheblichen Steigerung der gesamten Pflanzenproduktion, wodurch die Grundbesitzer wohlhabender wurden und das Bevölkerungswachstum gefördert wurde. Die hier vorgestellten Resultate ordnen diese Entwicklungen in die *longue durée* der Landwirtschaftsgeschichte in der Niederrheinischen Bucht ein, vom Neolithikum bis zum Mittelalter. Sie haben bedeutende Auswirkungen auf unser Verständnis der landwirtschaftlichen Produktion am Übergang von der römischen zur nachrömischen Zeit, der „Extensivierung" der Agrarwirtschaft und der Einführung der Fruchtfolge.

Résumé : La céréalisation de la Rhénanie : Extensification, rotation des cultures et « révolution agricole » médiévale sur la longue durée

Cet article présente les résultats choisis d'un projet de recherche conçu pour produire des preuves directes de la diffusion des cultures céréalières à bas niveau d'intrants et de la rotation des cultures, des éléments clés de ce que l'on appelle communément la ‹révolution agricole›, dans l'Europe du Haut Moyen-Âge. Ce type d'agriculture a considérablement accru la production agricole globale, enrichissant ainsi les propriétaires terriens et accélérant la croissance démographique.

Les résultats présentés ici placent ces progrès dans la longue durée de l'agriculture dans le bassin du Rhin inférieur du néolithique au Moyen-Âge central. Ces résultats ont aussi des implications importantes pour notre compréhension de la production agricole pendant la transition romaine à post-romaine, la diffusion des systèmes agricoles à bas niveau d'intrants et l'introduction de la rotation des cultures.

Adresses of authors:

Helena Hamerow
Institute of Archaeology
University of Oxford
34–36 Beaumont Street
GB–Oxford OX1 2PG
Helena.hamerow@arch.ox.ac.uk
https://orcid.org/0000-0001-5643-5888

Tanja Zerl
Labor für Archäobotanik
Institut für Ur- und Frühgeschichte
Universität zu Köln
Weyertal 125
DE–50931 Köln
tzerl@uni-koeln.de
https://orcid.org/0000-0003-3078-9922

Elizabeth Stroud
Institute of Archaeology
University of Oxford
34–36 Beaumont Street
GB–Oxford OX1 2PG
Elizabeth.stroud@arch.ox.ac.uk
https://orcid.org/0000-0003-4299-6638

Amy Bogaard
Institute of Archaeology
University of Oxford
34–36 Beaumont Street
GB–Oxford OX1 2PG
Amy.bogaard@arch.ox.ac.uk
https://orcid.org/0000-0002-6716-8890

References of figures:
Figs 1–2; 4–12: authors. – *Fig. 3:* authors after WEILER-RAHNFELD in prep., fig. 11 with some modifications. – *Tabs 1–7:* authors; graphics: O. Wagner (RGK).

Appendix

Period	Site	No. samples included in analysis
Neolithic (LBK)		166
	Aldenhoven 3	1
	Aldenhoven-Langweiler 1	2
	Aldenhoven-Langweiler 2	12
	Aldenhoven-Langweiler 3 & 6	5
	Aldenhoven-Langweiler 8	47
	Aldenhoven-Langweiler 9	11
	Aldenhoven-Niedermerz 1A	1
	Bedburg-Garsdorf	6
	Bergheim-Glesch	3
	Borschemich 1 und 6	1
	Eschweiler-Laurenzberg 7	28
	Eschweiler-Laurenzberg 8	2
	Eschweiler-Lohn	1
	Frimmersdorf 43	4
	Hambach 8	1
	Hochneukirch 33	5
	Inden-Lamersdorf	3
	Jüchen 65 B1	1
	Jülich-Wickrath 118	2
	Köln-Mengenich	1
	Meckenheim	3
	Morken-Harff	7
	Niederzier-Hambach (HA 382)	5
	Oekoven	2
	Rödingen	2
	Wanlo	8
	Würselen-Broichweiden	2
Neolithic (Grossgartach)		2
	Hambach 260	2
Neolithic (Rössen)		19
	Aldenhoven 1	3
	Aldenhoven-Langweiler 1	2
	Borschemich 5	1
	Frimmersdorf 2	1
	Gellep-Stratum, Ossumer Feld	1

Period	Site	No. samples included in analysis
	Inden 1	7
	Inden 3	1
	Inden-Pier, Güldenberg	2
	Wanlo 55	1
Neolithic (Bischheim)		5
	Hambach 502	1
	Jüchen-Garzweiler (2001/103)	1
	Jüchen-Garzweiler (FR 137)	1
	Jüchen-Garzweiler (FR 98/251)	2
Neolithic (Michelsberg)		2
	Hambach 11	1
	Hambach 32	1
Early Bronze Age		5
	Bedburg-Königshoven (FR 48)	4
	Jülich-Güsten (HA82/457)	1
Late Bronze Age		39
	Aldenhoven 1	1
	Aldenhoven-Langweiler 3 & 6	3
	Eschweiler-Lohn (WW 73/09)	1
	Eschweiler-Lohn (WW 14)	13
	Grevenbroich-Gustorf (FR 52)	1
	Inden-Altdorf (WW 127)	12
	Jülich-Bourheim (WW 93/53)	1
	Jülich-Bourheim (WW 111)	6
	Titz-Rödingen (HA514)	1
Early Iron Age		31
	Aldenhoven-Langweiler 1	1
	Aldenhoven-Langweiler 8	1
	Aldenhoven-Niedermerz (NM 16)	1
	Aldenhoven-Pattern (WW 94/7)	1
	Eschweiler-Lohn (WW 33 & 34)	2
	Frixheim-Anstel	1
	Jülich-Bourheim (WW 111)	2
	Köln-Worringen Blumenberg	5
	Nettesheim-Butzheim	1
	Niederzier-Hambach (HA 511)	2

Tab. 3. Sites and archaeobotanical samples included in the weed ecological analysis.

Period	Site	No. samples included in analysis
	Niederzier-Hambach (HA 512)	2
	Niederzier-Steinstraß (HA 513)	1
	Pulheim-Brauweiler	10
	Rommerskirchen	1
Middle Iron Age		27
	Aldenhoven-Pattern (WW 94/169)	2
	Bedburg-Königshoven (FR 3)	3
	Bedburg-Königshoven (FR 51)	1
	Bergheim (FR 74)	2
	Eschweiler-Lohn (WW 36)	1
	Eschweiler-Dürwiss	2
	Jüchen-Garzweiler (FR 84/88)	1
	Jüchen-Garzweiler (FR 137)	1
	Jülich-Bourheim (WW 111)	1
	Köln-Worringen Blumenberg	2
	Niederzier (HA 510)	1
	Niederzier-Hambach (HA 382)	1
	Niederzier-Hambach (HA 512)	1
	Niederzier-Steinstraß (HA 407)	2
	Pulheim-Sinthern	6
Late Iron Age		93
	Aldenhoven-Pattern (WW 88/131)	1
	Eschweiler-Laurenzberg (WW 51)	14
	Grevenbroich-Gustorf	8
	Jüchen-Garzweiler (FR 2000/89)	2
	Jüchen-Garzweiler (FR 2007/02)	3
	Jülich-Bourheim (WW 111)	2
	Jülich-Bourheim (WW 94/376)	2
	Jülich-Welldorf	1
	Niederzier-Hambach (HA 382)	34
	Niederzier-Hambach (HA 512)	6
	Niederzier-Hambach (HA 490)	7
	Niederzier-Steinstraß (HA 407)	1
	Niederzier-Steinstraß (HA 59)	12
Roman *(castra, vici)*		45
	Bonn, *Legionslager*	1

Period	Site	No. samples included in analysis
	Bonn, *vicus* IKBB	20
	Dormagen-Römerstraße	5
	Köln-Alteburg	8
	Krefeld-Gellep	9
	Moers-Asberg	2
Roman *(coloniae)*		28
	Colonia Claudia Ara Agrippinensium (CCAA)	9
	Colonia Ulpia Traiana (CUT)	19
Roman *(villae)*		24
	Aachen-Süsterfeldstraße	2
	Erftstadt-Friesheim	1
	Jüchen-Belmen	1
	Jüchen-Kamphausen	1
	Jüchen-Neuotzenrath	2
	Jülich-Bourheim (WW 94/376)	3
	Köln-Widdersdorf	4
	Morken-Harff, Am Messweg	1
	Niederzier-Hambach (HA 132)	1
	Niederzier-Hambach (HA 86)	1
	Niederzier-Hambach (HA 412)	6
	Niederzier-Steinstraß, München Busch	1
Medieval		131
	Bonn-Bechlinghoven	43
	Bornheim-Walberberg	56
	Duisburg Alter Markt	5
	Erkelenz-Tenholter Str.	8
	Inden-Pier	3
	Kaster	12
	Niederzier, Wüstweiler	4

Tab. 3. cont.

Analytical conditions:

Nitrogen and carbon elemental and isotopic compositions were determined using a Sercon 20-22 EA-GSL isotope mass spectrometer operating in continuous flow mode at the School of Archaeology's Research laboratory for Archaeology and the History of Art, at the University of Oxford. Stable carbon and nitrogen isotope compositions were calibrated relative to VPDB (δ^{13}C) and AIR (δ^{15}N) using IAEA-N1 and IAEA-N2 for nitrogen and IAEA-CH6 and IAEA-CH7 for carbon. Check standards of an internal alanine standard (δ^{15}N -1.56 ± 0.27 ‰ and δ^{13}C -27.11 ± 0.03 ‰) and EMA-P2 (δ^{15}N -1.57 ± 0.14 ‰ and δ^{13}C -28.19 ± 0.14 ‰) were used to determine analytical uncertainty as per Szpak et al. (2017; *Tab. 4* and *Tab. 5*). Every tenth sample was duplicated to help understand measurement precision (*Tab. 6* and *Tab. 7*; Szpak et al. 2017).

Standard	Number	Session	δ^{15}N mean	δ^{15}N SD
N1	5	190322	0.40	0.34
N2	6	190322	20.30	0.32
P2	5	190322	-1.12	0.06
ALANINE	12	190322	-1.20	0.2
N1	2	181126	0.40	0.03
N2	3	181126	20.30	0.1
P2	4	181126	-1.63	0.06
ALANINE	8	181126	-1.57	0.1
N1	4	180628	0.40	0.4
N2	4	180628	20.30	0.1
P2	4	180628	-0.77	0.24
ALANINE	8	180628	-1.49	0.34
N1	4	190405	0.40	0.36
N2	3	190405	20.30	0.4
P2	3	190405	-0.9	0.17
ALANINE	5	190405	-1.21	0.15

Tab. 4. The mean and standard deviation of the calibration standards and check standards from all nitrogen analytical sessions that contain data presented in this paper.

Standard	Number	Session	δ^{13}C mean	δ^{13}C SD
CH6	4	190308	-10.45	0.11
CH7	4	190308	-32.15	0.07
P2	4	190308	-28.27	0.11
ALANINE	8	190308	-27.14	0.03
CH6	4	180802a	-10.45	0.09
CH7	4	180802a	-32.15	0.04
P2	4	180802a	-28.35	0.04
ALANINE	8	180802a	-27.15	0.04
CH6	4	181119	-10.45	0.08
CH7	2	181119	-32.15	0.03
P2	4	181119	-28.26	0.08
ALANINE	8	181119	-27.14	0.07

Tab. 5. The mean and standard deviation of the calibration standards and check standards from all carbon analytical sessions that contain data presented in this paper.

ID	Session	δ^{13}C A	δ^{13}C B
RC2018	190308	-26.01	-26.14
WHXX3D	190308	-25.02	-25.02
BBV022	180802a	-25.48	-25.37
BBV051	180802a	-24.78	-24.9
BBV099	181119	-25.92	-25.89
BBV105	181119	-24.83	-24.86

Tab. 6. The δ^{13}C values of the duplicated samples within the analytical sessions from which the data in this paper derives from.

ID	Session	δ^{15}N A	δ^{15}N B
YAR010	190322	8.14	8.07
YAR020	190322	8.61	8.64
OAT230	190322	3.58	3.6
BAR0BD	190322	1.03	0.97
BBV099	181126	5.11	5.16
BBV105	181126	8.5	8.47
BBV022	180628	7.56	7.56
BBV029	180628	7.41	7.51
BBV051	180628	8.26	8.16
YAR004	190405	4.64	4.59
RC2018	190405	3.48	3.79

Tab. 7. The δ^{15}N values of the duplicated samples within the analytical sessions from which the data in this paper derives from.

Diskussionen

Passau zwischen Spätantike und Mittelalter: Die Ausgrabungsergebnisse in der Klosterkirche Niedernburg

Von Bernd Päffgen

Das Kloster in Passau-Niedernburg stellt mit seiner Kirche zum Heiligen Kreuz und der in den Gebäuden der 1802 aufgehobenen Abtei betriebenen Schule ein besonderes Denkmal in der traditionsreichen Bischofsstadt dar[1]. Dem heutigen Besucher erschließen sich als älteste erhalten gebliebene Bauteile aus romanischer Zeit das Erdgeschoss der beiden Westtürme, das Kirchenportal und die Vorhalle mit den aus der Zeit um 1200 stammenden Secco-Malereien[2]. Erste Ausgrabungen fanden bereits vor über 110 Jahren durch Wolfgang Maria Schmid (1867–1943) vom „Generalkonservatorium der Kunstdenkmale und Altertümer Bayerns" am Grab der seligen Gisela († 1060) statt und versuchten wenig später in der Zeit des Ersten Weltkriegs, die mittelalterlichen Bauphasen der Klosterkirche nachvollziehbar zu machen[3]. Als dagegen 1967 der Einbau von Heizungen stattfand, gab es bedauerlicherweise keine begleitenden Ausgrabungen, was andernorts in Bayern durchaus geschah. Die neue Heizungsanlage in der Regensburger Niedermünsterkirche führte bekanntlich zwischen 1963 und 1968 zu umfangreichen Ausgrabungen unter der Leitung des Landesarchäologen Klaus Schwarz (1915–1985), die nunmehr weitgehend ausgewertet vorliegen[4].

Die dann 1978 begonnenen Grabungsarbeiten in der ehemaligen Passauer Klosterkirche Heiligkreuz standen zunächst unter unguten Vorzeichen. Auftretende Statikprobleme der Kirche führten dazu, dass einzelne Grabungsflächen – vor allem im nördlichen Seitenschiff – unverzüglich und noch vor der Aufnahme der Grabungsprofile komplett mit Beton aufgefüllt wurden. Sogar wesentliche Daten, wie die erreichte Grabungstiefe im Seitenschiff vor der Verfüllung und die genaue Anlage der Schnitte, bleiben unklar. Danach musste sich die Ausgrabung ab 1979 auf den mittleren Teil des Kirchenschiffs beschränken. Ausgegraben wurden das gesamte Mittelschiff, ein großer Teil des Querhauses, das Westende des Chors und kleine Teilflächen in den beiden Seitenschiffen. Hinzu kommt außerhalb der Kreuzkirche eine kleine Fläche im Klostergarten. In der Gesamtheit kann die Untersuchungsfläche trotz der vorhandenen Verlustflächen also als aussagekräftig eingestuft werden. Eine zumindest annähernde Quadratmeterangabe zu Verlust- und Untersuchungsflächen wäre aber an gut zu findender Stelle der Publikation wünschenswert gewesen.

Die archäologischen Untersuchungen fanden von 1978–1980 unter der Leitung von Rainer Christlein (1940–1983) statt. Die Bedeutung der Ausgrabungen hatte Christlein im Hinblick auf die Frage nach der Kontinuität zwischen dem spätrömischen Reich und dem frühen Mittelalter formuliert und hier für Passau auf die historisch greifbare Zeit des heiligen Severin verwiesen[5]. Für den ersten Kirchenbau definierte Christlein im ersten Überblicksbericht zur Ausgrabung als

---

[1] SCHMID 1912; SCHMID 1927.
[2] MATZ 1955. Als Kurzfassung publiziert: MATZ-TUCZEK 1956; EWEL 1983; STEIN-KECKS 1993. Zu den Wandmalereien gehören auch Inschriften in romanischer Majuskel, die in die Zeit um 1200 datieren: STEININGER et al. 2006, 6 f. Nr. 5 Abb. 5–6.
[3] SCHMID 1912. Vgl. auch NIEMEIER 2001.
[4] SCHWARZ 1971. Als Aufarbeitung in Kooperation zwischen den dem Bayerischen Landesamt für Denkmalpflege und der Bayerischen Akademie der Wissenschaften: KONRAD 2007; KONRAD et al. 2011; WINTERGERST 2019.
[5] CHRISTLEIN 1980b; CHRISTLEIN 1982. Vgl. auch CHRISTLEIN 1979; CHRISTLEIN 1980a. – Vgl. zusammenfassend aus heutiger Sicht: LATER 2014.

terminus post quem „die erste Hälfte bis Mitte des 5. Jahrhunderts" und setzte dessen Errichtung zunächst vorsichtig „vielleicht erst um 700" an[6]. Danach kehrte er sich aber von dem Zeitansatz in die spätere Merowingerzeit ab und vertrat dezidiert die Frühdatierung der ersten Kirche in das 5. Jahrhundert[7]. Christlein stellte sich die spätantik gegründete Niederburger Kirche im 6. bis 7. Jahrhundert genutzt vor und nahm sie auch als Passauer Bischofskirche des vor der Mitte des 8. Jahrhunderts wirkenden Bischofs Vivilo an[8]. Die Deutung als spätantike Kirche wurde dann bald in Frage gestellt. Auch die Interpretation als Bischofskirche wurde als nicht haltbar kritisiert[9]. Der plötzliche Tod des charismatischen bayerischen Landesarchäologen Rainer Christlein verhinderte die rasche Bearbeitung der Ausgrabung.

Vielen galt schließlich ein Aufarbeitungsprojekt als unmöglich. Die Beharrlichkeit von Helmut Bender hat die Skeptiker nun eines Besseren belehrt. Vorgelegt wurden zum Jahreswechsel 2018/19 die eindrucksvollen Resultate einer elfjährigen Forschungsarbeit, die Bender nach seiner Entpflichtung als Professor für die Archäologie der römischen Provinzen an der Universität Passau mit kompetenten Mitautorinnen und -autoren realisieren konnte[10]. In seinem Aufarbeitungskonzept hat sich Bender einerseits in der Auswertung bewusst auf die spätrömische Zeit und den Übergang ins Mittelalter beschränkt, andererseits den diachronen Ansatz nicht ausgeblendet. Bearbeitet wurden sowohl die Befunde als auch die Funde wie Keramik, Glasgefäße und Münzen sowie die für die frühe Klostergeschichte relevanten historischen Zusammenhänge. Auf die einzelnen Beiträge im Detail soll hier nicht weiter eingegangen werden, vielmehr soll im Rahmen dieses Diskussionsbeitrags eine Annäherung an das mit der Publikation zu verbindende Wesentliche versucht werden. Nach der Behandlung der Forschungsgeschichte (S. 17–37) bietet Helmut Bender sehr ausführliche Befundbeschreibungen nach den Grabungsteilbereichen, die seine hohe Eindringtiefe in die Materie widerspiegeln (S. 38–200). Benders „Versuch einer Gesamtbewertung" beschließt den ersten Teilband (S. 201–216).

Der zweite Teilband bringt auswertende Einzelbeiträge überwiegend zum Fundmaterial. Die zumeist metallischen „Kleinfunde" behandelt Marcus Zagermann (S. 271–332). Der nordafrikanischen Sigillata widmet sich Michael Mackensen mit seiner besonderen Kennerschaft (S. 333–340). Als Experte für die rädchenverzierte Argonnensigillata wurde Lothar Bakker gewonnen (S. 341–352). Die überschaubare Anzahl an Amphoren bewertet Florian Schimmer (S. 353–356). Die Glasfunde des 4. bis 6. Jahrhunderts hat Sylvia Fünfschilling bearbeitet (S. 357–400). Emmi Federhofer beschäftigt sich als langjährige Mitarbeiterin Benders mit den für die Spätantike wichtigen Fundgruppen von Lavezgeschirr (S. 401–420) und glasierter Keramik (S. 421–470). Die eingeglättverzierte Ware wurde von Silvia Spors-Gröger behandelt (S. 471–496). Über die „Horreumkeramik" (S. 497–502) und die „germanische Keramik" (S. 503–514) haben Bender und sein Schüler Günther Moosbauer gearbeitet. Zu den spätantik-frühmittelalterlichen Beinfunden gibt es den Beitrag von Sabine Deschler-Erb (S. 515–536). Mit der früh- bis hochmittelalterlichen Keramik beschäftigt sich Eleonore Wintergerst (S. 537–554). Zu einigen ausgewählten frühmittelalterlichen Funden äußert sich Christian Later (S. 573–588). Im umfangreichen Beitrag von Bernward Ziegaus geht es um die Fundmünzen (S. 691–830).

---

[6] Christlein 1980b, 126.
[7] Christlein 1982, 229 f.
[8] Christlein 1982, 229 f.
[9] Boshof 1999, 63.
[10] Helmut Bender (Hrsg.), Die Ausgrabungen 1978– 1980 in der Klosterkirche zu Passau-Niedernburg. Materialhefte zur Bayerischen Archäologie Band 108,1–2. Verlag Michael Laßleben, Kallmünz 2018. € 149,–. ISBN 3-7847-5408-6. Teilbände 1–2, 835 Seiten und Mappe mit 21 Beilagen.

Nimmt man die Befunde und das Fundmaterial zusammen, gelingen trotz der problematischen Grabungsweise gut nachvollziehbare Aussagen zu Niedernburg in Spätantike und Frühmittelalter. In valentinianischer Zeit setzte auf dem Gelände eine umfangreiche Bautätigkeit ein. Christlein hatte hierbei an eine Art offenen Innenhof gedacht. Tatsächlich handelte es sich um einen unter der Klosterkirche gelegenen massiven Rechteckbau von 24,1 m Länge und 14,2 m Breite, der als Horreum zu interpretieren ist und fünf mächtige Pfeiler im Inneren aufweist *(Abb. 1)*. In der Einordnung verweist Bender auf die Speichergebäude der spätantiken Befestigungen vom Lorenzberg bei Epfach (Lkr. Landsberg am Lech), in Wilten (Bez. Innsbruck, AT) und dem Goldberg bei Türkheim (Lkr. Unterallgäu). Das Passauer Horreum ist mit einer Grundfläche von 342 m² besonders groß[11]. Der östliche Teil der Passauer Halbinsel dürfte in der Spätantike befestigt gewesen sein und u. a. den Donau-Hafen geschützt haben (heute der Bereich von Donaukai, Südende der Luitpoldbrücke und dem betriebenen Schiffsanleger). Es ist als das in Rätien gelegene Kastell *Batavis* zu identifizieren, das mit dem Kleinkastell *Boiotro* auf norischer Seite direkt am Innufer im 4. Jahrhundert eine Funktionseinheit bildete. Aufgrund von archäologischen Beobachtungen und der Kartierung von Fundmaterial kann die Größe der Befestigung von *Batavis* aber nur geschätzt werden. Bender nimmt eine große Ausdehnung auf 4 ha Fläche an (S. 210). Dann läge das Horreum relativ zentral innerhalb der Befestigung. Ältere Vorstellungen rekonstruierten das spätrömische Kastell lediglich gegenüber vom Ilz-Zufluss deutlich kleiner auf der Ostspitze der Halbinsel zwischen Donau und Inn, so dass das Horreum dann außerhalb gelegen hätte. Eine erste steinerne Befestigung dürfte nach der Analyse der Fundmünzen durch Bernward Ziegaus bereits in den 280er/290er Jahren erfolgt sein. Diese geschah nach einem deutlichen Zerstörungshorizont, der mit Barbareneinfällen in den 260er/270er Jahren in Verbindung zu bringen ist. Die bauliche Entwicklung der vermutlich in tetrarchischer Zeit angelegten Befestigung bis in die Zeit um 400 bleibt letztlich unklar.

Es bleibt ein gewisses Unbehagen bei der Rekonstruktion des Passauer Kastells vor allem im Hinblick auf die vermutete Größe. Diese wäre eher mit einem spätantiken Legionsstandort in Rätien zu vereinbaren, nicht aber mit dem hier belegten spätantiken Kohortenkastell. In Passau kommandierte ein Militärtribun im späten 4. und früheren 5. Jahrhundert die dem *Dux Raetiae* als Befehlshaber der Grenzarmee unterstehende Batavenkohorte, zu der auch Kavallerie und Marine gehörte[12]. Die Kastellgrundriss-Rekonstruktionszeichnung bleibt mit wenig konkreten Befunden zu verbinden *(Abb. 2)*. Wie sehr hier aber doch Unklarheit herrscht, spiegelt die nach Osten ganz anders aussehende Visualisierung des spätantiken Kastells auf der Passauer Halbinsel *(Abb. 3)*[13]. Für die Rekonstruktion bietet sich das knapp 1 ha große Kohortenkastell von Kellmünz (Lkr. Neu-Ulm) an, das wohl bald nach 297 n. Chr. angelegt und bis in das 5. Jahrhundert genutzt wurde[14].

Die Weiternutzung des Passauer Rechteckbaus im 5. Jahrhundert ergibt sich aus dem Fundmaterial, u. a. eine Schwertgriffhülse aus Hirschgeweih und nordafrikanische Terra sigillata der Formen Hayes 84 und 85, die in die zweite Hälfte des 5. Jahrhunderts gehörten. Hinweise auf bauliche Veränderungen sind nicht belegbar, was für eine Weiternutzung des Horreums im militärisch-zentralörtlichen Kontext spricht[15]. Nicht hinlänglich berücksichtigt wird hier der Fund eines Fingerrings mit Christogramm[16].

---

[11] BENDER 2018, 124 zusammenfassend zum Rechteckbau. Vgl. FUCHS 2011.
[12] Not. dign. occ. 35,24. Vgl. AIGN 1975; FISCHER 1995; BENDER 2003.
[13] SOMMER 2019.
[14] MACKENSEN 1995; MACKENSEN 1998.
[15] BENDER 2018, 127–134.
[16] Vgl. dazu PÄFFGEN 2016, 288. Versteckt im Beitrag von Zagermann in BENDER 2018, 276 Abb. 3,39 (ohne Datierungsangabe).

Abb. 1. Der durch die Grabungen 1978–1980 erfasste spätantike Rechteckbau in der ehemaligen Klosterkirche Passau-Niedernburg.

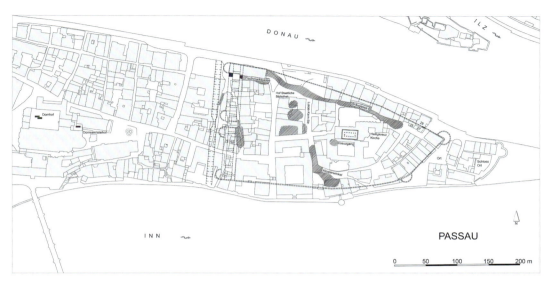

Abb. 2. Flächendeckend die Spitze der Passauer Inselsituation einnehmende Rekonstruktion der spätantiken Befestigung.

Abb. 3. Kleiner dimensionierter Rekonstruktionsvorschlag des spätrömischen Kastells in Rechteckform bei SOMMER 2019, 12 f. durch Martin Schaich / Arctron.

In der Bewertung des severinszeitlichen Horizonts der Niedernburg-Grabung bleibt Bender vorsichtig. Über die Severinsvita des Eugippius († nach 533)[17] gebe es zwar klare Hinweise auf kirchliche Organisation in Passau und geistliche Gemeinschaften auf beiden Innseiten, die Identifikation des als Horreum errichteten Rechteckbaus als ein von Severin genutztes Kirchengebäude sei jedoch nicht möglich[18].

[17] EUGIPPIUS, Vita Sev. [18] BENDER 2018, 127.

Freilich bleibt die Severinszeit in ihrer Bedeutung nicht zu marginalisieren. Die *Vita Severini* beschreibt *Batavis* als Oppidum zwischen Inn und Donau (*...inter utraque flumina Aenum atque Danuvium...*), das ummauert war (*...extra muros oppidi Batavini...*). Als militärische Einheit ist ein dort stationierter *numerus Batavinus* bezeugt, der nach dem Abzug berittener Einheiten *(turmae)* erfolglos versuchte, ausbleibende Besoldung in Italien zu reklamieren[19]. Severin erwies sich als Garant für Stabilität in der Krise. Er verhandelte 469/70 erfolgreich mit dem Alamannenkönig Gibuld vor dem befestigten Passau um die Unterlassung von Übergriffen und die Übergabe von Gefangenen. Es existierten mindestens eine Kirche und ein Baptisterium im Altstadtbereich sowie die Johannes dem Täufer geweihte Basilika in *Boiotro*. Außer Severin, dessen Stellung in der kirchlichen Hierarchie letztlich unklar bleibt, gab es in Passau den Presbyter Lucillius, den Diakon Amantius, mehrere Mönche und einen Vorsänger. Die in der Vita für *Batavis* erwähnte *cella* mit Baptisterium lässt sich nicht mit den Grabungsergebnissen in Niedernburg in Verbindung bringen. Alternativ wird man ihre Lokalisierung vielleicht eher am Domberg vermuten.

Die Bewohner des Oppidums betrieben überregionalen Handel, der über das Reichsgebiet hinausging. Dies ist daraus zu schließen, dass man Severin bat, sich bei Feletheus um Handelsprivilegien für den rugischen Herrschaftsbereich nördlich der Donau und das von den Rugiern kontrollierte Gebiet der Provinz *Noricum ripense* zu bemühen. Das Oppidum wurde nach Eugippius[20] – so wie es Severin befürchtet hatte – schließlich 476 bei einem von Hunimund geführten Barbarenangriff zerstört, die Bewohner getötet oder als Sklaven verschleppt. Mit Walter Pohl kann der donausuebische König Hunimund, der seinen Herrschaftsbereich 469/70 gegen die Ostgoten verloren hatte, zu diesem Zeitpunkt als eine Art „Räuberhauptmann" verstanden werden, der wenig organisiert handelte[21]. Alternativ kann man jedoch auch argumentieren, dass diese Bewertung erst durch den Gang der Entwicklung und der Etablierung des italischen Regnums Odoakers entstand und Hunimund stattdessen den rätisch-norischen Grenzraum in Kooperation mit Alamannen und Thüringern sehr wohl bewusst destabilisierte, um hier ein ähnliches barbarisch gentil strukturiertes Konstrukt zu realisieren, wie es etwas weiter östlich König Feletheus mit dem Rugier-Reich getan hatte.

Das von Eugipp beschriebene Oppidum stellte einen Zentralort im späteren agilolfingischen Herzogtum dar. Der Bereich von Niedernburg gilt in der historischen Forschung zumeist als Herzogsburg bzw. Herzogspfalz. Die merowingerzeitliche Weiternutzung des Gebäudes ergibt sich durch Fundkomplexe mit datierbaren Glasgefäßbruchstücken und Keramikresten[22].

In frühmittelalterlicher Zeit wurde der Ostabschluss des Rechteckbaus entfernt und in das ruinös bestehende (?) Gebäude ein etwas schmalerer Rechtecksaal von 13,5 m Breite eingebaut. Für die Errichtung des Neubaus wurde das Aufgehende des spätrömischen Speichers sukzessive abgebaut. Die stehengelassenen Fundamente des Vorgängerbaus stabilisierten den Neubau, der als Ostabschluss eine gestelzte, um halbe Mauerstärke eingezogene halbrunde Apsis erhielt *(Abb. 4)*. Der neue apsidiale Abschluss reichte etwas weiter nach Osten als beim Horreum[23].

In den Freiräumen zwischen Horreumsmauern und Neubau wurde eine besonders fundreiche schwarz-humose Lage mit älterem römischem Bauschutt und Ziegelbruch sowie Artefakten des 5. bis ins 7. Jahrhunderts festgestellt, die als *Dark Earth* zu klassifizieren ist. Wie und wann sich die *Dark Earth* bei noch bestehendem Speichergebäude bilden konnte, bleibt unklar[24]. Am ehesten

---

[19] Eugippius, Vita Sev. 20,1.
[20] Eugippius, Vita Sev. 22.
[21] Vgl. Pohl 1980, bes. 286.
[22] Bender 2018, 134–138.
[23] Bender 2018, 139–150 Abb. 35.
[24] Vgl. dazu Päffgen 2016, 287.

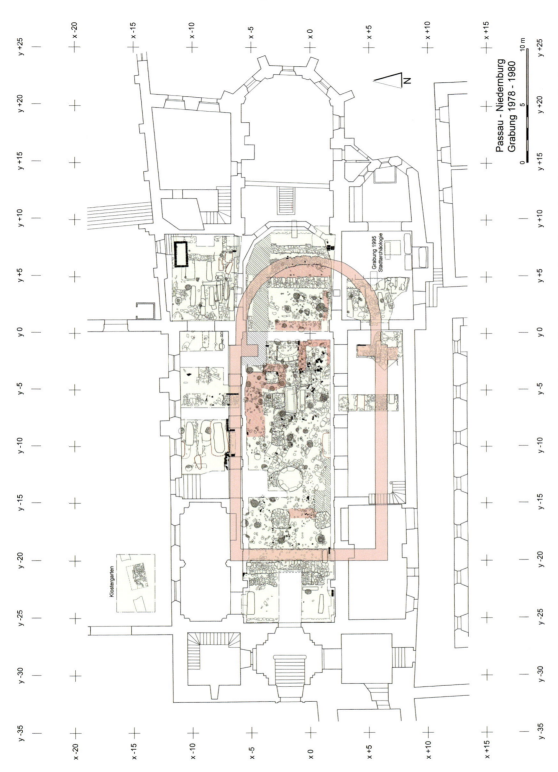

Abb. 4. Der durch die Grabungen 1978–1980 erfasste spätmerowingerzeitliche Kirchenbau in der ehemaligen Klosterkirche Passau-Niedernburg.

ist dabei wohl an eine Auffüllung mit Aushubmaterial aus der Umgebung beim Baugeschehen zu denken.

Das Baudatum des Apsidensaals, der naheliegend als der älteste Sakralbau unter der Klosterkirche gedeutet wird (Kirche I, *Abb. 4*), lässt sich archäologisch annähernd bestimmen. Christleins zuletzt favorisierte Frühdatierung des Apsidensaals in die Severinszeit (mittleres 5. Jahrhundert) kann ausgeschlossen werden. Drei Fundkomplexe mit Bruchstücken von rauwandiger Drehscheibenware belegen einen Baubeginn nach dem Ende des 7. Jahrhunderts. Holzkohleeinschlüsse aus Mörtelproben der Apsismauer konnten einer ^{14}C-Datierung unterzogen werden. Zwei ^{14}C-Daten geben mit 95,4 % Wahrscheinlichkeit die Zeitspanne von 632/642–726/775 n. Chr. an. In Abgleich mit der Keramikdatierung dürfte um 700 bis erste Hälfte des 8. Jahrhunderts als Gründungsdatum für Kirche I anzunehmen sein. Damit bestätigt sich im Grunde sogar Christleins zunächst bevorzugter Datierungsansatz „vielleicht erst um 700"[25]. In der Kirche und um sie wurde im Frühmittelalter bestattet[26].

Die eigentliche Grabungsaufarbeitung hätte an dieser Stelle auch von Helmut Bender für abgeschlossen erklärt werden können. Obwohl mit den jüngeren mittelalterlichen Phasen der Kirchengrabung die Befundlage und ihre Dokumentation schlechter werden, ist hier kein gänzlicher Einschnitt gesetzt, sondern zumindest perspektivisch weitergearbeitet worden. Eva Weiler, die sich im Rahmen ihrer kunsthistorischen Masterarbeit schon mit der Klosterkirche beschäftigt hat, werden „Überlegungen zur Gestalt der ottonisch-romanischen Kirche" verdankt (S. 589–624). Kenntnisreich behandelt der Passauer Mittelalterhistoriker Egon Boshof die „Geschichte des Klosters Niedernburg bis zur endgültigen Unterstellung der Abtei unter die bischöfliche Herrschaft" (S. 677–690). Dass damit aber auf gut 40 Seiten weder die erschöpfende Darstellung der Baugeschichte des Klosters noch seine Geschichte im 8. bis 12. Jahrhundert in Bezug auf die Grabungsergebnisse möglich sind, liegt auf der Hand.

Die Existenz des Klosters ist historisch durch ein Diplom König Arnulfs vom 8. Februar 888 erstmalig bezeugt, wo es um Abgaben ging, die dem *monasterium sancte Marie Batavie* weiterhin wie schon seit Generationen zustanden[27]. Es handelte sich zu diesem Zeitpunkt um ein herrschernahes Frauenkloster bzw. Damenstift. Für die Gründung gibt es aber keinen verlässlichen Nachweis. Spätere Quellen setzten die Gründung bereits agilolfingisch unter Herzog Odilo (736–748) oder Tassilo III. (748–788) an[28]. Daher kommt an dieser Stelle den Grabungsergebnissen besondere Bedeutung zu. Bender sieht als Bauherrn für die archäologisch gut erfasste Kirche I am ehesten Herzog Tassilo II. (715–719), da dieser nach der Herrschaftsteilung im bayerischen Herzogtum Passau als Residenz genommen hätte[29]. Stimmt man dieser Überlegung zu, könnte der Apsidensaal funktional als eine herzogliche Pfalzkapelle gegründet worden sein. Aus dieser könnte dann in der Karolingerzeit ein Frauenkloster hervorgegangen sein, wie dies auch für das Regensburger Niedermünster angenommen wird. Den Apsidensaal begleitende Nebengebäude, die für einen Kontext im Hinblick auf eine Herzogspfalz oder ein Kloster zu deuten wären, gibt es freilich nicht. Mit der Gründung des Bistums Passau vor dem Jahre 736 ist Niedernburg nicht in direkten Zusammenhang zu bringen. Fassbar ist der zu dieser Zeit amtierende, wohl angelsächsische Bischof Vivilo

---

[25] CHRISTLEIN 1981, 126.
[26] CH. LATER in: BENDER 2018, 555–557.
[27] E. BOSHOF in: BENDER 2018, 677 f.
[28] E. BOSHOF in: BENDER 2018, 678.
[29] BENDER 2018, 149. – Bei der sog. Landesteilung von 715? erhielt Theudebert / Theodo III. († 717?) als ältester Sohn Theodos II. Salzburg, während Regensburg dem Theudebald († 719) und Freising Grimoald († 724) zugesprochen wurde. Tassilo II. wird dabei *e silentio* mit Passau in Verbindung gebracht.

(† 746/747), der 739 von Bonifatius bestätigt wurde. Das Gründungsdatum vor 736 ist aus den Güterschenkungen von Herzog Hugbert (regierend 724–736) abzuleiten.

Einen Schritt weiter zurückgehend ist die Amtszeit von Herzog Theodo II. von Bedeutung, der von 680 bis 717 regierte. Theodo betrieb in der späteren Amtszeit eine starke Eigenpolitik im Merowingerreich. Hierzu gehört seine Verhandlung im Jahr 715 mit Papst Gregor II. in Rom über die Einrichtung einer eigenen bayerischen Kirchenprovinz mit mehreren Bistümern, unter denen auch Passau geplant gewesen sein dürfte[30]. Hinzu kommen die in der Korbiniansvita Arbeos von Freising überlieferte, den geplanten Bistümern entsprechende „Landesteilung" unter seine vier Söhne sowie die Sonderbeziehungen in das Langobardenreich.

Als verlässlich sehe ich die die Forschung oft verwirrende Überlieferung an, dass die fränkische Reichsregentin Plektrudis († nach 717) um 708 einen Kirchenbau in Passau initiiert oder für diesen gestiftet habe. Über die Namensgebung ist ein Verwandtschaftsverhältnis der bis 717 amtierenden und dann von ihrem Stiefsohn Karl Martell entmachteten Plektrudis mit den bayerischen Herzögen Theudebald († 719)[31], Grimoald († 724)[32] und Hugbert († 736)[33] ersichtlich. Theodo II. hatte in letzter Ehe möglicherweise Regintrudis, die jüngere Schwester der Plektrudis geheiratet. Alternativ gilt Herzog Theodebert / Theodo III. († 717?) als Ehemann der Regintrudis. Die Ehe und die Ansippung an die Pippiniden bzw. die Hugobertiner macht das bei den Agilolfingern fremde Namensgut nachvollziehbar. Die Verwandtschaft der Plektrudis mit den bayerischen Herzögen erklärt zumindest auch teilweise das Vorgehen von Karl Martell gegen Herzog Grimoald und seinen Sohn, die Verhaftung der bayerischen Herzogswitwe Pilitrudis[34] im Zuge seiner militärischen Intervention in Bayern 725 und seine Ehe mit deren Nichte Sunnichilde (Swanahild, † nach 743), die Ansprüche auf das Erbe der Plektrudis-Sippe (Hugobertiner) legitimieren konnte.

Auch die Passauer Patrozinien von St. Stephan und Maria verweisen eher in das östliche Frankenreich, wo man sie in Metz und Speyer kennt. Eine ähnliche Sakraltopographie besteht aber auch in Augsburg mit dem karolingisch nachweisbaren Mariendom und der 969 gegründeten Damenstiftskirche St. Stephan. Vor 1000 gegründete Damenstifte gehörten nicht nur in Passau und Augsburg, sondern auch in Salzburg, Regensburg, Freising und Eichstätt mit zur städtischen Sakraltopographie.

Unter dem Eindruck der Grabungsergebnisse dürfte man sich die Passauer Herzogspfalz eher im Bereich von Niedernburg als am alternativ diskutierten Standort südlich des Doms (Alte Residenz)

---

[30] MGH SS rer. Germ. 13, 203 (Vita Corbiniani 15) und die Anweisung von Papst Gregor II. (715–731), dass sich die künftige Bistumsorganisation in Bayern an der vorhandenen politisch-administrativen Gliederung des Herzogtums zu richten habe: MGH LL 3,3, 452 *(Litterae Gregorii II. papae decretales)*. Für Salzburg, Regensburg und Freising ist die Existenz agilolfingischer Herrschersitze quellenmäßig gesichert. Zur frühen Diözesanverfassung vgl. FREUND 2004.

[31] Mit Namensgleichheit zum vermutlich in Klosterhaft verstorbenen Sohn des Hausmeiers und Enkel der Plektrudis, der gemäß der Verfügung Pippins des Mittleren auf dem Totenbett unter Vormundschaft der Plektrudis zum Nachfolger als Hausmeier in Austrasien 714/715 bestellt wurde, um dann von Karl Martell abgesetzt zu werden. Vgl. SCHIEFFER 2006, 33–38.

[32] Er heißt wie der um 680 geborene, im April 714 erschlagene Sohn der Plektrudis, der neustrische und burgundische Hausmeier Grimoald. Vgl. SCHIEFFER 2006, 28–38.

[33] Den ersten gesicherten Schenker an den Passauer Stephansdom, mit gleichem Namen wie der Vater der Plektrudis, der Reichs-Seneschall und Pfalzgraf Hugbert († wohl 697), dem Enkel des Herzogs Theotar. Vgl. WERNER 1982, passim.

[34] Pilitrudis war die Tochter der Regintrudis und die Nichte der Plektrudis. Sie heiratete Herzog Theudebald und nach dessen Tod umstrittener Weise ihren Schwager Herzog Grimoald. Vgl. STÖRMER 1972, 21; 38.

vorstellen. Diese dürfte auch nach der Bistumsgründung weiter bestanden haben und nach 788 Königsbesitz geworden sein[35]. Danach erfolgte die Umwandlung von Niedernburg in eine geistliche Gemeinschaft für vornehme Damen. Das „Verschwinden der Pfalz und ihre Umwandlung in ein Kloster" dürfte wohl im Verlauf des 9. Jahrhunderts erfolgt sein[36]. Die spätmittelalterliche Passauer Tradition hielt dagegen bereits Herzog Odilo oder seinen Sohn Tassilo III. für den Klostergründer[37]. Die Ausgrabungsergebnisse geben keinen verlässlichen Anhaltspunkt in der landes- und kirchengeschichtlich wichtigen Frage nach dem Zeitpunkt der Klostergründung.

Die Zeit des Niedernburger Damenstifts im 9. und 10. Jahrhundert ist im Grabungsbefund nicht hinreichend ablesbar. Dieses war aber unzweifelhaft bedeutend. Christlein hielt die Basilika als nächste ablesbare Bauphase für karolingerzeitlich. Möglicherweise ist die *Notitia de servitio monasteriorum* von 819 mit der Nennung *Monasterium Altemburc* bereits auf das Kloster Niedernburg zu beziehen[38]. Zur ersten gesicherten urkundlichen Erwähnung Niedernburgs 888 ergeben sich zumindest Hinweise auf die Zugehörigkeit zum Krongut[39]. Urkundlich ist der Rechtsstatus als Königskloster 976 klar bezeugt, wenngleich Kaiser Otto II. zu dieser Zeit Rechte zugunsten des Passauer Bischofs Pilgrim (971–991) aufgab. Hier ist auf jeden Fall ein nicht erfasster bzw. erkannter, mindestens spätkarolingisch-ottonischer Klosterbau anzunehmen, was mit der eingangs geschilderten Problematik des wegen statischer Schäden missglückten Grabungsbeginns erklärbar ist. Überdies lassen sich für Passau Stadtbildungsprozesse und Fernhandel für diese Zeit über urkundlich genannten *possessores civitatis* erschließen[40].

Dennoch erbrachten die von Rainer Christlein verantworteten Ausgrabungen auch für die weitere Bauentwicklung der Kirche wichtige Erkenntnisse. Hier ist an erster Stelle auf die Existenz einer Krypta zu verweisen, die zuvor gänzlich unbekannt war und weiter östlich bei den Untersuchungen miterfasst wurde. Hierbei ist eine dreischiffige Hallenkrypta mit 2,50 m Raumhöhe anzunehmen, von der der nördliche Zugang erfasst wurde, während der Ostabschluss (wohl dem darüber liegenden Chorbereich entsprechend) sowie der Zugang seitlich von Süden unklar bleibt. Laut der Bearbeiterin der Keramik, Eleonore Wintergerst, ist „für den Bau der Krypta nur allgemein ein Baubeginn nach dem 10. Jahrhundert zu belegen"[41]. Ob die Krypta überhaupt fertiggestellt worden war, bleibt nach der Befundaufnahme unklar. Von ihrer Verfüllung wird im Zuge des weiteren Baugeschehens im 11. Jahrhundert ausgegangen. Hier dürfte m. E. an statische Probleme zu denken sein.

Anzunehmen ist ein im Bestand schwer ablesbarer spätottonischer Neubau der Kirche als dreischiffige Basilika mit Krypta und vermutlich Westbau mit Empore *(Abb. 5)*. Dieser dürfte mit den für das Jahr 1010 bezeugten Schenkungen durch Heinrich II. und seine Gattin Kunigunde zu verbinden sein[42]. Die erstaunlich reichen Schenkungen mit Königsforst, Zoll- und Marktrechten sowie die Bestärkung der Immunität haben schon Siegfried Hirsch daran denken lassen, dass hier ein „neuer, stattlicher Sitz für Damen aus königlichem Hause" geschaffen wurde[43]. In diesen Zusammenhang gehört die Überlieferung, dass Kunigunde aus ihrem *aerarium*, ihrem persönli-

---

[35] So zumindest mit STÖRMER 1972, 398–399 zu erschließen.
[36] BOSL 1966, bes. 56.
[37] BOSHOF 2011, 30–32. – Nicht zu halten ist die Vermutung, dass der amtsenthobene Herzog Tassilo III. in Niedernburg beigesetzt wurde (BAUERREISS 1931; BAUERREISS 1937; HEUWIESER 1936).
[38] WAGNER 1999, bes. 431.

[39] MGH DD Arnolf (1940) Nr. 13. Vgl. in diesem Sinne bereits HEUWIESER 1910, 34; TELLENBACH 1928, 20.
[40] MGH DD Otto II. (1888) Nr. 136–137.
[41] BENDER 2018, 157.
[42] MGH DD Heinrich II. (1900–1903) Nr. 214–217; siehe auch VEIT 1965.
[43] HIRSCH 1862, 247 f.

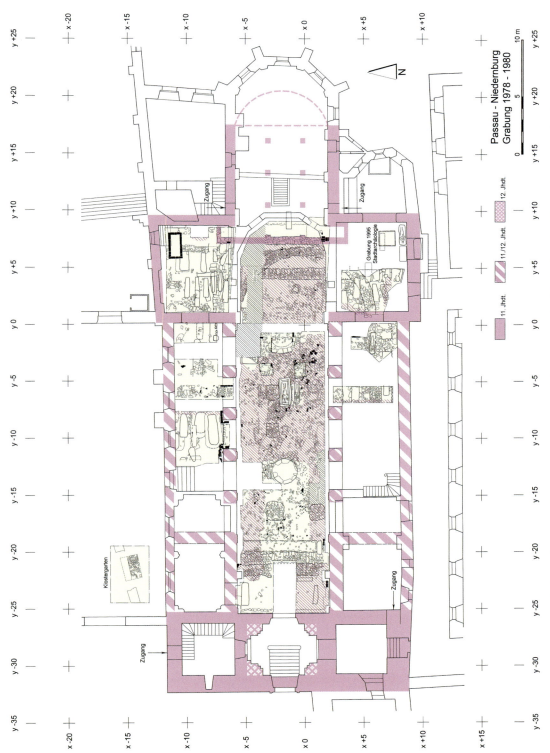

Abb. 5. Der durch die Grabungen 1978–1980 erfasste, vermutlich spätottonische Kirchenbau des Klosters Passau-Niedernburg.

chen Eigentum, Dotationen an das Stift vornahm und als besondere Reliquie einen Kreuzpartikel dorthin gab[44]. Dieser wurde aber besonders verehrt und – vielleicht zunächst in der Krypta verwahrt – in Verdrängung des Marienpatroziniums namensgebend für die Klosterkirche. Die wertvolle Goldschmiedearbeit ging in Passau verloren, eine gewisse Vorstellung mag aber Kunigundes Kreuzstiftung für den Bamberger Dom vermitteln, die sich heute in der Schatzkammer der Münchner Residenz befindet. Eine gewisse Vorbildhaftigkeit ist wiederum im Regensburger Damenstift Niedermünster zu sehen, wo die herzoglichen Großeltern sowie schließlich 1006/7 die Mutter Heinrichs II. bestattet wurden. Den dynastischen Gedenkort machte der König zum Amtsantritt 1002 zum Reichsstift und betonte besonders die Tätigkeit seiner Großmutter Judith als Stifterin *a fundamentis*[45].

Mit guten Gründen kann angenommen werden, dass die Kaiserin Kunigunde in Fortführung der dynastischen Tradition (Damenstifte Gandersheim, Quedlinburg und Essen) zunächst im Passauer Damenstift beigesetzt werden wollte. Dies änderte sich erst mit Kunigundes Klostergründung „Zum Heiligen Kreuz" am Königshof Kaufungen 1017, in die sie als Witwe 1024 eintrat. Auch für Kaufungen (Lkr. Kassel) ist eine Kreuzstiftung überliefert (das Reliquiar, zu dem detaillierte Beschreibungen vorliegen, ging im 16. Jahrhundert verloren). Die 1025 geweihte nordhessische Klosterkirche stellt einen spätottonischen Großbau mit Westempore dar. Eine Krypta besitzt sie nicht. Trotz der nicht vollzogenen Beisetzung Kunigundes bleibt das Passauer Damenstift als Memorialort für die kaiserliche Familie zu bewerten. Nach ihrer Kanonisation wurde Kunigunde im 13. Jahrhundert jedenfalls zeitweise auch offiziell als Mit-Patronin der Salvator-Kreuzkirche verehrt[46]. Hinzu kommt die Kirche als Bestattungsort nämlich noch für die mit großer Wahrscheinlichkeit mit Heinrich II. verwandte Äbtissin Heilika († 1020), die in den herrscherlichen Schenkungsurkunden als Empfängerin hervorgehoben wird[47]. Und schließlich zog sich 1045 die verwitwete Königin Gisela von Ungarn als Schwester von Kaiser Heinrich II. als Äbtissin nach Niedernburg zurück[48].

Die Krypta passt sehr gut in das Bauprogramm eines spätottonischen Damenstifts. Hinzuweisen bleibt auch auf den für Bischof Pilgrim (971–991) belegten Passauer Domneubau, von dem am 5. August 985 die Weihe des ersten Altars des Neubaus bezeugt ist; auch zu diesem Bauvorhaben gehörte eine Krypta. Bender spricht m. E. terminologisch zumindest nach der gängigen Definition durch das Corpus der vorromanischen Kirchenbauten nicht richtig von der „romanischen Krypta", wenn wir diese spätottonisch, d. h. noch vorromanisch ansetzen können. Beilage 21 der Publikation zu Niedernburg setzt die „Romanische Kirche mit Krypta ab 1010" an.

Aus heutiger Sicht bleibt schon im Hinblick auf die wohl doch noch spätottonische Krypta und dann erst recht im Hinblick auf die weitere bauliche Entwicklung zu bedauern, dass für die im Aufgehenden der Klosterkirche vorhandenen romanischen und gotischen Bauteile keine parallele historische Bauforschung durchgeführt wurde. So bleiben die von E. Weiler versuchten Überlegungen zur Gestalt der ottonisch-romanischen Kirche schwierig. Auch ein im Zuge der Renovierungsarbeiten der Kirche 1977–1982 vom Staatlichen Bauamt Passau über die statische Sicherung erstelltes Gutachten führt kaum weiter, sondern wirft im Hinblick auf eine Querschnittsänderung der Langhauspfeiler Fragen auf, die sich aus der Verwendung eines Mischmauerwerks aus Bruchstein

---

[44] VEIT 1965, 15 f.
[45] MGH DD Heinrich II (1900–1903) Nr. 29; 32.
[46] ACAD. SCIEN. BOICA 1829, 508.
[47] SCHMID 1912, 35 Abb. 1; STEININGER et al. 2006, 3 Nr. 1 Abb. 1 zur gotischen Heilika-Tumba der Zeit 1420/25.
[48] SCHMID 1912; STEININGER et al. 2006, 3 f. Nr. 2–3 Abb. 2–3 zur Grabplatte und der darüber befindlichen jüngeren Gisela-Tumba der Zeit um 1420.

und Ziegeln statt des üblichen reinen Bruchsteinmauerwerks und ihrer ursprünglich runden Form ergeben. Solche runden Stützen sind in Bayern im 12. Jahrhundert in Regensburg mit St. Leonhard und St. Kassian sowie in St. Laurentius in Künzing (Lkr. Deggendorf) zu belegen. Ob hier der Verweis auf Burgund mit der Vorhalle der Kirche von St. Philibert in Tournus (Dép. Saône-et-Loire, FR) und dem Vorkommen der runden Stützen im frühen 11. Jahrhundert angebracht ist, vermag ich nicht zu sagen.

Für die Romanik lassen sich mindestens zwei Bauphasen ablesen. Das Querhaus dürfte spätestens in der Mitte des 11. Jahrhunderts bestanden haben. Dies ergibt sich durch die im südöstlichen Winkel des Südquerhauses angelegte Bestattung der dort als Äbtissin verstorbenen Königin Gisela († 1060), die die zweitälteste Schwester Kaiser Heinrichs II. war und nach ihrer Vertreibung aus Ungarn 1045 dem Passauer Damenstift während der Zeit Heinrichs III. 15 Jahre lang vorstand. Die reichen Schenkungen der rasch verehrten Gisela dürften den Grundstock zu einem in der Mitte des 11. Jahrhunderts begonnenen, herrscherlich gewollten salierzeitlichen Neubau geliefert haben. Dazu gehörten doch wohl in Umsetzung eines einheitlichen Plans nach Aufgabe der Krypta die Baukörper von Chor, Querhaus, Langhaus und der möglicherweise schon bestehende Westbau mit Empore. Auch der Bischof *Gregorius aus Armenien* († 1093) wurde in dieser salierzeitlichen Kirche beigesetzt[49].

Hinzu kommt eine jüngere, stauferzeitlich anzusetzende romanische Umbauphase der Kirche. Hinzuweisen bleibt auf den Bedeutungsverlust des Klosters, das 1161 durch Friedrich Barbarossa an den Passauer Bischof Konrad übertragen[50] und durch den Verzicht seitens Heinrich VI. 1193 seine vorherige Reichsunmittelbarkeit verlor und ganz dem Bischof unterstellt wurde: Ende des 12. Jahrhunderts oder um 1200 wurde im Erdgeschoss der Vorhalle und im zentralen Emporenraum darüber ein Gewölbe eingezogen.

Die hier geäußerte Detailkritik im Hinblick auf die Probleme der mittelalterlichen Baugeschichte lässt sich freilich weniger auf die Bearbeitung als die Durchführung der Ausgrabungen selbst zurückführen, die doch 1978–1980 sehr stark auf die Römerzeit und das Frühmittelalter ausgerichtet gewesen sind. Immerhin wurden aber auch frühneuzeitliche Gräber untersucht, die Juliane Schenk in einem Beitrag behandelt (S. 625–676).

Gleichfalls als zeitbedingt bleibt anzuführen, dass man sich auf die Kirche beschränkte und nicht eine Strategie verfolgte, die auch Untersuchungen innerhalb der Immunität des ehemaligen Klosters ermöglichte. Diese ist immer noch relativ gut ablesbar. Nachdem das Kloster im Zuge der Säkularisation aufgelöst wurde und 1808 die letzten Nonnen auszogen, richteten die Englischen Fräulein 1836 in den Klostergebäuden eine bis heute in Trägerschaft der Diözese Passau betriebene Schule ein. Von daher dürften sich schützenswerte Strukturen bewahrt haben.

Die stets als wichtig eingestufte Ausgrabung vermittelte aber auch wichtige Einblicke in die Passauer Stadtgeschichte, die weit über die Zeit der Kirchennutzung und ihres spätantiken Vorgängerbaus, des Horreums, zurückgehen. Das Areal wurde nachweislich schon seit der Latènezeit besiedelt (Beitrag von Walter Irlinger zu den latènezeitlichen Funden aus der Grabung, S. 257–266). Die Keramik des 1. bis frühen 2. Jahrhunderts wurde von Helmut Bender und Günther Moosbauer bearbeitet (S. 267–270). Die danach einsetzende Bebauung und ihre festgestellte Brandzerstörung um 270 n. Chr. bleiben schwieriger zu beurteilen. Beilage 15 unterscheidet in der Bebauung eine

---

[49] CHRISTLEIN 1980c.
[50] In diese Zeit gehört die steinerne Bestätigungsinschrift der Zollprivilegien der Aachener Kaufleute von 1166 unweit vom romanischen Kirchenportal: STEININGER et al. 2006, 5 f. Nr. 4 Abb. 4.

erste sich gut abzeichnende Phase als schräg liegende Fachwerkbauten auf Schwellbalken oder -riegelkonstruktionen des späten 2. bis 3. Jahrhunderts, die an eine Art Vicus denken lassen. Danach wird eine schräge zweiphasige Bebauung des späten 3. und 4. Jahrhundert mit Öfen und Gräbchen unterschieden. Im mittleren Drittel des 4. Jahrhunderts existierte eine ebenfalls noch schräg zu den späteren Kirchenstrukturen verlaufende Bebauung in Trockenmauerwerk. Zu diesen römischen Nutzungsphasen vor der Errichtung des Horreums im späten 4. Jahrhundert fehlt bislang eine überzeugende Deutung. Dies gilt dann auch für die Frage der militärischen Nutzung und ihre Interpretation[51]. In spätconstantinischer Zeit, im zweiten Viertel des 4. Jahrhunderts, ist der wichtige Militärstandort mit Rädchensigillata aus den Argonnentöpfereien versorgt worden. Eine neuerliche Bautätigkeit dürfte in der Mitte des 4. Jahrhunderts mit der Trockenmauerperiode anzusetzen sein. Die Beschäftigung mit diesen Befunden und Funden bietet ausgedehnt auf die Gesamtfrage der spätrömischen Befestigung in Passau sicher Stoff für eine weitere und das bislang Vorgelegte ergänzende, im Umfang etwas kleiner anzusetzende monographische Studie, deren Realisierung man Helmut Bender und der Fachwelt ebenfalls nur wünschen kann. Eine solche Publikation würde auch das Verständnis der Entwicklung des Zentralorts Passau befördern, der als Militärstandort an der Provinzgrenze zu charakterisieren ist, der schlaglichtartig erhellt durch die Schilderung in der *Vita Severini* Fiskalbesitz in der quellenarmen Agilolfingerzeit werden konnte, auf dessen Grundlage Herzogspfalz und Bischofssitz im 8. Jahrhundert entstanden.

Literaturverzeichnis

Acad. Scien. Boica 1829
 Academia Scientiarum Boica (Hrsg.), Monumenta Boica. Diplomata Imperatorum authentica 28,1 (München 1829). http://digitalisate.bsb-muenchen.de/bsb10799619 (letzter Zugriff: 25.5.2022).

Aign 1975
 A. Aign, „Castra Batava" und die Cohors nona Batavorum. Ostbair. Grenzmarken 17, 1975, 102–157.

Bauerreiss 1931
 R. Bauerreiss, Wo ist das Grab Tassilos III.? Stud. u. Mitt. Gesch. Benediktinerorden u. seiner Zweige 49, 1931, 92–102.

Bauerreiss 1937
 R. Bauerreiss, Nochmals das Grab Tassilos III. Passau Gesch. Benediktinerorden u. seiner Zweige 55, 1937, 329–333.

Bender 2003
 RGA² 22 (2003) 496–499 s. v. Passau (H. Bender).

Bender 2018
 H. Bender (Hrsg.), Die Ausgrabungen 1978–1980 in der Klosterkirche zu Passau-Niedernburg. Materialh. Bayer. Arch. 108 (Kallmünz 2018).

Boshof 1999
 E. Boshof, Die Stadt im Früh- und Hochmittelalter: Unter der Herrschaft der Bischöfe. In: E. Boshof, Geschichte der Stadt Passau (Regensburg 1999) 63–96.

Boshof 2011
 E. Boshof, Das Kloster Niedernburg im Früh- und Hochmittelalter. In: F.-R. Erkens (Hrsg.), 1000 Jahre Goldener Steig. Vorträge der Tagung vom 24. April 2010 in Niedernburg. Veröff. Inst. Kulturraumforsch. Ostbaiern u. Nachbarregionen Univ. Passau 61 (Passau 2011) 29–46.

Boshof / Wolff 1994
 E. Boshof / H. Wolff (Hrsg.), Das Christentum im bairischen Raum. Von den Anfängen bis ins 11. Jahrhundert. Passauer Hist. Forsch. 8 (Köln, Weimar, Wien 1994).

Bosl 1966
 K. Bosl, Pfalzen, Klöster und Forste in Bayern. Zur Organisation von Herzogs- und Königsgut in Bayern. Verhand. Hist. Ver. Oberpfalz u. Regensburg 106, 1966, 43–62.

---

[51] Zur Gesamtentwicklung vgl. Mackensen 2018.

CHRISTLEIN 1979
R. CHRISTLEIN, Das spätrömische Kastell Boiotro zu Passau-Innstadt. Formen der Kontinuität am Donaulimes im raetisch-norischen Grenzbereich. In: J. Werner / E. Ewig (Hrsg.), Von der Spätantike zum frühen Mittelalter. Aktuelle Probleme in historischer und archäologischer Sicht. Konstanzer Arbeitskr. Mittelalterl. Gesch., Vorträge u. Forsch. 25 (Sigmaringen 1979) 91–123.

CHRISTLEIN 1980a
R. CHRISTLEIN, Romanische und germanische Funde des fünften Jahrhunderts aus den Passauer Kastellen Batavis und Boiotro. Ostbair. Grenzmarken 22, 1980, 106–118.

CHRISTLEIN 1980b
R. CHRISTLEIN, Ausgrabungen im römischen Batavis unter der Klosterkirche Niedernburg zu Passau, Niederbayern. Arch. Jahr Bayern 1980, 126–127.

CHRISTLEIN 1980c
R. CHRISTLEIN, Das Grab des Erzbischofs Gregorius von Armenien in der Klosterkirche Niedernburg zu Passau, Niederbayern. Arch. Jahr Bayern 1980, 174–175.

CHRISTLEIN 1982
R. CHRISTLEIN, Die rätischen Städte Severins. In: D. Straub (Hrsg.), Severin. Zwischen Römerzeit und Völkerwanderung. Ausstellung des Landes Oberösterreich, 24. April bis 26. Oktober 1982 im Stadtmuseum Enns (Linz 1982) 217–253.

Eugippius, Vita Sev.
Eugippius, Das Leben des heiligen Severin (lateinisch / deutsch). Einführung, Übersetzung und Erläuterung von R. Noll. Schr. u. Quellen Alte Welt 11 (Berlin 1963; Lizenzausg. Passau 1981).

EWEL 1983
M. EWEL, Die romanischen Fresken in der Vorhalle der Marienkirche zu Passau Niedernburg. Ostbair. Grenzmarken 25, 1983, 128–136.

FISCHER 1994
TH. FISCHER, Bemerkungen zur Archäologie in der Severinszeit in Künzing und Passau. In: BOSHOF / WOLFF 1994, 93–127.

FISCHER 1995
TH. FISCHER, Passau. In: W. Czysz / Th. Fischer / K. Dietz, Die Römer in Bayern (Stuttgart 1995) 494–498.

FREUND 2004
S. FREUND, Von den Agilolfingern zu den Karolingern. Bayerns Bischöfe zwischen Kirchenorganisation, Reichsintegration und karolingischer Reform (700–847). Schriftenr. Bayer. Landesgesch. 144 (München 2004) 8–42.

FUCHS 2011
J. FUCHS, Spätantike militärische *horrea* an Rhein und Donau. Eine Untersuchung der römischen Militäranlagen in den Provinzen Maxima Sequanorum, Raetia I, Raetia II, Noricum Ripense und Valeria [Diplomarbeit Univ. Wien] (Wien 2011). doi: https://doi.org/10.25365/thesis.17666.

HEUWIESER 1910
M. HEUWIESER, Die stadtrechtliche Entwicklung der Stadt Passau bis zur Stadtherrschaft der Bischöfe (Passau 1910).

HEUWIESER 1936
M. HEUWIESER, Ist Herzog Tassilo im Kloster Niedernburg zu Passau begraben? Zeitschr. Bayer. Landesgesch. 9, 1936, 412–416.

HIRSCH 1862
S. HIRSCH, Jahrbücher des Deutschen Reichs unter Heinrich II. Jahrb. dt. Gesch. 11,1–2 (Berlin 1862). https://www.mgh.de/de/bibliothek/digitale-angebote/quellensammlungen/jahrbuecher (letzter Zugriff: 25.5.2022).

KONRAD 2007
M. KONRAD, Die Ausgrabungen unter dem Niedermünster zu Regensburg 2. Bauten und Funde der römischen Zeit. Auswertung. Münchner Beitr. Vor- u. Frühgesch. 57 (München 2007).

KONRAD et al. 2011
M. KONRAD / A. RETTNER / E. WINTERGERST, Die Ausgrabungen unter dem Niedermünster zu Regensburg 1. Münchner Beitr. Vor- u. Frühgesch. 56 (München 2011).

LATER 2014
CH. LATER, Kontinuität seit Severin? Die Entwicklung Passaus vom bajuwarischen Zentralort zur bischöflichen Residenzstadt des späten Mittelalter aus archäologischer Sicht. In: P. Morsbach / I. Heckmann / Ch. Later (Hrsg.), Kreisfreie Stadt Passau.

Ensembles, Baudenkmäler, Bodendenkmäler 1. Denkmäler Bayern 2,25,1 (Regensburg 2014) XLVII–LXVIII.

Lotter 1976
F. Lotter, Severinus von Norikum. Legende und historische Wirklichkeit. Untersuchungen zur Phase des Übergangs von spätantiken zu mittelalterlichen Denk- und Lebensformen. Monogr. Gesch. Mittelalter 12 (Stuttgart 1976).

Mackensen 1995
M. Mackensen, Das spätrömische Grenzkastell *Caelius Mons* in Kellmünz an der Iller. Führer Arch. Denkmäler Bayern. Schwaben 3 (Stuttgart 1995).

Mackensen 1998
M. Mackensen, Das tetrarchische Kastell *Caelius Mons* / Kellmünz am raetischen Donau-Iller-Limes. In: C. Bridger / K.-J. Gilles (Hrsg.), Spätrömische Befestigungsanlagen in den Rhein- und Donauprovinzen. BAR Internat. Ser. 704 (Oxford 1998) 119–135. doi: https://doi.org/10.30861/9780860548874.

Mackensen 2018
M. Mackensen, Organization and development of the Late Roman frontier in the provinces of Raetia prima et secunda (ca. AD 270/300–450). In: C. S. Sommer / S. Matešić (Hrsg.), Limes XXIII. Proceedings of the 23rd International Congress of Roman Frontier Studies Ingolstadt 2015. Beitr. Welterbe Limes, Sonderbd. 4,1–2 (Mainz 2018) 47–69.

Matz 1955
S. Matz, Romanische Wandgemälde in Kloster Niedernburg-Passau [unpubl. Diss. Univ. Freiburg i. Br.] (Freiburg 1955).

Matz-Tuczek 1956
S. Matz-Tuczek, Romanische Wandgemälde im Kloster Niedernburg in Passau. Münchner Jahrb. Bildende Kunst 3,7, 1956, 32–48.

Niemeier 2001
J.-P. Niemeier, Die Erhebung der Gebeine der seligen Gisela. In: H. W. Wurster / M. Treml / R. Loibl (Hrsg.), Bayern – Ungarn. Tausend Jahre. Aufsätze zur Bayerischen Landesausstellung 2001. Vorträge der Tagung „Bayern und Ungarn im Mittelalter und in der frühen Neuzeit" in Passau 15. bis 18. Oktober 2000. Veröff. Bayer. Gesch. u. Kultur 43 (Passau 2001) 91–98.

Päffgen 2016
B. Päffgen, Kirchen in der *Raetia secunda*. In: K. Strobel / H. Dolenz (Hrsg.), Neue Ergebnisse zum frühen Kirchenbau im Alpenraum. Röm. Österreich 39 (Wien 2016) 277–319.

Pohl 1980
W. Pohl, Die Gepiden und die *gentes* an der mittleren Donau nach dem Zusammenbruch des Attilareiches. In: H. Wolfram / F. Daun (Hrsg.), Die Völker an der mittleren und unteren Donau im fünften und sechsten Jahrhundert. Berichte des Symposions der Kommission für Frühmittelalterforschung 24. bis 27. Oktober 1978, Stift Zwettl, Niederösterreich. Denkschr. Phil.-Hist. Kl. 145 = Veröff. Komm. Frühmittelalterforsch. 4 (Wien 1980) 239–305.

Schieffer 2006
R. Schieffer, Die Karolinger[4] (Stuttgart 2006).

Schmid 1912
W. M. Schmid, Das Grab der Königin Gisela von Ungarn, Gemahlin Stephans I. des Heiligen (München 1912).

Schmid 1927
W. M. Schmid, Illustrierte Geschichte der Stadt Passau (Passau 1927). doi: https://doi.org/10.11588/diglit.44010.

Schwarz 1971
K. Schwarz, Die Ausgrabungen im Niedermünster zu Regensburg. Führer Arch. Denkmäler Bayern 1 (Kallmünz / Opf. 1971).

Sommer 2019
C. S. Sommer, Der Donaulimes auf dem Weg zum UNESCO-Welterbe. Bayer. Arch. 3, 2019, 14–16.

Stein-Kecks 1993
H. Stein-Kecks, Die romanischen Wandmalereien in der Vorhalle zur ehemaligen Marienkirche des Klosters Niedernburg. In: K. Möseneder (Hrsg.), Kunst in Passau. Von der Romanik zur Gegenwart (Passau 1993) 30–59.

STEININGER et al. 2006
: Ch. Steininger / F. A. Bornschlegel / K. U. Högg, Die Inschriften der Stadt *Passau* bis zum Stadtbrand von 1662. Dt. Inschr. 67 (Wiesbaden 2006).

STÖRMER 1972
: W. Störmer, Adelsgruppen im früh- und hochmittelalterlichen Bayern. Stud. Bayer. Verfassungs- u. Sozialgesch. 4 (München 1972).

TELLENBACH 1928
: G. Tellenbach, Die bischöflich passauischen Eigenklöster und ihre Vogteien. Hist. Stud. 173 (Berlin 1928).

VEIT 1965
: L. Veit, Das Diplom König Heinrichs II. über die Schenkung der „portio silvae, quae vocatur Nortwalt" an die Abtei Niedernburg in Passau. Anz. Germ. Nationalmus. 1965, 7–32.

WAGNER 1999
: H. Wagner, Zur Notitia de servitio monasteriorum von 819. Dt. Archiv 55, 1999, 417–438.

WERNER 1982
: M. Werner, Adelsfamilien im Umkreis der frühen Karolinger. Die Verwandtschaft Irminas von Oeren und Adelas von Pfalzel (Stuttgart 1982).

WINTERGERST 2019
: E. Wintergerst, Die Ausgrabungen unter dem Niedermünster zu Regensburg 3. Befunde und Funde der nachrömischen Zeit. Münchner Beitr. Vor- u. Frühgesch. 66 (München 2019).

Anschrift des Verfassers:

Bernd Päffgen
Ludwig-Maximilians-Universität
Historicum – Zentrum für Geschichte und Archäologie
Institut für Vor- und Frühgeschichtliche Archäologie und
Provinzialrömische Archäologie
Schellingstraße 12
DE–80799 München
bernd.paeffgen@lmu.de

Abbildungsnachweis
Abb. 1: BENDER 2018, Beil. 16. – *Abb. 2:* BENDER 2018, 209 Abb. 1. – *Abb. 3:* Martin Schaich / Arctron. – *Abb. 4:* BENDER 2018, Beil. 17. – *Abb. 5:* BENDER 2018, Beil. 18.

Frankfurt zur späten Merowingerzeit:
Die Aussagen des Grabfunds in der ehemaligen Stiftskirche St. Bartholomäus

Von Bernd Päffgen

Von 1991 bis 1993 durchgeführte Ausgrabungen in der ehemaligen Stiftskirche St. Bartholomäus in Frankfurt am Main, die Andrea Hampel leitete, erbrachten wichtige Befunde, die bis in das Frühmittelalter zurückreichen und zu einer Revision der Baugeschichte des mehrphasigen gotischen Kirchenbaus führten, die ebenfalls im Frühmittelalter beginnt. Diese, mit der vorromanischen Königspfalz in Zusammenhang stehenden Befunde wurden von Magnus Wintergerst bearbeitet und 2007 als „Franconofurd 1" vorgelegt (Wintergerst 2007). Von besonderem Interesse ist das im Bereich des heutigen Kirchenmittelschiffs aufgefundene, reich ausgestattete Mädchengrab, das zur Verdeutlichung sogar im Kirchenfußboden durch eine Grabplatte gekennzeichnet wurde. Die Grabausstattung ist im Frankfurter Dommuseum ausgestellt.

Egon Wamers, der langjährige Leiter des Frankfurter Archäologischen Museums, hat sich intensiv mit diesem Grab beschäftigt. Dies fand bereits 2012/13 Ausdruck in der viel beachteten Sonderausstellung „Königinnen der Merowinger. Adelsgräber aus den Kirchen von Köln, Saint-Denis, Chelles und Frankfurt am Main" (Wamers 2012; Wamers / Périn 2013). Hier wurde eine vergleichende und vielleicht etwas hoch gegriffene Einordnung des Frankfurter Grabs versucht, die hinsichtlich einer Kontextualisierung mit den ungleich besser gesicherten merowingerzeitlichen Kirchenbauten westlich des Rheins manchem kritischen Besucher gewagt erscheinen musste. Existierte zur Merowingerzeit denn in Frankfurt überhaupt eine Kirche, die man Saint-Denis (Dép. Seine-Saint-Denis, FR) mit dem verehrten Bischofsgrab des Dionysius und den gesicherten Bestattungen der Merowinger mit Königin Arnegunde († um 580), König Chlothar II. († 629), König Dagobert I. († 638), Königin Nantechild († 642) und König Chlodwig II. († 657) auch nur annähernd vergleichend zur Seite stellen kann? Auch Chelles (Dép. Seine-et-Marne, FR) mit der von Königin Chrodechild († 544) gestifteten Georgskirche und dem 658 von Königin Bathilde eingerichteten Frauenkloster und der Beisetzung der Klostergründerin besitzt sicher andere Wertigkeit. Wieder anders zu bewerten ist der archäologisch nachgewiesene merowingerzeitliche Kirchenbau unter der Kölner Bischofskirche.

Tatsächlich ist schon die Interpretation der von Andrea Hampel aus geringen Fundamentresten auf knapp zwölf Metern Länge als Bau I unter der Frankfurter Stiftskirche rekonstruierte steinerne Saalkirche der Zeit der zweiten Hälfte des 7. Jahrhunderts schwierig. Ohne das Mädchengrab 95 und seinen Bezug zu besagten Fundamentresten hätte es diese Deutung kaum gegeben. Die Ausgräberin selbst führte dazu aus: „Der Zusammenhang der beiden Befunde ermöglicht eine eindeutige zeitliche Ansprache der Steinkirche in die zweite Hälfte des 7. Jahrhunderts nach Christus" (Hampel 1994, 174). Nicht geklärt sah die Ausgräberin das genaue chronologische Verhältnis von Steinbau und Grab. Sie betonte die enge Zusammengehörigkeit, schloss aber nicht aus, dass Bau I über dem Grab errichtet wurde. Magnus Wintergerst übte Kritik an Grabungsweise / Dokumentation und betonte bei seiner Befundaufarbeitung, dass das Mädchengrab nur im bereits bestehenden Gebäude angelegt worden sein kann (Wintergerst 2007). Weiterhin wandte er sich gegen die Deutung von Bau I als Kirche, da er die im Westteil vorhandene Hypokausteizung wegen einer darunter befindlichen Schicht mit Keramikscherben des 7. Jahrhunderts als später erkannte und richtig als im frühmittelalterlichen Kirchenbau fremdes Element herausstellte. Weniger überzeugend ist sein Argument, dass die Mädchenbestattung mit dem brettchengewebten Goldlahnkreuz nicht in eine Kirche passe, da die verwandten Goldblattkreuze nie in Kirchengräbern vorkämen (WINTERGERST 2007, 33 f.). Hier wäre zumindest das reiche Frauengrab der Zeit um 700 n. Chr. aus der Kirche St. Peter in Rommerskirchen im Rhein-Kreis Neuss zu diskutieren (PÄFFGEN / RISTOW 1996a; 1996b).

Diese Ausgangslage indiziert, dass die Beschäftigung mit Bau I und dem Kindergrab weiter angebracht ist. Dem geht Egon Wamers im ersten Hauptkapitel seines 2015 erschienenen Buchs „Franconofurd 2"[1] nach und widmet sich der Befundlage von Bau I und dem Mädchengrab (WAMERS 2015, 15–37). Wamers nimmt an, dass der Bau im Mittelschiff zu einer größeren Gebäudegruppe auf dem Domhügel gehörte und wegen des Heizungseinbaus im 7. Jahrhundert zunächst als Kleruswohnung diente (WAMERS 2015, 21–25). Nicht hinreichend geklärt ist, ob dieser Einbau nachträglich in ein schon bestehendes Gebäude erfolgte. Wamers wählt hierfür den Begriff *domus ecclesiae*. Da dies ja die kirchliche Versammlung generell und als archäologisch-kirchengeschichtlicher Terminus die frühen Hauskirchen meint, erscheint mir das nicht klärend. Auch der Wortgebrauch in den Schriftquellen des 6.–7. Jahrhunderts ist keineswegs eindeutig. Während das bei Gregor von Tours (Hist. Franc. 9,12) überlieferte *Oratorium in domus aecclesiastica* des 588 oder 591 verstorbenen Bischofs Agericus in Verdun dessen Hauskapelle im Kathedralbereich meinen dürfte[2], bezeichnet das Konzil von Toledo 610 damit das Gebäude, das Wohnungen für den Klerus und den Verwaltungsraum des Archidiakons enthielt (VIVES et al. 1963).

In einem nächsten Schritt sei die Kleruswohnung aufgegeben und zur *cella memoriae* umgenutzt worden (WAMERS 2015, 25 f.). Um dieses Gebäude wurden jedenfalls im Verlauf des 7. und 8. Jahrhunderts nach Ausweis von ^{14}C-Datierungen Gräber angelegt (WAMERS 2015, 26–28). Die Umnutzung zur *cella memoriae* sieht Wamers mit der Einbringung des Kindergrabs 95 erst im frühen 8. Jahrhundert in „die inzwischen aufgegebene oder gar verfallene domus ecclesiae" (WAMERS 2015, 29). Kindergrab 95 war als 2 m lange und 1,20 m breite Grabkammer angelegt, die auf den oberen Absätzen noch Reste von trocken gesetztem Bruchsteinmauerwerk aufwies *(Abb. 1)*. Dieses Faktum halte ich für wichtig. Steinumfassungen sind in der Grabarchitektur des frühen Mittelalters keineswegs nur konstruktiv von Bedeutung (z. B. PÄFFGEN 1992, 325–331). In der Rekonstruktion Abb. 11 liegen nur wenige längseinfassende Steine und deutlich anders als auf der Planumzeichnung Abb. 9,1.

An der Nordseite der Grabkammer befand sich ein auf Unterlegbalken ruhender Holzsarg von nur 1,20 m Länge. Parallelen zu solchen Unterlegbalken benennt Wamers ausschließlich aus alamannischen und bajuwarischen Gräberfeldern (WAMERS 2015, 31). Hier wären aber auch geographisch nähere Vorkommen aus dem Fränkischen anzuführen. Im Holzsarg befand sich der Leichnam eines vier- bis knapp fünfjährigen Kleinkinds (Infans I), das nach Schmuck und Kleidung weiblich war.

Überraschenderweise waren im Sarg auch der Leichenbrand eines zweiten Kindes und ein handgemachter Tontopf deponiert. Im Südteil der Grabkammer hatte man außerhalb des kleinen Sargs für die ausgehende Merowingerzeit erstaunlich umfangreiche Speisebeigaben deponiert. In zwei kleinen Kochtöpfen fränkischer Drehscheibenware fand man eine Rinderrippe mit Hiebspuren und

---

[1] EGON WAMERS, Franconofurd 2. Das bi-rituelle Kinderdoppelgrab der späten Merowingerzeit unter der Frankfurter Bartholomäuskirche („Dom"). Archäologische und naturwissenschaftliche Untersuchungen. Schriften des Archäologischen Museums Frankfurt 22,2. Verlag Schnell & Steiner, Regensburg 2015. Hbk. € 34,95. ISBN 978-3-7954-2762-7. 249 Seiten mit 185 Abb. – Auf Anregung von Alexander Gramsch wird hier die vor einiger Zeit übernommene Buchbesprechung zu einer Miszelle ausgeweitet.

[2] MGH SS rer. Merov. 1(Hannover 1937) 421, ed. B. Krusch; BUCHNER 1956, Bd. 2, 248 f.

Abb. 1. Frankfurt am Main, St. Bartholomäus. Rekonstruktionsvorschlag für das Kindergrab 95.

ein Hühnchen ohne Kopf. Daneben lagen – wohl auf vergangenen Holztabletts – Knochen von Kalb und Ferkel sowie Wirbel eines Lachses. In den Bereich der Trankbeigabe verweisen ein kleiner eisenbeschlagener Holzeimer, eine Glastasse und ein rundlicher Holzbecher mit Randbeschlägen aus Silber.

Ein zweites Hauptkapitel behandelt Analysen zu den Überresten der beiden menschlichen Individuen (WAMERS 2015, 39–50). Nils-Jörn Rehbach führte Untersuchungen zu den Skelett- und Leichenbrandresten der etwa gleichaltrigen Kleinkinder durch. Im Leichenbrand des Kindes (116 g) ließen sich acht Krallen eines Braunbären, verbrannte Überreste eines vermutlich jungen Schweins (Fersenbein) sowie Rippen- und Röhrenknochenfragmente mindestens eines Tiers der Größe von Schaf / Ziege / Hund nachweisen. Kulturgeschichtlich interessant ist die Feststellung, dass das körperbestattete Mädchen öfters „in den Genuss von vermutlich mit Honig gesüßten Speisen kam, da die kariöse Zerstörung besonders eines Milchzahnes bereits ein fortgeschrittenes Stadium erreicht hatte", andererseits ließ sich an den Dauerzähnen eine Wachstumsstörung diagnostizieren. Dies führt zur Vermutung, dass „es im 4. Lebensjahr auch Mangelernährung kennengelernt oder eine Erkrankung überstanden haben" dürfte (WAMERS 2015, 41). Alternativ sollte man auch daran denken, dass ein vornehmes Mädchen gut drei Jahre von einer Amme (?) gestillt worden sein kann und dann bei der Entwöhnung Probleme mit der Umstellung der Ernährung hatte. In seinem Kommentar S. 42 betont Wamers, dass die Annahme der Ausgräberin, dem Mädchen seien Kind, Ferkel und Bär gewissermaßen als Spielkameraden beigegeben worden, nicht haltbar sei. Stattdessen sei davon auszugehen, dass Leichenbrand und handgemachtes Gefäß gewissermaßen eine eigene Brandbestattung bildeten. Die in dem Leichenbrand enthaltenen Bärenkrallen dürften von einem Fell stammen, das als Unterlage des Kinderleichnams bei der Verbrennung diente. Ein weiterer Kommentar von Wamers (WAMERS 2015, 42 f.) stellt heraus, dass Brand- und Körperbestattung im Kammergrab als gleichzeitig anzusehen sind.

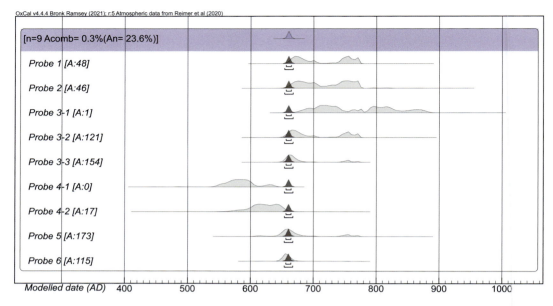

Abb. 2. Die neun ¹⁴C-Analysen aus Grab 95 der ehemaligen Stiftskirche St. Bartholomäus in Frankfurt am Main.

Die an fünf Proben durchgeführte ¹⁴C-Analyse von Knochenmaterial durch das Leibniz-Labor für Altersbestimmung und Isotopenforschung der Christian-Albrechts-Universität zu Kiel behandelt Matthias Hüls (in: WAMERS 2015, 44–47). Untersucht wurde Material aus der Körperbestattung (Probe 1: 1315 ± 21), Leichenbrand des zweiten Kindes (Probe 2: 1305 ± 30; Probe 3: 1245 ± 30), kremierte Menschen- oder Tierknochen (Probe 4,1: 1495 ± 25; Probe 4,2: 1430 ± 35) und eine angebrannte Bärenkralle (Probe 5: 1360 ± 30). Da die Proben 3 und 4 bei der Erstmessung 2006 deutlich anders datiert wurden, veranlasste Wamers 2013 und 2014 Nachmessungen an diesen Proben. Diese näherten sich mit 1330 ± 25 und 1345 ± 20 für Probe 3 an, blieben aber für Probe 4 mit der Datierung 1430 ± 35 abweichend. Im Ergebnis ergaben die Proben 1, 2, 3 und 5 „konsistente Radiokarbonalter, die auf eine Niederlegung in der zweiten Hälfte des 7. Jahrhunderts schließen lassen" (WAMERS 2015, 47). Etwas älter fiel die Messung der Probe 4 mit einer Datierung in die erste Hälfte des 7. Jahrhunderts aus. Da Wamers einen späteren Zeitansatz favorisiert, wurde eine Schädelprobe 6 der Körperbestattung 2014 zur Kontrolluntersuchung an das Curt-Engelhorn-Zentrum Archäometrie in Mannheim übergeben, die jedoch zum ähnlichen Ergebnis von 642–674 n. Chr. im 2 Sigmabereich führte (Beitrag Bernd Kromer in: WAMERS 2015, 48 f. Abb. 17).

Damit liegen für Grab 95 insgesamt neun ¹⁴C-Analysen an Knochenmaterial vor. Die Proben 1 und 6 stammen vom Skelett des körperbestatteten Mädchens. Vom kremierten Kind wurden vier Proben gemessen (Probe 2, Proben 3,1–3). Es ist äußerst selten, dass aus einem merowingerzeitlichen Grab so viele Datierungen vorliegen. Damit ergibt sich grundsätzlich eine herausragende Quelle zur Prüfung der Wertigkeit der Heranziehung von ¹⁴C-Analysen in der Frühgeschichtsforschung. Alle neun Proben aus dem Befund 95 zusammengenommen, ergibt sich die Darstellung in *Abbildung 2*. Lässt man die Proben 3,1 und 4,1–2 beiseite, ergibt sich mit sechs Messungen eine ebenso klares wie präzises Datierungsintervall, das mit dem dritten Viertel des 7. Jahrhunderts übereinstimmt *(Abb. 3)*. Im Abgleich mit den vorliegenden Grabbeigaben kann an einem Zeitansatz der Bestattung um 680 aus meiner Sicht kein Zweifel bestehen. Jede andere Argumentation müsste die generationsgenaue Heranziehbarkeit der ¹⁴C-Methode im ersten nachchristlichen Jahrtausend in Abrede stellen.

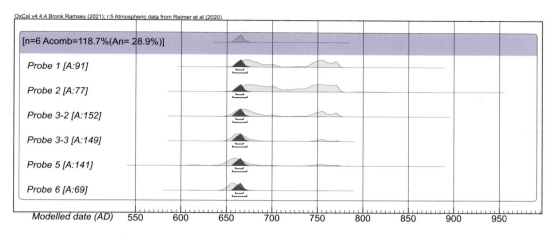

Abb. 3. Die ¹⁴C-Analysen aus Grab 95 wie in *Abbildung 2*, ohne die Proben 3,1 und 4,1–2.

Mike Schweissing untersuchte an der Staatssammlung für Anthropologie und Paläoanatomie in München die Strontiumisotope am Zahnmaterial der beiden Kinder, einer Bärenkralle sowie von Erdproben (WAMERS 2015, 49 f. Tab. 4). Ortsfremde Herkunft ist demnach eher auszuschließen, wenngleich zu bedenken gilt, dass auch in anderen Gebieten Isotopenwerte im Bereich von $^{87}Sr/^{86}Sr$ 0,708–0,709 vorkommen und letztlich der Raum zwischen der Donau und den Alpen sowie die Norddeutsche Tiefebene in Frage kommt.

Das dritte Hauptkapitel bringt „Untersuchungen zu den Gefäßbeigaben" (WAMERS 2015, 51–62). Hierbei handelt es sich um zwei scheibengedrehte Wölbwand-Töpfchen mit Rußspuren an der Außenwandung, die wegen der mineralogisch nachgewiesenen Rheinsand-Magerung aus rheinischen Töpfereien stammen dürften. Bereits Stamm hat die Gruppen 10 und 11 der spätmerowingischen bis karolingischen gelblichgrauen und grauen Ware mit Sandmagerung im Frankfurter Fundmaterial herausgestellt. Leider gibt Wamers weder Farbangaben noch Fassungsvermögen an. Die schöne Farb-Sammelaufnahme der Gefäße Abb. 18 bringt diese mit der Aufsicht von oben. Um das Gefäßprofil zu beurteilen, muss man leider umständlich auf die Zeichnungen in der Publikation der Ausgräberin zurückgreifen (HAMPEL 1994, Abb. 108–109). Zum grauschwarzen, handgemachten Topf hätte man sich eine Farbaufnahme gewünscht. Nach der Expertise von Gerwulf Schneider ist hier eine regionale Herkunft auszuschließen (in: WAMERS 2015, 53). Zur chronologischen Einordnung verweist Wamers auf die Parallelen der drei Gefäße aus dem Gräberfeld von Wenigumstadt (Lkr. Aschaffenburg), die den dortigen Keramikgruppen 16 und 18 und der Belegungsphase 12 (ca. 700–725 n. Chr.) der Gliederung durch Eva Stauch zuzuordnen sind. Der mit Eisenbeschlägen versehene konische Daubeneimer in Miniaturform von 11 cm Höhe bestand aus fast ganz vergangenem Nadelholz aus „höheren Gebirgslagen" (Beitrag Sigrun Martins in: WAMERS 2015, 53–55). In mehrfacher Hinsicht interessant ist ein laut Text S. 55 beutelförmiger Holzbecher mit Silberrandfassung, der aber in der Rekonstruktion Abb. 23 kugelig ausfällt (Beitrag Sigrun Martins in: WAMERS 2015, 55–58). Die Vergleiche solcher Holzbecher mit Tierstil II-Dekor behandelt Wamers im Anschluss S. 58–61, verweist auf das Schiffsgrab von Sutton Hoo (numismatischer *terminus post quem* 625 n. Chr.) oder das Kammergrab 165 aus Soest (erste Hälfte des 7. Jahrhunderts) und betont „die hohe wirtschaftlich-soziale Stellung der Familie des Kindes". Chronologisch sieht er das Frankfurter Exemplar als das jüngste in dieser Gruppe an, welches mit der Verzierung durch vier hängende Doppelvoluten auffällt. Die Einordnung der grünblauen Glastasse (WAMERS 2015, 61 f. Abb. 27) folgt weitgehend PÄFFGEN 1992, 363 f. Das Frankfurter Exemplar dürfte rheinischer Fabrikation der zweiten Hälfte des 7. Jahrhunderts entstammen. Für Wamers handelt es sich um ein Erzeugnis des mittleren Drittels des 7. Jahrhunderts, das aus „altem Familienbesitz" aber erst später beigegeben worden sein soll.

Das vierte Hauptkapitel stellt die durchgeführten Untersuchungen zu ausgewählten Gold-, Silber- und Buntmetallobjekten zusammen (WAMERS 2015, 62–120). Durchgeführt wurden Röntgenfluoreszenzuntersuchungen an Edelmetallobjekten, die Florian Ströbele behandelt (in: WAMERS 2015, 63–71). Im Detail behandelt WAMERS die Goldscheibenfibel (2015, 71–74), die vielleicht ursprünglich Bestandteil einer größeren Scheibenfibel war. Sein Vergleich rekurriert vor allem auf die Scheibenfibel von Fridingen (Lkr. Tuttlingen), die er ebenfalls als umgearbeitetes „»Alt«-Stück", als „Spolie von einem sakralen Objekt wie etwa einem Reliquiar oder Tragaltar" erkennt (WAMERS 2015, 74). Mit der Frankfurter Scheibenfibel beschäftigt sich dann weiterhin Susanne Greiff (in: WAMERS 2015, 74–78). Nach den materialkundlichen Untersuchungen stammt das Granatcloisonné der Scheibenfibel eindeutig aus Böhmen (Abb. 33); in der Mitte befand sich eine weitgehend vergangene weißliche Einlage, wohl eine Perle aus Elfenbein oder Knochen. Das Frankfurter Bommelohrringpaar ordnet Niklot Krohn vergleichend ein und stellt die Datierung in die zweite Hälfte des 7. Jahrhunderts heraus (in: WAMERS 2015, 78–84).

Für die Halskette des Mädchens benutzt Wamers den Begriff „Pektorale" (WAMERS 2015, 84f.), den ich im Frühmittelalter lieber für das Brustkreuz geistlicher Würdenträger verwendet sehen möchte. Mit den zum Halsschmuck gehörenden Filigrananhängern beschäftigt sich Niklot Krohn (in: WAMERS 2015, 85–92). An der Halskette war auch ein runder Anhänger befestigt, bei dem es sich um einen D-Brakteaten des 6. Jahrhunderts handeln könnte (Beitrag Alexandra Pesch in: WAMERS 2015, 92–97). Hinzu kommen 20 Goldblechperlen und zum Teil vergangene Silberblechperlen, die Niklot Krohn und Thomas Flügen einordnen (in: WAMERS 2015, 97–99).

Interessant sind dann die drei, an der rechten und linken Hand getragenen goldenen Fingerringe des Mädchens, mit denen sich wiederum Niklot Krohn befasst (in: WAMERS 2015, 99–106). Die kleine gleicharmige Bügelfibel der Form Thörle XB ist aus Silber gearbeitet und weist Vergoldung sowie Nielloeinlagen auf; Wamers sieht hier formenkundlich-chronologische Bezüge, die bereits in die Karolingerzeit verweisen. Er betont, dass „die Frankfurter Fibel kaum vor der ersten Hälfte des 8. Jahrhunderts entstanden sein kann" (WAMERS 2015, 109), was aber der ^{14}C-Datierung widerspricht. Drei Armreife runden die Ausstattung des Mädchens ab (WAMERS 2015, 110–113). Die „zylindrische Blechbüchse" (WAMERS 2015, 113–120) ordnet Wamers funktional nicht unter die von Tivadar Vida zusammengestellten Amulettkapseln / Reliquare, sondern erkennt hier eine „Riechdose" (VIDA 2009).

In Höhe der Taille des Mädchens befand sich eine eiserne Stangengürtelkette mit Gehänge (Roswitha Goedecker-Ciolek in: WAMERS 2015, 121–129; und Egon Wamers in: WAMERS 2015, 132–155). Zu dem an der linken Körperseite getragenen Gehänge gehörten eine silberne Riemenzunge auf einem 0,9 cm breiten Lederriemen, ein etwa 17 × 15 cm großes konisches (?) Objekt aus Mammut-Elfenbein (Tasche, Amulettanhänger, Reliquiar?) und ein 11,5 cm langes Eisenmesser in einer Ziegenlederscheide. Zum Gehänge als Beutelinhalt zugehörig oder als eigenes deponiertes Bündel können Schere, Nadel und Kamm angesehen werden. An den Kettengliedern hafteten Überreste von acht verschiedenen Textilien (WAMERS 2015, 129–131; Beitrag von Roswitha Goedecker-Ciolek). Das leinwandbindige Gewebe A dürfte zur Untertunika des Mädchens gehört haben, während ein weiteres leinwandbindiges Gewebe B als Übertunika gedeutet wird. Ein feineres leinwandbindiges Gewebe D wurde schleierartig über den Tuniken getragen. Das leinwandbindige Gewebe H dürfte zu einem Beutel gehört bzw. die Stoffumhüllung von Schere, Nadel und Kamm dargestellt haben. Textilrest G war ein Ripsband. Die Tote lag möglicherweise auf einem größeren Ripstuch. Anschließend formt Wamers Kleidung und Schmuckausstattung des Mädchens zu einem

Lebensbild, das als farbige Rekonstruktion gezeigt wird (Wamers 2015, 156–158; *Abb. 4*). Durch besondere Expertise überzeugt die Untersuchung des textilen Goldkreuzes durch Ina Schneebauer-Meißner und Britt Nowak-Böck, das auf der Kleidung des Mädchens oder einem Stoffbeutel angebracht gewesen sein kann (in: Wamers 2015, 159–172).

Obwohl die ¹⁴C-Datierungen in die zweite Hälfte des 7. Jahrhunderts (um 670 n. Chr.) und damit noch klar vor das Plateau der Kalibrationskurve um 700 n. Chr. verweisen, plädiert Wamers in seinem Beitrag „Die Zeitstellung des Grabes – ¹⁴C-Daten und antiquarische Analysen" (Wamers 2015, 173–177), mit Bezug auf die sekundär verwendete Scheibenfibel, die gleicharmige Fibel und die Keramikgefäße für einen Zeitansatz des Doppelgrabs „in die Jahre von etwa 700 bis 730" (Wamers 2015, 175).

Danach nimmt Wamers die Brandbestattung in den Fokus der Betrachtung (Wamers 2015, 177–198) und setzt diese als „völlig fremde Bestattungssitte heidnischen Charakters" aus einem „ánderen kulturell-ethnischen Hintergrund" von der Körperbestattung aus der „Familie des fränkischen *exactors / iudex*" ab (Wamers 2015, 179). Ein gewichtiges Argument stellt dabei für Wamers die Auffindung der acht verbrannten Bärenkrallen dar, die er als „Bestattung auf einem Bärenfell" (Wamers 2015, 179) bzw. „Bestattung mit einem Bärenfell" deutet (Wamers 2015, 180). Hier führt m. E. die Terminologie in die Irre, da doch nur

Abb. 4. Frankfurt am Main, St. Bartholomäus. Lebensbild des Mädchens aus dem Kindergrab 95.

die Verbrennung des Kleinkindes auf einem Scheiterhaufen mit Bärenfell oder seine Umhüllung zum Zeitpunkt der Kremation gemeint sein kann.

Im Kern ist Wamers Analyse der Bestattungen mit Bärenfell im ersten Jahrtausend (Wamers 2015, 180–193) dahingehend beizupflichten, dass diese aufgrund ihrer Verbreitung Abb. 98 eher als fremd einzustufen ist, aber durchaus einen „hohen Sozialstatus" (Wamers 2015, 193) anzeigt. Anschließend wendet sich Wamers der Sitte „bi-ritueller Doppelbestattungen" im 6. bis frühen 8. Jahrhundert zu, die hier als gleichzeitig erfolgte Körper- und Brandbestattungen zu definieren sind (Wamers 2015, 193–198). Warum auf der zugehörigen Verbreitungskarte dieses archäologischen Phänomens (Wamers 2015, Abb. 100) die vom Chronisten Willibald in der zwischen 763 und 765 verfassten *Vita Bonifatii* beschriebene, von Bonifatius bei Geismar im Jahre 723 gefällte sogenannte Jupiter-Eiche (Donar-Eiche) mit eingetragen ist, bleibt als so nicht zulässige, da gemischt archäologisch-historische Argumentation kritisch zu hinterfragen.

Anschließend beschäftigt sich Wamers mit der „Geschichte und Missionierung des ostfränkisch-thüringischen Raumes im 7. und 8. Jahrhundert" (Wamers 2015, 199–206). Ausgehend von seiner Datierung des Doppelgrabs in das erste Drittel des 8. Jahrhunderts interessiert ihn folgerichtig die

Einordnung in einen historischen Hintergrund. Hier referiert der Archäologe doch manches leichtfertig, was in der geschichtlichen Betrachtung stärker zu differenzieren wäre. So ist für Wamers der in der Nilkheimer Inschrift aus dem Beginn des 8. Jahrhunderts und bei Willibald genannte *dux* Theotbald der in Frankfurt amtierende Bruder des in Würzburg residierenden Herzogs Heden II. Es fehlt hier zum Verständnis der historischen Diskussion der Verweis auf Alfred FRIESE (1979), der Herzog Gosbert und Theotbald gleichsetzte und als Vater Hedens II. ansah. Mit Matthias Werner würde die heutige Mediävistik doch am ehesten Heden II. und Theotbald als nicht miteinander verwandte und gleichzeitig amtierende Herzöge ansehen (WERNER 1982, 148–156; 164–167). Wie auch immer, versucht Wamers das Doppelgrab in das Zeitgeschehen des frühen 8. Jahrhunderts einzuordnen und erkennt Zusammenhänge „mit der sächsischen Südexpansion Richtung Nordhessen (und Thüringen)", wodurch „Elemente des altsächsischen Heidentums in den Raum Hessen / Thüringen gelangten und hier ein Rest-Heidentum wiederbelebten, was dann zu dem pagan-christlichen Brauchtum führte, das die Bonifatiusüberlieferung so sehr beklagt" (WAMERS 2015, 206).

Die abschließende Synthese „Das bi-rituelle Kinderdoppelgrab unter der Frankfurter Bartholomäuskirche" (WAMERS 2015, 207–218) betont zunächst Frankfurts mögliche zentralörtliche Stellung zwischen ausgehender Merowingerzeit und der Karolingerzeit. Hinsichtlich der familiären Einordnung denkt Wamers nun weniger an die Adelsfamilie der Nantharinen, wie noch anlässlich der Frankfurter Ausstellung (S. 208), sondern sieht in dem körperbestatteten Mädchen eine Angehörige der Familie des Herzogs Theotbald (WAMERS 2015, 216) und Vorfahrin der 794 in Frankfurt verstorbenen Fastrada, der vierten Ehefrau Karls des Großen (WAMERS 2015, 209), die als Abkömmling der mainfränkisch-thüringischen Herzogsfamilie galt. Nur eine solche Genealogie macht nach Wamers erklärlich, dass die Frankfurter Pfalz Ludwigs des Deutschen im 9. Jahrhundert „die memoriale Verehrung eines Kleinkindes aus einer ostfränkischen Adelsfamilie [...] so prominent aufgriff und zum Fixpunkt seiner Pfalzkapelle machte" (WAMERS 2015, 211; ähnlich S. 217: „Wenn Ludwig nun dieses neue programmatische Sakral-Bauwerk seiner Hauptresidenz exakt über dem Kindergrab [nicht über dem gesamten Rechteckbau] ausrichtete, muss es sich bei der / den Kleinen um in dynastischer wie sakraler Hinsicht herausragende Figuren gehandelt haben"; WAMERS 2015, 217: „Tatsache der etwa 120–150 Jahre späteren zentralen Platzierung der neuen Frankfurter Pfalzbasilika durch Ludwig den Deutschen [...] macht deutlich, dass es hier [...] eine lange Tradition der Verehrung gegeben haben muss.").

Wamers geht von der Existenz eines fränkischen Königshofs des 7. Jahrhunderts aus, von dem eine aus drei Bauten bestehende sakral geprägte Gebäudegruppe erfasst sei (als Rekonstruktionsvorstellung Abb. 5). Dazu gehöre der beheizbare Rechteckbau „als Wohnhaus des örtlichen Klerikers" *(domus ecclesiae)*, für das es nach Wamers naheliegt, in ihm „eine Entlehnung aus Gallien zu sehen, vermutlich sogar einen direkten Hinweis auf einen Kleriker aus dieser Region, der sicherlich hochrangig war" (WAMERS 2015, 210). Wamers geht dann noch einen Schritt weiter und meint sogar, es könne sich hier um „einen Bischof gehandelt haben" (WAMERS 2015, 25; 210). Auch hier ist doch schärfer terminologisch zu trennen. Nirgends ist ein Königshof gleichzeitig als Bischofssitz nachweisbar. Da für Frankfurt keinerlei Überlieferung für einen Bischof existiert, bleibt eine solche Vorstellung auch nicht ernsthaft zu diskutieren. Wenig später beschreibt Wamers wieder ausschließlich „die Struktur eines merowingischen Königshofes des 7. Jahrhunderts mit Verwaltungs-, Sakral- und Wirtschaftsaufgaben", an den sich zur Mainfurt „am Ufer Anlegestellen, Boots- und Warenschuppen sowie Fischerhütten reihten" (WAMERS 2015, 210). Zur Aufnahme der Doppelbestattung habe man „etwa zwischen 700 und 720/30" das ehemalige Klerikerhaus zur „Memoria" umgenutzt (WAMERS 2015, 211). Wamers stellt sich vor, dass sogar der Mainzer Bischof Rigibert († 724) in Frankfurt persönlich anwesend gewesen sein könnte, der „das befremdliche Bestattungsritual" „durch ein Leichentuch mit aufgenähtem Kreuz aus Goldbändern" christlich signiert haben könnte (WAMERS 2015, 211).

Hinsichtlich der kulturhistorischen Stellung des Mädchengrabs betont Wamers die Zugehörigkeit „zum oberen Adel (Eliten) der ausgehenden Merowingerzeit" und geht dann noch einen Schritt weiter und erkennt m. E. so nicht mehr recht nachvollziehbar in „der Kombination aus edelmetallenen Ohrringen, Pektorale, Armreifen, Fingerringen und Fibeln" ein Schmuckensemble nach „altem höfischem Muster", was auch für den feinen Schleier zutreffe. Anstelle einer nachvollziehbaren Darlegung wird dann nur zur königlichen Hoftracht des frühen Mittelalters auf den Frankfurter „Königinnen-Ausstellungskatalog" verwiesen (Wamers 2015, 211). Die Besonderheit der golddurchwirkten Kleidung fällt hier in der Argumentation aus, da Wamers sie ja anders interpretiert und als Zutat des Mainzer Diözesans deutet. Die gleicharmige Fibel im Ensemble deutet Wamers im Hinblick auf historische Überlieferung als persönliches Geschenk von Willibrord, da dieser bei seinen Reisen „wohl in *Franconofurd* Station" machte: „Liegt es nicht nahe, dass ein solch rares Fremdstück am ehesten über die frühe angelsächsische Mission in die Hände der adligen Familie am Main kam?" (Wamers 2015, 213). Der D-Brakteat der Mitte des 6. Jahrhunderts ist für Wamers „von in Thüringen siedelnden Nordleuten gefertigt worden" und als „altes Familienerbstück" zu erklären (Wamers 2015, 213). Die Brandbestattung mit Bärenfell verweist nach Wamers in den sächsisch-thüringisch-skandinavischen Raum (2015, 213). Manche Beigaben wie Silberarmreif und das Bündel mit Schere, Nähzeug und Kamm möchte der Autor dann auch eher im Bezug zur Brandbestattung sehen (Wamers 2015, 214). Bei der Brandbestattung habe man „skandinavische Ethnizität" zum Ausdruck bringen wollen (Wamers 2015, 216). Dies stellt sich Wamers innerhalb einer mainfränkischen Adelsfamilie mit Bezügen nach Thüringen als möglich vor. Die Abdeckung der beiden verstorbenen Mädchen mit der kreuzverzierten Decke spiegelt nach Wamers „den Geist der Neuevangelisierung und -missionierung im Zuge der insularen Mission östlich des Rheins ab 700 n. Chr." (Wamers 2015, 215). Dieser Vorschlag widerspricht freilich in gewisser Weise der zuvor und dann auch wieder auf S. 216 geäußerten Deutung, der Mainzer Bischof Rigibert sei dafür verantwortlich gewesen. Für das Grab nimmt Wamers ohne jeglichen Quellennachweis, sondern einzig aufgrund der Lage eine „Verfestigung des Erinnerungskultes um das Kind oder die Kinder" an, die er mit der Person von Fastrada verbindet. Zudem hält er es für möglich, dass „sich am Grab der beiden Kinder eine lokale Tradition der Verehrung entwickelt" hatte, „die vielleicht mit Wunderaktivitäten und Pilgerbesuchen verbunden war und die dann bei den Bauplanungen für St. Salvator diese wichtige Rolle spielten", obwohl das „alte Geheimnis dieser beiden so fremden und gleichzeitig so vertrauten kleinen Kinder [...] gewiss schon vergessen" war (Wamers 2015, 218). Die von Wamers (2015, 199–206; 216) wohl nach Wilhelm Störmer (1993) referierte Meinung, Herzog Chrodobert sei wohl mit dem Würzburger Herzog Hruodi identisch, verdiente nähere Ausführung und kann so verkürzt nicht stehen bleiben. Auf S. 216 bezeichnet Wamers den Mainzer Bischof Rigibert als Erzbischof, was zumindest unter Verweis auf Daniel C. Pangerl und die zu dieser Zeit kaum noch existente Metropolitanverfassung etwas zu relativieren wäre[3].

Mit einer Datierung des Doppelgrabs in das spätere 7. Jahrhundert ergäbe sich freilich auch ein ganz anderer historisch-politischer Hintergrund, der unter den „mainfränkischen" Herzögen Heden I. und Gosbert anzusetzen wäre und für den als Quelle kaum mehr als die *Passio minor sancti Kiliani* zur Verfügung steht, d. h. obige kulturhistorische Überlegungen wären obsolet.

Die Fixierung auf das intensiv behandelte Grab lässt bisweilen den Gesamtzusammenhang der Sakraltopographie und die Einbeziehung der weiteren baulichen Entwicklung vermissen. Das Ende der römerzeitlichen Thermenanlage ist in der Mitte des 3. Jahrhunderts anzusetzen (Wahl 1982,

---

[3] Pangerl 2011 stellt die Wiedereinführung der Metropolitanverfassung als Neuerung unter Karl dem Großen heraus.

61–90). Festzuhalten bleibt der Wechsel der Bebauungsausrichtung, die römerzeitlich Südwest-Nordost verlief und in der jüngeren Merowingerzeit mit der Anlage des Rechteckbaus nach West-Ost geändert wurde. Von der ruinösen Thermenanlage des 2.–3. Jahrhunderts recycelte man in der jüngeren Merowingerzeit offenbar Bauteile und versuchte für den Rechteckbau eine Hypokaustierung als Fußbodenheizung anzulegen. Dies ist daraus zu erschließen, dass darunter spätantike und merowingerzeitliche Keramik bis in das 7. Jahrhundert aufgefunden wurde (HAMPEL 1994, 227 Taf. 10; WINTERGERST 2007, 31 mit Anm. 110). Auch wenn diese Hypokaustanlage sich wohl nicht als funktionsfähig erwies, bleibt ein solches Experiment während der ausgehenden Merowingerzeit kulturgeschichtlich interessant, zumal eine Schlauchheizung einfacher zu konstruieren und effektiver gewesen wäre. Der nach der Ausrichtung nachantik anzusetzende sogenannte Apsidenbau, von dem nur die Südseite fragmentarisch erfasst wurde, wurde von M. Wintergerst wegen der benutzten Qualität als vorkarolingisch und als noch vor dem Rechteckbau errichtet angesehen (WINTERGERST 2007, 26), während Wamers ihn für zeitgleich mit dem Rechteckbau ansieht (so erstmals WAMERS 2012, 162). Der Apsidensaal kann jedoch wohl mit größerer Wahrscheinlichkeit als jünger als der Rechtecksaal angesehen werden. Zu betonen ist, dass der frühmittelalterliche Apsidensaal (mit m. E. wahrscheinlicher Datierung erst in das 8. oder 9. Jahrhundert) für die weitere bauliche Entwicklung keine entscheidende Bedeutung besaß. Der Rechteckbau mit dem sog. bi-rituellen Doppelgrab der ausgehenden Merowingerzeit wurde von einem jüngeren kirchlichen Großbau der Karolingerzeit überbaut, der letztlich den Vorgänger der heutigen Kirche darstellt. Ob dieser karolingerzeitliche Großbau zweiphasig gewesen ist, kann derzeit nicht entschieden werden. Die von der Ausgräberin gesehene Zweiphasigkeit der karolingischen Pfalzkirche (HAMPEL 1994, 78–80) wird von M. Wintergerst nicht gesehen (WINTERGERST 2007, 68–71). Neueren Grabungsergebnissen zufolge könnte der sogenannte Apsidensaal durch das Atrium der Pfalzkirche überbaut worden sein oder war ein kapellenartiger Bestandteil im Atrium (HAMPEL 2017a; 2017b).

Einige weitere kritische Bemerkungen sind anzuschließen: Der Begriff „Frankfurter »Prinzessin«" (WAMERS 2015, 84) erscheint sehr problematisch, da etwas begrifflich suggeriert wird, das so nicht archäologisch zu klären ist, handelt es sich doch – historisch und rechtsgeschichtlich klar definiert – um den Titel für die Tochter eines regierenden Königs oder Fürsten. Etwas zu viel Begeisterung für den *genius loci* spricht aus der historisch sicher falschen Formulierung, dass Frankfurt die „eigentliche Hauptstadt" des Ostfränkischen Reiches gewesen sei (WAMERS 2015, 217)[4]. Auch Abbildungsunterschriften sind problematisch und vermutlich so nicht alle vom Autor verfasst[5].

Trotz aller hier im Detail angebrachten Kritik und manchen Zweifeln an der Deutungsebene bleibt Egon Wamers für die Gewinnung der kompetenten Mitautoren und die Beharrlichkeit bei der Realisierung des Buches zu danken.

---

[4] Weitere Punkte ließen sich anführen. So schreibt WAMERS (2015, 74) die Autorschaft der Fridinger Gräberfeld-Monographie Siegmar von Schnurbein zu; richtig muss es Alexandra von Schnurbein heißen. Falsch geschrieben und mit veralteter Kreisangabe versehen ist der Fundort Rommerskirchen (WAMERS 2015, 113 Anm. 346). Das Frauengrab von Rommerskirchen datiert Wamers m. E. zu spät in das 8. Jahrhundert statt um 700 (WAMERS 2015, 113 Anm. 346).

[5] So heißt es bei Abb. 2: „Blick in die ausgehobene Grube des Kindergrabes 95 [...] Auf den Absätzen nördlich und südlich der Grabkammer liegen Steine, die von der Nordmauer des »Baus I« (hier am oberen Bildrand) herabgefallen sind". Der Text zu Abb. 31 (WAMERS 2015, 73) verlegt den Fundort Großhöbing, d. i. ein Ortsteil der Stadtgemeinde Greding im mittelfränkischen Landkreis Roth, in einen ganz anderen Regierungsbezirk, nämlich in die Oberpfalz. Abb. 54 stellt nicht nur spätrömische tordierte Bronzearmreife zusammen, sondern mit Abb. 54,4 auch ein glattes Silberexemplar aus Aholming (Lkr. Deggendorf) der ausgehenden Merowingerzeit. Unsinnig ist es, wenn der Erläuterungstext zu Abb. 104 den im Wandfresko dargestellten adligen Stifter mit Schwert als „Stiftsherr von St. Benedikt Mals, Vinschgau" bezeichnet, da der deutsche Begriff Stiftsherr als Synonym für lat. *canonicus* eine definierte kirchliche Stellung bezeichnet, die hier sicher nicht vorliegt.

Literaturverzeichnis

BUCHNER 1956
R. BUCHNER, Gregor von Tours: Zehn Bücher Geschichten. 2 Bd. (Darmstadt 1956).

FRIESE 1979
A. FRIESE, Studien zur Herrschaftsgeschichte des fränkischen Adels. Der mainländisch-thüringische Raum vom 7. bis 11. Jahrhundert (Stuttgart 1979).

HAMPEL 1994
A. HAMPEL, Der Kaiserdom zu Frankfurt am Main. Ausgrabungen 1991–93. Beitr. Denkmalschutz Frankfurt am Main 8 (Nußloch 1994).

HAMPEL 2017a
A. HAMPEL, Aktuelle Ergebnisse der neuen Ausgrabungen im Archäologischen Garten auf dem Frankfurter Domhügel. In: P. Fasold / L. Giemsch / K. Ottendorf / D. Winger (Hrsg.), Forschungen in Franconofurd. Festschrift für Egon Wamers zum 65. Geburtstag. Schr. Arch. Mus. Frankfurt 28 (Regensburg 2017) 101–111.

HAMPEL 2017b
A. HAMPEL, Neue Grabungsergebnisse zur Pfalzanlage des 9. Jahrhunderts auf dem Frankfurter Domhügel. In: U. Recker (Hrsg.), *Iucundi acti labores*. Festschrift für Egon Schallmayer anlässlich des 65. Geburtstags. Hessen Arch., Sonderbd. 5 (Darmstadt 2017) 159–165.

PÄFFGEN 1992
B. PÄFFGEN, Die Ausgrabungen in St. Severin zu Köln. Kölner Forsch. 5 (Mainz 1992).

PÄFFGEN / RISTOW 1996a
B. PÄFFGEN / S. RISTOW, Christentum, Kirchenbau und Sakralkunst im östlichen Frankenreich (Austrasien). In: A. Wieczorek (Hrsg.), Die Franken – Wegbereiter Europas vor 1500 Jahren. König Chlodwig und seine Erben 1 [Ausstellung Reiss-Museum, Mannheim, 8. September 1996–2. März 1997 / Petit Palais, Paris, 23. April–22. Juni 1997 / Kulturforum, Berlin, 18. Juli–26. Oktober 1997] (Mainz 1996) 407–415.

PÄFFGEN / RISTOW 1996b
B. PÄFFGEN / S. RISTOW, Die Religion der Franken im Spiegel archäologischer Zeugnisse. In: A. Wieczorek (Hrsg.), Die Franken – Wegbereiter Europas vor 1500 Jahren. König Chlodwig und seine Erben 1 [Ausstellung Reiss-Museum, Mannheim, 8. September 1996–2. März 1997 / Petit Palais, Paris, 23. April–22. Juni 1997 / Kulturforum, Berlin, 18. Juli–26. Oktober 1997] (Mainz 1996) 738–744.

PANGERL 2011
D. C. PANGERL, Die Metropolitanverfassung des karolingischen Frankenreiches. MGH Schr. 63 (Hannover 2011).

STÖRMER 1993
W. STÖRMER, Zu Herkunft und Wirkungskreis der merowingerzeitlichen ‚mainfränkischen' Herzöge. In: K. Schnith / R. Pauler (Hrsg.), Festschrift für Eduard Hlawitschka zum 65. Geburtstag. Münchener Hist. Stud., Abt. Mittelalterl. Gesch. 5 (Kallmünz 1993) 11–21.

VIDA 2009
T. VIDA, Herkunft und Funktion von Privatreliquiaren und Amulettkapseln im frühgeschichtlichen Europa. In: U. von Freeden / H. Friesinger / E. Wamers (Hrsg.), Glaube, Kult und Herrschaft. Phänomene des Religiösen im 1. Jahrtausend n. Chr. in Mittel- und Nordeuropa. Akten des 59. Internationalen Sachsensymposions und der Grundprobleme der frühgeschichtlichen Entwicklung im Mitteldonauraum. Koll. Vor- u. Frühgesch. 12 (Bonn 2009) 261–280.

VIVES et al. 1963
J. VIVES / J. MARTÍNEZ TOMÀS / G. MARTÍNEZ DÍEZ (Hrsg.), Concilios visigóticos e hispano-romanos. España Crist. Textos 1 (Barcelona, Madrid 1963).

WAHL 1982
J. WAHL, Der römische Militärstützpunkt auf dem Frankfurter Domhügel. Mit einer Untersuchung zur germanischen Besiedlung des Frankfurter Stadtgebiets in vorflavischer Zeit. Schr. Frankfurter Mus. Vor- u. Frühgesch. 6 (Bonn 1982).

WAMERS 2012
E. WAMERS, Das Kinderdoppelgrab unter der Frankfurter Bartholomäuskirche. In:

E. Wamers / P. Périn (Hrsg.), Königinnen der Merowinger. Adelsgräber aus den Kirchen von Köln, Saint-Denis, Chelles und Frankfurt. Ein deutsch-französisches Ausstellungsprojekt des Archäologischen Museums Frankfurt und des Musée d'Archéologie nationale in Saint-Germain-en-Laye in Zusammenarbeit mit der Domschatzkammer Köln [Ausstellung in Frankfurt am Main: 10. November bis 26. Mai 2013, Ausstellung in Köln: 8. März bis 26. Mai 2013] (Regensburg 2012) 161–182.

WAMERS / P. PÉRIN 2013
E. WAMERS / P. PÉRIN (Hrsg.), Königinnen der Merowinger. Adelsgräber aus den Kirchen von Köln, Saint-Denis, Chelles und Frankfurt. Ein deutsch-französisches Ausstellungsprojekt des Archäologischen Museums Frankfurt und des Musée d'Archéologie nationale in Saint-Germain-en-Laye in Zusammenarbeit mit der Domschatzkammer Köln [Ausstellung in Frankfurt am Main: 10. November bis 26. Mai 2013, Ausstellung in Köln: 8. März bis 26. Mai 2013][2] (Regensburg 2013).

WAMERS 2015
E. WAMERS, Franconofurd 2. Das bi-rituelle Kinderdoppelgrab der späten Merowingerzeit unter der Frankfurter Bartholomäuskirche („Dom"). Archäologische und naturwissenschaftliche Untersuchungen. Schr. Arch. Mus. Frankfurt 22,2 (Regensburg 2015).

WERNER 1982
M. WERNER, Adelsfamilien im Umkreis der frühen Karolinger. Die Verwandtschaft Irminas von Oeren und Adelas von Pfalzel. Personengeschichtliche Untersuchungen zur frühmittelalterlichen Führungsschicht im Maas-Mosel-Gebiet. Vortr. u. Forsch. 28 (Sigmaringen 1982).

WINTERGERST 2007
M. WINTERGERST, Franconofurd 1. Die Befunde der karolingisch-ottonischen Pfalz aus den Frankfurter Altstadtgrabungen 1953–1993. Schr. Arch. Mus. Frankfurt 22,1 (Frankfurt a. M. 2007).

Anschrift des Verfassers:

Bernd Päffgen
Ludwig-Maximilians-Universität
Historicum – Zentrum für Geschichte und Archäologie
Institut für Vor- und Frühgeschichtliche Archäologie und
Provinzialrömische Archäologie
Schellingstraße 12
DE–80799 München

Abbildungsnachweis:
Abb. 1: Architectura Virtualis GmbH, Kooperationspartner der Technischen Universität Darmstadt / Archäologisches Museum Frankfurt. – *Abb. 2–3:* Ken Massy, Ludwig-Maximilians-Universität München, Institut für Vor- und Frühgeschichtliche Archäologie und Provinzialrömische Archäologie Geschwister-Scholl-Platz 1, 80539 München. – *Abb. 4:* Archäologisches Museum Frankfurt, Entwurf E. Wamers, Ausführung F. Vincent, Paris.

Korrigenda zu

Thomas Meier, Methodenprobleme einer Chronologie der Merowingerzeit in Süddeutschland. Germania 98, 2020 (2021), 237–290.
doi: https://doi.org/10.11588/ger.2020.85276.

Die Redaktion der Germania wurde von Herrn Matthias Friedrich, Autor von „Archäologische Chronologie und historische Interpretation: Die Merowingerzeit in Süddeutschland" (Friedrich 2016a), darauf aufmerksam gemacht, dass folgende Aussagen aus Meier 2020 einer Korrektur bedürfen (die Originalzitate sind kursiv gesetzt):

(1) Meier 2020, 277:

Die im Buch angegebenen Excel-Tabellen konnte ich nicht finden (Stand 20.8.2020) […].

Die Excel-Dateien der Korrespondenzanalysen stehen auf der Website von De Gruyter unter „Zusatzmaterial" dauerhaft zum Download zur Verfügung (https://doi.org/10.1515/9783110475340). Weiterhin sind die vollständigen Beilagen aus Friedrich 2016a als PDF-, Excel- sowie CSV-Dateien im Open Access bei Zenodo archiviert (Friedrich 2016b: https://doi.org/10.5281/zenodo.3936669).

(2) Meier 2020, 277 Anm. 197:

Der bei Friedrich 2016, 9 Anm. 15 angegebene Link scheint bereits jetzt (27.8.2020) nicht mehr zu funktionieren und führt lediglich auf die Verlagshomepage.

Der in Friedrich 2016a, 9 Anm. 15 abgedruckte Link[1] ist gültig und führt dauerhaft zu den Kontingenztafeln der Korrespondenzanalysen. Selbiger Link ist zusätzlich auf S. 56 Anm. 168 sowie S. 130 Anm. 204 abgedruckt.

(3) Meier 2020, 262:

Für die Datierung der termini post quos *seiner Münzen stützt sich Friedrich auf die unpublizierte und damit leider nur in Freiburg als Mikrofiche „zugängliche" Dissertation Josef Fischers von 2001. Fischer bewertet dort einige Münzen und ihre Prägezeiten offenbar anders, […] die Neudatierungen [bleiben] unüberprüfbar.*

Die Dissertation von Josef Fischer zum „Münzumlauf und Münzvorrat im Merowingerreich" (Fischer 2001) ist ordentlich publiziert und neben Freiburg i. Br. auch an weiteren Bibliotheksstandorten zur Aus- / Fernleihe verfügbar[2]: in der Deutschen Nationalbibliothek[3] sowie in Tübingen, Saarbrücken, Stuttgart[4], Frankfurt, Marburg[5], Hamburg, Göttingen, Hannover[6], Berlin[7],

---

[1] http://www.degruyter.com/view/books/9783110475340/9783110475340-bm/9783110475340-bm.xml (letzter Zugriff: 12.04.2022).

[2] Recherchegrundlage: Karlsruher Virtueller Katalog. https://kvk.bibliothek.kit.edu (letzter Zugriff: 12.04.2022).

[3] Deutsche Nationalbibliothek. https://d-nb.info/985789735 (letzter Zugriff: 12.04.2022).

[4] Quelle: Bibliotheksservice-Zentrum Baden-Württemberg (BSZ), K10plusPPN 1341389472. https://opac.k10plus.de/DB=2.299/PPNSET?PPN=1341389472&PRS=HOL&HILN=888&INDEXSET=21 (letzter Zugriff: 12.04.2022).

[5] Quelle: hebis-Verbundkatalog, PPN 194373339. http://cbsopac.rz.uni-frankfurt.de/DB=2.1/PPNSET?PPN=194373339 (letzter Zugriff: 12.04.2022).

[6] Quelle: Verbundzentrale des GBV (VZG), K10plusPPN 560034768. https://opac.k10plus.de/DB=2.299/PPNSET?PPN=560034768&PRS=HOL&HILN=888&INDEXSET=21 (letzter Zugriff: 12.04.2022).

[7] Quelle: Kooperativer Bibliotheksverbund Berlin

Bochum, Bonn, Köln, Münster, Trier[8]. Eine Überprüfbarkeit der in FRIEDRICH 2016a, 142–146 zitierten Passagen aus FISCHER 2001 ist grundsätzlich gewährleistet.

Literatur

FISCHER 2001
  J. F. FISCHER, Der Münzumlauf und Münzvorrat im Merowingerreich. Eine Untersuchung der zeitgenössischen Münzfunde aus dem Gebiet des Reihengräberkreises [Diss. Univ. Freiburg] (Freiburg 2001).

FRIEDRICH 2016a
  M. FRIEDRICH, Archäologische Chronologie und historische Interpretation. Die Merowingerzeit in Süddeutschland. RGA Ergbd. 96 (Berlin, Boston 2016). doi: https://doi.org/10.1515/9783110475340.

FRIEDRICH 2016b
  M. FRIEDRICH, Correspondence Analysis Data Set. Supplement to FRIEDRICH 2016a. Zenodo. doi: https://doi.org/10.5281/zenodo.3936669.

MEIER 2020
  TH. MEIER, Methodenprobleme einer Chronologie der Merowingerzeit in Süddeutschland. Eine Diskussion anhand von Matthias Friedrich „Archäologische Chronologie und historische Interpretation: Die Merowingerzeit in Süddeutschland" (2016). Germania 98, 2020, 237–290. doi: https://doi.org/10.11588/ger.2020.85276.

Brandenburg (kobv) sowie Universitätsbibliothek FU Berlin. https://fu-berlin.primo.exlibrisgroup.com/permalink/49KOBV_FUB/1v1tp5h/alma990032769180402883 (letzter Zugriff: 12.04.2022).

[8] Quelle: Hochschulbibliothekszentrum des Landes Nordrhein-Westfalen (hbz), hbz Verbund-ID: HT015302460. https://nrw.digibib.net/search/hbzvk/record/(DE-605)HT015302460 (letzter Zugriff: 12.04.2022).

Rezensionen / Reviews / Comptes rendus

SONJA B. GRIMM, Resilience and Reorganisation of Social Systems during the Weichselian Lateglacial in North-West Europe. An Evaluation of the Archaeological, Climatic, and Environmental Record. Monographien des Römisch-Germanischen Zentralmuseums Band 128. Verlag des Römisch-Germanischen Zentralmuseums, Mainz 2019. € 124,–. ISBN 978-3-88467-255-6. (Druckausgabe). doi: https://doi.org/10.11588/propylaeum.735. ISBN 978-3-948465-89-6 (PDF). 646 Seiten mit 96 Abbildungen, 86 Tabellen und 14 Tafeln.

Die vorliegende Arbeit ist die Kulmination der 2014 von der Johannes Gutenberg-Universität Mainz angenommenen und am Archäologischen Forschungszentrum und Museum für menschliche Verhaltensevolution des Römisch-Germanischen Zentralmuseums in Neuwied (MONREPOS) verfassten Dissertationsschrift von Sonja P. Grimm. Die Autorin unternimmt den ambitionierten, aber zeitgerechten und deshalb äußerst willkommenen Versuch, die klassische Archäostratigraphie Nordwesteuropas vom ausgehenden Pleniglazial bis zum Auftreten der Federmessergruppen und artverwandter Technokomplexe im Spätglazial einer umfassenden Synthese zu unterziehen und mit Hinblick auf drängende Fragen von Mensch-Umwelt-Klima-Interaktion und sozio-ökologischer Resilienz neu zu bewerten. Die Arbeit konzentriert sich dabei vor allem auf archäologische Schlüsselregionen in Westdeutschland, Nordfrankreich und Belgien und vergleicht die verfügbaren Informationen zum späteiszeitlichen Siedlungsverhalten und zur Steintechnologie mit lokalen und globalen klima- und umweltgeschichtlichen Archiven, um das komplexe Beziehungsgeflecht zwischen Mensch, Vegetation, Tierwelt und Klima besser zu verstehen.

Grimms Synthese beeindruckt durch Umfang (mehr als 600 Seiten), kompilatorische Sorgfältigkeit und einen kritischen Blick auf das Quellenmaterial, der andernorts neuerdings immer wieder dem Quantifizierungswahn und Datenfetischismus zum Opfer fällt. Formal und etwas überraschend folgt die Arbeit der in den Lebens- und Naturwissenschaften gängigen IMRaD-Struktur, die eine Präsentation wissenschaftlicher Ergebnisse anhand der idealtypischen Abfolge von Einleitung, Material und Methode(n), Resultat und Diskussion nahelegt. Die Einleitung (S. 1–5) ist zwar verhältnismäßig kurz gehalten, situiert die Arbeit aber in aktuellen fachübergreifenden Debatten des Klimawandels sowie der Resilienzforschung und Klimafolgenabschätzung. Die Autorin identifiziert die Pleniglazial-Spätglazial-Sequenz mit ihren vielgestaltigen und teils einschneidenden klimatischen und ökologischen Umbrüchen dabei als Modellszenario, in dem die Dynamiken sozialer Reorganisationsprozesse über viele Jahrtausende verfolgt und die Flexibilität und Trägheit *(inertia)* mobiler späteiszeitlicher Gesellschaften im Angesicht von Risiko und ökoklimatischer Unsicherheit untersucht werden können. Grimm interessiert sich insbesondere für das Tempo, die Modalitäten und die Synchronizität des Wandels am Ende der letzten Eiszeit und stellt dabei die Gretchenfrage, ob die archäologisch beobachtbaren Veränderungen menschlichen Verhaltens sich dabei als „evolutionäre" oder „revolutionäre" Prozesse qualifizieren lassen (S. 5).

Die Vorstellung der Materialien und Methoden umfasst numerisch fast die Hälfte der Druckseiten (S. 7–292) und liefert eine detaillierte Beschreibung der in den Blick genommenen klimageschichtlichen und chronostratigraphischen Archive (Eisbohrkerne mit Grönland-Provenienz, Tiefseebohrkerne und terrestrische Archive; S. 9–30), umweltgeschichtlichen Vergleichsdaten (Hydrologie, physische Geographie und Pollenstratigraphien; S. 31–48), archäologischen Fundstellen und übergeordneten taxonomischen Einheiten (S. 52–244) sowie belastbaren radiometrischen Datierungen von Pollen, Tierknochen und menschlichen Besiedlungsresten im Untersuchungsgebiet (S. 49–52). Methodisch arbeitet sich die Autorin am heiklen Problem der Korrelation von Eventstratigraphien und chronostratigraphischen Markern ab (S. 245–250). Zudem erweitert Grimm die CalPal-2007$_{HULU}$ Kalibrationskurve (B. WENINGER / O. JÖRIS, A ^{14}C age calibration curve for the last 60 ka: the Greenland-Hulu U/Th timescale and its impact on understanding the Middle to Upper Paleolithic transition in Western Eurasia. Journal of Human Evolution 55, 2008, 772–781. doi: https://doi.org/10.1016/j.jhevol.2008.08.017) um hochauflösende Umweltdaten aus dem Untersuchungszeitraum, z. B. dendrochronologisch fixierte Baumringinformationen aus dem Jüngeren Dryas-Komplex (S. 250–253). Dies ermöglicht die Konstruktion eines integrierten chronologischen Gerüsts, welches den direkten Abgleich mit anderen datierten Archiven erlaubt. Um die Landschaftsentwicklung im Untersuchungsgebiet zu analysieren, entwickelt die Autorin ein Verfahren zur Erstellung physischer Grundkarten mit kompilierten Informationen zum Verlauf von Paläoflusssystemen und Eisschildausdehnungen (S. 253–259). Des Weiteren werden die absolut datierten biotischen Landschaftskomponenten (Faunen- und Pflanzenreste) einer kritischen qualitativen Lektüre unterzogen und quantitativ hinsichtlich ihrer Wahrscheinlichkeits- und Häufigkeitsverteilungen untersucht (S. 259–264; 384–465).

Die archäologischen Informationen basieren auf 26 Fundstellen aus drei Regionen (zentrales Rheinland, westliches Hochland einschließlich Luxemburg und Teilen Belgiens sowie nordfranzösische Ebene, vom Amorikanischen Massiv bis ins Pariser Becken; S. 54; 75–244). Grimms Untersuchung beschränkt sich dabei auf zwei dem Tephrahorizont des Laacher See Vulkans vorgelagerte Makrokomplexe: das späte Magdalénien und die Federmessergruppen (FMG; S. 54; 56–74). Beide Komplexe werden von der Autorin als maximal inklusiv konzipiert, sodass der Begriff der FMG beispielsweise auch das französische Azilien umfasst (FMG *sensu lato*; S. 69–71). Methodisch evaluiert Grimm zunächst die chronologische und räumliche Integrität der so ausgewählten Schlüsselfundstellen (S. 75–244; 265–269) sowie deren Rohmaterialversorgung (S. 269–270) bevor die Steinartefaktinventare selbst näher in den Fokus rücken (S. 270–282). Auch wenn die Autorin diese Terminologie selbst nicht verwendet, folgt die Untersuchung der Lithik einer makroarchäologischen Analyselogik. Das Untersuchungsziel besteht weniger darin technologische und typologische Details oder Besonderheiten der zugrundeliegenden Inventare sowie deren technische Infrastruktur und Operationsketten zu erhellen, vielmehr werden Indizes und Verhältnisse bemüht und Klassifikationssysteme eingeführt, um *allgemeine* Inventartendenzen zu vergleichen und zeitlich zu kartieren (vgl. z. B. S. 271 Tab. 51; S. 274–275 Tab. 52–53; S. 277 Tab. 54; S. 282–283 Tab. 56–57; S. 285–287 Tab. 58–60).

Grimm extrahiert eine Reihe von spezifischen Variablen aus den vorliegenden Inventarinformationen, die sich zur Quantifizierung eignen oder zumindest qualitativ verglichen werden können, um Prozesse des Wandels auf unterschiedlichen Analyseebenen und in verschiedenen Verhaltensdomänen zu untersuchen (S. 269–282; 286–287; cf. S. 481–534). Die Autorin lässt sich dabei von einflussreichen theoretischen und empirischen Überlegungen zu Mobilität und Siedlungsorganisation von Jäger-Sammler-Fischer-Gruppen (L. R. BINFORD, Willow smoke and dogs' tails: hunter-gatherer settlement systems and archaeological site formation. Am. Ant. 45,1, 1980, 4–20. doi: https://doi.org/10.2307/279653), dem Verhältnis von bestimmten Werkzeugklassen mit Hinblick auf Werkzeugstatus und -funktion (L. LANG, [Hrsg.], Marolles-sur-Seine: Le Tureau des Gardes. Vestiges d'implantations du Paléolithique supérieur. Fouilles de sauvetage urgent [Saint-Denis 1998]), der Diversität von mobilen Werkzeugsätzen *(toolkits)* und deren Bezug zu Siedlungszyklus und -dauer (H. LÖHR, Der Magdalénien-Fundplatz Alsdorf, Kreis Aachen-Land. Ein Beitrag zur Kenntnis der funktionalen Variabilität jungpaläolithischer Stationen [Tübingen 1979] [Ungedr. Diss. Eberhard-Karls-Universität Tübingen]; J. RICHTER, Diversität als Zeitmaß im Spätmagdalénien. Arch. Korrbl. 20,3, 1990, 249–257) sowie Erwägungen zur besonderen Rolle von Projektilspitzen in der Steintechnologie (J. PELEGRIN, Sur les débitages laminaires du Paléolithique supérieur. In: F. Delpech / J. Jaubert [Hrsg.], François Bordes et la Préhistoire. Colloque international

François Bordes, Bordeaux, 22-24 avril 2009. Documents préhistoriques 29 [Paris 2011] 141–152 ; B. VALENTIN, Jalons pour une paléohistoire des derniers chasseurs [XIVe-VIe millénaire avant J.-C.]. Cahiers Arch. Paris 1 [Paris 2008]), sozialen Transmissionsprozessen (M. J. HAMILTON / B. BUCHANAN, The accumulation of stochastic copying errors causes drift in culturally transmitted technologies: Quantifying Clovis evolutionary dynamics. Journal Anthr. Arch. 28,1, 2009, 55–69. doi: https://doi.org/10.1016/j.jaa.2008.10.005) und kultureller Evolution (A. MESOUDI / M. J. O'BRIEN, The learning and transmission of hierarchical cultural recipes. Biological Theory 3, 2008, 63–72) leiten. In einem ersten Schritt werden die Größe und die Zusammensetzung der Inventare bestimmt sowie ein einfacher Dichte-Index (Anzahl an Artefakten pro m²) errechnet (cf. S. 486; S. 488–489 Tab. 83). Zudem werden diverse Indizes ermittelt, um die Handhabung von lithischen Rohmaterialeinheiten und die Ökonomisierung der Grundformherstellung zu eruieren (cf. S. 486–491), beispielsweise in Form eines generischen Ausbeutungs-Index (Anzahl aller Artefakte pro Anzahl an Kernen; cf. S. 488–489 Tab. 83). Grimms Analyse der Werkzeuginventare im engeren Sinne folgt Set-analytischen Prämissen, z. B. wenn die Gesamtzahl der dokumentierten lithischen Artefakte in fünf diskrete Fundstellenklassen überführt und mit dem Anteil an modifizierten Stücken, der Werkzeugdiversität gemessen am Vorhandensein gängiger Morphotypen sowie anderen Werkzeugklassen-Indizes konfrontiert wird (cf. S. 487–534; S. 514–515 Tab. 84). Ergänzt werden diese Informationen außerdem durch die metrische Analyse von 148 vollständig erhaltenen Projektileinsätzen aus den Schlüsselfundstellen (Taf. 1–14; cf. S. 529–532; S. 530 Abb. 83) sowie neu errechnete Projektil-Diversitäts-Indizes ausgehend von sieben idealtypischen Spitzenklassen (cf. S. 528–529, S. 518–519 Tab. 85).

In einem nächsten Schritt wird die Untersuchung durch die an den Fundstellen dokumentierten Faunenreste ergänzt, um das Subsistenzverhalten späteiszeitlicher Gruppen zu charakterisieren und mit den bereits gewonnen lithischen Daten zu verschneiden (S. 282–286; cf. S. 534–548). Auch der hier gewählte Ansatz basiert auf Set-analytischen Grundsätzen: Wenigers klassischer Studie des Magdalénien in Süddeutschland und der Schweiz folgend (G.-Ch. WENIGER, The Magdalenian in Western Central Europe: settlement pattern and regionality. Journal World Prehist. 3, 1989, 323–372) werden Herbivoren-Fauneninventare auf der Basis kalkulierter MNI-Werte in vier Größenklassen unterteilt (cf. S. 535; S. 536–537 Tab. 86), wobei die resultierenden Klassen von der Autorin auf der Grundlage ethologischer Informationen zu einzelnen Tierarten wie beispielsweise Saisonalität und Herdengröße weiter präzisiert werden (z. B. S. 554–555). Analog zur Auswertung der Steinartefaktinventare wird zudem ein Diversitäts-Index für die Fauneninventare ermittelt (cf. S. 536–537 Tab. 86; S. 541 Abb. 85). Genau wie für die Herstellung und Nutzung lithischer Artefakte lassen sich daraus auch für die Ausbeutung tierischer Ressourcen Erwartungen für zugrundeliegende Fundstellentypen ableiten. Während Grimm für die Lithik eine Differenzierung von *base camp*, *workshop*, *hunting camp* und *short-term habitation* als Ausdruck des Verhältnisses von Werkzeugdiversität und Kernanzahl in archäologischen Fundstellen postuliert (S. 275 Tab. 53), schlägt sie eine Auftrennung von *provisioned / opportunitic episode*, *short episode*, *hunting camp* und *base or agglomeration camp* Fundstellen als Ausdruck der Beziehung von Faunendiversität und korrigierter MNI-Größe vor (S. 286; S. 287 Tab. 60). Aus der Überlappung dieser Lithik- und Faunenindikatoren wird schließlich ein allgemeines fünfgliedriges Modell relevanter archäologischer Fundstellentypen am Übergang vom Plenigazial zum Spätglazial in Nordwesteuropa entwickelt (S. 556 Abb. 93), welches die Rekonstruktion und Konfrontation von Landnutzungsstrategien und Siedlungssystemen erlaubt (cf. S. 554–559).

Die Resultate der bis hierhin skizzierten Analysen sowie deren synthetische Zusammenführung werden auf 271 Seiten ausführlich dargelegt (S. 293–564). Grimm präsentiert zunächst ihre spezifisch auf die Anforderungen des Spätglazials in Nordwesteuropa zugeschnittene ^{14}C-Kalibrationskurve, die strukturell zwar der ursprünglichen CalPal-2007$_{HULU}$ Kalibrationskurve sehr ähnlich ist, die Einhängung lokaler und globaler Umwelt- und Klimaarchive aus dem Untersuchungszeitraum aber deutlich vereinfacht und eine insgesamt präzisere Chronologie des spätglazialen Interstadials ermöglicht (S. 358–364). Der wichtigste Beitrag der Arbeit besteht aber zweifelsfrei in der sukzessiven und umfassenden Synthese der Entwicklung von physischer Landschaft, Vegetation, Tierökologie und menschlichem Verhalten vom späten Pleniglazial bis ins Spätglazial (S. 365–465), die wesentlich durch zusammenfassende Tabellen und synthetische Abbildungen erarbeitet wird (insb. S. 434–435 Abb. 63; S. 445 Abb. 64). Die meist numerischen Ergebnisse werden zu diesem Zweck qualifiziert und in diskrete Verhaltens-, Landschafts-, Umwelt- und Klimakategorien überführt. Kategorienübergänge werden entsprechend als Regimeverschiebungen gedeutet (cf. S. 445 Abb. 64; S. 483 Abb. 72; S. 508 Abb. 78; S. 533 Abb. 84; S. 547 Abb. 87; S. 550 Abb. 88 und insb. S. 560–561 Abb. 95; S. 562 Abb. 96). Auch wenn hier nicht auf die reichhaltigen Details dieser Zusammenschau eingegangen werden kann, gelingt der Autorin auf dieser Basis schließlich der Nachweis einer fundamentalen Asynchronität des Wandels – sowohl *innerhalb* als auch *zwischen* den verschiedenen Archiven und Verhaltensdomains.

Die resultierende Chronologie ist verschachtelt und gestaffelt und entzieht sich daher einer strikt korrelativen Erklärung. Grimms Synthese lässt erkennen, dass die Dynamiken und Komplexitäten an der Mensch-Umwelt-Klima-Schnittstelle am Übergang vom Pleistozän ins Holozän bisher vermutlich unterschätzt worden sind und damit zumindest den gängigen, mehr oder weniger strikt linearen und / oder deterministischen Interpretationen sozioökologischen Wandels im Untersuchungszeitraum den Boden entziehen. Nicht nur ist die so offengelegte Sequenzierung der Veränderungen für sich bereits instruktiv (S. 560–561 Abb. 95; S. 562 Abb. 96), es wird ebenso deutlich, dass einschneidende Zäsuren im Verhaltensspektrum der betroffenen späteiszeitlichen Menschen dem klimageschichtlichen Pleniglazial-Spätglazial-Übergang entweder um viele Jahrtausende vorgelagert sind oder erst viele Jahrhunderte danach erkennbar werden (cf. S. 559–564). Etliche Transformationsprozesse, sowohl im Bereich von Umwelt- und Landschaftsparametern als auch im Geltungsbereich menschlichen Verhaltens, lassen darüber hinaus Phasen des graduellen Umbruchs oder der mosaikartigen Überlappung und Verschneidung erkennen. Die meisten dieser Übergangsphasen setzen gleichermaßen viele Jahrtausende vor der spätglazialen Erwärmung ein.

Die Analyse der zeitlichen Akkumulation von Veränderungen, welche die Autorin als Proxy für Evolutionsraten *(rates of evolution)* liest, unterstützt diese These und demonstriert, dass gradueller, inkrementeller Wandel zwar als *modus operandi* ausgewiesen werden kann, nichtsdestotrotz aber ein sprunghafter Anstieg der dokumentierten Veränderungsrate zwischen ca. 14,2 und 13,6 ka cal. B. P. zu verzeichnen ist (S. 568) – ein Zeitraum, der ebenfalls nicht mit dem epochalen Klimaeinschnitt am Pleniglazial-Spätglazial-Übergang zusammenfällt. Veränderungsraten sind ferner nicht gleichmäßig über die untersuchten Archive und Verhaltensdomains verteilt, was stark divergierende, substratabhängige Tempi des Wandels nahelegt, die Grimm mit *slow* bzw. *fast changing variables* assoziiert (S. 575). Für die Autorin ergibt sich insgesamt das Bild eines eng verflochtenen aber dekorrelierten Transformationsprozesses, der die leitende Eingangsfrage vordergründig zu Gunsten eines weitgehend „evolutionären" Vorgangs – wenn auch mit „revolutionärem" Moment – beantwortet (cf. S. 563–564; 587). Der Zusammenbruch des späten Magdalénien am Übergang vom Pleniglazial zum Spätglazial und die Herausbildung des FMG-Komplexes sind der Autorin zufolge dann als emergentes Produkt dieses revolutionären Moments zu deuten (insb. S. 568; 587–589). Die Asynchronität des Wandels von Klima-, Landschafts-, Umwelt- und Humanvariablen wird darüber hinaus als Nachweis für die erhöhte und häufig unterschätzte Flexibilität und Resilienz adaptiver späteiszeitlicher Sozialsysteme ins Feld geführt (S. 569–571).

Resilience and Reorganisation of Social Systems during the Weichselian Lateglacial in North-West Europe leistet damit einen wichtigen Beitrag zur Revision unseres Verständnisses vielgestaltiger

Mensch-Klima-Umwelt-Interaktionen am Ende der letzten Eiszeit und mobilisiert eine beeindruckende Datensammlung, die zukünftigen Untersuchungen zum Spätglazial nur Vorschub leisten kann. Die Achillesferse der Arbeit ist aber zweifelsohne in der fehlenden theoretischen Kontextualisierung von Fragestellung, Ansatz und Interpretation sowie in der unterentwickelten und oftmals zu kleinteiligen Diskussion der Ergebnisse zu suchen. Ein Teil des Problems ist hier m. E. auch die gewählte IMRaD-Gliederung, die einer monographischen Aufarbeitung nur selten gerecht wird. Nicht nur ist der Umfang von Einleitung, Hauptteil und Diskussion unausgewogen, was die Lektüre deutlich erschwert und die Destillation der Kernbefunde behindert, es fehlt ferner ein eigenständiger Theorieteil, der eine explizite Auseinandersetzung mit Resilienz, Vulnerabilität, Flexibilität, sozioökologischen Systemen, adaptiven Zyklen und komplexen Ungleichgewichtssystemen eröffnet und damit auch eine überzeugendere Interpretation späteiszeitlicher Transformationsdynamiken autorisiert hätte. Auffallend ist in diesem Zusammenhang auch die häufig ungenutzte Möglichkeit zur diskursiven Abarbeitung an einschlägigen Fachdiskussionen zu Mensch-Umwelt-Dynamiken im Untersuchungszeitraum (vgl. z. B. G. Marchand, Préhistoire atlantique. Fonctionnement et évolution des sociétés du Paléolithique au Néolithique [Paris 2014]; Valentin 2008) und der insgesamt sparsame, teils sehr selektive und oftmals allenfalls punktuelle Einsatz von Literaturverweisen. Allein eine Auseinandersetzung mit neueren archäologischen Arbeiten und Konzepten zur komplexen Heteronomie von Mensch, Umwelt und Klima hätte die Diskussion bereichert und die Einsichten fundiert (cf. S. T. Hussain / F. Riede, Paleoenvironmental humanities: challenges and prospects of writing deep environmental histories. WIREs Climate Change 11,5, 2020, e667. doi: https://doi.org/10.1002/wcc.667). Dessen ungeachtet markieren die Ergebnisse von Grimms beachtlichem kompilatorischem Kraftakt einen Paradigmenwechsel von klimadeterministischen hin zu interaktiven und Eigendynamiken betonenden Erklärungsmodellen in der Erforschung von Mensch-Umwelt-Beziehungen in der Altsteinzeit. Es ist zu hoffen, dass dieser Impuls von anderen Arbeiten aufgenommen und weitergetragen wird. Auch wenn viele Fragen und Probleme am Ende unbeantwortet bleiben, lohnt sich eine Lektüre von Grimms 600 Seiten starkem Opus allein aus diesem Grund sowohl für Spätglazial-Expert*innen als auch für all jene, die sich für eine *Deep History* der Interrelationalitäten von Mensch, Umwelt und Klima interessieren.

DK–8270 Højbjerg	Shumon T. Hussain
Moesgård Allé 20	Aarhus Universität
E-Mail: s.t.hussain@cas.au.dk	Department of Archaeology and Heritage Studies
Orcid: https://orcid.org/0000-0002-6215-393X	

Silviane Scharl, Innovationstransfer in prähistorischen Gesellschaften. Eine vergleichende Studie zu ausgewählten Fallbeispielen des 6. bis 4. Jahrtausends vor Christus in Mittel- und Südosteuropa unter besonderer Berücksichtigung temporärer Grenzräume. Kölner Studien zur Prähistorischen Archäologie Band 10. Verlag Marie Leidorf GmbH, Rahden / Westf. 2019. € 54.80. ISBN 978-3-86757-370-2. 251 pages with 50 figures and 13 tables.

The theme of this book has become the focus of many culture-historical discussions and has been extended to the important turns of prehistory in the past decades, especially connected to the spread of metallurgy and in many cases connected to the advent of the Bronze Age. Silviane Scharl sets out from similar research questions, like the physical and mental path leading from invention to innovation and finally to the distribution and established state, in which the innovation becomes an everyday practice. Yet, she chose three case studies from earlier, "pre-Bronze-Age" prehistoric periods, of the turn of the 6th / 5th to the early centuries of the 4th millennia cal BC. The nature of the three case studies is also fairly different: the innovations discussed include the spread of the copper metallurgy in the Carpathian basin and westwards; a special example of the belated Neolithic transition north of the loess area in Northern Central Europe; and, finally, the distribution of circular ditches in the Lengyel-Stichband-Gatersleben circle and its possibly shared social, ritual background. The declared research questions are to detect any patterns in the transfer and also possible causes for variations.

The book consists of six chapters. It starts with the introductory part (pp. 11–19), setting the research questions, the goals, the history of research into knowledge transfer in cultural history, ethnography, sociology, and archaeology – the latter cross-checked with the meaning and contemporary use of 'archaeological culture', all in some thirty pages. The consequences and summaries take the last twenty pages (pp. 210–217), so the core body of the text is taken by the three case studies. The first part of Chapter five part devotes 50 pages for the innovation and the spread of copper artefacts in the 5th millennium cal BC in the eastern and western Carpathian basin (pp. 40–97). The remaining hundred pages are divided between the second case study, the formation of the Funnel beaker community out of the Mesolithic Ertebølle groups (pp. 98–143), and the third example, the emergence of the circular ditches in southern Germany, their possible origin and contacts (pp. 144–180).

The author was certainly free to choose the topics: these three very different examples, innovations that originated from social processes and then enhanced further social changes, seem to be fruitful and promising to be studied. The sequence of them, though, raises questions. If the geographic regions were taken as basis, e. g. from the southeast to the northwest, case study 3 on circular ditches should be placed in between the Carpathian basin and the northern glacially shaped landscape. In case the chronological order would be followed, the earliest phenomenon of the ditches, starting at the turn of the 6th to 5th millennium cal BC, could have been discussed first, the Lengyel and Tisza-Tiszapolgár processes were to set second and the late 5th, early 4th millennium changes in the north as last. If the nature of the innovation had been set in focus, so the turn to sedentary life and food production in the northern German plateau were to set first. But possibly, the longest and most detailed case study on a more conventional theme of innovation has a special stress in the text, and also, in the argumentation of the author.

The targets and the research questions are summarised in Chapters 2 and 3. The focus has been set on the distinction between invention and innovation, all embedded in a rather complex social (and sometimes even ritual) context, with a short research historical background. For the author, not only the geographic situation, transfer routes and the contacts that made the transfer possible, were important, but also barriers, called "temporary borders". These are regions, through which the innovation transfer became difficult, or was even halted for a certain period of time.

Chapter 4 is devoted to methodology, with distinguishing constant, independent and dependent variations of the possible transfer of innovation. The flow of information might well be influenced by the actual demographic situation of a given area, where a higher density on population is always a positive factor, although it is more effective when combined with a certain cultural complexity. Higher mobility is certainly also a triggering effect. So is previously existing information, perhaps also an acceptance of the values that eventually became transferred and adapted in the recipient community.

This factor, the mobility among knowledgeable individuals ("agency"), and the resulting exchange between people, smaller or larger groups, up to the grade of mobility among whole population groups are considered to be key factors, which are underpinned with rich sets of examples. As it is highlighted, the author accepts the view by Colin RENFREW (Approaches to Social Archaeology [Cambridge 1984] 396), that knowledge alone rarely leads to the spread of any innovation. The circumstances must match a certain chain of information, which, however, is more effective when it is bound together with prestige and social gain (p. 33). Signs of high value and prestige go together with the desire for taking over, accepting the given new technology, and the author cites good examples for these: e.g. making copies, replacements of the original object prepared with the new technology are interpreted as signs for the community getting ready for adopting the innovation. S. Scharl agrees with those who consider peers, family ties or a network by extended families to be the most important agents for knowledge transfer (pp. 33–39).

Chapter 5, the core part of the volume, contains the three case studies mentioned above. The first study concentrates on the spread of copper metallurgy over Central Europe (pp. 40–97). The earliest finds, as Scharl emphasises, are clearly connected to, and rooted in the southerly Vinča copper sources and early metallurgy (p. 65). Setting out from this fact, it is no surprise that copper metallurgy (i.e. besides the finds of traces for local copper melting) reaches the northwards and westwards lying Lengyel distribution area with a certain delay. In order to explain this delay, the hypothesis of barriers, "temporary borders" in between Eastern Hungary and the Transdanubian Lengyel culture on the one hand, and between the Lengyel culture and its neighbours in Moravia, Eastern Austria, and Bavaria on the other, is understandable.

Scharl goes one step further and states that the depopulation of large and concentrated settlements, which is part of a series of changes parallel with the spread of copper metallurgy, happened in the Alföld considerably earlier than with Lengyel settlements in Transdanubia. Yet, also the late phase of the Lengyel cultural circle, characterised by unpainted pottery, seems to reveal – one can admit, in a less spectacular way – some hidden but definite traces of the changes towards "Chalcolithisation", i.e. a more mobile society and a settlement pattern consisting of many small sites instead of large centres. This happened practically coeval with the eastern part of the Carpathian basin. Signs of a cultural change (and possible genetic impact from the south) can be observed within the late (III.) Lengyel phase (4300 cal BC), and continuously onward in the Middle Copper age. Here, differences were caused only in the intensity of the southern impacts that reached Transdanubia: stronger in the south (Balaton-Lasinja culture), moderate in the Balaton Upland, and weak in the north (Ludanice or Lengyel V phase – e.g. p. 75). This is discussed in detail in works also cited by the author several times (e.g. E. Bánffy, South-west Transdanubia as a mediating area. On the cultural history of the Early and Middle Chalcolithic. Antaeus 1995, 157–196), yet, Scharl's interpretations of these studies are apparently different. She even gives absolute dates to underpin this alleged chronological difference, the delayed "Chalcolithisation" of the Western Carpathian basin: 4500 cal BC for the Alföld and 4100 cal BC (pp. 76; 206) for the end of the Lengyel culture. The consequence is clearly a large gap regarding communication, connections, and networks, and also the emergence of copper metallurgy in the western Carpathian basin. However, the absolute dates seem to be mistaken and thus the main pillar of her argumentation fades away. The late Lengyel settlements are dated to the 44th century cal BC and the Balaton-Lasinja and Ludanice settlements are dated to 4300–4220 (e.g. K. Oross et al., Die Siedlung der Balaton-Lasinja-Kultur in Balatonszárszó-Kis-Erdei-dűlő. In: J. Šuteková et al. [eds], Panta rhei. Studies on the Chronology and Cultural Development of South-Eastern and Central Europe in Earlier Prehistory. Presented to Juraj Pavúk on the occasion of his 75th birthday [Bratislava 2010] 379–405), and so the temporary difference between these and the Alföld (Tiszapolgár-Bodrogkeresztúr culture) is not meaningful. Thus, a possibility emerges which is different from the temporary borders and delay. This calls for more attention to the Northern Balkans and the Vinča culture and its complex long-distance networks which reached the southern part of the Carpathian basin again and again in the 6th–5th millennium BC. Notably, the above drafted process is impressively depicted in Figure 16 (p. 92).

The next case study is a special Neolithisation story in the northern Central European plain. The main question discussed here is the long-lasting (personal) contact between the hunter-gatherer communities and the southerly settled farmers, before the spread of the innovation (in this case, the sedentary lifestyle and food production) happened. The result has an enormous impact on Central European prehistory, since the one-time fishing communities, who eventually became cattle breeders, the people of the Trichterbecher (TRB, Funnel Beaker) culture, distributed south in the heartland of modern Germany and became later the communities leaving magnificent megalithic monuments behind.

Scharl leads the reader into fine details of e.g. palaeobotany for seeking the first domesticated plant remains in the early TRB sites, to detect the first signs of food production – or even preceding that, the traces of the vivid contacts with farming communities. For the irreversible changes in the life of these groups, the author discusses issues of climate change and also, the demographic estimations and calculations, so that the issue of the density of the population becomes important in the possible scenarios discussed, for a better understanding of hunter-gatherers adopting the Neolithic "package". Figure 18 (p. 99) is a good summary of the chronology beginning with the final Ertebølle and Swifterband to the end of the 3rd millennium cal BC between the Low Countries and Jutland. Unfortunately, culture names occur only in the Abbreviations, not in the chart itself.

The third case study focuses on the concentration of circular ditches in the first half of the 5th millennium cal BC, especially on its western distribution area, the Großgartach culture. This region receives a special attention with the detailed presentation of the ditch found in Ippesheim (DE), and the Bavarian development of the post-LBK societies where the enclosures mostly occur (pp. 146–151). This time, the impressively meticulous discussion on the southern German Danubian area concentrates on the transfer of innovation that belongs to the ideological – according to the author, ritual – sphere. Beyond this particular case study, the mechanism, the ways (and possible halts) of the innovation getting adopted is strikingly similar in terms of time and pace, with those of other nature.

There might be only one interesting shortcoming of this third case study on innovations, and it is related to the origin of circular ditches, connected to the chronology given by the author. According to this, the emergence of the idea of building circular enclosures happened in the post-LBK world, beginning with 4850/4750 cal BC, with centres in Bavaria, called "Middle Neolithic" in Austria and Germany, with "further ditches" occurring in Eastern Germany, Poland, and Hungary (p. 144). The fact is that several circular ditches already can be found in the LBK world ca. 5300 cal BC. To name some from its area of origin: Becsehely, Balatonszárszó; moreover, circular enclosures were found in the Vinča-related Sopot culture, dated to the turn of the 6th/5th millennium cal BC (K. Oross et al., Midlife changes: the Sopot burial ground at Alsónyék. Ber. RGK 94, 2013 [2016], 151–178. doi: https://doi.org/10.11588/berrgk.1938.0.37153; J. P. Barna, The Formation of the Lengyel Culture in South-Western Transdanubia [Budapest 2017]). Further east and south, beginning with the 6th millennium cal BC, tell settlements were surrounded with circular ditches of the same or very similar kind, beginning with a well-known example in Okolište (Z. Kuljundžić-Vejzagić et al., Okolište – Grabung und Geomagnetik eines Zentralbosnischen Tells aus der ersten Hälfte des 5. vorchristlichen Jahrtausends. In: B. Hänsel [ed.], Parerga Praehistorica. Jubiläumsschrift zur Prähistorischen Archäologie. 15 Jahre UPA. Univforsch. Prähist. Arch. 100 [Bonn 2004] 69–81). The late 6th millennium LBK enclosures and also the 5th millennium cal BC post-LBK ditches are built outside of settlements, and probably by an effort of communities coming from more than one settlement. The tracking of demographic trends and contact networks are convincing and open interesting avenues as compared to the examples of the other case studies.

It is exactly the aforementioned comparison of the three case studies that brings novel inferences, mainly based on the phenomena triggering innovation in their complexity. One of the conclusions is that no innovation would be transferred at the time of the first contact, be this personal or achieved by migrating groups. Yet, this prior knowledge is necessary for an information transfer at a much later stage. Common mechanisms are mentioned which all contain this triggering effect such as a favourable situation leading to demographic increase. Also, climatic circumstances can foster the process. The ways of innovation transfer itself can be varied in terms of how and when they become daily practice, but in all the cases the outcome influences the society at large and leads to a certain transformation of the innovation itself (p. 214).

The volume is illustrated with several maps; some of these are very informative (e. g. fig. 8, pp. 66–67). Yet, it must be noted that some of these seem to be far from being correct. For example, Figure 4 (p. 46) is supposed to show the oldest copper finds in Central Europe and Italy; in the text in the given section mentions ample and justified examples of finds from western Hungary, Czechia, and Slovakia (pp. 46–52), yet these are completely missing from the map (and from the tables, although latter with right, since the table claims to contain only finds from the northern and southern Central Europe). Figure 7a and b is essential, if interpreted the right way, since it shows the Kernel density estimation of copper mining centres in southeast and Central Europe before and after 4200 BC. Alas, the figure caption is not aware of the map cut and claims to show Eurasia. Figure 11 (p. 70) showing cultural formations of the early 5th millennium cal BC has a legend that does not fully correspond with the depicted distribution areas. A thorough checking of the orthography would have done good to the text.

Despite some factual uncertainties and uncertain inferences drawn, this approach, i. e. comparing cases of different innovations, taken from different temporal and chronological backgrounds, seem to be innovative itself. Thus, details may be argued, but the frames are rightly drawn and, in most cases, thoroughly underpinned with relevant literature. In the end, the reader may have more questions than answers, but as I am sure, Silviane Scharl would take these questions as exciting and triggering effects for further research. Hopefully including her own further research.

DE–60325 Frankfurt a. M.
Palmengartenstr. 10–12
E-Mail: eszter.banffy@dainst.de
Orcid: https://orcid.org/0000-0001-5156-826X

Eszter Bánffy
Römisch-Germanische Kommission
des Deutschen Archäologischen Instituts

Nico Fröhlich, Bandkeramische Hofplätze. Artefakte der Keramikchronologie oder Abbild sozialer und wirtschaftlicher Strukturen? Frankfurter Archäologische Schriften Band 33. Verlag Rudolf Habelt GmbH, Bonn 2017. € 129.00. ISBN 978-3-7749-4012-3. XIX + 682 pages with 412 figures, 1 CD-ROM with 2 appendices and 3 inserts.

This massive volume is in the author's words a "slightly edited" version of his 2016 Frankfurt dissertation. The driving force behind the work is the *Hofplatz* model and its relevance for our understanding of Neolithic *Linearbandkeramik* (LBK) settlement and socio-economy, a theme succinctly expressed in the book's subtitle. Indeed, ceramic chronology and social interpretation are closely intertwined in this model, since it was originally devised – on the basis of presuppositions about the organisation of domestic space and residence practices – as a procedure for working out internal settlement chronology. Ideally, a LBK house is dated through the decorated ceramics from its lateral pits *(Längsgruben)*, enabling a relative chronology of houses to be established through seriation of the various house assemblages. The *Hofplatz* model, however, dates houses with few or no finds from lateral pits by assigning other more distant pits to these houses. It also provides a convenient way of fitting completely undatable houses into a site sequence, since the model stipulates that a household always built a new house on the same plot of land, forming through time the distinct groups of houses called *Hofplätze*. The next logical step is to look for household-specific traditions attached to these groups, and this is the main goal of Nico Fröhlich's study. Such traditions could be visible in the characteristics of the buildings themselves or, more particularly, in finds distributions within the settlement. In short, can the groups of houses defined by applying the *Hofplatz* model produce information that goes beyond the simple chronological ordering of features? The author addresses these issues by presenting a detailed analysis of two major LBK sites: Schwanfeld in lower Franconia and Langweiler 8 in the Rhineland (both DE). Already well known from a long series of publications, the two settlements were chosen because they cover most of the timespan of the LBK. Nevertheless, the sites are 300 km apart and exhibit considerable differences in size, duration, and layout, rendering their comparison difficult.

With more than 600 pages of text and around 1500 footnotes, "Bandkeramische Hofplätze" is a challenging read. There are also over 400 figures, mostly tables and distribution plans, the latter notably without any illustration of the finds themselves. Some further tables listing finds and statistical data are provided on CD-ROM, together with digitised versions of the two site plans. After a short introduction (I, pp. 1–9) discussing the premises, methods, and drawbacks of the *Hofplatz* model, the author proceeds to the main section (II, pp. 11–662) dealing with the analysis of the settlements, first Schwanfeld and then Langweiler 8. This section is split fairly evenly between the two sites, with around 300 pages devoted to each. The last section (III, pp. 663–668) offers some concluding remarks.

Schwanfeld dates to the earliest LBK and was excavated in the late 1970s and early 1980s as part of a research project. The estimated surface area of the site is just over 1 ha, at least half of which was investigated, producing seven complete and four incomplete houseplans, mostly grouped into two closely spaced and slightly staggered rows. Following previous studies of the site, each row is interpreted here as a *Hofplatz*. The houses are clearly associated with lateral pits, although there are also six other pits in the areas between the houses, seen as "west" pits. An initial assessment of the occurrence of the main finds categories (flint, stone, ceramics, and fauna) in features reveals no significant spatial variation and mainly shows that a large majority of the material comes from the lateral pits, including here the so-called *Vorbautengruben* (p. 35 fig. 5).

The more detailed study of finds distribution is first approached through the ceramics, extremely abundant on this site, with a total weight of 209 kg, representing an average of 19 kg per house. Using a wider selection of decoration motifs, N. Fröhlich builds on previous studies, mainly by Maria Cladders, to undertake new seriations of the house assemblages and define the most likely building sequence. This is divided into five "house generations" (phases), with one house in use per phase and per row. In the southern row the houses generally shift westwards, whilst the pattern is more irregular in the northern row. In addition, an attempt is made to relate the decorated material to two supra-regional groups within the earliest LBK, termed A and B. The reasoning behind this classification is not easy to follow, especially in the absence not only of illustrations of decoration motifs but also of distribution maps. There follows a lengthy study of the distribution of decoration types within the settlement, for both coarse and fine wares. Figure 74 (p. 136) summarises the main results, listing types varying in time and types possibly of social significance, either related to house rows or the supra-regional groups. In terms of the proposed *Hofplätze*, no clear picture emerges here, although some individual preferences can be identified. For instance, graphite surface treatment is not attested in the southern row and occurs in four out of five houses in the northern row. Vessel shape is also examined in the same perspective. Here again, no significant differences emerge between the two house rows. The spatial distribution of potsherds in terms of varieties of temper and natural inclusions in the clay reveals no clear patterning on a long-lasting basis. Interestingly, correspondence analysis of these technological attributes tends to group together pits belonging to the same house (pp. 189–190 figs. 108–110). This raises the question of modes of discard round the houses, an aspect briefly dealt with in the following section on refitting sherds (see especially p. 196 fig. 113). The author notes that only two house assemblages were intensively searched for refits. In his opinion, the fact that sherds from some vessels are found quite widely scattered in and between lateral pits on either side of a house is evidence in support of the idea that the pits filled in quite slowly.

Fröhlich then turns to lithic finds, dealing first with flint artefacts (pp. 197–281). The total weight here is only 2.5 kg, indicating that the settlement was not intensively involved in flint processing activities. This is probably why there are no clear results from the various distributional analyses of raw materials and production techniques, although house 15 does appear to stand out from the rest. Aspects such as the dimensions of flakes and blades are examined in detail with the help of statistics, but no patterns emerge. The discussion here of possible Mesolithic blade production techniques, relying heavily on previous work on the earliest LBK by Detlef Gronenborn and Inna Mateiciucová, will be of interest to lithic specialists. Lastly the spatial variation in distributions of tool types on the site is difficult to interpret, given the small sample size. One can refer here for example to the distribution of arrowheads (p. 279 fig. 170), more frequent in the southern row. Stone artefacts include grinding, polishing or abrading equipment in sandstone, as well as polished adze blades in other materials. The primary study of these finds was undertaken by Britta Ramminger (Zur wirtschaftlichen Organisation der ältestbandkeramischen Siedlung Schwanfeld, Landkreis Schweinfurt am Beispiel der Felsgesteinversorgung. In: J. Lüning [ed.], Schwanfeldstudien zur Ältesten Bandkeramik. Univforsch. Prähist. Arch. 196 [Bonn 2011] 219–221). The quantitative data summarised in figure 171 (p. 285) reveal no obvious patterning related to house row. The overall conclusion on the lithic artefacts is that households were basically autonomous as regards activities involving these materials. Reference could have been made here to recent work on LBK sites in the Aisne valley, where smaller houses appear more involved in abrading activities, as well as hunting (L. Hachem / C. Hamon, Linear pottery culture household organisation. An economic model. In: A. W. R. Whittle / P. Bickle [eds], Early Farmers, the View from Archaeology and Science. Proc. British Acad. 198 [Oxford 2014] 159–180).

This comment leads us to the following section on faunal remains (pp. 318–337). Unlike the other finds categories from Schwanfeld, these are published here in detail for the first time, using the identifications originally made by Marion Uerpmann. The site is broadly characterised by a high percentage of wild animals (c. 42 %), with a clear predominance of caprines over cattle in the domestic fauna. Although the assemblage is small (815 identified bones), Fröhlich wisely looks for variations within the settlement. One notes that two small and early houses (18, 19) were possibly engaged in more hunting activities than others. The paucity of faunal remains in the pits of house 11 is also intriguing, given the size of the building and the large numbers of other categories of find. This is seen as possible evidence for food sharing between households at an early stage of the settlement's development. These new data from Schwanfeld recall the huge potential of faunal remains for investigating different focuses in LBK household economies, as has already been shown for Cuiry-lès-Chaudardes. Surprisingly in this context, no reference is made here to the monograph on the faunal remains (L. Hachem, Le site néolithique de Cuiry-lès-Chaudardes – I. De l'analyse de la faune à la structuration sociale. Internat. Archäologie 120 [Rahden 2011]).

After a brief mention of plant remains, the section on Schwanfeld closes with a chapter summarising results (pp. 341–362). This starts with an assessment of relations with other regions, analysed in terms of eight "contact directions", ranging from Transdanubia to Württemberg, with some discussion again of possible interaction with unidentified Mesolithic groups. The various lines of evidence, summarised in figures 211 and 212, do not show clear patterning in the house rows and the overall picture is one of a settlement integrated in multiple interacting networks. The remainder of this chapter is a long overview of the observed variations in finds distribution within the settlement, with some additional interpretation of the settlement's history. Ultimately, in view of all the evidence presented for Schwanfeld, one concludes that the most relevant unit for study is the house itself and not the supposed *Hofplatz* rows.

Langweiler 8 is the largest of the seven LBK settlements located along the Merzbach valley on the Aldenhovener Platte. Covering around 10 ha, the site was extensively investigated in the early 1970s in advance of opencast mining. Just over 100 houseplans were identified, as well as a ditched enclosure on the southern edge of the settlement. As Fröhlich underlines, the general context is quite different from Schwanfeld, since Langweiler 8 starts later but has a much longer occupation sequence, producing extensive and often dense clusters of buildings with no obvious spatial organisation. Furthermore, we are reminded that many features were badly eroded and that only relatively small numbers of pits were completely excavated, through lack of time under rescue conditions.

The *Hofplatz* model played a key role in previous work on the structure of the settlement, since the dating of many houses is based on ceramics from pits other than lateral pits and the numerous (40!) undatable houses simply attributed to phases in their respective *Hofplätze*. The site is divided spatially into twelve *Hofplätze* and chronologically into fourteen phases. This scheme, based on Petar STEHLI's 1988 seriation (Zeitliche Gliederung der verzierten Keramik. In: U. Boelicke / D. von Brandt / J. Lüning [eds], Der bandkeramische Siedlungsplatz Langweiler 8, Gemeinde Aldenhoven, Kreis Düren. Rheinische Ausgr. 28,1 [Köln 1988] 441–482), with later modifications by Ulla Münch, provides the main framework for the study. However, reference is made to two further possible divisions of the site, either into seven *Lagegruppen*, which are larger groups of houses than the *Hofplätze*, or into four quadrants (p. 389 fig. 225).

The quantity of houses at Langweiler 8 naturally leads Fröhlich to search initially for spatial patterns in house type and orientation. No correlation is observed with the *Hofplätze*, but there are chronological trends, notably with the occurrence of most of the trapezoidal houseplans in the southern quadrants (p. 405 fig. 236), as well as a slight shift in orientation westwards after the early LBK. This architectural section is followed by a series of analyses of the number, weight, and proportion of the major finds categories (see also annexe 1d on CD-ROM). The average weight of ceramics per house is 5 kg, substantially less than the amount already mentioned for Schwanfeld. No clear results emerge at this stage.

The next chapter (pp. 421–520) is devoted to ceramics, dealing successively with decoration and shape and then briefly with "foreign" (i. e. non-LBK) types. The question of tempering materials is not addressed. Many decoration motifs reveal interesting distributional patterns, although Fröhlich acknowledges that most of these relate to the chronological development of the settlement. One possible exception is Bandtyp 37 (band motif filled with short incised lines), mostly linked to *Hofplatz 1* (p. 459 fig. 277). The distribution of variants of V- or U-shaped secondary motifs (p. 471 fig. 281) is perhaps significant, too. Characteristic of the early phases, these seem to divide the settlement into two sectors. Yet there are no truly *Hofplatz*-specific motifs, apart from rare types that only occur once. As regards vessel shapes and sizes, the author concludes that there is no evidence for spatially delimited ceramic traditions. One might add here that this is hardly surprising, as recent studies on the LBK have shown that such traditions are more likely to be detected in technological attributes, in particular forming techniques (L. GOMART, Traditions techniques et production céramique au Néolithique ancien. Étude de huit sites rubanés du nord est de la France et de Belgique [Leiden 2014]). Lastly, very few sherds can be attributed to "foreign" types. These include one probable La Hoguette vessel, four sherds of Limburg pottery and two or three sherds attributed in earlier studies – quite mistakenly, this reviewer emphasises – to the Blicquy group.

The following chapter (pp. 521–624) deals in turn with flint and stone finds, originally studied by Andreas Zimmermann (Steine. In: Boelicke et al. 1988, 569–787). The flint assemblages from pits represent a total of about 126 kg, which signifies that the average per house is five times greater than at Schwanfeld. However, this relative abundance does not apparently lead to more conclusive results in terms of recurrent spatial patterns within the settlement, whether involving raw materials, production, or tool categories. Although differences between house assemblages are observed, relating for example to aspects of procurement and production, no uniform picture emerges for the various *Hofplätze* (see notably p. 580 fig. 371). These remarks also apply to the distributional analyses of stone finds. The most common raw material here is a local sandstone, mostly used for grinding equipment. Fragments are particularly abundant in the enclosure ditches (p. 600 fig. 384). The numbers of abrading and polishing tools are relatively small, throughout the settlement.

Lastly, the botanical and faunal remains are mentioned (pp. 625–639). The site was extensively sampled for carbonised plant remains and charcoal, analysed respectively by Karl-Heinz Knörzer and Lanfredo Castelletti. In particular Fröhlich takes a fresh look at the distribution of plant remains, applying correspondence analyses to the data. No patterning emerges at *Hofplatz* level, although there is a hint that the larger spatial divisions (*Lagegruppen* and quadrants) may be more relevant here, at least as far as cereals are concerned (p. 630 fig. 405). Preservation of faunal remains on the site was poor and no conclusions can be drawn from the very small sample.

The final chapter on Langweiler 8 is a long overview of results (pp. 640–662). Of special interest here is the author's "contact directions" approach, again applied to assess possible relations with other regions. Eight such directions are proposed, either pointing westwards or to the south-east and integrating a variety of ceramic and lithic data (p. 643 fig. 410; p. 648 fig. 411). Flint raw materials are a major component of western contacts at all times, reflecting sources in Dutch Limburg and to a lesser extent in Belgium. South-eastern contacts are attested by ceramic decoration motifs and stone adze raw material, particularly in the early LBK phases. The appearance of comb decoration is understood as a sign of western contacts in the later phases. This is not altogether correct, since comb decoration is particularly common to the south in the Moselle basin, and Bandtyp 90 (Leihgestern style incised comb decoration) is typically found to the east in Hessia. Even more contentious is the author's integration of the "foreign" La Hoguette, Limburg and Blicquy ceramics, speculatively associated here with lithic data. In this reviewer's opinion, the rare Limburg sherds at Langweiler 8 are much more likely to represent contacts with other LBK settlements using this pottery than with late Mesolithic groups. The Blicquy group is seen as a potential western contact with the late LBK, but the author's references here are not in line with current research that firmly places the Blicquy group after the LBK (e.g. V. Blouet et al., Le Néolithique ancien en Lorraine. Soc. Préhist. Française, Mém. 55 [Paris 2013]). All in all, however, the "contact directions" proposed for Langweiler 8 are more linked to chronology than to the *Hofplatz* units.

Yet Fröhlich is able to provide a plausible narrative for the Langweiler 8 settlement, despite the unsuccessful search for long-lasting social units related to the proposed *Hofplätze*. He suggests that households were self-sufficient in terms of economic activities and although certain households at various times may have been more actively engaged in particular activities, no consistent patterns emerge. There are indications that an analysis using larger spatial divisions would in some respects have been more relevant. Thus the four quadrants reflect to some extent the chronological structure of the settlement, since the built-up area gradually shifted from the northern to the southern quadrants. One suspects that this shifting pattern would be even clearer if one eliminated or re-attributed some of the undatable houses that were assigned to phases by the *Hofplatz* model, since in their current temporal positions they may well artificially extend the duration of occupation of certain parts of the site.

In the last, concluding section (III, p. 663–668), the author reiterates that neither Schwanfeld nor Langweiler 8 provide clear results for distribution patterns, but at the same time considers that the *Hofplatz* model can still be a useful tool for the spatio-temporal analysis of LBK settlements. Long-lived settlements with dense clusters of features are always going to be difficult to analyse, especially in the absence of sufficient finds from lateral pits. The longer a site is occupied, the greater the risks involved in using finds from other kinds of pit to search for spatial patterns. One might also add that, on LBK sites with few or no faunal remains, there is little chance of detecting meaningful patterns relating to household economic practices.

Nico Fröhlich has left few stones unturned in his painstaking search for spatial patterns in the finds from Schwanfeld and Langweiler 8. When such a wide range of material is examined, there are inevitably some shortcomings in references to recent research. Many readers will be discouraged by the sheer length of the text. All but the most hardened specialists will be put off by the total absence of illustration of the decoration motifs and flint artefacts that feature in so many of the distributional analyses. And on the whole, readers who are fundamentally sceptical about the *Hofplatz* model are unlikely to be persuaded by Fröhlich's study to think otherwise. Nevertheless, "Bandkeramische Hofplätze" is a remarkably versatile achievement and will surely be a landmark for many years in the field of LBK settlement studies.

FR–75004 Paris
9 rue Malher
E-Mail: michael.ilett@univ-paris1.fr
Orcid: https://orcid.org/0000-0002-2226-7967

Michael Ilett
Université Paris 1 – Panthéon-Sorbonne
UMR 8215 Trajectoires

Fritz Jürgens, Der bandkeramische Zentralort von Borgentreich-Großeneder (Kr. Höxter). Universitätsforschungen zur prähistorischen Archäologie Band 340. Aus dem Institut für Ur- und Frühgeschichte der Universität Kiel. Verlag Dr. Rudolf Habelt GmbH, Bonn 2019. € 83.00. ISBN 978-3-7749-4199-1. 260 pages with 80 figures, 75 tables and three plans as supplements.

This book presents traces of the Linear Pottery Culture (LBK) occupation discovered at Borgentreich-Großeneder, in the region of Warburger Börde in Eastern Westphalia (DE). This peripheral region of the LBK *oecumene* has not been the focus of intensive archaeological research so far. The work is a printed version of a PhD thesis prepared at the University of Kiel under the supervision of Johannes Müller.

The book is divided into eight chapters of very various length. Chapter 1 (pp. 17–26) is a broad introduction to the subject. After a presentation of the state of research on the LBK, especially in Eastern Westphalia, the complicated history of the research on the site itself is outlined. It was discovered in the 1940s and since that time numerous surveys have been conducted there which yielded thousands of finds. In the 1990s small rescue excavations due to a road construction took place; unfortunately, the entire documentation was lost. In 1993 the MIDAL *(Mitte-Deutschland Anbindungs-Leitung)* gas pipeline project led to larger rescue excavations. Altogether an area of 14,700 sqm was uncovered; it was divided into two sections of a total length of ca. 300 m and a width of 20 m, running from the northwest to the southeast. The northern MIDAL 30 and the southern MIDAL 31 areas were divided by the Ederbach valley. In preliminary reports each of these areas is interpreted as a separate LBK settlement (H.-O. Pollmann, Frühe Ackerbauern und Viehzüchter in Westfalen. Borgentreich-Großeneder und das Gräberfeld von Warburg-Hohenwepel. In: T. Otten et al. [ed.], Revolution Jungsteinzeit. Archäologische Landesausstellung Nordrhein-

Westfalen. Schr. Bodendenkmalpfl. Nordrhein-Westfalen 11,1 [Darmstadt 2015] 330–333), and a critical examination of this hypothesis is one of the main goals of Fritz Jürgens' publication. Between these two main areas, south of Ederbach, there was a small, irregular area MIDAL 32, which was also excavated in 1993.

In 2005, 2006 and 2016 magnetic surveys were conducted in both parts of the site, while in the south small trenches were opened as well. Additionally, ca. 500 m west of MIDAL 31 a large cluster of stone adzes was registered during fieldwalking in the 1980s and 1990s. It was interpreted as traces of a graveyard and this hypothesis was confirmed by excavations conducted between 2011 and 2017, when ca. 150 graves were discovered. However, finds from this research were not analysed in the present work.

In the second part of chapter 1 the method of analysis of features and finds is presented. Unfortunately, some field documentation was lost, which led to a very general association of artefacts with features, without any information on their internal layers, which would have been useful because the author implies on the basis of pottery decoration that at least some features could have been used during more than one phase. He does not analyse features other than postholes connected with houses and other constructions, limiting their presentation to a catalogue at the end of the book. The analysis of longhouses is based on Pieter Modderman's well-known typology (P. J. R. Modderman, Linearbandkeramik aus Elsloo und Stein. Analecta Praehist. Leidensia 3 [Leiden 1970]) with additional modifications made mainly for the Aldenhovener Platte. However, the description in this book is not purified from interpretation, for example when the author names southwest parts of houses granaries. The pottery analysis was conducted almost exclusively on the basis of Jürgen Kneipp's scheme for the LBK in the Rhine, Weser and Main area (J. Kneipp, Die Bandkeramik zwischen Rhein, Weser und Main. Studien zu Stil und Chronologie der Keramik. Univforsch. Prähist. Arch. 7 [Bonn 1998]) and it was restricted to reconstructed vessel entities *(Gefäßeinheiten)*, while the remaining "total mass" *(Gesamtmasse)* was only counted and weighed, without any additional division, for example between fine and coarse ware. In this introductory part the author also discusses local chronological schemes based on pottery, paying special attention to the division into ten stylistic groups *(Stilgruppen)* by Kneipp (confusingly named in other parts of this book also stylistic phases – *Stilphasen* – and stylistic stages – *Stilstufen*), which was applied as a basis of relative dating in this work. Little attention was paid to other categories of finds such as chipped or ground stones and thus reflections on daub imprints, albeit only descriptive and not quantitative, surprise in a positive way.

Chapter 2 (pp. 27–32) presents quite briefly the geology and the landscape of the loess area of Warburger Börde and the topographic location of the site. The author deals here with such issues as environmental conditions in the Early Neolithic and the extent of erosion since that period, although in the latter case he does not rely on any detailed analysis and does not try to reconstruct the relief from the LBK, which would have been helpful for the interpretation of areas MIDAL 30 and 31. He implies *a priori* that they represent a single settlement.

This settlement is the subject of the most comprehensive part (more than 100 pages, 52 % of the text excluding references and appendices), chapter 3 (pp. 33–140), which is divided into two subchapters, each of them for one part of the site: the northern part in subchapter 3.1 and the southern in subchapter 3.2. Both are organised in a similar way. They begin with the information on the spatial extent of finds and features for both parts. The size of the northern part can be estimated on the basis of fieldwalking and magnetic survey to ca. 300 m along the north-south axis and 500 m along the east-west axis. For the southern part these measurements are ca. 400 m for the north-south axis and 550–750 m for the east-west axis, respectively. Unfortunately, these areas are not presented on a plan and it is not possible to estimate their spatial relation. Excavated features are presented in the next part of this chapter; in the MIDAL 30 area a total of 340 features was registered, most of them dated to the LBK, 116 constituting elements of timber constructions. Altogether four longhouses and four other structures were identified, although only one complete house was unearthed within the excavated area. Magnetic survey conducted to the north and east of the trench indicated the existence of at least 30 additional houses. In the MIDAL 31 area ca. 666 features were unearthed, with 391 of them connected with 16 longhouses. Six additional houses were discovered in small test trenches to the west of this area and seven others further west could be identified on the basis of magnetic anomalies. Unfortunately, these houses are presented only on small and unclear plans and the magnetic survey was not integrated with excavation results on a common plan.

The presentation of other features was restricted to some outstanding ones. In the case of the northern part, it was the feature 301 with a deposit of flint blades, although unfortunately, information of its location was lost, and a grave containing a flexed skeleton unearthed within the area MIDAL 34a located to the northwest of MIDAL 31. According to the text it should be marked on figure 19 (p. 45); however, it is not.

In the southern part of the site excavations as well as magnetic survey revealed the existence of an enclosure consisting of four ditches and some postholes of a palisade. In the southern section of the MIDAL 31 trench a puzzling circular enclosure with a diameter of only 15.5 m was discovered as well.

From other, more regular features the author selected only pits with outstanding finds for presentation: feature 109 – a hollow with construction rubbish; feature 346 – a refuse pit with a rich inventory; feature 361 – a deposit of vessels; and feature 527 – a refuse pit with charred cereal grains and numerous daub fragments. Other features are presented very briefly although the author implies that some of them could be connected with undetected longhouses where postholes were not preserved.

The following parts of chapter 3 present artefacts found at Borgentreich-Großeneder. Altogether 5010 were found in the MIDAL 30 and 5157 in the MIDAL 31 and these were mainly pottery and daub. These finds were obtained from 99 features from MIDAL 30 (12.2% of all features) and 81 from MIDAL 31 (30% of all features). The author pays particular attention to vessel entities of the pottery. He identifies 350 of them for MIDAL 30, 283 decorated; for MIDAL 31 there are 327 entities, consisting of 279 "real vessels", 200 of them decorated, and 49 collections of undecorated rim sherds. For some vessels the temper is described; organic and grog were the most common types. Preservation of vessels, methods of their production, wall thickness, vessel forms as well as the morphology of rims and bases are presented here as well. The description of decoration is divided into rim, band, and secondary motifs *(Zwickel)* as well as plastic elements grouped into handles, knobs, and other applications. The coarse pottery is presented as a separate category, although in the text various band types are mentioned: it is not clear here if they were included in the band type category or not. The whole analysis is mainly descriptive: simple bar charts presenting the amount of respective analytical categories are the only form of quantitative analysis applied.

The analysis of flint artefacts is reduced to a basic classification into flakes, cores and tools, the latter including blades. The raw material, so essential in the LBK research, was not analysed due to a high degree of fragmentation. The presentation of ground stone artefacts is similarly basic.

In the case of animal bones and botanical remains special studies were conducted before (W. D. BECKER, Von verkohlten Nahrungsvorräten, geheimnisvollen Wällen und bitteren Mahlzeiten. Archäobotanische Untersuchungen in Westfalen. In: H. G. Horn / H. Hellenkemper [eds], Ein Land macht Geschichte. Archäologie in Nordrhein-Westfalen. Schr. Bodendenkmalpfl.

Nordrhein-Westfalen 3, 1995, 191–194; H.-J. Prilloff, Archäozoologische Analysen der Tierreste von zwei Fundplätzen der Linienbandkeramik von Borgentreich-Großeneder, Kr. Höxter. In: H.-O. Pollmann [ed.], Archäologische Rückblicke. Festschrift für Daniel Bérenger. Univforsch. Prähist. Arch. 254 [Bonn 2014] 21–28) and their main results are described in this book.

Unfortunately, survey finds were not included in the analysis. The author presents them very briefly at the end of each subchapter about finds, focusing mainly on some random, outstanding flint and stone artefacts.

The following subchapters deal with "the chronology and the dating". They begin with stratigraphic analysis which was difficult to conduct due to some missing field documentation. Some houses overlap, thus indicating a temporal depth. Houses were also dated according to their typological traits and in rare cases also on the basis of diagnostic finds connected with them, even more rarely on ^{14}C dates. Much attention is placed on stratigraphic relations between separate ditches of the enclosure.

The very brief chapter 4 (pp. 141–143) is a comparison of finds between two parts of the settlement: their number, weight, form of vessels and proportion of decorated vs plain vessels as well as basic types of chipped and ground stone artefacts, demonstrated in the form of simple box charts. This data is the basis for the verification of the hypothesis from preliminary excavation reports about the existence of two separate LBK settlements at Borgentreich-Großeneder. The author tackles this challenge in chapter 5 (pp. 145–163) on the settlement history and settlement structure. Based on the chronological estimations he suggests that a single settlement unit (Siedlungsverband) existed there instead, and that the occupation shifted gradually from the north to the south. In the following section the author joins the controversially discussed debate, especially in German archaeology, on the microregional settlement organisation of the LBK as either consisting of house wards (Hofplatz) or rows. He opts unequivocally for the latter model, based on false assumptions that the continuity of place is an argument against the house ward model (p. 149), although the opposite is the case. His reconstructions of rows at Borgentreich presented in figure 118 (p. 150) therefore cannot be taken seriously. After some remarks on the size and orientation of houses discussed in comparison with other regions, the author attempts to estimate the size of the whole settlement using as a proxy the mean number of houses per hectare and applying it to the whole settlement area, which is 30 hectares. The impressive total number of 500 houses is a naive fallacy because it neither takes into account different house densities, visible already within the studied area (e.g., in p. 45 fig. 19 there seems to be a boundary of houses in the southern part of the northern settlement), nor relief variations such as the river valley which can influence the structure of occupation. Nevertheless, this extrapolation serves as a basis for further demographic and economic estimations.

In the further part of this chapter the author compares the site with other large LBK settlements and looks for analogies for the shifting of occupation in other regions of this culture. He also discusses the relationship of the settlement with a cemetery and the enclosure, which he similarly declares as the largest within the whole LBK although its northern boundary can only be estimated. The chapter ends with some remarks on the LBK subsistence at Borgentreich, based mainly on botanical remains from the feature 527.

Chapter 6 (pp. 165–179) places the site in the regional context of the Warburger Börde. The author interprets the settlement as a central place in a regional network. He also discusses whether the peripheral location could have influenced the construction of a monumental enclosure and what the relations of the farmers were like with the local hunter-gatherers.

The subject of chapter 7 (pp. 181–187) is the absolute dating of the LBK in the Warburger Börde based on ^{14}C dates from the site, the first ones in this region. They range between 5100–4800 cal BC.

The author explains the very late end of the LBK with the local resistance to change and innovation known as "Westfälische Zeitverschiebung". However, these dates, which are at least 100 years later than the generally assumed demise of the LBK (e. g. K. Riedhammer, The radiocarbon dates from Herxheim and their archaeological interpretation. In: A. Zeeb-Lanz [ed.], Ritualised Destruction in the Early Neolithic: The Exceptional Site of Herxheim [Palatinate, Germany]. Forsch. Pfälz. Arch. 2 [Speyer 2019] 285–303), definitely deserve much more serious discussion. If they are correct, how could this community survive unchanged when most of the previous networks (data on flint raw material would be so useful here!) had collapsed?

The most important conclusions are summarised in the final chapter 8 (pp. 189–190). In the appendix one can find a catalogue of analysed variables and features as well as 74 plates with drawing of finds (pl. 1–28) and schematic profiles of features (pl. 29–75). Plans of MIDAL 30, 31 and 32 are also attached.

Regarding the bad state of research on the LBK in Eastern Westphalia a publication of this important site must be greeted positively, at least on the data level. Doubts appear at the interpretation level: the author definitely tends to spectacular but not seriously founded assumptions such as the largest settlement, the largest enclosure etc. The interpretation of the settlement history with an impressive shift of occupation also relies on very weak data. Why was the pottery from the survey not used to support the dating, which is based on a small selection of the site? Additionally, this dating relies to a large degree only on the typology of houses, which does not allow a precise assignment to one of ten phases which the author proposed. The chronological scheme by Kneipp (1998) is rejected by most researchers working on the LBK (e. g. J. Ritter-Burkert, Die Bandkeramik in Mittelhessen und angrenzenden Gebieten – Typologie, Chronologie, Kontaktszenarien [Kaarst 2019] 301–305, further references therein). The author ignores these controversies and Kneipp's work is the main reference for him, which raises additional doubts on his conclusions.

And although I am aware that I kick a man when he is down, I must stress again the bad quality of the figures in this book. They are not only confusingly imprecise (no clear general plan presented in the whole book), but sometimes also erroneous: for example, figure 113 is duplicated while figure 114 is missing. In figure 125 applied from Pollmann (2015) the author left a dashed line (the boundary of loess) without any explanation in the captions.

Summing up: even if Borgentreich-Großeneder is not the largest LBK site ever found, it is interesting and important. That is why I can recommend this book to scholars interested in the material of the LBK in Eastern Westphalia, with a remark: read with caution.

PL–80-851 Gdańsk
ul. Bielańska 5
E-Mail: joanna.pyzel@ug.edu.pl

Joanna Pyzel
Instytut Archeologii i Etnologii
Uniwersytet Gdański

Dieter Kaufmann, Die Rössener Kultur in Mitteldeutschland. Die rössenzeitlichen Geräte aus Felsgestein. Veröffentlichungen des Landesamtes für Denkmalpflege und Archäologie Sachsen-Anhalt Band 72/V and 72/VI = Die Rössener Kultur in Mitteldeutschland Band 5. Landesamt für Denkmalpflege und Archäologie Sachsen-Anhalt, Halle (Saale) 2020. € 79.00. ISBN 978-3-948618-05-6. 645 pages with 58 illustrations and 120 plates.

Following the publication of "Die Rössener Kultur in Mitteldeutschland (I und II) – Katalog der Rössener und rössenzeitlichen Funde – Altkreise Altenburg bis Gotha" in 2017, the catalogue of the stone artefacts referenced in this study has now been published. The double volume presents 2825 tools from 1087 sites, 1030 of which are known sites in Saxony-Anhalt. The catalogue also includes artefacts from unclear contexts ("site unknown"). The majority of the finds, 2509 out of 2825, consist of axes or axe fragments. The catalogue (pp. 307–640) includes, after a brief introduction to the structure of the catalogue and a list of sites attached as a conclusion (pp. 636–640), the most extensive compilation of Rössen period flint tools to date. With this publication, Dieter Kaufmann partially fills a gap in Central German research, since similarly comprehensive studies on either the *Rössen* or *Linear-* and *Stichbandkeramik* periods have yet to be published. The only exception so far has been one of D. Kaufmann's own previous contributions to the subject, a presentation entitled *"Rössenzeitliche Amphibolithgeräte aus Mitteldeutschland"*, which he delivered at the 2010 International Conference on Central Europe in the 5th Millennium BC in Münster. A colour-contrasted reprint of the presentation can be found in Volume 72/V under Appendix 1 (pp. 161–182). At the time of this presentation, however, he was "only" able to include 2172 finds in his investigations. A reread of this initial publication is certainly recommendable, though it lacks an analysis of the rare *Rössen*-Age stone club heads (there is a brief explanation on p. 47 and 74, as well as some depictions in the plate section, pl. 30,7; 41,5; 49,3). The flat adzes which, in contrast to the aforementioned maceheads, are extremely common were also explicitly excluded from his extensive research (pp. 12; 41; 47). In this case, however, the lack of in-depth analysis is understandable due to the generally large amounts of material and the frequent occurrence of these artifacts outside of the framework of the *Rössen*-Age. As an exception the *"senkrecht durchlochte, flachen und breiten, dickblattigen Dechseln"* (vertically perforated, flat and wide, thick-leafed adzes) are presented in their own separate chapter (pp. 53–76) with their own corresponding catalogue (see below). Rather than providing a strict and exclusive definition of the *Rössen* Culture, the author includes chronologically and geographically adjacent phenomena (such as the late *Stichbandkeramik* Culture, *Schiepziger* and *Gatersleben* groups) under the umbrella of the *Rössen*-Age. A graphic representing this taxonomy, however, does not appear until page 34 (fig. 3; see below).

In *Einführung und Danksagung* (Introduction and Acknowledgments, pp. 7–12), the author describes in detail which museums and collections were visited as part of the research for the catalogues (the effort must have been considerable), as well as which Central German journals and other publications were evaluated for inclusion in the catalogue. This section already contains extensive critical comments on available sources, as well as initial explanations on terminology and research history. These subjects are also elaborated upon in later chapters.

The *Anmerkungen zu den Fundumständen* (Notes on the context of the finds, pp. 13–23) primarily contain a comprehensive description of the various uses of adzes as "thunderbolts" in folklore contexts. These rather entertaining explanations are supplemented by an illustration of the probably oldest known literary example of a "thunderbolt" in Saxony (p. 14 fig. 1) which dates back to a text by Conrad Gessner from 1565 (for details on the subject see also: M. Meinecke, Cerauniae – Donnerkeile. In: U. Veit / M. Wöhrl / M. Augstein, Donnerkeil – Opfermesser – Thränengefäß. Die archäologischen Objekte aus der Sammlung der Leipziger Apothekerfamilie Linck [1670–1807] im Naturalienkabinett Waldenburg / Sachsen. Leipzig Forsch. Ur- u. Frühgesch. 8 [Leipzig 2014] 48–51). Conclusions regarding the frequency of finds without clear context are certainly as accurate as they are disillusioning. In-depth examinations of find contexts provide indispensable information; however, lost finds outside of settlement areas or contact finds with *hunter-gatherer societies* are certainly not to be dismissed out of hand. The circumstances of these types of distributions are discussed in detail later on in chapter 11 (pp. 109–119); perhaps the "thunderbolt-discussion" would have been better suited here, rather than grouped in the chapter on find contexts. In his analysis, Kaufmann suspects that some of the finds were lost during transit by river or, conversely, deposited intentionally (p. 20). The hoard finds discussed subsequently are less problematic in their location, although here the original intention of the deposition remains open to discussion as well (pp. 20–23 fig. 2). As a side note in this chapter (p. 23) but detailed in chapter 11, the author concludes that the relative frequency of contemporaneous hoard finds could indicate specialisation and trade.

The chapter on the context of finds is rounded off with the few stone tools which were found in burial contexts. All other early and middle Neolithic analogies (e. g. burial grounds of Linearbandkeramik in the Rhineland, Stichbandkeramik in Bohemia or Großgartach in Alsace) mentioned in this section also reflect the regular wear and tear of the grave goods (p. 23). This information is especially worth noting, as this sort of criterion can also be used to evaluate other finds from suspected burials.

As the author himself admits (p. 25), the chapter *Zur Forschungsgeschichte* (On the history of research) does not take into account all relevant authors, nevertheless covers the period between 1841 and the present day. Somewhat inevitably, differences in terminological, functional, technological and chronological concepts and interpretations between the authors involved are mentioned here, though the issue is also revisited their own separate chapters.

The aptly named chapter *Zur Nomenklatur* (On Nomenclature) is dealt with on pages 33–41. Since nomenclature always consists of terms that are strictly pertinent to a specific subject, the choice of words has a certain humorous smugness about it; precisely the confusion of terms relating to the *Rössen*-Age stone tools that were discussed at the beginning of the chapter. In particular, the author goes into great detail about the adjunct *"Donauländisch"* (Danubian) culture (pp. 33–36). For symmetrical axes, some of which also have typological features of High Shoe-last Celts (*"hohe Schuhleistenkeile"*), he sees connections to a distinct *"Donauländisch"* tradition, citing a few examples from a *Lengyel* cultural context and Central German parallels (fig. 4). Nonetheless, he sees a distinction between these and the broad, crooked-nosed axes, which occur in the *Hinkelstein*- and *Großgartach*-Cultures (fig. 5–6). However, in the text (pp. 35–36), it seems there is an unintended comparison drawn to Austrian / Moravian Painted Ware. Kaufmann concludes his discussion of the nomenclature of these Middle Neolithic axes and wedges, widespread in Western and Central Europe, by recommending the use of the umbrella term *"Rössenzeitliche Geräte"* (*Rössen*-Age devices). He thereby also refutes the seemingly narrow scope which the chosen title of this publication suggests.

A chronological sequence of the included archaeological cultures is shown in Figure 3, along with some of the corresponding ^{14}C-dates. The frequently mentioned Hinkelstein- and Großgartach-Cultures could have been included at this point, if only as an external or trade influence. The demarcation of "Donauländisch", suggesting a geographically cohesive origin, is as straight-forward as it is sensible. It is, however, worth discussing whether a designation based on chronological or stylistic aspects of these cultures could potentially also offer a suitable comparison. In addition, the question remains open as to whether, for example, the "Rössen-Age" adze (see lists 5 and 9 of the appendix) can or should continue to be referred to as "Donauländisch". The author compares his relatively neutral designations, devised and intended so as to not imply any (erroneous) function (e. g. "Plättbolzen"), to those given by Karl Heinz Brandt (Studien über steinerne Äxte und Beile der Jüngeren Steinzeit und der Stein-Kupferzeit Nordwestdeutschlands. Münster. Beitr. Vorgeschforsch. Veröff. Seminar Vor- u. Frühgesch. Univ. 2. [Hildesheim 1967] 36–37). This comparison is shown in a table. A more extensive elaboration of these distinctions is given in the next section, Formen der im Katalog beschriebenen rössenzeitlichen Felssteingeräte (Forms of Rössen-Age stone devices described in the catalogue, pp. 45–47). A total of 13 categories are shown, but the graphic in Figure 9 focuses on categories 1–9, which are regarded as typical of the Rössen-Age.

The *Exkurs zu den senkrecht durchlochten, flachen und breiten, dickblattigen Dechseln* (Detour to vertically perforated, flat and broad adzes, pp. 53–76) contains a further catalogue of 104 corresponding sites, or 118 finds (pp. 56–73), with nine illustrations of individual objects (figs. 19–27) and a distribution map (p. 75 fig. 28). Maybe, the small additional catalogue would have better been integrated into the main catalogue for this volume, with only a reference list shown within the chapter. The interesting question of whether Mesolithic or *Rössen*-Age tool makers actually produced the devices (possibly even for Mesolithic "customers") is discussed extensively, but – as expected – cannot be answered definitively.

The chapter *Anmerkungen zum Rohmaterial rössenzeitlicher Felsgesteingeräte* (Notes on the raw materials used for *Rössen*-Age stone tools, pp. 77–81) also begins with a short outline of research history, which justifiably emphasises the importance of research into the raw materials, particularly with regard to the geological origin. The author shows this innate archaeological and economic importance with his own research: the vast majority of finds (86.62 % of 403 specimens) consists of North Bohemian amphibolite (p. 78). Further remarks concern the predominant practice of creating a cutting edge across the direction of foliation (p. 80). The increasing robustness of these tools proves the skills and expertise of the toolmakers, but it also raises the question, how the raw stone blocks weighing up to 20 kg were transported, which, however, is not addressed (p. 81).

Only now the core subject of the publication is discussed, *Technologische Aspekte der rössenzeitlichen Felsgesteinbearbeitung* (Technological aspects of *Rössen*-Age stone working, pp. 84–92). The author first reviews the work of Hans Quitta (Ein Verwahrfund aus der Bandkeramischen Siedlung in der Harth bei Zwenkau. In: Institut für Vor- und Frühgeschichte der Karl-Marx-Universität Leipzig [Hrsg.], Leipziger Beiträge zur Vor- und Frühgeschichte: Festschrift zum 70. Geburtstag von Friedrich Behn. Forsch. Vor- u. Frühgesch. 1. [Leipzig 1955] 20–59), who draws similar conclusions like Kaufmann. The following analysis describes the saw marks found on particular artefacts (pp. 83–86); an important chronological observation is that tools from the *Rössen*-Age, unlike those from the later Neolithic, hardly have any perpendicular saw cuts. The author also elaborates on the boreholes in axes. These were usually achieved with crown (hollow) drilling, rather than full drilling (pp. 86–91). In the latter case, a two-sided approach to drilling seems to have dominated; perforations that are continuous from one side are only found on thinner tools. For this, too, several lists with extensive examples are given.

The next chapter 9 (pp. 93–99) deals with the uses for axes and stone wedges. The fact that many axes are broken along the shaft hole indicates extensive use. This is also supported by frequent reworking and reshaping seen on many of these tools (examples on p. 96). An exhaustive discussion on their potential use as splitting wedges, as well as felling devices, is ultimately fruitless; likewise without resolution is the proposition of the tools as status symbols and offerings. "Woodworking" as a commonplace explanation remains a recent theory. Unfortunately, one must agree with the author when he says that there are still more questions than useful answers (p. 97).

The last two chapters 10 (pp. 101–107) and 11 (pp. 109–119) both discuss the chronology of Rössen-Age stone tools. While the focus is initially limited to finds from closed Central German settlements, the last chapter also deals extensively with the distribution of stone tools outside of rural settlement areas; here, however, the reviewer would have liked to see referenced the work of Leo Verhart (Contact in stone: adzes, Keile and Spitzhauen in the Lower Rhine Basin. Neolithic stone tools and the transition from Mesolithic to Neolithic in Belgium and the Netherlands, 5300–4000 cal BC. Journal Arch. Low Countries 4,1, 2012, 5–35). With regard to the chronological classification, the reader can find a large number of relevant references (e.g. that symmetrical axes are first found in the late Stichbandkeramik Culture, that large stone wedges […] enjoyed a special preference at the end of the Rössen Culture [p. 102], the use of flat adzes and high, non-pierced adzes [shoe last wedges]) during the Rössen Cultural development can be explained with long-lasting Bandkeramik traditions [p. 105] etc.). Here, however, apart from the inventories listed (figs. 34–38), a graphic representation of the tool types with potential timelines and distribution would have been a helpful complement. Some distribution maps would have been another useful addition to the remarks on export goods (figs. 39–44).

The text concludes with some thought- and discussion-provoking considerations on possible trading posts and the influence of logistical connections via water and / or land routes during the process of Neolithisation. This is followed by the list of abbreviations (p. 120), the bibliography (pp. 121–128) and the list of figures (p. 129), as well as the appendix with 29 thematic lists referred to in the text (pp. 132–160), the above-mentioned reprint (pp. 161–182), and the plate section (pp. 184–304).

Overall, it can be said that the extensive references to further finds and sources supplied in the text form a good basis for further research and that the extensive, critical, and knowledgeable discussion of individual aspects made a positive impression on this reviewer. On the other hand, precisely this vast scope requires some prior knowledge on the subject in order for the reader to maintain context. It is therefore not a monograph suitable for "beginners". For this reason, in the reviewer's opinion, a summary at either the beginning or end of the text is necessary to provide helpful background information for the reader. This reviewer would have also preferred a slightly differently structured text and less bulky headings, in order to optimise readability; but personal stylistic preferences are not the deciding factor in this context. Conclusion: the wealth of details, technical facets and dissemination aspects provided within this publication speak to the fact that here – at long last – we have a strong body of work that has been long overdue. The monograph arouses the hope of serving as a suggestion to other colleagues to close further knowledge gaps in the subject area. In light of the great effort the author had to make to complete these volumes (and thankfully he did), the need to further simplify and facilitate the accessibility of primary sources (e. g. N. Kemle / L. Reichel, Open Access in der Archäologie – Rechtliche Voraussetzungen und Rahmenbedingungen. Kunstrechtsspiegel 1, 2018, 2–10. doi: https://doi.org/10.11588/krsp.2018.1.72813), which are so fundamentally important for research in the future, becomes clearly evident.

Translated from the German by Steven Joel Hubbard.

DE–53545 Linz am Rhein　　　　　　　　　　　　　　　　　　　　　　　Eric Biermann
Neustraße 1
E-Mail: biermann.eric@web.de
Orcid: https://orcid.org/0000-0001-9918-3262

Milena Vasić, Personal Adornment in the Neolithic Middle East: A Case Study of Çatalhöyük. Studies in Early Near Eastern Production, Subsistence, and Environment 22. ex oriente, Berlin 2020. 54,–€. ISBN 978-3-944178-17-2. x + 234 Seiten mit 110 Abbildungen.

Çatalhöyük in der Türkei ist einer der auch über die archäologische Fachwelt hinaus bekanntesten neolithischen Fundorte. Seit den 1960er-Jahren eröffnete sich dort eine reiche Bilderwelt in Form von Figurinen, Wandmalereien und Gipsinstallationen mit Tierschädeln, die einen Einblick in die religiöse Vorstellungswelt der frühesten Ackerbauern zu erlauben schien. Aufgrund der Schwerpunkte der Ikonographie wurden zwei Kernthemen identifiziert: eine überwiegend weibliche Bilderwelt, die um die oft gebärend dargestellte „große Göttin" zu kreisen schien und, komplementär dazu, den Stier als männliches Symbol. Diese Interpretationslinie wirkt bis heute nach, obwohl der Fundort über die letzten Jahrzehnte einer Neuinterpretation unterzogen worden ist. Hatte der erste Ausgräber (1961–1965) James Mellaart gemeint, eine „Stadt der Steinzeit" mit Arbeitsteilung, Spezialisierung und ausgeprägter Hierarchisierung gefunden zu haben (J. Mellaart, Çatal Hüyük. Stadt aus der Steinzeit² [Bergisch Gladbach 1973]), so zeichnen die Arbeiten des neueren Grabungsprojekts (1993–2017) unter der Leitung von Ian Hodder das Bild einer weitgehend egalitären und wenig städtischen Gemeinschaft. Die reich verzierten Schreine J. Mellaarts wurden dabei teils zu *history houses*, immer wieder an derselben Stelle neu errichteten und mit wichtigen Spolien früherer Bauten sowie Ahnenschädeln / Bestattungen ausgestatteten Gebäuden, die zentral für die Vergegenwärtigung von Genealogien und die Aufrechterhaltung der Identitäten gesellschaftlicher Subgruppierungen gewesen seien (I. Hodder / P. Pels, History houses: a new interpretation of architectural elaboration at Çatalhöyük. In: I. Hodder [Hrsg.], Religion in the Emergence of Civilization: Çatalhöyük as a Case Study [Cambridge 2010] 163–186). Seit 2018 ist die Grabungsleitung an das Museum von Konya und die Ege Universität Izmir übergegangen (Ç. Çilingiroğlu, Introducing the new Çatalhöyük Project. Neo-Lithics 2020. https://www.exoriente.org/repository/NEO-LITHICS/NEO-LITHICS_2020.pdf [letzter Zugriff: 06.05.2022]), man darf auf neue Ergebnisse und Interpretationen gespannt sein. In die zweite Untersuchungsphase und Deutungslinie fügt sich die hier zu besprechende Arbeit ein, die auf einer an der Freien Universität Berlin 2018 angenommenen, von Susan Pollock betreuten Dissertation beruht. Sie behandelt die Belege für „personal adornment", worunter Schmuckstücke, aber auch Kleidung und Körperbemalung verstanden werden.

Das erste Kapitel (S. 1–5) umreißt die Grundlage und Zielrichtung der Arbeit. „Personal adornment" sei Ausdruck von Identitäten, die im Einklang mit der postmodernen Theoriebildung als sozial determiniert, dabei fluide und potentiell multipel aufgefasst werden, als situationsgebundenes soziales Kommunikationsmittel im Rahmen der „cultural values of a society" (S. 3). Interpretationen gelten damit für den konkreten archäologischen Kontext und können nur begrenzt verallgemeinert werden.

Kapitel 2 (S. 6–20) bietet Hintergrundinformationen zum südwestasiatischen Neolithikum, zum Forschungsstand in Çatalhöyük und zu früheren Arbeiten zu Schmuck, Kleidung und Körperbemalung von diesem Fundplatz. Der erste Punkt wird knapp abgehandelt. Der Abschluss des Übergangs zu permanenter Sesshaftigkeit, Ackerbau und Viehzucht im Präkeramischen Neolithikum B (*Pre-Pottery Neolithic B*, PPNB) falle zusammen mit Veränderungen in der Architektur, die einen Wechsel von gemeinschaftlicher Produktion hin zu individuell wirtschaftenden Einzelhaushalten anzeige; genannt wird insbesondere der Wechsel von kommunaler (Präkeramisches Neolithikum A bzw. *Pre-Pottery Neolithic A*, PPNA) zu individueller (PPNB) Vorratshaltung. Dieser Wechsel zeige möglicherweise den Beginn von sozialer Differenzierung an, wovon die Verfasserin jedoch nicht überzeugt ist, denn „Neolithic sites across the Middle East do not show evidence of hierarchy, social differentiation in terms of power, or the existence of an ‚elite'" (S. 6). Die Interpretation der Gesellschaft von Çatalhöyük als egalitär ist die Grundlage der späteren Deutung des behandelten Materials. Eine ausführlichere Diskussion wäre daher willkommen gewesen. Die markanten Unterschiede in Anzahl und Qualität der teils intentionell zerstörten Beigaben der PPNA-zeitlichen Gräber von Körtik Tepe (TR, inklusive reichen Schmucks) hätten zum Beispiel an dieser Stelle besprochen werden können. Die Zerstörung von Reichtum an diesem Fundplatz ist als Maßnahme zur Unterdrückung beginnender sozialer Unterschiede in einer noch-egalitären Gemeinschaft gedeutet worden (M. Benz / Y. S. Erdal / F. Şahin / V. Özkaya / K. W. Alt, The equality of inequality – social differentiation among the hunter-fisher-gatherer community of Körtik Tepe, south-eastern Turkey. In: H. Meller et al. [Hrsg.], Rich and Poor-Competing for Resources in Prehistoric Societies [Halle 2016] 147–164). Folgt man diesem Modell, dann würde die Notwendigkeit solcher Maßnahmen bereits im PPNA eine starke soziale Differenzierungstendenz im Rahmen der Neolithisierung nahe-legen. Es wäre zu fragen, wo das wesentlich spätere Çatalhöyük in diesem Prozess steht, der natürlich nicht unbedingt linear und einheitlich abgelaufen sein muss. Erwähnt werden auch die großen und teilweise noch PPNA-zeitlichen Gemeinschaftsbauten an Orten wie Jerf el Ahmar (SY) oder Göbekli Tepe (TR). Mit Blick auf egalitäre Gesellschaften müsste diskutiert werden, wie solche Großprojekte organisiert wurden, und ob die reiche Bilderwelt und die Hinweise für rituelle Handlungen nicht zumindest auf religiöse Spezialist*innen hindeuten, die gebrannten Kalkestrichböden und elaborierten steinernen Bauteile, Skulpturen und Reliefs nicht vielleicht auf eine handwerkliche, zumindest temporär arbeitsteilige Spezialisierung und welche sozialen Rückwirkungen solche Differenzierungstendenzen auf frühneolithische Gesellschaften gehabt haben mögen.

Kapitel 3 (S. 21–40) umreißt die Materialgrundlage der Arbeit. Einleitend werden die behandelten Fundgruppen eingegrenzt. Artefakte wurden über Grabfunde als zum „personal adornment" zugehörig definiert, wenn ihre Position nahelegte, dass sie an Kleidung oder Körper getragen wurden. Für auffällige Gegenstände wie Flintdolche oder Obsidianklingen wird teilweise eine entsprechende Rolle erwogen. Letztlich werden auf diesem Wege aber – durchaus analog zu den gängigen funktionalen Klassifikationsschemata – primär Textilien, Perlen, Ringe, Armringe, Kragen („collars") aus Eberzähnen, Gürtelschließen / Knebel („fasteners"), Armschutzplatten und Pigmente als „personal adornments" verstanden und auch in Fundkontexten über die Gräber hinaus verfolgt. Es wird bereits einleitend zu Recht angemerkt, dass dieses Vorgehen die Gefahr birgt, primär Totenkleidung zu erfassen, die möglicherweise nicht der Alltagskleidung entsprach. Dies ist ein generelles Problem bei entsprechenden archäologischen Rekonstruktionen, die häufig auf Grabfunden beruhen. Eine Korrektur können nur andere Fundkategorien bieten. Aus Çatalhöyük liegen relevante Darstellungen auf Figurinen sowie Wandmalereien vor. Zudem gibt es Textilfragmente aus Gräbern, bei denen jedoch unklar bliebe, ob sie zur Kleidung der Bestatteten gehörten oder es sich um Leichentücher o. Ä. handelte (Mellaart hatte hier eine Reihe konkreter Kleidungsstücke rekonstruiert). Nach Betrachtungen zu den Rohstoffquellen, die meist in der Nähe der Siedlung lokalisiert werden können (mit Ausnahme besonders von Meeresmuscheln und -schnecken), folgt die Betrachtung der einzelnen Fundgruppen.

Bei dem besprochenen Buch handelt es sich nicht um eine umfassende Materialvorlage. Es wird nur eine Auswahl an Funden abgebildet und mit Fundkontexten in Tabellenform vorgelegt. Wie Tabelle 7 zeigt, sind Perlen mit 38.547 Funden am häufigsten, gefolgt von Ringen, die allerdings nur in 173 Exemplaren vorliegen. Die übrigen Fundgruppen überschreiten die Anzahl von 20 Stücken nicht. „Personal adornment" meint also primär Perlen und Perlenarrangements und es wird auch nur für diese Fundgruppe eine detaillierte Gliederung in 31 Typen vorgenommen. Die Typengliederung wird dabei nicht im Text beschrieben, sondern findet sich in Tabelle 11. Die Tabellen sind vor den Abbildungen am Ende des Bandes platziert. Möchte man die Typengliederung und die zahlreichen Auswertungen zu Rohmaterial, Kontexten etc. nachvollziehen, muss man also permanent zwischen mindestens drei Stellen des Buches blättern. Benutzerfreundlicher wäre eine Platzierung etwa der Tabelle zur Typengliederung und der Abbildungen zu den Typen auf einer Doppelseite im Text gewesen.

Die Perlentypen wurden teils aufgrund der Form, teils aufgrund des Rohmaterials gebildet. Bei den drei Typen T.26–28 handelt es sich, wie auch angemerkt wird, nicht um Typen, sondern um Gruppen von Perlen verschiedener Formen. Zudem wird in Tabelle 11 für einzelne Typen auf Varianten verwiesen, die nicht genauer definiert werden. Das Ziel dieser Gliederung sei gewesen, den Eindruck zu erfassen, den die Perlen zu Ketten aufgefädelt ergeben hätten. Daher seien zum Beispiel alle Muschelformen, die komplett aufgefädelt wurden, als ein Typ erfasst worden. Dies ist nachvollziehbar, doch sind zum Beispiel unter T.21 („button beads") nach Abb. 15,1–4 zu urteilen unterschiedliche Formen (rundlich, trapezoid, ovaloid) zusammengefasst, die dann hätten differenziert werden müssen. Typ T.17 umfasst nach Tabelle 11 „irregularly shaped pebbles or rocks that were naturally or artificially perforated", der Gesamteindruck ist damit ähnlich zu Typ T.22 „beads mainly made of Unio shell. The majority are large flat roughly circular beads with one or two perforations", wenn man die Abb. 11, 14 und 18 vergleicht.

Die übrigen, weniger häufigen Fundgruppen werden knapp mit Verweisen auf Vergleichsfunde behandelt. Sie sind in den Tabellen 18–21 meist mit Kontextinformationen zusammengefasst, die verdeutlichen, dass nur wenige Stücke aus den relevanten Fundlagen in Gräbern stammen. Unter den Farbpigmenten sind rot (Ocker) und blau (Malachit) sowie grün (Azurit) in Bestattungen belegt, ihre potentielle Rolle wird in Kapitel 5 genauer erörtert. Interessant ist der Hinweis, dass möglicherweise einige Perlen gefärbt worden waren.

Als letzte Quellengruppe werden Figurinen und Wandmalereien besprochen. Anthropomorphe Figurinen sind mit 7% Gesamtanteil in Çatalhöyük wesentlich seltener als zoomorphe und die meisten zeigen keine Kleidung. Gelegentlich werden Frisuren, Kopfbedeckungen und Ketten angedeutet, Leopardenhäute / -flecke verweisen wohl auf Kleidungsstücke. In neun Häusern gibt es Wandmalereien mit Menschen. Kleidung ist hier in Form von Lendenschurzen belegt, die in einigen Fällen Leopardenflecke zeigen. Insgesamt sind weder Figurinen noch Wandmalereien ausgesprochen aufschlussreich für Rekonstruktionen von Bekleidung, auch weil die Darstellungen oft schematisch sind. Abschließend werden Fundkategorien besprochen, deren Ansprache als „personal adornment" unklar ist, darunter insbesondere Spiegel und Stempelsiegel.

Kapitel 4 (S. 41–62) behandelt Kontexte, Verteilung und „social geography" des Fundmaterials. Die Kontextinformationen zu den weniger häufigen Fundgruppen werden knapp behandelt. Komplette Armbänder und Gürtelhaken stammen aus Gräbern, Fragmente aus Abfalldeponierungen und Raumfüllungen. Für Ringe ist die Tendenz ähnlich, Stempelsiegel stammen hingegen hauptsächlich aus den Siedlungsarealen. Zerbrochene Schmuckstücke wurden also entsorgt. Der Hauptteil des Kapitels ist den Perlen gewidmet, die überwiegend aus Gräbern und Abfallschichten stammen, in Gebäudekontexten aber selten sind. Ausführlich werden die Gründe für das konzentrierte Auftreten von kompletten Perlen in den Bereichen außerhalb der Häuser erörtert, wobei angenommen wird, dass sie entweder bewusst entsorgt worden seien, weil sie aus einem nicht näher bestimmbaren Grund als unbenutzbar angesehen wurden, oder aber die Zusammenstellung zu Ketten außerhalb der Häuser erfolgte und überschüssige Perlen weggeworfen wurden (S. 47–48). Perlen brechen aufgrund ihrer geringen Größe allerdings auch seltener als andere Gegenstände und werden vermutlich auch öfter übersehen, wenn Fußböden gereinigt und die anfallenden Abfälle entsorgt werden. Als weitere Überlieferungskategorie werden intentionelle Deponierungen angeführt. Der Aussage, dass das Konzept der „structured deposition" in der britischen Archäologie entwickelt wurde (S. 48), würde vermutlich ein Großteil der kontinentaleuropäischen Bronzezeitforschung widersprechen, die solche Konzepte seit über 150 Jahren für Hortfunde diskutiert. Hier würde man auch methodisch fündig werden, um zwischen „forgotten storage", „dump" oder Funden zu unterscheiden, die auf „special events" verweisen. Interessant ist, dass die „history houses" die höchste Funddichte an Perlen aufweisen.

Kapitel 5 (S. 63–84) behandelt die Gräber als primäre Quelle zur Rekonstruktion von Schmuckensembles, wobei einleitend auf die vielen Bedeutungsebenen von Grabbeigaben hingewiesen wird. Für Çatalhöyük kommt erschwerend eine Kontroverse um den Ablauf der Bestattungen hinzu. Während seiner Ausgrabungen hatte Mellaart zahlreiche Bestattungen unter Plattformen im Nordosten der Häuser beschrieben, die scheinbar aus dem anatomischen Verband gerissen waren. Dies schien zu mehreren Wandmalereien zu passen, die Geier zeigen, die auf kopflose menschliche Körper herabstoßen – die Idee eines mehrphasigen Bestattungsrituals mit einer Phase der Exkarnation durch Vögel lag nahe. Zwischenzeitlich wurde diese Rekonstruktion kritisch gesehen (P. ANDREWS /

T. Molleson / B. Boz, The human burials at Çatalhöyük. In: I. Hodder [Hrsg.], Inhabiting Çatalhöyük. Reports from the 1995–1999 seasons [Cambridge 2005] 261–278), dann jedoch aufgrund neuer Belege rehabilitiert (M. A. Pilloud / S. D. Haddow / C. J. Knüsel / C. S. Larsen, A bioarchaeological and forensic re-assessment of vulture defleshing and mortuary practices at Neolithic Çatalhöyük. Journal Arch. Scien. Reports 10, 2016, 735–743). Viele (teilskelettierte) Körper scheinen zudem zu Bündeln geschnürt worden zu sein, um in schmale Grabgruben zu passen.

Solche Bestattungsrituale könnten Rekonstruktionen auf Grundlage der 440 betrachteten Gräber erschweren, doch sollen von 9568 Perlen 98 % als intentionelle Beigaben bestimmbar und immerhin 60 % zu Ketten gehört haben, die direkt mit Individuen assoziiert waren (S. 65–66). 52 Individuen haben Beigaben von Perlen erhalten. Je älter die Bestatteten waren, desto höher ist die Wahrscheinlichkeit dieser Beigabe. Auch sind Frauen tendenziell öfter mit Perlen bestattet worden als Männer. Es ergeben sich keine Korrelationen von bestimmten Perlenfarben mit Altersgruppen oder dem Geschlecht, einige Typen könnten aber an Altersgruppen und Geschlecht gebunden sein. Auch sind erschließbare Auffädelungen von Perlen keinen Regeln bezüglich Form- und Farbkombinationen unterworfen. Nach Form, Farbe und Material einheitliche Kombinationen sind selten. Rote, grüne und blaue Pigmente kommen in den Gräbern vor, doch bleibt unsicher, ob es sich um Reste von Körperbemalung handelt. Hier hätten die Befunde vom Körtik Tepe mit Gewinn diskutiert werden können, wo in PPNA-zeitlichen Gräbern mehrstufige Rituale mit Entfleischung, Überziehen der Knochen mit Kalkputz und Bemalung klar nachgewiesen sind (Y. S. Erdal, Bone or flesh: Defleshing and post-depositional treatments at Körtik Tepe [Southeastern Anatolia, PPNA period]. European Journal Arch. 18,1, 2015, 4–32).

Aus dem Fehlen eindeutiger Regeln bei den Beigaben wird der Schluss gezogen, es habe „no apparent inequalities" (S. 80) gegeben, und „as males and females were adorned in the same way in burials, there is no way to assume that they were not similarly adorned during their lives" (S. 82). Dies sind mögliche Erklärungsansätze für das Fehlen von eindeutiger Strukturierung in dem betrachteten Fundgut; zwingend erscheinen sie nicht. Gleichheit im Grab (die aber in Çatalhöyük angesichts sehr unterschiedlich ausgestatteter Gräber gar nicht gegeben ist) muss nicht Gleichheit im Leben bedeuten, wie der europäische Kulturraum klar zeigt.

Kapitel 6 (S. 85–96) ist der chronologischen Entwicklung der betrachteten Fundkategorien gewidmet, die von Kontinuitäten über längere Zeiträume geprägt zu sein scheint. Bei den Perlen kommen nur langsam neue Rohmaterialien und Formen hinzu; auch die Nutzung von Pigmenten bleibt konstant, wird aber durch blau und grün als neue Farben erweitert. Klarere chronologische Gewichtungen deuten sich bei den weniger häufigen Fundgruppen an, was aber mit der schwerpunktmäßigen Ausgrabung von Befunden bestimmter Zeitstellungen zu tun haben könne.

Kapitel 7 (S. 97–115) zieht ein Resümee und versucht eine vorsichtige Rekonstruktion von Kleidung und Schmuckensembles auf Grundlage der Textilreste, der bildlichen Darstellungen und Funde (Abb. 110). Die chronologischen Differenzen zwischen den herangezogenen Elementen werden als hinderlich angesprochen. Trotzdem ist es begrüßenswert, dass eine Rekonstruktion gewagt wird. Bekräftigt wird noch einmal die Deutung der Gesellschaft von Çatalhöyük als egalitär, auch angesichts des Umstands, dass einige Häuser deutlich elaborierter seien als andere, Unterschiede in Menge und Qualität der Grabbeigaben bestehen und einige Menschen offenbar mit wesentlich reicheren Schmuckensembles ausgestattet waren als andere. Das Buch fügt sich mit dieser Sicht in die von I. Hodder vorgegebene Interpretationslinie ein. Die durchaus anregende Diskussion der Befunde hätte noch zusätzlich gewonnen, wenn diese Deutung stärker hinterfragt worden wäre.

Wie auch in der besprochenen Arbeit mehrfach betont, suchen Archäolog*innen meist nach sich wiederholenden Mustern und Korrelationen im Fundgut, um zu Schlüssen zu gelangen. Dieser Ansatz ist bei dem hier betrachteten Material, für das wenig entsprechende Bezüge festgestellt werden konnten, schwierig. Der Fokus und die Stärken des Bandes liegen auf der Interpretation der Perlen aus Grabkontexten. Aus dieser begrenzten Grundlage destilliert das Buch eine Reihe interessanter Ergebnisse. Zu nennen sind hier insbesondere die Abhängigkeit der Perlenbeigaben von Alter und teils vom Geschlecht und ihre lange chronologische Kontinuität ebenso wie die durchaus gelungenen, bislang noch viel zu seltenen Rekonstruktionen von Schmuck- und Kleidungsensembles auf einer breiten Quellenbasis. Das Buch stellt eine Bereicherung der Diskussion insbesondere zu neolithischem Perlenschmuck dar und bietet zahlreiche Anknüpfungspunkte für weiterführende Fragen.

DE–06114 Halle (Saale)
Richard-Wagner-Straße 9
E-Mail: odietrich@lda.stk.sachsen-anhalt.de
Orcid: https://orcid.org/0000-0001-7013-3317

Oliver Dietrich
Landesamt für Denkmalpflege und Archäologie
Sachsen-Anhalt –
Landesmuseum für Vorgeschichte

Refik Duru / Gülsün Umurtak, Bademağacı Höyüğü Kazıları I. Neolitik ve Erken Kalkolitik Çağ Yerleşmeleri. Excavations at Bademağacı Höyük I. The Neolithic and Early Chalcolithic Settlements. Mit Beiträgen von Aslıhan Yurtsever Beyazıt, Elisabeth Smits, Yılmaz Selim Erdal, Bea De Cupere, Jan Baeten, Dirk De Vos, Hadi Özbal, Andrew Fairbairn und Ahmet Güleç. Ege Yayınları, Istanbul 2019. TL 320,00 (ca. € 41,00). ISBN 978-6057673-13-8. 274 Seiten und 134 Tafeln.

Neben Hacılar, Höyücek und Kuruçay Höyük im Seengebiet stellt Bademağacı Höyük, am Übergang vom Seengebiet zur Antalya-Ebene, einen wichtigen Fundort für die Erforschung des Neolithikums im Gebiet des südwestlichen Anatoliens dar. Der seit 1993 untersuchte mehrphasige Fundort wird immer wieder im Zusammenhang mit der chronologischen Entwicklung des Neolithikums diskutiert (vgl. L. Clare / B. Weninger, The dispersal of neolithic lifeways: absolute chronology and rapid climate change in Central and West Anatolia. In: M. Özdoğan / N. Başgelen / P. Kuniholm [Hrsg.], The Neolithic in Turkey 6. 10500–5200 BC: Environment Settlement, Flora, Fauna, Dating, Symbols of Belief, with views from North, South, East, and West [Istanbul 2014] 1–65). Von besonderer Relevanz ist seit einigen Jahren eine absolute Datierung aus der ersten Hälfte des 7. Jahrtausends v. Chr. (Schicht FN I/8), welche neben einem etwa vergleichbaren Datum aus Hacılar VII Fragen zu einem eventuell frühen Neolithisierungsprozess der Region aufwirft. Daher ist eine monographische Vorlage der neolithischen und frühchalkolithischen Ausgrabungen am Bademağacı Höyük immens wichtig, um anhand der Stratigraphie und der verschiedenen Materialstudien die Entwicklung in diesem Raum zu bewerten.

Das hier besprochene zweisprachige Buch (Türkisch: S. 1–152; Englisch: S. 153–274) gliedert sich in vier große Kapitel mit Unterkapiteln und nachfolgend angehängter Literatur sowie Tafelabbildungen. Der Band fügt sich in die Reihe der bereits erschienenen Endpublikationen der Ausgrabungen von Refik Duru und Gülsün Umurtak zum Neolithikum und Frühchalkolithikum der Fundplätze Kuruçay Höyük (R. Duru, Kuruçay Höyük I. 1978–1988 kazılarının sonuçları. Neolitik ve Erken Kalkolitik Çağı yerleşmeleri / Kuruçay Höyük I. Results of the Excavations 1978–1988. The Neolithic and Early Chalcolithic Periods [Ankara 1994]) und Höyücek (R. Duru / G. Umurtak, Höyücek. 1989–1992 yılları arasında yapılan kazıların sonuçları / Höyücek. Results of the Excavations 1989–1992 [Ankara 2005]) ein. Positiv hervorzuheben ist bereits an dieser Stelle der grundlegende Ansatz von Autor und Autorin, dass die Endpublikationen ihrer Ausgrabungen durchweg in zwei Sprachen publiziert werden, wodurch eine größere Verbreitung der Resultate ermöglicht wird.

Im ersten Kapitel (S. 1–14; 159–166) gibt R. Duru eine Einführung zur Topographie sowie Entdeckung des Fundplatzes Bademağacı Höyük (dt. „Mandelbaumhügel") und bettet diesen in seine langjährigen Forschungen und Ausgrabungen, die bereits 1976 in der Burdur-Region begonnen haben, ein. Duru ist damit zurecht der wichtigste Experte für die Archäologie dieser Region. Die ausführliche Darlegung des Grabungsverlaufs und der beteiligten Personen sowie die Erwähnung der beindruckenden Menge an finanziellen Unterstützern lassen der Leser*innenschaft die enorme Arbeit und den Einsatz der beteiligten Personen während des 17-jährigen Ausgrabungsprojektes (1993–2010) erahnen. Anschließend folgen grundlegende und wichtige Informationen zu den Ausgrabungen, speziell den gewählten Grabungsarealen, der Stratigraphie und den erfassten Perioden. Abgerundet wird das Kapitel durch eine Schilderung, wie der Fundort geschützt und der interessierten Öffentlichkeit zugänglich gemacht wurde sowie einer vollständigen Auflistung der bislang erschienenen 57 Publikationen.

Das zweite Kapitel (S. 15–86; 167–212) behandelt die archäologischen Befunde sowie das Fundmaterial und gliedert sich in vier Unterkapitel. Duru beschreibt einführend die architektonischen Überreste (Kap. II. A, S. 15–29; 167–182) der neolithischen und frühchalkolithischen Siedlungen. In den ältesten Siedlungsphasen (FN I/9–8) wurden lediglich Reste von terrazzoartigen Fußböden, bestehend aus einer kalkhaltigen Mischung, angetroffen. Hierbei ist jedoch anzumerken, dass die Grabungsflächen in diesen Bereichen sehr klein waren. Das Ende des Frühneolithikums I markiert, ihm folgend, eine mächtige Brandschicht (FN I/5). Im darauffolgenden Frühneolithikum II (FN II/4B–1) erkennt Duru einen klaren Wandel, da nun reichlich Architekturbefunde in Form von freistehenden Bauten zutage kamen. Es handelt sich hierbei um abgerundete, rechtwinklige Architektur, welche aus einem Steinfundament mit einem Aufbau aus unregelmäßig geformten „Lehmziegeln" *(kerpiç)* konstruiert wurde. Im Inneren fanden sich Lehmstampfböden mit Installationen, wie an die Wände gebaute Öfen, Herdstellen und Plattformen. Interessanterweise gibt es ebenfalls Hinweise auf mögliche Lageraktivitäten (ab FN II/2). Hierauf deuten freistehende Installationen mit Kammern oder Einbauten in Räumen. Möglicherweise sind in diesem Zusammenhang ebenfalls Steinreihenstrukturen zu sehen (S. 27; 180), die eventuell zum Schutz vor Feuchtigkeit oder sogar als Trockenplattformen gedient haben könnten. Aus dem Spätneolithikum (SN 2–1) sind im Gegensatz zur vorherigen Zeit nur spärliche Befunde ausgegraben. Die erfassten Bauten besitzen eine rechteckige Form, und auch hier finden sich gesetzte Steinreihen unklarer Funktion innerhalb eines Baus. Aus dem Frühchalkolithikum kann keine gesicherte Architektur angeführt werden. Am Ende des Architekturteils folgt eine Zusammenschau und Interpretation der Befunde. Problematisch bei der Interpretation der ausgegrabenen Befunde ist die Schlussfolgerung sowohl für das Frühneolithikum (II) als auch für das Spätneolithikum. Duru sieht in den frühneolithischen Befunden einen Übergang vom Dorf zur Stadt („transition from village to town", S. 28; 181) und bezeichnet die spätneolithischen Überreste sogar als vorstädtisch („Proto-Town", S. 28; 181). Zwar finden sich in den frühneolithischen Siedlungen Hinweise auf Lagerungstätigkeiten, jedoch handelt es sich hier immer noch um bäuerliche Gemeinschaften (vgl. B. S. Düring, The Prehistory of Asia Minor. From Complex Hunter-Gatherers to Early Urban Societies [Cambridge 2011] 198–199). Daher sollte hier eine klare Abgrenzung zu den Termini der späteren proto-urbanen und urbanen Gesellschaften des 3. Jahrtausends v. Chr. hergestellt werden.

Neben der Architektur wurden bei den Ausgrabungen insgesamt 74 Bestattungen (Kap. II. B, S. 30–31; 183–184) angetroffen, von denen die meisten in das Frühneolithikum II datieren. Duru geht jedoch davon aus, dass die meisten Individuen außerhalb des Siedlungsbereichs bestattet wurden. Die große Anzahl an Gräbern von Bademağacı Höyük stellt für diesen Horizont in Westanatolien eine wichtige neue Datenquelle dar und lässt spannende neue Erkenntnisse zu derzeit laufenden Forschungen wie z. B. der aDNA-Debatte erwarten.

Die Keramik (Kap. II. C, S. 32–73; 185–203) der neolithischen und frühchalkolithischen Kontexte wurde von G. Umurtak bearbeitet. Das Subkapitel gliedert sich in eine Beschreibung der Warengruppen und Formen mit einer anschließenden Bewertung des Inventars. Für die Publikation wurden 3500 Scherben herangezogen, welche zwölf Hauptwarengruppen zugeordnet werden. Das Spektrum reicht von beigen / grauen bis roten / braunen Oberflächen. Die Formen spiegeln klassische neolithische Typen wider, die eine gewisse kontinuierliche Entwicklung im Frühneolithikum I (FN 9–5) mit einer Tendenz zu einem differenzierteren Formenspektrum ab dem Frühneolithikum II (ab FN 4) zeigen. Diese Veränderung hat auch Ulf-Dietrich Schoop hervorgehoben (U.-D. Schoop, Das anatolische Chalkolithikum. Eine chronologische Untersuchung zur vorbronzezeitlichen Kultursequenz im nördlichen Zentralanatolien und den angrenzenden Gebieten. Urgesch. Stud. 1 [Remshalden 2005] 171; 180–181). Die im Keramikteil angeführten Diagramme (S. 41–52) unterstreichen diese Entwicklung und deuten auf eine Kontinuität und eine gewisse zeitliche Nähe zwischen dem Frühneolithikum I und II am Bademağacı Höyük hin. Die Keramik aus dem Spätneolithikum / Frühchalkolithikum des Fundplatzes lässt eine noch spätere Zeitstellung erkennen, worauf insbesondere das Auftreten von Fingernagelimpressodekor hinweist (vgl. Ç. Çilingiroğlu, The appearance of impressed pottery in the Neolithic Aegean and its implications for maritime networks in the eastern Mediterranean. Türkiye Bilimler Akad. Ark. Dergisi 13, 2010, 9–22). Für die Einordnung des Materials zieht Umurtak naheliegende Vergleiche aus dem Seengebiet (Hacılar, Höyücek und Kuruçay Höyük) heran. Eine zusammenfassende relativchronologische Auswertung findet sich in diesem Subkapitel nicht, wird jedoch von Duru am Ende des Buches gegeben (S. 144–146; 262–263). In diesem Zusammenhang findet Duru einen Vergleich mit Kontexten Westanatoliens nicht zielführend, da es sich am Bademağacı Höyük um frühere Kontexte handele (S. 146; 263). Dennoch spricht bislang nichts gegen die von Ulf-Dietrich Schoop (2005, 190; Abb. 4,9) postulierte Einordnung der Keramik vor allem in die zweite Hälfte des 7. Jahrtausends v. Chr. Eine Einbettung in einen größeren Kontext wäre jedoch wünschenswert gewesen, hat sich doch in den letzten Jahren gezeigt, dass gerade die Daten zum Neolithikum des Seengebietes unter Berücksichtigung Zentralanatoliens, der ägäischen Küstenregion und Nordwestanatoliens immer wieder breit in der Literatur diskutiert werden (vgl. z. B. M. Brami / V. Heyd, The origins of Europe's first farmers: The role of Hacılar and Western Anatolia, fifty years on. Prähist. Zeitschr. 86,2, 2011, 165–206; s. o. Clare / Weninger 2014, 11–29).

Die Kleinfunde (Kap. II. D, S. 74–86; 204–212) umfassen Figurinen, Tonobjekte, eine Bandbreite von Knochen- sowie Steinobjekten und spiegeln somit ein klassisches Siedlungsinventar des Neolithikums wider. Die Figurinen folgen den bekannten neolithischen Typen und Duru verweist auf gute Vergleiche besonders im Inventar von Höyücek. Auch Stempel aus Ton (Pintadera) stellen eine gängige Fundgruppe dieser Zeit dar. Duru unterscheidet hierbei jedoch zwischen Siegeln und Pintadera (S. 77; 207). Zwar kann eine Verwendung als Siegel nicht gänzlich ausgeschlossen werden, jedoch wurde bereits gegen eine solche Interpretation in neolithischer Zeit argumentiert (vgl. C. Lichter, Neolithic stamps and the neolithization process. A fresh look at an old issue. In: R. Krauß [Hrsg.], Beginnings. New Research in the Appearance of the Neolithic between Northwest Anatolia and the Carpathian Basin. Papers of the International Workshop, 8th–9th April 2009, Istanbul. Menschen – Kulturen – Traditionen. Stud. Forschcluster DAI 1 [Rahden / Westf. 2011] 35–44). Unter den weiteren von Duru angeführten Tonobjekten, wie kleine Tischchen, Boxen, Löffel, Schleudergeschosse, fällt besonders eine Gruppe von kleinen runden oder bikonisch durchlochten Tonobjekten auf, welche Duru als Perlen oder mögliche Spinnwirtel interpretiert (S. 78; 208; Taf. 125,8). Vergleiche von Spinnwirteln aus den spätneolithischen Schichten des Çukuriçi Höyük in der zentralwestanatolischen Küstenregion unterstützen anhand der Form und der Maße die Interpretation Durus (vgl. Ch. Britsch, Early Textile Technologies in the Anatolian-Aegean World. From Neolithic to Early Bronze Age [ungedr. Diss.] [Wien 2018]). Ebenfalls ist die Deponierungspraxis von Schleudergeschossen im Wohnbereich (S. 78; 208; Taf. 19,6) interessant und lässt sich wiederum gut mit spätneolithischen Befunden im westlichen Küstengebiet (vgl. Ulucak Höyük, Çukuriçi Höyük) vergleichen. Die Objekte aus Knochen, Mollusken und Stein wurden von Aslıhan Yurtsever Beyazıt bearbeitet. Neben Geräten, wie beispielsweise Löffel und Ahlen, wurden aus Knochen auch Ornamente und Anhänger gefertigt. Zu den Gesteinsobjekten zählen Beile, Keulenköpfe, Glättsteine, Klopfsteine, Reibsteine, Perlen und Steingefäße. Gerade letzte sind interessant, da sie aus Marmor gefertigt wurden und derartige Gefäße auch aus den näheren Fundorten Höyücek, Kuruçay Höyük und Hacılar bekannt sind. Weiterhin erwähnt Duru die vorläufigen Ergebnisse der geschlagenen Steine aus Obsidian und Flint. Anhand des Materials kann von einer lokalen Klingenproduktion aus beiden Rohstoffen ausgegangen werden. Beidseitig retuschierte Pfeil- / Speerspitzen deuten zusätzlich auf wahrscheinliche Importe aus Zentralanatolien hin. Zwar bleibt die endgültige Materialvorlage – gerade für Details zur chronologischen Stellung – noch abzuwarten, jedoch zeichnet sich insbesondere durch die Menge an „bullet cores" (Taf. 134,7–8) aus beiden Materialen eine klare Standardisierung der lokalen Produktion ab. Hier wäre es für die Zukunft wünschenswert, die technologischen Aspekte weiter zu untersuchen und mit Kappadokien und der Izmir-Region zu vergleichen.

Das dritte Kapitel (S. 87–127; 213–246) beinhaltet unterschiedliche Berichte zu analytischen Detailstudien organischer und anorganischer Fundgruppen, welche von verschiedenen Spezialistinnen und Spezialisten durchgeführt wurden. Im ersten Subkapitel (III. A, S. 87–111; 213–217) werden Ergebnisse der anthropologischen und demographischen Studien ausgehend von den menschlichen Skelettfunden von Bademağacı Höyük behandelt. Insgesamt wurden 28 Individuen (hiervon drei aus der Frühbronzezeit) anthropologisch bestimmt: zehn Erwachsene, drei Jugendliche und 15 Neugeborene. Elisabeth Smits gibt zwar zu bedenken, dass die Datenmenge relativ gering ist, dennoch folgert sie, dass es sich um eine Bevölkerung mit zumeist jungen Individuen handelte. Weitere Untersuchungen an 48 Individuen aus neolithischer Zeit wurden von Yılmaz Selim Erdal durchgeführt, wodurch sich laut ihm die Gesamtzahl auf 74 Individuen neolithischer Zeitstellung erhöht (S. 90; 216). Diese Zahl verwirrt ein wenig, da Smits lediglich 25 Individuen aus dem Neolithikum und drei aus der Frühbronzezeit anführt (S. 213). In der türkischen Übersetzung ihres Textes werden die drei frühbronzezeitlichen Skelette jedoch als neolithisch eingeordnet. Erdal geht in seiner Auswertung somit von insgesamt 76 Individuen aus, von denen er zwei aufgrund der mangelnden Aussagefähigkeit vernachlässigt (S. 90; 216). Ausgehend von Erdals Datenbasis liegt der Anteil der Kinder bei 60 % und bei den Erwachsenen überwiegen die Frauen mit zwei Dritteln gegenüber den Männern. Im Hinblick auf die Anzahl der Individuen, die ausgegrabene Siedlungsfläche und die Anzahl der Bauphasen folgert Erdal, dass der Großteil der Toten wahrscheinlich extramural bestattet wurde. Die hohe Anzahl an Kinder im Siedlungsbereich scheint somit wohl die gängige Bestattungssitte zu dieser Zeit für diese Altersgruppe widerzuspiegeln (vgl. C. Lichter, Burial customs of the Neolithic in Anatolia – an overview. In: Ü. Yalçın [Hrsg.], Anatolian Metal VII. Anatolien und seine Nachbarn vor 10.000 Jahren. Anschnitt, Beih. 31 = Veröff. Dt. Bergbau-Mus. 214 [Bochum 2016] 71–83).

Das zweite Subkapitel (III. B, S. 112–119; 218–232) behandelt die archäozoologischen und weitere biologischen Studien. Die Auswertung der Tierknochen wurde von Bea De Cupere durchgeführt. Ausgehend von der Gesamtknochenanzahl handelt es sich bei etwa der Hälfte der Säugetierknochen um Schafe und Ziegen (51 %), gefolgt von Rindern (23 %) und Schweinen (17 %). Wünschenswert wäre hier ein Diagramm mit prozentualen Anteilen der einzelnen Siedlungsperioden gewesen, um diese besser vergleichen und in einen breiteren Kontext eingliedern zu können. Wichtig für die Diskussion des Neolithisierungs- und Adaptionsprozesses vor Ort wäre die Frage, wie groß der Anteil der Schweine im Inventar der jeweiligen Zeitstellung ist (vgl. B. S. Arbuckle, The late adoption of cattle and pig husbandry in Neolithic Central Turkey. Journal Arch. Scien. 40, 2013, 1805–1815; B. Horejs et. al., The Aegean in the early 7th millennium BC: Maritime networks and colonization. Journal of World Prehist. 28,4, 2015, 310–311). Im anschließenden

Bericht diskutieren De Cupere, Jan Baeten und Dirk De Vos Hinweise auf Milchproduktion im Neolithikum anhand archäozoologischer Daten und Rückstandsanalysen. Die Schlachtalter der Schafe und Ziegen liegen bei 60 % der Individuen bei über zwei Jahren, weshalb davon ausgegangen wird, dass die Tiere nicht vordergründig für ihr Fleisch, sondern als Milch- und Felllieferant gedient haben. Rückstandsanalysen wurden an elf Scherben durchgeführt, von denen sieben verwertbar waren. In drei Fällen fanden sich tierische Fettsäuren, die auf Milch hindeuten, jedoch muss festgehalten werden, dass nicht unterschieden werden kann, ob es sich dabei um Milch von Schafen, Ziegen oder Rindern handelt. Der Frage nach organischen Rückständen auf neolithischer Keramik geht auch Hadi Özbal nach. Sieben von 31 Gefäßen erbrachten Ergebnisse, welche auf Bienenwachs, tierische Fette von Wiederkäuern und ebenfalls auf Milchfette hindeuten, und stellen somit wichtige Daten – leider ohne genaue Phasenzuordnung – aus dem südwestanatolischen Gebiet dar.

Im dritten Subkapitel (III. C, S. 120–122; 233–242) fasst Andrew Fairbairn die Resultate der archäobotanischen Studien zusammen. Es handelt sich hierbei um Daten aus dem Frühneolithikum (FN II), dem Frühchalkolithikum und der Frühbronzezeit 2. Zwar sind die Daten übersichtlich, aber anhand des Berichts nicht exakt zu quantifizieren, jedoch überwiegt zumindest im Neolithikum der Anteil an Hülsenfrüchten und vermehrt findet sich Emmer, Einkorn und Weizen.

Das vierte Subkapitel (III. D, S. 123–127; 243) befasst sich mit Materialanalysen der Fußböden von Bademağacı Höyük und Hacılar. Anhand von mikroskopischen und chemischen Untersuchungen konnte Ahmet Güleç feststellen, dass sich die Fußböden der beiden Fundorte unterscheiden. Interessant sind besonders die Terrazzo-Böden. Am Bademağacı Höyük bestehen die Terrazzo-Böden aus gelöschtem Kalk mit einem Kalkstein-Gemenge, wohingegen sich in Hacılar ein Marmor-Kalkstein-Gemenge findet. Auch bei der Zusammensetzung des Mörtels finden sich Unterschiede, wodurch Güleç auf eine andersartige Herstellungstechnik schließt.

Als letztes Subkapitel (III. E, S. 128–130; 244–246) werden die Daten der 13 Radiokarbondatierungen des Fundortes angeführt, ohne weiter auf diese einzugehen. Die Besprechung der Daten geschieht im anschließenden, auswertenden Kapitel.

Das abschließende und auswertende Kapitel IV (S. 131–152; 247–270) beinhaltet zwei Unterkapitel zur Datierung der neolithischen Schichten von Bademağacı Höyük im Kontext der Befunde im Seengebiet sowie eine Bewertung der neolithischen Kultur des Fundplatzes.

Im ersten Teil (IV. A, S. 131–133; 247–250) gibt Duru einen Überblick zu den vorhandenen Radiokarbondaten des Fundortes und weiteren neolithischen Fundplätzen im Seengebiet. Interessanterweise unterscheiden sich die kalibrierten Daten von Bademağacı Höyük im türkischen und englischen Teil voneinander. Für Bademağacı Höyük geht Duru anhand eines Datums aus dem Frühneolithikum I/8 und den nächstfolgenden Daten aus dem Frühneolithikum II/4B von einer Besiedlungsdauer von ca. 7100/6900–6500/6400 v. Chr. für den frühen Abschnitt des Frühneolithikums (I) aus (S. 132; 248). Das Frühneolithikum II setzt er zwischen ca. 6400 und 6080 v. Chr. an. Darauf folgt ein anschließendes Spätneolithikum am Ende des 7. und Beginn des 6. Jahrtausends v. Chr. (S. 132–133; 248–249). Insbesondere der große Zeitraum des Frühneolithikums I verwundert und es kann hier nicht genau bestimmt werden, ob es sich um eine durchgehende Besiedlung handelt oder nicht, da die Radiokarbondaten auf dem kritischen Plateau (ca. 7000–6600 v. Chr.) der Kalibrationskurve liegen. Hierdurch sind sie nicht genau fixierbar und es ergibt sich eine größere Ungenauigkeit bei der Datierung. In diesem Zusammenhang wäre eine Angabe der 2-Sigma-Werte der Radiokarbondaten wünschenswert, damit hier kein verzerrtes Bild der Chronologie entsteht. Hingegen lassen sich im Kontext der bekannten Radiokarbondaten im Seengebiet die Daten des Frühneolithikums II von Bademağacı gut mit den Daten der anderen Fundorte in Einklang bringen und datieren in die zweite Hälfte des 7. Jahrtausends v. Chr.

Lediglich die zwei bereits eingangs erwähnten Daten aus Bademağacı und Hacılar deuten auf eine frühere Besiedlung hin. Zwar kann – gerade mit Blick auf Zentralanatolien – eine derartige Entwicklung nicht ausgeschlossen werden, ohne weitere, konkrete Daten muss diese Frage jedoch weiterhin unbeantwortet bleiben (vgl. B. HOREJS, Long and short revolutions towards the Neolithic in western Anatolia and Aegean. Doc. Praehist. 46, 2019, 68–83). Auffallend ist in diesem Zusammenhang das neolithische Keramikinventar des Fundplatzes, welches sich, wie SCHOOP zeigen konnte (s. o. 2005, 180–181; 190), recht gut in das anatolische Spätneolithikum einordnen lässt und terminologische Unterschiede erkennen lässt (s. o. CLARE / WENINGER 2014, 27–28).

Der zweite Teil (IV. B, S. 134–152; 251–270) umfasst eine Zusammenschau und Synthese der präsentierten Befunde und Funde unter Berücksichtigung zeitgleicher Fundplätze der Region. Duru führt hierzu mehrere Punkte an: die Architektur, Hinweise zur Religion und Glaubensvorstellungen, Bestattungssitten, Keramik, sowie Kleinfunde. Diese bettet er vor allem in das Neolithikum des Seengebietes ein. Auffallend ist jedoch, dass vordergründig die Literatur bis 2007 (vgl. S. 135; 252) berücksichtigt wurde, wodurch eine Vielzahl von neuen Forschungsergebnissen der letzten Jahre, wie der aktuelle Stand des Prozesses der Neolithisierung und der Chronologie, bei seiner Bewertung nicht miteinbezogen wurden. Problematisch ist somit auch seine Annahme, dass die neolithische Lebensweise bereits gegen 7500 v. Chr. im Seengebiet präsent war (S. 150–151; 268–269). Ausgehend vom derzeitigen Stand der Forschung kann ein mögliches Auftauchen bereits in der ersten Hälfte des 7. Jahrtausends v. Chr. im Seengebiet nicht ausgeschlossen werden, muss jedoch als „unsicher" betrachtet werden (vgl. z. B. E. ROSENSTOCK, Dot by dot: Phase-mapping the Central / Western Anatolian farming treshold. In: M. Brami / B. Horejs [Hrsg.], The Central / Western Anatolian Farming Frontier. Oriental and European Arch. 12 [Wien 2019] 103–126). Eine Datierung um 7500 v. Chr. erscheint anhand der Datengrundlage daher deutlich zu hoch angesetzt und sollte kritisch betrachtet werden.

Dem Autor und der Autorin Refik Duru und Gülsün Umurtak ist für ihre außerordentliche Leistung zu gratulieren, da sie bis auf die jüngeren Perioden von Bademağacı Höyük (in Vorbereitung) alle ihre Ausgrabungen publiziert und somit der Wissenschaft zugänglich gemacht haben. Nicht nur in Anatolien, sondern auch in der gesamten Archäologie können sie daher als Paradebeispiel angesehen werden. Nach den Ausgrabungen von James Mellaart in Hacılar (J. MELLAART, Excavations at Hacılar [Edinburgh 1970]) haben sie mit ihren über 30 Jahren Feldarbeit maßgeblich zur Erforschung der prähistorischen Archäologie Südwestanatoliens beigetragen.

A–1020 Wien
Hollandstraße 11–13
E-Mail: christoph.schwall@oeaw.ac.at
Orcid: https://orcid.org/0000-0002-6310-4056

Christoph Schwall
Abteilung Prähistorie & Westasien /
Nordostafrika-Archäologie
Österreichisches Archäologisches Institut
Österreichische Akademie der Wissenschaften

CHRISTOPH GUTJAHR / GEORG TIEFENGRABER (Hrsg.), Beiträge zur Kupferzeit am Rande der Südostalpen. Akten des 4. Wildoner Fachgesprächs am 16. und 17. Juni 2016 in Wildon / Steiermark (Österreich). Materialhefte zur Archäologie des Südostalpenraumes Band 1 = Hengist-Studien Band 5 = ISBE-Forschungen Band 1. Verlag Marie Leidorf, Rahden / Westf. 2020. € 59,80. ISBN 978-3-86757-143-2. 280 Seiten mit zahlreichen Abbildungen und Tafeln.

Im vorliegenden Band präsentieren die beiden Veranstalter die Akten des 4. Wildoner Fachgesprächs am 16. und 17. Juni 2016 in Wildon / Steiermark (Österreich). Sie vertreten den Kulturpark

Gleirscher: Gutjahr / Tiefengraber (Hrsg.), Kupferzeit am Rande der Südostalpen   249

Hengist bzw. das Institut für südostalpine Bronze- und Eisenzeitforschung (ISBE) und deren Interesse zur archäologischen Erforschung eines als „südostalpine-transdanubische-nordwestbalkanische Kulturkoiné" (S. 7) bezeichneten Raumes. Gemeint ist anders formuliert der südostalpine Raum zwischen dem Caput Adriae und der pannonischen Tiefebene. Ziel der 17 Referate des Fachgesprächs im Sommer 2016 war eine Zusammenfassung des Forschungsstandes zur Kupferzeit einschließlich der Präsentation aktueller Grabungsbefunde. Zwölf Beiträge von elf Autorinnen und Autoren gelangten nunmehr zum Druck.

Judit Regenye (S. 11–22) erörtert mehrere Fundstellen in der Region Bakony nördlich des Plattensees (HU), die mit dem Abbau von Radiolarit in Zusammenhang stehen. Das Fundgut ist quantitativ und qualitativ gesehen bescheiden. Sie erwägt, ob die spätlengyelzeitlichen Betriebsstätten nicht bis in die Zeit der Balaton-Lasinja-Kultur fortbestanden haben könnten, ohne von deren kulturellem Wandel erfasst worden zu sein. Derartige Retentionsphänomene wurden auch im Südostalpenraum wiederholt erwogen, konnten aber noch nie bestätigt werden (P. Gleirscher, Frühe Bauern in Kärnten und in der Steiermark. In: Ch. Gutjahr / M. Roscher / G. P. Obersteiner [Hrsg.], Homo effodiens – der Grabende. Festgabe Helmut Ecker-Eckerhofen zum 70. Geburtstag. Hengist-Studien 1 [Wildon 2006] 10–20, bes. 15). Im Zusammenhang mit Bergbautätigkeit wird man derlei umso weniger erwarten und von einer dynamischen kulturgeschichtlichen Entwicklung auszugehen haben.

Samo Sankovič (S. 23–37) präsentiert weitgehend kleinteiliges Fundmaterial von der Fundstelle Na Plesi in Murska Sobota (SL), das in Verbindung mit mehreren grubenartigen Vertiefungen steht, deren seichte Überreste sich erhalten haben. Die Kleinfunde sind der Lasinja-Kultur und der Furchenstichkeramik zuzuordnen und fanden sich infolge späterer Umlagerung(en) gewissermaßen in verkehrter stratigraphischer Lagerung. Das zeigt einmal mehr die Problematik der Schichtung auch in Siedlungen der Kupferzeit, die immer wieder als Befund missinterpretiert wurden und werden (Gleirscher 2006, 15; Gleirscher [Rez. zu]: G. Tiefengraber, Der Wildoner Schlossberg. Die Ausgrabungen des Landesmuseums Joanneum 1985–1988. Schild von Steier Beih. 7 = Forsch. Gesch. Landeskde. Steiermark 80 [Graz 2008]. Carinthia I, 2020, 739–742).

Branko Kerman (S. 39–52) gibt einen Überblick zu den kupferzeitlichen Idolen im Nordosten Sloweniens (Prekmurje), die aus Fundzusammenhängen der Kultur mit Furchenstichkeramik (Typus Retz-Gajary) stammen. Die Anzahl ist mittlerweile stattlich, wodurch mehrere Typen unterschieden werden können, die auch im Umfeld Analogien finden. Kerman nennt Statuetten mit betontem Gesäß, Statuetten von pyramidaler Grundform, flache Statuetten mit Fettsteiß, ovale Statuetten mit Brüsten oder betontem Gesäß sowie Statuetten mit Brüsten und Stummelbeinen (zum herausragenden spätkupferzeitlichen „Idol" aus Ig im Laibacher Moor vgl. P. Gleirscher, Mensch oder Vogelmensch? Zur Deutung eines spätkupferzeitlichen Ritualgefäßes aus Ig [Slowenien]. Rudolfinum. Jahrb. Landesmus. Kärnten 2016, 2018, 16–32).

In einem umfangreichen Beitrag geht Bine Kramberger (S. 53–89) Fragen zur absoluten und relativen Chronologie zwischen Save und Mur im 5. Jahrtausend v. Chr. nach, womit er sich seit seiner Dissertation beschäftigt (vgl. B. Kramberger, The Neolitic-Eneolitic sequence and pottery assemblages in the fifth millenium BC in north-eastern Slovenia. Documenta Praehist. 41, 2014, 237–282. doi: https://doi.org/10.4312/dp.41.13; B. Kramberger, Forms, function and use of early Eneolitic pottery and settlement structures from Zgornje Radvanje, Slovenia. Documenta Praehist. 42, 2015, 231–250. doi: https://doi.org/10.4312/dp.42.16). Dabei stehen und fallen die Einschätzungen mit der Frage, inwieweit sich die Stratigraphie der jeweiligen Fundplätze für derlei Fragen überhaupt eignet (vgl. oben) bzw. ob die Forschung bereits ausreichend zu differenzieren vermag, wenn einzelne spätneolithische und kupferzeitliche Fundstellen im Laufe der Jahrhunderte immer wieder besiedelt wurden. Vergleichsweise scheint es bei weitem einfacher zu sein, hallstattzeitliche Siedlungsphasen von spätkeltischen zu unterscheiden als neolithisch / spätkupferzeitliche Gemengelagen aufzulösen. Das führt wohl auch immer noch dazu, dass – wie Kramberger festhält (S. 60) – „die Keramik der Sava-Gruppe in Bezug auf Formenspektrum und Verzierungen keine Einheit bildet". Nur der Zuwachs von Referenzfundstellen mit einphasiger Belegung – wie schon die Altfunde aus Bad Gleichenberg (AT) erhellen (GLEIRSCHER 2006, 13–14, Abb. 2) – wird aus diesem Dilemma herausführen und typenchronologische Überlegungen verlässlich schärfen können. Dementsprechend bleiben ^{14}C-Daten aus Gemengelagen problematisch. Auch zu den Fundorten der Lasinja-Kultur muss Kramberger in diesem Sinn festhalten (S. 68), „dass bestimmte Typen und Ornamente über längere Zeit in Gebrauch waren. […] und es nur wenige Fundplätze mit einer vertikalen Stratigrafie und mit sog. geschlossenen Kontexten gibt bzw. von diesen nur wenige veröffentlicht sind". Zudem „ist das Material der Sava-Gruppe II der Lasinja-Kultur in diesem Raum ähnlich, was die Interpretation zusätzlich erschwert" (S. 77).

Marko Sraka (S. 91–132) erörtert unter Zugrundelegung des Bayesianischen Modells Fragen der Dynamik der kulturellen Entwicklung im heutigen Slowenien am Übergang vom Neolithikum zur Kupferzeit, also während des 5. Jahrtausends v. Chr. Angesichts der angesprochenen Probleme um die kulturgeschichtliche Definition der Kulturgruppen bleibt das in hohem Maße theoretisch.

Martin Bertha (S. 133–165) stellt zum einen eine Reihe kleinteiliger Tonscherben vom Burgberg von Eppenstein bei Judenburg (Steiermark, AT) vor (vgl. nunmehr ausführlich M. BERTHA, Der Burgberg vor der Burg. Die urgeschichtliche Besiedlung des Eppensteiner Burgberges anhand der Surveyfunde der Jahre 2011 bis 2013. Forsch. Gesch. Landeskde. Steiermark 90 [Graz 2021]). Die Lesefunde belegen, dass die markante Kuppe am Zugang zum Obdacher Sattel in Richtung Lavanttal vom mittleren Neolithikum bis in die späte Kupferzeit – und darüber hinaus – immer wieder besiedelt war. Zusammen mit Georg Tiefengraber (S. 239–259) kommt er zum anderen auf die Ausgrabungen am Wauberg am Faaker See östlich von Villach (Kärnten, AT) zu sprechen. Von einer hochmittelalterlichen Burg überlagert bzw. weitgehend gestört zeigen die Kleinfunde, dass die markante Kuppe während der gesamten Kupferzeit (immer wieder) besiedelt war. Das setzt sich ähnlich wie in Eppenstein über die Spätbronzezeit in die ältere Eisenzeit fort. Im Gegensatz zum nahe gelegenen Kanzianiberg bei Finkenstein (AT; A. PEDROTTI, L'insediamento di Kanzianiberg: rapporti culturali fra Carinzia ed Italia Settentrionale durante il neolitico. In: P. Biagi [Hrsg.], The Neolithisation of the Alpine Region. Monogr. Natura Bresciana 13 [Brescia 1990] 213–226) zeichnen sich am Wauberg derweil keinerlei Kulturkontakte ins östliche Oberitalien ab.

Christoph Gutjahr (S. 167–197) beschäftigt sich mit verlagerten Grabfunden der Lasinja-Kultur, die 2012 am Bockberg, einem westlichen Ausläufer des Buchkogels bei Wildon (Steiermark, AT), in der Schüttung eines hallstattzeitlichen Hügelgrabes ans Licht kamen. Gutjahr geht jedenfalls von der Brandbestattung einer vermutlich männlichen erwachsenen Person in einer Knickwandschüssel aus; eine direkte Zusammengehörigkeit erscheint angesichts der Verlagerung nicht nachvollziehbar. Weitere Knochenreste stammen von einer jugendlichen Person sowie von einem Kind. Michael Brandl (S. 199–210) ergänzt diesen Beitrag mit einer Analyse von mehreren Artefakten aus Stein, die jedenfalls Siedlungscharakter haben. Sie machen außerdem ein Netzwerk im Tausch von Rohmaterial bis zu den Karpaten sichtbar.

Jakob Maurer führt in seinem Beitrag an den Attersee in Oberösterreich (S. 211–222). Vor dem Hintergrund der Auszeichnung als transnationale Welterbestätte „Prähistorische Pfahlbauten um die Alpen" sollte im Rahmen der Erforschung der sogenannten Mondsee-Gruppe auch das Hinterland der Pfahlbauten im Salzkammergut erforscht werden. Am Burgstall bei Lenzing, nur rund 2 km von der Seeufersiedlung Seewalchen entfernt, wurden bei schlechter Erhaltung 15 Grubenbefunde sowie ein Abschnittswall erfasst. Die spärlichen Kleinfunde datieren mondseezeitlich (Keramik mit Furchenstich) und chamzeitlich. Neue relevante Erkenntnisse zur Mondsee-Gruppe ergaben sich nicht. Anton Velušček (S. 223–238) steuert einen kurzen Überblick zu seinen umfangreichen und vielseitigen Forschungen zu den kupferzeitlichen Pfahlbausiedlungen im Bereich des Laibacher Moores (SL) bei. Die Gleichzeitigkeit einzelner spätkupferzeitlicher Stationen stellt er anhand einer Typentafel dar. Umfangreiche dendrochronologische Analysen ermöglichen es, beispielswiese im Pfahlbau von Ig (SL) Hausgrundrisse wahrscheinlich zu machen.

Georg Tiefengraber (S. 261–280) befasst sich in seinem, den Band abschließenden Beitrag mit dem Forschungsstand zur Vučedol-Kultur im Südostalpenraum. Dabei geht er von seinen, inzwischen als Monographie erschienenen Forschungen zum Schlossberg von Wildon (AT) aus (G. Tiefengraber, Der Wildoner Schlossberg. Die Ausgrabungen des Landesmuseums Joanneum 1985–1988. Schild von Steier Beih. 7 = Forsch. Gesch. Landeskde. Steiermark 80 [Graz 2018]; vgl. Gleirscher 2020). Von dort stammt ein umfangreiches Fundspektrum der Vučedol-Kultur (Horizonte VIII und IX), allerdings aus einem durchaus komplexen Schichtverband (vgl. S. 264). Wie für die älteren Perioden hat sich auch für die Spätkupferzeit gezeigt, dass es mitunter erhebliche Divergenzen zwischen den ^{14}C-Daten gibt, die – wie bereits gesagt – auch Fragen zur Auswertbarkeit der Schichtung hervorrufen (vgl. S. 274 u. 277). Die Zahl der Fundstellen mit Gefäßfragmenten der Vučedol-Kultur hat sich auch im Alpeninneren verdichtet (S. 275; Abb. 14). Sie liegen vielfach auf kleinen, steil abfallenden Kuppen. Man wird treffender an „Gehöfte" denn an befestigte Höhensiedlungen zu denken haben. Wie Ufer für die Siedlungen an Gewässern, boten Anhöhen beste Voraussetzungen, der dichten Waldlandschaft zu entkommen.

Der Band bietet in ansprechender Form Einblick in eine Reihe aktueller Forschungen zum ausgehenden Neolithikum und zur Kupferzeit im Südostalpenraum und dessen Umfeld. Der Problematik, dass sich am Ende nach wie vor nur wenige Fundplätze auch auf Grund ihrer Schichtung für typenchronologische Studien eignen, wird man mehr und mehr Beachtung schenken müssen. Fundvorlagen und an modernen Landesgrenzen orientierte Studien sind eine Sache, Studien zu Kulturgruppen und deren territorialen und chronologischen Bezügen eine andere. In diesem Sinn wünscht man eine Nachfolgetagung, die darauf den Fokus legt.

AT–9020 Klagenfurt a. W.   Paul Gleirscher
Liberogasse 6   Landesmuseum für Kärnten
E-Mail: paul.gleirscher@landesmuseum.ktn.gv.at   Sammlungs- und Wissenschaftszentrum
Orcid: https://orcid.org/0000-0002-7003-7963

Karsten Wentink, Stereotype. The Role of Grave Sets in Corded Ware and Bell Beaker Funerary Practices. Sidestone Press, Leiden 2020. € 40,–. ISBN 978-90-8890-938-2 (Softcover). € 120,–. ISBN 978-90-8890-939-9 (Hardcover). Open Access: https://hdl.handle.net/1887/123270 (letzter Zugriff: 05.05.2022). ISBN 978-90-8890-940-5 (E-Book). 296 Seiten mit 67 farbigen und 30 Schwarz-Weiß-Abbildungen.

Mit „Stereotype", der Publikation seiner 2020 an der Universität Leiden verteidigten Dissertation, legt Karsten Wentink ein Werk vor, das die kulturhistorische Aussagekraft von Bechergräbern über eine holistische Betrachtung zu erfassen sucht. Dabei geht er bewusst über primär typologisch, chronologisch oder materialkundlich orientierte Behandlungen einzelner Objektgruppen hinaus und fokussiert auf das Zusammenwirken von Grabausstattungen als Ensembles („sets") und hinter ihrer Komposition stehende Intentionen. Im Zentrum stehen Fragen nach der Identifikation von Objektbiographien, Standardisierung und Entwicklung der Sets, sowie der Erkennbarkeit von Identitäten und Konventionen. In theoretischer Hinsicht stützt sich K. Wentink dabei zur

Identifikation von in der Grabausstattung deutlich werdender Eigenrepräsentation des Individuums als Ausdrucksform sozialer Identität auf die Arbeiten des Soziologen Erving Goffmann aus den 1950er-Jahren. Dieser verwendet dazu das Konzept der „front", also Mittel, die einer Person dazu dienen, ein bestimmtes Bild von sich anderen gegenüber nach außen hin sichtbar werden zu lassen. Hierzu gehören persönliche Eigenheiten und Verhaltensweisen wie auch Accessoires materieller Art. Mittels des von Anthony Cohen 1985 beleuchteten Begriffs der „communities", der auf die Betonung von realen oder vermeintlichen Gemeinsamkeiten und Konventionen innerhalb der eigenen Gemeinschaft als Kontrast gegenüber der Andersartigkeit von anderen abzielt, lässt sich dieses Identitätskonzept dann auch auf Gruppen übertragen. Der Umstand, dass sich „Fronten" unter bestimmten Bedingungen zu Konventionen entwickeln können, ermöglicht Formen der Kommunikation damit verbundener Inhalte über Kulturgrenzen hinweg. Ein wichtiges Element dabei ist die Unschärfe in der genauen Bedeutung solcher Symboliken, wodurch oft ein interpretativer Spielraum für deren Anwendung entsteht und damit eine große Zielgruppe angesprochen wird. Eine solche Simplifizierung führt zu einer hohen Bedeutung von Symbolen, da sie weithin verstanden werden und damit eine verbindende Ebene schaffen können, trotz bestehender kultureller Eigenheiten und Unterschiede. Hier sieht Wentink eine wichtige Anwendungsmöglichkeit dieses interpretativen Ansatzes für das Studium der Becherkulturen, da er die großen überregionalen Ähnlichkeiten in ihrem kulturellen Erscheinungsbild als Ausdruck der Existenz solcher Fronten begreift. Er erkennt darin ein überregional verständliches Zeichensystem, zu dem die von uns identifizierbaren materiellen Hinterlassenschaften in den Grabfunden gehören. Dies wird jedoch von regionalspezifischen Eigenheiten im übrigen Fundmaterial begleitet, über die lokale Identitäten und Traditionen sichtbar werden. Materielle Kultur und insbesondere Objektbiographien können auf diese Weise als Indikatoren für solcherart soziale Strukturen und Interaktionen dienen und mit den Mitteln der Archäologie analysiert werden.

Die Arbeit beginnt mit einer Einführung in die Forschungslage zu spätneolithischen Gräbern in Mittel- und Westeuropa (S. 11–19), der Darlegung der grundlegenden theoretischen Konzeptionen der Arbeit (S. 21–30) und der bisherigen Modelle der Entwicklung der Becherkulturen (S. 31–46). Es folgen drei Kapitel mit jeweils einer detaillierten Darstellung der materiellen Grundlage der Arbeit: Becher allgemein (S. 47–83), Grabfundmaterial des Spätneolithikums A (S. 85–136) und des Spätneolithikums B (S. 137–200). Im Anschluss werden in zwei Kapiteln zu spätneolithischen Gräbern generell (S. 201–217) und mit Überlegungen zum Zustandekommen der Grabensembles (S. 219–228) die Beobachtungen synthetisierend zusammengefasst. Der interpretative Teil der Arbeit findet sich in den letzten drei Kapiteln, die auf Erwägungen zur Selbstdarstellung der Toten im Grab jeweils im Spätneolithikum A und B (S. 229–238), die Präsentation der Verstorbenen als Reisende (S. 239–247) und Zeitreisende (S. 249–252) zielen. Den Abschluss bilden ein umfangreiches Literaturverzeichnis sowie eine detaillierte Liste der in die Untersuchung einbezogenen Grabfunde (S. 253–284).

Grundlage von Wentinks Arbeit bildet eine Aufnahme niederländischer Bechergräber. Dabei stützt er sich in chronologischer Hinsicht auf die von Louwe P. Kooijmans, Peter W. van den Broeke, Harry Fokkens und Annelou L. van Gijn (L. KOOIJMANS et al. [Hrsg.], The Prehistory of the Netherlands [Amsterdam 2005]) erstellte Gliederung der Becherzeit in ein Late Neolithic A (LNA), das die erste Hälfte des 3. Jahrtausends v. Chr. umfasst und durch die Präsenz der Schnurkeramik und der *All Over Ornamented* (AOO)-Becher charakterisiert ist, sowie ein Late Neolithic B (LNB). Dieses wird durch das Auftreten von Glockenbechern kulturchronologisch charakterisiert und datiert in die 2. Hälfte des 3. Jahrtausends v. Chr. In einer Übersicht über den bisherigen Forschungsstand konstatiert er, trotz der offensichtlichen Unterschiede in den Bestattungssitten zum vorangehenden Trichterbecherkomplex mit seinen zumeist megalithischen Kollektivgräbern, mehr kulturelle Kontinuitäten als Diskontinuitäten vom 4. zum 3. Jahrtausend und auch innerhalb der

Becherzeit. Hinsichtlich der Frage, ob dies auch eine Konstanz der Bevölkerungsbasis bedeute oder Veränderungen durch externe Einwanderung verursacht wurden, bleibt Wentink etwas undeutlich. Es findet sich hierzu lediglich ein recht kurz gefasster Bezug zu dem in den letzten Jahren intensiv diskutierten Thema des Nachweises von Migration und dem Zusammenhang von Kulturwandel mit neuen Bevölkerungsgruppen (S. 45–46). Auch wenn leichte Kritik an simplifizierenden Modellen deutlich wird, werden die Ergebnisse entsprechender öffentlichkeitswirksamer Publikationen wiedergegeben und nicht kontrovers diskutiert.

Der Hauptteil der Arbeit widmet sich dem Fundmaterial der Bechergräber sowohl im Hinblick auf die Herstellung und Verwendung als auch der Biographie der Stücke, sofern dazu klare Anhaltspunkte vorliegen. Auf diese Weise werden alle Beigabenkategorien detailliert diskutiert. Es finden sich dabei immer wieder gut reflektierte Detailbeobachtungen aus der Produktions- und Nutzungsgeschichte, wie beispielsweise im Falle des Ursprungs der Schnureindrücke auf den Bechern des LNA. Wentink bestätigt die auf der Basis technologischer Analysen von Sander Ernst Van der Leeuw (Neolithic Beakers from the Netherlands: the potter's point of view In: J. N. Lanting / J. D. van der Waals [Hrsg.], Glockenbecher Symposium Oberried 1974 [Haarlem 1976] 81–139) geäußerte Vermutung, dass sie ursächlich mit der Herstellung der Becher verbunden sind (S. 88). Nach seiner Darstellung wurden mit Schnüren die Wände der Becher in deren oberer Hälfte stabilisiert. Die dort als funktionale Spuren übrig gebliebenen Eindrücke wären als gewöhnliche Reminiszenzen daran später durch dekorative Eindrücke in den noch feuchten Ton ergänzt. Dies ist als Neuerung gegenüber der früheren Technik der Herstellung von Trichterbechern anzusehen, bei der zwar ebenso wie bei den Schnurbechern Lehmwülste übereinandergelegt und verstrichen wurden, aber die Nutzung von Bändern oder Schnüren zu deren Stabilisierung nicht nachweisbar ist. Der Nachweis von stabilisierenden Schnüren, Riemen oder Bändern ist nicht überall gegeben. Zumeist sind die Eindrücke nur als dekorative Elemente erkennbar. Dennoch ist die Annahme plausibel, dass ein funktionaler Einsatz der Schnüre am Anfang stand.

Die Diskussion der nichtkeramischen Beigaben der schnurkeramischen Bechergräber (LNA) umfasst vor allem solche aus Stein (Silex und Felsgestein), die nach den Bechern die häufigste Fundkategorie (Dolche, Beile, Äxte und Abschläge) in den Gräbern bilden (S. 85). Eine Übersicht über das Vorkommen in den Gräbern widmet sich der Platzierung im Grab, der Identifizierbarkeit von Gebrauchsspuren (bei der Mehrzahl der Objekte waren keine feststellbar) und der Herkunft der Rohmaterialien. Bezüglich derjenigen mit „nördlicher" Provenienz (65 von 84 Dolchen) wird ein höchstwahrscheinlich südskandinavischer oder norddeutscher Ursprung postuliert. Des Weiteren ließen sich auch Importe von französischen Rohmaterialien aus Grand Pressigny (14 Dolche) feststellen. Interessant ist die Beobachtung, dass diese in den Gräbern gleich wie die nordischen Silexdolche behandelt wurden, auch wenn die Dolche aus Materialien französischen und nordischen Ursprungs sich in Grabfundensembles jeweils generell ausschließen. Auch wenn andere Austauschnetzwerke dahintersteckten, ist der Charakter als fremdes Importgut im Grabkontext der gleiche.

Einen bemerkenswerten kulturgeschichtlichen Befund stellen die Ergebnisse von Wentinks experimentalanalytischer Untersuchung der LNA-Steinäxte dar (S. 120–126). Während er sich skeptisch über den weiterführenden Nutzen elaborierter typologischer Gliederungen zum Verständnis des Charakters der Geräte äußert, widmet er sich intensiv der Frage nach der potentiellen Nutzung in der Vorgeschichte. Da Steinäxte, sowohl der Trichterbecher- als auch der schnurkeramischen Zeit, gemeinhin als Waffen angesehen werden, nicht selten auch als Statusanzeiger von Kriegern (im Englischen werden sie deshalb auch als „battle axes" bezeichnet), untersuchte er sie zunächst auf ihre Nutzbarkeit als Waffen. Dazu wurden mit einem nachgearbeiteten Stück insgesamt 18 Schädel von Wildtieren mit insgesamt 315 Schlägen traktiert. Es zeigte sich, dass sich die Geräte sehr gut dazu eignen, potentiell tödliche Schläge auf Schädel auszuführen. Dabei entstanden allerdings keine

Spuren an den Schneiden, die denjenigen auf den archäologischen Stücken entsprechen. Versuche, mit den Äxten Bäume zu fällen, erwiesen sich als mühsam, da die Äxte aufgrund ihrer mechanischen Eigenschaften und der Art der Schäftung dazu ungeeignet waren. Angaben zum für die Schäftung der Äxte verwendeten Holz sowie zur Auswahl der zu fällenden Bäume und damit verbundene technische Überlegungen fehlen allerdings. Auch bei diesen Versuchen entstanden nicht die charakteristischen Rillenspuren an den Schneiden. Erst der Einsatz als Werkzeug, um Wurzelstöcke zu roden und dabei vor allem Wurzeln zu zertrennen, zeigte Gebrauchsspuren, die denjenigen prähistorischer Exemplare glichen. Zudem eigneten sich die Äxte für diese Tätigkeiten sehr gut. Wentink weist in seiner Bewertung dieses Befundes auf den interessanten zeitlichen Zusammenhang mit der Öffnung der Landschaften in Mittel- und Nordeuropa während des 4. und 3. vorchristlichen Jahrtausends hin, die mit dem verstärkten Einsatz von Pflug und Wagen einhergeht, und charakterisiert die Äxte als ein wichtiges Utensil der Urbarmachung von Land. Ihr Vorkommen vor allem in jenem Zeithorizont und später seltener könnte dazu als ein wichtiges Indiz herangezogen werden. Zweifellos konnten Steinäxte wie auch Steinbeile als Waffe eingesetzt werden, die starke Abnutzung vieler der gefundenen Exemplare spricht jedoch für eine primäre Nutzung als Werkzeug. Inwiefern dies Rückschlüsse auf eine weiterführende, durch die Beigabe zum Ausdruck gebrachte Bedeutung von Äxten als Symbole gestattet, sei hier dahingestellt. Möglicherweise spiegelt sich hier die Bedeutung des Holzhandwerks im Zuge der vielen Rodungstätigkeiten im 4./3. vorchristlichen Jahrtausend wider, aber vielleicht stellten sie auch einfach nur die Lieblingsgeräte der Verstorbenen dar, die man ihnen aus Pietät mitgeben wollte.

Neben der Keramik sind Äxte und Beile aus Felsgestein und Silex die häufigsten und auffälligsten Beigaben in Grabfunden und Wentink betont die vermutlich vorrangige Nutzung für die Holzbearbeitung. Daraus ergibt sich ein Hinweis, wie stark Holz als Werkstoff präsent gewesen ist, wovon uns auch Feuchtbodenfundplätze einen Eindruck vermitteln. Wentink hebt hier den massiven Einsatz in zahlreichen Infrastrukturprojekten hervor, wie den Bohlenwegen durch Sumpfgebiete, die gerade in jenem Zeithorizont einen großen Ausbau zusammen mit dem intensiveren Einsatz von Wagen und Zugtieren als Transportmitteln erfahren. Daneben ist anzunehmen, dass Holz (und andere organische Materialien) auch in signifikantem Umfang in die Gräber mitgegeben worden ist, sofern uns die skandinavischen Grabhügel der älteren Bronzezeit hier ein repräsentatives Bild geben, das auch auf das 3. Jahrtausend v. Chr. in anderen Teilen Nord- und Mitteleuropas übertragbar ist. Hierdurch deutet sich wieder einmal an, dass uns vermutlich in den Gräbern ein Großteil der Beigabenausstattung verlorengegangen ist und uns mit den Objekten aus haltbaren Materialien nur einen reduzierten Ausschnitt des ehemaligen Repertoires überliefert wurde.

In ähnlich detaillierter Weise analysiert Wentink die Gräber des nachfolgenden Late Neolithic B (S. 137–200). Dabei konstatiert er, dass im LNB die Ausstattung der Gräber gegenüber dem LNA in allem wechselt, außer in der Sitte Becher beizugeben. LNB-Gräber zeigen sich in ihrer Ausstattung deutlich weniger einheitlich als die des LNA. Auffällig ist in Männergräbern nun die Dominanz von mit dem Bogenschießen assoziierten Accessoires, neben Schmuck, was von der primär durch die Beigabe von Silexdolchen sowie Beilen und Äxten dominierten Ausstattung von LNA-Männergräbern abweicht. Hierin und auch in der übrigen Ausstattung von Männergräbern folgt das niederländische Glockenbecherphänomen größeren europäischen Trends, was Wentink auch deutlich herausstreicht (S. 232). Die Diskussion der verschiedenen Beigabentypen und ihrer Verwendung ist auch hier sehr detail- und kenntnisreich. Viele kleine Beobachtungen zu den Herstellungstechniken bereichern dabei die Darstellung. Hinsichtlich der Interpretation der Funktion der Objekte tritt immer wieder Wentinks Fokus auf ihren kommunikativen Nutzen als non-verbale Zeichen hervor. Dabei betrachtet er die Grabausstattungen nicht so sehr als Spiegel der individuellen Identität der Verstorbenen, sondern mehr als Ausdruck eines kulturellen Ideals. Hierzu gehören Überlegungen wie die zum Kontext oder zur Trageweise von Schmuckobjekten, wodurch z. B. mit diesen Codes Vertraute durchaus Informationen über die Tragenden und ggf. deren sozialen Status erhalten konnten. Bei einer reinen materialfixierten Betrachtung der Stücke würden solche wichtigen Konnotationen und Bedeutungen unentdeckt bleiben. Hier kommt die Beobachtung zum Tragen, die Wentink gleich zu Beginn seines Buches anekdotenhaft präsentiert und später verschiedentlich wiederholt, nämlich, dass es keine Bechergruppengräber in den Niederlanden gibt, die exakt einer Normausstattung entsprechen, sondern stets eine gewisse Varianz vorliegt. Hierin vermutet er die Materialisierung von Codes, die via des Konzepts der „Fronten" auf diese Weise Informationen über die Bestatteten vermittelten, die die Hinterbliebenen anhand bestimmter Regelsysteme sichtbar machten. Dieser Ansatz bildet eine interessante Alternative zu dem weit verbreiteten Interpretationsschema von Grabfunden, bei dem anhand von Quantität und Qualität der Beigaben, wofür die Kriterien in der Regel aus unserer heutigen Welt in das Altertum übertragen werden, lediglich auf die mögliche Identifikation sozial niedriger oder höher stehenden Personen fokussiert wird. Hierbei bietet auch die Einbeziehung potenziell weiterer Objekte aus vergänglichen Materialien, deren ursprüngliches Vorhandensein in Fundkontexten mit besonderen Erhaltungsbedingungen immer wieder dokumentiert wird, in die Überlegungen eine sinnvolle Erweiterung von positivistischen Ansätzen zur Rekonstruktion von Sozialverhältnissen in der traditionellen Gräberarchäologie.

Das Buch ist insgesamt gut lesbar geschrieben. Immer wieder werden vorrangig theoretisierende oder deskriptive Teile durch anekdotische Exkurse illustriert und damit belebt. Auch für das selektive Lesen hilfreich sind kurze Einführungen in die Inhalte der Kapitel sowie deren Verknüpfung mit dem vorherigen. Am Ende eines jeden Kapitels zieht der Autor zudem Schlussfolgerungen aus dem Inhalt des vorher Diskutierten und präsentiert diese in konziser Form.

Ob man Wentink insgesamt in allen interpretativen Tendenzen folgen möchte, die er für die Erklärung des Zustandekommens des Spektrums an Grabausstattungen spätneolithischer Gräber in den Niederlanden bietet, oder nicht, ist letztlich von sekundärer Bedeutung. Maßgeblich ist der erfrischende Charakter seines Ansatzes, sich mit den Grabausstattungen aus der Perspektive der Objektgeschichte(n), der Kommunikation und der „personal front" in einer Form auseinanderzusetzen, die darauf fokussiert einen Beitrag zu einer Ideengeschichte prähistorischer Gesellschaften zu leisten und dabei deren Kommunikationskonzept zu ergründen. Als dominantes Element vermutet Wentink dabei die Absicht, hier vorrangig die Repräsentation von Idealen von Personen zu vermitteln.

DE–72070 Tübingen
Schloss Hohentübingen
Burgsteige 11
E-Mail: martin.bartelheim@uni-tuebingen.de
Orcid: https://orcid.org/0000-0002-7745-9712

Martin Bartelheim
Institut für Ur- und Frühgeschichte
und Archäologie des Mittelalters
Eberhard Karls Universität Tübingen

Neil Carlin, The Beaker Phenomenon? Understanding the Character and Context of Social Practices in Ireland 2500–2000 BC. Sidestone Press, Leiden 2018. € 95,–. ISBN 978-90-8890-464-6 (Hardcover). € 34,95. ISBN 978-90-8890-463-9 (Paperback). € 9,95. ISBN 978-8890-465-3 (E-Book). 244 Seiten mit 68 Schwarz-Weiß- und 45 Farbabbildungen.

Schon der von Neil Carlin gewählte Titel „The Beaker Phenomenon?" formuliert die zentrale Frage seines Buches: nämlich die Deutung und Ausprägung des sog. Glockenbecher-Phänomens sowie seiner Merkmale in Irland. Hierbei bezieht sich N. Carlin auf die Definition des

Glockenbecher-Phänomens u. a. nach Colin Burgess und Stephan J. Shennan von 1976 (vgl. S. 13 bzw. C. Burgess / S. Shennan, The Beaker phenomenon: some suggestions. In: C. Burgess / M. Miket [Hrsg.], Settlement and Economy in the Third and Second Millennia BC. BAR British Ser. 33 [Oxford 1976] 309–331). So möchte die Arbeit von N. Carlin im Vergleich mit Nachbarregionen (v. a. Großbritannien) das Becher-Phänomen interpretieren, wobei er vom Fund und dessen spezieller Deutung unter besonderer Berücksichtigung des Befundkontexts ausgeht. Die grundlegende Fragestellung nach dem „Wie" und „Warum" Glockenbecher und die typischen mit ihnen vergesellschafteten Objekte in Irland verwendet wurden (vgl. Kap. 1, S. 13 u. 20).

Das Buch ist die überarbeitete Fassung seiner Dissertation, welche der Autor am University College Dublin im Jahr 2011 abgeschlossen hat. Während der Stand der Doktorarbeit die Datengrundlage bildet, wurde das Buch durch aktuelle Literatur ergänzt. Vor allem hat der Verfasser die Interpretation seiner Untersuchungsergebnisse noch um die aktuelle Forschungsdiskussion um die auf aDNA-Analysen basierenden Migrationsbewegungen im 3. Jahrtausend ergänzt (vgl. Kap. 10.1, S. 198–200). Die Arbeit von Carlin basiert neben Altgrabungen vor allem auf den zahlreichen Neuentdeckungen, die im Zuge baubegleitender Ausgrabungen der großen Infrastrukturprojekte in Irland zwischen 1997 und 2007 gemacht wurden (vgl. S. 30 Abb. 2.2). Diese Grabungen haben die Kenntnisse über die prähistorische Landschaft umfangreich verändert und zu unzähligen neuen Fundstellen aus allen Zeiten geführt. So kann Carlin für seine Untersuchung auf 150 neue Fundstellen zurückgreifen, welche nach modernen Standards untersucht und dokumentiert wurden.

Die Arbeit ist die erste umfassende Vorlage der becherzeitlichen Funde und Befunde Irlands und berücksichtigt alle Hinweise auf „Glockenbecher" bis auf Einzelfundebene, welche in die Interpretation einbezogen wird. Kapitel 1 (S. 13–20) gibt den groben Rahmen der Analyse wieder und stellt die allgemeine Datengrundlage und das methodische Vorgehen vor. Des Weiteren wird am Ende des Kapitels eine Erklärung für die Ausprägung, Verbreitung und Übernahme des Glockenbecher-Phänomens in Irland in Aussicht gestellt (S. 20).

Im zweiten Kapitel (S. 21–37) wird vor allem die Forschungsgeschichte zur Glockenbecherkultur in Irland detailliert rezipiert. Auch wenn Carlin selbstverständlich die irische Forschungsgeschichte mit ihrem teils historischen Hintergrund einer Abgrenzung gegenüber Großbritannien in den Vordergrund stellt, wird hier auch die britische Forschung miteinbezogen. Ein „Kontinentaleuropäer" würde sich allerdings an dieser Stelle eine deutlichere Berücksichtigung der z. B. iberischen, französischen oder mitteleuropäischen Forschung wünschen, zumal der Autor später (Kap. 10.2, 200–202) wieder den Bezug auf die kulturellen Verbindungen zum Kontinent aufnimmt.

Ein allgemeiner Überblick über die Befundsituation und die Verbreitung der Spuren des Glockenbecher-Phänomens in Irland wird in Kapitel 3 (S. 39–63) vorgestellt, während in den folgenden Kapiteln 4 bis 7 (s. u.) noch detaillierter auf den Siedlungs- oder Grabkontext sowie Depots und sog. „natürliche Orte / Plätze" eingegangen wird. Wie erwähnt, genügt ein einzelner Fund eines als charakteristisch glockenbecherzeitlich definierten Objektes zur Aufnahme einer Fundstelle in die Datenbank, die dem Lesenden zwar nicht zur Verfügung steht, aber über die Homepage der *University College Dublin* als PDF-Datei abrufbar ist (http://hdl.handle.net/10197/9438 [letzter Zugriff: 29.04.2022]). Es zeigt sich schnell, dass – anders als in den meisten Regionen Europas – das Gros der Glockenbecherfunde bzw. mit der Glockenbecherkultur in Verbindung gebrachter Funde in Irland überwiegend aus Siedlungskontexten stammt (S. 46 Abb. 3.7). Ein möglicher Grund für dieses abweichende Befundbild kann sein, dass die überwiegende Zahl der berücksichtigten Fundstellen bei Grabungen im Zuge von Infrastrukturprojekten entdeckt worden ist und somit auch einen Querschnitt durch die Fundlandschaft liefert. Fundstellen wurden aufgedeckt und gründlicher untersucht, welche wohl ohne Ausgrabungen während der Infrastrukturprojekte nur als Lesefunde erfasst worden wären. Möglicherweise wären diese Einzelfunde auch als Reste von bereits zerstörten Gräbern gedeutet worden. Außerdem widmet sich der zweite Teil des Kapitels einigen lange bekannten Fundorten, wie Newgrange, und stellt diese nochmals vor.

Nach einem Überblick über die Befundsituation und die breite Datengrundlage, geht Carlin in den Kapiteln 4 bis 7 ausführlich auf die unterschiedlichen Quellengattungen ein. Zuerst werden die Siedlungsbefunde vorgestellt (Kap. 4, S. 65–93). Das heißt, er stellt die Einzelbefunde vor, aus denen Glockenbecher bzw. glockenbechervergesellschaftete Funde (Objekte des sog. Glockenbecher-Sets oder Glockenbecher-Ensembles) stammen. Dabei handelt es sich vorwiegend, wie zu erwarten war, um die üblichen Siedlungsgruben, wie Abfall- oder Pfostengruben, aus welchen aber teils nur eine Scherbe aus einer Grube einer Siedlung bekannt ist (S. 71). In Kapitel 5 (S. 95–133) beschreibt der Autor die verschiedenen Grabformen. Die auf dem Kontinent typischen Einzelbestattungen in Flachgräbern kennt man aus Irland kaum. Megalith- und Steinkistengräber wurden in Irland bereits zur Zeit der *Grooved Ware*-Keramik angelegt. Diese Bestattungsweise fand zur Zeit des Glockenbechers weiterhin Verwendung, denn entsprechende Keramikfunde kennt man aus diesen Gräbern. Eine besondere Befundart sind *timber cycles*, d. h. hölzerne Kreisanlagen, die in Kapitel 6 (S. 135–151) vorgestellt werden. Diese Art der Befunde sind für Großbritannien und Irland bereits aus dem Kontext der *Grooved Ware* bekannt. Auch hier greifen die Träger des Glockenbecher-Phänomens also auf Elemente vorangegangener archäologischer Kulturen zurück. So ist anzunehmen, dass viele Traditionen des Spätneolithikums beibehalten und vor allem eine neue Keramikform genutzt wurde (S. 151). Letztlich widmet Carlin das Kapitel 7 (S. 153–160) den Deponierungen in *natural spaces*, d. h. besonderen, möglicherweise als Naturheiligtümer zu interpretierenden, natürlichen Orten, wie Mooren und Seen.

Nach ausführlichen Befundbeschreibungen wird die Chronologie des irischen Glockenbecher-Phänomens diskutiert (Kap. 8, S. 161–171). Hierfür kann der Autor auf 61 Radiocarbondaten von insgesamt 40 Fundplätzen zurückgreifen, wobei sich die Daten in zwei verschiedene Qualitätsstufen unterscheiden lassen (vgl. S. 162–164). Mittels Bayesianischer Modellierung werden die ^{14}C-Daten statistisch ausgewertet und auf dieser Grundlage interpretiert. Es kristallisieren sich zwei Peaks heraus: 2580–2468 cal. BC und 2204–2050 cal. BC. Aufgrund der Datenmodellierung sieht der Autor ein relativ plötzliches Auftreten von All Over Ornamented (AOO)- und von All Over Corded (AOC)-Bechern vom Kontinent um ca. 2580 cal. BC. Insgesamt datieren keine der Befunde mit dem Glockenbecher-Phänomen zugeschriebenen Funden nach 2000 cal. BC in Irland, während es in Großbritannien Hinweise auf eine Verwendung bis mindestens 1800 cal. BC gibt. Die ^{14}C-Daten aus Irland weisen außerdem auf eine teilweise Gleichzeitigkeit von einerseits der älteren *Grooved Ware*-Keramik und andererseits der jüngeren *Food Vessel*-Keramik (um ca. 2000 BC) hin. Jedoch hinterfragt Carlin zu Recht die Datengrundlage und die Anwendung statistischer Methoden für diese kleine Datengrundlage. So würde eine größere Datenmenge, vor allem aus verschiedenen Befundkontexten, eine klareres Bild liefern (S. 171). Die vorliegenden Daten stammen überwiegend aus Gräbern, die wie vorher gezeigt, nur einen kleinen Teil der Gesamtzahl des Fundniederschlags liefern. Letztlich wäre eine weitere Analyse zur Chronologie wünschenswert, die alle Befundgattungen und überdies auch die vorangehenden und nachfolgenden neolithischen Kulturgruppen berücksichtigt. Eine typochronologische Diskussion der Keramik bzw. eine gründliche Diskussion zur inneren Chronologie des Glockenbecher-Phänomens in Irland, basierend auf den absolut-chronologischen Daten, fehlt in dem Buch. Dies dürfte aber darin begründet sein, dass, wie erwähnt, die ^{14}C-Daten vor allem aus den verhältnismäßig wenigen Gräbern stammen und die Mehrzahl der Keramikfunde nur kleinteilig fragmentiert aus Siedlungsbefunden vorliegt.

In Kapitel 9 (S. 173–196) stehen die charakteristischen mit Glockenbechern assoziierten Funde im Mittelpunkt, die in der Forschung als Glockenbecher-Set bekannt sind. Auch hier steht weniger eine typologische oder funktionale Beschreibung und Diskussion der Objekte im Vordergrund, sondern mehr der Befundkontext. So wird ausführlich deren Verbreitung in Irland beschrieben und der archäologische Kontext, in welchem zum Beispiel die typische Becherkeramik (Kap. 9.2, S. 173–177), Armschutzplatten (Kap. 9.5, S. 181–185), Lunulae (Kap. 9.8, S. 189–191) oder Äxte (Kap. 9.10, S. 192–193) gefunden wurden, dargestellt. Abschließend wird in Kapitel 9.11 (S. 193–196) nochmals der Befundkontext der jeweiligen Objekte zusammengefasst und mögliche Gründe für ihre Deponierung besprochen. Somit bildet Kapitel 9 eine Klammer um die vorherigen Kapitel 3 bis 7. Es zeigt sich, dass viele Objekte, die wir aus Mitteleuropa als Teil des Glockenbecher-Sets in Gräbern kennen, in Irland vor allem als Einzelfunde bekannt sind (z. B. Dolche und Armschutzplatten). Carlin sieht hier intentionelle Deponierungen (vgl. S. 194–195). Man muss aber berücksichtigen, dass es sich bei den nicht-keramischen Funden überwiegend um Einzelfunde handelt, die v. a. aus den sogenannten *„natural spaces"* wie Mooren stammen (S. 195 Tab. 9.6), was eben zu ihrer Interpretation als Deponierungen und nicht Verlustfunde führt.

Am Ende seines Buches beleuchtet Carlin das Glockenbecher-Phänomen Irlands nochmals von allen Seiten. Hier integriert der Verfasser die nach Abschluss seiner Dissertation erschienenen Forschungsergebnisse zu aDNA-Analysen (z. B. I. Olalde et al., The Beaker Phenomenon and the genomic transformation of northwestern Europe. Nature 555, 2018, 190–196. doi: https://doi.org/10.1038/nature25738). Was schon seit Beginn der Forschungen zum Glockenbecher-Phänomen viel diskutiert wurde, unterstreichen die neuen Untersuchungen. Durch Migrationsbewegungen werden Objekte und Ideen verbreitet und gelangen eben auch auf die irische Insel. Jedoch erklärt das nicht die Akzeptanz des Neuen. Hier sind, so Carlin richtig, weitere soziale und kulturelle Faktoren zu berücksichtigen, denn auch wenn durch die aDNA-Analysen ein „Zuzug" auffällig ist, so warnt er vor einer Überinterpretation dieser Daten (S. 199–200). So zeigt er in der Folge verschiedene externe Einflüsse auf, die sich überwiegend im Fundmaterial niederschlagen. Hier wie so oft steht leider der Vergleich mit Großbritannien im Vordergrund. Insbesondere aufgrund der langen Forschungsdiskussion über die kulturellen Verbindungen entlang der europäischen Atlantikküste wäre an dieser Stelle eine umfassendere Diskussion des Glockenbecher-Phänomens in Kontinental-Europa wünschenswert. Dieses Thema kommt trotz einiger Hinweise des Autors auf die Verbindungen mit zum Beispiel Dänemark, Frankreich oder Portugal zu kurz. Abschließend zeigt der Autor verschiedene Aspekte und Interpretationsansätze des Glockenbecher-Phänomens in Irland auf, ohne aber eine abschließende Hypothese für die Verbreitung des Glockenbecher-Phänomens liefern zu können. Es handelt sich hierbei zwar um eine äußerst inspirierende Zusammenstellung verschiedener Facetten, die letztlich aber auf das Motto der internationalen Glockenbecher-Forschung seit mindestens den 1990er- / 2000er-Jahren – „Similar but Different" – abzielt und eben wieder in einzelnen Punkten die Unterschiede und Gemeinsamkeiten zu anderen Regionen des sogenannten Glockenbecher-Phänomens aufzeigt (vgl. auch Ch. Strahm [Hrsg.], Das Glockenbecher-Phänomen: Ein Seminar. Freiburger Arch. Stud. 2 [Freiburg 1995]; J. Czebreszuk [Hrsg.], Similar but Different: Bell Beakers in Europe [Poznan 2004]).

Die Arbeit von Neil Carlin ist ein umfassendes Werk auf Grundlage vor allem zahlreicher modern gegrabener Fundstellen. Ob insbesondere diese Fundstellen, wenn kaum glockenbechertypisches Fundmaterial vorhanden ist, tatsächlich die kulturelle Signifikanz für die Geschichte Irlands haben, müsste im Vergleich mit anderen neolithischen Kulturen diskutiert werden. Eine große Stärke der Arbeit ist die Aufnahme aller potentiellen Belege und Hinweise auf das Glockenbecher-Phänomen und ihre detaillierte Analyse unter besonderem Fokus auf den Befundkontext. Allerdings fehlt dem Buch ein Katalogteil bzw. eine beiliegende CD mit der Datenbank, um künftigen, auf Carlins Arbeit aufbauenden Forschungen einen schnellen Zugang zu den Daten und eine Weiterverarbeitung zu ermöglichen. Allerdings ist die Dissertation online als PDF-Datei abrufbar (http://hdl.handle.net/10197/9438). Dieses Dokument enthält einen Katalogteil, der entsprechend auf Stand der Dissertation ist und nicht mehr ergänzt wird (vgl. *Preface*, S. 11). Betrachtet man die detaillierte

Fund- und Befundaufnahme und den Aufwand der statistischen Erhebung und Auswertung, so ist das Ergebnis seiner Interpretation leider etwas ernüchternd. Schließlich kann der Autor mittels seiner Datenbank (vgl. z. B. Tab. 3.1. o. 3.2) sicher jede Scherbe einem Befund zuordnen. Dennoch fehlt am Ende der Leserschaft der Rückschluss auf diese detaillierte Erfassung. Inwiefern einzelne Scherben helfen können, das Glockenbecher-Phänomen zu klären, bleibt offen.

Möglicherweise kann Irland, das an der Peripherie Europas gelegen ist, helfen, einige Fragen zum sogenannten Glockenbecher-Phänomen zu beantworten. Seine Zusammenfassung verschiedener Interpretationsansätze für die Verbreitung und Akzeptanz des Glockenbechers und letztlich des Glockenbecher-Phänomens ist eine gute Inspiration für andere Regionalstudien (vgl. Kap. 10.1–10.10, S. 198–215). Die Arbeit von Carlin ist somit nicht nur für die angelsächsische Glockenbecher-Forschung wichtig. Sie bietet eine hervorragende Basis für weiterführende Untersuchungen, allerdings bleibt sie Erklärungen schuldig. Es deutet sich wie schon in anderen Studien der letzten 10–20 Jahre an, dass es eine europaweite monokausale Erklärung für die Verbreitung und die (regionale) Ausprägung des Glockenbecher-Phänomens nicht gibt. Stattdessen verweist der Autor auf die Komplexität der Interpretation des Glockenbecher-Phänomens und meint, dass in weiten Punkten das „Beaker ‚problem'" aufgrund des Wissensstandes von der Forschung auch hausgemacht ist (S. 215). So ist dieses Buch ein wichtiger Baustein im Versuch das Glockenbecher-Phänomen zu verstehen, auch wenn wir das Glockenbecher-Problem wahrscheinlich nie gänzlich lösen können. Ein Blick nach Irland und die Lektüre seines Buches liefern nicht nur den Vergleich Irlands mit Großbritannien und Kontinentaleuropa, sondern können vor allem die Glockenbecher-Forschung erweitern, denn das Glockenbecher-Phänomen in Irland ist aus (mittel-)europäischer Perspektive in vielen Punkten „different". Durch die zahlreichen und gut dokumentierten Ausgrabungen im Zuge der Baumaßnahmen zwischen 1997 und 2007 liegt – bis auf die Ebene der Einzelfunde – ein dichtes Informationsnetz zum Glockenbecher-Phänomen und seiner Verbreitung in Irland vor, wie es aus anderen Regionen noch fehlt.

DE–96117 Memmelsdorf bei Bamberg Matthias Merkl
Schloss Seehof Bayerisches Landesamt für Denkmalpflege
E-Mail: Matthias.Merkl@blfd.bayern.de Dienststelle Schloss Seehof

David Fontijn, Economies of Destruction. How the Systematic Destruction of Valuables Created Value in Bronze Age Europe, c. 2300–500 BC. Routledge, London 2020. £ 34,99. ISBN 978-1-138-08839. ISBN 978-1-138-08839-9 (Softcover). 202 Seiten mit 44 Schwarz-Weiß-Abbildungen.

Destruction – gleich zweimal kommt das wirksame Schlagwort im Titel von David Fontijns neuestem Buch vor. Dabei geht es weniger um das *Zerstören* im Sinn einer substanziellen Veränderung zur Unbrauchbarmachung als vielmehr um das *Vernichten*, also das bewusste, systematische und zielgerichtete Beseitigen. Das Beseitigen von Wertgegenständen manifestiert sich im archäologischen Befund in sogenannten *Deponierungen* (auch: Depots, Horte), wobei es sich um vergrabene, niedergelegte, versenkte oder versteckte Objekte handelt. Am eindrücklichsten zeigt sich diese Praxis in der Bronzezeit, wo sie mit einer hohen Frequenz, größeren Ansammlungen von Gegenständen (v. a. aus Bronze) und außergewöhnlichen Objekttypen aufwartet. Genau darum dreht sich das Buch. Im Rahmen des vom Niederländischen Forschungsrat (NWO) geförderten Projekts *Economies of destruction. The emergence of metalwork deposition during the Bronze Age in Northwest Europe, c. 2300–1500 BC* (2015–2020, Universität Leiden) ist David Fontijn der bewussten Aufgabe von Wertgegenständen in der Bronzezeit auf den Grund gegangen, dies im wirtschaftlichen Kontext.

Während soziökonomische Theorien die Interpretation bronzezeitlicher Deponierungen schon früh beeinflusst haben („Thesaurierung zur Statusregulierung" und „im Wettbewerb zerstörtes Vermögen"; K. KRISTIANSEN, The consumption of wealth in Bronze Age Denmark. A study in the dynamics of economic processes in tribal societies. In: K. Kristiansen / C. Paludan-Müller [Hrsg.], New Directions in Scandinavian Archaeology. Stud. Scandinavian Prehist. and Early Hist. 1 [Copenhagen 1978] 158–190; M. J. ROWLANDS, Kinship, alliance and exchange in the European Bronze Age. In: J. C. Barrett / R. Bradley [Hrsg.], Settlement and Society in the British Later Bronze Age. British Arch. Reports, British Ser. 83 [Oxford 1980] 15–55; R. BRADLEY, The Social Foundations of Prehistoric Britain. Themes and Variations in the Archaeology of Power [London, New York 1984] bes. 104–105; R. BRADLEY, The Passage of Arms. An Archaeological Analysis of Prehistoric Hoards and Votive Deposits [Cambridge 1990]; S. HANSEN, Studien zu den Metalldeponierungen während der Urnenfelderzeit zwischen Rhônetal und Karpatenbecken 1. Univforsch. Prähist. Arch. 21 [Bonn 1994]; C. HUTH, Westeuropäische Horte der Spätbronzezeit. Fundbild und Funktion. Regensburger Beitr. Prähist. Arch. 3 [Bonn 1997]; A. TESTART [Hrsg.], Les armes dans les eaux. Questions d'interprétation [Paris, Arles 2012] bes. 299; 323–324; 384), wartet man seit langem auf eine differenzierte Auseinandersetzung mit dem archäologischen Phänomen des ostentativen *Beseitigens*. Diesem Desiderat ist das Buch gewidmet.

D. Fontijn eröffnet das Kapitel 1 (S. 1–21) mit dem spektakulären Fund von Ommerschans in den Nordost-Niederlanden, einer Ansammlung von Bronzegegenständen aus einem Torfmoor, darunter ein eigenartiges, überdimensioniertes Schwert. Davon ausgehend, dass das Deponieren von Dingen „selektiv" sei, also nicht zufällig und irrational, sondern einer bewussten Systematik folgend, fragt der Autor nach dem Sinn hinter der Aufgabe von Wertgegenständen. Im Schnelldurchlauf erläutert Fontijn das Wirtschaftssystem der Bronzezeit, wobei er dieses grundsätzlich vom namengebenden Werkstoff abhängig macht, und neben dessen materiellem und ideellem Wert auch den Aspekt der Wiederverwertung betont. Aus einer modernen Wirtschaftslogik betrachtet, sei die Aufgabe von Bronzeobjekten eine fundamentale Antithese zur Herstellung und Zirkulation ebendieser, was es näher zu untersuchen gelte. Ausgehend von der Gabentheorie Maurice GODELIERS (The Enigma of the Gift [Cambridge 1999]) und Michael LAMBEKs Wertekonzept (Value and virtue. Anthropological Theory 8,2, 2008, 133–157), sowie der Gegenüberstellung etablierter theoretischer Modelle zur Bronzezeitwirtschaft (KRISTIANSEN 1978; ROWLANDS 1980; BRADLEY 1984; T. EARLE, Bronze Age Economies. The Beginnings of Political Economies [Boulder 2002]) und Ideen zur gesellschaftlichen Bedeutung von Deponierungen, entwickelt der Autor ein Modell zweier gegenseitig abhängiger „Sphären": einerseits die „politische Wirtschaft" *(political economy)*, gekennzeichnet durch quantifizierbare Werte, einer Preissetzung, individuellem Wettbewerb und individueller Gewinnmaximierung, einem Grad an Interaktion zwischen Individuen, sowie überregionalen Beziehungen, einer kurzfristigen Logik folgend, und andererseits die „moralische Wirtschaft" *(moral economy)*, gekennzeichnet durch qualitative, kulturelle und kollektive Werte, Bemühungen zur Aufrechthaltung ebendieser, gesellschaftlicher Relevanz, sowie Regionalbezug, einer längerfristigen Logik folgend. Das Definieren dieser zwei Sphären sei der Diskussion um die Aufgabe von Bronzen insofern dienlich, als dass sie die Umwandlung von Preiswerten in Kulturwerte offenlege (s. Kap. 8). Das Kapitel wird mit einem Rückgriff auf das Ommerschans-Schwert geschlossen: Während jenes als Sonderform und v. a. zuletzt in seiner Deponierung einer „moralischen" Wirtschaftslogik entspreche, sei es zumindest zu Beginn seiner Existenz kurzfristig Teil einer „politischen" Transaktion gewesen.

In Kapitel 2 (S. 22–43) stellt Fontijn das Konzept der *Selective deposition* vor, wie er es in seiner vielzitierten Dissertation entwickelt und etabliert hat (D. R. FONTIJN, Sacrificial Landscapes. Cultural Biographies of Persons, Objects and 'Natural' Places in the Bronze Age of the Southern Netherlands, c. 2300–600 BC. Analecta Praehist. Leidensia 33/34 [Leiden 2002]). Dabei bringt er zusätzlich den Aspekt der doppelten Exklusivität ins Spiel, welche sich in einer Kombination aus herausragenden Funden und herausragenden Orten manifestiere. In der Forschung zu Deponierungen kamen in den vergangenen Jahren wiederholt handlungstheoretische Ansätze zur Anwendung (A. BALLMER, Zur Topologie des bronzezeitlichen Deponierens. Von der Handlungstheorie zur Raumanalyse. Prähist. Zeitschr. 85, 2010, 120–131; A. BALLMER, Topografie bronzezeitlicher Deponierungen. Fallstudie Alpenrheintal. Univforsch. Prähist. Arch. 278 [Bonn 2015]; D. NEUMANN, Depositions of the Bronze Age. Perception and cultural Practice in Prehistoric Landscapes. In: Kiel Graduate School "Human Developments in Landscapes" [Hrsg.], Landscapes and Human Development: The Contribution of European Archaeology. Univforsch. Prähist. Arch. 191 [Bonn 2010] 237–248; D. NEUMANN, Landschaften der Ritualisierung. Die Fundplätze kupfer- und bronzezeitlicher Metalldeponierungen zwischen Donau und Po. Topoi: Berlin Stud. Ancient World 26 [Berlin 2015]; nicht zuletzt auch: FONTIJN 2002, insbes. 24–25). Dabei hat sich v. a. Pierre Bourdieus „Habitus"-Konzept und damit die „soziale Praxis" zum Verständnis von Deponierungsmustern bewährt (P. BOURDIEU, Esquisse d'une théorie de la pratique, précédé de trois études d'éthnologie kabyle [Genève 1972]). Im vorliegenden Fall wird alternativ mit dem Begriff „Durchschnittsverhalten" *(average behavior)* operiert. So stünde das „Durchschnittsverhalten" für eine richtige Art zu Handeln *(the right way to act)* und äußere sich im regelhaften Erscheinungsbild einer Deponierung: der Objektzusammensetzung, -behandlung und -anordnung, sowie dem Deponierungsort. Dieses Durchschnittsverhalten müsse indes keinesfalls auf gleiche Beweggründe zurückführen. Damit würde eine vergleichende, kulturübergreifende Perspektive auf das Phänomen möglich.

Im dritten Kapitel (S. 44–62) setzt sich Fontijn theoretisch mit dem Thema „Wert" auseinander, insbesondere mit dem Graeberschen Konzept zu „kulturellen Werten" *(cultural value)* und „Preiswerten" *(value-as-price)* – beide nur sinnvoll innerhalb eines relationalen Systems und beide Ergebnis konstanten Aushandelns (D. GRAEBER, Toward an Anthropological Theory of Value: The False Coin of our own Dreams [New York 2001]; D. GRAEBER, Value. Anthropological theory of value. In: J. G. Carrier [Hrsg.], A Handbook of Economic Anthropology [Cheltenham 2005] 439–454). In der Folge geht es darum, inwiefern das Deponieren von Gegenständen die Wahrnehmung von Permanenz und Umlauf und schließlich den Objektwert an sich beeinflusst. Zunächst wird zwischen „unveräußerbaren" *(inalienable)* und „veräußerbaren" *(alienable)* Dingen unterschieden. Der Hauptunterschied liege in der persönlichen bzw. übertragenen Bedeutung der Objekte für den Besitzenden oder die Gemeinschaft: Während unveräußerbare Objekte bedeutungsvoll und singulär seien und Verbindungen zu Personen, Identitäten und sozioreligiösen Werten aufwiesen (wie eben das Schwert von Ommerschans, oder auch die Himmelsscheibe von Nebra), hätten veräußerbare Objekte (z. B. Ösenringe oder Beile) einen allgemeinen, geläufigen Charakter und würden in ihrer Wertigkeit v. a. auf andere Objekte Bezug nehmen. Die Bewertung der Gegenstände sowie der Ablauf der Tauschgeschäfte sei im Sinne von Maurice Bloch und Jonathan Parry stets im Zusammenhang sozialer Vereinbarungen zu verstehen (M. BLOCH / J. PARRY, Introduction: money and the morality of exchange. In: M. Bloch / J. Parry [Hrsg.], Money and the Morality of Exchange [Cambridge 1989] 1–31). Obschon unveräußerbare und veräußerbare Dinge unterschiedlich wahrgenommen würden, läge die Definition beider im Sozialen und beide würden direkt oder indirekt auf ein universelles bronzezeitliches Weltbild verweisen. Hier kommt dann erstmals die Praxis des *Vernichtens (destruction)* zur Sprache, nämlich wenn Objekte mit ihrer Deponierung endgültig aufgegeben und damit dem weltlichen Kreislauf entzogen werden.

Kapitel 4 (S. 63–85) ist der Deponierungspraxis vormetallzeitlicher Gesellschaften gewidmet. In einem Kurzabriss bespricht Fontijn die prominentesten vorbronzezeitlichen Vertreter des Deponierungsphänomens: Breitkeile der Linearbandkeramischen Kultur, alpine Jadeitbeile ab 5300 v. Chr., osteuropäisches Kupfer im 5.–4. Jahrtausend v. Chr., Jade und Kupfer der Trichterbecherkultur im 4. Jahrtausend v. Chr. Auffällig ist die Unterbrechung der Deponierungsaktivität im 3. Jahrtausend

v. Chr. Die Deponierungen des darauffolgenden Schnurkeramikkomplexes werden vom Autor als eigentliches Vermächtnis der bronzezeitlichen Ausprägung bezeichnet. Das selektive Deponieren von Dingen sei konsequenterweise als zeit- und kulturübergreifende Praxis zu sehen. Als Vergegenständlichungsstrategie stünde jene stets im Spannungsfeld zwischen Werten – symbolischen und weltlichen, heimischen und fremden, persönlichen und allgemeinen.

In Kapitel 5 (S. 86–111) geht es um Dinge und Werte im ganz konkreten Sinn. Fontijn bezeichnet den Umstand, dass vermeintliche Warenbestände (sogenannte „Rücklager von Handwerkern und Händlern") in einer „unökonomischen" Logik permanent weggegeben werden, als einen der rätselhaftesten Aspekte von Metalldeponierungen. Seiner Meinung nach hätten Objekte in solchen Deponierungen durchaus einen Warenwert *(commodity)*, der sich allerdings auf ganz spezifische Austauschsphären beziehen würde. Das Deponieren von Bronzegütern ist dem Autor zufolge ein wesentlicher Teil der bronzezeitlichen Wirtschaft, unabhängig davon ob permanent oder vorübergehend. Eine spezielle Rolle spielten Modellobjekte oder Stellvertreter, beispielsweise die in der Amorika zu hunderten deponierten früheisenzeitlichen Tüllenbeile, die einen derart hohen Bleianteil aufweisen, dass sie weder als Werkzeuge funktionierten noch zu Bronze eingeschmolzen werden konnten. Diese hätten also zu sozialen Transaktionen gedient. Das Kapitel schließt Fontijn mit Erläuterungen zum Konzept der *Sacrificial Economy*, das er in Anlehnung an Susanne KÜCHLERS Werk (Sacrificial Economy and its Objects. Rethinking Colonial Collecting in Oceania. Journal Material Culture 2,1, 1997, 39–60) bereits 2002 eingeführt hat (FONTIJN 2002, bes. 274–275): Demnach würden deponierte Bronzen einem symbolischen Tauschgeschäft übergeben. Dass die betreffenden Objekte nicht zur Schau gestellt wurden, sondern außer Sichtweite vergraben, versenkt oder versteckt werden, würde die kulturellen und materiellen Werte einerseits definieren und andererseits ihre konzeptuelle Unterscheidung manifestieren.

Gifts to familiar gods? – in Kapitel 6 (S. 112–134) hinterfragt Fontijn die Forschungstradition Deponierungen mit Weihegaben an Gottheiten in Verbindung zu bringen. Dabei steht er dem Studium religiöser Motive hinter Bronzedeponierungen offensichtlich kritisch gegenüber. Alternativ dazu schlägt er vor, aus den Deponierungen die bronzezeitliche Konzeptualisierung des Übernatürlichen zu lesen. Dabei vertritt er die Meinung, dass sich Deponierungsrituale auf kosmologische Narrative beziehen würden, wobei er wieder auf den Tausch zurückkommt: Ähnlich wie die Güter in einer zeremoniellen Transaktion hätte das deponierte Material eine vermittelnde Funktion zwischen imaginierten Sphären eingenommen.

In Kapitel 7 (S. 135–152) wird die Rolle der Landschaft behandelt. Wie in den vorangehenden Kapiteln wiederholt angekündigt, weisen Deponierungen einen auffälligen Bezug zur Landschaft auf. Diese sei nicht bloßer Handlungsrahmen, sondern vielmehr aktive Empfängerin der deponierten Dinge. Die betreffenden Orte selber würden auf das Vorhandensein einer imaginierten Landschaft verweisen, welche auf Empirie beruhe, relational funktioniere und tief im kollektiven Gedächtnis verankert sei (s. a. FONTIJN 2002). Zum Schluss des Kapitels regt Fontijn an, Deponierungsbereiche mittels *Predicitive Modeling* statistisch ausfindig zu machen.

Im letzten Kapitel 8 (S. 153–176) entfaltet Fontijn schließlich seine Theorie zur *Economy of Destruction* – der Wirtschaft des Vernichtens. In Anlehnung an Anette B. WEINER (Inalienable Possessions: The Paradox of Keeping-while-giving [Berkeley, Los Angeles, Oxford 1992]) bildet er das Schlagwort *Keeping-while-destroying*. Gemäß dem Autor manifestiere sich im Deponieren von Wertgegenständen sogar eine Verschränkung der „politischen" und der „moralischen" Ökonomie (s. Kap. 1 u. 2). Im Sinn von M. Lambek versteht Fontijn das Deponieren als *Transformation* eines Werts in einen anderen, bzw. würden durch die Aufgabe von (ökonomischen bzw. „politischen") Wertgegenständen neue (soziale bzw. „moralische") Werte erzeugt (s. Kap. 1). Er schließt mit der Feststellung – die man auch als Empfehlung lesen kann – dass manchmal Dinge aufgegeben werden müssten, um gesellschaftlich zu avancieren.

Das knapp über 180-seitige Buch aus dem britischen Verlagshaus Routledge präsentiert sich in handlichem Format. Der Inhalt ist übersichtlich gegliedert, und jedes Kapitel verfügt über eine eigene Bibliografie. Schematische Darstellungen bringen die theoretischen Überlegungen visuell auf den Punkt und unterstützen die Erfassung und das Verinnerlichen der komplexen Zusammenhänge. Sehr nützlich ist das Stichwortverzeichnis am Buchende.

Man ist überrascht, dass eine Thematik, zu der schon derart viel Tinte geflossen ist, immer noch in innovativer Weise diskutiert werden kann. Dass dies ausgerechnet Fontijn gelingt, ist derweil weniger überraschend. So hat er seine originelle Sichtweise und attraktive Präsentation vermeintlich ausdiskutierter Themen schon zahlreiche Male exemplarisch vorgeführt. Im vorliegenden Fall setzt er die bronze- und früheisenzeitlichen Deponierungen in ein Spannungsfeld von Sozial-, Wirtschaftswissenschaften und Archäologie, um letztendlich einen Neuentwurf der Bronzezeitwirtschaft vorzustellen. Fontijns Bestreben, sich von der polemisch geführten Diskussion der 1980er- und -90er Jahre und deren Epilog entschieden abzugrenzen, ist dabei mehr als deutlich (vgl. L. Pauli, Einige Anmerkungen zum Problem der Hortfunde. Arch. Korrbl. 15, 1985, 195–206; W. Torbrügge, Über Horte und Hortdeutung. Arch. Korrbl. 15, 1985, 17–23; B. Hänsel, Gaben an die Götter. Schätze der Bronzezeit Europas. Eine Einführung. In: A. Hänsel / B. Hänsel [Hrsg.], Gaben an die Götter. Schätze der Bronzezeit Europas. Ausstellung der Freien Universität Berlin in Verbindung mit dem Museum für Vor- und Frühgeschichte, Staatliche Museen zu Berlin Preußischer Kulturbesitz. Staatl. Mus. Berlin, Bestandskat. 4 [Berlin 1997] 11–22; M. K. H. Eggert, Das Materielle und das Immaterielle. Über archäologische Erkenntnis. In: U. Veit / T. L. Kienlin / C. Kümmel / S. Schmidt [Hrsg.] Spuren und Botschaften. Interpretationen materieller Kultur. Tübinger Arch. Taschenbücher 4 [Münster, New York, München, Berlin 2013] 423–461). Alternative Zugänge zum Thema wurden in jüngster Zeit – wohlgemerkt von Fontijn motiviert, begleitet und gefördert – von einer Nachfolgegeneration beschritten (Ballmer 2015; Neumann 2015; T. Vachta, Bronzezeitliche Hortfunde und ihre Fundorte in Böhmen. Topoi: Berlin Stud. Ancient World 33 [Berlin 2016]). Fontijn schlägt mit seinem Buch wiederum einen anderen Weg ein, bzw. einen, den er zu einem früheren Zeitpunkt bereits maßgeblich vorgespurt hat (Fontijn 2002, bes. 30–33; 253–255; 274–275). Dieser ist offensichtlich wirtschaftsanthropologisch ausgerichtet, und obschon der Autor sich nicht explizit zu seiner eigenen Position äußert, ist seine theoretische Orientierung an David Graebers anarchistischer Anthropologie sozialer Ungleichheit und an der neomarxistischen Wirtschaftsethnologie M. Godeliers unübersehbar.

D. Fontijn beherrscht die Kunst der stilistischen Komplexitätsreduktion definitiv, was den dargestellten Sachverhalt gleichzeitig fesselnd und auf weiten Strecken leicht nachvollziehbar macht. Die stellenweise großen Sprünge in der Diskussion und die oftmals nur vagen Hinweise auf bestehende Werke, Konzepte und Theorien bedingen allerdings Assoziationskompetenzen von Experten und Expertinnen. Der Autor arbeitet mit einem dichten Kondensat aus Grundlagenforschung, Schlüsseltexten, Konzepten und Theorien aus mehreren Dekaden Forschung in verschiedenen Disziplinen. In der Folge wirken Inhalt und Argumentation stellenweise eklektisch. Wenngleich Fontijn mit seiner ökonomischen Annäherung tatsächlich eine vielversprechende Perspektive auf die Deponierungspraxis eröffnet, ist die Vision von einem unruhigen Flimmern aus Nebenschauplätzen und Verweisen auf andere Arbeiten gestört. So entsteht der Eindruck, es werde angestrebt, das Phänomen bronzezeitlicher Deponierungen möglichst gesamthaft abzudecken und sämtliche Facetten anzusprechen, eine Absicht, die weder umsetzbar noch in der Sache unbedingt weiterbringend scheint.

D. Fontijns Auseinandersetzung ist temporeich, energetisch, reflektiert, wortgewandt, und dabei angenehm zu lesen. Das Buch wartet mit einer Serie neuer Ideen und Konzepte auf und inspiriert ab dem ersten Kapitel. Auch der subtile Brückenschlag zur gegenwärtigen Kapitalismuskritik gelingt recht gut und regt an. Wieder einmal ist es Fontijn in seiner geschätzten Art gelungen, ein vieldiskutiertes Thema von einer neuen, erfrischenden und faszinierenden Seite zu beleuchten. Dass bei der Erstlektüre der eine oder andere Zusammenhang auf der Strecke bleibt, tut dem Lesegenuss keinen Abbruch. Fontijns Buch ist auf jeden Fall als richtungsweisender Beitrag zur Europäischen Bronzezeit zu werten.

CH–3012 Bern
Mittelstrasse 43
E-Mail: ariane.ballmer@iaw.unibe.ch
Orcid: https://orcid.org/0000-0001-8210-7837

Ariane Ballmer
Universität Bern
Institut für Archäologische Wissenschaften,
Abteilung Prähistorische Archäologie &
Oeschger-Zentrum für Klimaforschung (OCCR)

Aleksandar Kapuran, Velebit, a Tumulus Culture Necropolis in the Southern Carpathian Basin (Vojvodina, Serbia). BAR Internat. Ser. Band S2942. BAR Publishing, Oxford 2019. £ 25,–. ISBN 978-1-40732-378-7 (Paperback). 112 Seiten mit 3 Tabellen, 81 Schwarz-Weiß-Abbildungen, 77 Tafeln, 2 Landkarten und 2 Plänen.

Dieses Buch präsentiert die Ausgrabungen der Velebit-Nekropole, einer Schlüsselstätte für die Mittel- und Spätbronzezeit Südosteuropas, die im Herzen des Balkans und am Rande der Pannonischen Ebene liegt. Diese Ausgrabungsstätte ist für mehr als ein halbes Jahrhundert unveröffentlicht geblieben. Dank der Arbeit von Aleksandar Kapuran werden nunmehr die erhaltenen Funde und die archäologische Dokumentation in diesem Buch publiziert und diskutiert.

Das Buch beginnt mit einer kurzen Einführung (1. *Introduction*, S. 1–2), in der die Entdeckung und Ausgrabung der Velebit-Nekropole im Kontext der archäologischen Praxis in Jugoslawien von den 1950er- bis in die 1970er-Jahre beschrieben wird. Das folgende Kapitel (2. *History of Research*, S. 3–5) befasst sich eingehender mit den verschiedenen Ausgrabungsphasen und stellt zwei Lagepläne der Ausgrabungsstätte vor (S. 4 u. 5). Beide liefern wichtige synthetische Informationen zur Position der Gräber innerhalb der Nekropole, zur Chronologie der einzelnen Befunde und zum Bestattungsritual.

In Kapitel 3 *Origin of the Tumulus (Hügelgräber) Culture and its Influence on the Bronze Age Cultures in the Central Balkans* (S. 6–8) werden kulturhistorische Ansätze und Interpretationen der Hügelgräberkultur und ihrer Bedeutung diskutiert. Veränderungen in der materiellen Kultur werden als Folge der Migration von Trägern der Hügelgräberkultur von Mitteleuropa auf den Balkan interpretiert. Nach A. Kapuran folgte die Nord-Süd-Bewegung der Hügelgräber-Kultur im Gebiet des heutigen Serbiens zwei Korridoren: dem nördlichen durch Bačka-Banat und dem südlichen entlang der Flüsse Drina und Zapadna Morava. Diese Durchdringung zeige sich im Verschwinden von zwei Keramikstilen: dem Vatin-Stil und dem inkrustierten Keramikstil. Auf der Grundlage von Nikola Tasić (Die Pannonische Tiefebene und der Zentralbalkan am Übergang von der Mittleren in die späte Bronzezeit. Balcanica III, 1972, 93–115) formuliert der Autor die These, dass sich zwei Gruppen von Menschen friedlich verschmolzen haben, wie man anhand der materiellen Kultur beobachten könne (S. 7). Interessanterweise unterstreicht der Autor, dass im Gegensatz zu Westserbien eigentliche Hügelgräber in der Vojvodina fehlen, wo die Nekropolen in der Tat aus Flachgräbern bestehen. Dieser Unterschied ist hier nur angedeutet, da die materielle Kulturtypologie als kultureller Indikator in diesem Kapitel wichtiger zu sein scheint als die Grabarchitektur.

Kapitel 4 *Catalogue of the Graves and Finds from Velebit* (S. 9–68) beinhaltet den Katalog der erhaltenen Funde der Nekropole von Velebit. Die Funde werden in chronologischer Reihenfolge von den ersten bis zu den jüngsten Ausgrabungskampagnen besprochen. Durch die Analyse der erhaltenen Dokumentation rekonstruiert Kapuran – wenn möglich – Grabinventare. Für jedes Objekt werden eine Beschreibung, Maße und eine Zeichnung präsentiert. Die Körperbehandlung und die Lage des Grabes werden angegeben und ebenso die Beschreibung der Ausgrabung und die Erhaltung jedes Kontextes. Die photographische Dokumentation, die während der Ausgrabungen gemacht wurde, ist auch publiziert. Die Dokumentationsarbeit ist sehr zuverlässig und homogen, und man muss sagen, dass in diesem Katalog der Hauptwert des Bandes liegt. Die vollständige Publikation von Ausgrabungen – insbesondere der alten – ist äußerst zeitaufwändig und in einigen Fällen nicht lohnend, da die Veröffentlichung von Artikeln das Format ist, das heute auf dem akademischen Markt allgemein bevorzugt wird. Dennoch sind Veröffentlichungen wie die vorliegende für die Weiterentwicklung der Forschung von grundlegender Bedeutung, da sie der wissenschaftlichen Gemeinschaft große Mengen neuer Daten zur Verfügung stellen.

Bestattungsriten werden im Kapitel 5 *Burial rites* (S. 69–89) diskutiert. Nach dem Katalog ist es der umfangreichste Teil des Buches. Der Unterschied zwischen Architekturtypen – tatsächlichen Hügelgräbern und Flachgräberfeldern – wird nicht auf kulturelle Entscheidungen, sondern auf geografische Einschränkungen zurückgeführt. In Velebit scheint die Brandbestattung etwas beliebter gewesen zu sein als die Körperbestattung, aber dies ist nicht die Regel auf zeitgleichen Friedhöfen in benachbarten Gebieten. Um kulturelle Ähnlichkeiten zwischen Velebit und anderen Hügelgräber-Gruppen zu bestimmen, wird die Vergesellschaftung von Funden als Hauptmerkmal angesehen. Analogien bei den Grabbeigaben und der Körperorientierung in den Bestattungen werden zur Bestimmung des Geschlechts verwendet. Interessanterweise haben die Körperbestattungen mehr Bronzegegenstände, während die Brandbestattungen meistens Tongefäße als Beigaben haben. In einem Fall (Grab 80) sind auch Gussformen als Grabbeigabe dokumentiert (S. 88–89). Die Brandbestattungen sind in der Regel, was die Beigaben betrifft, ärmer als die Körperbestattungen. Das Kapitel enthält für ausgewählte Bestattungen eine genaue Rekonstruktion der Position der Beigaben in Bezug auf den Körper. Bei einigen Brandbestattungen ist die Urne mit einer Deckel-Schüssel zugedeckt worden. Es folgt die Beschreibung und typologische Einordnung der Objekte. Die Beigaben sind in drei Kategorien unterteilt: Schmuck, Waffen und Keramik. Schmuck ist die am häufigsten vertretene Kategorie der Metallobjekte; dazu gehören Nadeln, Ringe, Armbänder, Anhänger, Beinschienen und einige weitere Objekte aus Metall. In diesem Kapitel werden ihre chronologische, kulturelle und typologische Bedeutung im Rahmen der südosteuropäischen Bronzezeit diskutiert. Waffen sind hingegen nur mit drei Dolchen vertreten, zwei als Beigaben in Brandbestattungen und einer in einer Körperbestattung. In Velebit ist Keramik überwiegend in Brandbestattungen zu finden, obwohl die Ausgrabungen von 1970 zeigen, dass Keramik in fast allen Gräbern als Beigabe oder als Urnen zu finden ist (S. 84). Einige Schalen könnten die Funktion von Deckeln gehabt haben (S. 87). Die Gefäße sind typologisch klassifiziert; die häufigsten Typen sind Urnen, Becher und Deckel-Schüssel. Bemerkenswert ist das Vorhandensein von Steingussformen als Grabbeigaben. Leider stammen diese Objekte aus den Ausgrabungen von 1954 und ihr Fundkontext kann nicht mehr rekonstruiert werden.

Kapitel 6 *Analogies with Neighbouring Necropolises and Cultures* (S. 90–92) gibt einen Überblick über die benachbarten Nekropolen. Die Kontakte zwischen der einheimischen Beliegiš-Cruceni Kultur und der fremden Hügelgräberkultur sind am besten in der Keramik zu beobachten. Kapuran postuliert, dass die größere Zahl an Brandbestattungen in Velebit im Vergleich zu den anderen Nekropolen nördlich der Vojvodina den starken Einfluss der einheimischen Kultur zeige. Kapitel 7 *Relative and Absolute Chronology* (S. 93) schließt das Buch mit der Darstellung des relativen und absoluten chronologischen Rahmens für die Velebit-Nekropole ab. Leider sind keine organischen Überreste erhalten, für die man ein absolutes Datum hätte bestimmen können. Eine ^{14}C-Datierung liegt für das zentrale Grab des Grabhügels XVIII in Paulje (Nordwestserbien) vor und datiert dieses in das 14. Jahrhundert v. Chr. Grab 107 ist das einzige aus Velebit, von dem das Skelett noch erhalten ist, da es ins Museum von Senta gebracht wurde und sich seit 1970 unverändert dort befindet. Da die Urne zur Makó-Kultur gehört, ist es nicht ausgeschlossen, dass dieses Grab zu einer früheren Phase der Nekropole gehört.

Das Buch ist zweifellos eine bedeutsame Veröffentlichung, da sie einen wichtigen Fundplatz vorlegt und das Verständnis für die Bronzezeit im Balkanraum erweitert. Die Publikation von alten Grabungen ist eine dankenswerte Aufgabe, besonders in solchen Fällen, in denen die Forschung so lange unterbrochen war. Es gibt jedoch einige Mängel, auf die hingewiesen werden muss. Der Text leidet unter der unzureichenden Bearbeitung und enthält mehrere Fehler; in einem Fall gibt es einen Satz, der unvollendet erscheint (S. 69). Während Zeichnungen, Maße und Dokumentation äußerst präzise sind, könnten einige Abbildungen und Tabellen verbessert werden. Dies ist der Fall bei Tabelle 3, die einen sehr nützlichen Überblick über die Kapitel des Buches darstellt, jedoch zu kurze und verwirrende Beschriftungen enthält.

Ein weiterer problematischer Aspekt ist der Versuch, Annahmen und Interpretationen aus der jugoslawischen und serbischen archäologischen Tradition mit neueren Ansätzen der Bestattungsarchäologie zu kombinieren. Meiner Meinung nach ist es ein veraltetes Konzept, vor allem auf Migration zurückzugreifen, um Veränderungen in der materiellen Kultur und in den kulturellen Mustern zu erklären. Dies wurde in der Tat durch archäologische, anthropologische und soziologische Untersuchungen zu Migrationen in Frage gestellt. Diese Kritik mindert jedoch nicht den Wert des Buches. Es ist eher ein allgemeiner Kommentar zur Notwendigkeit, neue Interpretationsparadigmen zu übernehmen, um das reiche und vielfältige archäologische Erbe des Balkans zu erklären.

IT–00015 Monte Rotondo Scalo (Rom) Maja Gori
Area della Ricerca Roma 1 Istituto di Scienze del Patrimonio Culturale
Via Salaria Km 29,300 Consiglio Nazionale delle Ricerche (ISPC-CNR)
E-Mail: maja.gori@cnr.it
Orcid: https://orcid.org/0000-0002-8106-4801

Miriam Hauser, Der Rest vom Fest. Eine spätbronzezeitliche Grube voller Scherben vom Seckeberg in Frick. Archäologie im Aargau, Brugg 2019. € 25,–. ISBN 978-3-906897-35-6 (Softcover). doi: https://doi.org/10.19218/3906897356 (PDF). 199 Seiten mit 92 farbigen Abbildungen und 20 Tafeln.

Bei der sehr lesenswerten Studie Miriam Hausers über eine mit den keramischen Überresten eines spätbronzezeitlichen Festmahls dicht verfüllte Grube handelt es sich um die Drucklegung einer an der Universität Basel von Brigitte Röder betreuten Masterarbeit. Die 199 Seiten umfassende Studie ist umfänglich, zumeist farbig, illustriert. 126 Seiten widmen sich der Vorstellung des Fundstoffs; die restlichen Seiten enthalten im sogenannten Anhang die Dokumentation des Ausgrabungsbefunds, den tabellenförmigen Fundkatalog sowie das auf 20 Tafeln im großzügigen Maßstab 1 : 2 abgebildete keramische Fundmaterial in Auswahl. In den einleitenden Kapiteln stellt M. Hauser in klassischer Manier den Fundplatz, den Befund und das keramische Material ausführlich vor (S. 19–67). Den Hauptteil der Studie nimmt die Interpretation ein (S. 68–117). Sie gliedert sich zunächst in die funktionale Ansprache des Gefäßrepertoires der Grube, die Diskussion der Funktion von Gruben im archäologischen Befund im Allgemeinen sowie schließlich – und dies macht die zu besprechende Studie interessant – den Versuch, die besondere Zusammensetzung des Grubeninventars zu deuten.

Der Fund auf dem Seckeberg in Frick im Kanton Aargau in der nordwestlichen Schweiz wurde im Zuge der Verlegung einer Gasleitung entdeckt und anschließend im Rahmen einer Notbergung von der Kantonsarchäologie ausgegraben. Durch diesen Umstand der begrenzten Grabungsfläche konnte nicht ermittelt werden, in welchen weiteren archäologischen Kontext der Grubenbefund einzuordnen ist, worauf die Verfasserin im auswertenden Teil eingeht (S. 84–89). Die Grube mit den Maßen 1,35 × 1 m enthielt in dichter Packung 3267 Scherben im Umfang von 60,4 kg, die sich zu mindestens 68 in Teilen erhaltenen Gefäßindividuen rekonstruieren ließen (S. 99). Wenige kalzinierte Tierknochen (Analyse durch Barbara Stopp, Kap. 3.2, S. 67) befanden sich zwischen den Scherben. Der Fragmentierungsgrad und der Anteil der Scherben, deren ursprüngliche Oberfläche nicht mehr erhalten ist, sind hoch, wie Hauser durch Detailaufnahmen sowie diverse Diagramme anschaulich verdeutlicht. Sie kann zeigen, dass die Gefäße bereits vor ihrer Deponierung zerschlagen worden waren und zudem alle, bis auf lediglich 2,5 bis 4 %, Spuren einer sekundären Brandeinwirkung aufweisen, wobei die über 50 % beidseitig sekundär gebrannten Scherben als ein wichtiger Hinweis dafür dienen, dass die Gefäße in fragmentiertem Zustand dem Feuer überantwortet wurden. So wichtig diese Erkenntnis in ihrer detaillierten Dokumentation ist, bleibt doch zu bedenken, dass bei im Meilerbrand hergestellter Keramik unregelmäßige Hitzezufuhr sowie Rußentwicklung während des Brandes auch bei intakter Grabkeramik häufig zu Farbflecken bzw. Schmauchspuren führen können. Auch Küchenkeramik kann diese Gebrauchsspuren aufweisen. Da jedoch nur 18 % dieser Kategorie 2 nach Hauser dieses Kriterium aufweisen, kann dieser Befund für die abschließende Deutung des Materials weitgehend vernachlässigt werden. Schließlich wird die Suche nach Passscherben (S. 31–33) als Basis für Gefäßrekonstruktionen auch mit Blick auf die Rekonstruktion der Handlungsabläufe, die zur Verfüllung der Grube führten, bedeutsam. Wie Hauser anmerkt, ist die Rekonstruktion von Gefäßeinheiten mit insgesamt maximal 238 sehr hoch und ließe auf einen starken Selektionsvorgang schließen. Die in den anschließenden Abschnitten des Kapitels 3 folgenden Betrachtungen widmen sich mit großer Akribie der Beschaffenheit der Scherben (Oberflächenbeschaffenheit, Magerung: S. 33–43). Diese Unterkapitel sind für künftige Bearbeitungen von Keramik eine vorbildliche Grundlage, die auch über die Region hinaus sowie für andere Perioden gern genutzt werden wird. Möchte man jedoch die besondere inhaltliche Bedeutung des vorgestellten Befunds erschließen, sollte man diese Seiten zunächst überspringen. Eine Unterscheidung in für die Deutung hoch relevante Aspekten des Umgangs mit Keramik (Zerscherbungsgrad, Oberflächenerhaltung, Hitzeeinwirkung, Anpassungen) hätten von diesen eher allgemeinen Beschreibungen der Beschaffenheit getrennt werden können, um die argumentative Kraft der Studie noch stärker zu machen.

Die Rekonstruktion der Gefäßformen offenbart erneut die hervorragende Durcharbeitung eines eher spröden Fundmaterials. Bei der Einteilung in sogenannte Grundformen mit jeweiligen Varianten – der Begriff „Typ" wird bewusst vermieden – überzeugt, auch in der graphischen Darstellung. Der Kunstgriff, die Grundformen exemplarisch entsprechend der Durcharbeitung im Text auf den Tafeln anzuordnen, ist überzeugend. Die Reduktion auf ausgewählte Stücke ist angesichts des Zerscherbungsgrads und der im beschreibenden Teil angegebenen Anzahl der den Grundformen und Varianten zugeordneten Gefäßfragmente gerechtfertigt.

Das Kapitel 3.1.7 (S. 55–67) widmet sich der chronologischen Bestimmung der Keramik. Die im Anhang 8 (S. 164) in Tabellenform mit Angabe der Datierung angeführten Vergleiche weisen eine erhebliche chronologische Spanne auf. Um sie im Einzelnen nachvollziehen zu können, müsste man das Vergleichsmaterial und seine jeweilige chronologische Einordnung überprüfen. Dies kann eine Rezension nicht leisten. Es wird jedoch deutlich, dass sich Hauser sehr intensiv mit der Literatur beschäftigt hat und ihre Arbeit für künftige Bearbeiter*innen vergleichbaren Materials eine wichtige Referenz bieten wird. So stellt sie heraus, dass die exakte zeitliche Bestimmung des Materials schwierig ist, da z. B. Zierelemente wie die in Reihen angeordneten Dreiecksstempel allein sich nicht für eine chronologische Unterscheidung in die Stufen Bz C und D eignen. Die durch Paul Reinecke und Herrmann Müller-Karpe vorgegebene Nomenklatur, die gerade für den Übergang von der späten Mittel- zur Spätbronzezeit eine scharfe Zäsur postulierte, erklärt zumindest in Teilen der nordalpinen Region die Dynamik kultureller Entwicklung nicht in befriedigender Weise. Die Autorin führt die Schweiz und das Elsass bzw. das zentrale Westfrankreich an (S. 58), Süddeutschland ließe sich ergänzen. Nach wie vor wird, wie Hauser ausführt, der absolutchronologische Übergang der späten Mittelbronzezeit (Bz C2) zur frühen Spätbronzezeit / frühen Urnenfelderzeit kontrovers diskutiert. Ob die von ihr favorisierte traditionelle, d. h. späte Datierung des Übergangs im 13. Jahrhundert v. Chr. zu halten ist, ist immer auch eine Frage regional unterschiedlich verlaufender Entwicklungen. Das Material der Grube vom Seckeberg wird dazu nur bedingte Erkenntnisse liefern können. Unabhängig davon ändert sich dadurch nicht die Problematik der phänomenologischen Einordnung stilistischer Merkmale in eine relativchronologische Nomenklatur. Man kann die Bearbeiterin nur darin bestärken, diesem Problem künftig weiter nachzugehen. Entsprechende Ansätze wurden kurz vor Erscheinen ihrer monographischen Studie als Ergebnis einer Tagung publiziert (Th. LACHENAL / C. MORDANT / Th. NICOLAS /C. VÉBER [Hrsg.], Le Bronze moyen et l'origine du Bronze final: en Europe Occidentale, de la Méditerranée aux pays nordiques. Actes du Colloque International du 17 au 20 juin 2014 à Strasbourg. Mém. Arch. Grand-Est 1 [Dijon 2017]).

Kapitel 4 (S. 68–117) befasst sich in umfassender Weise mit der Interpretation des Befundes der Grube. Zunächst widmet Hauser ihr Augenmerk der Funktionsanalyse der keramischen Formen. Sie rekonstruiert aus dem hohen Anteil an Trinkgefäßen aus Feinware ein Trinkgelage, für ca. 30 Personen, das sie jedoch überzeugend in einen Handlungsablauf mit weiteren Komponenten wie Serviergefäßen (von Speisen) sowie „Aufbewahrungsgefäßen" integriert und damit eine komplette Mahlzeit ableitet. Beachtung sollte ihre Feststellung finden, dass Großgefäße u. U. als in den Boden eingetieft vorgestellt werden müssen (S. 75 Abb. 70–71).

Der Handlungsablauf des gewaltsamen Zerschlagens der Keramik, die anschließend einem Feuer überantwortet wurde, und die Auswahl weniger kalzinierter Tierknochen als Reste des Mahls bedürfen der Interpretation. Ihr Ansatz, das Grubeninventar mit Ensembles aus Siedlungs- und Grabkontexten sowie mit intentionellen Deponierungen intakter Gefäßensembles, sogenannten Gefäßdepots, mit ähnlicher Zeitstellung zu vergleichen, liefert das schöne und in dieser Form neue Ergebnis, dass die größte, nahezu deckungsgleiche Übereinstimmung mit letzterer Fundgattung besteht (S. 83 Abb. 78).

Der folgende Vergleich unterschiedlicher Grubenarten bestätigt die Nähe zu den rituellen Gefäßdeponierungen, über die ein überregionaler und diachroner Überblick gegeben wird (S. 91–104). Dieses Kapitel ist sehr informativ, kann jedoch nur einen ersten Ansatz liefern; eine umfassende Bearbeitung wäre eine eigene Studie wert. Die ausgewählten Beispiele werden jedoch sehr ausführlich diskutiert. Hauser kommt zu dem Schluss, dass Gefäßdepots materielle Zeugnisse besonderer Ereignisse seien, und schlägt jahreszyklische Feste, Feiern anlässlich besonderer sozialer Ereignisse oder Götterfeste vor, die von einem Festmahl als Teil ritueller Handlungsabläufe begleitet waren (S. 104). Auch Alexandra KRENN-LEEB hat bronzezeitliche Gefäßdeponierungen als intentionelle und rituelle Handlungen verstanden und als „unsichtbare Inszenierungen" von Festgelagen gedeutet (Tabuisierung – Inszenierung – Transformierung. Bemerkungen zum Phänomen deponierter Gefäßensembles im Ritualkontext. Arch. Österreich 25,1, 2014, 26–31). Die von ihr beschriebenen Deponierungen wie auch die meisten der von Hauser ausgewerteten 29 Beispiele (teils auch bei Krenn-Leeb behandelt) unterschieden sich jedoch durch die in der Regel komponierte Anordnung ganzer Gefäße von dem Befund aus Frick. Das wesentliche Unterscheidungsmerkmal ist die intentionelle Zerschlagung, selektive Deponierung sowie die absichtliche Verwendung von Feuer. Ein weiterer gut mit dem Seckeberg vergleichbarer Befund stammt aus der (älter-)urnenfelderzeitlichen Siedlung von München-Grünwald. Es handelt sich um eine Grube mit dicht gepackter, stark zerscherbter Keramik sowie dem nahezu vollständigen Skelett einer Ziege (L. GEISWEID, Die vorgeschichtlichen Siedlungen von München-Grünwald. In: C. Metzner-Nebelsick [Hrsg.], Einblicke in die Vorgeschichte Grünwalds [München 2016] 69–79).

Hauser gibt als Exkurs in Kapitel 4.6 (S. 105–117) der ausführlichen Darstellung antiker schriftlicher Zeugnisse zu festlichen Mahlzeiten oder mit Opferpraktiken assoziiertem Speisegenuss, insbesondere anhand von Beispielen aus den homerischen Epen sowie dem Alten Testament, sehr viel Raum. Dieses für Leser*innen, die mit der Thematik nicht vertraut sind, nützliche Kapitel führt jedoch nicht mittelbar zur Deutung des Befundes von Frick-Seckeberg. Das von Hauser zuvor als heterogen erkannte Erscheinungsbild der Gefäßdeponierungen bringt sie schließlich zu dem Vergleich mit den zunächst von Werner Krämer 1966 beschriebenen alpinen Brandopferplätzen, insbesondere den für Südbayern bemerkten „reinen Scherbenhaufen und Scherbendepots" (W. KRÄMER, Prähistorische Brandopferplätze. In: R. Degen et al. [Hrsg.], Helvetia Antiqua. Festschrift für Emil Vogt. Beiträge zur Prähistorie und Archäologie der Schweiz [Zürich 1966] 111–122, bes. 118), die dieser als Reste von, seiner Deutung nach, blutigen Speiseopfern ansah. Auch hier gilt, dass es „einen" einheitlichen Typus des Brandopferplatzes nicht gibt, sondern sich hinter dieser über Jahrhunderte im Alpenraum verfolgbaren Denkmälergruppe sehr verschiedene Erscheinungsformen und mit ihnen assoziierte Opferpraktiken verbergen. Hauser verweist angesichts der Komplexität der Materie auf die umfassende Behandlung der Brandopferplätze durch Hubert STEINER (Alpine Brandopferplätze. Archäologische und naturwissenschaftliche Untersuchungen. Forsch. Denkmalpfl. Südtirol 5 [Trento 2010]). Hauser deutet an, dass die Ablehnung Steiners, zerscherbte Keramik in einen rituellen Zusammenhang zu stellen, für die Deutung des Befundes von Frick-Seckeberg zu keinem Erkenntnisgewinn führt. Überzeugender ist für sie die Deutung Andrea STAPELs (Bronzezeitliche Deponierungen im Siedlungsbereich. Tübinger Schr. Ur- u. Frühgesch. Arch. 3 [Münster 1999]), stark fragmentierte Keramikdeponierungen als Zeugen intentioneller Gewalt anzusehen, welche die bei besonderen religiös oder rituell aufgeladenen Anlässen verwendete Keramik einer Wiederverwendung und damit Profanierung entziehen sollten. Zu ergänzen wäre die Bearbeitung der Brandopferplätze in Bayern durch Rainer-Maria WEISS (Prähistorische Brandopferplätze in Bayern. Internat. Arch. 35 [Espelkamp 1997]), der ebenfalls die Deutung dieser Befundgattung als dingliches Zeugnis ritueller Handlungen vorschlug.

Im 5. und letzten Kapitel „Fazit und Ausblick" (S. 118–123) werden die Ergebnisse noch einmal knapp zusammengefasst, gleichzeitig jedoch ein wichtiger und neuer Aspekt angesprochen, der bei dem Thema rituelle Mahlzeiten im aktuellen Diskurs die wichtigste Rolle spielt: den der sozialen Interaktion und der Gemeinschaft stiftenden und stärkenden Komponente des gemeinsamen Mahls. Erneut werden vielfältige, auch ethnologische Beispiele eingeflochten, wodurch die Stringenz der Argumentation etwas verloren geht.

Am Ende gelingt Hauser eine sinnvolle und überfällige Unterscheidung der in komponierter Manier in intaktem Zustand niedergelegten Gefäße in den sogenannten Keramikdepots, die zweifelsfrei in einen rituellen Zusammenhang mit religiös motivierter Intention gehören, und dem Inventar der Grube aus Frick-Seckeberg oder vergleichbarer Befunde. Man wird ihr gern zustimmen, in den intentionell zerstörten Gefäßresten das dingliche Zeugnis eines Festmahls zu sehen. Da ein Kontext mit religiöser Bedeutungsbelegung nicht zwingend nachgewiesen werden kann, ist der Begriff „Festgrube" zwar inhaltlich überzeugend, die der deutschen Sprache eigene Substantivierung komplexerer Sachverhalte klingt jedoch etwas sperrig und bedarf außerhalb des Kontextes weiterer Erläuterung.

Die am Anfang einer wissenschaftlichen Laufbahn stehende Autorin Miriam Hauser hat es in dieser bemerkenswerten Studie verstanden, eine phänomenologische und damit terminologische

Unterscheidung keramischer Deponierungen vorzunehmen. Die Arbeit liefert somit wichtige Anregungen im Diskurs zum *ritual feasting*. Darüber hinaus werden in der Analyse stark fragmentierter Keramikensembles interessante Ansätze aufgezeigt, die sicher die Forschung weiter anregen werden.

Trotz des sehr positiven Eindrucks sei am Schluss milde Kritik erlaubt. Im auswertenden Teil finden sich einige Längen, der Text mäandriert mit mehreren Zwischen-Fazits und wirkt bisweilen nicht wirklich glücklich strukturiert. Trotz des sehr ansprechenden Layouts hätte das Lektorat bei der unbeholfen wirkenden graphischen Gestaltung der Verzierungselemente (S. 52 Abb. 58) mit einem computergestützten Zeichenprogramm der Autorin zur Hand gehen können. Das Bild des Buchcovers erzeugt zumindest bei der Rezensentin einen eher negativen ersten Eindruck. Die Darstellung ist eindeutig auf den Inhalt bezogen und hat die Absicht, den Inhalt des Buchs in optischer Verkürzung zu vermitteln. Die beabsichtigte Wirkung gelingt jedoch nicht überzeugend. Dies liegt an der naiv anmutenden, an Kinderbücher erinnernden Visualisierung der imaginierten Szene. Durch die spielenden / tanzenden Kinder entsteht der Eindruck einer harmlosen, fröhlichen Handlung, was ebenso wie die Kleidung der dargestellten Personen eine nicht belegbare Wertung darstellt. Die Art der Darstellung birgt die Gefahr, dem Inhalt des Buches intellektuelle Schlichtheit zu unterstellen, die Prähistoriker*innen im Vergleich mit anderen archäologischen Disziplinen bisweilen attestiert wird. Dies ist schade, denn das Buch beweist auf eindrückliche Weise das genaue Gegenteil. Hauser hat es verstanden, im Rahmen ihrer Masterarbeit eine gedanklich scharfsinnige und kreative Behandlung einer zunächst unscheinbar anmutenden Fundgattung – „Festgruben", wie sie es nennt, d. h. intentionelle Deponierungen von Rückständen gemeinschaftlicher Mahlzeiten – in den Blick der (nicht nur spätbronze- / urnenfelderzeitlichen) Forschung zu rücken. Analysen organischer Rückstände oder die gezielte Beachtung ähnlicher Befunde werden sicher weitere Erkenntnisse zu dieser Befundgruppe liefern; auf die Studie von Miriam Hauser wird man sich daher künftig berufen müssen.

DE–80539 München
Geschwister-Scholl-Platz 1
E-Mail: Metzner-Nebelsick@vfpa.fak12.uni-muenchen.de

Carola Metzner-Nebelsick
Ludwig-Maximilians-Universität München
Institut für Vor- und
Frühgeschichtliche Archäologie
und Provinzialrömische Archäologie

Enrico Lehnhardt, Die Anfänge der Eisenverhüttung im Bereich der Przeworsk-Kultur. Berlin Studies of the Ancient World Band 62. Edition Topoi, Berlin 2019. € 59.90. ISBN 978-3-9819685-2-1. doi: https://doi.org/10.17171/3-62. 404 pages.

Iron production has undoubtedly been a major area of manufacturing for over 3000 years, essentially determining the civilisational development as well as political and military importance of European societies. It is all the more surprising that the beginnings of iron smelting in the Przeworsk culture – one of the largest and longest functioning (end of the 3rd century BC to mid-5th century AD) cultural formations in Poland – has not yet been the subject of a monographic study. This was even despite achievements in studies on large production centres in the Świętokrzyskie Mountains and Western Mazovia or numerous discoveries of metallurgical sites in Silesia and other regions of Poland. This is partly understandable, given the complexity of technical and technological issues, discouraging for archaeologists-humanists, combined with the scarcity of sources and their poor state of preservation, typical of dawns of any industry. To date, Szymon Orzechowski's monograph on iron smelting centres of the Przeworsk culture (Region żelaza. Centra hutnicze kultury przeworskiej [Kielce 2013]) has been the most thorough one on this topic. Still, it leaves numerous uncertainties. Therefore, Enrico Lehnhardt's attempt at this challenge is even more welcome, especially taking the major linguistic barrier caused by majority of writing being available in Polish. The book is the slightly revised version of his dissertation, which was submitted to the Department of History and Cultural Studies at the Freie Universität Berlin in December 2015 and defended in June 2016.

The work was inspired by research carried out in 2008–12 under the international research structure "Excellence Cluster Topoi. The Formation and Transformation of Space and Knowledge in Ancient Civilisations", within research group A-1. The study focused on the secondary distribution settlement of the Przeworsk culture population in the foothills of the Southern Harz in the younger pre-Roman period, which was shown to be closely related to the presence of iron ore in that area. The author aimed at verifying this thesis. Thus, the earliest traces of iron making had to be examined against the background of settlement processes occurring in the native areas of the discussed culture, with particular emphasis on Silesia as a probable starting point area. As a result, an original concept was created which provides a new perspective on the emergence of iron smelting in the Przeworsk culture.

Geographically, the study has not been limited to this culture unit only. E. Lehnhardt examined a much wider area on multiple levels (p. 11), starting from large areas on the European continent and adjacent Asian areas known for their early iron production (global perspective), to then move on to increasingly small units (local perspective). Apart from literature data on excavation and surface research conducted since the beginning of the 20th century, the author also used archives and documents from AZP (Archaeological Picture of Poland) research as a source base at the meso- (Silesian area) and micro-regional levels (a fragment of the Widawa valley).

When characterising the Przeworsk culture in the pre-Roman period, Lehnhardt quotes a well-established view that high consumption of iron, noticeable from the very beginning, contributed to the parallel development of the local production of this metal based on native ores. Nearly from the outset of archaeology, a paradigm has prevailed that the technology transfer in both iron producing and its processing resulted from contacts with the La Tène culture. However, this view, too, is increasingly being criticised, with the Jastorf culture being indicated as an alternative direction.

In chapter 2 (pp. 31–96) the author, referring mostly to theoretical findings, tries to explain various processes that took place in the initial stages of development of iron metallurgy in a specific area and reveals motivations for craftsmen's activities. He is primarily concerned with innovation, the concept which has recently gained popularity also in archaeology (p. 34 figs. 17–18). When considering iron as an innovation, the reference to the work of Vincent C. Pigott (The innovation of iron. Cultural dynamics in technological change. Expedition Magazine 25,1, 1982, 20–25) could not be omitted. According to this author the production of iron may be seen as "an innovative stage within a pyrotechnological continuum which began with the earliest intentional smelting of metallic ores" (Pigott 1982, 20). Lehnhardt points out that the iron-smelting process required profound knowledge and experience in terms of raw materials, construction of devices and subsequent production stages. It allowed, through continuous practice and learning processes (p. 40 fig. 23), to develop a certain set of production and technological rules (p. 40 fig. 22). Discussing the problem of the origin of innovation and the mechanism of its diffusion in prehistoric societies, the author shares opinion of Holger Braun-Thürmann (Innovation [Bielefeld 2005] 35) about the need to combine linear models describing them on the basis of feedback (p. 40 fig. 24). The spread of iron-smelting technology depended on several natural, social, and economic factors. Above all, it could only be established where mineral resources were available. Moreover, on the basis of the theory of innovation by Everett M. Rogers (Diffusion of Innovations [New York, London 1983] 247–250), in prehistoric societies specific groups of recipients can be distinguished, who accepted technical or technological novelties faster or slower, or who were unable or unwilling to accept them for various reasons. For example, easy access to iron products through exchange or import meant that the local population was not interested in iron producing and processing on their own. If, however, there was a technology transfer, it had to take place only through cultural and interpersonal contacts, including migration or mobility of craftsmen. Theoretical conclusions made here will play an important role in building the concept of the beginnings of iron smelting both in the discussed culture and in the wider context.

The author devoted the next subchapter to presenting the earliest manifestations of iron metallurgy in several selected areas, which he describes as model regions: Georgia (Kolkhida), Levant (Jordan, Israel), Iberian Peninsula, Germany (North Black Forrest, Siegerland, Brandenburg), Denmark (Zealand, Central Jutland), England (East Yorkshire). He includes technical, social and cultural points of view, seeking to clarify mechanisms for diffusion and adaptation of iron smelting technology. This leads to the conclusion (p. 68 tab. 2) that this technology was adapted in different communities and cultures. It was predetermined by a readiness to accept novelties resulting from the demand for iron. In addition to cultural contacts, population migration was certainly an important factor in technology transfer. In general, there are clear economic and organisational similarities. There are differences in the raw material base, as well as the technical sphere.

In the last part of this chapter Lehnhardt discusses canal-pits, which are typical technical phenomena in the Przeworsk culture iron smelting. Simultaneously, they are quite widespread in Central Europe and beyond. The chronological aspect of their occurrence is very interesting, too. The author argues here with S. Orzechowski's thesis according to which furnaces with this construction represent an early stage of iron making in its local dimension (S. ORZECHOWSKI, The canal-pit and its role in the bloomery process: the example of the Przeworsk culture furnaces in the Polish territories. In: J. Hošek / H. Cleere / L. Mihok [eds], Archaeometallurgy of Iron. Recent Developments in Archaeological and Scientific Research. [Prague 2011] 41–54). Their occurrence in some areas of the *Barbaricum* only in the late Roman period clearly contradicts this.

The main part of the study (chapter 3, pp. 97–297) opens with an analysis of the use of iron in Silesia in the pre-Roman period. The presence of iron objects marks this whole period starting from the Ha C phase. They appear in variable saturation and assortment (p. 131 tab. 11). The author presents a detailed statistics and spectrum of iron objects and their forms successively in the Lusatian (north-eastern group of the Hallstatt culture), Billendorf, Pomeranian, La Tène and Przeworsk cultures. The development of the Przeworsk culture started the most iron-rich settlement period in this region, whereas types of iron artefacts and their forms match those of the La Tène culture.

Another aspect important for the study are the results of numerous chemical analyses of ferrous objects related to phosphorus content carried out by Jerzy Piaskowski (p. 132). In the whole pre-Roman period, including the Przeworsk culture area, the vast majority (about 80%) of samples show low content of this element (below 0.2%). This may indicate that it was mainly imported raw material produced from low-phosphorus "mountain" ores which was used.

Then Lehnhardt conducts a detailed analysis of selected cemeteries from the Przeworsk and Oksywie culture located across Poland, focusing on occurrence, number and assortment of iron artefacts in particular chronological phases (pp. 132–179). To estimate the total weight of iron coming from these sites, and thus enable a comparative analysis, he assigns model values to statistically most significant or heaviest categories of artefacts: from 1 to fibulas to 40 to swords. Comparisons between the individual necropolises reveal that factors determining the amount of iron might have included their geographical location, or more precisely connections with the trade and transport network based on major rivers. Another significant fact is that raw material for different product groups came from different sources. Weapons and larger items were mainly made from low-phosphorus iron. For smaller products, however, high-phosphorus iron was mostly used.

Considering iron production in the Iron Age in Poland further on, the author states that the thesis that the Lusatian, Billendorf and Pomeranian cultures were engaged in iron making cannot be proved (pp. 179–185; 237). Settlement structures of the La Tène culture which developed in southern Poland since the Lt B1 phase do not provide any convincing evidence for the existence of iron production, either. However, it is difficult to agree with this opinion taking the research results from Sułków E site (Upper Silesia), dated to the Lt C1b–C2 phases. As apart from traces of a smithing workshop (p. 191 fig. 187), a relatively small excavation revealed over 1000 kg of slag morphologically typical for slag-pit furnaces (B. Czerska, Celtycki ośrodek hutniczy w Sułkowie w powiecie Głubczyce. Acta Univ. Wratislaviensis 157 = Stud. Arch. 5 [Wrocław 1972] 6) and big slag-cakes resulting from the refining of blooms (p. 190 fig. 185). This discovery is particularly valuable as no traces of any younger settlement were found either in or around the site. Moreover, hopes are high that a discovery made in 2019 in Warkocz 12 (Lower Silesia) – a sunken-floored bloomery ironwork with 12 slag-pit furnaces – can provide an explanation concerning the technology and organisation of iron production in the eastern zone of the La Tène culture (unpublished research by Przemysław Dulęba).

The situation, however, is different in the Gubin group of the Jastorf culture which occupied the western part of Silesia until the A2 phase. Iron production in this culture is undisputable and the prevalence of slag (perhaps only partially bloomery slag) at settlement sites is astonishing. For this reason, involvement of this group in the shaping of iron metallurgy in the Przeworsk culture should be seriously considered.

Conversely, the assessment of the dawn of the Przeworsk culture iron smelting is highly controversial. The author lists only two sites in the Świętokrzyskie Mountains and the settlement enclave on the Nida River (pp. 197–200; 241): Gardzienice II and Pokrzywnica III, which could possibly be associated with the younger pre-Roman period. With reference to production centres in Mazovia, only the Falenty site can be dated based on pottery finds exclusively to the phases A2 and A3 (p. 207). Taking the scale of the research, on the other hand, there was very little radiocarbon dating. Like in the case of the Świętokrzyskie Mountains, the obtained dates include both the pre-Roman and the Roman period. Considering the equally broad artefact dating, it makes them useless in determining the chronology of the production activity. Focusing on the area of Silesia, Lehnhardt analyses 40 sites where traces of iron production and material from the younger pre-Roman period were found (pp. 212–218; 241–244; 242–243 tab. 56–57). For all six excavated sites, on which remains of bloomery furnaces were discovered (Domasław 10–12, Namysłów 69, Polwica-Skrzypnik site complex, Psary 1, Radwanice 2 and Tarchalice 1), it is virtually impossible to date iron production to the pre-Roman period due to the multi-phase character of the settlement. The series of ^{14}C datings made only for the Psary and Polwica-Skrzypnik sites and covering also the Roman period are not conducive to this, although in the former case the author allows the beginning of the iron production in the A3 phase. In general, however, iron smelting is automatically associated with the Roman period, if only because of the predominance of ceramic material. The situation is similar on the remaining 34 sites, where only surface finds of slag or possibly loose pieces of it were found in the fillings of settlement features. Most sites yielded also finds from the Roman period or the Middle Ages, but in some of the locations, known mainly from the AZP research, the slag was found only with the pre-Roman sherds. Most of them form a cluster in the Widawa valley near Namysłów (Upper Silesia). For a long time researchers had high hopes related to excavating and verifying it, possibly even discovering the "cradle" of the Przeworsk culture metallurgy. However, the comprehensive field work undertaken by Lehnhardt in this area did not confirm iron production in the younger pre-Roman period. Essential data were provided by geophysical investigations and excavations at Pielgrzymowice 5 site (pp. 250–291). Two smelting furnaces were discovered there (pp. 272–275 fig. 313–318; 326–334). They belong to the category of devices with a 'very large' slag-pit, and based on the ceramic finds and the ^{14}C analysis they were dated to the middle and late Roman period (p. 289 tab. 60; p. 290 fig. 343). However, no traces of iron production from the younger pre-Roman period were found. The results of this work have been carefully documented and provide valuable input to settlement research and study on the smelting technology in this part of the region.

In an extensive chapter 4 (pp. 299–332) Lehnhardt reviews sources concerning the beginnings of iron use and production in the eastern part of Central Europe. Phenomena similar to those characteristic of the pre-Roman Przeworsk culture can be observed in all of the examined areas. Thus, in the author's opinion, the widespread use of iron on the one hand, and the scarcity (the example of Bohemia) or absence of traces of iron smelting clearly dated back to the La Tène period on the other, are a supra-regional feature. Indeed, it is only in the Roman period that the number of the ironmaking sites clearly increased.

The study also includes a reference to technology transfer in the Przeworsk culture (chapter 5, pp. 333–336). The key issue is the origin of the slag-pit single-use furnaces, which highly relies on interpretation of the available data. The author believes that they cannot derive from the La Tène patterns, as they were virtually unknown in the La Tène culture, at least in its eastern zone and single examples from Bohemia may raise doubts as to dating. It is equally improbable that this technology was transferred from the Jastorf culture, while the involvement of the Gubin group must be ruled out because it disappeared before the beginning of iron smelting in the Przeworsk culture. Thus, it must have been the Elbe-Germanic tribes who were responsible for the transfer of the new technology to Silesia, as well as to Bohemia and Slovakia, as they had already mastered the secrets of iron production at the time in question.

Finally, the author returns to the initial thesis concerning the motives for the appearance of the Przeworsk culture settlement in the earlier phases of the younger pre-Roman period in Thuringia (pp. 337–342). Excavations in Nordhausen-Himmelgarten and Leimbach (DE) did not, however, yield traces of iron production in the A1 and A2 stages. The fact that settlers had no interest in smelting iron in favourable environmental conditions, visible in the archaeological material, may indirectly testify to the ignorance of this technology in their home area.

The multifaceted, detailed and consistently conducted analysis resulted in a new, extremely interesting concept concerning the beginnings of iron production activity in the Przeworsk culture, which stands in opposition to the views that have been established for years in the literature. It is based on the thesis that there is no conclusive evidence of iron smelting in the younger pre-Roman period. The author can accept the existence of local production only from the A3 phase and just in few selected areas in Silesia and Mazovia. The demand for iron, both finished products and raw material for blacksmith manufacturing, was satisfied by imports from the metallurgical centres of the La Tène culture, most probably located within the zone where phosphorus-poor ores occurred. Vast transport and exchange networks with La Tène communities were used for this purpose, especially along the Amber Road. Extensive iron production appeared in Silesia and Mazovia only in the early Roman period. Lehnhardt links it with the fact that at the turn of the La Tène and the Roman period the Elbe-Germanic population moved to Bohemia, Moravia and Slovakia, which were previously occupied by Celtic tribes. That coincided with civilizational and military pressure from the Roman Empire. These changes may have disrupted iron supplies and encourage own production. Thus, the technology transfer to the Przeworsk culture area might have taken place through contacts with Marcomanni and Quadi people, who pursued the idea of self-sufficiency and the use of local raw material sources, while in terms of technical equipment they preferred slag-pit furnaces.

Notably, the author does not limit his study exclusively to the emergence of iron smelting in the Przeworsk culture. It might even appear that it was just a pretext for presenting a much broader issue, namely the history of adaptation of this innovation in vast areas of Central Europe, including Poland, the Czech Republic, Slovakia and parts of Austria, Hungary and Romania. The researcher thus referred to a number of well-known publications relating to areas of Scandinavia, including Denmark and northern Germany, covering, however, a narrower territorial scope and much less factual data.

Notwithstanding his contribution, it must be noted that given the current state of research the author could only present a hypothetical picture of the beginnings of iron production. Despite its consistency, a number of counter-arguments can be pointed out in several aspects, which result from ambiguity of the available data and the successive influx of new ones. The presented concept may therefore be subject to some adjustments. For example, a recent, more thorough analysis of unpublished sources concerning Psary and Polwica-Skrzypnik casts a different light on ^{14}C dates from these sites. Obviously, the broad artefact dating in both cases, with predominance of early Roman material (especially from the B2 phase), generates the above-mentioned problem of placing the production activity on a time scale. However, the fact remains that the radiocarbon dating of some furnaces from Psary includes with high probability the oldest phases of the Przeworsk culture (p. 218 fig. 231–233; 235). It cannot be disregarded especially when taking into account Marek Wróbel's work (Ceramika z osady hutniczej kultury przeworskiej w Psarach, stanowisko 1, gmina Jemielno, województwo leszczyńskie. [Unpubl. master thesis, Institute of Prehistory, Adam Mickiewicz University] [Poznań 1983]) devoted to ceramic finds from this site. Namely, in the group of sherds bearing mid- and late La Tène period features, which constitutes about 18 % of the whole collection, forms typical for the A1–A2 phases were clearly manifested (Wróbel 1983, 104). What is more, this chronology is confirmed by the presence of a brooch of F-type according to Kostrzewski, dated to the A2 phase (Wróbel 1983, 105, tab. XI:2). The case is similar for Polwica-Skrzypnik, where two out of seven ^{14}C dating measurements from slag-pits include the A2 phase (P. Madera, Ze studiów nad piecami dymarskimi z kotlinką ,bardzo dużą' na Śląsku. In: E. Błażejewski [ed.], Labor et patientia. Studia archaeologica Stanislao Pazda dedicata [Wrocław 2008] tab. 3). Simultaneously, as many as 51 settlement features dated by means of ceramic material indicate the younger pre-Roman period (L. Berduła / M. Dobrakowski, Osada hutnicza z okresu wpływów rzymskich na stanowiskach: Polwica 4–5, Skrzypnik 8, woj. Dolnośląskie. In: S. Orzechowski [ed.], Hutnictwo świętokrzyskie oraz inne centra i ośrodki starożytnej metalurgii żelaza na ziemiach polskich [Kielce 2002] 108). A direct insight into this material revealed that it comes mostly from the A2 phase. In this context, it is essential these features occurred mainly in the part of the site where the oldest of the analysed bloomeries were discovered. Lehnhardt's suggestions concerning low relevance of ^{14}C measurements for an earlier dating of iron production in Silesia may therefore turn out to be wrong. On the other hand, the thesis that in few places iron production started as early as in phases A1–A2, to continue after a period of settlement breakdown in the A3 phase on a much larger scale far into the early Roman period, would gain credibility. Consequently, the possibility that there had been technology transfer from the area of the La Tène and Jastorf cultures should be reconsidered. Undoubtedly, however, more reliable solutions can be provided only by further excavations, long series of ^{14}C dates and metallographic expert opinions, and finally the widespread application of osmium isotope analyses, which are extremely promising in provenance studies.

Regardless of any remarks and reservations, it must be admitted that E. Lehnhardt created a valuable work, unrivalled by any previous literature on the eastern part of Central Europe. It is a real challenge and inspiration for a group of archaeometallurgists, but also a powerful source of knowledge for all those who study the history of civilisation, not only in terms of raw materials.

PL–50-136 Wrocław
ul. Cieszyńskiego 9
E-Mail: pmadera@mmw.pl
Orcid: https://orcid.org/0000-0003-0983-9171

Paweł Madera
Museum of Archaeology Wrocław

Tom Moore, A Biography of Power. Research and Excavations at the Iron Age *oppidum* of Bagendon, Gloucestershire (1979–2017). Mit Beiträgen von Sophia Adams, Michael J. Allen, Sam Bithell, Loïc Boscher, Cameron Clegg, G. B. Dannell, Lorne Elliott, Elizabeth Foulds, Freddie Foulds, Christopher Green, Derek Hamilton, Colin Haselgrove, Yvonne Inall, Tina Jakob, Mandy Jay, Sally Kellett, Robert Kenyon, Mark Landon, Marcos Martinón-Torres, Edward McSloy, Janet Montgomery, J. A. Morley-Stone, Geoff Nowell, Charlotte O´Brien, Chris Ottley, Cythia Poole, Richard Reece, Harry Robson, Ruth Shaffrey, John Shepherd, Jane Timby, Dirk Visser, D. F. Williams und Steven Willis. Archaeopress, Oxford 2020. £ 85,–. ISBN 978-1-78969-534-2. 626 Seiten mit zahlreichen Abbildungen und Tabellen.

Mit „A Biography of Power" legt Tom Moore eine umfassende und reich illustrierte Darstellung zum Oppidum von Bagendon in Gloucestershire (GB) vor. Obwohl Colchester, Stanwick, Saint Albans oder Hengistbury Head wohl die bekannteren britischen Oppida sind, wird in diesem Band deutlich, welche Bedeutung einem derart vorbildlich untersuchten – und nun komplett vorgelegten – Platz wie Bagendon zukommt. Wie umfänglich die enthaltenen Informationen sind, wird bereits beim Blick auf die, neben dem Hauptautor, 34 weiteren Autor*innen aus verschiedensten Disziplinen (Prähistorische und Römische Archäologie, Archäobotanik, Archäozoologie, Anthropologie, Geowissenschaften, Umweltrekonstruktion etc.) deutlich. Daher verwundert es nicht, dass im Vorwort auf drei Seiten etlichen Personen und ganzen Familien für die Unterstützung des Projekts gedankt wird. So bedankt sich Tom Moore auch bei Richard Reece und Stephen Trow für die Möglichkeit, über die Ausgrabungen 1979–81 in Bagendon zu schreiben, was schließlich der Anlass war für seine weiteren Grabungs- und Prospektionskampagnen vor Ort, die von 2012 bis 2017 andauerten. Auch der Dank an die mehr als zehn verschiedenen Mittelgeber der zahlreichen hier aufgearbeiteten Grabungskampagnen nimmt einigen Platz ein.

Das Buch ist in sechs größere Abschnitte *(parts)* unterteilt, zu denen insgesamt 25 Kapitel gehören. Der erste Abschnitt befasst sich mit dem Begriff Oppidum, der Topographie und Forschungsgeschichte des Platzes (S. 1–17) und stellt so eine sinnvolle Einleitung dar. Genau wie dieser wurde auch der zweite Abschnitt komplett von T. Moore verfasst. Hier stehen nun die Befunde des *Bagendon complex* – also des Oppidums und seines Umlandes – im Fokus, welche durch geophysikalische Prospektionen (Kap. 2; S. 21–98), Ausgrabungen an den Vorgängersiedlungen (Kap. 3; S. 99–133), im Oppidum (Kap. 4; S. 134–172) und einem nach-oppidumzeitlichen Komplex (Kap. 5; S. 173–193) während der Jahre 1979–2017 untersucht wurden. Dabei werden die Grabungsergebnisse der Altgrabungen sehr gut mit denen der neuen Untersuchungen zusammengeführt und mit den aus den Prospektionen gewonnen Daten kontextualisiert. Besonders die beiden untersuchten „banjoförmigen" Vorgängersiedlungen sind höchst interessant für die Frage nach den Ursprüngen des Oppidums von Bagendon, während andererseits die beiden vorgestellten römischen Villen für die Nachnutzung des Areals Zeugnis ablegen. Im dritten Abschnitt behandeln zahlreiche Autor*innen auf über 150 Seiten die breite Palette an fast ausschließlich eisen- und kaiserzeitlichen *(Roman)* Funden und beleuchten so u. a. handwerkliche Aktivitäten und Tauschnetzwerke (S. 197–355). Zu den wichtigsten diskutierten Fundgattungen zählen hier Keramik, Fibeln, Metallfunde, Schlacke, Münzen, Tüpfelplatten, Glas-, Knochen- und Steinartefakte. Ebenfalls in diesem Abschnitt diskutiert Derek Hamilton die Ergebnisse der ^{14}C-Daten bzw. des *Bayesian modelling* (S. 347–353). Diese sind vor allem in Hinblick auf die feinchronologische Fixierung der beiden Vorgängersiedlungen *(Cutham and Scrubditch enclosures)* interessant.

Abschnitt IV ist den Menschen- und Tierknochen sowie der Umweltrekonstruktion (Archäobotanik) gewidmet. Im Falle der Menschenknochen fällt vor allem deren relative Seltenheit auf, was auf Bestattungsformen hinweist, die keine archäologisch fassbaren Spuren hinterlassen haben. Dieser Umstand wird durch Moore sinnvoll mit dem aktuellen Forschungsstand zu lokalen und überregionalen eisen- und kaiserzeitlichen Bestattungssitten kontextualisiert, in die sich Bagendon nahtlos einfügen lässt (S. 365–367). Die archäozoologischen Daten hingegen sind deutlich komplexer und lassen zwischen Eisenzeit und Römischer Kaiserzeit keine Diskontinuitäten erkennen. Auffällig ist hier auch der gleichbleibend hohe Anteil an Schweineknochen, was auf spezielle Vorlieben oder Schweinehaltung vor Ort zurückgeführt wird (S. 384). Die folgenden Isotopenanalysen an Menschen- und Tierresten zeichnen das Bild mobiler Menschen und Tiere und verweisen mehrfach nach Wales (S. 386–409). Die Rekonstruktion der Paläo-Umwelt zeichnet das Bild einer offenen, menschengemachten Landschaft, in welcher vor allem Viehzucht eine große Rolle spielte (S. 410–460). Die überraschend geringen Hinweise auf Ackerbau sprechen dafür, dass landwirtschaftliche Produkte aus ertragreicheren Gegenden bezogen wurden, wofür das obere Themsetal vorgeschlagen wird (S. 460). Der folgende Abschnitt trägt den Titel „Landscape Studies" und enthält verschiedene geoarchäologische und GIS-gestützte Untersuchungen zum Umland des Oppidums sowie geophysikalische Prospektionen einiger Fundorte. Hierbei wird explizit auf die Veränderungen von Landschaft und Siedlungsintensität am Übergang zwischen Eisenzeit und Römischer Kaiserzeit eingegangen, wobei Fragen nach wechselnden Identitäten und einer „Landscape of Power" stets mitschwingen (S. 463–538). Dementsprechend werden wie allgemein üblich auch die vorgenommenen Sichtbarkeitsanalysen interpretiert. Während *Least Cost Analyses* die generell verkehrsgünstige Lage von Bagendon belegen, wird anhand statistischer Analysen die vermehrte Aufsiedlung des Umlands in der Römischen Kaiserzeit deutlich (Fig. 23.11). Generell folgt Bagendon den regionalen Trends der Siedlungsentwicklung in Eisen- und Kaiserzeit. Lediglich sein Ende im späten ersten Jahrhundert n. Chr. ist ungewöhnlich, spricht aber für eine gewisse soziopolitische Rolle, welche mit der Etablierung römischer Infrastruktur in dieser Form nicht mehr gefragt war (S. 538). Der letzte Abschnitt wurde erneut von Moore verfasst und widmet sich den Narrativen – wie z. B. der Ansprache der Bewohner als die schriftlich überlieferten *Dobunni* – und der Diskussion der Ergebnisse (S. 541–596). Hier wird die im Titel angekündigte Biographie des Fundplatzes gezeichnet, welche auf ansprechende Art die wichtigsten Forschungsfragen aufgreift. Somit stellt dieser Abschnitt eine sinnvolle Zusammenfassung der zentralen Aspekte der vorigen Kapitel dar und gibt einen Ausblick auf zukünftige Forschungsfragen – z. B. das Überdenken gängiger Narrative zu sozialen Modellen der späten Eisenzeit (S. 595). Nach den Anhängen und dem weitestgehend englischsprachigen Literaturverzeichnis folgt ein umfangreiches Glossar, welches das Nachschlagen bestimmter Aspekte deutlich einfacher macht und so eine Bereicherung für jedes derart umfangreiche Buch darstellt. Beim Durchsehen der dortigen Lemmata wird jedoch auch schnell ein Schwachpunkt des Bandes deutlich: Trotz der Masse an Untersuchungen bleibt man gedanklich sehr auf sich selbst fokussiert. Während gelegentlich noch Vergleiche zu anderen britischen Fundorten unternommen werden, wird die kontinentale Oppidaforschung fast vollständig ausgeblendet. Der einzige nicht-britische Fundort im Glossar ist Bibracte (FR), was sicher vor allem auf Moores dortige Forschungen zurückgehen dürfte (z. B. T. Moore et al., Oppida, agglomerations and suburbia. The Bibracte environs and new perspectives on Late Iron Age urbanism in central-eastern France. European Journal Arch. 16,3, 2013, 491–517). Gerade in den einleitenden und zusammenfassenden Kapiteln hätte man sich eine überregionale Einordnung der Forschungen und ihrer Ergebnisse gewünscht, zumal die Ansprache der britischen Siedlungen als Oppida durchaus umstritten ist (vgl. M. FERNÁNDEZ-GÖTZ, A world of 200 oppida. Pre-Roman urbanism in temperate Europe. In: L. de Ligt / J. Bintliff [Hrsg.], Regional Urban Systems in the Roman World. 150 BCE–250 CE [Leiden 2019] 35–66 mit weiterführender Literatur). Ferner wäre auch ein Vergleich der Kleinfunde und der naturwissenschaftlichen Daten mit denen gut erforschter kontinentaler Oppida an mancher Stelle eine Bereicherung gewesen. Des Weiteren weist der Paperback-Einband leider bereits nach kurzem Gebrauch die üblichen Ermüdungserscheinungen auf.

Nichtsdestotrotz stellt „A Biography of Power" eine vorbildliche Vorlage umfassender Untersuchungen des Oppidums von Bagendon dar, an deren Qualität sich zukünftige Forschungen messen müssen. Die versammelte Fachkompetenz, gute Lesbarkeit und die zahlreichen qualitätvollen Abbildungen werden sicher dazu beitragen, dass dieser Fundort auch international mehr Beachtung finden wird.

DE–18233 Schliemannstadt Neubukow
Am Brink 1
E-Mail: winger@neubukow.de
Orcid: https://orcid.org/0000-0002-3984-0635

Katja Winger
Heinrich Schliemann-Gedenkstätte

TINNA MØBJERG / ULLA MANNERING / HANS ROSTHOLM / LISE RÆDER KNUDSEN (Hrsg.), The Hammerum Burial Site. Customs and Clothing in the Roman Iron Age. Jutland Archaeological Society Publications Band 103. Jutland Archaeological Society, Museum Midtjylland, Højbjerg 2019. 300 DKK. ISBN 978-87-93423-23-7. 223 Seiten mit zahlreichen Farbabbildungen.

Die archäologische Textilforschung kann in Skandinavien auf eine lange Tradition zurückblicken, nicht zuletzt begründet durch die bekannten bronzezeitlichen Baumsargfunde wie von Egtved (DK) oder Kleidungsstücke, die in eisenzeitlichen Mooren wie Huldremose in der Nähe von Ramten (DK) entdeckt wurden (M. HALD, Ancient Danish Textiles from Bogs and Burials. A Comparative Study of Costume and Iron Age Textiles. The National Museum of Denmark 11 [Kopenhagen 1980]; U. MANNERING / M. GLEBA / M. BLOCH HANSEN, Denmark. In: M. Gleba / U. Mannering [Hrsg.], Textiles and Textile Production in Europe from Prehistory to AD 400. Ancient Textiles Ser. 11 [Oxford 2012] 91–121). Die teils bereits im 19. und beginnenden 20. Jahrhundert entdeckten Objekte werden immer wieder ergänzt durch bei archäologischer Forschung in Dänemark auftauchende spektakuläre neuere Funde, wie z. B. jene aus Hammerum.

Die nun erschienene reich bebilderte monografische Vorlage der Gräber mit Kleidungs- und Haarresten von Hammerum wurde von der Jutland Archaeological Society als 103. Band ihrer gleichnamigen Publikationsreihe veröffentlicht. „The Hammerum Burial Site. Customs and Clothing in the Roman Iron Age" stellt einen weiteren Meilenstein dar – herausgegeben von Autor*innen, die jeweils als ausgewiesene Expert*innen ihres Fachgebietes bekannt sind:

Ulla Mannering, langjährig tätig am renommierten *Centre for Textile Research* in Kopenhagen und nun als *Senior Researcher* am Dänischen Nationalmuseum Kopenhagen, kann mit Recht als eine Koryphäe im Bereich prähistorischer Textil- und Kleidungsreste in Europa bezeichnet werden. Die Expertise von Lise Ræder Knudsen liegt neben ihrem Hauptaufgabengebiet am *Conservation Centre Vejle* zu konservatorischen Aspekten vor allem auch in ihrem tiefen Verständnis von textilen Fertigungsprozessen, und sie ist eine der führenden Expertinnen in Europa für die Rekonstruktion prähistorischer Webtechniken. Zu den Textilspezialistinnen sind von Seiten des Museum Midtjylland jene zu nennen, die maßgeblich für diesen Fundort, seine Erforschung und auch die öffentliche Präsentation der Objekte verantwortlich sind, namentlich Tinna Møbjerg, die in diesem Museum als *Senior researcher* tätig ist, sowie der Emeritus des Museums, Hans Rostholm. Letzterer war langjähriger Direktor der archäologischen Abteilung des Midtjylland Museum in Herning und war für die Ausgrabungen am Fundort Hammerum verantwortlich. Zu diesen Hauptautor*innen, die das Werk auch herausgegeben haben, gesellen sich Berichte weiterer Spezialist*innen, die bei der Besprechung der einzelnen Kapitel ihre Erwähnung finden werden.

Die Monografie zu „The Hammerum Burial Site" erfüllt nicht nur deshalb ein wichtiges Desiderat in der Forschung, weil es sich um einen sehr wichtigen dänischen Fundplatz handelt. Vor allem wird hier das für unser Verständnis der Geschichte der Kleidung wichtige Grab 83 neben sechs anderen Gräbern mit Textil- und teils Menschenhaarresten in seinen archäologischen Komponenten vorgestellt, wobei auch dem interdisziplinären Forschungsansatz voll Rechnung getragen wird.

Dementsprechend gliedert sich das vorliegende Buch in mehrere Bereiche, die den archäologischen Fundort in seinem Kontext, die in den Gräbern aufgefundenen Textilien und Kleidungsstücke, sowie Funde von Menschenhaar umfassen. Einen sehr großen Teil in diesem Buch nehmen die interdisziplinären Analysemethoden ein, nach denen auch experimentalarchäologische und kulturhistorische Aspekte besprochen werden. Nachfolgend soll nun auf die einzelnen Kapitel näher eingegangen werden.

Nach einer Einführung zur Struktur und Zielsetzung des Buches (Kap. 1 von T. Møbjerg, S. 13–14) erfährt in Kapitel 2 (S. 15–47) von H. Rostholm und L. Ræder Knudsen der Fundort Hammerum eine Darstellung, wobei nach der Kurzcharakterisierung von Fundgeschichte, Topografie und der in die römische Eisenzeit um AD 200 datierenden Gräbergruppe vor allem auf die Gräber mit reichen Textil- und Menschenhaarfunden eingegangen wird. Die Ausgrabung erfolgte im Jahr 1993, dabei wurde jedoch die Bedeutung der organischen Reste erkannt, weshalb die Gräber teils als Blockbergung gesichert wurden. Dies ermöglichte dann sowohl (vor allem zwischen 2009 und 2010) eine detaillierte Ausgrabung im Labor als auch viele begleitende naturwissenschaftliche Detailanalysen (s. Kap. 5). Die in diesem Kapitel erfolgte, mit zahlreichen Bildern unterlegte, sehr plastische Darstellung der Arbeiten an den Blockbergungen führt dabei das große Potenzial dieser Methoden gut vor Augen.

Die beiden Textilspezialistinnen U. Mannering und L. Ræder Knudsen widmen sich im Kapitel 3 „Textile and clothing production" (S. 49–81) der intensiven Analyse der Textilreste vom Fundort Hammerum. Durch die hervorragende Konservierung vor allem des komplett erhaltenen Kleidungsstücks in Grab 83 können wertvolle Informationen zur Gestaltung und zu technischen Details an Kleidungsstücken in der dänischen Römischen Eisenzeit gewonnen werden, die unser Bild zur Kleidungsgeschichte wesentlich ergänzen. Dazu gehören webtechnische Details genauso wie generelle Gestaltungstechniken, Zierborten oder auch die Nähtechnik. Die Erhaltung des Gewandes aus Grab 83 ist so gut, dass selbst Gebrauchsspuren entdeckt werden konnten und somit der Konnex gegeben ist, dass dieses Gewand nicht eine reine Totentracht darstellt, sondern auch zu Lebzeiten getragen worden ist und dadurch Verschleißerscheinungen aufweist.

Ein sehr spannendes Detail, weil höchst selten an anderen Fundstellen erhalten, sind die Funde von Menschenhaar, vor allem da noch Frisuren erkennbar sind. Diese Haarfunde aus den Gräbern 43, 83 und 100 werden in Kapitel 4 (S. 83–95) von Ræder Knudsen und Møbjerg detailliert besprochen, wobei auch Rekonstruktionen der Frisuren am „lebenden Modell" in einem experimentalarchäologischen Ansatz zur Entschlüsselung der Funde beitragen. Rekonstruiert werden Frisuren mit verdrehten, geflochtenen Elementen ebenso wie Haarknoten.

Ein wesentliches Element dieses Buches ist das knapp 70 Seiten starke Kapitel 5 (S. 97–165) zu den interdisziplinären Analysen, die in ihrer Vielfalt und den sowohl wissenschaftlichen als auch konservatorisch-restauratorischen Fragestellungen zunächst von Ræder Knudsen erläutert werden. Dabei wird auch diskutiert, welche davon nicht destruktiv sind und aus welchen Überlegungen heraus dann an welchen Stellen Proben genommen wurden. Solche Erläuterungen einzubinden ist ein gutes Beispiel für eine State-of-the-art-Studie.

Die Analysen selbst beginnen mit Holzuntersuchungen von Peter Hambro Mikkelsen (Kap. 5.2, S. 101–102), der die hölzerne Abdeckung von Grab 83 durch Holzartenanalyse als Birke bestimmen konnte. Danach folgt die AMS ^{14}C-Datierung (Kap. 5.3, S. 103–107), bei der Marie Kastrup und Jan Heinemeier sowohl ihre Methodik als auch die Ergebnisse mit detaillierten Tabellen und Grafiken erläuterten. Die Proben aus verschiedenen Bereichen in den Gräbern 8, 83 und 100 (Holz, Textilien, Haar und Tierhaut) stellen das Gesamtensemble der Gräber in eine Zeit um AD 132–224.

Vor allem Grab 83 mit dem „Hammerum girl" war Gegenstand von aktuellen naturwissenschaftlichen Methoden, wie z. B. die „Soil thin section analysis" durch Nina Helt Nielsen (Kap. 5.4, S. 109–114). Dabei wurden vor allem Daten zu Vorgängen bei der Bestattung selbst und nach der Deponierung des Leichnams und der Beigaben erfasst. Die Textilien aus diesem Grab waren auch Gegenstand von Strontiumisotopenanalysen, (Kap. 5.5 von Karin Margarita Frei, S. 115–120). Diese hatten zum Ziel, die Herkunft der Wolle zu bestimmen – wobei als Bezugssystem auch die Haare des „Hammerum girl" herangezogen wurden, um zu klären, ob das Gewand (bzw. die Wolle, aus dem es gefertigt wurde) und die Person aus derselben geografischen Region stammen. Auch bei dieser sehr modernen Analyse wird zunächst detailliert auf die Methodik eingegangen. Da aufgrund der spezifischen Bodenchemie an dem Fundort die Knochen des Skelettes vergangen waren, zielten chemische Analysen an Proben, die vom Bereich der Kleidung und des Erdreiches genommen wurden, darauf ab, die chemische Signatur des Leichnams selbst zu finden (Kap. 5.6 von Michelle Taube und Jens Glastrup, S. 121–130). Weitere biologische Beobachtungen (Kap. 5.7 von Franz Jensen, S. 131–133) wurden während der Konservierung der Kleidung durchgeführt. Es konnten jedoch keine Kleiderläuse oder Ähnliches entdeckt werden. Zu den verschiedenen Analysemethoden, die zur Untersuchung von Grab 83 herangezogen wurden, gehört auch die Pollenanalyse (Kap. 5.8 von Renée Enevold, S. 135–141). Die Zusammensetzung von Pollen im Grab sollte Aufschluss geben über die Vegetation im Umfeld des Grabes während der Grablegung, wodurch der Vegetationsbestand vor 2000 Jahren rekonstruiert werden konnte. Die detaillierten Pollentabellen und zahlreiche Bilder geben hier gut Aufschluss, dass eine semi-offene Landschaft mit Hasel und Erle sowie trockene Wiesen und Heide vorhanden war. Aufschlussreich war die Konzentration an kultivierten Kräutern, die direkt in Verbindung mit der Kleidung entdeckt wurden – sie bestätigen, dass das „Hammerum girl" in der Kleidung bestattet wurde, die sie auch für ihre alltäglichen Arbeiten getragen hatte.

aDNA-Analysen an den Fasern (Kap. 5.9 von Luise Ørsted Brandt, S. 143–148) sollten Aufschluss geben über die Tierart. Leider war die Methode in diesem Fall nicht erfolgreich, was jedoch Anlass zu einer intensiven Diskussion zur Herausforderung von aDNA Analysen an archäologischem Textilmaterial ergab, die wichtige Impulse für zukünftige Forschungen bringen wird. Zu den in der Textilarchäologie bereits seit einigen Jahrzehnten angewendeten Standardverfahren gehört die Faseranalyse mittels Wollfeinheitsmessungen (Kap. 5.11 von Irene Skals, S. 151–158), deren Zielrichtung es ist, anhand der Fasern auch die Entwicklungsgeschichte der Schafrassen fassen zu können. Auch geben derartige Analysen Aufschluss zu verschiedenen Vorgängen während der Herstellung des Textils (v. a. zu den Aufbereitungsarbeiten der Wolle vor dem Spinnen und Weben). Bereits bei der Auffindung des Gewandes von Grab 83 war ein rot-weißes Farbmuster sichtbar, was eine Farbstoffanalyse (Kap. 5.12 von Ina Vanden Berghe, S. 159–162) logisch erscheinen ließ. Bedauerlicherweise erbrachte sowohl die Farbstoffanalyse als auch die Pigmentanalyse kein positives

Ergebnis. Damit reiht sich der Fund in eine Reihe anderer ein, bei denen zwar optisch ein Farbmuster erkennbar war, jedoch aufgrund der Degradationsprozesse kein naturwissenschaftlicher Nachweis mehr glückte.

CT-Scans des kompletten Textils in der Blockbergung (Kap. 5.10 von Niels Lynnerup und Chiara Villa, S. 149–150) wurden im Lillebælt Hospital in Vejle durchgeführt. Dabei sollten die verschiedenen Lagen des im Grab befindlichen flach gedrückten Gewandes virtuell voneinander getrennt werden. Obwohl dies bei dem Versuch nicht gelang, ist es auch hier wesentlich, über solche fehlgeschlagenen Methoden in einer derartigen Monografie zu berichten, da dies wiederum der Fortentwicklung des wissenschaftlichen Methodenspektrums dient.

Neben den naturwissenschaftlichen Analysen, die ein gutes Spektrum des derzeit in der Textilarchäologie Möglichen aufzeigen, wurde auch die Experimentelle Archäologie angewandt, um eine Replik des Textils 1 (Kleid) herzustellen (Kap. 6 von Ida Demant, S. 167–185). Im Sagnlandet Lejre gibt es dazu eine jahrzehntelange Expertise, auch ein theoretisch-methodisches Grundgerüst, um bei solchen Rekonstruktionen sowohl im handwerklichen Prozess als auch in Trageversuchen vielfältige Aussagen in Bezug auf kulturwissenschaftliche Fragestellungen generieren zu können. Dabei wird bereits bei der Auswahl des Rohmaterials (der Wolle) als auch der verschiedenen Geräte, mit denen gearbeitet wird, großer Wert darauf gelegt, so weit wie möglich dem archäologischen Original zu entsprechen. Fragestellungen zu Details in der *chaîne opératoire*, wie auch zum Zeitaufwand sind so möglich.

Ein so bedeutender Fund wie Grab 83 von Hammerum, liebevoll als das „Hammerum girl" personifiziert, stellt auch Herausforderungen an die museale Präsentation und Öffentlichkeitsarbeit. Tinna Møbjerg vom Midtjylland Museum in Herning, in dem seit 2009 der Fund ausgestellt ist, präsentiert in Kapitel 7 „The Hammerum Girl in the public space" (S. 187–202). Verschiedene Konzepte zur Vermittlung und Öffentlichkeitsarbeit kommen hierbei zum Tragen, wobei selbst die Forschungs- und Konservierungsaktivitäten rund um den Fund Teil der musealen Aktivitäten sind. Onlineauftritte etwa über Facebook sollen ebenfalls ein Kanal zur breiten Öffentlichkeit weltweit sein. Zur Öffentlichkeitsarbeit gehören auch Workshops, die den Fund und die spezifischen Forschungsergebnisse mit der heutigen Welt verknüpfen, so ein Workshop mit Kindern zu den Frisuren, oder ein Projekt mit Studierenden von Mode- und Kunstschulen, die eigene Entwürfe präsentierten oder sogar den Fund künstlerisch umsetzten. In der Landschaft um den Fundort wurde mittels einer Smartphone-App ein eigener Wanderweg gestaltet. Dies sind nur einige der Aktivitäten in der Öffentlichkeitsarbeit, die dem regionalen Museum in Herning einen Aufschwung gaben, und diese in der vorliegenden Monografie zu verschriftlichen ist ein wichtiger Weg, auch in akademischen Kreisen die Wichtigkeit der Öffentlichkeitsarbeit zu positionieren.

Mit dem Kapitel 8 „Perspectives and conclusions" von den Herausgebern dieser Monografie, Møbjerg, Mannering, Rostholm und Ræder Knudsen, schließt diese in jeder Hinsicht bemerkenswerte Publikation (S. 203–216). Noch einmal werden die Gräber und insbesondere Grab 83 reflektiert und in Beziehung gesetzt zu anderen zeitgleichen Funden, wobei hier mit dem typochronologischen Vergleich des Fundmaterials die klassischen Methoden der Archäologie genauso zum Tragen kommen wie eine Diskussion der Grabtypen. Es werden auch Überlegungen angestellt, inwieweit sich in den Funden vor allem von Grab 83 auch römische Einflüsse abzeichnen. Gesamt gesehen können aus diesem Fund vielerlei neue Erkenntnisse zum Bestattungswesen in der frühen Römischen Eisenzeit in Dänemark gewonnen werden, basierend auf den zahlreichen, in diesem Band hervorragend dargestellten, interdisziplinären Studien.

Interdisziplinäre Forschung im Sinne der von Kristian Kristiansen so definierten „Third Science Revolution (K. Kristiansen, Towards a new paradigm? The Third Science Revolution and its possible consequences in archaeology. Current Swedish Arch. 22, 2014, 11–34) zeichnet sich nicht nur dadurch aus, dass verschiedene neueste naturwissenschaftliche Ansätze und Analysemethoden an einem Fundensemble angewandt werden, sondern auch dadurch, dass diese Erkenntnisse wieder zurückbezogen werden auf den Kontext, die Funde und die sich daraus ergebenden kulturhistorischen Aussagen. Dies ist m. E. bei diesem Werk vorzüglich gelungen.

Der an Textiltechnologie und Kleidungsgeschichte interessierten Leserschaft sei dieses Buch wärmstens ans Herz gelegt. Das Buch wendet sich auch an alle Archäolog*innen, Kunst- und Kulturgeschichtler*innen, wie durch das am Ende des Buches abgedruckte Glossar zu textiltechnologischen Begriffen angezeigt wird, das einen niederschwelligen Zugang zu den in dem Werk behandelten Themen bietet. Dieses Buch kann daher mit Recht als Standardwerk weit über das Forschungsfeld der Textilarchäologie hinaus aufgefasst werden.

AT–1010 Wien
Burgring 7
E-Mail: Karina.groemer@nhm-wien.ac.at
Orcid: https://orcid.org/0000-0001-5711-8059

Karina Grömer
Naturhistorisches Museum Wien

Falko Weis, Der Goldmünzhort und die spätlatènezeitlichen Münzen aus Riegel am Kaiserstuhl. Freiburger Beiträge zur Archäologie und Geschichte des ersten Jahrtausends Band 19. Verlag Marie Leidorf GmbH, Rahden / Westf. 2019. € 45.80. ISBN 978-3-89646-779-9. 148 pages with 37 figures, 14 tables and 14 plates.

This slim volume publishes the Iron Age coins, including a hoard of gold ones, found in the excavation of a Late Iron Age settlement at Riegel am Kaiserstuhl (DE) in 2000/01. The site, which was occupied in the later second and earlier first centuries BC (La Tène C2–D1), is located close to the confluence of the rivers Elz and Dreisam and within 10 km from the Rhine, and was part of a well-developed settlement network in the Upper Rhine region. The volume is based on a master's thesis submitted in 2014 to the Albert-Ludwigs-Universität Freiburg supervised by Christoph Huth, assisted by Michael Nick of the *Inventar der Fundmünzen der Schweiz*. The work is divided into three parts. "Teil I" (pp. 9–22) introduces the settlement at Riegel and gold coins and gold coin hoards of the La Tène period. "Teil II" (pp. 19–62) comprises the bulk of the work and is devoted to accounts of the different types of coins that are supported by a detailed catalogue, 1:1 illustrations of the coins in colour and in high-contrast black and white, and details of the findspots of the types and distribution maps. The gold coins were analysed with Energy Dispersive X-Ray Fluorescent (EDXRF) by Andreas Burkhardt (p. 26 and tab. 9). "Teil III" (pp. 63–84) presents an evaluation of the study and an interpretation of the significance of the coins from Riegel in their regional context.

The 27 coins in the hoard comprise almost equal numbers of the widely distributed ostgallischen Radstatere and the much less common oberrheinische Statere, whose distribution is much more localised. No east Gaulish quarter-staters, which are rare, were included in the hoard. The other 40 coins are interpreted as casual losses and comprise cast potin and struck bronze issues in equal numbers, as well as a single silver one. The potins are all well-known types attributed to the Leuci, Sequani and Lingones and the silver coin is a well-known KALETEDOY quinarius issue. In contrast, the struck bronzes, which Weis christens the Riegel type, are known from only one other site, the settlement at Kirchzarten-Zarten 'Rotacker' (DE) near Tarodunum, c. 30 km away. A miniature bronze wheel, sometimes considered to be a form of currency, is also catalogued but not discussed further. The accounts of the different coin types largely follow Michael Nick (Die keltischen Münzen vom Typ „Sequanerpotin". Eine Studie zu Typologie, Chronologie und geographischer Zuweisung eines ostgallischen Münztyps. Freiburger Beitr. Arch. u. Gesch. erstes Jahrtausend 2 [Rahden / Westf. 2000]; M. Nick, Gabe, Opfer, Zahlungsmittel. Strukturen keltischen Münzgebrauchs im westlichen Mitteleuropa. Freiburger Beitr. Arch. u. Gesch. erstes Jahrtausend 12,1–2 [Rahden / Westf. 2006]) but Weis develops new typologies for the oberrheinische Statere and the Riegel types (pp. 31–47). As 20 Riegel type coins were found, compared to the four at Kirchzarten, Weis reasonably suggests that the type was issued at Riegel (p. 35) and that, because the settlement appears to have passed out of use by the second quarter of the first century BC (i. e. by La Tène D2), they are also the earliest struck bronze issues in the Upper Rhine. Although the Riegel type coins are not well-preserved, a little more could perhaps have been said about origins of the designs on them, which largely comprise separate symbols, some of which recall those on Rolltierestatere-type Regenbogenschüsselchen. On page 35 a piece of bronze which is suggested to be a coin blank may in reality simply be a piece of manufacturing waste although this does not affect the suggestion that Riegel type coins were made there. A failed casting is also suggested to indicate that potin coins were also made at Riegel but it is also not clear that the fragment is from a coin mould and all the potins found at Riegel are of well-known types with the site lying at the edge of most of their distributions.

The book is well-written and well-produced in the familiar *Freiburger Beiträge zur Archäologie und Geschichte des ersten Jahrtausends* format, and it follows two earlier volumes in the series on Iron Age coins by M. Nick (2000; 2006). Both the colour and high contrast black and white photographs of the coins are well reproduced but the location map, which shows principally soil types, is too small and the plan of the excavation is informative but does not show the location of the hoard. The appendices of findspots, which largely repeat information published by Nick, are printed in a larger font than the main text.

At present coinage provides the best evidence for the nature of the Riegel settlement as the reports on the 2000 and 2001 excavations and subsequent ones in 2003 and 2004 have yet to be published. It is clear that there was intensive coin use as the 40 site losses were found, presumably mainly in pits and postholes (their contexts are not given) in an area of only approximately 1200 m². In the final section Weis suggests that Riegel was a central place in the Upper Rhine settlement network, like the one at nearby Limberg-Sasbach (DE), and that these centres were linked to each other and to more distant ones such as Basel-Gasfabrik (CH) by a system of intensive production and exchange (cf. pp. 53–58). He argues that in La Tène C2–D1 there was a market economy in the Upper Rhine region that employed a trimetallic coinage of gold, silver, and bronze (initially only of potin but then also including struck bronzes). This would imply that gold coinage, which was previously a very high-value unit of wealth with a limited range of uses, had now become a general-purpose money. This is a tempting conclusion, but unlike the potin and bronze coins, the gold coins found at Riegel were not casual losses; they were placed in a pot and buried and so, despite the discovery of a plated *oberrheinische Stater* with an iron core at Basel-Gasfabrik, this could also be interpreted as indicating that gold coins were never a general-purpose money. Thanks to this publication by Falko Weis, the coins from Riegel will play a part in this long-running debate.

UK–Leicester LE1 7RH
University Road
E-Mail: af215@leicester.ac.uk
Orcid: https://orcid.org/0000-0002-9545-9417

Andrew P. Fitzpatrick
University of Leicester
Archaeology and Ancient History

Markus Schussmann, Die Kelten in Bayern. Archäologie und Geschichte. Verlag Friedrich Pustet, Regensburg 2019. € 39,95. ISBN 978-3-7917-3093-6. 415 Seiten mit zahlreichen Verbreitungskarten, Fotos und graphischen Abbildungen von Plänen, Rekonstruktionen und Artefakten.

Es ist eine schwierige Aufgabe, nach jetzt schon unzähligen Übersichtswerken über „die Kelten" eine neue, spannende Zusammenfassung zu liefern. Ich möchte nur einige solcher Werke – in chronologischer Reihenfolge ihres Erscheinens – erwähnen, die auch oft das Ergebnis von großen und erfolgreichen Ausstellungen waren (eine Vollständigkeit ist natürlich nicht gegeben). Beginnen möchte ich mit dem Katalog der Landesausstellung „Die Kelten in Mitteleuropa" 1980 in Hallein (Hallein 1981), der umfassenden Ausstellung „I Celti" (Venedig 1991) und der gleichzeitig stattfindenden Ausstellung mit dem Begleitbuch „Die Kelten im Osten Österreichs" (St. Pölten 1992) von Johannes-Wolfgang Neugebauer – eine „Neuauflage" zur Latènekultur im Osten Österreichs ist bereits erschienen (P. Trebsche [Hrsg.], Keltische Münzstätten und Heiligtümer. Die jüngere Eisenzeit im Osten Österreichs [ca. 450 bis 15 v. Chr.]. Archäologie Niederösterreichs [Wien 2020]). Es folgten „Das keltische Jahrtausend" (Rosenheim 1993) und der Band „Die Schweiz vom Paläolithikum bis zum frühen Mittelalter: Vom Neandertaler bis zu Karl dem Großen. 4. Eisenzeit" (Basel 1999) von Felix Müller, Gilbert Kaenel und Geneviève Lüscher, die „Encyclopedie Keltů v Čechách" (Praha 2001) von Jiří Waldhauser und „Kelten in Deutschland" (Stuttgart 2001) von Sabine Rieckhoff und Jörg Biel. Im Jahre 2004 erscheinen die „Encyclopedie Keltů na Moravě a ve Slezsku" (Brno 2004) von Jana Čižmářová und „Kelten in der Schweiz" (Stuttgart 2004) von Felix Müller und Geneviève Lüscher. Die nächste Großausstellung in Bern bzw. Stuttgart bedingt den Begleitkatalog „Kunst der Kelten" (Stuttgart 2009). Schließlich folgen im östlichen Mitteleuropa „Die keltische Besiedlung der Slowakei" (Nitra 2010) von Karol Pieta und „The Eastern Celts" (Koper 2011) von Mitja Guštin und Miloš Jevtić. Atemlos folgen „Die Welt der Kelten" (Stuttgart 2012) und der Band „Iron Age" aus der Serie „The Prehistory of Bohemia" (Praha 2013) von Nathalie Venclová und ihrem Team. Abgeschlossen werden soll die Liste mit dem Band zur Keltenausstellung im Prager Nationalmuseum „The Celts. Bohemia from the 8th Century to the 1st Century BC" (Prag 2019), hrsg. von Jiří Militký, Jan Kysela und Marika Tisucká.

Der Band „Die Kelten in Bayern" ist als allgemeiner Überblick zu werten, wendet sich also v. a. an interessierte Fachfremde, kann aber sicher auch für Studierende als Einstiegsliteratur gut verwendet werden. Er folgt der Struktur von „Die Kelten in der Schweiz" oder „Die Kelten in Mitteleuropa", indem allgemeine Kapitel von Quellenkunde bis Kunst behandelt und die jeweiligen lokalen Bezüge und Fundorte miteinbezogen werden. Ein Katalog mit einer kurzen Beschreibung der Fundorte, wie in „Encyclopedie Keltů na Moravě a ve Slezsku" oder „Kelten in Deutschland", ist in diesem Buch nicht vorgesehen, die wichtigsten sind in den Kapiteln eingearbeitet und ausgeführt.

Die genaue Struktur sieht folgendermaßen aus: Nach den obligatorischen Einleitungskapiteln wird die ebensolche Frage nach den Kelten gestellt (S. 10–11), es folgen die Quellen der antiken Autoren und der Archäologie (S. 12–17) und die Forschungsgeschichte (S. 18–26). Bei den Quellen sticht die treffende Bemerkung, dass „nicht alle keltischen Männer von der Iberischen Halbinsel bis ins Anatolische Hochland ungestutzte Schnauzbärte und karierte Hosen getragen hätten" heraus – ein erster Hinweis auf die große Regionalität der „Latènekultur". Bemerkenswert bei der Forschungsgeschichte ist der dreiseitge Abriss über die Chronologie in Bayern für die Vertiefung in die lokale Materie (S. 22–24).

Es folgt das Kapitel über „Archäologie und Geschichte" (S. 27–51), in dem der Zeitraum von der Hallstattzeit bis zur römischen Eroberung aufgerollt wird. Die oft gezeigte Karte mit der flächenmäßigen Ausbreitung der „Latènekultur" (Abb. 24) ist schwer in Diskussion (J. Collis, The

Celts. Origins, Myths and Inventions [Stroud 2003]) und vermittelt einen falschen Eindruck, weil es sich nicht um eine einheitliche Kulturerscheinung bzw. ein „Volk" handelt, sondern um lokale Kulturen, die durch bestimmte, archäologisch definierte Faktoren miteinander verbunden sind. Darauf folgt „Aussehen, Wesen und Gesellschaft" (S. 52–81), wo einer obligaten Aufzählung von antiken Quellen die archäologischen Quellen gegenübergestellt werden. Dies wird in die Unterkapitel „Tracht und Schmuck" und „Kriegshandwerk und Bewaffnung" unterteilt, wobei zweiteres Kapitel die erhöhte Aufmerksamkeit des Autors erfährt. Zahlreiche Beispiele von Funden aus Bayern illustrieren die Ausführungen. Die schon häufig abgedruckten Abbildungen von Peter Connolly (Abb. 62; 76; 79; 80) hätten besser durch Umzeichnungen ersetzt werden sollen. Einen sehr großen Teil nimmt das Kapitel „Siedlungswesen" (S. 82–188) ein. Dabei werden neben den dörflichen Flachlandsiedlungen, befestigte Höhensiedlungen, Großsiedlungen sowie Oppida, Refugia und „Viereckschanzen" aber auch übergreifende Aspekte wie „Veränderungen der Siedlungsschwerpunkte" behandelt. Auch ein Ausblick in die ausgehende Latènezeit (S. 175–181) und schließlich noch ein kurzer anschaulicher Überblick über Hausbau und Architektur in der Latènezeit wird gegeben.

Wie oben erwähnt, schöpft der Autor in diesem Kapitel voll aus dem Fundus seiner Erfahrung und gibt diesem Kapitel eine eigene Richtung, die sich beispielsweise in Fallbeispielen wie zu den Palisadengehöften und „Herrenhöfen" wie in Niedererlbach und Kyberg wiederfindet. Bei den Höhensiedlungen stechen natürlich der Staffelberg (mit der extra geschützten Akropolis) und die höchst interessante Ehrenbürg hervor. Auch der einzige „Fürstensitz" in Bayern, der Marienberg, wird hervorgehoben. Schließlich sind es die unbefestigten Großsiedlungen mit vorindustriellem Charakter wie Berching-Pollanten (Salz) oder Steinebach (Glas), die als treffende Fallbeispiele gebracht werden. Bei den Oppida („Städte keltischer Prägung") und den Refugien stechen natürlich das allzeit berühmte Manching in der Schotterebene mit seiner annähernd kreisförmigen Ummauerung, der Staffelberg und Kelheim hervor, die den Charakter dieser Siedlungsform in Latène C2/D1 hervorragend darstellen. Den Todesstoß erhielten diese Städte (unter anderem) durch die Vernichtung des gallischen Systems und der daraus folgenden Unterbrechung der lebensnotwendigen Fernhandelskontakte.

Das ebenfalls umfassende Kapitel „Totenwelten" (S. 189–243) widmet sich den Grab- und Bestattungssitten in ihren vielfältigen Ausprägungen. Dabei handelt es sich um eine der wichtigsten Quellen der Archäologie der Eisenzeit, um sich dem Individuum an sich zu nähern.

Angefangen bei den Grab- und Bestattungssitten der Hallstattzeit geht der Autor zu denen der Frühlatènezeit über, wobei auch die Nachbestattungen in alten Grabhügeln, wie z. B. in Drosendorf, erwähnt werden. Dass zu Beginn der Latènezeit auch eigene Grabhügel angelegt wurden, wie beispielsweise in Höresham (S. 219) oder Heroldsberg (S. 215), fügt sich in ein bekanntes Bild (das auch aus Ostösterreich, beispielsweise in Rassing, bekannt ist: P. C. Ramsl, Tracht und Schmuck der Frühlatènezeit. In: P. Trebsche [Hrsg.], Keltische Münzstätten und Heiligtümer. Die jüngere Eisenzeit im Osten Österreichs [ca. 450 bis 15 v. Chr.]. Arch. Niederösterreich 2 [Wien 2020] 334–345; 402–423). Neben den regulären Bestattungen finden sich zahlreiche Skelette in Siedlungsgruben (wie z. B. in Unterpleichfeld). Ob es sich dabei um Entsorgungen oder um „verkehrte" Bestattungen handelt (P. Trebsche, Latènezeitliche Leichen im Keller? Überlegungen zur Deutung von Siedlungsbestattungen im österreichischen Donauraum. In: L. Husty / K. Schmotz [Hrsg.], Vorträge des 34. Niederbayerischen Archäologentages [Rahden / Westf. 2016] 79–117) ist noch schwer in Diskussion. Auch Schachthöhlen wie der Dietersbergschacht und die Kirschbaumhöhle mit ihren mannigfaltigen Funden werden zur Diskussion gestellt. Schließlich folgt der (einst von Jan Filip) postulierte „Flachgräberhorizont" mit den bayrischen Gräberfeldern, wie beispielsweise in Manching, Rieckofen oder Dornach (S. 227–235), um nur einige wenige hervorzuheben.

Bemerkenswert sind die spätlatènezeitlichen Gräber (S. 237–243) wie in Manching, Kelheim, Grünwald und Erding (die wir beispielsweise in Ostösterreich vermissen).

Schließlich folgt das Kapitel „Fernbeziehungen und Eliten" (S. 244–271), welches sich in zeitlicher Abfolge gliedert. Angefangen wird mit der Älteren Eisenzeit mit den hallstattzeitlichen Gräbern mit Wagenbeigabe (Abb. 322), bei denen sich der Autor mit verschiedenen Aspekten der damaligen Gesellschaft, wie Güteraustausch, Tempelbezirken (Abb. 324) sowie „Besitz- und Machtansprüchen", Verkehrsanbindungen und Fernverbindungen, die zum damaligen Güteraustausch notwendig waren, auseinandersetzt. Als außerordentliche Beispiele für verhandelte Güter bzw. südlichen Vorbildern nachempfundene Artefakte sollen Elfenbein und Bratspieße mit eisernen Feuerböcken genannt werden, aber auch Bernsteincolliers und italische Figurinen wie in Ehringen (Abb. 337). Schließlich folgt der Abschnitt über die Übernahme der Fibelmode aus dem italischen Raum und auch der Bronzegefäße wie Situlen und Becken. In der Jüngeren Eisenzeit dünnen anscheinend die Kontakte und damit die Importe aus. Sklavenketten, Silberfibeln, einige Bronzegefäße, Gemmenringe und Reste von hellenistischen Glasgefäßen geben einen Eindruck der Verbindungen.

Im Kapitel „Wirtschaftsleben" (S. 272–331) wird ein Überblick über die Produktion von Gütern jeder Art in der Eisenzeit geboten. Nach der landwirtschaftlichen Produktion (Pflugscharen, Sensen, Mühlsteine) werden das Schmiedehandwerk und seine vielfältigen Produkte, das Handwerk mit Bronze und Edelmetallen (wie Münzen), Glas und die Töpferei sowie Holz- und Geweih- / Knochenbearbeitung vorgestellt. Schließlich finden sich noch kurze Abschnitte über chirurgische Instrumente, Ressourcennutzung und Handel sowie Maße und Gewichte und Schriftlichkeit.

Danach folgt das für die „keltische" Periode so wichtige Kapitel „Kunst" (S. 332–363). Nach einigen grundsätzlichen Worten zum Terminus Kunst und einer Einschätzung zu Kunst in vergangenen Zeiten beginnt dieser Abschnitt mit der Hallstattzeit. Hier wirft der Autor die Frage nach dem „Hallstatt-Stil" auf. Außer einem starken Hang zur Geometrie ist dieser nicht zu erkennen, auch durch die oft kleinregionalen Variationen quer über Europa (S. 333). Andererseits dürfen auch die figürlichen Darstellungen nicht vergessen werden, die zum Beispiel als tönernes Pferdchen aus Prächting oder mit dem menschlichen Figürchen aus Pfaffenhof (Abb. 438) auftreten. Der nächste Abschnitt widmet sich den Latène-Stilen, beginnend mit dem „Frühen Stil". Nach einer kurzen Bemerkung zur Entstehung der Latènekunst wird beispielsweise über die figürlichen Fibeln (Tier, Vogelkopf und Masken) ausgeführt und mit Beispielen aus Bayern veranschaulicht. Weitere prominente Beispiele aus Bayern wie die Trense von Donauwörth, die mit Tieren verzierte Linsenflasche aus Matzhausen, die Tonschnabelkanne von der Ehrenbürg und die Schale von Thalmässing (Abb. 456) werden ausführlich abgehandelt. Die Prachtstücke aus Parsberg und Ostheim werden extra vorgestellt. Die Verbreitungskarte dazu ist leider etwas ungenau. Bei dem ansprechenden Abschnitt über die durchbrochenen Gürtelhaken fehlt leider bei Abb. 450 die Ansprache als „Typ Dürrnberg" (erstmals Th. STÖLLNER, Kontakt, Mobilität und Kulturwandel im Frühlatènekreis – das Beispiel Frühlatènegürtelhaken. In: E. Jerem / M. Schönfelder / G. Wieland [Hrsg.], Nord-Süd, Ost-West Kontakte während der Eisenzeit in Europa. Archaeolingua [Main Ser.] 17 [Budapest 2010] 277–319). Auch bei der Verbreitungskarte der Schwertscheiden mit „Drachenkopfpaar" (Abb. 451) fehlen leider zahlreiche Fundorte (vgl. z. B. N. GINOUX, Le theme symbolique de « la paire de dragons » sur les fourreaux celtiques [4ᵉ–2ᵉ siècles avant J. -C.]. Etude iconographique et typologie. BAR Internat. Ser. 1702 [Oxford 2007]). Als weiterer Stil der Latènekunst wird der Waldalgesheimstil vorgestellt und mit Beispielen aus dem Gräberfeld von Manching und einem unikaten Schleudergeschoss von der Ehrenbürg veranschaulicht. Der sich aus dem vorher genannten Stil heraus entwickelnde „Plastische Stil" kann in Bayern mit zahlreichen Beispielen aufwarten, wie den beinahe schon abstrakt anmutenden Hohlbuckelringen aus Erding, Straubing-Alburg (Abb. 461) und Aholming. Der mit Pseudofiligran verzierte Reif aus München-Moosbach verweist in den östlichen Bereich. Aus der figürlichen Kategorie sind als Beispiele die Achsnägel und eine Gürtelkette aus Manching bebildert. Schließlich befasst sich der Autor kurz mit dem „Schwertstil", bei dem vor allem die gegenständig angeordneten Drachen- oder Greifenmotive hervorgehoben werden. Der sogenannte „Späte Stil", der auch mit der Oppida-Kultur in Verbindung gebracht wird, ist durch einen Hang zum Naturalismus gekennzeichnet, das Ornament an sich tritt in den Hintergrund.

Ein höchst interessantes, doch schwer zu fassendes Thema wird im Kapitel „Religion" (S. 364–384) behandelt. Wie der Autor treffend bemerkt, lassen sich „nur im bescheidenen Umfang" Aussagen hierzu treffen und nur durch „Schlaglichter" einzelne, mögliche Indizien enttarnen. Einerseits bieten „naturheilige", besondere Orte mit Deponierungen Hinweise auf kultische Handlungen. Bei den Gräberfeldern finden sich zeitweise Umfassungen ohne Grablege (wie in Litzendorf-Naisa), die zeremoniellen Zwecken gedient haben können, wie auch in Ostösterreich z. B. in Franzhausen angenommen wird (P. C. RAMSL, Des sanctuaires de l'âge Du Fer en autriche. In: P. Barral / A. Daubigney / C. Dunning / G. Kaenel / M.-J. Roulière-Lambert [Hrsg.], L'âge du Fer dans l'arc jurassien et ses marges. Dépôts, lieux sacrés et territorialité à l'âge du Fer. Actes du XXIXe colloque international de l'AFEAF; Bienne, 5-8 mai 2005 [Besançon 2007] 831–837). Gewisse außergewöhnliche Strukturen in Siedlungen werden Tempelbezirken zugeordnet, wie in Kösching, Velburg und natürlich Manching. Der Frühlatènezeit zugewiesen werden der „Altar von Kosbach" (Abb. 487) oder der Befund von Greding-Günzenhofen mit einem Hirschgeweih (Abb. 489), bei dem kultisch-religiöses Verhalten postuliert wird. Hier werden auch die Ausprägungen der plastisch gestalteten Fibeln wie Fabelwesen und Köpfe mit oft übergroßen Augen als Indizien für religiöses Handeln zitiert. Amulette und andere Anhänger aus den verschiedensten Materialien sollen unheilabwehrende Wirkung gehabt haben. In der mittleren und späten Latènezeit scheint sich ein tiefgreifender Wandel im Bestattungsbrauchtum und den Jenseitsvorstellungen vollzogen zu haben, der sich (zumindest in Bayern, nicht aber in Ostösterreich, anders als oft dargestellt – P. C. RAMSL, Cremation burials, weapon burials and biritual burials of the Latène period in North-Eastern Austria. In: M. Karwowski / B. Komoróczy / P. C. Ramsl [Hrsg.], Archaeological Studies of the Late Iron Age in Central Europe. Spisy Arch. Ústavu Av Čr Brno 71 [Brno 2021] 25–34) in der Durchsetzung der Brandbestattung zeigt. Daneben werden allerdings noch andere Formen der Bestattung neu kreiert, wie das Deponieren von Leichenteilen in sogenannten „Heiligtümern", die dann oft als Menschenopfer angesprochen werden. Deponierungen von verschiedensten Fundgattungen, wie z. B. Waffen und Kleinplastiken von Tieren, werden ebenfalls zahlreich.

Im letzten Kapitel „Eine alte Frage zum Schluss", das ich als „Nachleben (?)" (S. 385–388) bezeichnen möchte, wird wieder einmal die Frage bemüht, ob die Bayern von den Boiern abstammen, die der Autor kurz und bündig negativ beantwortet. Schließlich wird noch ein kurzer Abriss der historischen Entwicklungen über das Regnum Noricum bis zur römischen Okkupation geboten.

Abgeschlossen wird das umfassende Werk mit einem umfangreichen Literaturverzeichnis (S. 389–406) und einem praktischen Namens- und Ortsregister (S. 407–412).

Leider fehlen Zitate im oder unter dem Text, zumal auch das Literaturverzeichnis nicht in Kapitel eingeteilt, sondern durchgehend ist. Auch in einem Sachbuch wäre hier eine andere Struktur womöglich lesefreundlicher gewesen. Eine durchnummerierte Verbreitungskarte (zumindest) der erwähnten Fundorte wäre ebenfalls sehr hilfreich gewesen – vielleicht kann diese ja noch vom Verlag nachgedruckt und als Faltblatt beigelegt werden bzw. online zur Verfügung gestellt werden. Zahlreiche Verbreitungskarten erleichtern dem geneigten Leser*innen das Verstehen gewisser Themen und Problematiken, bei manchen überregionalen Karten (z. B. Abb. 328; 345; 346) scheint mir jedoch das östliche Mitteleuropa etwas vernachlässigt worden zu sein.

Zusammenfassend kann aber gesagt werden, dass dieses Buch eine akribisch recherchierte, lang erwartete Zusammenstellung des Wissens über die ausgehende Hallstattzeit und die Latènezeit in Bayern darstellt, auf die viele Latèneforscher*innen (nicht nur in Österreich) sehnsüchtig gewartet haben, auch um es Studierenden als reich bebildertes Nachschlagwerk empfehlen zu können! Auch für interessierte Laien stellt es sicher ein umfassendes Nachschlagewerk dar. Es ist mir aus eigener Erfahrung bewusst, dass ein solcher Überblick Schwerstarbeit und einen erheblichen Zeitaufwand (auch bei der Beschaffung der Abbildungen) bedeutet. Gewisse angedeutete Schwächen und Fehler stellen daher nur marginale Mängel in diesem Werk dar.

A–1190 Wien
Franz-Klein-Gasse 1
E-Mail: peter.ramsl@univie.ac.at
Orcid: https://orcid.org/0000-0002-1906-3875

Peter C. Ramsl
Universität Wien
Institut für Urgeschichte und Historische Archäologie

Andrzej Kokowski, Illerup Ådal 15. **Kleinfunde zivilen Charakters.** Jutland Archaeological Society Publications = Jysk Arkæologisk Selskabs Skrifter 25. Aarhus Universitetsforlag, Aarhus 2019. 400 DKK. ISBN 978-87-93423-39-8. 235 Seiten mit 21 Fundlisten, 121 Abbildungen und einer Tafel.

Die Aufarbeitung der Ergebnisse der Grabungsarbeiten, die in den Jahren 1950–56 unter der Leitung von Harald Andersen und seit 1975 von Jørgen Ilkjær auf der Moorfundstelle im Illerup Ådal (DK) im östlichen Teil der Kimbrischen Halbinsel durchgeführt wurden, in der Publikationsreihe ist eine der bedeutendsten Errungenschaften der Archäologie des „barbarischen" Europa in den letzten dreißig Jahren. In der Römischen Kaiserzeit war die hier erwähnte Fundstelle ein See, in den die von besiegten Angreifern erbeuteten Waffen und persönlichen Gebrauchsgegenstände hineingeworfen wurden. Wir haben es somit mit Überbleibseln der sogenannten lebendigen Kultur zu tun, die nicht selten gleichzeitig deponiert wurden, was im Hinblick auf die archäologischen Quellen lediglich sporadisch vorkommt. Seit 1990 erschienen 15 Bände monographischer Aufarbeitung der Ergebnisse von Grabungen im Illerup Ådal, herausgegeben in der Serie Jutland Archaeological Society Publications. Die Redakteur*innen dieser Bände sind Spezialist*innen für die Römische Kaiserzeit im nördlichen Barbaricum. In den bisherigen Bänden wurden Lanzen- und Speerspitzen, Gürtelgarnituren (Schnallen, verschiedene Beschläge und am Gürtel hängende Geräte), Prachtausrüstungen der Krieger, Beschläge der Schilde, Schwerter, Bogen und Pfeilspitzen, Äxte, sowie Münzen, die in am Gürtel befestigten Beuteln getragen wurden, aufgearbeitet und vorgelegt. Der letzte Band, aus der Feder von Andrzej Kokowski, widmet sich den sogenannten Kleingegenständen „zivilen Charakters", die also keine Militaria sind.

Die Analyse umfasst 153 Funde, die man in der Mehrzahl nicht als charakteristisch für die Ausrüstung der Krieger des europäischen Barbaricums erachten kann; im Gegenteil, sie sind erkennbar als Elemente weiblicher Tracht, wie z. B. dekorative Halsketten aus Glas- und Bernsteinperlen. Aufgearbeitet wurden verschiedene Arten von Anhängern (eimerförmige Anhänger, durchbrochen gearbeitete Anhänger, Kapselanhänger), außerdem verschiedene Typen von Glasperlen und aus Bernstein gefertigte Gegenstände (Rohmaterial, Perlen, Spielwürfel) sowie S-förmige Schließhaken der Halsketten und Fragmente von Glasgefäßen. Es erscheint in diesem Zusammenhang ein methodisch schwer zu lösendes Problem, die Frage zu beantworten, unter welchen Umständen diese Gegenstände in den Besitz eventueller Krieger gelangten und in welchen Regionen des Barbaricums sie geraubt wurden.

Entsprechend der von Jørgen Ilkjær vorgeschlagenen Methode der Aufarbeitung der im Illerup Ådal deponierten Funde wird im ersten Kapitel (S. 9–26) des Buches der archäologische Fundkontext der Objekte dargestellt. Infolge einer sehr genauen Analyse der Fundstelle wurde festgestellt, dass die Gegenstände zivilen Charakters in Konzentrationen auftreten, die in den meisten Fällen als Überbleibsel der Beutel interpretiert werden, die die Krieger am Gürtel trugen. In diesem Fall knüpft der Verfasser der Arbeit an die Ergebnisse der Rekonstruktion der Gürtel aus dem Illerup Ådal aus der Feder von J. Ilkjær aus dem Jahr 1993 an (J. ILKJÆR, Illerup Ådal 3–4. Die Gürtel. Bestandteile und Zubehör [Aarhus 1993]). Die graphische und photographische Dokumentation der Konzentrationen von Artefakten ermöglicht der Leserschaft die problemlose Ermittlung der Standorte der untersuchten Gegenstände auf der Fundstelle und ihres Auftretens gemeinsam mit anderen Elementen der Ausrüstung.

In den nachfolgenden Kapiteln (2–17) wird die antiquarische Untersuchung von Gegenständen zivilen Charakters dargestellt. Der Verfasser bespricht einzelne Objektkategorien und stellt knapp die Geschichte ihrer Erforschung dar. Dabei verwendet er die in der Literatur gängigen Klassifikationen, die er stellenweise zutreffend ergänzt. Dies gilt insbesondere für die metallenen Anhänger, die Ines BEILKE-VOIGT (Frühgeschichtliche Miniaturobjekte mit Amulettcharakter zwischen Britischen Inseln und Schwarzem Meer. Univforsch. Prähist. Arch. 51 [Bonn 1998]) aufarbeitete. Die Bestimmung der Herkunft der untersuchten Gegenstände, die im Illerup Ådal deponiert waren, bedurfte der Zusammenstellung eines enormen Vergleichsmaterials. Es entstanden imposante Fundlisten mit gleichartigen Artefakten aus verschiedenen Regionen des europäischen Barbaricums, einschließlich der Gebiete am Schwarzen Meer. Berücksichtigt wurden die neuesten Daten, die in den von der Römisch-Germanischen Kommission herausgegebenen Bänden „Corpus der römischen Funde im europäischen Barbaricum" und in den Bänden der Serie „Monumenta Archaeologica Barbarica", deren Herausgeber das Archäologische Museum Warschau ist, enthalten sind. Beachtenswert sind auch neue Verbreitungskarten, die die räumliche Ausdehnung der untersuchten Funde zeigen und auf ihre Chronologie eingehen. Eine Ergänzung zu den Untersuchungsergebnissen sind Tabellen und Diagramme. Zu nennen ist noch eine sehr umfangreiche Bibliographie, die die neuesten einschlägigen Veröffentlichungen umfasst.

Eine beträchtliche Serie bilden im untersuchten Material eimerförmige Anhänger aus Eisen sowie aus Kupfer- und Silberlegierungen (Kap. 2, S. 27–48). Der Verfasser unterscheidet hier Anhänger, die über einen Einzelkörper (Gruppe I), und solche, die über einen Doppelkörper (Gruppe II) verfügen. Die Form des Körpers ist in der Gruppe I Grundlage für die Einteilung in einzelne Typen: röhrenförmig (Typ A: Untertypen A1 – schlank und A2 – flach), trapezoid (Typ B), sanduhrförmig (Typ C) und vielkantig (Typ D). Die Analyse der Verbreitung der genannten Typen von eimerförmigen Anhängern (unter Berücksichtigung der verwendeten Rohstoffe) führte zu wichtigen Feststellungen. Sie erlaubte dem Verfasser nachzuweisen, dass die Anhänger, die dem Typ IA1 und IA2 entsprechen, hauptsächlich im westlichen Teil des Ostseebeckens einschließlich der dänischen Inseln getragen wurden. Die im Illerup Ådal entdeckten eisernen Anhänger stammen möglicherweise aus dem Verbreitungsgebiet der Przeworsk-Kultur, wo die aus diesem Rohstoff gefertigten Exemplare dominieren. Das Auftreten des Anhängers mit dem Doppelkörper (Typ II) kann wiederum ein Hinweis auf Kontakte zu den Sarmaten sein. Darauf deutet auch der im Material aus dem Illerup Ådal befindliche durchbrochen gearbeitete Anhänger aus einer Kupferlegierung hin (Kap. 3, S. 49–62). Zum ersten Mal wird im vorliegenden Buch eine Klassifikation der durchbrochen gearbeiteten Anhänger entwickelt, die nicht nur Exemplare aus dem Gebiet des mitteleuropäischen Barbaricums, sondern auch aus dem Gebiet Osteuropas – hauptsächlich von der Krim – umfasst (Typ I – Illerup; Typ II – Hansdorf; Typ III – Ust'-Al'ma; Typ IV – Alma-Kermen; Typ V – Bel'bek; Typ VI – Nejzac). Das Exemplar aus dem Illerup Ådal weist eine Ähnlichkeit mit den Anhängern aus der Krim auf und kann eine Anregung für die nähere Erforschung der skandinavisch-sarmatischen Kontakte werden. Ein weiteres Fundstück zivilen Charakters aus dem Illerup Ådal ist ein silberner Kapselanhänger mit gewölbten Wänden und trapezförmiger Öse (Kap. 4, S. 63–67), der typologisch vermutlich mit dem Elbgebiet verbunden ist. Ziemlich wenige, ähnlich geformte Anhänger treten zerstreut auf dem Gebiet des Barbaricums auf.

Im untersuchten Material aus dem Illerup Ådal kommen relativ häufig Glasperlen vor, die sich meist in den rekonstruierten Beuteln befanden (Kap. 5–12). Bei ihrer Aufarbeitung stützte sich der Verfasser auf die Klassifikation von M. Tempelmann-Mączyńska (Die Perlen der römischen Kaiserzeit und der frühen Phase der Völkerwanderungszeit im mitteleuropäischen Barbaricum. Röm.-German. Forsch. 43 [Mainz 1985]). Auf der Fundstelle Illerup Ådal sind Perlen folgender Gruppen vertreten: I (einfarbige Perlen), XIV (kubooktaedrische Perlen), XVIII (gerippte Perlen), XXI (Perlen mit Schichtaugen), XXII (Perlen mit Streifen) und der Gruppe XXIX (Perlen mit Metalleinlage). Bei der Analyse der Perlen berücksichtigte man nicht nur ihre Form, sondern auch die Art der Glasmasse (durchsichtig, undurchsichtig) und die Farbe. Der Verfasser fordert, dass bei der Analyse der Glasperlen auch die Glaswerkstätten berücksichtigt werden sollen. Diese Bemerkung des Verfassers betrifft vor allem die Werkstätten in den Städten am Schwarzen Meer, aber auch in Tibiscum in Dakien (RO) und auf dem Gebiet anderer Provinzen.

Unter den Perlen, die im Illerup Ådal auftreten, widmet der Verfasser sich besonders den Perlen mit Metalleinlage vom Typ 387 (Gruppe XXIX; Kap. 6, S. 83–95). Im Gebiet des mitteleuropäischen Barbaricums treten diese Perlen sehr häufig im gotischen Kulturkreis auf (Fundlisten 8–10). Ihre größte Konzentration wurde allerdings im baltischen Kreis dokumentiert (Fundliste 11). Der Verfasser äußert die Vermutung, dass diese zwei Kulturkreise dazu beigetragen haben, dass die erwähnten Perlen nach Jütland und auf die dänischen Inseln gelangten (Fundliste 12). In der älteren Fachliteratur begegnet man auch der Hypothese, dass die Perlen mit Metalleinlage in Werkstätten am Rhein und in Gallien produziert wurden, von wo sie zur Ostseezone und nach Südskandinavien gelangten (J. Okulicz, Cmentarzysko z okresu rzymskiego w miejscowości Bogaczewo, na przysiółku Kula, pow. Giżycko. Rocznik Olsztyński 1, 1958, 47–116). Es ist nicht auszuschließen, dass dabei all die hier genannten Verbindungen von Bedeutung waren. Außerdem bestimmt der Verfasser präzise die Chronologie dieser Perlen und weist nach, dass sie vor allem zwischen der Stufe B1 der frühen Römischen Kaiserzeit und der Stufe C1b der jüngeren Römischen Kaiserzeit auftraten und auch in der späteren Zeit bezeugt sind, bis hin zur Stufe C3/D1.

Im Zuge der Analyse der gerippten Perlen des Typs 171 (Gruppe XVIII) – unterstreicht der Verfasser zu Recht die Notwendigkeit von deren erneuter, eingehender Analyse (Kap. 7, S. 97–100). In der Literatur nennt man sie nämlich oft Fayenceperlen und den Stoff, aus dem sie hergestellt wurden, bezeichnet man als ägyptische Fayence. Neuere Untersuchungen zeigen jedoch, dass diese Perlen aus Quarzsand produziert wurden, man kennt sie unter dem Namen Melonenperlen aus Quarzkeramik (vgl. S. Fünfschilling, Die römischen Gläser aus Augst und Kaiseraugst. Kommentierter Formenkatalog und ausgewählte Neufunde 1981–2010 aus Augusta Raurica. Text und Formenkatalog. Forsch. Augst 51 [Augst 2015] 209, Abb. 288,6). Diese Perlen kommen häufig im mitteleuropäischen Barbaricum in der Wielbark-Kultur, in der Przeworsk-Kultur und im Elbgebiet vor. Es wird angenommen, dass sie aus dem Schwarzmeergebiet stammen.

Im Illerup Ådal befinden sich auch längliche und kurze gerippte Perlen, die den Typen 181–183 ähneln und in der Wielbark-Kultur am Unterlauf der Weichsel und in der Masłomęcz-Gruppe häufig anzutreffen sind. In der Zone an der unteren Weichsel und in der Masłomęcz-Gruppe treten auch röhrenförmige Perlen mit Streifen auf, die den Typen 304, 307 und 309 ähneln. Die kugelförmige Perle mit Pflanzenornament (Typ 347), das in diesem Fall als Lebensbaummotiv bezeichnet wird, wurde wiederum aller Wahrscheinlichkeit nach in einer Werkstatt im Schwarzmeergebiet produziert und von dort nach Nordeuropa transportiert.

Die nächsten Fragen, die in der Monographie besprochen werden, hängen mit der Anwesenheit von Rohbernstein, Bernsteinperlen und eines Spielwürfels aus Bernstein auf der Fundstelle im Illerup Ådal zusammen (Kap. 13, S. 119–129). Nach der Ansicht des Buchautors stammen die Bernsteinklümpchen mit hoher Wahrscheinlichkeit aus dem Gebiet zwischen der Mündung der Weichsel und der Kurischen Nehrung oder aus einer nicht näher bestimmten, ausgeraubten Bernstein-Werkstatt. Die handgefertigten (tonnenförmigen, Typ 392; doppelkonischen, Typ 395) und auf der Drehbank gefertigten (scheibenförmigen, Typ 429; doppelkonischen, Typ 433) Perlen seien hingegen für den gotischen Kulturkreis und für die skandinavischen Gebiete charakteristisch, und es ist durchaus möglich, dass sie dort hergestellt wurden. Der erwähnte Spielwürfel vertritt wiederum den Typ Westerwanna, der für das Gebiet zwischen der Mündung der Elbe und der Weser und für die Jütische Halbinsel charakteristisch ist.

Eine Ergänzung der detaillierten Besprechung der Perlen aus dem Illerup Ådal ist das kurze Kapitel 14 (S. 131–133) über Perlen aus anderen Moorfundplätzen. Der Verfasser unterscheidet drei Gruppen derartiger Fundstellen: 1. Fundplätze, auf denen die Perlen im militärischen Kontext auftreten; 2. Fundplätze, auf denen die Perlen nicht im oben erwähnten Kontext oder nur mit einzelnen Elementen der Bewaffnung auftreten; 3. nicht konkreter definierbare Funde. Die Fundstelle im Illerup Ådal gehört zur ersten Gruppe, zu der auch berühmte Moorfundplätze im nördlichen Deutschland und in Skandinavien zu rechnen sind, z. B. Thorsberg (DE), Nydam, Vimose, Kragehul, Ejsbøl, Porskjær (alle DK) und Skedemosse (SE).

In einem der rekonstruierten Beutel im Illerup Ådal entdeckte man zwei Fragmente eines Glasgefäßes, das vermutlich im Feuer des Scheiterhaufens geschmolzen war. Sie bilden den Ausgangspunkt zu Erörterungen im Kapitel 15 (S. 135–138). Nach der Ansicht des Verfassers stammen sie mit hoher Wahrscheinlichkeit aus einem (ausgeplünderten) Brandgrab. Er unternahm die mühsame Arbeit der Identifikation der Region, in der Brandbestattungen dominieren und wo die Grundsätze ihrer Ausstattung es zulassen, Glasgefäße auf den Scheiterhaufen zu legen (Fundliste 20). Es wurde festgestellt, dass solche Bestattungen in der Wielbark-Kultur sowie in der Masłomęcz-Gruppe stattfanden. Vor allem aber praktizierte man sie an der südwestlichen Küste der Ostsee, an der unteren Elbe und auf der Jütischen Halbinsel. Der Autor unterstreicht jedoch, dass das zerschmolzene Glas möglicherweise aus einer der Glaswerkstätten stammt, die in solchen Siedlungen wie Lundeborg auf der Insel Fyn arbeiteten, wo das Glas umgeschmolzen wurde.

Unter den Gegenständen zivilen Charakters auf dem Fundplatz Illerup Ådal befinden sich auch S-förmige Schließhaken aus Silber oder aus Kupferlegierung und aus Eisen (Kap. 16, S. 139–142). Sie besitzen nach außen gebogene, einmal (Typ Illerup I) oder mehrmals (Typ Illerup II) zusammengerollte Enden. Solche S-förmigen Schließhaken treten – wie der Verfasser feststellt – vor allem im Einzugsgebiet der Elbe, auf der Jütischen Halbinsel, auf den dänischen Inseln und auf dem Gebiet der Wielbark-Kultur auf.

Aufgrund der Annahme, dass der Inhalt der Beutel einen geschlossenen Komplex bildet, unternimmt der Verfasser einen Versuch der Rekonstruktion der Halsketten (Kap. 17, S. 143–145). Er unterscheidet drei Gruppen: Halsketten aus einfarbigen Perlen, aus vielfarbigen Perlen sowie aus Perlen und metallenen Elementen (Anhänger und S-förmige Schließhaken). Laut Verfasser sind reiche Halsketten für die Bevölkerung der Wielbark-Kultur (Gebiet am Unterlauf der Weichsel) und für die Bevölkerung auf der Insel Seeland, der Insel Bornholm und im südlichen Teil der Jütischen Halbinsel charakteristisch. Bei der Analyse der Halsketten aus dem Illerup Ådal bemerkt der Verfasser aber, dass in ihnen im Gegensatz zu den Halsketten aus den oben genannten Gebieten keine achtförmigen Bernsteinperlen vorkommen. Die rekonstruierten Halsketten zeugen von einer regionalen Differenziertheit der Tracht in der nördlichen Zone des mitteleuropäischen Barbaricums und in Skandinavien.

Die vom Verfasser durchgeführte gründliche und komplexe Analyse der Gegenstände zivilen Charakters, die auf dem Fundplatz im Illerup Ådal deponiert waren, ermöglicht es die Gebiete zu ermitteln, zu denen die skandinavischen Krieger gelangten (Kap. 18, S. 147–153). Diese Raubzüge galten der Insel Bornholm, dem östlichen Holstein und dem Gebiet der Ansiedlung der Bevölkerung der Wielbark-Kultur. Eine wesentliche Rolle spielte dabei vor allem Bornholm – als Verbindungspunkt zwischen Skandinavien und Mitteleuropa. Wichtig ist die Beobachtung, dass die im Illerup Ådal gefundenen Gegenstände vor dem Jahr 205 n. Chr., also der Periode der intensivsten Deponierung der Militaria im Illerup-See, auf dem Gebiet Skandinaviens kaum auftreten. Dies stimmt mit den Ergebnissen der Analyse der Münzfunde aus dem hier besprochenen Fundplatz überein (A. Bursche, Illerup Ådal 14. Die Münzen [Aarhus 2011]). Die Zeit der Deponierung verschiedener Gegenstände im Illerup Ådal kann ansonsten für eine präzisere Bestimmung der chronologischen Position analoger Funde aus anderen Teilen des Barbaricums von Bedeutung sein. Als neuartig ist die Interpretation einzustufen, nach der die für die weibliche Tracht charakteristischen Gegenstände „zivilen" Charakters aus ausgeraubten Bestattungen stammen können.

Besonders zu betonen ist der enorme Arbeitsaufwand, den die Analyse des gesammelten Materials, die Zusammenstellung und Auswertung des Vergleichsmaterials, die Aufarbeitung der Fundlisten und des kartographischen Materials von Andrzej Kokowski verlangte. Besondere Beachtung verdienen die auf der Grundlage des gesammelten Materials ausgearbeiteten Schlussfolgerungen. Der hier besprochene Band ist ein wichtiger Teil der epochalen Aufarbeitung der historischen Materialien aus dem Illerup Ådal.

Übersetzt ins Deutsche von Wieńczysław Niemirowski

PL–31-007 Kraków
ul. Gołębia 11
E-Mail: renata.madyda-legutko@uj.edu.pl
Orcid: https://orcid.org/0000-0001-6210-7450

Renata Madyda-Legutko
Instytut Archeologii UJ
Uniwersytet Jagielloński w Krakowie
Zakład Archeologii Epoki Żelaza

Alex R. Furger, Antike Schmelztiegel. Archäologie und Archäometrie der Funde aus Augusta Raurica. Mit Beiträgen von M. Helfert. Beiträge zur Technikgeschichte 1. Librum Publishers & Editors, Basel / Frankfurt a. M. 2018. € 85,–. ISBN 978-3-9524542-3-7 (Hardcover). doi: http://dx.doi.org/10.19218/3952454237. 386 Seiten mit 164 Abbildungen und 30 Tafeln.

Alex R. Furger, Antike Stahlerzeugung. Ein Nachweis der Aufkohlung von Eisen aus Augusta Raurica. Beiträge zur Technikgeschichte 2. Librum Publishers & Editors, Basel / Frankfurt a. M. 2019. € 65,–. ISBN 978-3-906897-28-8 (Hardcover). doi: http://dx.doi.org/10.19218/3906897288. 176 Seiten mit 122 Abbildungen.

Alex Furger hat vor einigen Jahren etwas eher Ungewöhnliches und Bemerkenswertes getan, indem er vorzeitig von seiner Leitungsposition als Direktor von *Augusta Raurica* zurückgetreten ist, um sich seinen Forschungsprojekten widmen zu können. Seither erscheinen regelmäßig Bücher aus seiner Feder zu den unterschiedlichsten Themen. Die Manuskripte scheinen allerdings schon seit Jahren in der Schublade gelegen zu haben, weshalb sie nun in kurzer Abfolge erscheinen. Mit den Schmelztiegeln hat er sich, wie er selbst schreibt, einer „unattraktiven" Fundgattung gewidmet, die genauso wie Schlacken sonst wenig Beachtung findet. In England hatten vor allem Mike Tite und Ian Freestone in den 1980er-Jahren einige wegweisende Publikationen zu technischer Keramik unterschiedlicher Zeitstellungen veröffentlicht (I. A. Freestone / M. S. Tite, Refractories in the ancient and preindustrial world. In: W. D. Kingery / E. Lense [Hrsg.], High-Technology Ceramics: Past, Present, and Future. Ceramics and Civilization III [Westerville 1986] 35–63). Im deutschsprachigen Raum fand das Thema erst ab den 1990er-Jahren durch die Arbeiten von Thilo Rehren (Tiegelmetallurgie – Tiegelprozesse und ihre Stellung in der Archäometallurgie. Habilitationsschrift TU Freiberg [Freiberg 1998]) etwas Beachtung, weshalb dieses Buch „Antike Schmelztiegel" für die archäologische Forschung sicherlich eine große Bereicherung ist.

Das Buch beginnt mit einem kurzen, jedoch sehr interessanten Kapitel über die Forschungsgeschichte zur Metallverarbeitung in *Augusta Raurica*, in dem auf alle durchgeführten Untersuchungen und publizierten Ergebnisse hingewiesen wird. Mit fast 500 Literaturzitaten bietet der Band insgesamt eine akribische Zusammenstellung von Veröffentlichungen über römische Tiegel, Tiegel und Keramik im Allgemeinen und über römische Metallverarbeitung. Wer sich erstmals mit diesen Themen beschäftigen möchte, findet hier eine gute Übersicht über die Literatur und damit einen schnellen Einstieg. Die gleiche Akribie zeigt sich vor allem im Hauptkapitel über die Tiegel selbst, die dort anhand ihrer Form und Farbe gruppiert werden und tabellarisch erfasst sind. Bei insgesamt 884 Tiegeln, neun Tiegeldeckeln und vier Reguli, die zusätzlich alle am Ende des Bandes in einem Katalog erfasst sind, ist das eine beträchtliche Arbeitsleistung. Sehr schön ist auch, dass alle Tiegel gezeichnet und teilweise fotografisch dargestellt sind. Dies zeigt eine Wertschätzung, die üblicherweise solch einem Material nicht zukommt und hoffentlich Nachahmer*innen findet. Der Eifer, die Begeisterung und der Fleiß, die sich überall offenbaren, sind aber nach Ansicht des Rezensenten auch eine der großen Schwachstellen des Buches.

Der Wunsch, alles zu erfassen, zu beschreiben, zu erklären und möglichst Beispiele aus der Literatur anzuführen, macht das Lesen mühsam und kann für jemanden, der nicht mit der Materie technischer Keramik und der Literatur dazu vertraut ist, verwirrend sein. Es wird dabei munter zwischen Vorgeschichte und Neuzeit hin und her gesprungen, um die verschiedensten Angaben aus der Literatur zusammenzutragen, und ohne Kenntnis der zitierten Literatur sind die Zusammenhänge oft nicht erkennbar. Wenn z. B. Brenntemperaturen von Tiegelkeramik zitiert werden, die sich in mehreren hundert Grad unterscheiden, ist es auch erforderlich, den Grund dafür zu nennen. Das Wissen, dass ein prähistorischer Tiegel aus sandgemagertem Blähton zwischen 1300 und 1400 °C üblicherweise nicht mehr stabil ist, während ein neuzeitlicher kaolinitischer Tontiegel bei solch hohen Temperaturen vorgebrannt wurde um stabil zu werden, kann von der Leserschaft eines solchen Buches nicht vorausgesetzt werden und noch weniger, wenn die Information über die unterschiedlichen Tonqualitäten nicht mitgeliefert, sondern nur die Brenntemperaturen aufgelistet werden. Den meist rein phänomenologischen Beschreibungen fehlt die Vermittlung der für das Verständnis notwendigen materialkundlichen Grundlagen und so hetzt man als Leser*in dem Autor von einer Beschreibung zur nächsten Beobachtung hinterher. Es werden sehr komplexe Sachverhalte angeschnitten, wie z. B. die Unterscheidung zwischen Schmelz- oder Zementationstiegeln für die Messingproduktion, die sich in der Praxis oft schwierig gestaltet und trotz materialkundlicher Untersuchungen nicht immer eindeutig ist. Obwohl sich für diese und andere Fragen mit den analytischen Methoden, die für die Publikation eingesetzt wurden, nicht oder nur bedingt gesicherte Antworten finden lassen, geht der Autor recht leichtfertig und teilweise hemdsärmelig mit seinen Interpretationen und Schlussfolgerungen um. Diese können in einer Rezension nicht alle einzeln besprochen und kommentiert werden, der Rezensent hätte sich jedoch insgesamt etwas mehr Zurückhaltung gewünscht.

Sehr schön ist der Vergleich der Augster Tiegelformen mit Tiegeln von anderen Fundorten, die jeweils in den Abbildungen zusammengestellt sind. Das ist sehr hilfreich und könnte, wie ein Handbuch für Tiegelbestimmung benutzt werden, wenn Form und Funktion stets eindeutig in Zusammenhang gebracht werden könnten. Das ist leider auch hier nicht gelungen und konnte vermutlich durch die gewählte Vorgehensweise auch nicht erreicht werden. Andererseits wurde technische Keramik oft mehrfach verwendet, so dass sich Relikte aus unterschiedlichen Prozessen finden lassen. Wenig benutzerfreundlich ist die Vorgehensweise bei dem Tafel- und Abbildungsnachweis, in welchem auf die in den Fußnoten zitierten Publikationen verwiesen wird, die man dann wiederum aus dem Literaturverzeichnis heraussuchen muss. Man ist dadurch gezwungen ständig zwischen den einzelnen Verzeichnissen hin und her zu blättern.

Der Band enthält auch einen Beitrag von Markus Helfert, der Tiegelkeramik und lokale Tonvorkommen mit einem portablen Röntgenspektrometer (pRFA) untersucht hat. Leser*innen ist dabei zu raten, sich parallel auch die Dissertation von Daniela K. KÖNIG (Roman Metallurgical Ceramics. An Archaeometrical Approach. GeoFocus 36 [Freiburg i. d. Schweiz 2014] https://folia.unifr.ch/unifr/documents/304221 [letzter Zugriff: 02.05.2022]) über römische Schmelztiegel anzusehen, auf die auch im Buch von A. Furger Bezug genommen wird, da auch Tiegel aus *Augusta Raurica* untersucht wurden. Portable Röntgenspektrometer sind seit den 1960er-Jahren in der Archäometrie im Einsatz, haben jedoch erst mit der Entwicklung der Mikrochips, Wafer-Detektoren und kleinen, leistungsstarken Röntgenröhren breitere Anwendung erfahren, weil sie kleiner, kostengünstiger und einfacher zu handhaben sind. Es ist hier nicht der Ort, diese Entwicklung und die Anwendung der pRFA allgemein zu kommentieren, nichtsdestotrotz erfordert die Vorgehensweise im vorliegenden Beispiel ein paar grundlegende Anmerkungen. Grundsätzlich ist bei Provenienzbestimmungen immer nur ein negatives Ergebnis eindeutig, während bei einer positiven Übereinstimmung eine weitere positive Übereinstimmung mit einer anderen Lagerstätte nicht ausgeschlossen werden kann. Im vorliegenden Fall hat man diese Grundvoraussetzung auszuhebeln versucht, indem anfänglich postuliert wurde, dass alle Tone lokalen Ursprungs sind, und dass es ein feuerfester Spezialton sein müsse. Da die Tiegelkeramik jedoch im direkten Vergleich mit lokaler Gebrauchskeramik und Ziegeln keine Übereinstimmung aufweist, wurden auch weit entfernte Lagerstätten beprobt und verglichen. Der auf diese Weise vorgenommene Vergleich zwischen Gebrauchskeramik und Tiegelkeramik ist zulässig und sinnvoll, während der direkte Vergleich zwischen Tiegelkeramik und Tonlagerstätten fragwürdig ist. D. König hat in ihrer Arbeit festgestellt, dass alle Tiegel mit Sand gemagert sind, wie dies bei Tiegeln üblich ist, was aber zu einer Veränderung der chemischen Zusammensetzung führt. Durch die Magerung mit Quarz und Feldspäten können u. a. sogenannte geochemisch inkompatible Spurenelemente wie Rubidium oder Strontium eingebracht werden, die auch bei der chemischen Klassifizierung der Tiegel herangezogen werden. Diesen Zusammenhang kann man allerdings nur bei einer geringen Anzahl der Tiegel erkennen, während die Mehrheit der Tiegel niedrige Rubidium- und Strontium-Gehalte aufweisen, obwohl die Quarzanteile hoch sind. Dennoch muss die durch einfache bivariate lineare Darstellungen gewonnene positive Korrelation des Großteils der Tiegel mit dem sogenannten Weißen Hupperlehm von Châtelat (CH) in Frage gestellt werden, zumal dies im Wesentlichen auf der Übereinstimmung von Rubidium- und Strontium-Gehalten beruht. Ein wesentliches Argument für den Einsatz der pRFA ist die schnelle und kostengünstige Analyse großer Probenmengen. Dafür hat man vor Ort die frisch erzeugten Bruchkanten an den Scherben analysiert, wodurch allerdings Abschattungs- und Streueffekte auftreten, die die Röntgenfluoreszenzintensität beeinflussen. Die Ergebnisse wurden teilweise mit fünf signifikanten Nachkommastellen angegeben, was eine Präzision vortäuscht, die mit dieser Methode im Allgemeinen und unter diesen Messparametern im Speziellen nicht erreicht werden kann. Möchte man den Datensatz mit anderen Daten vergleichen, so kann man diese kostenfrei auf der Webseite des Verlags herunterladen, muss sie jedoch zuvor selbst filtern und auf die richtige Stelle runden.

Den Abschluss bildet ein experimenteller Teil, der sehr gut veranschaulicht, welchen Spannungen solche Tiegel im Feuer ausgesetzt waren und was alles dabei schiefgehen kann. Wie schon im Textteil ist nach Meinung des Rezensenten auch hier der Bogen teilweise überspannt worden, indem alle an den Tiegeln gemachten Beobachtungen auch experimentell nachzustellen versucht wurde, statt sich ausführlicher und statistisch relevant mit einzelnen Phänomenen zu beschäftigen. Ungeachtet dieser Einschränkung ist es ein sehr anschauliches Kapitel, mit dem das Buch abgerundet wird.

Insgesamt ist es ein gelungenes Buch und wird hoffentlich dazu anregen die metallurgischen Relikte einzelner Fundorte ebenso gewissenhaft zusammenzustellen, auch wenn die Präsentation teilweise Schwachstellen aufweist. Alex Furger wäre gut beraten gewesen, sich an einigen Stellen etwas auszubremsen und sich stattdessen ausführlicher auf einige wenige Details zu stürzen. Weniger ist bekanntlich oftmals mehr.

Der zweite Band über „Antike Stahlerzeugung" ist dagegen ein wahrhaft schwieriges Buch. Der Aufhänger sind mehrere Lehmformen unbekannter Funktion aus *Augusta Raurica*, die von A. Furger als Lehmumhüllungen für das Aufkohlen von Eisenbarren interpretiert werden. Das ist normalerweise eine interessante These für einen Zeitschriftenaufsatz, aber der Autor hat daraus ein fast zweihundertseitiges Buch gemacht, das den Leser*innen von der Eisen- und Stahlgewinnung im Rennofen, über die neuzeitliche Tiegelstahlerzeugung in Zentralasien und Europa, nach Afrika und Nepal, zu den Eisenbarrenformen von der Vorgeschichte bis ins Frühmittelalter, zu den Lehmformen selbst sowie der experimentellen Nachstellung der These, hin zu einem irritierenden Fazit führt. Entgegen der Überzeugung des Autors erschließt sich nicht, wofür die Formen tatsächlich verwendet worden sind. Alle Lehmformen haben unterschiedliche Durchmesser und Querschnitte, wobei kein Querschnitt einer bekannten römischen Barrenform entspricht. Betrachtet man die oftmals stereotypen Formen römischer Handelsbarren, deren Materialqualität bereits durch die unterschiedlichen Formen mitgeteilt wird (s. G. Pagès et al., A study of the Roman iron bars of Saintes-Maries-de-la-Mer [Bouches-du-Rhône, France]. A proposal for a comprehensive metallographic approach. Journal Arch. Science 38,6, 2011, 1234–1252. doi: https://doi.org/10.1016/j.jas.2010.12.017), so kann man mit ziemlicher Sicherheit ausschließen, dass die in Augst gefundenen Lehmformen mit solchen Barren in Verbindung stehen. Der Autor führt stattdessen ein Eisenstück aus dem 6. Jahrhundert v. Chr. aus Griechenland an, das in Form und Größe den Lehmformen entsprechen würde, was aber mit keiner bekannten römischen Barrenform kompatibel ist und zudem die Funktion dieser Lehmformen nicht erklärt, weil dieses Stück gar nicht aufgekohlt ist. Es wäre einfacher und zielführender gewesen petrographische oder strukturellen Untersuchungen an den Lehmformen selbst durchführen zu lassen, die zeigen könnten, inwieweit der Lehm überhaupt größerer Hitze ausgesetzt war oder nicht. Die rein äußerliche optische Beurteilung dazu durch den Autor fällt widersprüchlich aus, da einerseits von „leichten Versinterungen", andererseits vom Fehlen von „Spuren starker Hitzeeinwirkung" berichtet wird (S. 88–93). Eine geeignete naturwissenschaftliche Untersuchung wäre dabei hilfreicher gewesen.

Stattdessen hat sich der Autor auf die Suche nach Parallelen gemacht und mehrere wikingerzeitliche versinterte Lehmformen aus Skandinavien gefunden. Weiterhin interpretiert er eine 1932 publizierte keramische Anlage als Zementationsofen für Eisen. Dieser in der Tat merkwürdige Befund ist seit seiner Erstpublikation mehrfach unterschiedlich interpretiert worden, wobei tatsächlich auch einmal der Vorschlag für einen Zementationsofen im Raum stand (z. B. R. F. Tylecote, Metallurgy in Archaeology. A Prehistory of Metallurgy in the British Isles [London 1962] 230–231; R. F. Tylecote, The Prehistory of Metallurgy in the British Isles [London 1986] 164–165). Die wikingerzeitlichen Lehmformen werden in der angegebenen Literatur (A. Söderberg, Metallurgical clay packages. In: H. Clarke / K. Lamm [Hrsg.], Excavations at Helgö 17 [Stockholm 2008] 1–11) vorwiegend als Lehmumhüllungen für das Hartlöten von kleinen Eisenteilen und nur untergeordnet auch zum Aufkohlen von Eisenteilen interpretiert. Diese Formen sind jedoch im Gegensatz zu den Formen aus Augst eindeutig verglast oder versintert und reduzierend gebrannt.

Letztendlich führt alles, was in diesem Buch akribisch zusammengetragen wurde, zu keiner Beweisführung der zentralen These. Es steht völlig außer Frage, dass Eisen von der Vorgeschichte bis in die Gegenwart zementiert, also aufgekohlt worden ist. Dafür gibt es genügend metallographisch untersuchte Beispiele aus allen Epochen (z. B. S. 30–34) sowie die auch von A. Furger zitierten historischen Überlieferungen. Die meisten dieser historischen Verfahren betreffen jedoch Eisen, das in einem indirekten Verfahren, also über die Herstellung von flüssigem Roheisen in einem Hochofen und anschließender Raffination in einem oxidierenden Frischfeuer hergestellt wurde. Beim Frischen verbrennt der Kohlenstoff und ein Großteil weiterer unerwünschter Bestandteile (Si, P, S, Mn) wird in die Schlacke überführt, so dass gefrischtes Eisen wieder sekundär aufgekohlt werden muss. Wir wissen durch die Untersuchungen an Luppen und Barren jedoch, dass kohlenstoffreicher Stahl bis hin zum flüssigen Roheisen direkt im Rennofen produziert und danach verhandelt worden ist, und wir kennen vor- und frühgeschichtliche Werkzeuge und Waffen, für die primärer Stahl – wenn auch nicht durchgehend – verwendet worden ist (s. R. Pleiner, Iron in Archaeology. Early European Blacksmiths [Prag 2006]). Im vorliegenden Buch werden die entsprechenden Untersuchungen neben einer Vielzahl an weiteren Themen angerissen, der Zusammenhang mit dem Kernthema, nämlich dem sekundären Aufkohlen in Lehmformen während der römischen Kaiserzeit, besteht aber nur lose. Es gibt z. B. ein eigenes Kapitel über die Zementation, in dem eine Tabelle über Temperatur, Einsatzdauer und Einsatztiefe aus der Literatur zusammengestellt ist und weitere Angaben in den Fußnoten zitiert werden. Eine gutgemeinte aber wenig sinnvolle Fleißarbeit, weil die Angaben ohne erklärenden Text und einer ansatzweisen Erläuterung der physikalischen Grundlagen für eine unbedarfte Leser*innenschaft unverständlich sein können, zumal es sich teilweise um völlig unterschiedliche Prozesse handelt. Ein durch das Frischfeuer vollständig entkohlter mehrere Zentimeter dicker Eisenbarren muss, um vollständig aufgekohlt zu werden, bei einer Temperatur über 911 °C mehrere Tage geglüht werden, während ein heterogenes Rennofeneisen mit 0,2 bis 0,4 % Kohlenstoff, der mit einer 2 bis 3 mm dicken Aufkohlungsschicht versehen werden soll, bei einer Temperatur über 800 °C nur einige Stunden geglüht werden muss. Die notwendige Mindesttemperatur hängt hierbei in erster Linie vom Ausgangkohlenstoffgehalt ab und lässt sich problemlos aus dem Zustandsschaubild Eisen-Kohlenstoff ablesen, während sich Einsatztiefe und Dauer durch das parabolische Zeitgesetz und dem Boltzmann-Faktor bzw. mit der Arrhenius-Gleichung errechnen lassen (vgl. R. Schwab / M. Senn, Recycling von Alteisen. Berliner Beitr. Archäometrie 21, 2008, 206–226). Da die Temperatur exponentiell in die Gleichung eingeht, ist sie der bestimmende Faktor. Das Aufkohlen kann daher mehrere Stunden oder nur Minuten dauern, was dann ja auch in einer gewissen Weise aus Tabelle 1 im Buch entnommen werden kann, die jedoch für einen Leser ohne Vorkenntnisse der physikalischen Zusammenhänge wenig hilfreich ist. Wie schon beim Buch über die Tiegel ist der Band über die „Antike Stahlerzeugung" von der Ambition geprägt möglichst viele Beispiele aus der Literatur anzuführen, wobei auch hier munter zwischen verschiedenen Prozessen unterschiedlicher Zeiten und Kulturen hin und her gesprungen wird und der Leser mit einer unstrukturierten Informationsflut konfrontiert wird, die hohe Sachkenntnis erfordert, um die wahllos miteinander vermengten Inhalte in den richtigen Kontext setzen zu können. Auch das Glossar ist sehr fehlerhaft. Dieses Buch ist deshalb keinem unbedarften Neueinsteiger zum Thema „Antike Stahlerzeugung" zu empfehlen, wenngleich das Literaturverzeichnis eine wahre Goldgrube ist. Wer z. B. zum Thema Barren zu forschen beginnen möchte, erhält hier eine gute und aktuelle Übersicht.

Wie schon für das Buch über die Tiegel hat der Autor eigene Experimente mit selbsthergestellten Lehmhüllen und im Lehmtiegel durchgeführt. Diese wenig effektiven Versuche werden dabei über 37 Seiten ausgebreitet und lassen erahnen, dass diese umständliche Prozedur in dieser Form kaum ein Standardverfahren gewesen sein kann. Seit Jahrzehnten überprüfen Studierende der Materialwissenschaften häufig in einem Praktikum, neben den Vorlesungen über Diffusion, inwieweit die berechnete Konzentrationskurve von einer experimentellen Kurve abweicht. Dabei wird in der Regel eine handelsübliche unlegierte Weicheisenprobe (ARMCO-Eisen) zusammen mit einem kohlenstoffhaltigen Gemisch geglüht, worauf anschließend die Eindringtiefe ermittelt wird. Dies ist ein standardisiertes, praktisches Experiment, das nach der Vermittlung der physikalischen Grundlagen unter kontrollierten Bedingungen durchgeführt wird. Auch die im Buch angeführten historischen Beispiele stammen weitgehend aus frühindustrieller Zeit und setzen ein wenngleich empirisch ermitteltes, aber standardisiertes und reproduzierbares Verfahren voraus, um Schmiedestahl bei gleicher Qualität in möglichst großen Stückzahlen herstellen zu können. Viele der Beispiele aus vor- und frühgeschichtlichem Kontext zeigen hingegen, dass oft sehr schnell und unkontrolliert zementiert wurde und die Objekte deshalb häufig überkohlt wurden (z. B. Schwab / Senn 2008). Das gezielte Aufkohlen von Eisen war bekannt und wurde, wenn auch nicht häufig, praktiziert. Es war aber nach heutigem Forschungsstand mit Sicherheit kein standardisiertes Verfahren vor der Einführung des indirekten Verfahrens im Mittelalter und konnte ohne Lehmhüllen oder spezielle Öfen einfach im Schmiedefeuer ausgeführt werden. Die Idee, die gut organisierten römischen Metallurgen könnten ein standardisiertes Verfahren für die Aufkohlung von Stahl entwickelt haben, ist sicherlich eine interessante These, aber das ganze Buch folgt in erster Linie dieser Idee, die sich den Leser*innen jedoch nicht überzeugend erschließt und für die es keine zwingende Beweisführung liefert. Es bleibt also die Frage wofür diese Lehmformen tatsächlich verwendet worden sind.

DE–68159 Mannheim
D6, 3
E-Mail: roland.schwab@ceza.de
Orcid: https://orcid.org/0000-0002-0593-7746

Roland Schwab
Curt-Engelhorn-Zentrum Archäometrie gGmbH

Andrew Lawrence, Religion in Vindonissa. Kultorte und Kulte im und um das Legionslager. Mit Beiträgen von Örni Akeret, Sabine Deschler-Erb und Simon Kramis. Veröffentlichungen der Gesellschaft Pro Vindonissa Band 24. Kantonsarchäologie Aargau, Brugg 2018. € 55,–. ISBN 978-3-906897-29-5. doi: https://doi.org/10.19218/3906897295. Digitale Supplemente: https://doi.org/10.19218/3906897296 und https://doi.org/10.19218/3906897297. 240 Seiten mit zahlreichen Abbildungen.

Das Legionslager in *Vindonissa* und seine Zivilsiedlung, die im Verlauf von 120 Jahren ausgegraben worden sind, liefern zahlreiche und wichtige Zeugnisse über Kultorte und Kulte der römischen Welt. Diese Quellen sind nicht etwa von sensationellem Inhalt, sondern bieten in ihrem archäologischen Zusammenhang mit den Gebäuden viele Informationen zum Thema Religion in einem Legionslager und seiner Umgebung in der Zeit vom 1.–3. Jahrhundert n. Chr. Mit der Aufarbeitung der zahlreichen Funde hat Andrew Lawrence in seiner Dissertation, die von der *Vindonissa*-Professur der Universität Basel betreut und im Januar 2016 abgeschlossen wurde, einen Einblick in die verschiedenen sozialen Zusammenhänge der öffentlichen wie der privaten Kulte während dieser drei Jahrhunderte vermittelt. Dass alle archäologischen Kontexte nicht gleich gut erhalten und ausgegraben sind, ist verständlich, wenn man die über ein Jahrhundert andauernden Ausgrabungen und ihre methodologische Entwicklung in den Blick nimmt.

Die Arbeit von A. Lawrence untersucht die Entwicklung von Kulten in und um ein römisches Lager sowie in der Zivilsiedlung, die auf das Lager folgt. Die Arbeit ist in drei Teile gegliedert, wobei der erste mit Hilfe von anthropologischen, archäozoologischen und archäobotanischen Untersuchungen die Sakral- und Kultbauten *intra* oder *extra muros* betrachtet, mit dem Ziel Kulthandlungen festzustellen. Der zweite Teil untersucht weitere Manifestationen der rituellen Kommunikation, und das Buch endet, vor einer Synthese, mit der Besprechung weiterer oder vermuteter Orte der rituellen Kommunikation *intra* und *extra muros*. Die Einleitung zum Buch bespricht die Quellenlage und den Forschungsstand sowie den methodischen Zugang zu den epigraphischen und archäologischen Quellen der Untersuchung. Es handelt sich nicht um die Aufnahme einer „topographischen Verbreitung des Sakralen" auf einer Karte „mit mehr oder weniger ‚sakralen' Orten" (S. 28), da die Realität der Religionsausübung in der Antike komplexer war. Der Verfasser versucht eher, alle zugängigen Zeugnisse zur Rekonstruktion der lokalen Kulthandlungen zu verwerten, als in *Vindonissa* generelle Vorstellungen von römischer oder Provinzialreligion „wiederzufinden". Er zitiert als Beispiel seiner Methode den Aufsatz von S. HANSEN (Archäologie zwischen Himmel und Hölle. Bausteine für eine theoretisch reflektierte Religionsarchäologie. In: M. Heinz / M. K. H. Eggert / U. Veit [Hrsg.], Zwischen Erklären und Verstehen? Beiträge zu den erkenntnistheoretischen Grundlagen archäologische Interpretation. Tübinger Arch. Taschenbücher 2 [Münster 2003] 113–148), wonach religionsarchäologische Gegenstände nicht von vornherein als solche aufgenommen werden können, sondern vorerst unter religionsarchäologischen Aspekten befragt werden müssen. Dies bedeutet, dass die religionsgeschichtlich relevanten Quellen erst zu erschließen sind. Denn diese Gegenstände oder Orte sollen, wo möglich, der Rekonstruktion der für vorchristliche Religionen zentralen Kulthandlungen dienen.

So ist die erste Aufgabe, die sich Lawrence stellt, die religiösen Quellen in ihren jeweiligen historischen Zusammenhang einzufügen und vor allem ihren Unterschied zu moderner, westlich-christlicher Auffassung von Religion herauszustellen. In diesem Rahmen unterstreicht er zu Recht, dass man im individuellen wie im gemeinschaftlichen Kult normativ geregelte Handlungen erwarten muss, wobei jeweils der soziale Rahmen entscheidend war (S. 28–32). Denn diese Kulthandlungen definierten und stärkten die Identität und die Kohäsion dieser sozialen Gruppen. Wobei zu beachten ist, dass die Quellen zu einer solchen Studie sich nicht von selbst anbieten, sondern von dem Forscher und der Forscherin durch ein möglichst quellenbasiertes induktives Vorgehen aufgearbeitet werden müssen. Dabei ist in fast jedem Fall eine quellenkritische Analyse der Fundsituation unumgänglich. So identifiziert Lawrence nach den Quellen drei Kategorien von Kulthandlungen: Kultpraktiken, die in einer architektonischen Form lokalisiert werden können; Manifestationen der rituellen Kommunikation (Statuen, Statuetten, Kultgefäße, Inschriften); und schließlich Orte der rituellen Kommunikation, bei denen zwar befundbasierte Argumente für ein Kultareal fehlen, die aber durch eine Konzentration von archäologisch fassbaren Zeugnissen von Kulthandlungen als solche identifiziert werden können. Die Arbeit berücksichtigt nur die Funde des 1.–3. Jahrhunderts n. Chr., d. h. weder die Gräberfelder oder -straßen, es sei denn in Bezug auf publizierte Resultate, noch die Quellen zum frühen Christentum.

Man kann hier nicht auf alle Einzelheiten der kritischen Sammlung und Bearbeitung des reichen Fundmaterials eingehen. Es sei nur global gesagt, dass Lawrences Arbeit in ihrer methodologischen Basis durchaus überzeugt und er eine präzise und sehr informierte Studie von Religion in einem Legionslager und einer darauf folgenden Zivilsiedlung der frühen Kaiserzeit vorlegt. Wobei auch die auf Deutsch, Französisch, Englisch und Italienisch verfasste Zusammenfassung den anderssprachigen Leser*innen sehr nützlich sein wird. Ich füge hinzu, dass die Korrektheit der lateinischen Zitate erfrischend ist (nur muss das *numen praesenti* [S. 59–60] in *numen praesens* korrigiert werden). In einem Punkt finde ich die Terminologie etwas künstlich. Der Unterschied zwischen Sakral- und Kultbauten scheint nicht einleuchtend, denn alle Kultbauten sind eigentlich Sakralbauten und umgekehrt, egal ob öffentlich oder privat. Wichtig ist jeweils, ob der Kultort im römischen Sinn öffentlich, also dem Lager oder der Zivilsiedlung zugehörig ist oder nicht; alle anderen Kultorte sind dann privater Natur, so wie auch verschiedene private Kulthandlungen in öffentlichen Kultorten.

Die Kultorte, die besprochen werden, liegen einerseits innerhalb des Lagers, in dem seit Beginn der Kaiserzeit bis zum Anfang der flavischen Zeit drei Legionen standen, andererseits außerhalb dieses Ortes. Leider sind nicht alle Perioden gleich gut belegt. In den *principia* identifiziert der Verfasser einen Raum mit einer Apsis, in dem wahrscheinlich die *aedes* der Feldzeichen der 21. Legion zu erkennen ist. Leider aber sind hier keine Inschriften und Spuren von Altären erhalten.

Viel besser bezeugt ist ein Tempel im Lagerzentrum, der durch eine genaue Rekonstruktion der Grabungszeugnisse in das Ende des 1. Jahrhunderts. n. Chr. datiert wird, aber schon vor 49 n. Chr., etwa in der mittelaugusteischen Zeit, in diesem Hof stand, dessen Funktion nicht erkennbar ist. In der 2. Hälfte des 1. Jahrhunderts steht der Tempel wahrscheinlich in einem mit Portiken ausgestatteten Hof. Es besteht leider keine öffentliche Inschrift, die uns über den Tempel selbst informiert. Die Grabung hat ihrerseits einen Tempel mit Pronaos bezeugt. In diesem Bezug ist es unnötig, über die römische Form dieses Tempels zu rätseln, denn wir sind hier in dem Lager einer römischen Legion, also im römisch öffentlichen Bereich, wo es keinen Grund gab, einen „Umgangstempel" wie in den Städten Galliens zu bauen. Man kann beachten, dass in der Zivilsiedlung des 1. bis 3. Jahrhunderts ein solcher bezeugt ist, der aber auch von Soldaten benutzt wurde (s. u.). Neben Statuetten sind eine Anzahl von *tabulae ansatae* und Fragmente von Steinaltären anscheinend im Tempelhof begraben worden. Die Inschriften zeugen vom Kult des Mars, was in diesem Kontext nicht verwunderlich ist, und von Gottheiten, die mit dem Militär zu tun haben: dem *Genius legionis*, der Minerva, die gewöhnlich von den Militärschreibern und den Exerziermeistern im Heer verehrt wird, dem Silvanus, Gott des Draußen und der Grenze, und den *Dii Deae*. Die Dedikanten sind Soldaten oder ein Veteran der 11. Legion. Ein Sklave hat zudem der den Sklaven zugeneigten Fortuna ein privates Gelübde beglichen. All diese Weihungen entsprechen der römischen Tradition.

Weitere Kultgebäude sind außerhalb des Lagers gefunden worden. An der Straße nach *Aventicum* ist, neben einem vorrömischen Fundort, ein Tempel belegt, der den Münzfunden nach von der republikanischen bis in die frühkaiserzeitliche Zeit besucht wurde; leider gibt es keine Hinweise auf Kultaktivitäten. Daneben ist im 2. Jahrhundert ein Umgangstempel mit einer *aedicula* und einer Halle gebaut worden. Verschiedene Gruben mit Keramik zeugen von Opfertätigkeiten. Auf diesen Tempel bezieht sich eine in einer Grube mit Architekturfragmenten und Ziegeln gefundene private Votivinschrift, nach der ein gewisser *[…] Iuvenis* wahrscheinlich in der Mitte des 2. Jahrhunderts dem *Deus Mercurius* dieses *templum [ad] facie(m) novam* (S. 88) hat bauen lassen, was heißt, dass er den Tempel neu erbaut hat. Nach den Keramik- und Münzfunden waren die Kultgebäude bis ins 4. Jahrhundert frequentiert. In der spätrömischen Deckschicht wurde eine Miniaturkultaxt gefunden (S. 90 Abb. 69), die Apollo geweiht ist; die Dedikantin ist eine gewisse Iulia, nicht Iul*l*a, denn der Punkt rechts neben dem L gehört klar zu dem linken Bein des letzten Buchstabens von *IVLIA*.

Da es sich hier um neuere Grabungen handelt, wurden wichtige archäozoologische Erkenntnisse gewonnen und ausgewertet. Sie bezeugen Reste von Rind, Schaf / Ziege, Schwein und Huhn. Da man nicht viel von Hühneropfern spricht, möchte ich in diesem Zusammenhang auf die Inschrift *AE* 1926, 69 aus dem Tempel im Lager (S. 216 Nr. 1) hinweisen, nach der ein Soldat dem Genius der Legion einen *pullus*, ein (junges) Huhn, als Weihgabe darbrachte. Ich glaube nicht, dass er von der Weihung einer Terrakottadarstellung eines Huhnes spricht, sondern eher, wegen der einfachen Terminologie, dass er ein Huhnopfer meinte, was eben auch durch die Knochenfunde bestätigt wird. Lawrence diskutiert die Präsenz von Knochen in und um die Kultbauten, wobei nicht immer klar ist, ob es sich um Spuren eines Opfers oder eines Opfermahls handelt.

Ein weiterer Umgangstempel, der zwischen die tiberische Zeit und die Mitte des 3. Jahrhunderts zu datieren ist, befindet sich außerhalb des Lagers. Die Inschriften beziehen sich auf Römer, darunter ein Legionär der 21. Legion und entweder der Legat oder ein an seinen Dienst gebundener Legionär. Weiter sind Fragmente einer gepanzerten Statue – eines Mars oder einer Kaiserstatue – gefunden worden. Im Osten der Zivilsiedlung sind auch Altäre an Apollo und die Nymphen entdeckt worden, bei Wasserleitungen, die also wahrscheinlich zu einem Nymphäum gehörten. Schließlich erörtert Lawrence auch alle Zeugnisse der Hauskulte.

Wir haben es also mit einem anspruchsvollen Werk zu tun, in dem die Leserschaft keine pauschalen und oberflächlichen Beschreibungen der Religion in einem und um ein Legionslager erhält, so wie die allgemeine Doxa sie erwartet, die einerseits in der Kaiserzeit nur die sogenannten orientalischen Kulte als interessant ansieht oder aber die Kultorte und Handlungen in den Siedlungen mit der vorrömischen Zeit verbindet. Auch wenn natürlich nicht alles zu klären ist, können wir Schritt für Schritt quellenkritische Rückschlüsse ziehen auf das, was in dieser Welt des 1. bis 3. Jahrhunderts zum Bereich des Religiösen gehörte, und auch was man in der antiken Welt darunter verstand. Lawrence vergleicht die Befunde im Lager und in der späteren Zivilsiedlung mit den Kulthandlungen, die in anderen Lagern, Provinzialsiedlungen und in Italien bezeugt sind. Seine Arbeit widmet sich der schwierigen Erstellung von Interpretationen der verschiedenen Befunde und nicht, wie das noch oft geschieht, z. B. der Beschreibung von Religion als individueller Tätigkeit, die irgendwie die exklusive Wichtigkeit des Bezugs des Individuums zu einer Gottheit hervorhebt oder vor allem die sogenannten orientalischen Kulte als noch einzig lebendige Religion bevorzugt. Solche Einstellungen sind von der christlichen Deutung der antiken Religionen bestimmt, und man muss Andrew Lawrence dankbar sein, dass er die mühsame Arbeit an der Erschließung der archäologischen Quellen nicht gescheut und versucht hat, sie in ihrem historischen, rituellen Kontext zu deuten. Wie er oft bemerkt, ist noch viel Arbeit nötig, um die Resultate dieser Art von Religionsarchäologie zu verbessern, zu bekräftigen und zu erweitern. In dieser Hinsicht ist seine präzise Studie der Religion in *Vindonissa* eine richtungweisende Bereicherung.

FR–75005 Paris
11, place Marcelin-Berthelot
E-Mail: john.scheid@college-de-france.fr

John Scheid
Collège de France

JANKA ISTENIČ, Roman Military Equipment from the River Ljubljanica. Typology, Chronology and Technology / Rimska Vojaška Oprema iz Reke Ljubljanice. Arheološke in naravoslovne raziskave. Katalogi in Monografije 43 / Catalogi et monographiae 43. Narodni muzej Slovenije, Ljubljana 2019. € 58,–. ISBN 978-961-6981-35-4. 394 Seiten mit 146 Abbildungen einschließlich 92 Seiten Katalog mit Farbabbildungen der Objekte und 20 Fundtafeln.

Mit der hier zu besprechenden Arbeit legt die Autorin Janka Istenič, die Kuratorin für die römische Epoche und Leiterin der archäologischen Abteilung am Slowenischen Nationalmuseum, eine überzeugende Zusammenfassung ihrer jahrzehntelangen Forschungen zu den republikanischen und kaiserzeitlichen Militaria aus dem Fluss Ljubljanica in Slowenien vor. Die Publikation ist komplett zweisprachig (englisch / slowenisch) gehalten und außergewöhnlich gut illustriert. Besonders hervorzuheben ist der umfassende Einbezug der Materialanalytik, die nicht nur in Form eines Anhangs abgedruckt ist, sondern aktiv bei der Besprechung der einzelnen Objektgruppen mit in die Diskussion einbezogen worden ist.

Die Autorin hat ihr Werk in insgesamt 19 Kapitel mitsamt anschließendem Katalog sowie Tafeln mit Fundzeichnungen und umfangreicher Literaturliste gegliedert. Im Rahmen meiner Besprechung werde ich dieser Gliederung folgen.

Die Kapitel 1–3 sind dem Vorwort (S. 12–15), der Einführung (S. 16–21), einer kleinen Forschungsgeschichte (S. 22–25) und den Zielsetzungen der Arbeit (S. 26–29) gewidmet. Die vorgelegten Objekte stammen aus dem Abschnitt der Ljubljanica (antiker Name *Flumen Nauportus*) zwischen Vrhnika / *Nauportus* und Ljubljana / *Emona*. Aus dem nicht besonders tiefen und auch nicht außergewöhnlich rasch strömenden Fluss konnten neben den hier näher besprochenen Militaria zahlreiche weitere Fundstücke geborgen werden (S. 16 Anm. 1; S. 23 Abb. 8), die aber von der Autorin im Zusammenhang dieser Publikation nicht weiter Berücksichtigung finden; gerne hätte man zu dieser Auswahl eine nähere Begründung gelesen. Vorgestellt wird Militärausrüstung der römischen Republik und der Kaiserzeit. Fibeln fanden zu Recht keine Berücksichtigung, da deren alleinige Zweckzuweisung zum römischen Militär nicht zu belegen ist.

Die Sammlungsgeschichte zu den Objekten umfasst mittlerweile 200 Jahre und ist somit begreiflicherweise ziemlich komplex (Kap. 2, S. 22–25). Derzeit werden die hier vorgestellten Militaria zum einen im *National Museum of Slovenia* (NMS) und zum anderen im *City Museum of Ljubljana* (MM) aufbewahrt. Daneben wird von einer gewissen Anzahl an Objekten in Privatsammlungen auszugehen sein. Von diesen wurde der Autorin aber bisher einzig eine Speerspitze (E4, S. 101 Abb. 44) bekannt gemacht und hier im Text mit Abbildung übernommen. Leider schlägt sich die komplexe Fund- und Sammlungsgeschichte auch im Text nieder. Insgesamt stellt die Autorin 85 Militaria vor, von denen 79 in Kapitel 18 (S. 208–231) in die weitere Analyse genommen werden. Davon stammen 58 Objekte aus dem *National Museum of Slovenia* und sind im Katalog- sowie Tafelteil aufgeführt. Die Stücke aus dem *City Museum of Ljubljana* sind im Katalog nicht enthalten. Diese erscheinen nur im Textteil der Arbeit mit jeweils vorgestelltem „MM" und werden bei Bedarf mit Foto oder Zeichnung im Text abgebildet. Für die Leserschaft wäre es einfacher gewesen, wenn die Autorin alle von ihr behandelten Militaria in einem einzigen Katalog aufgeführt und dokumentiert hätte. Auch aus diesem Grund der unterschiedlichen Katalogisierungsweisen wird bis zum Ende der Arbeit nicht klar, von wieviel Objekten exakt die Rede ist.

In den Kapiteln 4 bis 15 (S. 30–143) erfolgt die Vorlage und typochronologische Einordnung der Funde. Dafür erstellte die Autorin eine Aufgliederung des Materials in zehn Kategorien mit jeweils vorangestellten Buchstaben. Zur besseren Übersicht dieser Gliederung und den darin aufgeführten Katalognummern sei auf die hier beigefügte *Tabelle 1* verwiesen. Die Ausführungen der Autorin zu den einzelnen Kategorien belegen beispielhaft ihre umfassende Expertise im Bereich der Militariaforschung und sind neben Abbildungen der Stücke aus dem *City Museum of Ljubljana* durch zahlreiche weitere Beispiele / Parallelen der Region illustriert.

Gleich zu Beginn (Kap. 4, S. 30–65) steht die Präsentation von insgesamt 33 Schwertteilen (Klingen und Scheiden), die im Rahmen dreier Unterkategorien behandelt werden. Ganz besonders wichtig sind dabei die Ausführungen zu den Klingen- und Scheidenteilen spätrepublikanischer Schwerter (Kap. 4.1, S. 30–40), die zu Recht von der Autorin dem *gladius hispaniensis* zugewiesen werden. Insbesondere die Klinge mit zugehöriger Netzscheide A1 (S. 150 Tab. A1.1–9; S. 151 Abb. 61; Taf. 1) kann mit Fug und Recht als Typ-definierend bezeichnet werden. Den umfangreichsten Teil nehmen dann die Erörterungen zu den Klingen- und Scheidenteilen vom Mainzer Typ (Kap. 4.2, S. 40–57) ein. Dieser Gruppe können insgesamt 23 Teile zugewiesen werden, wobei die Scheidenklammer A13 vom *National Museum of Slovenia* und die Schwertklinge mit Mundblech MM A24 vom *City Museum of Ljubljana* zu ein und demselben Schwert gehören. Die Erläuterungen und Beschreibungen zu den verschiedenen Klingen und Scheidenteilen sind sehr instruktiv und geben der Leserschaft neue Einblicke zum Schwert Typ Mainz, dessen Produktion anscheinend in großem Umfang standardisiert verlaufen ist. Das abschließende Kapitel zu den Schwertern (Kap. 4.3, S. 58–65) widmet sich weiteren Schwertformen jenseits vom Typ Mainz. Zu nennen sind u. a. der Typ Pompeji (MM A32) und der obere Abschluss eines Ringknaufschwerts (A21), beides Formen / Typen, die erst ab der Mitte des 1. Jahrhundert n. Chr. und später zu datieren sind.

Kapitel 5 (S. 66–87) widmet sich den insgesamt vier Dolchen aus dem Fluss, von denen zwei zum Typ Dangstetten (B3–4) und zwei zum Typ Mainz mit Emailverzierungen auf Griff und / oder Scheide gehören (B1–2). Die Autorin nutzt den Platz für einen größeren Exkurs zu den frühen Dolchformen (Kap. 5.1, S. 66–69) und ergänzt ihre Ausführungen zum Typ Dangstetten (Kap. 5.2, S. 69–80) mit einer Liste aller derzeit bekannten Exemplare dieses Typs (S. 72–80, Liste 1 mit

Kategorie	Unterkategorie	Katalog	Bemerkungen
A. Schwerter / Scheiden	Vorläufer Typ Mainz	A1–A4, MM A23 = 5	
	Typ Mainz	A5–A18, A35, MM A24–30, MM A34 = 23	A13 und MM A24 von einem Schwert
	Andere Schwerttypen	A19–A21, MM A31–33 = 6	
B. Dolche	Typ Dangstetten	B3–4 = 2	
	Dolche mit verzierten Scheiden	B1–2 = 2	
C. Helme	Montefortino	C1	
	Buggenum / Hagenau	C2	
D. Pila	Zungenpila	D1–8, MM D10 = 9	3 Pila Herkunft unsicher
	Tüllenpilum	D9	
E. Speerspitzen	Mit facettierter Tülle	E1–3, E4, E5 = 5 (4)	1 Spitze verloren
F. Dolabrae	Große Form	F1–2, F4–5, (F6) MM F7–8 = 7 (6)	1 Dolabra Herkunft unsicher
	Kleine Form	F3, MM F9 = 2	
G. Torfstecher		G1–3, MM G4–5 = 5	
H. Gürtelteile	Schnalle / Gürtelblech	H1–2 = 2	
	Doppelösenknopf	H3	
	Ösenknöpfe	H4–5 = 2	
	Einfache Schnalle	H6	
Schuhnägel		H7–8 = 2	
I. Militärische Abzeichen	Medaillon	I1	
	Torques	I2	
J. Zeltnägel	Kopföse	J1, MM J3–4 = 3	
	Seitenöse	MM J2, MM J5 = 2	
SG. Schildbuckel		MM SG	
P. *stimuli* / Fußangeln (?)		P01–06 = 6	

Tab. 1: Römische Militaria aus der Ljubljanica zwischen Vrhnika / *Nauportus* und Ljubljana / *Emona*. Gliederung anhand der Angaben in Text und Katalog. MM = City Museum of Ljubljana.

Abb. 38). Auch die Analyse der beiden Dolche B1–2 mit Emailleverzierungen (Kap. 5.3+4, S. 80–87) auf Griff oder Scheide ist angefüllt mit guten Beobachtungen und weiterführenden Überlegungen zu Parallelen aus der Region (S. 84 Abb. 39; S. 84–85).

Die beiden Helme aus Bronze (Kap. 6, S. 88–93) gehören zum Typ Montefortino (E1) und Typ Buggenum / Hagenau (E2). Beide Exemplare werden sorgfältig beschrieben, wobei ein besonderes Augenmerk auf den Herstellungsspuren liegt. Mit dem Helm E1 dürfte eines der ältesten Stücke (mittlere Republik) der gesamten hier vorgelegten Flussfunde vorliegen.

Die Kapitel 7 und 8 (S. 94–101) sind den Wurfwaffen gewidmet. Neben den maximal zehn Pila (Kategorie D) liegen vier gesichert frühe Speerspitzen (Kategorie E) vor. Gerade bei den Pila ist vor allem ihre meist vollständige Erhaltung zu beachten. Insgesamt handelt es sich bis auf ein Pilum mit Tüllenschäftung (D9) um Pila mit Zungenschäftung. Leider fallen die Erläuterungen zu dieser Kategorie etwas spärlich aus, bei der Einordnung dieses außergewöhnlichen Ensembles hätte die Autorin ausführlicher sein können. Dies holt J. Istenič bei den Speerspitzen nach. Charakteristisch bei den präsentierten Stücken ist die facettierte Schafttülle. Eigentlich wird eine solche Tülle eher bei frühmittelalterlichen Speertypen erwartet. Mit Hilfe der Vorlage eines umfangreichen Vergleichsspektrums kann die Autorin aber eindrücklich und überzeugend die frühkaiserzeitliche Einordnung ihrer Exemplare belegen.

In die Kategorie der weiteren Ausrüstung bzw. dem Gerät für Pioniere (Kap. 9 und 10, S. 102–107) gehören die Kategorie F der Dolabrae und die Kategorie G der Torfstecher. Die Dolabrae liegen in zwei Ausprägungen vor, die aufgrund ihrer Maße in eine große, schwere und eine kleine, leichte Variante unterteilt werden. Auch wenn das im Text nicht ausdrücklich genannt wird, so ist doch der militärische Bezug dieser Geräte offensichtlich. Etwas schwieriger ist das bei den sogenannten Torfstechern zu belegen, zu denen es nur sehr wenige Parallelen gibt. Doch auch bei dieser Objektgruppe dürfte der militärische Bezug unzweifelhaft sein.

Kategorie H, die in Kapitel 11 (S. 108–117) abgehandelt wird, umfasst sechs Gürtelteile und zwei Schuhnägel. Der Einbezug der Schuhnägel in diese Kategorie ist dabei nicht besonders überzeugend. Für diese beiden Objekte hätte auch eine eigene Abteilung geschaffen werden können. Unter den Gürtelteilen fallen besonders die beiden fein verzierten Stücke H1 und H3 aus Silber auf. Dieses Edelmetall ist bei der militärischen Ausrüstung eher selten nachgewiesen und könnte auf einen Nutzer höheren militärischen Rangs hinweisen. Zum Doppelösenknopf H3 überlegt sich die Autorin eine Nutzung als Gürtelverschluss oder zur Aufhängung eines Schwerts (S. 113 Abb. 49). In letzterem Fall müsste ein zweiter Doppelösenknopf eingesetzt gewesen sein, der sich aber natürlich noch im Fluss befinden könnte.

Schuhnägel zählen zum umfangreichsten Fundgut aus spätrepublikanisch-frühkaiserzeitlichen Zusammenhängen. Die geringe Zahl aus der Ljubljanica verwundert aber nicht, immerhin handelt es sich um Flussfunde und nicht um Funde aus einer Ausgrabung. Aufgrund der Kreuz- und Warzenzier auf der Unterseite (H7) bzw. dem Kopfdurchmesser (H8) lassen sich beide Exemplare am ehesten in die späte Republik datieren.

Kapitel 12 (S. 118–129) ist den militärischen Abzeichen gewidmet, einem Medaillon (I1) und einem mutmaßlichen Torques (I2). Dem Medaillon mit Kaiserbüste widmet die Autorin einen größeren Exkurs. Dabei kann sie recht wahrscheinlich machen, dass eine sogenannte *phalera* vorliegt, die Augustus zeigt und als Teil einer militärischen Auszeichnung genutzt wurde. Vergleichbares wird mit dem tordierten Reif I2 aus Zinn versucht, der sich aber in Form und vor allem Materialzusammensetzung mit keinem anderen antiken Objekt direkt vergleichen lässt. Bei diesem Fund sollte eine nachrömische (mittelalterliche?) Datierung nicht ganz außer Acht gelassen werden.

Die insgesamt fünf Zeltheringe (Kategorie J) werden in Kapitel 13 (S. 130–133) den beiden bekannten Formen mit Kopföse oder mit Seitenöse zugewiesen, die beide aus der frühen Kaiserzeit bekannt sind. Interessanter ist danach in Kapitel 14 (S. 134–139) die umfassende Präsentation eines Schildbuckels (Kategorie SG) aus Messing. Aufgrund seiner Form und anhand von Vergleichsfunden kann die Autorin diesen Schildbuckel überzeugend ins 3. Jahrhundert n. Chr. datieren. Er ist damit das mit Abstand jüngste Objekt römischer Militärausrüstung, das in den vorliegenden Katalog aufgenommen worden ist. Zum Abschluss der Materialvorlage (Kap. 15, S. 140–143) präsentiert die Autorin noch sechs mögliche einarmige Fußangeln (Kategorie PO), deren sichere Zuweisung sie im Verlauf des Textes eher wieder anzweifelt. Den Zweifeln kann sich angeschlossen werden, vielleicht könnte eine Nutzung als Karst- bzw. Rechenzinken überlegt werden.

In Kapitel 16 (S. 144–189) legt die Autorin Materialanalysen zu einer großen Anzahl der in den vorangehenden Kapiteln 4–15 typochronologisch eingeordneten Militaria vor. Dieses Kapitel hätte gut auch direkt zur Materialvorlage gepasst. So ergeben sich im Text ab und an Redundanzen, die hätten vermieden werden können. Ausgewählt wurden insgesamt 35 Stücke, die bis auf den Schildbuckel MM SG aus dem *City Museum of Ljubljana* allesamt aus dem *National Museum of Slovenia* stammen. Eingesetzt wurden bei diesen Analysen zum einen die Proton-induzierte Röntgenemission (PIXE) und zum anderen die Untersuchung mit Partikel-induzierter Gamma Emission (PIGE), letztere vor allem für eine exakte Materialbestimmung der Oberflächen. Die Beschreibung der Untersuchungen sind detailliert aufgeführt mitsamt Elementnachweistabelle und exakter Bebilderung (Foto und Zeichnung), anhand der die genauen Messpunkte der Materialbestimmung zu sehen sind. Leider scheinen bei der Abbildung von Schwert A19 (S. 166 Abb. 87) Teile der Zeichnung (Griff und Klinge) vergessen gegangen zu sein. Der Analyse der einzelnen Objekte schließt sich im Kapitel 17 (S. 190–207) eine Gesamtbeurteilung der Nutzung einzelner Legierungen bzw. Metalle beim antiken Produktionsprozess an. Im Einzelnen werden die Buntmetalllegierungen Messing, Bronze und Zinn-Bleilegierung sowie die Metalle Kupfer, Silber, Gold und Zinn analysiert. Dabei gehen die Aussagen weit über eine Analyse der Militaria aus der Ljubljanica hinaus. Zu jeder Legierung und zu jedem reinen Metall werden die Verarbeitung und die Nutzung in der Antike allgemein besprochen und dies in einer Vollständigkeit, die einem Eintrag in einem Handbuch gleichkommt. Kapitel 17 allein lohnt bereits die Anschaffung der gesamten hier vorgestellten Monografie.

Das Werk schließt mit einer auswertenden Synthese der Materialvorlage in Kapitel 18 (S. 208–231) und weiterführenden Schlussfolgerungen zur Ljublianica als Fundplatz in Kapitel 19 (S. 232–257). Das Fundensemble wird datiert (mehrheitlich republikanisch-frühkaiserzeitlich), kategorisiert und einzelnen Truppeneinheiten (mehrheitlich reguläre römische Armee) zugewiesen (Kap. 18.1–3, S. 208–215). In einem zweiten Schritt (Kap. 18.4–5, S. 215–223) geht es um den Erhaltungszustand der Objekte und deren Verteilung im Flussbett (eher im westlichen Abschnitt). Diese Verteilung wird danach im Vergleich mit anderen kaiserzeitlichen Fundgattungen angeschaut und auch mit der Fundverteilung anderer Epochen (Eisenzeit und Frühmittelalter) verglichen (Kap. 18.6–7, S. 222–231). Im Kapitel 19 (S. 232–257) stellt die Autorin die Fundverteilung der römischen Militaria und anderer Fundgattungen in der Ljubljanica in ihren soziokulturellen und historischen Zusammenhang. Während ein gewisser Teil des Fundniederschlags wohl dem normalen Verkehr auf dem Wasser geschuldet sein dürfte, fällt J. Istenič eine Häufung von Material an einem Punkt (Fundort eines antiken Grenzsteins) entlang der Strecke auf, der wahrscheinlich in der späten Republik und der frühen Kaiserzeit die Grenze zwischen der geordnet verwalteten römischen Provinz *Italia* und dem zu erobernden Grenzland ab *Emona* und weiter zur Donau hin markierte. Die römische Armee hätte bei Überschreiten der Außengrenze des Reichs Waffen geopfert, um danach in feindlichem Land erfolgreich zu bleiben. Dies ist eine interessante These, die aber sicher noch weiter zu prüfen und anhand anderer Beispiele zu verifizieren sein wird.

Den Abschluss der Arbeit bildet ein umfangreicher Katalog (S. 258–369) aller Funde aus dem *National Museum of Slovenia*. Die insgesamt 57 Objekte werden ausführlich beschrieben, sorgfältig im Bild dokumentiert und auf insgesamt 20 Tafeln mit Zeichnungen präsentiert.

Fazit: Mit dem hier besprochenen Katalog krönt Janka Istenič ihre Forschungen zu den römischen Militaria aus der Ljubljanica und legt eine Arbeit vor, die weit über eine Materialvorlage hinausgeht. Die Publikation ist allen zu empfehlen, die sich für die Ausrüstung der römischen Armee und die Erforschung römischer Metallfunde interessieren.

E-Mail: edeschle@uni-koeln.de
Orcid: https://orcid.org/0000-0003-2420-8685

Eckhard Deschler-Erb
Universität zu Köln
Archäologie der Römischen Provinzen

Martial Monteil / William Van Andringa (Hrsg.), **Monumentum fecit: Monuments funéraires de Gaule romaine**. Gallia 76,1. CNRS Éditions, Paris 2019. € 49,–. ISBN 978-2-271-12974-1. doi: https://doi.org/10.4000/gallia.4515. 276 Seiten mit 268 Abbildungen und 10 Tabellen.

Der Sammelband beinhaltet zehn Beiträge unterschiedlicher Verfasser*innen, die sich einzelnen, meist neu entdeckten römischen Grabmonumenten in den gallischen und germanischen Provinzen widmen. In den Beiträgen werden dabei die Ergebnisse jüngerer Forschungen präsentiert.

Vorangestellt ist den Beiträgen eine allgemeine, von den Herausgebern des Bandes verfasste Einleitung zu den Grabmonumenten im Untersuchungsgebiet (S. 1–8). Hier wird einerseits eine Definition und Abgrenzung der Begriffe „*monumentum*", „*sepulcrum*", „*mausoleum*" und „*heroum*" im antiken Sprachgebrauch sowie nach damaligen rechtlichen Kriterien gegeben. Anderseits kommt das vielfältige Spektrum bezüglich der Standorte, Gestaltung und Inhaberinnen oder Inhaber der Monumente zur Sprache. Untermauert werden beide Themenblöcke durch antike Quellen und archäologisch-epigraphische Beispiele, wobei einzelne in den Beiträgen behandelte Befunde ebenfalls eine Erwähnung finden. Erweist sich das Gesagte grundsätzlich als richtig, finden sich im zweiten Themenblock einzelne allzu pauschale Aussagen. So ist die Annahme (S. 3), dass die räumliche Verbindung von Monument und Villa etwas mit eisenzeitlichen Traditionen lokaler Eliten zu tun hat, als heikel einzustufen. Derartige Vergesellschaftungen besitzen in Mittelitalien bereits seit spätestens spätrepublikanischer Zeit eine starke Tradition (vgl. M. Verzár-Bass, A proposito dei mausolei negli horti e nelle villae. In: M. Cima / E. La Rocca [Hrsg.], Horti romani. Atti del Convegno Internazionale, Roma 4–6 maggio 1995. Bull. Comm. Arch. Roma, Suppl. 6 [Rom 1998] 401–424). Monumente im Untersuchungsgebiet mit entsprechenden Standorten könnten daher auch dieser römischen Sitte gefolgt sein. Problematisch erweist sich ferner die Aussage, nach der monumentale Grabmonumente im Untersuchungsgebiet ein Phänomen der „*élites gauloise*" und reicher Freigelassener darstellen würden (S. 1 f.; 3; 6). Die Sachlage zeigt vielmehr, dass solche Grabbauten von allen Gesellschaftsgruppen errichtet wurden, die über die hierfür erforderlichen finanziellen Grundlagen verfügten; vgl. z. B. das monumentale Grab des *Q. Calvius Turpio* in Lyon *(libertus)*, des *[—?] Vedianus* in Köln *(dispensator Augusti)*, der *Secundinii* in Igel (Tuchhändler), des *C. Poblicius* in Köln (einfacher Soldat), des *Q. Acceptus Venustus* in Lyon (munizipaler *decurio*), des *D. Domitius Celer* in Rognes *(tribunus militum)* und des *Sex. Iulius Verus* in Aix-en-Provence (Angehöriger des *ordo senatorius*).

Die darauf folgenden Beträge zu den Grabmonumenten sind entsprechend der Lage des Bauwerks in folgende Themenblöcke geordnet: Au plus près de la ville. Monumentalité des nécropoles suburbaines (S. 9–70); *Sepultus in villa*. Monuments funéraires et *villae* (S. 71–184); Sur le territoire des cités. Des mausolées marqueurs du paysage (S. 185–254). Diese Einteilung ist wenig vorteilhaft, da die in den zwei letzten Kapiteln besprochenen Monumente allesamt im näheren Umfeld oder auf dem Grundstück der Villen der Grabinhaberinnen und Grabinhaber lagen und wohl auffällige „Landmarken" gebildet haben. Selbst für die Monumente in den Nekropolen im unmittelbaren Vorfeld der Städte ist vorstellbar, dass ihr Standort durch Villen der Grabinhaber im Umfeld bestimmt wurde. Als Kriterium für das Ordnungsprinzip der Beiträge bietet sich der Standort der Monumente daher wenig an.

Der erste Beitrag von Yvan Maligorne, Serge Février und Jean-Noël Castorio beschäftigt sich mit den Resten einer monumentalen, architektonisch gegliederten und mit mythologischen Reliefs geschmückten Fassade des späten 1. / 2. Jahrhunderts n. Chr. in Langres (S. 11–44). Die erhaltenen Blöcke dieser Fassade, die in der Stadtmauer von Langres wiederverwendet wurden, lassen sich einer monumentalen Grabeinfriedung zuordnen, die von lokalen Handwerkern ausgeführt wurde. Den im Beitrag angeführten Vergleichsbeispielen solcher Architekturen wären noch die Umfriedungen der frühkaiserzeitlichen Grabbauten der *Plautii* in Tivoli und der *Titecii* in Trasacco hinzuzufügen. Bei letztgenanntem Beispiel werden die Zwischenräume der Pilaster mit gegenständlichen Reliefs ausgefüllt, worin sich der Bau besser mit dem Monument in Langres vergleichen lässt. Der Grabbau der *Plautii* zeigt hingegen, dass Umfriedungen der betreffenden Art auch in Kombination mit Baukörpern errichtet wurden, die das eigentliche Grabmonument bildeten. Dies wäre gleichsam für das Monument in Langres in Betracht zu ziehen. Inwiefern die registrierten Reliefmotive in Langres als apotheotische Bilder zu verstehen sind, wie vorgeschlagen wird (S. 39), sei dahingestellt. Darstellungen von Neptun und mythologischen Meereswesen fügen sich jedenfalls gut in das allgemeine Motivrepertoire römischer Sepulkraldenkmäler ein und sind hauptsächlich als Allegorien eines fröhlich-unbeschwerten Daseins im retro- wie prospektiven Sinn zu verstehen. Mängel redaktioneller Art finden sich in der Erläuterung und Legende zur Tabelle I (S. 14–16 mit Tab. I). Hier werden Informationen zu den Maßen und bautechnischen Aspekten der überlieferten Quader der Fassade in Aussicht gestellt, die in Tabelle I nicht geliefert werden.

Im zweiten Beitrag von Olivier Ginouvez und Sandy Gaulandi wird ein Grabmonument aus der 2. Hälfte des 1. Jahrhunderts n. Chr. vorgestellt, das im Bereich des Hôtel-Dieux in Narbonne freigelegt wurde (S. 45–54). Nach den geringen erhaltenen Resten wird es sich um einen Tumulus italischer Art oder ähnlichen Bau gehandelt haben.

Das sog. ‚Mausolée d'Herrane' in Saint-Bertrand-de-Comminges aus dem 2. Jahrhundert n. Chr. ist Untersuchungsgegenstand des dritten Beitrages von William Van Andringa (S. 55–70). Dieses Grabmonument erhob sich innerhalb eines durch eine Mauer umschlossenen Bezirks von mindestens 1 ha Fläche. Der Bezirk erstreckte sich direkt vor dem Stadtgebiet von *Lugdunum Convenarum* und wohl in der Nähe der Villa des Grabinhabers. Ausgerichtet war der Bezirk auf das Stadtgebiet. Diese Bezugnahme sowie die Größe und Gestaltung des Bezirks führen den Verfasser zur Vermutung, dass der Bezirk einer Persönlichkeit gehörte, die in *Lugdunum Convenarum* wichtige munizipale Ämter innehatte (S. 66–68). Hierfür liegen aber keine stichfesten Argumente vor. Das Bestreben, sich mit der Grabrepräsentation an die Bevölkerung der Stadt zu wenden, die im Leben des Grabinhabers eine zentrale Rolle spielte, ist vielmehr bei allen Bevölkerungsgruppen feststellbar. Lediglich in den finanziellen Möglichkeiten, dieses Anliegen auf möglichst vorteilhafte Weise umzusetzen, sind deutliche Unterschiede erkennbar.

Der vierte Beitrag von Philippe Mellinand und Elsa Sagetat-Basseuil beschäftigt sich mit einem Grabbau in der Lokalität Ussol in Saint-Rémy-de-Provence, der zwischen dem frühen 3. und mittleren 4. Jahrhundert n. Chr. etwa 50 m neben einer Villa errichtet wurde (S. 73–89). Wahrscheinlich ist der rechteckige Grabbau mit halbunterirdischer Grabkammer, in der sich zwei gemauerte, zu unterschiedlichen Zeitpunkten entstandene Sarkophage befanden, als Tempelgrab mit Säulenfront zu rekonstruieren. Gewinnbringender als der Abschnitt des Beitrages, in dem Vergleichsbeispiele von Grabkammern im Kontext von Villen genannt werden, wäre eine Suche nach gemauerten Sarkophagen gewesen, die mit ihrer Lage im Zentrum der Grabkammer ein außergewöhnliches Ausstattungselement darstellen.

Der fünfte Beitrag von Richard Pellé fokussiert auf ein an das Ende des 1. Jahrhunderts n. Chr. datierendes Grabmonument in Carcassonne, das innerhalb eines Villengrundstücks vor der Fassade des Wohnhauses lag (S. 91–104). Dieser auch von Verkehrswegen aus sichtbare, rechteckige Grabbau mit unterirdischem Bestattungsraum ist wohl am ehesten als Tempelgrab mit Podium und Säulenfront zu ergänzen. Dies zieht der Verfasser als Möglichkeit auch zögernd in Betracht. Der für das Untersuchungsgebiet und den relevanten Zeitraum fehlende Nachweis solcher Tempelgräber muss nicht viel bedeuten. So stand gerade die *Gallia Narbonnensis* als Gebiet, aus dem bereits in der frühen Kaiserzeit zahlreiche Ritter und Senatoren rekrutiert wurden, in einem engen Kontakt zu Rom. Hier kamen Tempelgräber im späten 1. Jahrhundert n. Chr. bei Angehörigen des *uterque ordo* in Mode. Ein frühes Aufkommen von Tempelgräbern in der *Gallia Narbonnensis* wäre somit durchaus vorstellbar.

Thema des sechsten Beitrages von Claire Barbet, Muriel Pardon-Labonnelie, Clémence Chalvidal und Marlène Aubin ist ein Bestattungsplatz in Marquion, der wohl zu einer ca. 150 m entfernt liegenden Villa gehörte und von einer Straße aus wahrgenommen werden konnte (S. 105–125). Dieser Bestattungsplatz setzte sich aus sieben in den anstehenden Boden eingegrabenen Grabkammern mit Holzkonstruktionen zusammen, die zwischen dem späten 1. und frühen 2. Jahrhundert n. Chr. für jeweils eine Brandbestattung angelegt wurden. Alle Grabkammern, die Wandnischen für die Bestattungen und Beigaben aufwiesen, verfügten über eine Zugangstreppe, die nach Beisetzung des Verstorbenen zugschüttet wurde. Zwei der Gräber waren oberirdisch durch ein gemauertes Monument markiert und zusammen mit einem weiteren Grab durch eine gemauerte Umfriedung vom restlichen Bestattungsplatz separiert. Unter den Beigabeninventaren fallen vor allem die kosmetisch-medizinischen Objekte aus vier Gräbern auf, die z. T. der Herstellung von Augensalben gedient haben dürften. Nach Meinung der Verfasser könnten diese Objekte einen Hinweis auf das Tätigkeitsfeld der bestatteten Personen liefern (S. 120–122). Es ist aber zweifelhaft, dass gleich vier Familienmitglieder, die innerhalb von weniger als 50 Jahren verstorben sind, im kosmetisch-medizinischen Bereich tätig waren. Möglicherweise sind die fraglichen Objekte eher als symbolische Beigaben zu verstehen, die einer familiären Beigabensitte folgten.

Der siebte Beitrag von Maxence Segard, Rémi Corbineau, Cécile de Seréville-Niel und Antoinette Rast-Eicher beschäftigt sich mit einem Komplex in der Commune déléguée Jaunay-Clan (S. 127–184). Dieser Komplex, der als Bestattungsplatz einer in der Nähe gelegenen Villa zu interpretieren ist, setzt sich aus einem Grabbau, einem *ustrinum* sowie einem quadratischen Bauwerk unbekannter Art zusammen. Der quadratische, im 3. oder frühen 4. Jahrhundert n. Chr. entstandene Grabbau barg in seiner Kammer die sterblichen Überreste eines Knaben und eines Mannes. Beide Individuen wurden jeweils in einem Bleisarkophag beigesetzt, der wiederum durch einen Steinsarkophag umschlossen war. In beiden Fällen lassen sich detaillierte Informationen zur Bekleidung der Verstorbenen und Bestattungssitte im Allgemeinen gewinnen. Inwiefern die im Sarkophag Bestatteten als Mitglieder der lokalen Aristokratie anzusprechen sind, wie vorgeschlagen wurde (S. 177–178), muss ohne konkrete Indizien offenbleiben. Erkenntnisreich erweisen sich außerdem die Forschungsergebnisse zu dem *ustrinum* aus dem 3. Jahrhundert n. Chr., die Aussagen zur Bestattungszeremonie und den Grabriten erlauben. Das *ustrinum* selbst bildete eine rechteckige Grube, welche mit Ziegelplatten verkleidet und durch einen Graben eingefasst wurde. Neben dem *ustrinum* lag eine Grube, die 70 Keramikgefäße sowie weitere Fundstücke enthielt und durch ein Mal mit gemauertem Sockel markiert wurde.

Der Rekonstruktion eines Grabmonuments in Vervoz ist der achte Beitrag von Catherine Coquelet, Jean-Luc Schütz und Fabienne Vilvorder schwerpunktmäßig verpflichtet (S. 187–212). Dieses Monument bildete den Mittelpunkt eines wohl zu einer Villa gehörigen Bestattungsplatzes, um das sich sechs Gräber gruppierten, darunter ein kleiner Tumulus für ein Kind und eine aufwendige Bestattung einer Frau. Von dem Monument haben sich einige Architekturfragmente erhalten, die um 1900 geborgen wurden. Der Bau ist als zweistöckige Aedicula zu rekonstruieren, die dem Grabdenkmal des *L. Poblicius* in Köln ähnelte. Es ist aber fraglich, ob die Skulpturen einer Sphinx, einer Raubkatze, eines Greifs sowie mythologischer Meereswesen allesamt dem betreffenden Monument zuzuweisen sind, wie von den Verfassern angenommen wird (S. 206–208). An vergleichbaren Grabmonumenten lassen sich jedenfalls nur Skulpturen von maximal zwei der genannten Motivgruppen belegen, die immer zum Dachbereich gehörten. Ferner ist die von den Verfassern geäußerte Annahme spekulativ, dass in der Aedicula eine Porträtstatue des Kindes und der Frau aufgestellt gewesen seien, die in den Gräbern zu Seiten des Monuments bestattet wurden (S. 204). Zumindest finden sich ansonsten keine Belege für die Repräsentation von Verstorbenen, die in benachbarten autonomen Gräbern bestattet wurden. Außerdem ist das Verhältnis der Frau und des Kindes zum Inhaber des Grabmonuments unklar. Nicht nachvollziehbar ist die von den Verfassern postulierte Errichtung des Monuments im 3. Viertel des 1. Jahrhunderts n. Chr. So werden für die Datierung des erwähnten Tumulus, aus dem sich der *terminus ante quem* für das Grabmonument ergeben soll, keine Erklärung oder Literaturzitate geliefert. Abgesehen davon ist die zeitliche Relation zwischen Monument und Tumulus ungewiss. Vage bleibt die Vermutung, nach welcher der Grabmonumentinhaber ein Militär gewesen sein müsse (S. 204 f; 210). So beinhalten das ‚Attis tristis'-Relief und der Waffenfries des Monuments, die als Argumente für die These angeführt werden, mehrere Aussagemöglichkeiten. Folglich überrascht es nicht, dass sich ähnliche Motive auch auf Sepulkraldenkmälern wiederfinden, deren Inhaber nichts mit dem militärischen Bereich zu tun hatten; vgl. z. B. das Waffenkonglomerat auf dem Aschealtar eines designierten *tribunus plebis* aus Fabrica di Roma (I. Di Stefano Manzella, Falerii Novi. Suppl. Italica 1, 1981, 140 Nr. 17) und die ‚Attis tristis'-Darstellungen auf der Grabstele des peregrinen *Demiuncus* aus Dunaújváros (A. Schober, Die römischen Grabsteine von Noricum und Pannonien. Sonderschr. Österr. Arch. Inst. 10 [Wien 1923] 119–120, Nr. 261).

Im neunten Beitrag von Frédéric Mercier wird ein Grabbezirk in Saint-Herblain behandelt, der bereits in der Latènezeit eine Nutzung unbekannter Art erfuhr (S. 213–225). Dieser unregelmäßig rechteckige, wohl um 100 n. Chr. eingerichtete Grabbezirk wurde durch einen Graben umgrenzt. Wahrscheinlich gehörte der Bezirk, der von einer Straße aus sichtbar gewesen ist, zu einer in der Nähe gelegenen Villa. Innerhalb des Bezirks lagen ein tempelförmiger Bau, mehrere Gruben, die wohl z. T. als *ustrina* oder Grablegen zu interpretieren sind, sowie vier wohl bronzezeitlichen Grabstätten, an denen rituelle Handlungen in römischer Zeit vollzogen wurden. Römische Fundstücke in den bronzezeitlichen Grabgruben, darunter mehrere Terrakottafiguren der Venus und von Tieren, sprechen jedenfalls dafür. Die kultische Bedeutung dieser vorgeschichtlichen Bestattungen zeigt sich aber vor allem darin, dass der römische Grabbezirk genau an dieser Stelle fernab einer Siedlung und mit Abstand zur Straße errichtet wurde. Die Sachlage führt den Mercier zu dem Schluss, in dem Befund eine Grab- und Verehrungsstätte für die Eigentümer der benachbarten Villa und deren Ahnen zu erkennen (S. 223–225).

Ein Grabbezirk in Boinville-en-Mantois aus der 2. Hälfte des 2. / 1. Hälfte des 3. Jahrhunderts n. Chr. ist Untersuchungsgegenstand des zehnten Beitrags von Aurélie Laurey, Vanessa Brunet, Mélanie Demarest und Céline Mauduit (S. 227–254). Dieser Bezirk wurde in unmittelbarer Nähe zu einer Villa und direkt neben dem Brandgrab eines Erwachsenen der 2. Hälfte des 1. / 2. Jahrhunderts n. Chr. eingerichtet, das wohl über eine Libationsvorrichtung verfügte. Mittelpunkt des fast quadratischen, durch eine Mauer umschlossenen Bezirks bildete ein Monument, das vermutlich in der Art eines Pfeilergrabes zu rekonstruieren ist. Innerhalb des Bezirks und auf zwei gegenüberliegenden Seiten des Monuments verteilt lagen je ein Brand- und ein Körpergrab. Die Brandgräber, davon eines mit hölzerner Konstruktion, beinhalteten die sterblichen Überreste von drei Erwachsenen und einem Kind. Eine der Körperbestattungen lässt sich einem Individuum perinatalen Alters zuschreiben, das in einem Keramikgefäß beigesetzt wurde. In dem anderen Körpergrab wurde ein Kind in einem hölzernen, durch Ziegelplatten umschlossenen Sarkophag bestattet. In dem Grabbezirk existierten zudem zwei Gruben, davon eine mit Kalksteinblock, die mit rituellen Praktiken in Verbindung zu bringen sind. Die These der Verfasserinnen (S. 239–240; 251), nach welcher der als Grabbeigabe verwendete Klappstuhl eine *Sella castrensis* gewesen ist, die auf einen munizipalen Magistraten als Grabinhaber hindeuten würde, muss jedoch bestritten werden. So waren *Sellae castrenses*, deren genaue gestalterische Definition unklar ist, ausschließlich für senatorische Amtsinhaber mit *imperium* und militärischen Aufgabengebieten bestimmt; vgl. RE II A 2 (1923) 1311

s. v. Sella curulis (B. KÜBLER). Klappstühle der vorliegenden Art finden sich dagegen auch in bildlichen Kontexten, die nichts mit senatorischen oder munizipalen Ämtern zu tun haben; vgl. z. B. den Weihaltar des *L. Minucius Optatus* aus Este (IT), auf dem der Dedikant bei seiner Tätigkeit als Schmied auf einem solchen Stuhl sitzend dargestellt wird (s. G. ZIMMER, Römische Handwerker. In: H. Temporini / W. Haase [Hrsg.], Aufstieg und Niedergang der römischen Welt [ANRW] / Rise and Decline of the Roman World 12,3 [Berlin 1985] 205–228, insbes. 211).

Den Abschluss des Sammelbandes bildet der Epilog von Thomas Creissen, der sich dem spät- und nachantiken Schicksal der Grabmonumente sowie den frühchristlichen Mausoleen in Frankreich widmet (S. 257–274). Viele pagane Monumente wurden vor allem im 5.–13. Jahrhundert als Lieferant von Werkstoffen oder Baumaterial genutzt. Andere Grabbauten sind in spätrömischer Zeit oder im Mittelalter zu christlichen Kultstätten um- oder ausgebaut worden. In der Regel bleibt unklar, ob es sich dabei um eine simple Wiederverwendung einer älteren Baustruktur oder eine Umwandlung in eine Verehrungsstätte des Grabinhabers im christlichen Sinn handelt. Schwierig erweist sich ferner die Deutung der frühchristlichen Grabbauten, die häufig an christliche Kultbauten gekoppelt oder mit jenen errichtet worden sind. Wurde in dem Kultbau der Grabinhaber verehrt oder suchten die Grabinitiatoren die Nähe zu christlichen Kultstätten? Für all diese Handlungsweisen werden übermäßig viele Beispiele genannt, die meist jedoch nicht eindeutig zu interpretieren sind.

Dem Anspruch des Sammelbandes, die Perspektive zu den Grabmonumenten in den gallisch-germanischen Provinzen zu bereichern, wird die Publikation mit ihren oft interdisziplinären Untersuchungen zu ausgewählten Befunden vollkommen gerecht. Weitergehende Betrachtungen, die über den jeweiligen Befund hinausgehen, sind im Band allerdings kaum enthalten. Ausnahmen stellen der siebte und zehnte Beitrag des vorliegenden Buches dar. Hier werden bestimmte Aspekte zu den Bestattungssitten, Grabriten und Verhaltensweisen in der Grabrepräsentation, die sich am jeweiligen Befund erfassen lassen, eingehender und im überregionalen Zusammenhang diskutiert (S. 164–178; 233; 239–240; 242–246). Solche weiterführenden Analysen wären auch für die übrigen Beiträge gewinnbringend gewesen und hätten wichtige Impulse für die Gräberforschung auf überregionaler Ebene liefern können. In gegebener Form beschränkt sich der Erkenntnisgewinn der Publikation aber vor allem auf den regionalen Bereich.

DE–60629 Frankfurt a. M.
Norbert-Wollheim-Platz 1
E-Mail: t.knosala@gmx.de

Thomas Knosala
Goethe-Universität
Institut für Archäologische Wissenschaften-
Klassische Archäologie

ANDRÁS MÁRTON, Les pratiques funéraires en Pannonie de l'époque augustéenne à la fin du 3e siècle. Archaeopress Roman Archaeology 62. Archaeopress, Oxford 2019. £ 70,–. ISBN 978-1-78969-335-5 (gedruckte Textausgabe). £ 16,–. ISBN 978-1-78969-336-2 (E-Book). doi: https://doi.org/10.2307/j.ctvwh8c7h. 338 Seiten mit 382 Tafeln (ausschließlich Karten), ein digitaler Katalog mit 868 Seiten und ein digitaler Band mit 116 Tabellen.

Bei der hier zu besprechenden Publikation handelt es sich um die Druckfassung der siebenbändigen Dissertation von András Márton, die dieser 2013 an der *Université de Bretagne Occidentale*, Brest eingereicht hat. Für die Drucklegung wurde die Arbeit nicht überarbeitet und neuere Literatur wurde lediglich in Fußnoten ergänzt, aber nicht mit in die Auswertung einbezogen.

Der untersuchte Raum umfasst das gesamte Gebiet der beiden Pannoniae (ab 106 n. Chr. *Pannonia Inferior* und *Pannonia Superior*). Da die Kolonie von Ljubljana / *Emona* (Slowenien) nach neueren Forschungen wahrscheinlich nie Teil von Pannonien war, sind die Nekropolen von *Emona* und die auf ihrem Gebiet gefundenen Bestattungen nicht in die Untersuchung miteinbezogen worden. Der analysierte Zeitraum reicht von der augusteischen Zeit bis vor die Herrschaft Diokletians.

Ziel der Arbeit ist es, zunächst auf dem Gebiet der römischen Provinzen *Pannonia Inferior* und *Pannonia Superior* eine möglichst vollständige Übersicht über alle publizierten römischen Grabfunde zu gewinnen, um dann in einem zweiten Schritt eine detaillierte Analyse der Grabbehandlungen und der Grabausstattungen zu erarbeiten. Am Ende der Arbeit steht eine Synthese (S. 234–238), die als Grundlage für spätere Arbeiten dienen soll. Die Datenbasis der Arbeit besteht aus insgesamt 1107 Fundeinheiten, die mindestens 11 421 Bestattungen repräsentieren, von denen 6343 individualisierbare Assemblagen sind (S. 27; 234). Die zwei Hauptschwierigkeiten, denen sich der Autor bei seiner Arbeit gegenübersah, war einmal die Ungleichheit der quantitativen und qualitativen Daten innerhalb des Bearbeitungsgebietes und die Uneinheitlichkeit der Nomenklatur, die A. Márton versucht hat zu standardisieren (S. 1).

Dem gedruckten Auswertungsteil (auch als E-PDF beziehbar) und dem auswertenden Kartenteil sind ein Online-Katalog (https://tinyurl.com/MartonCatalogue) und eine digitale Zusammenstellung aller Tabellen (https://tinyurl.com/MartonTableaux [beide letzter Zugriff: 05.05.2022]) beigegeben, die im Open Access abrufbar sind. Als Anhang zum gedruckten Teil der Arbeit findet sich eine Übersicht über die Ossuarien- und Sarkophagfunde Pannoniens.

Die Arbeit ist sehr kleinteilig, aber sinnvoll gegliedert. Im Weiteren soll der Aufbau der Arbeit nur grob skizziert werden. Nach einer allgemeinen Einführung folgt zunächst ein systematischer Teil, in dem verschiedene Begrifflichkeiten und deren Verwendung geklärt, die räumlichen und zeitlichen Grenzen gezogen und weitere Punkte erläutert werden (S. 1–24). Nach einer Forschungsgeschichte (S. 25–26) widmet sich die Studie dann der Darstellung der Dokumentationslage und der Datenbasis, bevor sie im Einzelnen auf die Bestattungen als archäologische Befunde eingeht (S. 30–47). Darauf folgt ein umfangreicher Abschnitt zum Thema der Kremation der Verstorbenen. Dieser reicht von der Ausrichtung der Scheiterhaufen und Einäscherungsgruben, dem Ort von Kremationen oder der Behandlung des Leichenbrandes nach der Verbrennung, über die Verwendung von einzelnen Urnengefäßen (Keramik, Glas oder Metall) bis hin zu den einzelnen Typen von Brandbestattungen (S. 49–81). Der Autor widmet sich dann in einem eigenen, kurzen Abschnitt den Praktiken am Grab (S. 81–82), bevor er sich in einem umso umfangreicheren Kapitel den Beigaben zuwendet (S. 82–233). Die Leichenbrandgefäße ausschließend, die ja vorher schon abgehandelt wurden, reicht das Repertoire von Keramik über Glas, Lampen, Fibeln, Schmuck, Militaria, Jagd- und Fischfanggeräte bis hin zu Nahrungsmittelbeigaben oder Kuriositäten, wie z. B. prähistorische Werkzeuge oder einem Bergkristall (S. 227), als Beigaben in den Gräbern.

Den einzelnen Abschnitten sind umfangreiche statische Grafiken direkt im Text beigegeben. Wer weitere Informationen benötigt, ist auf die separaten Tabellen (im separaten digitalen Tabellenband!) angewiesen, auf die jedoch immer verwiesen wird.

Abgeschlossen wird die Arbeit durch eine kurze Synthese der beobachteten Befunde und Funde (S. 234–238), eine englischen Übersetzung dieser Synthese (S. 239–243), einen Anhang der Sarkophagfunde (Annexe I, S. 244–271) und einem Anhang der Ossuarien (Annexe 2, S. 272–282). Eine umfangreiche Bibliographie (S. 283–338), der erwähnte Kartenteil (S. 339–520) und eine Einführung in den Katalog und Tabellenteil beschließen den Auswertungsteil (S. 521–525).

In seiner Zusammenfassung betont Márton die Vielfältigkeit der bezeugten Bestattungspraktiken in seinem Arbeitsgebiet. Sicher eine Folge der vielfältigen Bevölkerungselemente, die sich im römischen Pannonien über die Zeit hinweg vermischten. In vorrömischer Zeit sind noch wenige mediterrane Einflüsse in den Bestattungspraktiken fassbar, auch wenn es Gegenstände mediterranen

Ursprungs oder mit mediterranen Vorbildern im Gebrauch vor Ort gab. Mit der römischen Eroberung in augusteischer Zeit kamen dann in großen Mengen nicht einheimische Personen, vor allem Militärs, in den Raum, die ihre eigenen Bestattungssitten mitbrachten. Begleitet wurden sie von vielen (männlichen wie weiblichen) Migranten, Kaufleuten und Siedlern, die sich ein neues Leben erhofften und ebenfalls zunächst an ihren vertrauten Bestattungsweisen festhielten. Vor allem die Bevölkerung der neugegründeten Städte wie *Colonia Claudia Savaria* (Szombathely), *Scarbantia* (Sopron) und später *Aquincum* (Budapest, alle Ungarn) bestand aus Zugezogenen. Aber auch die einheimische Bevölkerung begann sich zu romanisieren. Keimzelle der Romanisierung, auch bei den Bestattungsbräuchen, war die römische Armee. Ihre Angehörigen gaben direkt und indirekt ihre Lebensweise an ihre Umgebung weiter und hatten auch die Kaufkraft, von weither importierte Waren zu erstehen.

So lassen sich in Pannonien zwei Tendenzen mit unterschiedlichen Vorstellungen von Bestattungspraktiken unterscheiden. Einmal, im militärischen und städtischen Umfeld, „römische" Strukturen der Bestattungen (Grabdenkmäler, Ziegelgräber, Sarkophage) und „römische" Beigaben (Lampen, Münzen, Balsamaria usw.). Dagegen sind für die indigene Aristokratie / Eliten die autochthonen Traditionen wichtiger. Die oder der Verstorbene wird in einem imposanten Bauwerk (Tumulus, Steinkammer) mit pompöser Ausstattung (Bronzegeschirrservice, Waffen, Streitwagen) bestattet. Je nach dem, zu wem die wohlhabende Mittelschicht in den ländlichen Gebieten mehr Kontakt hat, richtet sie sich in ihren Bestattungspraktiken aus. Während dies überregionale Beobachtungen innerhalb der Provinz sind, gelingen dem Autor auch kleinräumige Unterscheidungen, die häufig auf unterschiedliche Bevölkerungsstrukturen vor Ort zurückgeführt werden (z. B. auf Germanen in römischen Diensten). Der Autor betont jedoch, dass die Ergebnisse seiner Arbeit und die beobachteten Trends von der Interpretation einiger weniger, gut dokumentierter Befunde abhängig sind. Es wird Aufgabe zukünftiger Forschungen sein, unter Verwendung moderner Ausgrabungs- und Dokumentationstechniken, die in dieser Arbeit gemachten Annahmen zu bestätigen oder zu widerlegen, wie er betont.

Der umfangreiche Katalog bietet nur spärliche Angaben zu den einzelnen Fundorten und Gräbern. Die Einträge bestehen aus dem Fundort mit dem Verwaltungsbezirk, einem Hinweis, wo die Örtlichkeit innerhalb des Fundortes liegt, einer allgemeinen Bibliographie und einer Datierung der Gräber von – bis. Sind individuelle Gräber vorhanden, werden diese im Folgenden aufgelistet. Hierbei ist die Literatur zum individuellen Befund angegeben, gefolgt von einer Datierung des Grabes und der Angabe, in welcher Tabelle das Grab erwähnt ist. Ist man neugierig und möchte man weitere Informationen, ist man gezwungen sich diese aus der angegebenen Literatur zusammenzusuchen. Zwar sind in den Tabellen viele Informationen aufgelistet, Fragen, wie z. B. die Befundqualität oder die Frage nach den Kriterien der Datierung eines Befundes, bleiben jedoch weitestgehend unbeantwortet. Leider erschloss sich dem Rezensent die Konkordanz zwischen Katalog / Tabellen und den Karten im Auswertungsteil nicht. Da die Karten bei den Fundpunkten keine Beschriftung aufweisen, ist es bei wenigen Fundorten auf den Karten schwierig, bei vielen Fundorten so gut wie unmöglich, von den Karten zu einzelnen Fundorten in den Katalog zu gehen. Der gedruckte Auswertungsteil ist sinnvoll nur mit Hilfe der E-PDF der Auswertung, des digitalen Kataloges und den digitalen Tabellen nutzbar.

Als Bearbeiter der augusteischen Nekropole von Haltern hätte sich der Rezensent gewünscht, in diesem Band Parallelen zu den Befunden und Funden dieser Gräberstraße zu finden. Doch trotz der umfangreichen und personalintensiven Feldzüge der augusteischen Zeit im Bearbeitungsraum, die denen in das Innere Germaniens in nichts nachstanden, gibt es nur wenige sicher augusteische Grabfunde, die sich vor allem in Südpannonien gefunden haben (S. 29). Aus *Emona* und *Colatio* gibt es einige wenige Hinweise auf Klinen. Die Abwesenheit der entsprechenden Befunde und

Funde im Material des Gebietes, die sich der Rezensent im Moment nur schwer erklären kann, mag auch das Fehlen entsprechender Titel im Literaturverzeichnis erklären.

Die vorliegende Arbeit führt uns wieder ein Dilemma der Archäologie vor Augen, auf das man nicht genug hinweisen kann. Es gab und gibt viele Ausgrabungen, die dem Stand der Dokumentationstechnik und den Möglichkeiten, daraus Erkenntnisse zu gewinnen, nicht standhalten und man wird selbstkritisch fragen müssen: Gilt dies nicht in einigen Jahrzehnten generell für unsere heutige Arbeitsweise und unsere Standards? Kann es richtig sein, Jahr für Jahr die Denkmalsubstanz auszugraben, die Funde ins Magazin zu legen und die Dokumentation zu archivieren und zu wissen, wie wenig man damit nach Jahrzehnten bei einer Auswertung anfangen kann? Vor allem, wenn man den rasanten Anstieg der Möglichkeiten bei den Auswertungstechniken in den letzten Jahren bedenkt.

Trotz einzelner Kritikpunkte muss man zusammenfassend konstatieren: András Márton hat eine immense Materialsammlung zusammengetragen und eine beeindruckende Arbeit vorgelegt. Diese Materialsammlung wird unverzichtbar bei zukünftigen Forschungen zum Thema römische Bestattungen in den pannonischen Provinzen sein und als wichtige Referenz für andere geographische Räume des Imperiums dienen.

DE–54296 Trier
Universitätsring 15
E-Mail: Berke@uni-trier.de
Orcid: https://orcid.org/0000-0002-4031-7614

Stephan Berke
Klassische Archäologie
Universität Trier

Katharina Mohnike, Das jüngerkaiser- bis völkerwanderungszeitliche Gräberfeld von Uelzen-Veerßen. Materialhefte zur Ur- und Frühgeschichte Niedersachsens Band 55. Verlag Marie Leidorf GmbH, Rahden / Westf. 2019. € 64.80. ISBN 978-3-89646-847-5. 683 pages with 127 figures, 4 tables, 4 lists, 199 plates and 1 supplement.

The first impression: it is a heavy book, written by Katharina Mohnike about the late Roman to Migration Period cemetery of Veerßen, in the urban district of Uelzen (Lower Saxony, DE). This book is based on her PhD thesis, which she finished in the winter of 2012/13. Her academic supervisor was Jan Bemmann at Bonn University. Publishing this work took over six years.

The series' editor Henning Haßmann states that the book is more than its title says. Based on the core study on the burial ground of Veerßen, the extended work is a regional, comparative, and chronological study concerning the late Roman to Migration Period graves of the Ilmenau river region (pp. 7; 11; p. 20 fig. 2). The bibliography shows that the latest text additions were carried out in the year 2016.

The content is divided into three main parts: text (225 pages including 101 figures and 4 tables), catalogue (244 pages including 26 figures, bibliography, and lists), and plates (200 pages). The text begins with topographical information and the state of research and continues with information about the excavations and the quality of documentation, as well as the two main features of the site – cremations and inhumations. In chapter 2 (pp. 33–159) analysis of the grave inventories is dominated by typological and chronological studies on ceramic vessels (94 pages), which is then followed up by a comprehensive analysis (chapter 3, pp. 159–205) on ceramic vessels with glass inlays (window urns). Chapter 4 (pp. 205–232) is, again, a study on cremations (especially "Buckelgräber") and inhumations, focusing on the Ilmenau-region and Lower Saxony. In the last chapter 5 (pp. 232–235), a short summary is given which includes critical thoughts concerning chronological results, burial customs, cultural clusters, and settlement history.

The state of research in the Ilmenau-region is characterised by the publication of basic research data by Ole Harck in the 1970s and more recent studies by Dagmar B. GAEDTKE-ECKARDT (Hügelgräber des 4. Jahrhunderts nach Chr. aus Bad Bevensen. Die Urnenfriedhöfe in Niedersachsen 16 [Oldenburg 2001]) and K. MOHNIKE herself (Das spätkaiser- bis völkerwanderungszeitliche Brandgräberfeld von Lüneburg-Oedeme, Stadt Lüneburg. Bonner Beitr. Vor- u. Frühgesch. Arch. 9 [Bonn 2008]), which is why the state of research cannot be described as deficient ("mangelhaft", p. 11). However, there is indeed a lack of research on the studies of settlements (pp. 23–24 with fig. 3), with the publication of the important Rullstorf settlement only having just begun.

The most important guideline for the author was Babette LUDOWICI's study on "Frühgeschichtliche Grabfunde zwischen Harz und Aller. Die Entwicklung der Bestattungssitten im südöstlichen Niedersachsen von der jüngeren römischen Kaiserzeit bis zur Karolingerzeit. Materialh. Ur- u. Frühgesch. Niedersachsen 35 (Rahden / Westf. 2005)". There are also other regions to compare with, for example, figure 4 (p. 27) visualises "selected" studies on surrounding regions, but recent studies of the nearby situated Altmark are missing. Furthermore, the reader should keep in mind that LUDOWICI (2005) only deals with grave finds, whereas others deal with grave and settlement finds.

The burial ground of Veerßen is situated on an east-slope above the Stederau brook (p. 33 fig. 5; p. 40 fig. 11; p. 41 fig. 12). Since it was not fully excavated, the expanse of the burial site remains unknown. The reason for excavating this heritage was a ring road that was to be constructed. Although finds of "various periods" (p. 36) were known of in this area, the relevant authorities saw no necessity to act. Stadtarchäologie Uelzen even called it an "unknown" site (F. MAHLER, Das Gräberfeld im Veerßer Wald bei Uelzen. Ausgrabungen im Bereich der künftigen Ortsumgehung Uelzen. Heimatkalender für Stadt und Kreis Uelzen 1998, 125–134; here 125). That is why in the year 1995, the excavations began only after volunteers found archaeological objects at the construction zone. Until 2001, a total of 1023 graves were excavated. There are only 110 cremations with an anthropological examination (p. 38). While Mohnike points out the modern excavation techniques (pp. 11; 219), various facts cast doubt on this statement; there are no descriptions of the features ("Befundbeschreibungen"), there are only a few documented profile-ditches and only 320 photographs, and there is no original document recording the boundary of the excavation field (pp. 275–276). Two percent of the ceramic vessels were missing after the excavation (p. 45), and a lot of finds, especially metal finds, were lost. Additionally, a great deal of grave-coordinates was missing, and for some of the graves, the find context is stated as unknown.

Figure 11 on p. 40 illustrates graves with different distances between them, as well as clusters of graves, but there is no site plan for locating the grave numbers. A site plan is needed not only for understanding conclusions, but also for the simple documentary purpose of this monograph, and its absence is a big drawback.

Within the excavation field, 19 circular ditches were found (pp. 36; 42; 205–213; p. 38 fig. 9; p. 206 fig. 98). These incomplete circles with diameters between 3,5 m and 7,0 m are not only typical for the Ilmenau-region (p. 205), but also for the "ostniedersächsische Buckelgräbergruppe" (p. 42). An illustrating distribution map is provided by MOHNIKE (Die Buckelgräber der jüngeren römischen Kaiser- und Völkerwanderungszeit in Ostniedersachsen. In: B. Ludowici / H. Pöppelmann, Das Miteinander, Nebeneinander und Gegeneinander von Kulturen: Zur Archäologie und Geschichte wechselseitiger Beziehungen im 1. Jahrtausend n. Chr. Neue Stud. Sachsenforsch. 2 [Stuttgart 2011] 68–79; here p. 68 fig. 1). It was finally determined by the author that there is no burial ground with a chronological succession of "Buckelgräber" and mount-less graves (p. 207).

The Veerßen graves can be classified into 1004 urn-graves, two or three inhumation graves, and 17 concentrations of cremated remains ("Leichenbrandkonzentrationen") (p. 39). Inhumation graves are of special interest (pp. 42–44; 220–232), since due to soil conditions in Veerßen and most other places, bones do not normally survive (p. 220). Mohnike therefore brought together all late Roman to Migration Period inhumation graves of Lower Saxony (pp. 220–223). She concludes that a greater variety of skeletal orientation and positioning existed since stage C 3 (p. 224). There is an obvious cluster of inhumation graves in the Elbe-Weser-region (p. 224 fig. 101). According to the inhumation graves of the Harz-Aller-region, it should be pronounced that they show a close connection to the north-eastern Harz foreland and Middle Germany (p. 230). This is reinforced by a recent inhumation grave discovery at Hiddestorf (D. Winger, Gemeinsam in den Tod. Der Krieger von Hiddestorf und seine Begleiter. In: B. Ludowici [ed.], Saxones. Neue Stud. Sachsenforsch. 7 [Darmstadt 2019] 203–215). Compared with many other regions, it seems that people of the Ilmenau-region started inhumation rite with delay (p. 231), namely during the fifth century (p. 233). This result is confirmed by the inhumation grave 1456, yielding a ceramic bowl dated to the 5th/6th century (p. 43).

The most frequent finds from the graves, comprising 1086 units (p. 46), are ceramic vessels. Mohnike deals with this in chapter 2.4.1 (pp. 44–137), and again in chapter 3 (pp. 159–205). At the beginning (again on pp. 121–122), she examines the tempering and surface treatment. In both cases, it would have been better to display the numbers in diagrams. As in the Harz-Aller-region, in the Ilmenau-region, black pottery with bright, clearly visible quartz temper particles are known (p. 45.). This pottery is typical for the Migration Period (pp. 45; 53; 79 and 131).

A total of 832 ceramic vessels (p. 46) are distinguished in a detailed typology. The basic forms can be divided into 681 vessels with structured shapes (676 wide-mouthed and five narrow-mouthed vessels) and 151 vessels with unstructured shapes. There is no generally accepted typology, and Mohnike did not define her terms "structured shape" and "unstructured shape", or "narrow mouthed", and so on. Furthermore, when discussing the 151 unstructured vessels (pp. 83–87), she did not distinguish between opened forms (for instance, 1210.1) and those that are closed (for instance, 2290.1). Summarised in a positive way: Mohnike is looking for common features but not for differences, which then leads to similar features being subsumed under different "forms" (for instance, vessel 1739.1 on fig. 15 [p. 53] compared to vessel 1409.1 on fig. 16 [p. 55]) and many vessels of different shape in the same type ("Form") (for example, vessels 1123.1 and 1570.1 compared to vessel 1879.1 [fig. 15 on p. 53]). She did not separate a third basic type that other authors would call a "pot" ("*Topf*"; p. 48). Additionally, her typology evens out differences in proportion and robustness (sherd thickness).

Perhaps this generalising way of typological treatment is one reason for the wide-ranging chronological results spanning between the late Roman Period and the 6th/7th, even the 8th century (pp. 49–87 passim, 127; 132; 135). Nevertheless, most burials are said to date to the 4th and 5th centuries (pp. 219; 232–233). Continuity between the early Roman and late Roman Period cannot be proved (pp. 26; 232).

More precise chronological results are based on studies of special decoration types (p. 49) or bottom styles of the ceramic vessels; however, definitions of types of decoration and vessel bottoms are missing (e.g., "Ährenzier" [p. 62], "Auslassungsrosetten" [p. 56], "Buckel- und Fransenverzierung" [pp. 54; 76], "abgesetzter Fuß" [p. 49] or "angesetzte Standringe"). The reader is advised to consult the extensive, but displaced studies on decorations (pp. 89–121) and bottom styles (p. 89). The identification of some ornaments is doubtful (e.g., seemingly different types of stamp negatives ["Stempeleindrücke"; p. 113 fig. 46] dated to the Migration Period [p. 114], which, however, are a result from the same circular stamp.)

"Keilstichdekor", which is quite frequent in Veerßen (70 vessels; see pp. 114; 134 and 117 fig. 49), as well as in the Ilmenau-region (p. 115 with note 132), is dated to the Migration Period and to the 6th century (p. 73), but Mohnike misquotes Joachim WERNER (Die Langobarden in Pannonien. Beiträge zur Kenntnis der langobardischen Bodenfunde vor 568. Bayer. Akad. Wiss., Phil.-Hist. Kl., Abhandl. N. F. 55 [München 1962]), who did not link "Keilstichdekor" with the Langobards (p. 114), but called it an example of "elbgermanischen Dekor". Another terminological imprecision is the use of "twin vessels" ("Zwillingsgefäße"; pp. 66; 76; 161; 210) for vessels with great similarity, so that they seem to be made by one hand. The term "Zwillingsgefäße" is better known for coupled vessels from all prehistoric times, especially the Hallstatt Period.

The cremation of grave 958 was buried in a wheel-made vessel with a sieve bottom (p. 67 and 68 fig. 20 [unfortunately this figure is not coloured]). Aside from that one, there are seven, maybe nine, graves which delivered sherds of wheel-thrown pottery (p. 67). These sherds were interpreted as burial gifts (p. 70). The complete vessel of grave 958 belongs to "Braunschweiger Drehscheibenware". The corresponding distribution map (p. 69 fig. 21) only considers grave finds from Lower Saxony, excluding finds from neighbouring Saxony-Anhalt (for instance: B. BERTHOLD et al., Germanische Funde der römischen Kaiserzeit. In: H. Meller [ed.], Quer-Schnitt. Ausgrabungen an der B 6n 1. Benzingerode-Heimburg. Arch. Sachsen-Anhalt, Sonderbd. 2 [Halle a. d. Saale 2005] 107–125; esp. 120). Furthermore, distinguishing between "Braunschweiger" and "Hannoversche" wheel pottery is a controversial discussion that is still going on, and unfortunately Mohnike did not examine vessels by autopsy, even the one from the Bad Bevensen burial ground (p. 68).

Deviating from her typological rules (p. 46) which are based on shapes and forms, on pp. 81–82 (with fig. 25) the author separates seven vessels dating back to the Early Roman Period. These vessels are called "Terrine" (p. 81; catalogue also), a term she previously criticised (p. 48). The exact difference between a wide-mouthed vessel and a "Terrine" remains unexplained.

The burial ground of Veerßen delivers four "Fenstergefäße" (window urns). On pages 159–205, Mohnike gives an extensive study on window urns from all over Europe dated from the 2nd to the 6th/7th century, displaying a lot of examples, and four representative distribution maps. It should be kept in mind, however, that some vessels with openings or holes (p. 203) may result from searching graves by drilling a pole in the ground (s. E. CZIESLA / J. HOGARTH, Wildes Urnenstechen. Nachuntersuchungen auf einem bronzezeitlichen Bestattungsplatz bei Bergholz-Rehbrücke, Lkr. Potsdam-Mittelmark. Arch. Berlin u. Brandenburg 2012, 2014, 44–46).

In chapter 2.4.2 (pp. 138–159), the grave inventories are presented. Diverse items and materials were found, including pottery (spindle whorl), glass (molten beads), bone / antler / ivory (combs, comb cases, rings, a disc, a stick ["*Orakelstäbchen*"]), metal (rivets, arrow heads, brooches, sheets), stone (fossil), and organic substances (resin). Items made of ivory are of special interest (pp. 151–155 – this chapter is largely identical to K. MOHNIKE, Eborarii in Uelzen? Beobachtungen zu elfenbeinernen Objekten aus ostniedersächsischen Brandgräbern der jüngeren Römischen Kaiserzeit bis Völkerwanderungszeit. Nachr. Niedersachsen Urgesch. 84, 2015, 45–58). The discussion of certain types of objects often lacks precise numbers; Mohnike rather refers to imprecise phrases such as "a few" or "a rich spectrum". The reviewer counted 286 graves (28 % of 1023 graves) containing grave inventories apart from the cremation. That means in this case, that Veerßen – contrary to the author's statement on pages 158 and 233 – clearly differs from Bad Bevesen (80 % – reviewers count) as well as from Oedeme (62 %; p. 158).

The neighbouring Altmark region is said to be less connected to the Ilmenau-region (p. 132). Looking at some of the connecting aspects – narrow-mouthed vessels, structured vessels, vessels with facets, window urns, sieve vessels, wheel made pottery, similar dating for the end of the burial grounds, burial grounds with large number of graves, etc. – this statement seem to be questionable. Considering recent Altmark studies (F. Gall, Siedlungen der Römischen Kaiser- und Völkerwanderungszeit in der westlichen Altmark, ausgehend von den Siedlungen bei Benkendorf, Chüttlitz, Klötze und Stappenbeck. Veröff. Landesamt Denkmalpfl. u. Arch. Sachsen-Anhalt 65 [Halle a. d. Saale 2012]), it would have been possible to find "published Migration Period material" (p. 132) from the Altmark.

Coming to the final chapter, it is remarkable to note that the Saxons are not mentioned, even though the study deals with late Roman to Migration Period finds. The material seems to give no connection to the Langobards either, even though we know about the presence of this tribe in the Ilmenau-region only during the early Roman Period (p. 13). Instead, Mohnike prefers to discuss the "Ilmenau-group", which is more characterised by differences rather than similarities (pp. 232–233). Taking these differences into consideration, the reviewer misses an explanation for the alleged homogeneous end of burial grounds all over the Ilmenau-region around the year 500 (pp. 219; 233), as well as a discussion of whether the Veerßen burial ground belonged to the Elbe circle.

Together with the monographs of Gaedtke-Eckardt 2001 and Mohnike 2008, the present work is completing the Ilmenau-region-"puzzle". Thanks to Mohnike's diligent, careful, and richly illustrated book, we get to know in detail the Veerßen burial ground and others like Boltersen and Lüneburg-Ochtmissen, the pottery types and ceramic chronology, the inhumation graves in Lower Saxony, window-urns all over Europe, and "Buckelgräber" between the Harz mountains and lower Elbe region. The Ilmenau region is closely connected to surrounding areas, most of all the Harz-Aller-region, even if the Ilmenau-region is said to be of minor importance (p. 235). Graves that clearly indicate an elite are missing. The most characteristic feature seems to be the 200 year-long use of the burial grounds analysed in the Ilmenau-region and the (questionable) end of use around the year 500. It is to Mohnike's merit to have dealt with material over the years that others would have characterised as brittle and tricky. This makes this book an important study on the late Roman and Migration Period between the Harz mountains and the river Elbe – and, as the editor states, indeed an important contribution to the early history of Lower Saxony.

DE–Halle (Saale) \
E-Mail: f-gall@gmx.de

Fabian Gall

Peter Kos, Das spätrömische Kastell Vemania bei Isny III. Auswertung der Fundmünzen und Studien zum Münzumlauf in Raetien im 3. und 4. Jahrhundert. Münchner Beiträge zur Vor- und Frühgeschichte Band 65. Verlag C. H. Beck, München 2019. € 38.00. ISBN 978-3-406-10766-5. 240 pages with 63 figures and 89 tables.

This important study by Peter Kos discusses the coins found at the late Roman fort *Vemania* (Isny im Allgäu, DE) during the excavations of the years 1966–70. Far more than being just a presentation and discussion of this material, the author presents both a discussion of the appropriate methods to quantify and compare coin finds and an extensive comparison of the Vemania material with coins found in Roman Raetia and beyond. Thus, this work offers both thoughtful insights in coin supply and circulation in third and fourth century Raetia and a state-of-the-art overview of the coins in their archaeological contexts on the site.

After a very brief overview of the site and the history of excavations (pp. 9–10), the author addresses the various quantitative methods to compare coin finds from various sites (pp. 11–16). A standard practice is to sort the coins into issue periods and calculate the number of coins per year per issue period per thousand, thus taking the varying lengths of the issue periods and the total number of coins from a given site into account. Though P. Kos in the end predominantly uses this method, he clearly explains why in some cases it might be more informative to just use simple percentages or coins per year (p. 14). Furthermore, he clearly explains why it is important to study the coin profile of a site always against the backdrop of a wider region (p. 16). Only deviations from this backdrop are related to the particular site-history and have to be politically or economically explained. What he does not address however, is where to put the threshold of what still aligns to the standard pattern and what constitutes a significant deviation.

After a brief chapter on the coins from the first and second centuries, which are interpreted as residual material in the coin circulation of the late third century (pp. 17–18), Kos addresses from all possible angles the coin finds of the third century at Isny (date of issue, authority, mint, denomination; pp. 19–63). The question in how far the coin finds can shed light on the construction date of the fort takes centre stage, but is always thoughtfully embedded in wide-ranging comparisons with other sites. As the first peak in coin finds from Isny can be dated to the period 260–268 it has been suggested in the past that the fort had been founded in that period. Kos demonstrates that coins of this period kept circulating well into the late third century and that the coin profile of Isny shows a number of characteristics that make a construction date around 270–275 far more plausible (pp. 41; 48–49). Furthermore, Kos convincingly argues that in Raetia – in contrast to the Upper Rhine region – there are no indications of a drop-off in coin supply between 260 and 294 (the year of a major coin reform), which is indicative of a fully functioning defense system on the Donau-Iller limes (pp. 56–60).

The major part of the book is taken up by a full discussion of the fourth-century coins (pp. 63–117). As in the previous chapter on the third century, the coins found at Isny are compared in respect to their chronology, place of mint, coin type and issuing authority with sites in Raetia and beyond. Kos advances step by step and discusses all these aspects period by period. Slightly confusing is figure 37, which presents all coins from Isny by period, as the periods are not discrete units. Thus, he lists e. g. 28 coins from period 320–324, 13 from period 324–330, but four from period 318–337. In the presentation of the material period by period in the rest of the chapter, this plays no further part, however.

The major achievement of this chapter is that it provides a wonderful overview of the characteristics of fourth century coin circulation in Raetia and how this differs from regions further to the west and east. To highlight a few points: in the period 294–305 a number of sites in Raetia, and Isny in particular, show high ratios of coins minted in Carthage (up to forty percent), which is contrary to the standard pattern that coins are predominantly supplied by the nearest mint. Kos explains the presence of large numbers of Carthaginian coins by the movement of troops from Africa to Raetia, who took their savings with them. Both in the period 313–324 and 341–348 the political strife in the empire becomes visible in the coin circulation. In the earlier period, coins of Licinius, who controlled the East, barely add up to twenty percent of the coin pool in Raetia, but already reach forty percent in modern day Slovenia. Similarly, the sharp decline in coins minted at the Balkan mints in the period 341–348 reflects the conflict between Constantius II, who controlled the East, and Constans, who controlled the West, after the death of Constantinus II in 340, which somehow impeded the unhindered circulation of coins across the demarcation lines.

Of particular interest for the habitation history of Vemania is a Theodosian coin in an archaeological context, indicating a *terminus post quem* of 388 for the final building phase of the fort. Generally speaking, there is only a negligible proportion of coin imitations of fourth century coins among the fourth century coin pool in Raetia, which is markedly different from more western areas. Kos argues that this implies that Raetia was well supplied with fresh specie for the entire period.

A separate chapter is dedicated to the question of when coin supply to Raetia ended and how long bronze coins remained in circulation (pp. 118–128). As has often been observed, the production of bronze coins almost completely ceased in the western mints after 403 and coins from eastern mints failed to arrive in the West. Although Kos stresses that very few bronze coins postdating 403 have been found in Raetia, it is nevertheless a quite consistent phenomenon even if the numbers per site are almost insignificant to what went on before. Taken together with his analysis of the longevity of bronze coins issued in the period 388–403 in the Eastern Empire, where they often dominated well into the sixth century, it is absolutely plausible that coin circulation at Vemania, and other sites in the region, continued at least until the middle of the fifth century. Kos goes one step further though and postulates that "die raetischen Fundplätze mit einer für eine objektive Analyse ausreichenden Anzahl von Münzen der Prägeperiode 388–403 […] alle Merkmale eines kontinuierlichen Geldzuflusses bis zur Mitte des 5. Jahrhunderts zeigen" (p. 125). His main argument is the ratio of the VICTORIA AVGGG-type (minted in the western mints) versus the SALVS REI PVBLICAE-type (minted in Italy, the Balkans and further east). The latter type was produced for a few more years after the former had ended. The higher the proportion of the youngest type, the later the coin assemblage presumably is. As SALVS REI PVBLICAE was already produced from 388 onwards and Raetia generally was supplied more from the Balkan and Italy-mints than from the west, a dominance of this coin type not necessarily implies a later date for an assemblage, but above all, it does not indicate a continued *supply* of this coin type well into the 5th century.

The final chapter lists, rather than discusses, coins from chronologically relevant archaeological contexts like burnt layers and postholes (pp. 129–143). Importantly, it also lists all archaeological contexts which yielded more than one coin find, which gives a good insight in how long coins could remain in circulation (or not).

After the summaries in German and English and the bibliography, the book closes with a catalogue of all coin finds. Apart from the numismatic description, from which surprisingly the size and weight as well as the state of wear are missing, the x-, y- and z-coordinates of the find location as well as a brief statement on the archaeological context are provided.

To sum up, this is an exemplary publication of coin finds, giving both ample thought to the distribution on site and coins from archaeological context and to coin circulation in the wider region. Furthermore, we now have a solid baseline for late Roman coin circulation in Raetia and all further studies will profit from it.

DE–60323 Frankfurt a. M.
Norbert Wollheim-Platz 1
E-Mail: Kemmers@em.uni-frankfurt.de
Orcid: https://orcid.org/0000-0001-9962-7812

Fleur Kemmers
Institut für Archäologische Wissenschaften
Goethe-Universität Frankfurt

Nikolas Hächler / Beat Näf / Peter-Andrew Schwarz, Mauern gegen Migration? Spätrömische Strategie, der Hochrhein-Limes und die Fortifikationen der Provinz *Maxima Sequanorum* – eine Auswertung der Quellenzeugnisse. Verlag Schnell & Steiner GmbH, Regensburg 2020. € 45,00. ISBN 978-3-7954-3511-0. doi: https://doi.org/10.5167/uzh-187452. 382 pages avec 88 illustrations en noir et blanc et 92 en couleur.

Depuis quelques années, on assiste à un important regain de l'intérêt pour l'étude des régions frontalières du monde romain. Cause ou conséquence de ce phénomène, l'effervescence créée par les reconnaissances successives du mur d'Hadrien en 1987, du *limes* de Germanie supérieure et de

Rhétie en 2005 et du mur d'Antonin en 2008, comme un seul Patrimoine mondial par l'UNESCO, sous l'appellation *Frontières de l'Empire romain* (https://whc.unesco.org/fr/list/430 [dernier accès: 12 mai 2022]), ne lui est certainement pas étrangère. En outre, l'intérêt pour le *limes* européen est aujourd'hui alimenté par l'effort des États concernés pour faire connaître ce patrimoine, non seulement du point de vue scientifique, mais aussi au grand public, de même que par la candidature à venir de ses parties centrales et orientales (http://danubelimesbrand.org [dernier accès: 12 mai 2022]), pour qu'elles rejoignent la partie occidentale au sein d'un même Patrimoine mondial unitaire.

Le livre ici recensé (qui est disponible en libre accès sur la plateforme *Zurich Open Repository and Archive* : https://www.zora.uzh.ch [dernier accès: 12 mai 2022]) s'inscrit donc dans une sorte de mouvement européen, pour ne pas dire mondial, qui est parfaitement illustré par la vitalité et le dynamisme de la communauté scientifique qui travaille sur le monde romain frontalier – il suffit de consulter les réseaux sociaux pour le constater –, dont témoigne la progression de la participation à chaque édition du *Limes Congress*. Pour autant, l'étude que nous offre Nikolas Hächler (Université de Vienne), Beat Näf (Université de Zurich) et Peter-Andrew Schwarz (Université de Bâle) est pleinement originale, en ce sens qu'elle s'intéresse avant tout à l'Antiquité tardive et aux sources textuelles. Le prétendu « *limes* » est, en effet, un sujet qui est plus souvent abordé dans l'optique de la romanisation pendant le Haut-Empire ainsi que principalement via le prisme des témoignages matériels. « Mauern gegen Migration? » n'est rien de moins que le recueil analytique et critique des principaux textes anciens, littéraires, juridiques et épigraphiques, en traduction allemande, qui sont utiles à l'étude d'une province romaine tardive issue de la division de la Germanie supérieure à l'époque de Dioclétien, en l'occurrence la *Maxima Sequanorum*.

L'ouvrage est divisé en onze chapitres, qui sont précédés d'une introduction générale (« Einleitung » – pp. 11–65), proposant un court tableau du patrimoine tardo-romain sur le territoire de cette province, tout en dressant un bilan historiographique de l'étude dudit patrimoine, autant des points de vue historique qu'archéologique. La mise en valeur la plus récente par les pouvoirs publics, y compris pour les touristes non-initiés (jusqu'à servir de publicité pour des entreprises locales, comme c'est le cas à Yverdon-les-Bains, dans le canton suisse de Vaud, qui a fait faire à l'organisme *Mobile Tour Information System* un petit film dans lequel deux curistes en peignoir nous font la visite de la reconstitution du *castrum Eburodunum* – cf. p. 58 ; p. 60 fig. 42), est aussi évoquée dans le propos introductif.

Le premier chapitre, « Römische Strategie » (pp. 66–94), est divisé en deux grandes parties inégales. La première se distingue quelque peu du reste du livre, car, même si le prisme de lecture demeure la *Maxima Sequanorum*, les textes latins et grecs qu'elle rassemble et qui nous informent sur la stratégie militaire romaine, y compris du point de vue architectural, ne portent pas tous strictement sur cette province, mais parfois sur d'autres contextes frontaliers similaires. On y lit ainsi dans l'ordre des extraits de : Vitruve, Frontin, l'auteur anonyme du *De munitionibus castrorum* (Pseudo-Hygin), Procope de Césarée, le *Compendium* ou *Strategikon* de Syrianus Magister (ici qualifié d'Anonyme byzantin), Ammien Marcellin, le *De rebus bellicis*, Végèce, Ptolémée, Festus, Eutrope, la *Vie des Pères du Jura* et l'Anonyme de Ravenne, à quoi s'ajoutent des renvois à d'autres sources comme Polybe, la *Notitia dignitatum*, le *Code Justinien* ou la *Table de Peutinger*. La deuxième partie de ce premier chapitre, beaucoup plus courte (à peine quatre pages), s'intéresse prétendument à l'action stratégique de la figure impériale. Néanmoins, elle est vraiment très générale et annonce plutôt la suite du livre. Si la première des deux dresse indubitablement un tableau qui permet de mettre en place tous les fondements nécessaires au reste de l'étude, on se demande bien quelle peut être l'utilité de la seconde, tant son contenu est pauvre. Tout au plus, il aurait été préférable qu'elle soit présentée simplement comme une transition et rien de plus.

Les deuxième et troisième chapitres, « Limites, Strategie und Kriegschauplätze in der Kaiserzeit » (pp. 95–116) et « Die Erneuerung des Kaisertums durch die Tetrarchie » (pp. 117–149), se concentrent sur l'histoire événementielle, de même que sur les enjeux et sur le processus de la romanisation et de l'occupation du territoire, respectivement de César à Probus (58 av. J.-C. à 282 ap. J.-C.) et de Dioclétien à Constantin (284–337 ap. J.-C.). D'emblée il est question du terme « *limes* » que les auteurs proposent de définir, en remontant à ses origines – sans toutefois en donner une interprétation claire –, afin de justifier l'utilisation qu'ils en font. Étant donné l'importance quantitative de la littérature sur le sujet, marquée par plus d'un siècle de débats scientifiques, l'appui bibliographique à cette tentative de définition semble largement insuffisant. Par exemple, où sont les travaux fondamentaux de Giovanni Forni (Esercito e marina di Roma antica. Raccolta di contribute [Stuttgart 1992] 213–262)? Quant à la contribution de Theodor Mommsen au débat, elle n'est évoquée qu'en introduction, dans la partie historiographique générale (pp. 50–51). Pour ainsi dire, si plusieurs historiens et archéologues contemporains acceptent pleinement aujourd'hui, surtout par convention et commodité, l'utilisation du terme « *limes* » pour qualifier les secteurs frontaliers militarisés sous le Haut-Empire, il faut savoir qu'environ les deux-tiers des attestations de ce mot dans la littérature latine, tout sens confondu, sont postérieurs au IVe siècle (à paraître : D. Moreau, The concept of "*limes*" in the textual sources. A short preliminary study. In: M. Korać et al. [ed.], Limes XXIV: 24. International Limes Congress, Serbia, September 2018 [Belgrade en prép.]). Pour plusieurs autres raisons bien décrites par Benjamin Isaac, qui est cité dans l'introduction (p. 67), on est sérieusement en droit de se demander s'il s'agit vraiment d'une réalité proprement militaire avant l'Antiquité tardive. Quoi qu'il en soit, la question du sens réel du concept de « *limes* » est ici contournée. On comprend qu'il ne s'agit pas du sujet central du livre, mais quelques éléments supplémentaires auraient été nécessaires pour justifier davantage son utilisation tout au long de celui-ci.

En conclusion de ce premier ensemble de chapitres chronologiques, les auteurs, dans leur souci d'enquête historique et patrimoniale globale, reviennent rapidement sur un sujet récurent de l'étude (pp. 14–16 ; 65 ; 126 ; 148–149 ; 279 ; 299–302 ; 304 ; 309 et 314), à savoir les prétendus éléments historiques dans la légende du massacre de la légion thébaine ainsi que la réception de son culte, jusqu'à aujourd'hui, dans la région correspondant à l'antique *Maxima Sequanorum*. Il semble toutefois à l'auteur des présentes lignes que l'approche et l'analyse de cette légende ne sont pas ici suffisamment critiques et qu'il y a trop la volonté de rattacher à l'histoire un récit hagiographique, apparu dans l'Antiquité tardive et développé au Moyen Âge, qu'une grande partie de littérature scientifique de la seconde moitié du XXe siècle considère comme une pure fiction (absents de la bibliographie : D. van Berchem, Le martyre de la légion thébaine. Essai sur la formation d'une légende [Bâle 1956]; D. F. O'Reilly, The Theban legion of St. Maurice. Vigiliae Christianae 32,3, 1978, 195–207; D. Woods, The origin of the legend of Maurice and the Theban legion. Journal of Ecclesiastical Hist. 45, 1994, 385–395).

Le quatrième chapitre, « Strategie, Verwaltung, Versorgung und Militär-, Provinz- und Truppenorganisation » (pp. 150–178), propose moins de textes en traduction que les deux précédents. L'objectif de cette partie est d'expliquer les grands principes de l'évolution de la présence et de l'organisation militaire sur le territoire de la *Maxima Sequanorum* depuis César, en opérant une distinction nette entre histoire théorique de l'organisation des troupes, plutôt à partir des sources textuelles, et présence réelle sur le terrain, à travers les témoignages archéologiques. L'accent étant mis sur l'Antiquité tardive, la *Notitia dignitatum* sert de fondement à une grande partie du propos, ce qui est un peu déroutant au regard du *terminus ante quem* du troisième chapitre, c'est-à-dire l'année 337. C'est que la *Notitia dignitatum*, bien qu'étant difficilement datable, lui est postérieure. Elle aurait été composée en plusieurs étapes, avec une version finale pour sa section la plus ancienne, l'*Orient*, qui ne serait pas antérieure à Théodose Ier (379–395), alors que la partie consacrée à l'*Occident*, à laquelle appartient la province ici étudiée, n'aurait vu le jour que pendant les premières décennies du V⁰ siècle, peut-être même aussi tardivement que 425, voire 437/8 (le mariage de Valentinien III à Licinia Eudoxia, de même que la promulgation du *Codex Theodosianus* sont les deux éléments qui mettent un terme définitif au débat ouvert par la *partitio imperii* et la *Notitia dignitatum* pourrait n'être que l'illustration allégorique de ce résultat final, voulu par Théodose II). En outre, les études les plus récentes sur la question concluent toutes qu'il ne s'agit pas d'un document administratif et le texte, tel qu'il nous est parvenu, cumulerait plusieurs situations anachroniques (cf. en particulier les travaux de P. BRENNAN, également absents de la bibliographie, parmi lesquels : The *Notitia dignitatum*. Entretiens sur l'Antiquité classique 42, 1996, 147–178). En ce sens, on se demande à quel moment exact correspond la situation décrite dans ce document pour la *Maxima Sequanorum* et si l'on peut vraiment s'en servir comme fondement d'une description générale de la situation dans l'Antiquité tardive. De manière inusitée, attendu qu'il était question d'armée jusqu'ici, ce quatrième chapitre se termine sur quelques lignes concernant la diffusion du christianisme et la création d'une organisation épiscopale comme conséquence de la politique impériale dans la région. Était-il vraiment pertinent de parler de ce sujet alors que les règnes postérieurs à Constantin n'ont pas encore été abordés ? N'aurait-il pas été plus intéressant de traiter ici de l'impact de l'armée romaine sur la diffusion des cultes en général ? D'ailleurs, où est le mithraïsme dans ce livre, cette religion qui a été si importante dans le milieu militaire rhénan ? Pour la *Maxima Sequanorum* on pense immédiatement au mithréum de Biesheim en Alsace (voire notamment E. KERN, Le mithraeum de Biesheim-Kunheim [Haut-Rhin]. Rev. Nord Arch. 292, 1991, 59–65).

Les cinquième et sixième chapitres, « Neue Bürgerkriege nach dem Tode Constantins: Der Silberschatz von Kaiseraugst und das Ringen um legitime Herrschaft » (pp. 179–182) et « Die Usurpation des Magnentius und das geplünderte Kaiseraugst » (pp. 183–186), se concentrent spécifiquement sur Augst *(Augusta Raurica)*, dans le premier cas sur le célèbre trésor en argent qui y aurait été enterré à l'époque de Constance II, dans le deuxième sur le sort de l'agglomération à l'époque de Magnence. Sans que l'on conteste l'intérêt du sujet de ces très courts chapitres, qui semblent avoir été écrits pour servir de transition avec ce qui suit, on ne comprend pas très bien pourquoi la matière qu'ils traitent n'a pas été intégrée aux parties subséquentes. Les cinq chapitres finaux reprennent effectivement la suite de l'histoire événementielle là où le troisième chapitre s'était arrêté : « Constantius II » (chapitre 7, pp. 187–201), « Julian » (chapitre 8, pp. 202–230), « Valentinian und die Fortsetzung und Verfestigung der Alemannenpolitik » (364–375) (chapitre 9, pp. 231–266), « Von Gratian zu Theodosius » (chapitre 10, pp. 267–280) et « Der Fall Roms und die Folgen: Vom Kindkaiser Honorius zu den Burgundern » (chapitre 11, pp. 281–311). Dans ce bloc final, qui couvre les années 337 à 534 ap. J.-C., l'analyse est richement accompagnée de textes littéraires et épigraphiques en traduction, de résultats de fouilles, de plans, de cartes et de schéma, avec « l'originalité » de dépasser le cadre romain et de s'intéresser également, dans le dernier chapitre, à la stratégie d'occupation du territoire par les Burgondes et les Francs.

L'ouvrage se termine d'abord par une conclusion (« Schluss / Ausblick », pp. 312–316) qui propose une courte synthèse de l'ensemble et dans laquelle on peut lire, à la toute fin, une sorte d'appel à préserver le patrimoine romain régional, relativisant l'impact des grandes migrations sur sa destruction. S'ensuit la liste des nombreuses cartes et illustrations (« Verzeichnis der Karten und Abbildungen », pp. 317–320), celle des principales sources textuelles traduites, chapitre par chapitre (« Wichtigste Testimonia im Überblick », pp. 321–324) et celle des références bibliographiques (« Bibliographie », pp. 325–382). Cet ultime élément du livre mérite une très courte analyse. La bibliographie, qui intègre les abréviations utilisées, est divisée en quatre sous-parties : a) les éditions et traductions de sources (pp. 325–334) ; b) les recueils de sources (p. 334) ; les études (pp. 335–347) ; un catalogue des sites concernés par l'étude, dont chaque notice est accompagnée de plans et donne la littérature afférente. Notons cependant quelques lacunes, par exemple les travaux de Séverine Blin sur l'abandon du sanctuaire de Mandeure (voire par exemple, S. BLIN / C. CRAMATTE, Du sanctuaire civique à l'église paléochrétienne de Mandeure [cité des Séquanes]. Gallia 71,1, 2014, 51–63). Si l'utilité de chacune de ces parties – en particulier celle du catalogue – est indéniable, un des choix opérés pour la présentation des références bibliographiques est particulièrement malcommode : le classement est certes alphabétique et par nom, mais ledit nom est systématiquement précédé du prénom, ce qui n'aide vraiment en rien à la lecture. On comprendra néanmoins que c'est là un choix de l'éditeur et non des trois auteurs.

Malgré toutes les critiques qui peuvent être formulées, en particulier celle concernant l'agencement de la matière, « Mauern gegen Migration? » est un très bel ouvrage, tout en étant un bel objet, largement illustré et en couleur, proposant un intéressant panorama de l'histoire et de l'archéologie d'une province romaine tardo-antique, qui peut intéresser autant la communauté scientifique qu'un grand public averti.

FR–59653 Villeneuve d'Ascq cedex
Campus « Pont-de-Bois », BP 60149
E-Mail: dominic.moreau@univ-lille.fr
Orcid: https://orcid.org/0000-0003-3350-6203

Dominic Moreau
Faculté des Humanités, Département d'Histoire
Université de Lille / UMR 8164-HALMA

Martin Rundkvist, At Home at the Castle. Lifestyles at the Medieval Strongholds of Östergötland, AD 1200–1530. Östergötland County Administration / Länsstryelesen Östergötland, Linköping 2019. ISBN 978-91-7488-477-7. 137 Seiten mit 77 Abbildungen und 16 Tabellen.

Bei der vorliegenden Arbeit handelt es sich um eine Untersuchung von befestigten Adelssitzen des Mittelalters in der Provinz Östergötland und der Lebensumstände auf diesen. Östergötland ist eine Region im Osten von Schweden, südlich von Stockholm gelegen. Zahlreiche Seen sind durch Flüsse untereinander und so schließlich mit der Meeresküste im Osten verbunden. Seit dem 12. Jahrhundert gehört es zu den Kernprovinzen der schwedischen Krone und gilt als gut erschlossenes Altsiedelgebiet mit Kirchen, Klöstern, Marktflecken und stadtartigen Ansiedlungen. Wenngleich keine Siedlungskammer, so handelt es sich doch um einen gut umrissenen Raum, in dem alle befestigten Adelssitze bzw. burgartige Befestigungen („strongholds") systematisch erfasst wurden, sodass der vorliegenden Untersuchung durchaus ein besiedlungsarchäologischer Ansatz zu Grunde liegt. Aus der Feder des Autors stammen gemäß seiner Literaturliste bereits zahlreiche Publikationen zu diesen und anderen Burgen, sodass er ein ausgewiesener Kenner ist. Dabei versteht er unter burgartigen Herrschaftssitzen Objekte, die eine oder mehrere Voraussetzungen aufweisen: einen mehrstöckigen steinernen Wohnturm („keep"), eine steinerne Ringmauer, Graben, erhöhte Lage, gegebenenfalls auch nur ein Steingebäude auf einer schmalen Halbinsel oder Insel. 25 Objekte erfüllen diese Definition. Fast alle sind weniger als 100 m vom Zugang zu Gewässern (See, Fluss) entfernt, einige liegen auf kleinen (Halb)inseln. Die Lage der befestigten Adelssitze in Östergötland war dabei meist so gewählt, dass zwar kein täglicher direkter Kontakt mit den Wirtschaftsbetrieben bestand, aber diese sowie weitere Siedlungsanlagen wie Kirche und stadtartige Ansiedlungen leicht zu erreichen waren. Im Kontrast zu den größeren Burgen der Krone oder der Kirche stehen die kleineren privaten Herrschaftssitze. Diese waren häufig nur kurzzeitig bewohnt, sodass die Lebensumstände stärker individuell geprägt waren. In einer Feldstudie wurden vor allem zwischen 2014 und 2016 Ausgrabungen durchgeführt, darüber hinaus ältere Grabungen ausgewertet. Sieben besonders fundreiche Burganlagen stehen im Zentrum der Untersuchung (Stegeborg, Skällvik, Bjärkaholm, Ringstadaholm, Stensö, Landsjö, Munkeboda) und werden in einzelnen Kapiteln (Kap. 4–10, S. 56–115) ausführlicher vorgestellt. Ein achter gut untersuchter Sitz, Birgittas udde, erbrachte kaum Fundmaterial und scheint daher nur periodisch genutzt worden zu sein (Kap. 11, S. 116–124). Anderseits erklärt sich der Fundreichtum von Bjärkaholm, Ringstadaholm und Skällvik auch dadurch, dass sie ein gewaltsames Ende fanden.

Der Aufbau der Arbeit ist systematisch: Zunächst werden Forschungsgeschichte, Quellenlage (Kap. 1, S. 9–14) sowie Landschaft und Lage (Kap. 2, S. 15–16) erläutert. Dann beschreibt der Autor die zahlreichen Ergebnisse zur Rekonstruktion des alltäglichen Lebens in einzelnen Kurzkapiteln (Kap. 3, S. 17–55). Anschließend werden die acht wichtigsten Fundplätze ausführlich vorgestellt (Kap. 4–11, S. 56–124), bevor sich die beiden letzten Kapitel mit der Schleifung der Befestigungsanlagen in nachmittelalterlicher Zeit (Kap. 12, S. 125–126) und den Ergebnissen (Kap. 13, S. 127–129) beschäftigen. Hilfreich ist auch die abschließende umfangreiche Übersicht über die Literatur zum Alltagsleben auf Burgen. Im Vordergrund der Untersuchung steht somit nicht die architektonische Gestaltung der Anlagen. Ziel ist es vielmehr, aus den ergrabenen archäologischen Funden in Kombination mit schriftlichen Quellen möglichst umfassende Hinweise auf die spätmittelalterlichen Lebensumstände auf diesen Burgen zu erhalten. Insbesondere sind hier drei wichtige historische Quellen zu Burgen in Östergötland zu nennen: Das Testament mit Inventar der Kristina Fastesdotter (Landsjö, um 1280), das Geschäftsbuch bzw. das Ausgabenbuch für Lebensmittel und Futter von Gregers Mattsson (Stegeborg, um 1490) und die Wirtschaftsbücher von Probst Hans Brask (Linköping, um 1510). Alle diese Quellen behandeln bedeutende Steinburgen der Krone. Zudem wurden noch zwei königliche Burgen in der Nachbarschaft von Östergötland, von denen Steuerlisten (Nyköpningshus 1365–67) bzw. Inventare (Stegeholm 1506) vorliegen, mit in die Betrachtung einbezogen. Als Mittelalter wird in Schweden die Zeit von um 1100 bis zum Beginn der Reformation um 1530 verstanden. Als Datierungsgrundlage dienten vor allem Keramik, Münzen und schriftliche Quellen. Älteste Anlage ist demnach der küstennahe, große freistehende Rundturm („kastaler") in Stensö mit einem Beginn um 1200. Im Laufe des 13. Jahrhunderts wurde offenbar Birgittas udde errichtet, wenn auch nur zeitweilig genutzt. Birgittas udde, eine Anlage des Hochadels, besteht aus einer Gruppe von Gebäuden auf einer schmalen, in den Boren-See ragenden Halbinsel. Ein paralleles Graben-Wall-System riegelte die Landzunge ab. Unter den wenigen Funden sollen an dieser Stelle ein venezianisches (?) Glasfragment und eine Münze (Ende 13. Jahrhundert) genannt werden. Mit einem zeitlichen Abstand eines halben Jahrhunderts setzt um 1270 eine Art „Burgenboom" ein. So wurde der Backsteinturm von Biskopsholmen um 1270 erbaut. Der königliche Palast in Vadstena wurde ebenfalls um 1270 errichtet, zunächst noch unbefestigt. Auch die mit mehreren Türmen ausgestattete, auf einer Halbinsel gelegene Burg Landsjö wurde zwischen 1260 und 1275 errichtet. 1280 wird sie im Testament der Kristina Fastesdotter erstmals genannt, die dort ihren herrschaftlichen Sitz hatte. Konungsberg ist nur historisch erwähnt, da König Magnus dort (im „castrum") in den 1280er-Jahren mehrere Urkunden ausstellte. Das herrschaftliche Gebäude ist aber nicht ausgegraben worden. Linköping war schon um 1100 eine bischöfliche Residenz. Die Burg selbst wurde um 1290 angelegt. Die meisten Anlagen wurden vor Ende des Mittelalters wieder aufgegeben und verlassen. Nur sechs blieben auch nach 1480 in verteidigungsbereitem Zustand, noch weniger, darunter Munkeboda, bestanden über 1520 hinaus. Dabei kam es während der Nutzungsphase zu Standortverlagerungen. So hat die Befestigung von Munkeboda vom 14. bis frühen 16. Jahrhundert gleich drei zeitlich aufeinanderfolgenden Standorte gehabt (Übersicht, S. 10 Tab. 1,1; des Weiteren S. 109–115; Karte Abb. 10,1). Der gesamte Untersuchungszeitraum reicht somit über ca. 330 Jahre.

Hauptziel der Untersuchung von Martin Rundkvist war es, Aussagen zu den alltäglichen Lebensumständen auf den untersuchten Burgen zu erlangen. Dazu wurden zum einen die schriftlichen Zeugnisse, zum anderen das archäologische Fundmaterial herangezogen. Sowohl die Schriftzeugnisse als auch das Fundmaterial der Burgen von Östergötland zeigen, dass dort vielfältige

Tätigkeiten ausgeübt wurden, darunter viele spezialisierte. Beide ergänzen sich und liefern im Idealfall ein schlüssiges Bild. Einen Hauptteil der Untersuchung von Rundkvist nimmt folglich die systematische Vorstellung der einzelnen Lebensbereiche auf den Burgen ein, die je nach Quellenlage unterschiedlich ausführlich behandelt und hier in Auszügen beispielhaft besprochen werden.

Die Burgen in Östergötland lagen meist nicht direkt an ackerbaulich nutzbaren Flächen. Die verteidigungstechnisch bevorzugten Insel- oder Höhenbereiche sind dazu meist zu ungünstig. Dementsprechend gering sind auch die Zeugnisse von landwirtschaftlichen Funden von den Burgen selbst. Lediglich eine Sichel aus Ringstadaholm gehört in diese Kategorie. Einzige Hinweise auf die Ernährung geben wenige Handmühlen und vor allem zwei Backstuben, die in den Burgen Skällvik und Linköping gefunden wurden, während eine weitere in Stegeborg indirekt erwähnt ist. Für das auf vielen Burgen ausgeübte Brauen von Bier findet sich kaum Niederschlag im Fundmaterial. Immerhin werden in den Inventaren von Stegeborg und Linköping Brauer genannt.

Zahlreiche Tierknochenfunde geben Hinweise auf die Nahrungsgewohnheiten, insbesondere einen häufigen Fleischkonsum. Die Knochenanalysen erfolgten durch Rudolf Gustavsson und Lena Nilsson. Üblicherweise dominieren bei den Knochenfunden Rind oder Schwein, bis auf Landsjö, wo Schaf und Ziege vorherrschen. Zu jeder Burg gehörten offenbar ein oder mehrere Landgüter in der Umgebung (z. B. Stegeborg und Linköping). So wurden die Tiere selten auf den Burgen direkt gehalten, das Fleisch stammt überwiegend wohl von den nahegelegenen Wirtschaftshöfen. Dies bestätigt Gregers Mattson, der um 1490 Abgaben auflistet, die auf seiner Burg gesammelt wurden. Er nennt lebendes Vieh, darunter Schweine, ebenso Pökelfleisch, Hecht, Gerste, Roggen, Butter. Nur in Stegeholm ist schriftlich bezeugt, dass Vieh, darunter sieben Schweine, auf der Burg gehalten wurde. Geschlachtete Jungschweine sind ein Hinweis auf Eliten, ebenso zahlreiche Wildtiere wie z. B. Reh, Hirsch, Elch, aber auch Hase, Enten und anderes Geflügel (an der Tafel von Probst Brask sind Haselhuhn, Birkhuhn und Auerhuhn erwähnt). In Stegeborg wird 1490 ein Jäger genannt.

Wie bereits erwähnt liegen in Östergötland alle Burgen in Wassernähe. Entsprechend wurde Fisch reichlich verzehrt, wie vor allem die Schriftquellen bezeugen (an Fundmaterial ist nur ein Angelhaken aus Munkeboda I anzuführen). Stegeborg führt Fischer und Netzmacher in den Verzeichnissen auf. Es lassen sich sowohl Süß- als auch Salzwasserfische belegen. Dabei kommen gelegentlich auch importierte Nordatlantikfische wie der große Kabeljau vor. Umfangreich behandelt werden die Bereiche Kochen, Essen und Trinken. Neben wenigen Kochtöpfen und – häufigeren – Bechern geben hier wieder die Schriftquellen interessante Detailhinweise. Letztlich gehören zur Ernährung auch die Bereiche Müllentsorgung und Abortanlagen, die kurz dargelegt werden.

Ein anderer großer Komplex des täglichen Lebens sind die Raumausstattung und das eigentliche Leben auf den Burgen. So widmen sich Kurzkapitel den Bereichen Beleuchtung, Beheizung, Gesundheit bzw. Körperpflege, Textilien und Schmuck. In den Wirtschaftsbüchern von Probst Brask sind für seine persönliche Toilette Kamm, Schere, Kleiderbürste, Taschentücher und Handtücher erwähnt. Funde von Kammfragmenten gibt es aus Skällvik (Mitte 14. Jahrhundert, S. 32 Abb. 3,8) und Bjärkaholm. Interessant sind bei den Textilien Funde von Bleiplomben, mit denen die Warenballen gesichert waren. Ihr Siegelfeld gibt gute Hinweise auf die Herkunft: Zwei stammen aus Helmond in Brabant (S. 33 Abb. 3,10; S. 34 Abb. 3,11), eines aus dem benachbarten 's-Hertogenbosch (S. 34 Abb. 3,13).

Ein weiterer Komplex des täglichen Lebens sind Ritterlichkeit und Reiter, die sich im archäologischen Material durch verschiedene Sporentypen und Steigbügel, aber auch Zaumzeugverzierung und vor allem Hufnägel niederschlagen. Dass auf den Burgen auch Hochzeiten stattfanden, belegen wiederum die schriftlichen Quellen.

Auch der Soldatenalltag spiegelt sich wider, beispielsweise in Funden von Blankwaffen für den Nahkampf, aber auch von Fernwaffen. Die Schriftzeugnisse (Anweisungen zur Herstellung der Kampfbereitschaft, Inventarlisten) unterstreichen die herausragende Bedeutung der Armbrust. Dies bestätigen die archäologischen Funde, da Armbrustbolzen von nahezu allen ausgegrabenen Burgen Östergötlands zahlreich belegt sind. In Ringstadaholm wurde zudem ein Spannhaken gefunden. Für Ringstadaholm (1470 niedergebrannt) und Stegeborg (mehrfach belagert) sind Kämpfe schriftlich bezeugt. Aber auch Artilleriewaffen, die seit dem fortgeschrittenen 15. Jahrhundert zunehmen, entsprechen dem Fundbild von vielen anderen Burgen in Europa. Interessant sind zudem die schriftlichen Nennungen von Soldaten. So werden in Linköping um 1510 Wächter, Torhüter, Schießpulvermeister, Kanoniere und Knappen erwähnt. Bemerkenswert ist ein Befund aus Skällvik: In einem als Backstube angesprochenen Raum wurden fünf Würfel zusammen mit Armbrustbolzen und Münzen gefunden. Nach Ansicht des Autors könnte dies vermuten lassen, dass hier Soldaten ihre Langeweile in der warmen Backstube mit Würfelspielen überbrückt haben. Vielleicht sind auch die in diesem Zusammenhang gefundenen beiden Pferdezähne als einfache Spielsteine zu interpretieren.

Auf den Burgen in Östergötland sind Schmiedearbeiten naheliegend und nachgewiesen. Dort wurde für den Eigenbedarf produziert oder es wurden Reparaturen ausgeführt. Ketten und Handfesseln beleuchten den Aspekt der Gefangenschaft bzw. des Sklavenhandels, der im Ostseeraum bis Anfang des 14. Jahrhunderts ein wichtiger Wirtschaftszweig war.

Interessant ist es, abschließend einen Blick darauf zu werfen, welche Tätigkeitsbereiche auf den Burgen Östergötlands nicht üblich waren. So sind die Hinweise auf Religiosität dürftig. Keine Hinweise gibt es auf handwerkliche Überschussproduktion und auf weiträumige Handelstätigkeit. Darin sieht der Autor einen deutlichen Unterschied zu den Burgen anderer Regionen Schwedens wie Småland und Värmland, vor allem aber zum europäischen Kernland. Nach seiner Interpretation könnte dies daran liegen, dass die Region von Östergötland vergleichsweise reich mit ländlichen oder stadtartigen Siedlungen versehen ist, sodass diese Tätigkeiten nicht auf Burgen ausgeübt wurden.

Zusammenfassend ist festzustellen, dass es ein wichtiges, herausragendes Charakteristikum der Studie ist, dass sowohl schriftliche (Wirtschaftsbücher, Inventare) als auch archäologische Quellen herangezogen und miteinander verglichen wurden. Im Idealfall stützen und bestätigen sie sich gegenseitig. Wo andererseits die eine Quellengattung wenig Aussagemöglichkeiten bot, konnte die andere dies trefflich ergänzen. Das Zusammenwirken beider Quellengattungen stellt sicher, dass alle greifbaren Informationen zur Rekonstruktion der spätmittelalterlichen Lebensumstände ausgeschöpft und miteinander verknüpft wurden. Insgesamt scheinen die schriftlichen Quellen in dieser Untersuchung mehr und detailliertere Hinweise zu den Lebensumständen zu geben. Andererseits liefert die Archäologie wichtige Ergänzungen und beleuchtet einzelne Bereiche intensiver. So nehmen unter den archäologischen Funden die Tierknochen einen großen Anteil ein, ihre Auswertung ergab zahlreiche wichtige Erkenntnisse.

Ein Manko stellt allerdings die Tatsache dar, dass bei den einzelnen Burgen das archäologische Fundmaterial zwar aufgelistet wird, es aber an den zur Überprüfung und vor allem zum Vergleich wichtigen Abbildungen mangelt. Es gibt keinen für die Archäologie so wichtigen Tafelteil. Immerhin werden bedeutende Funde in einer (repräsentativen?) Auswahl als Fotos vorgelegt. Die Qualität der eigentlich recht nützlichen Übersichtskarte an den Innenseiten des Einbandes ist leider nicht optimal, die landschaftlichen Gegebenheiten sind nur schwer zu erschließen. Stellenweise ergeht sich der Text auch in Allgemeinplätzen. Trotz dieser – geringen – Kritikpunkte ist das Gesamtergebnis der Studie als voll gelungen zu bezeichnen: Insgesamt ergibt sich durch diese wertvolle vergleichende Untersuchung – vor allem durch die Kombination von detaillierten schriftlichen Quellen und archäologischen Funden – ein hochinteressanter Einblick in den spätmittelalterlichen Alltag der unterschiedlichen Burgbewohner. Sie ermöglichte eine größtmögliche Rekonstruktion der Lebensumstände auf den Burgen in Östergötland.

DE–56338 Braubach
Schlossstr. 5
E-Mail: ebi.leiter@deutsche-burgen.org

Reinhard Friedrich
Europäisches Burgeninstitut
Einrichtung der Deutschen
Burgenvereinigung e. V.

Christina Schmid, Ergrabene Kontexte. Interpretationen archäologischer Fundzusammenhänge auf Burgen. Formate – Forschungen zur Materiellen Kultur Band 2. Böhlau Verlag, Wien, Köln, Weimar 2020. € 85.00. ISBN 978-3-205-20979-9 (Hardback). € 69.99. ISBN 978-3-205-21180-8 (E-Book). doi: https://doi.org/10.7767/9783205211815. 585 pages with 105 mostly monochrome find tables and 87 coloured figures.

The work under review emerged from the PhD team project "RaumOrdnungen – Raumfunktionen und Ausstattungsmuster auf Adelssitzen im 14. bis 16. Jahrhundert", supervised by Sabine Felgenhauer-Schmiedt, and funded by the Austrian Academy of Sciences. The project was hosted by the Institute for Medieval and Early Modern Material Culture (IMAREAL) in Krems between 2007 and 2010. The team project also included a historian's doctoral thesis (Josef Handzell) and a doctoral thesis in German Studies (Gabriele Schichtag née Klug), which sought in parallel spatial approaches to aristocratic residential culture during the late Middle Ages and early modern period in southern Germany and Austria. Christina Schmid's thesis consists of a voluminous text component (pp. 15–407) with a concise German summary and a rather short English abstract, as well as a catalogue of finds (pp. 469–583) and tables.

The "Introduction" (pp. 15–17, all translations by RA) presents, as an overarching research goal, to describe and understand the castle as a place of residence along the coordinates of "space", "person / figure", "object", and "activity". This archaeological dissertation consistently works object-centered: the basis consists of numerous finds unearthed with poor documentation on the noble residences of Reichenstein and Prandegg in the Eastern Mühlviertel in Upper Austria. Without an explicit mention, the dissertation is focussed – apart from a few particular types – on non-ceramic housewares and excludes drinking glasses and coins (which first becomes apparent in a passing comment on p. 153 and p. 227). Thus, the study sheds light on a central issue for European research, where large assemblages have been exposed in castles without sufficient documentation. Until now, it has not been possible to analyse these finds beyond a bare typological and chronological identification mapping their distribution.

The next chapter "Theoretical Basics: Architecture and its Meaning" (pp. 19–27), discusses the interdependence between built space, its inhabitants, and the fixed, as well as the movable special features we encounter as archaeological finds. "The Castle as Built Environment and a System of Settings" (pp. 29–34) reconsiders the possibility of identifying spatial functions and underlines the necessity of a holistic approach of a "Household Archaeology" (p. 34–35), which takes into consideration a castle's structure, access, and inventory. The difference between the original building with its intended function and later changes of use is, however, a research problem that is somewhat exaggerated here (p. 29). After all, the perception of later uses is hardly distorted by the knowledge of the original configuration, if the inventory is subjected to stratigraphic building research, which certainly allows the complete biography of the architectural shell to be written (G. Eriksdotter, The stratigraphy of buildings: examples of the methodology of buildings archaeology. In: H. Andersson / P. Carelli / L. Ersgård, Visions of the past. Trends and traditions in Swedish medieval archaeology [Lund 1997] 741–761).

The chapter "Space and Activity on Castles from an Archaeological Point of View" (pp. 37–69) defines central terms used in the thesis. "Context" denominates features that underwent a primary or a secondary formation in the soil. A "single find" designates both a single object and an assemblage without known provenance. A concise discussion considers which human activities can leave archaeological traces, i. e. those leaving remnants surviving taphonomical processes and which an excavator recognises – and, we might add, publishes. The understanding of these traces as a reflex of historical reality in the sense of "New Archaeology" or also as a consequence of anthropologically determined behaviour in the sense of "Post-Processual Archaeology" is, however, rejected in favour of a multifactorial approach. The fundamental hypothesis is the readability of traces deriving from repetitive actions with a defined topographical setting. Against this background, a review of the find-bearing features on Swiss, German, and Austrian castle sites follows (pp. 52–56), in which historical function are consistently inferred from the presence or absence of certain groups of finds. The Chapter "The Interpretation of Single Finds without a Documented Context" (pp. 71–73) underlines these finds' relevance as neglected source material. Schmid rightly points out the importance of interpretation during the registration process and develops a new approach comparing similar objects from known functional contexts. The following thoughts about the contextual understanding of archaeological finds underpin her argument (pp. 75–92). She structures the descent conditions in four *patterns* describing the relationship between the object and its provenance: "Pattern 1 – Intentionally and Contemporary Deposited Finds" comprises grave goods and deposits. The somewhat misleading title, "Pattern 2 – Topographically Significant Objects" gathers objects unintentionally enclosed due to a sudden incident (fire, collapse), which might include older items left or stored on-site without any relationship to the activity. The reviewer counters that a careful excavation can identify these old objects – and even useless waste does belong to the "accepted" contents of a room. Moreover, this pattern explicitly includes glacier corpses and sunken ships – both are comparatively seldom in castles! 'Pattern 3 – Objects in Relationship to their Context of Use" describes all other features documented during excavation with a known provenance but possibly containing re-deposited material. "Pattern 4 – Only Vague Context Known" summarises all objects from a place without an archaeological context. "Pattern 5 – Unknown Context" designates all finds without a provenance, and surprisingly includes metal detector finds that usually ought to be discovered at known coordinates today; even a plough is not able to change the find spot of an object significantly, as Walter Janssen's study on the deserted village of Königshagen (DE) has proven (Königshagen: Ein archäologisch-historischer Beitrag zur Siedlungsgeschichte des südwestlichen Harzvorlandes [Hildesheim 1965]). Consequently, the latter pattern should be limited to objects without origin from a museum or other collections.

The actual interpretation of the finds starts with the traditional typo-chronological classification based on dated comparative finds and features, mostly from castles, but also including urban objects. In a second step, the reference objects are contextualised in identifying their provenance "pattern 1–4".

The chapter "Contextual Interpretation Applied on the Assemblages from Reichenstein and Prandegg Castle – Spatial and Historical Circumstances" (pp. 93–124) gives a shocking review of the archaeological state of research on castles in Upper Austria. Until today, apart from a few modern studies, research is based on monographs written in the first half of the 20th century, which long for an update. Complete excavations of castles are either absent or unpublished (Water castle

Neyharting: "meanwhile, the excavation documentation seems to be lost", p. 94). Since the 1990s, excavation activities accompanying construction work on castles have been considerably intensified, but Austrian monument law does not offer any practicable means for serious excavations. For example, in 2011 and 2012, only small sondages were possible to prepare the new planned museum building in Reichenstein Castle's courtyard (p. 97). This sounds more like a mid-20th century approach than modern archaeology. We read about "sondages, surveillances", and heart-touching efforts by "amateur historians and treasure hunters" (p. 98) to save and preserve things during "restorations". The Alfred Höllgruber collection, which formed the material basis of the dissertation, also falls into this category. It was created in the course of field work and factually undocumented excavations by the primary school teacher on the slopes and grounds of many castle sites, including the Reichenstein und Prandegg castles. The collection became a part of the Oberösterreichisches Museum. A brief summary of the castles' owner and building history completes the background.

The dissertation's core is formed by the chapter "Contextualized Interpretations of Find Assemblages in Reichenstein and Prandegg Castles – Finds as Evidence for Areas of Life and Activity" (pp. 125–380) that discusses the finds structured by their function. After an intensive typo-chronological classification of each find category, the contexts of reference finds are discussed in each case. Apart from apparent identifications, we meet some surprising, but well-argued stipulations: Spoons are by no means clearly table utensils, but could also belong to the field of pharmacy (p. 143). Pans would be expected in the kitchen, but they also seem to belong to the brewery (p. 146). Buttons and other appliqués primarily appear in graves (pp. 259–260; 262), probably due to rough excavation techniques in castles and towns. Horseshoes and their nails are found in castle courtyards, cellars, and collapsed buildings (p. 294), while book clasps are more common in monasteries than in castles (pp. 309–311). Most of the medieval marbles used for comparison come from the Brandenburg Cistercian convent of the Marienwerder (DE; p. 320), but supplementary reference should be made here to the exhibiton of the Heilbronn City Museum (Spielzeug in der Grube: lag und schlief. Allerlay kurtzweil. Ausstellung der Städtischen Museen Heilbronn 1993) or to Verena Hoffmann's analysis of Saxonian toy finds (Allerlay Kurtzweil. Mittelalterliche und frühneuzeitliche Spielzeugfunde aus Sachsen, Arbeits- u. Forschber. Sächs. Bodendenkmalpfl. 38, 1996, 127–200) which tend to support the expected image of marbles as children's toys.

"Space – Function – Fitting: Result and Perspective" (pp. 381–402) initially repeats the theoretical premises of the introductory chapters in an avoidable duplication. While the chapter about owner and building history assumed Reichenstein's erection in the early 13th century (p. 108), here, the find analysis argues for an earlier date "after about 1150" (p. 387), which is a remarkable discrepancy that would deserve a further discussion. The number of finds increases in the late period (1450 until 1650), signifying its intensified use. Also, Prandegg is, according to the findings that start "about 1150" (p. 388), considerably older than its first mention in written sources 1287 (p. 116) or its oldest preserved buildings from the late 12th century (p. 121). Like Reichenstein, Prandegg flourished between 1460 and 1650, also showing an increased quality in the objects. In the next step, the households' position in social networks is analysed. Schmid does not use formal network analysis or other multivariate tools that would have been able to "scrutinise all connected parts in a society" (p. 390) if she had defined and examined archaeological variables.

The systematic analysis of the comparative contexts differentiates the interpretation of the two castles: The finds from "Kitchen and Table" mark up the living room and the adjacent (?) kitchen. "Husbandry and Agriculture" do not play a significant role, which is a crucial result that indicates an outsourcing of these funtions. Christof Krauskopf interpreted this as an indicator for a lord belonging to the higher nobility (Tric-Trac, Trense und Treichel. Untersuchungen zur Sachkultur des Adels im 13. und 14. Jahrhundert. Veröff. Dt. Burgenvereinigung B 11 [Braubach 2005]). Not surprisingly, weapons and armour appear in the living space or in the cellar, which also applies to chests and locks. Horse stables are also to be expected in a castle. The living area comprises tools for craft and textile production, the latter usually in heated rooms. The assumed bathhouse at Reichenstein Castle (fig. 19) is not a singularity: the Schlössel Castle close to Klingenmünster also provided such a luxury (D. Barz, Das „Schlössel" bei Klingenmünster. Erkenntnisse zum Alltag auf einer salierzeitlichen Burg. In: C. Müller [ed.], Burg und Stadt. Forsch. Burgen u. Schlössern 11 [München 2008] 217–226). Religious objects are not restricted to the castle chapel but were also personal and mobile belongings.

All in all, this is a commendable and successful research project: the approach of not only drawing conclusions about the chronology of a castle and its integration into social networks from more than 14,000 (!) unstratified finds, but also using the finds themselves as a source for spatial functions via comparative finds, is extremely innovative and effective. We cannot blame Schmid for the sparse state of research concerning structures and functional spaces on Southern German and Austrian castles that set narrow limitations to her work. A more detailed analysis of the archaeology and history of construction of the two castles would have been useful, but this would certainly have gone beyond the sope of the project.

Minor editorial weaknesses should be noted, such as certain textual redundancies or the lack of an overview map, which would have facilitated the localisation of the castles in the Lower Mühlviertel. The path from the text section to the object depiction only through the catalogue is impractical. The ground plan (fig. 20) does not show the 13th century period, and the full citation of Olsen 1990 (p. 72 fn. 10) is missing in the bibliography. Until the last page, it remains unclear to the reviewer why the title of the book is actually "Excavated Contexts" – the finds under discussion neither derive from a regular excavation nor known contexts. *Erschlossene Kontexte* / "Investigated Contexts" would have made a better match. Yet, these are small details; the volume is a piece of methodological pioneer work and essentially contributes to the research on medieval material culture. It deserves a broad perception, even beyond the study of medieval castles.

DK–8270 Højbjerg
Moesgaard Allé 22
E-Mail: rainer.atzbach@cas.au.dk
Orcid: https://orcid.org/0000-0002-3823-0616

Rainer Atzbach
School of Culture and Society
Aarhus University

Wayne D. Cocroft / John Schofield, Archaeology of the Teufelsberg. Exploring Western Electronic Intelligence Gathering in Cold War Berlin. Routledge Archaeologies of the Contemporary World. Routledge, London 2019. £ 44,99. ISBN 978-1-13833-7-107 (Hardback). £ 16,99. ISBN 978-0-36767-184-6 (Paperback). £ 22,50. ISBN 978-0-42944-2-629 (E-Book). doi: https://doi.org/10.4324/9780429442629. 162 Seiten mit 123 Schwarz-Weiß-Abbildungen.

Dieses Buch, veröffentlich bei Routledge im Jahre 2019, hat eine komplexe Geschichte, da bereits 2016 eine deutsche Fassung erschien. Ich gehe auf diese Umstände am Ende des Reviews nochmals näher ein. In dieser Rezension beziehe ich mich auf die englische Fassung von Wayne D. Cocroft und John Schofield samt ihrer Kapitelzählung: Nach einer kurzen Einführung (S. 1–5) folgt in Kapitel 2 eine auf unterschiedliche Orte fokussierte Geschichte der Abhöranlagen der West-Alliierten in West-Berlin (S. 6–39), sodann eine näher auf den Teufelsberg eingegrenzte Geschichte der Zeit des Kalten Kriegs (S. 40–59). Ein kurzes Kapitel 4 geht auf archäologische Methoden und Ansätze ein (S. 60–65), um dann im bei weitem längsten Kapitel 5 die einzelnen Gebäude bzw.

deren Reste zu beschreiben (S. 66–139). Gefolgt ist dies von zwei kurzen Endkapiteln, bestehend aus einer Übersicht zur Struktur des Ortes und seiner Architektur (S. 140–143) und schließlich Vorgängen auf dem Teufelsberg nach Verlassen des Militärs im Jahre 1992 (S. 144–150). Bibliographie und Index schließen das Werk ab. An dieser Kurzübersicht zeigt sich die umfassende Zielsetzung des kurzen Werks. Meine Besprechung richtet sich daher aus an den Ansprüchen, die ich an jede „Endpublikation" eines archäologischen Platzes stellen würde, egal, aus welcher Zeit er stammt.

Was ist nun daran „archäologisch"? Nach deutschen Amtsdefinitionen eigentlich kaum etwas, denn die analysierten Materialien sind allesamt Baudenkmale, nicht aber Bodendenkmale. Um „Archäologie" im amtsdefinitorischen Sinne handelt es sich also nicht. Dazu passt, dass mobile Funde, gar Ausgegrabenes nicht erörtert werden. Der Band ist jedoch in doppelter Hinsicht typisch für eine internationale Tendenz der Archäologie, sich in Richtung einer „Wissenschaft des Materiellen" zu entwickeln. Erstens löst sich das Fach von der Bindung an das „Altertum". Die „Contemporary Archaeology", als deren Teil das Buch sich versteht, ist ein hauptsächlich im anglo-amerikanischen Raum sich entfaltender Wissenschaftszweig, der vor allem Orte der Zeitgeschichte mit archäologischen Herangehensweisen erforscht. Chronologisch interessiert dabei der Zeitraum etwa ab Mitte des 20. Jahrhunderts bis heute. Zweitens beschäftigt sich Archäologie immer mehr mit dem Dinglichen nicht nur als Basis für eine Geschichtsschreibung, sondern als an sich untersuchenswerte Materie, ob dies naturwissenschaftliche Methoden betrifft oder eher philosophische. Behandelte Themen rangieren dabei in einem extrem weiten Bereich, von ganzen Flughäfen über ein einzelnes Büro bis zu Treibholz auf dem Meer.

Allein aufgrund des Ortes ist die hier vorgenommene Untersuchung von großem Interesse. Es handelt sich um einen Gebäudekomplex zur massiven Datensammelei, noch dazu unter Geheimhaltungsbedingungen. Eine Konstellation, die einer archäologischen Analyse nicht oft zur Verfügung steht. Ich hätte mir allerdings gewünscht, dass die methodische Frage, die sich bei diesem Charakter des untersuchten Materials stellt, deutlicher formuliert und ihre Antworten hätten überprüft werden sollen: Was sagt die mit archäologischen Mitteln durchgeführte Analyse über einen der wichtigsten Orte der Informationsbeschaffung des Kalten Kriegs aus? Erwartbar ist, dass Strukturen zutage kommen, die Alltagsabläufe erhellen – doch wie sieht es aus mit den aus dem Äther abgegriffenen Informationen selbst? Bleibt der Teufelsberg archäologisch eine „Black Box", deren Input und Output vielleicht in den Archiven in den Vereinigten Staaten von Amerika und Großbritannien, nicht aber am Ort selbst erschließbar werden? Wo genau liegt der Erkenntnisgewinn der materiellen Erforschung? Und schließlich: Gibt es über die historische Spezifizität dieses Horchpostens hinaus generelle Einsichten in eine „archaeology of the contemporary world", wie der Titel der Serie lautet, in der das Buch erschienen ist?

Den rein archäologischen Untersuchungen sind zwei historische Kapitel vorangestellt, die eine allgemeine Geschichte der Spionage und des Abhörens in West-Berlin und dann eine spezifischere, auf den Teufelsberg zugeschnittene beinhalten. Die Textstruktur betont die Abgrenzung der westlichen Geheimdienste voneinander. Gatow und die britischen Einheiten, die Abhöranlagen der Vereinigten Staaten von Amerika im Stadtteil Marienfelde und französische Einrichtungen in Berlin-Reinickendorf werden nacheinander beschrieben. Sicher entwickelten sich diese Abhöreinrichtungen separat. Man wüsste aber doch gerne mehr über deren Zusammenhänge, die getrieben waren durch den Grundkonflikt mit der Sowjetunion und dem Warschauer Pakt – ohne diesen wären auch die Anlagen auf dem Teufelsberg nicht notwendig gewesen. Für eine internationale Leser*innenschaft, für die dieses Werk bestimmt ist, mangelt es zudem in Kapitel 2 an einer Karte, die die eigenartige Lage Berlins in der östlichen Hälfte der ehemaligen Deutschen Demokratischen Republik (DDR) und die drei Luftkorridore nach Frankfurt, Hamburg und Bückeburg in West-Deutschland dargestellt hätte, die aber auch verdeutlicht hätte, warum gerade West-Berlin ein idealer Ort zum

Abhören jeglicher „Ostblock"-Kommunikation war. Leider findet sich in der Berlin-Karte ebenfalls ein gewichtiger Fehler, denn die US-amerikanischen Andrews Barracks sind im britischen Sektor eingezeichnet statt im amerikanischen. Dies vermittelt den falschen Eindruck, als seien neben dem Teufelsberg weitere größere amerikanische Militäranlagen im britischen Sektor gewesen.

Einige Elemente der Ereignisgeschichte fließen in die historische Darstellung ein, wie etwa der Fall des Überläufers Brian Patchett (* 1939) der britischen Abhöreinheit in Gatow, der sich Anfang Juli 1963 nach Ost-Berlin absetzte, oder der Absturz eines sowjetischen Jak28-Bombers im West-Berliner Stößensee im Jahr 1966, dessen technische Einzelheiten britische Einheiten auskundschaften konnten, bevor das Wrack an die Sowjetunion überstellt wurde. Diese eingestreuten Bemerkungen betreffen auch den Überläufer Hüseiyn Yıldırım (* 1932), der nicht nur selbst als Agent tätig war, sondern vor allem andere Personen als Agenten anwarb. Solche konkreten Ereignisse beleben eine manchmal etwas sperrige historische Darstellung, die gespickt ist mit Abkürzungen vor allem militärischer Art. Wie schon gesagt, hätte die Geschichte der Nutzung des Teufelsbergs mit der Gesamtgeschichte der Spionage seitens der westlichen Alliierten zu einer klareren Übersicht zusammengebracht werden können.

Kapitel 4 berührt die archäologischen Methoden, besonders die auf eine Archäologie der Zeitgeschichte zugeschnittenen. Dieses wichtige Kapitel ist zu kurz und hätte meines Erachtens weiter ausholen müssen. Hat die zeitgeschichtliche Archäologie spezifische, von anderen Epochen abweichende Methoden der Befund- und Fundaufnahme? Was sind ihre spezifischen Eigenheiten und Probleme sowie mögliche Lösungen hierfür? Der Verweis auf die britischen Anleitungen zur Beschreibung historischer Bauten – herunterladbar aus dem Internet (https://historicengland.org.uk/images-books/publications/understanding-historic-buildings/ [letzter Zugriff 05.05.2022]) – ist insofern instruktiv, als diese „Rezeptur" zur Bauaufnahme bei weitem nicht so gründlich ausfällt wie eine architektonische Aufnahme. Denn Maße sind weitaus weniger relevant als etwa Funktionszuweisungen. Man erahnt, dass das Vorgehen daraus bestand, eine an der Technischen Universität Berlin abgeschlossene Magisterarbeit zurate zu ziehen. Diese bildet den Grundstock für bautechnische Bemerkungen und ist publiziert (und von W. D. Cocroft und J. Schofield zitiert: K. Beckmann et al., Field Station Berlin. Geheime Abhörstation auf dem Teufelsberg [Berlin 2013]).

Die Feldarbeit der beiden Autoren selbst fand im Jahre 2011 statt und umfasste eine Woche. Ob Archivrecherche und eine Sichtung sekundärer Quellen danach oder davor betrieben wurden, bleibt unklar. Wir erfahren allerdings gleich im Vorspann des Bandes, dass der Vater eines der Autoren als „Wing Commander A. E. Schofield" auf dem Teufelsberg tätig gewesen war, und dass die Autoren wohl den einen oder anderen Zeitzeugen kontaktiert hatten. Leider werden den Leser*innen allerdings allein Ergebnisse der Forschungen präsentiert, sodass der Prozess der Erlangung der Erkenntnisse im Dunkeln bleibt.

Das Hauptkapitel 5 dient einer Beschreibung aller Bauten des Teufelsbergs, was Kapitel 6 nochmals rekapituliert. Die Gebäude werden in unterschiedlich gründlichem Ausmaß beschrieben, auch die Herkunft zweier parallel genutzter Gebäudezeichnungen (Nummern und Großbuchstaben) bleibt den Leser*innen unbekannt. Die britischen Strukturen erregen bei den Autoren deutlich mehr Interesse als die amerikanischen, was damit begründet wird, dass ein Teil der amerikanischen nach Verlassen des Militärs stark umgestaltet wurde für ein nie vollendetes Bauprojekt, aufgegeben im Jahr 2002. Ich beschränke meine Kommentare bezüglich dieses Kapitels hier auf einige wenige Aspekte. Die Autoren arbeiten sehr anschaulich heraus, welcher Aufwand betrieben werden musste, um die Abhör-Gebäude funktionsadäquat zu gestalten. Die damaligen Computer liefen so heiß, dass eine leistungsstarke Klimaanlage eingebaut werden musste, deren Zu- und Ableitungen in einer abgehängten Decke und einem aufgeständerten Boden dem Blick verborgen blieben; allerdings muss hier auch berücksichtigt werden, dass außer der Kantine keines der Gebäude Fenster besaß und somit *air conditioning* auch für Menschen notwendig war. Was die technischen Geräte, auch elektrische Leitungen, Steckdosen und sogar Fernschreiber angeht, so stellen die Autoren heraus, dass vieles von deutschen Firmen stammte. Zugangswege und unterschiedliche Zugangsrechte werden anhand von Indizien ebenfalls eingängig rekonstruiert und auf zwei schwer lesbaren Plänen dargestellt (S. 92–93).

Andere Teile der Analyse führen zu offenen Fragen. Warum gab es in der Südwest-Ecke des Gebäudes Toiletten für Männer und Frauen? In dem Buch kommen Frauen praktisch nicht vor, auch nicht auf einem Gruppenfoto von Mitarbeitern mit geschwärzten Gesichtern, allesamt Männer (S. 38). Hingegen muss man nicht lange nach Quellen suchen, um beispielsweise in „Die Welt" vom 11.03.2013 herauszufinden, dass Colonel Carol Hemphill die letzte US-Kommandantin der US-amerikanischen Army Intelligence Einheit am Teufelsberg war (https://www.welt.de/geschichte/article121457272/So-belauschte-die-NSA-Berlin-im-Kalten-Krieg.html [letzter Zugriff: 27.09.2022]). Das Buch gibt keine Informationen darüber preis, ob auch britische Frauen auf dem Teufelsberg arbeiteten. Da jedoch die Gebäude und sogar innerhalb derselben Stockwerke und ganze Raumfluchten voneinander abgeschottet waren, deuten die Toiletten auf die Anwesenheit sowohl von Abhör-Spezialistinnen als auch -Spezialisten hin.

Ebenso interessant sind Anlagen zur Dokumentenvernichtung, deren Kontexte und Konsequenzen mir nicht ausreichend interpretiert zu sein scheinen. Auf dem Teufelsberg befand sich in Gebäude 1455B eine Verbrennungsanlage und in Struktur 1469 standen zwei kalifornische Dokumentenschredder, die verbunden waren mit Maschinen, die aus den Fetzen Papierbrei machten, der dann zum Verbrennen in Würfel gepresst wurde. Unklar bleibt, ob die Verbrennungsanlage in Bau 1455B für diese Papiermasse da war oder dort andere Arten von Dokumentresten inziniert wurden, etwa Tonbänder und später Disketten. Jedenfalls aber lässt sich eine ganze *chaîne opératoire* der automatisierten Dokumentenvernichtung rekonstruieren. Dieser komplexe Zerstörungsapparat kann mit der Dokumentenherstellung verbunden werden. Das Einfangen der Wörter ist illustriert in ein paar Innenraumfotos des britischen Hauptgebäudes mit seinen Funkschreibern und Tonbandgeräten. Geräte dieser Art wurden samt und sonders vor Verlassen von den Abhör-Einheiten entfernt. Dennoch fällt es nicht schwer, sich den Teufelsberg als eine riesige, multilinguale Wortsammelstelle, eine Transformationsmaschine dieser Wörter in materielle Dinge (geschriebene, magnetographisch oder digital festgehaltene) und gleichzeitig als eine massive Wortvernichtungsanlage vorzustellen. Der materielle und technologische Aufwand für diesen Zweck ist, wenn man sich die ideologischen und militärischen Frontstellungen des Kalten Kriegs vor Augen führt, keineswegs erstaunlich. Der Berg selbst und die Gebäudehüllen existieren noch, ebenso wie die Skelette der technischen Anlagen. Die dort beschäftigten Militärs sind längst verschwunden, ebenso wie die eingefangenen und wieder vernichteten oder an anderer Stelle in geheimen Archiven versteckten Worte, die wir gerne als „Information" bezeichnen.

Der Teufelsberg ist damit eigentlich ein idealer Ort für ein Nachdenken über ein Teilfach der Archäologie, dass wir – m. E. unsinnigerweise – als „Prähistorie" bezeichnen: Es ist ein Ort, an dem Handlungen abliefen, über deren allgemeinen Inhalt wir Bescheid wissen – Abhören von Kommunikation der politischen und militärischen Gegner –, deren Einzelheiten uns aber völlig abgehen. Wir haben nur mehr die materielle Hülle, um daraus zu rekonstruieren, was hier einmal gehört und aufgeschrieben worden sein mag. Die Analyse führt zur Erkenntnis einer zerklüfteten Struktur, in der die Routinehandlungen des Abhörens von Feindgesprächen jeweils unter Abschottungskriterien stattfanden. „What it [the archaeological analysis] cannot reveal are the secrets of the software, nor what was intercepted", schreiben die Autoren gegen Ende des Buches (S. 140). Man ist versucht zu fragen: Ist es nicht mit jedem bandkeramischen Gehöft ebenso? Wir wissen um die Subsistenz- und Bestattungspraktiken, die dort durchgeführt wurden, wir kennen Gebäudegrößen und Siedlungsstrukturen, wir wissen, dass dort Menschen lebten, sich fortpflanzten, Feste feierten, und sich vor allem miteinander verbal austauschten – über ihre eigene Geschichte, über Nachbarn, möglicherweise Feinde und transzendentale Mächte. Doch jeder wirkliche Inhalt, das Diskursive, geht uns ab. Wie gehen wir mit dieser Situation um? Schmerzlich wird uns das fehlende Wissen bewusst, welches wir gerne hätten, um die Geschichte besser zu verstehen. Wir enden in einer auf das Fehlen von Sprache ausgerichteten Analogie.

Doch bieten die materiellen Reste des Teufelsbergs in genau dieser Hinsicht auch eine andere Analogie. Wie Cocroft und Schofield berichten, war auf dem Teufelsberg auch die *National Security Agency* (NSA) präsent, ein US-Geheimdienst, der heutzutage allein aus einer riesigen Metadatensammlung große Teile der Erdbevölkerung überwachen kann, wie man durch Edward Snowdens Enthüllungen weiß. Relevant hieran ist, dass Strukturen der Welt und Praktiken von Personen sich offensichtlich allein aus den Metadaten zu signifikanten Erkenntnissen verknüpfen lassen, ohne dass irgendwelche konkreten Inhalte bekannt sein müssten. In dieser Art des Metadaten-Wissens geht es nicht mehr ums Individuum, sondern darum, wie gut sich ein Exemplar (Personen, aber auch z. B. die Teufelsberg-Gebäude mit ihren Resten an Installationen) in einen größeren Rahmen fügt. Das Einmalige, Persönlichkeiten, Eigenheiten werden *a priori* als uninteressant ausgesondert. Vielleicht ist ja eine solche extrem kollektivierte Historiographie unserem Zeitalter angemessener als die Suche nach Partikularitäten? Der Band hätte gerade durch einen Bezug auf die durchaus bekannten Abhörinteressen und -praktiken an dieser Stelle deutlich gewinnen können.

Es ist weiterhin schade, dass die Autoren nur an einer Stelle und ganz am Ende des Bandes darauf eingehen, dass der Teufelsberg an einen westasiatischen Tell erinnert, besteht er doch ausschließlich aus Schutt, der sich allerdings wesentlich schneller zur beträchtlichen Höhe von 120 m ansammelte – nämlich innerhalb von nur etwas mehr als 20 Jahren – als die antiken Siedlungshügel, zumal dieser Schutt nicht vor Ort entstand, sondern in Lorenbahnen und Lastwagen antransportiert wurde. In diesem Zusammenhang hätte auch etwas mehr Detail eingefügt werden können, was die untersten Schichten dieses „Tells" angeht. Zwar wird an einer einzigen Stelle kurz die von Albert Speer, Hitlers Lieblingsarchitekten und späterem Rüstungsminister, geplante sog. „Wehrtechnische Fakultät" erwähnt, auf deren unfertigen Bauresten der Teufelsberg seit 1950 aufgeschüttet worden war. Die bereits von den Nazis ausgeführten Bauteile bestanden aus einem quadratischen, bis zu vierstöckigen Bau mit hervorspringenden Ecken. Allein hier hätten weitere Nachforschungen schnell ergeben können, dass es zwischen der NS-Zeit und 1950, als man anfing, hier Bauschutt abzuladen, eine kurzfristige Zwischennutzung gab: In den Jahren 1948 bis 1950 wurden die wuchtig-bedrohlichen Mauern der besagten Rudimente der „Wehrtechnischen Fakultät" als Untergrund für zwei 40 m hohe Richtfunk-Masten verwendet. Dies war notwendig geworden, da die Berlin-Blockade von Juni 1948 bis Mai 1949 von der Gefahr begleitet war, dass die sowjetische Militäradministration die Überland-Telefonverbindungen nach West-Deutschland kappen könnte. Nur wenig später wurden dort jedoch Trümmer aufgeschüttet, was zum Verdacht eines Zusammenhangs zwischen der künstlichen Herstellung eines Berges und der Möglichkeit der späteren drahtlosen Kommunikation zu zivilen als auch militärischen Zwecken beiträgt. Dieser wird ebenfalls in Cocroft und Schofields Buch angesprochen, jedoch nicht weiter elaboriert. Bedenkt man, dass zwischen der Zeit der Richtfunk-Station in den späten 1940er-Jahren und der initialen Nutzung durch britisches und US-Militär nur ca. zehn Jahre liegen, ist ein Zusammenhang zwischen den beiden Episoden durchaus möglich.

Ich habe mich beim Lesen gefragt, wo die auf dem Teufelsberg tätigen Abhörspezialist*innen eigentlich ihren Feierabend verbrachten, der immerhin aus 16 Stunden nach den 8-Stunden-Schichten bestand. Fündig wird man auch dazu nicht in dem Buch, sondern eher in journalistischen Quellen, etwa dem Welt-Artikel über die oben erwähnte Kommandantin Carol Hemphill.

Offensichtlich wurden z. B. die US-Belegschaften für jede Schicht mit einem Militär-Bus aus ihren Kasernen in Lichterfelde zum Arbeitsort gebracht, ein Transport, der gefolgt war von Kontrollen an den einzelnen Schleusen zu Raumkomplexen mit jeweils steigender Geheimhaltungsstufe. Nimmt man die vorhandenen Schriftzeugnisse und die Erkenntnisse des Buches zusammen, ergibt sich ein weit lebendigeres Bild dessen, was auf dem Teufelsberg im Kalten Krieg ablief.

Zum Schluss sei die merkwürdige Geschichte des Buchs nochmals aufgegriffen. Als Leser*in erfährt man gleich am Anfang, dass das Buch zuerst im Jahre 2016 auf Deutsch publizierte wurde. Kurioserweise, nachdem es vom Englischen ins Deutsche übersetzt worden war. Wir können mit relativ großer Wahrscheinlichkeit davon ausgehen, hier einen eventuell leicht modifizierten Urtext vor uns zu haben. Die deutsche Fassung mit dem Titel „Der Teufelsberg in Berlin. Eine archäologische Bestandsaufnahme des westlichen Horchpostens im Kalten Krieg" erschien im Verlag Christoph Links. Unterschiede bestehen unter anderem darin, dass der deutschsprachige Band eine wesentlich bessere Druckqualität hat, mit Farb- statt verwaschenen Schwarz-Weiß-Abbildungen versehen ist, der Text weitaus besser Korrektur gelesen wurde und das Ganze zudem wesentlich weniger kostet (5,- €). Man kann also einem deutschen Lesepublikum auf keinen Fall zuraten, die Version des renommierten Verlags Routledge zu erstehen.

Auch insgesamt bin ich von diesem Band einigermaßen enttäuscht. Es fehlt nicht nur die Auseinandersetzung mit der zeitlichen Tiefe des Teufelsberges, einschließlich der letzten 30 Jahre nach Abzug der britischen und US-Abhöreinheiten, sondern auch der breitere Kontext. Zum sogenannten Kalten Krieg wird kaum ein einschlägiges Werk zitiert (etwa die Arbeiten von Odd Arne Westad, stellvertretend sei The Cold War: A World History [London 2017] genannt; oder Bernd Stövers Der Kalte Krieg, 1947–1991. Geschichte eines radikalen Zeitalters [München 2007]). Damit ähnelt der Band eher einem Reiseführer als einem archäologischen Werk, das in einen Fachdiskurs eingebettet ist. Als Begleitbuch zu einer intensiven Besichtigung des Teufelsbergs eignet sich das Buch, nicht aber als Einstiegsband für eine Reihe mit dem Titel *Routledge Archaeologies of the Contemporary World*.

DE–14195 Berlin
Fabeckstr. 23–25
E-Mail: rbernbec@zedat.fu-berlin.de
Orcid: https://orcid.org/0000-0002-8062-3384

Reinhard Bernbeck
Institut für die Vorderasiatische Archäologie
Freie Universität Berlin

David Reich, Who We Are and How We Got Here. Ancient DNA and the New Science of the Human Past. Oxford University Press, Oxford 2019. £ 10,99. ISBN 978-0198821267 (Paperback). Pantheon Books, New York 2018. Vergriffen. ISBN 978-1101870327 (Hardback). Knopf Doubleday Publishing Group, New York 2018. € 15,64. ISBN 978-1101870334 (e-Book). xxv und 335 Seiten mit 28 Abbildungen.

David Reich ist einer der wichtigsten Protagonisten der gegenwärtigen „ancient DNA-Revolution" (S. xiii), die unser Bild von der Vergangenheit an vielen Stellen in teils spektakulärer Weise ergänzt und verändert haben. Von der Entdeckung des Denisova-Menschen über die Entschlüsselung des Neandertaler-Genoms bis zur genetischen Erschließung einer massiven Steppenvölker-Einwanderung nach Europa am Ende der Jungsteinzeit: Wann immer im letzten Jahrzehnt Aufsehenerregendes auf der Grundlage von DNA aus archäologischen Funden publiziert wurde, war er meistens führend mit dabei. Gleichsam im Alleingang hat er mit seinem Labor in Harvard den „Ancient DNA-Trenngraben" beseitigt, der noch 2016 beklagt wurde (A. Gibbons, Ancient DNA divide. Science 352,6292, 2016, 1384–1387. doi: https://doi.org/10.1126/science.352.6292.1384), also den Rückstand der USA gegenüber europäischen Instituten in diesem Forschungsfeld. Auch in der Öffentlichkeit ist der Archäogenetiker inzwischen recht bekannt. Die Veröffentlichung des hier zu besprechenden Buches im Frühjahr 2018 begleitete die Wissenschaftsredaktion der New York Times mit einer regelrechten Kampagne: Es erschien ein Porträt (C. Zimmer, David Reich unearths human history etched in bone. New York Times Online-Version 20.04.2018. https://www.ncbi.nlm.nih.gov/search/research-news/1813/ [letzter Zugriff: 27.09.2022]; Printversion in der New York Edition, Section D, S. 1, unter dem Titel „Uncovering ancient DNA") samt einem Artikel, welcher die Thematik gleich in eine Lehreinheit für den Schulunterricht umsetzte (C. C. Gilpin, Teaching activities for: 'David Reich unearths human history etched in bone'. New York Times 22.03.2018. https://www.nytimes.com/2018/03/22/learning/teaching-activities-for-david-reich-unearths-human-history-etched-in-bone.html [letzter Zugriff: 27.09.2022]), ferner eine enthusiastische Besprechung durch Jared Diamond, dem Doyen der naturwissenschaftlichen Forschung zur Menschheitsgeschichte (J. Diamond, A brand-new version of our origin story. New York Times Online-Version 20.04.2018. https://www.nytimes.com/2018/04/20/books/review/david-reich-who-we-are-how-we-got-here.html [letzter Zugriff: 27.09.2022]; Printversion in der New York Times Sunday Book Review unter dem Titel „Origin story" 22.04.2018), sowie zuvor bereits ein von Reich selbst verfasster Beitrag (D. Reich, How genetics is changing our understanding of ‚race'. New York Times Online-Version 23.03.2018. https://www.nytimes.com/2018/03/23/opinion/sunday/genetics-race.html [letzter Zugriff: 27.09.2022]; Printversion nur in der New York Edition, Section SR, S. 1 unter dem Titel „'Race' in the age of modern genetics"). Darin rief er dazu auf, auf wissenschaftlicher Basis offen über genetische Unterschiede zwischen menschlichen Populationen zu sprechen, anstatt dieses Thema zu tabuisieren, zu vereinfachen und dem Rassismus zu überlassen. Die Reaktion auf diesen Vorstoß fiel groß und kontrovers aus, wie kaum anders zu erwarten. So warfen zahlreiche Wissenschaftler in einer gemeinsamen Erklärung Reich vor, selbst zu simplifizieren und gefährlich zu argumentieren (D. Reich, How not to talk about race and genetics. BuzzFeed.News 30.03.2018. https://www.buzzfeednews.com/article/bfopinion/race-genetics-david-reich [letzter Zugriff: 10.05.2022]). Auch die Leserschaft der New York Times hatte viele Fragen und Einwände. Reich beantwortete diese in einem erneuten Beitrag in der Zeitung (D. Reich, How to talk about race and genetics. New York Times 30.03.2018. https://www.nytimes.com/2018/03/30/opinion/race-genetics.html [letzter Zugriff: 10.05.2022]). Mehrere Monate später berichtete die New York Times in ihrem Sonntagsmagazin noch einmal ausführlich über Reich. Eine lange Reportage mit dem suggestiven Titel „Game of Bones" widmete sich ihm, jedoch diesmal nicht hymnisch, sondern mit schweren Vorwürfen (G. Lewis-Kraus, Game of bones. New York Times Magazine 17.01.2019; Online-Version unter dem Titel „Is ancient DNA research revealing new truths – or falling into old traps?". https://www.nytimes.com/2019/01/17/magazine/ancient-dna-paleogenomics.html [letzter Zugriff: 27.09.2022]). Reich soll in einer Studie über die Besiedlung Ozeaniens auf schmalster Grundlage äußerst weitreichende Schlussfolgerungen getroffen haben, mit denen er auf arrogante Weise den bisherigen interdisziplinären Forschungskonsens für obsolet erklärt habe. Ferner soll die veröffentlichende Zeitschrift, keine geringere als „Nature", massiv gegen übliche Begutachtungsstandards verstoßen haben. Auch hier widersprach Reich deutlich (D. Reich, Letter in response to Jan. 17 article in The New York Times. https://reich.hms.harvard.edu/letter-response-jan-17-article-new-york-times [letzter Zugriff: 08.04.2022]; D. Reich, Five corrections to The New York Times. https://reich.hms.harvard.edu/five-corrections-new-york-times [letzter Zugriff: 08.04.2022]).

Doch auch ohne diese Kontroversen (ausführlicher dazu J. Feuchter, David Reich in der Kritik: Die Frühgeschichte Ozeaniens umschreiben? Frankfurter Allgemeine Zeitung 30.01.2019. https://www.faz.net/aktuell/karriere-hochschule/david-reich-in-der-kritik-ozeanische-stichprobe-16013092.html [letzter Zugriff: 27.09.2022]) wäre das Buch Pflichtlektüre für alle in den Archäologien und Geschichtswissenschaften, die sich genauer über genetische Zugänge zur

Vergangenheit informieren wollen. Denn selbst wenn Reich v. a. auf seine eigenen Forschungen eingeht, decken diese *de facto* die Breite des Feldes ab. So ist das Buch ganz ohne Zweifel die beste aktuelle ausführliche Überblickslektüre zu diesem Thema, noch dazu gut und spannend geschrieben. Doch es bleibt nicht an der populärwissenschaftlichen Oberfläche wie viele andere Bücher von Naturwissenschaftlern zum Thema (etwa A. RUTHERFORD, Eine kurze Geschichte von jedem, der jemals gelebt hat. Was unsere Gene über uns verraten [Hamburg 2018]; Originalausgabe: A Brief History of Everyone Who Ever Lived: The Stories in Our Genes [London 2016]); deutlich weniger im negativen Sinne populärwissenschaftlich, aber doch auch nicht so vertiefend wie Reichs Monographie, ist die des führenden deutschen aDNA-Forschers: Johannes KRAUSE (mit Thomas TRAPPE, Die Reise unserer Gene. Eine Geschichte über uns und unsere Vorfahren [Berlin 2019]; vgl. die Rezension von D. HOFMANN in Germania 97, 2019, 432–435. doi: https://doi.org/10.11588/ger.2019.78878). Vielmehr geht Reich stark in die Einzelheiten, sowohl methodisch als auch hinsichtlich der Details der vielen von ihm vorgestellten Studien zu verschiedensten Perioden und Problemen der Menschheitsgeschichte, die er in der Regel selbst geleitet hat. Er will tatsächlich möglichst genau vermitteln, was er über die Vergangenheit herausgefunden hat, auf welche Weise und unter welch widrigen Umständen – und was dies alles für unsere Gegenwart und Zukunft bedeutet. Für diese Bemühung um Offenlegung gebührt ihm große Anerkennung.

Die Einleitung (S. xi–xxv) reißt kurz die Geschichte der genetischen Vergangenheitsforschung an und ehrt vor allem deren Pionier Luigi Luca Cavalli-Sforza, dessen „Vision" von der Genetik als einem „Fenster in die Vergangenheit" dank der aDNA-Technologie erfüllt werden könne. Anschließend ist das Buch in drei Teile gegliedert: Der erste, „The Deep History of Our Species" (S. 1–74), gibt einen grundsätzlichen Einblick in die Forschungsgeschichte und die Methodik des Faches (Kap. 1 „How the Genome Explains Who We Are", S. 3–22) und seine revolutionären Beiträge zur Erforschung der Neandertaler (Kap. 2 „Encounters with Neanderthals", S. 24–50) und der überhaupt nur durch aDNA entdeckten Denisova-Menschen (Kap. 3 „Ancient DNA Opens the Floodgates", S. 52–74). Der zweite und bei weitem umfangreichste Teil, „How We Got to Where We Are Today" (S. 77–225), enthält sechs Kapitel zu Themen der jüngeren Menschheitsgeschichte. Erst der dritte Teil „The Disruptive Genome" (S. 229–286) enthält jenes Plädoyer, das für so viel Kontroverse gesorgt hat.

Die sechs Kapitel des zweiten Teils im Einzelnen: Kapitel 4, „Humanity's Ghosts" (S. 76–97), widmet sich den sogenannten „ghost populations", also solchen vergangenen und bisher unbekannten Menschengruppen, für die es keine eigenen aDNA-Funde gibt (und auch keine sonstigen archäologischen Evidenzen), die aber indirekt dennoch aus dem Erbgut erschlossen werden können – wobei im Falle der „Ancient North Eurasians" später doch noch ein Fund getätigt wurde, der die Methode validierte. Kapitel 5, „The Making of Modern Europeans" (S. 98–121), widmet sich v. a. der bereits eingangs erwähnten Steppeneinwanderung, die mit der indoeuropäischen Sprache verbunden gewesen sein soll. Kapitel 6, „The Collision that Formed India" (S. 122–153), behandelt die Herkunft der Einwohner Indiens und ist eines der interessantesten hinsichtlich der Beschreibung von Vorbehalten gegenüber genetischen Forschungen und der ambivalenten Haltung, die Reich dazu einnimmt. Er berichtet nämlich ausführlich über seine von zwei indischen Kollegen, Lalji Singh und Kumarasamy Thangaraj, motivierten Bemühungen, neutrale Namen für die erschlossenen Herkunftspopulationen Indiens zu finden. Zugleich lässt er aber durchblicken, dass er dies eher für eine Übung in *political correctness* bzw. Rücksicht auf „cultural resonance" hält als für ein wissenschaftlich, aus interdisziplinärer Kooperation gebotenes Verfahren, auch wenn er durchaus einen Lernprozess beschreibt: „[…] At the time I felt that we were being prevented by political considerations from revealing what we had found. […] The cultural resonances of our findings gradually became clear to us. So we groped toward a formulation that would be scientifically accurate as well as sensitive to these issues" (S. 135). Mit „issues" bezieht sich Reich auf den von den indischen Kollegen und Partnern geäußerten Unwillen, eine der beiden Vorfahrenpopulationen als „West Eurasians" zu bezeichnen, wie ursprünglich von Reich und seinem Team vorgesehen, und damit eine entsprechende Herkunft eines großen Teils der Vorfahren der heutigen Inder direkt zu benennen. Reich beschreibt zuvor, wie die indischen Kollegen es vermieden hätten, offen auszusprechen, dass eine solche Bezeichnung „politically explosive" (S. 134) gewesen wäre. Stattdessen wurde dann Singhs und Thangarajs Vorschlag „Ancestral North Indian" umgesetzt. Bemerkenswert sind auch Reichs Vergleiche des Kastensystems und der Position des Judentums in der europäischen Diaspora, denn er reflektiert hier ausdrücklich seine eigene jüdische Abstammung und Identität („When I started my work on Indian groups, I came to it as an Ashkenazi Jew, a member of an ancient caste of West Eurasia", S. 145; vergleichbare Passagen auch S. 271–273 und S. 284–286).

Kapitel 7, „In Search of Native American Ancestors" (S. 154–185), und Kapitel 8, „The Genomic Origins of East Asians" (S. 186–204), sind jeweils umfassende Darstellungen der Forschungsgeschichten und der eigenen Beiträge zu diesen Themen, die auch nur anzudeuten den Rahmen einer Rezension sprengen würde. Kapitel 9, „Rejoining Africa to the Human Story" (S. 206–225), widmet sich der oft beschworenen „Wiege der Menschheit" Afrika, die bekanntlich die größte genetische Vielfalt beherbergt. Auch hier breitet Reich zugleich ein großes Panorama und die neueren Erkenntnisse aus, die zu vielen Thesen über die Geschichte Afrikas und der Menschheit führen.

Kommen wir nun zum letzten, so umstrittenen Teil des Buches. „The Disruptive Genome" besteht aus drei Kapiteln. Kapitel 10, „The Genomics of Inequality" (S. 229–246), ist gleichsam nur ein Vorlauf zu diesen Ausführungen in Kapitel 11, „The Genomics of Race and Identity" (S. 247–273), das Anlass zu der großen Kontroverse gab. Es versucht zu erklären, dass der seit den 1970er-Jahren etablierte Konsens über die viel größere genetische Varianz innerhalb von Populationen als zwischen Populationen, wie er maßgeblich von dem Genetiker Richard Lewontin geprägt wurde, auf dem heutigen Stand der Forschung der Ergänzung bedürfe, z. B. zu medizinisch relevanten Unterschieden. Reich geht es bei seiner Erschütterung dieser „orthodoxy" aber nun gerade darum, Rassismus keine neue Grundlage zu geben. Er distanziert sich auch ausdrücklich von plumpen Versuchen, die Archäogenetik dafür in Anspruch zu nehmen. Er sieht jedoch die Gefahr, dass andere das tun, wenn man die neuen Ergebnisse nicht selbst thematisiere. Seine Forderung dazu sei hier ausführlich zitiert: „If as scientists we wilfully abstain from laying out a rational framework for discussing human differences, we will leave a vacuum that will be filled with pseudoscience, an outcome that is far worse than anything we could achieve by talking openly" (S. 258). Abgeschlossen wird das Buch von Kapitel 12, „The Future of Ancient DNA" (S. 274–286). Hier fasst Reich noch einmal die Bedeutung der aDNA-Forschung zusammen, die auf eine „second scientific revolution in archaeology", nach der „radiocarbon revolution", hinauslaufe (S. 274). Bereits die erste naturwissenschaftliche Revolution, markiert durch die Radiokarbondatierung, habe aus der Kulturwissenschaft Archäologie eine Disziplin mit „equally strong roots in the sciences" (S. 275) gemacht. Doch die Disruption durch das immense Potential der aDNA-Technologie sei noch ungleich größer. Reich vergleicht es mit der Entdeckung des Lichtmikroskops im 17. Jahrhundert und wagt auch einige Prognosen, wohin das Feld sich bewegen werde (mehr aDNA-Analysen von außereuropäischen Befunden, mehr Studien zu den letzten 4000 Jahren, eine „industriellere" und mehr als Dienstleistung für die Archäologie fungierende Arbeitsweise in den Laboren, wieder vergleichbar der Entwicklung bei der Radiokarbondatierung). Außerdem schließt er in diesem Kapitel den Kreis zur im eigentlichen Sinne biologischen Forschung, aus der die historische aDNA-Analyse ursprünglich eher zufällig entstand, wie Reich bereits anfangs (Kap. 1) dargelegt hatte. Neue Erkenntnisse seien etwa zu Pandemien zu erwarten.

Dass Reichs Buch für Archäologen wie Geschichtswissenschaftler ein ebenso an- wie manchmal aufregender und oft auch fordernder Lesestoff ist, braucht an dieser Stelle wohl kaum noch ausdrücklich betont zu werden. Gerade in Deutschland, das mit den Max-Planck-Instituten für

Menschheitsgeschichte in Jena und für Evolutionäre Anthropologie in Leipzig (die in Zukunft im Wesentlichen in Leipzig vereint sein werden) ein führender Standort der aDNA-Forschung ist, lohnt sich die Auseinandersetzung mit der „new science of the human past" besonders. Erfreulicherweise findet sie hierzulande inzwischen auch tatsächlich statt. So erschienen Anfang 2021 in deutscher Sprache gleich drei kurze Monographien von Historikern und einer Archäologin, die sich aus ganz unterschiedlichen Perspektiven mit der „Genetic History" beschäftigen: Patrick J. Geary (Herausforderungen und Gefahren der Integration von Genomdaten in die Erforschung der frühmittelalterlichen Geschichte [Berlin 2021]); Stefanie Samida (Molekularbiologie und Archäologie. Eine ungewöhnliche Beziehung [Wien 2021]) und Mischa Meier / Steffen Patzold (Gene und Geschichte. Was die Archäogenetik zur Geschichtsforschung beitragen kann. Zeitenspiegel Essay 2 [Stuttgart 2021]). Das sechzigseitige Büchlein des Historikers Geary, der selbst führend an aDNA-Projekten mitwirkt, ist auch eine sehr gute Kurzeinführung ins Thema, die Neueinsteiger sinnvollerweise der Lektüre von Reichs Buch voranschalten können.

Abschließend seien einige grundsätzliche Bemerkungen erlaubt. Sie stützen sich auf einen gemeinsamen Beitrag (E. Bösl / J. Feuchter, Genetic History – Eine Herausforderung für die Geschichtswissenschaften. Neue Polit. Lit. 64,2, 2019, 237–268. doi: https://doi.org/10.1007/s42520-019-00111-6) der Münchner Wissenschaftshistorikerin Elsbeth Bösl, die das Feld im Entstehen begleitet hat und darüber eine vorzügliche Monographie veröffentlicht hat (E. Bösl, Doing Ancient DNA. Zur Wissenschaftsgeschichte der aDNA-Forschung [Bielefeld 2017]; vgl. die Rezension von M. Sommer in Germania 97, 2019, 428–431. doi: https://doi.org/10.11588/ger.2019.78877) und des Autors dieser Rezension, der sich als Mittelalterhistoriker seit längerem für eine Auseinandersetzung mit der Herausforderung der „Genetic History" einsetzt (zuletzt: J. Feuchter, The Middle Ages in the genetics lab. In: Ch. Jones / C. Kostick / K. Oschema [Hrsg.], Making the Medieval Relevant. How Medieval Studies Contribute to Improving our Understanding of the Present. Das Mittelalter. Perspektiven mediävistischer Forsch., Beih. 6 [Berlin, Boston 2020] 99–111. doi: https://doi.org/10.1515/9783110546316-004). Wenn naturwissenschaftliche Fächer Vergangenheitsforschung betreiben, kann das für die Geistes- und Kulturwissenschaften grundsätzlich sowohl eine Ressource bedeuten als auch eine neue Konkurrenz. Mitunter wird dies sogar als Übergriff erlebt, denn schließlich war den Geisteswissenschaften bereits im 19. Jahrhundert das Verstehen des Sinns der Phänomene in der kulturellen und sozialen Welt und darauf aufbauend die soziokulturelle Sinnstiftung überlassen worden. Doch es gibt immer wieder epistemische Neusortierungen. Archäologen sowie Historiker sollten hier durchaus selbstbewusst Position beziehen. Denn molekulare Quellen und Methoden können nicht per se mehr oder gewissere Informationen liefern als beispielsweise das Sachgut oder Schriftquellen. Es handelt sich einfach um andere Informationen. Die Herausforderung im interdisziplinären Miteinander besteht darin, sich über die jeweiligen Methoden und Interessen zu verständigen und die gewonnen Informationen sinnvoll und kritisch zu verknüpfen. Wir haben daher im genannten Beitrag vorgeschlagen, eine Art „kritische Freundschaft" (Bösl / Feuchter 2019, S. 264–265; Begriff nach Julia Adeney Thomas bzw. Nikolas Rose) aufzubauen, d. h. eine grundsätzlich bejahende Einstellung zu den Erkenntnisangeboten der Naturwissenschaften einzunehmen, dabei aber immer wieder nach deren Bedingtheiten und Grenzen zu fragen. Statt in „science envy" zu verfallen oder begeistert alles zu akzeptieren, was die Naturwissenschaften offerieren, sollte so ein komplementäres Verhältnis entwickelt werden, in das die Geistes- und Kulturwissenschaften ohne Komplexe ihre Erkenntnis- und Deutungsmöglichkeiten einbringen.

DE–10117 Berlin
Jägerstr. 22–23
E-Mail: feuchter@bbaw.de
Orcid: https://orcid.org/0000-0003-0402-1805

Jörg Feuchter
Berlin-Brandenburgische Akademie der Wissenschaften

Jannis Kozatsas, The Dialectic of Practice and the Logical Structure of the Tool. Philosophy, Archaeology and the Anthropology of Technology. Praehistorica Mediterranea 7. Archaeopress Publishing LTD, Oxford 2020. € 22,50. ISBN 978-1-78969-404-8. 90 Seiten.

Der Titel lässt zunächst nur erahnen, welche Aufgabe sich Jannis Kozatsas gestellt hat: Georg Wilhelm Friedrich Hegels Theorie des Werkzeugs fruchtbar zu machen für ein archäologisches Verständnis von Technik als einem Zusammenwirken von materieller Kultur und menschlicher Praxis. Bislang habe die Archäologie Technik mit zwei unterschiedlichen Ansätzen zu begreifen versucht: einem dualistischen, von zwei ontologisch geschiedenen Sphären (Subjekt / Objekt bzw. Geist / Natur) ausgehenden, und einem monistischen, nur einen Seinsbereich unterstellenden, in welchem menschliche und nichtmenschliche Entitäten gleichsam auf Augenhöhe interagieren. Die daraus entstehende metatheoretische Dichotomie von Dualismus und Monismus provoziere die Frage: „[…]) is it possible to conceive technology (...) in such a way that would neither absolutise the subject-object opposition nor eliminate it by postulating an equally axiomatic monism?" (S. 11). Vor dieses Problem der Vermittlung von Dualismus und Monismus sah sich auch Hegel in seiner Jenaer Zeit (1801–1807) gestellt, und die von ihm gefundene Lösung könne, so J. Kozatsas, die gegenwärtige Theoriediskussion bereichern.

Das Buch besteht aus drei, durch eine Einleitung (S. 9–13) und einen Epilog (S. 71–73) gerahmten Teilen. Auf eine kurze Sichtung der Forschungsgeschichte folgt eine Exposition der Hegelschen Dialektik und ihrer Bedeutung für das Verständnis von Praxis und Technik, und schließlich wird der aus Hegels Philosophie zu gewinnende Zugang zu materieller Kultur dargestellt.

Die forschungsgeschichtliche Rekapitulation im ersten Teil (S. 15–40) orientiert sich an der Differenz Dualismus / Monismus und hebt mit der „New Archaeology" an. Als von Stichwortgebern wie Karl Popper und Carl Gustav Hempel angeleiteter Empirismus reproduziere sie den Dualismus von Natur und Kultur im Dualismus von Funktionalität und Stil. Technik werde als weitgehend vor- oder außersoziales Phänomen begriffen und auf das Ausnutzen von Naturgesetzen reduziert. Die sich in Reaktion auf postmoderne Strömungen seit ca. 1980 konstituierende und als Gegenentwurf zur New Archaeology verstehende postprozessuale Archäologie wertet J. Kozatsas nicht als Paradigmenwechsel, sondern als Akzentverschiebung hin zu einem subjektivistischen Empirismus, welcher sich auf „the empirical subject and its mental capacity to impose meanings on a meaningless material substratum" (S. 20) konzentriere und damit den Aspekt der Technik vernachlässige. Neue Impulse verdankten sich dann der französischen Tradition einer anthropologischen Technikforschung, die mit Namen wie André Leroi-Gourhan, Pierre Bourdieu oder Pierre Lemonnier verbunden sei. Bei der Analyse von materieller Kultur liege der Fokus hier auf sozialer Praxis, verstanden als Prozess und auch die Dimension der Materialität umfassend. Zwar fänden sich Ansätze zu einer Synthese des Sozialen und Materiellen, in ihnen sei aber, analog zu den Synthesen Immanuel Kants, der Dualismus noch nicht überwunden – vielmehr müsse das Soziale und das Materielle nicht im Sinne einer nachträglichen Zusammenfügung begriffen werden, sondern als vorgängige Einheit des Gegensätzlichen, als Einheit sich wechselseitig konstituierender Momente, wie dies in der Hegelschen Dialektik der Fall ist.

Die gegenwärtigen Diskurse seien geprägt durch ein wiedererwachtes Interesse an Materialität und durch phänomenologische Zugänge, verbunden mit einem posthumanistischen Impetus, der die ontologische und kategoriale Unterscheidung von Subjekten und Objekten aufzuheben strebe. Derartige den Menschen dezentrierende und eine Symmetrie von Menschen und Dingen postulierende Theorien seien unmittelbar folgenreich für den Technikdiskurs, und J. Kozatsas schließt sich Ian Hodder an, welcher feststellt, dass eine „symmetrische Archäologie" mit dem Verwerfen des Dualismus von Mensch und Ding zugleich auch die Dynamik dieser Beziehung ignoriere, während es darauf ankomme, die Dialektik dieser Beziehung als Einheit von Gegensätzen zu begreifen

(I. Hodder, The asymmetries of symmetrical archaeology. Journal Contemporary Arch. 1, 2014, 26–28).

Das leitet zu dem zweiten Teil (S. 41–55) über, in welchem das Hegelsche Verständnis von Praxis dargelegt wird. J. Kozatsas bezieht sich vor allem auf die „Phänomenologie des Geistes" (G. W. F. Hegel, Phänomenologie des Geistes. Gesammelte Werke 9 [Hamburg 1980]), insbesondere die Passagen zum Begriff der Arbeit im Abschnitt über Herrschaft und Knechtschaft (G. W. F. Hegel, Phänomenologie des Geistes. Gesammelte Werke 9 [Hamburg 1980] 114–116). Er diskutiert Diskursverengungen, die in marxistischen Hegelrezeptionen aus einer Überbetonung von Arbeit zulasten anderer Praxiselemente resultierten, und fasst Hegels Praxisbegriff in drei Thesen zusammen. Erstens werde der von der philosophischen Tradition als primordial angesehene Subjekt-Objekt-Dualismus erst dann ontologisch bedeutsam, wenn sich der Mensch als handelnde Entität zur Welt verhalte. Diese Praxis sei zweitens als Selbstbewusstsein ermöglichend epistemisch relevant: „Knowledge of the thing and self-knowledge are mutually conditioned and anchored in the practical activity itself" (S. 47). Und drittens bildeten Subjekt und Objekt eine Einheit des Gegensätzlichen, weil sie durch wechselseitige Negation aufeinander verweisen und nur durch ihren negativen Bezug auf das Andere bestimmt werden. Ihre Einheit erfordere daher keine nachträgliche Synthese, sondern sie seien immer schon durch ihr dialektisches Verhältnis verbunden.

Auf dieser Grundlage erfolgt im dritten Teil (S. 57–70) die Auseinandersetzung mit Hegels Theorie des Werkzeugs, wie er sie in seiner Jenaer Zeit formulierte. Neben ihm habe es mit Martin Heidegger in der Moderne nur einen weiteren Philosophen gegeben, der sich mit dem Werkzeug als Konstitutivum menschlicher Praxis befasst habe. In Heideggers Ansatz, erläutert in § 16 von „Sein und Zeit" (M. Heidegger, Sein und Zeit[16] [Tübingen 1986] 72–76), werde das in praktischen Verwendungszusammenhängen gebrauchte Werkzeug dem Bewusstsein erst dann zugänglich, wenn es seine Funktion nicht (mehr) erfüllt. Das führe in eine logische und epistemologische Sackgasse, „hence its transformation into a logically inconsistent pragmatic agnosticism according to which the only possible knowledge of the tool *as a tool* is its knowledge *as not a tool*" (S. 60–61; Hervorhebungen in Zitaten stets wie im Original). Diesen Fallstricken entgehe Hegels Theorie des Werkzeugs, und J. Kozatsas legt seiner Auseinandersetzung mit dieser die folgenden Schriften zugrunde: das in Reinschrift überlieferte „System der Sittlichkeit" von 1802/03 (G. W. F. Hegel, System der Sittlichkeit. In: G. W. F. Hegel, Schriften und Entwürfe. Gesammelte Werke 5 [Hamburg 1998] 277–361), die Fragmente des in Vorbereitung einer Vorlesung im Wintersemester 1803/04 verfassten „Systems der speculativen Philosophie" (G. W. F. Hegel, Das System der speculativen Philosophie. Jenaer Systementwürfe I. Gesammelte Werke 6 [Hamburg 1975]) sowie das Vorlesungsmanuskript „Naturphilosophie und Philosophie des Geistes" aus den Jahren 1805/06 (G. W. F. Hegel, Naturphilosophie und Philosophie des Geistes. Jenaer Systementwürfe III. Gesammelte Werke 8 [Hamburg 1976]). Hegel charakterisiert das Werkzeug folgendermaßen:

„Das *Werkzeug* ist die existirende, vernünftige Mitte existirende Allgemeinheit des praktischen Processes, es erscheint auf der Seite des thätigen gegen das passive; ist selbst passiv nach der Seite des arbeitenden, und thätig gegen das bearbeitete. Es ist das worin das Arbeiten sein Bleiben hat, was von dem arbeitenden und bearbeiteten allein übrig bleibt, und worin ihre Zufälligkeit sich verewigt; es pflanzt sich in Traditionen fort, indem sowohl das begehrende, als das begehrte nur als Individuen bestehen, und untergehen" (Hegel 1975, 300).

Damit bestimmt er das Werkzeug nicht als einen Gegenstand und damit als eine dritte ontologische Entität zwischen Subjekt und Objekt, sondern als Ausdruck ihrer Beziehung. „If the subject, in the immediacy of productive praxis, is the negation of the object, the tool is the negation of the negation. It is a firm expression of a subject's return to itself that includes in its concept and awareness its own relation to the object, not in the form of an abstract opposition, but as its own constitutive determinacy" (S. 69). Zugleich transzendiere das Werkzeug die Partikularität der Zufälligkeit seiner Entstehung insofern, als es ein Allgemeines und Bleibendes ist, das seine Entstehungskonstellation überdauert. Mit dieser in eine dialektische Theorie der Praxis eingebetteten relationalen Konzeption des Werkzeugs habe Hegel die Grundlage für eine anthropologische Techniktheorie vorgelegt, welche auch für die archäologische Diskussion einen Ausweg aus der Dichotomie von Dualismus oder Monismus weise.

Es ist in der Tat erstaunlich, dass in der archäologischen Theoriediskussion das Werk Hegels weitgehend unbeachtet geblieben ist, während Theoreme etwa von Karl Marx, Martin Heidegger oder Ludwig Wittgenstein zum geläufigen Repertoire zumindest anglophoner Archäologiediskurse zählen. Gewiss ließe sich auf die mit der Hegel-Lektüre verbundenen Schwierigkeiten verweisen, zu welchen Theodor W. Adorno bemerkte, im Bereich großer Philosophie sei Hegel wohl der einzige, „bei dem man buchstäblich zuweilen nicht weiß und nicht bündig entscheiden kann, wovon überhaupt geredet wird" (T. W. Adorno, Drei Studien zu Hegel. In: T. W. Adorno, Gesammelte Schriften 5 [Frankfurt am Main 1970] 326). Außerdem haben die erst posthum publizierten Systementwürfe aus der Jenaer Zeit, verglichen mit dem entwickelten philosophischen System Hegels, häufig den Charakter des Unfertigen, Fragmentarischen und Tentativen. Andererseits aber sind die intellektuellen Anstrengungen, die das Verständnis Heideggers erfordert, sicher nicht geringer, was in seinem Fall einer archäologischen Rezeption nicht im Wege stand. Offensichtlich ist der Geist der Zeit einer objektiv idealistischen Philosophie wie der Hegels nicht günstig, für welche objektiver Sinn und objektiver Geist zentral sind, die sich nicht auf Subjektives oder Materielles reduzieren lassen. So haben sämtliche der in dem forschungsgeschichtlichen Abriss (S. 15–40) erwähnten theoretischen Positionen keinerlei Affinitäten zu einem objektiven Idealismus, während umgekehrt Theorien, die solche aufweisen – wie beispielsweise die von Claude Lévi-Strauss oder Noam Chomsky – in der archäologischen Diskussion allenfalls eine marginale Rolle spielen.

Wie ist das Buch einzuordnen? Zu lesen ist es primär als Programmschrift, die auf Aporien der gegenwärtigen Theoriediskurse eingeht und einen Lösungsvorschlag unterbreitet. Es enthält dagegen keine materialen Analysen, welche die forschungslogische Bedeutung der Hegelschen Werkzeug-Theorie für das archäologische Handeln exemplarisch veranschaulichen würden. Aus einer archäologischen Perspektive wären einige prägnante und kontrastive Fallbeispiele wünschenswert, die aufzeigen, wie sich Forschungsprobleme *in concreto* mit dem Hegelschen Ansatz bearbeiten und wie sich Strittigkeiten bezüglich unterschiedlicher Lesarten archäologischer Objekte im Rekurs auf Hegel klären lassen; die Erläuterungen des Ansatzes anhand der Töpferscheibe (S. 65) fallen denkbar knapp aus. Außerdem stellt, bezogen auf die Gesamtheit der materiellen Kultur, das Werkzeug einen Sonderfall dar, weil es ein Gerät ist, das der Herstellung anderer Geräte dient und eben wegen dieser vermittelnden Funktion die Beziehung von tätigem Subjekt und passivem Objekt repräsentieren kann. Lässt sich aber die Bedeutung des Werkzeugs verallgemeinern im Hinblick auf Materialität und Technik insgesamt? Kann Werkzeug paradigmatisch für materielle Kultur stehen?

Auch aus einer philosophischen Perspektive sind einige Desiderata zu konstatieren. Nicht thematisiert werden die Hintergründe der Genese von Hegels Werkzeugtheorie, insbesondere die Potenzenlehre Friedrich Wilhelm Joseph Schellings, der die frühen Systemversuche Hegels konzeptionell und terminologisch verpflichtet waren (siehe W. Ch. Zimmerli, Schelling in Hegel. Zur Potenzenmethodik in Hegels System der Sittlichkeit. In: L. Hasler [Hrsg.], Schelling. Seine Bedeutung für eine Philosophie der Natur und der Geschichte. Problemata 91 [Stuttgart, Bad Cannstatt 1981] 255–278). In seinen naturphilosophischen Schriften um 1800 verstand Schelling die Ausdrucksgestalten der Natur als sich aufstufende Potenzen, und Hegel unternahm es, dieses Vorgehen in den Gegenstandsbereich der sozialen Welt zu transponieren. Daher erscheint, im „System der Sittlichkeit" und im „System der speculativen Philosophie" unterschiedlich akzentuiert, auch das Werkzeug als eine solche Potenz, während in „Naturphilosophie und Philosophie des Geistes" von Potenzen nicht mehr die Rede ist. Spätestens mit der „Phänomenologie des Geistes" gab Hegel, zumindest hat es diesen Anschein, seine Theorie des Werkzeugs auf – das Werkzeug findet späterhin höchstens in sporadischen Reminiszenzen Erwähnung, spielt aber keine systematische Rolle mehr. Irritierend bleibt die Ungleichzeitigkeit, mit der Hegel zunächst die Form seiner Ausführungen über das Werkzeug, die Potenzenlehre, und erst danach auch ihren Inhalt dispensierte. Bezüglich der Form liegt die Überlegung nahe, dass die Ausarbeitung der Fülle der mit humaner Sozialität verbundenen Aspekte sich nicht mehr in das Prokrustesbett eines apriorischen Schemas wie der Potenzenmethodik Schellings zwingen ließen. Schwieriger ist die Frage nach der inhaltlichen Bedeutung des Komplexes der Technik in Hegels Werk nach der Jenaer Zeit zu beantworten. Einerseits wird Hegel als exemplarisch für die Ignoranz der neuzeitlichen Philosophie gegenüber der Technik angeführt (V. Hösle, Warum ist die Technik ein philosophisches Schlüsselproblem geworden? In: V. Hösle, Praktische Philosophie in der modernen Welt [München 1992] 87), andererseits wird aber auch auf eine „verborgene" Technikphilosophie Hegels verwiesen, die sein Gesamtwerk durchziehe und sich insbesondere an Stellen artikuliere, „denen eine wesentliche ‚Gelenkfunktion', ein Schlüsselcharakter für die Modellierung der Übergänge im Prozeß der Selbsterschließung (Phänomenologie) und Selbstentfaltung (Logik, Rechtsphilosophie) der Vernunft zukommt" (Ch. Hubig, Macht und Dynamik der Technik. Hegels verborgene Technikphilosophie. In: R. Bubner / W. Mesch [Hrsg.], Die Weltgeschichte – das Weltgericht? Veröffentlichungen der Internationalen Hegel-Vereinigung 22 [Stuttgart 2001] 334). Damit wird zugleich die übergeordnete Frage nach der Stellung der Jenaer Arbeiten in Hegels Gesamtwerk virulent. Sind sie als Vorarbeiten zu qualifizieren und stehen mithin in Kontinuität zu dem entwickelten System, oder aber gab es einen konzeptionellen Bruch? Für letztere Lesart votiert Jürgen Habermas: Bei den drei Potenzen Kind, Werkzeug und Rede (Hegel 1998, 290–293), welche für die Bereiche Familie, Arbeit und Sprache stehen, handele es sich „noch nicht um Stufen, die nach der gleichen logischen Form konstruiert wären, sondern um verschiedene Formen der Konstruktion selber", woraus folge, dass Familie, Arbeit und Sprache nicht (wie in späteren Systemkonzeptionen) Manifestationen des Geistes seien, „sondern erst der dialektische Zusammenhang von sprachlicher Symbolisierung, Arbeit und Interaktion bestimmt den Begriff des Geistes" (J. Habermas, Arbeit und Interaktion. Bemerkungen zu Hegels Jenenser ‚Philosophie des Geistes'. In: J. Habermas, Technik und Wissenschaft als ‚Ideologie' [Frankfurt am Main 1968] 9–10). Solche für das Verständnis von Hegels Theorie des Werkzeugs wichtigen Kontextuierungen und Implikationen, die für ihre Geltungsreichweite und damit auch für ihre archäologische Anwendung relevant sind, bleiben in dem Buch unberücksichtigt. Freilich berührt die Frage nach der philosophiehistorischen Einordnung von Hegels Überlegungen zum Werkzeug nach Ansicht des Rezensenten nicht die Berechtigung, sie im Kontext aktueller Diskurse auch dann aufzugreifen, wenn sie von ihm selbst verworfen wurden – wie ja auch Theoreme aus den frühen Theorien Heideggers und Wittgensteins, von denen sich ihre Urheber später distanzierten, nach wie vor in der Forschung präsent sind.

Seiner Monita ungeachtet sieht der Rezensent in dem Werk einen bemerkenswerten Beitrag, dessen Programmatik, würde sie in archäologischen Diskurszusammenhängen forschungspraktisch umgesetzt, einen substanziellen Erkenntnisfortschritt bedeuten könnte. Gerade der Tatsache eingedenk, dass die Gegenstände der Archäologie besonders anschauliche Zeugnisse der „Schädelstätte des absoluten Geistes" (Hegel 1980, 434) bieten, ist dem Buch eine breite Rezeption zu wünschen.

DE–97070 Würzburg
Residenzplatz 2, Tor A
E-Mail: ma.jung@em.uni-frankfurt.de
Orcid: https://orcid.org/0000-0002-1573-5865

Matthias Jung
Lehrstuhl für Vor- und Frühgeschichtliche Archäologie
Institut für Altertumswissenschaften
Julius-Maximilians-Universität Würzburg

Oliver Nakoinz, Zentralität. Theorie, Methoden und Fallbeispiele zur Analyse zentraler Orte. Berlin Studies of the Ancient World Band 56. Edition Topoi, Berlin 2019. € 33.90. ISBN 978-3-9819685-4-5. doi: https://doi.org/10.17171/3-56. 238 pages.

To review Oliver Nakoinz' 2019 book *Zentralität* (engl. *Centrality*) for *Germania* was a challenging task – mostly because O. Nakoinz' theoretical and methodical approaches are based on a long-standing discourse in the field of quantitative and qualitative archaeology. It soon became clear that this book not only includes a discussion about Central Place Theory, but is much more than that: besides its functionalist-like segmentation of theoretical and methodological details about the origin and subsequent development of Christaller's work from the early 1930's, this book further provides a tool to understand the author's own scientific development, which has significantly influenced digital and quantitative archaeological research for over two decades now. What is more important, this volume offers the reader a broad spectrum of theoretical (but not only) approaches to model, visualise, and interpret distributions of archaeological material. It is not surprising that Nakoinz, who completed his PhD and his habilitation at the Christian-Albrechts-University at Kiel, spiced up his thoroughly theoretical book, written during a Senior Fellowship at the Excellence Cluster Topoi in Berlin, with a significant number of case studies and applications, which help the reader to understand the applicability of these methods to elucidate site distribution patterns and to enable the interpretation of large (spatial) datasets. The book is available online (doi: https://doi.org/10.17171/3-56) and as printed version and was edited by the *e-topoi* edition of the *Berlin Studies of the Ancient World* (Vol. 56) in 2019.

A broad theoretical and methodical part is divided into a short introduction, followed by a more detailed presentation of the evolution and reception of Christaller's work and a summary of international as well as recent approaches to Central Place Theory. Nakoinz then introduces what he calls *Modifikation der Zentralitätstheorie* (chapter 3, Modification of the theory of centrality, p. 51). This is the moment where the book begins to develop its own characteristic appearance – mostly because the theoretical discourse increases in complexity and at the same time starts to connect with mathematical formulas, pointing towards the actual modelling approach of the author. It is also the part, which basically defines the terminological environment of centrality, albeit in an extraordinarily broad way. The strength of Nakoinz' work here is the very comprehensive discussion of the manifold variables and parameters underlying centrality, intensity, and interaction, which testifies that this book is the result of many years of continuous work in archaeological method and theory. As a result, the definitions can be considered dense – or rather condensed – simplifications of the broader theoretical discourse, which makes it sometimes difficult to follow the author's thoughts (particularly if the reader is not familiar with the theory behind quantitative models). Nakoinz does not attempt to provide an economic theory of centrality in the very sense of Christaller, but rather to emphasise a more generalised approach. In this context, his definitions are important steps towards a meaningful explanation of centrality. The first statement defines *Zentralitätsintensität* (intensity of centrality), which is understood as "relative concentration of interaction" (p. 53). With this basic definition, Nakoinz emphasises the relative and gradual nature of intensity of centrality compared to population density and the structure of the surrounding complementary region. Shortly afterwards, he defines *Interaktion* (interaction) as a "mutual action of at least two interaction partners" (p. 57), which includes information exchange (communication), exchange of goods, mutual activities, physical manipulations, and their various subtypes. It now becomes clear that interaction represents a major hub in the concept of centrality, and the author acknowledges this by including a broad discussion about interaction systems and structures, which eventually leads to the construction of interaction models (p. 61) and interaction organisation (p. 62). There, distance-based "gravity models" and the concept of "entropy" are introduced, which represent potential tools to evaluate distance-related meaning of a particular location or to identify those interactions that enable optimised interaction within the entire system. In such a system, transportation *(Transportkost)* and route costs *(Wegekost)* increase in significance in the moment of increased frequency of the interaction intensity. That leads to attempts towards minimization / optimisation of these costs in the moment or over a temporal interval of mutual interaction. Using collective action theory to build synergies, these considerations trigger the development of main route axis and infrastructure or high transport capacities. However, as Nakoinz points out correctly, environmental prerequisites play a decisive role as factors influencing the location of a settlement itself and as the major determinant of local accessibility and terrain permeability (pp. 64; 98).

It is not very surprising that these well-known variables show up quite frequently in the book; however, I would like to highlight one particular section in which Nakoinz compares demographic dispersal, the concentration of interaction, and potential environmental suitability for human occupation (chapter 4.7, Strategy of analysis, p. 155). In this section, he states that centrality is not accomplished if a population is maximally dispersed according to the immediate environmental parameters. If the empirically observed distribution is significantly different from the theoretically ideal distribution, we can conclude that a particular interaction was necessary and that centrality is achieved in the core density area. This furthermore takes into account the organisational structure of the place itself in relation to the surrounding places and settlements, which enables centrality (p. 160).

From this point of view, it is easier to understand that centralisation processes can be observed in settlement systems, and that these systems follow optimised parameters to maintain persistence (p. 87). The reconstruction of supraregional settlement systems, however, requires the knowledge of each single hub in the system – a rather optimistic assumption, considering the scattered and incomplete nature of the archaeological record (p. 97). To overcome this limitation, Nakoinz refers to the implementation of *models* to compare the observed archaeological distribution to a theoretical distribution. A *model* is an *icon*, which represents relevant characteristics of an object in terms of a particular parameter (p. 82). He aims at constructing a most simplified (comprehensive and efficient) theoretical and deductive model, which most accurately predicts an empirical and inductive model (pp. 83–85). The general differentiation between inductive and deductive models is also an important feature to understand two major aspects of site distribution analyses (p. 99): in principle, the inductive approach tries to build up a model from the evidence, while a deductive approach builds a model from a theory and then tries to see if the evidence fits. In reality, theory always lies behind the inductive process of building a model from evidence, and evidence always lies behind the theory that you try to fit the model to.

Apparently, empirical data (nodes, edges, structures) is basically what makes archaeology quantifiable. Nakoinz introduces *centrality indices* to determine weighted and / or directed "networks", based on "nodes" (or vertices, *Knoten*) and "edges" *(Kanten)*, which are the two units that construct the network (graph) (p. 75). In such a network, the centrality of each node is a measure of its relationships to all the other nodes in the network (p. 139). The above-mentioned differentiation into nodes (in this case: points) and edges (the connection between two points) forms the respective "interaction structure", which can help to reconstruct interaction spheres and so-called "territories" (pp. 97–98). In an inductive model, this structure is built by the environmental prerequisites and the individual and group affordances of the local population. From the site distribution and the interaction edges, the prevailing physical characteristics can be derived, which form the respective territorial composition of one region, the central places dispersed therein, and their complementary areas. Of course, this is a reductionist approach (just like the model itself), and one can argue to what extent human-made landscapes are the construct of merely physical interaction processes or whether they are conceptualisations of both environmental factors and individual affordances in the moment of mutual interaction. Broadly speaking, landscape development (and thus also settlement patterning) is the result of the mental perception of spatio-temporal environmental variability and not simply a manifestation of topography, hydrologic system, and climate determinants. Modelling such cognitive variability in the development of landscapes and ecosystems, however, can be considered a major challenge – particularly in archaeological research, due to the limitations described above.

Nakoinz further offers a broad variety of methods to analyse, visualise, and interpret site distribution, mostly based on previous work and well-established approaches of point pattern analysis (chapter 4.3.4, Distribution, and 4.3.5, Density, pp. 103–111). His major focus lies on the analyses of interaction node concentrations, which is mirrored in the exemplary performance of sequential nearest-neighbour analysis, CSR-test (Complete Spatial Randomness), KDE (Kernel Density Estimation), and Monte-Carlo-Simulations with a specific emphasis on moving-window operations and Voronoi-densities. With these technically sound operations, the spatial properties of a point pattern (nodes) can be analysed. The methods (such as the G-Function in a Monte-Carlo-Simulation) evaluate whether the observed point pattern is different from a theoretical distribution (tested many times against a random comparison dataset) or if they are drawn from the same (random) sample. This allows for the detection of clustered behaviour, regular dispersal, or random point distribution. Eventually, this results in a density map of the point pattern, from which density anomalies (p. 110), interaction node densities (p. 111), and local density maximum values (p. 114) can be derived. From these analyses, the author suggests centrality of specific places. In a next step, he also includes distance-based measures to evaluate whether the degree of overlap of the single interaction regions (complementary region, *Ergänzungsgebiet*) is high or low. In the very sense of Christaller's approach, an ideally tessellated distribution of complementary regions equals non-overlapping interaction regions, which Nakoinz defines as territories (p. 119). Such territories can be calculated using spatial analysis technique implemented in QGIS and GRASS GIS, which produce a two-dimensional distance-based Voronoi-diagram (pp. 119–120). Nakoinz further refers to weighted Voronoi-diagrams, which integrate specific parameters pre-processed in a so-called cost-surface (e. g., terrain roughness, accessibility, hydrologic system) and enable the calculation to leave the two-dimensional level in favour of multivariate statistics.

The book then starts to dive deeper into network analysis and the construction of "ideal" and the reconstruction of "real" networks (chapter 4.5, Methods to analyse interaction networks, p. 132), and Nakoinz lists important aspects of how to set up optimal pathways, including transportation and route costs. The ultimate goal is to achieve a combination of a minimal "spanning tree" *(Spannbaum)* and the entire graph. This means a weighted hierarchical differentiation into directed long-distance transportation between the central places and an all-channel-network between the lower local classes and their nearest central place (pp. 133–134). As mentioned earlier, the author uses centrality indices to determine whether there is interaction between two nodes (pp. 140–142) (see also L. C. Freeman, Centrality in social networks conceptual clarification. Social Networks 1,3, 1978, 215–239. doi: https://doi.org/10.1016/0378-8733(78)90021-7). Among other indices, Degree Centrality (tZI_1, t=theoretical) measures the number of neighbours of each node in particular distances and/or relations around the node. The index Closeness Centrality (tZI_2) can be used to identify the nodes, which are capable of spreading information through the graph in a most cost-effective way. It is the inverse-distance of the node to all other nodes in the graph, which produces a short-distance ranking and enables one to measure interdependency of nodes. The so-called Betweenness (tZI_3) assesses the degree to which a node lies on the shortest path between two other nodes (see also T. Opsahl / F. Agneessens / J. Skvoretz, Node centrality in weighted networks: Generalizing degree and shortest paths. Social Networks 32,3, 2010, 245–251. doi: https://doi.

org/10.1016/j.socnet.2010.03.006). A high degree of Betweenness enables a central place to control information-flow in a network. This selection of centrality indices, however, does not include the degree of interaction between two places and thus represents only a potential centrality (p. 142). For this reason, Nakoinz redefines the centrality indices to weighted centrality indices that consider weighted edges within the graph (pp. 142–145). For example, the Weighted Degree Centrality (rZI_1, $r=real$) represents the sum of all edge-weights in relation to all neighbours. It is the sum of the weights assigned to the direct connections of the node and represents the node strength (L. Candeloro / L. Savini / A. Conte, A new weighted degree centrality measure: The application in an animal disease epidemic. PloS One 11,11, 2016, e0165781. doi: https://doi.org/10.1371/journal.pone.0165781). (rZI_1) can further be split into incoming (rZI_1e) and outgoing (rZI_1a) Weighted Degree Centrality, which determine the sum of the edge-weighted interactions incoming from and all outgoing interactions towards all neighbours. Similarly, the Weighted Closeness Centrality (rZI_2) measures the sum of the minimum edge weight of the edges in the shortest paths divided by the path length for the other points – and can be distinguished accordingly. Nakoinz further differentiates the Weighted Betweenness (rZI_3) into (rZI_{31}), which is the sum of the minimum edge weights of the shortest paths between all points on which the observed point is situated, and (rZI_{32}), which is the sum of the minimum edge weights of all edge-disjoint paths between all points on which the considered point is located.

None of these indices is a universal indicator of centrality, but they allow one to identify different types of centrality in the nodes of a network (p. 145). The comparison of the different aspects of centrality – interaction intensity (I), interaction outreach (R), hierarchical level (H), interaction control (K) – can then be described as a vector of total centrality (I,R,H,K) (p. 146). Based on the interaction intensity of a node, (I) is defined as the sum of all interactions, and the integration of distance relations enables one to draw conclusions about (R). (H) is derived from the comparison of neighbouring indices, and (K) is basically represented by Betweenness and the ability to allow or prevent contact between potential interaction partners. Depending on the character of the network (free, bound, weighted, directed, hierarchical etc.), the Closeness parameter can be used to determine the degree of site location intervention and optimisation.

This section (chapter 4.5.3, Network Analyses, p. 138) can be considered a major result of the volume. Nakoinz introduces a great many potential algorithms to calculate and interpret total centrality of different kind of networks (pp. 148–153), which can be used in manifold ways. The very detailed summary of centrality theory, which accompanies the discussion during the first 150 pages of the book, culminates in these seemingly simple considerations about potential centrality of places within certain networks. However, as Nakoinz points out on page 146, the theoretical approaches to centrality theory are often lacking. Furthermore, stand-alone manifestations of theoretically derived definitions are neither useful nor reproducible for a broad readership in archaeological research.

This book provides a highly suitable manual for understanding centrality and network theory and further enables the reader to reproduce the models based on their own archaeological point data. Although the book itself does not appear very attractive to a merely superficial reader who wants to gloss over theoretical details and methodical approaches of quantitative modelling and certainly meets with some editorial inadequacies related to the final stage of the Excellence Cluster Topoi, it can be considered a major advance in computational archaeology and summarises quite sufficiently the scientific approaches of Oliver Nakoinz.

CZ–60200 Brno
Arne Nováka 1
E-Mail: kempf@phil.muni.cz
and

Michael Kempf
Department of Archaeology and Museology
Masaryk University

DE–79085 Freiburg
Schreiberstr. 20
E-Mail: michael.kempf@geographie.uni-freiburg.de
Orcid: https://orcid.org/0000-0002-9474-4670

Physical Geography
Institute of Environmental Social Science and Geography
University of Freiburg

Guido Furlan, Dating Urban Classical Deposits. Approaches and Problems in Using Finds to Date Strata. Archaeopress, Oxford 2019. £ 48,–. ISBN 978-1-78969-252-5 (Paperback). ISBN 978-1-78969-253-2 (E-Book; im Open Access verfügbar: https://www.archaeopress.com/Archaeopress/download/9781789692525 [letzter Zugriff: 20.05.2022]). xiv + 288 Seiten, 153 Abbildungen und 6 Tabellen, davon 71 Seiten in Farbe.

Die stratigraphische Grabung nach natürlichen, meist anthropogenen Schichten gehört heute zum modernen Standard der Grabungstechnik. Optimal durchgeführt und publiziert, lässt sich jede Stratigraphie vom Schreibtisch aus nachvollziehen. Während die Grabungsmethoden längst standardisiert wurden, könnten die Auswertung und Publikation von Grabungsdaten oft expliziter und nachvollziehbarer aufbereitet werden. Dabei stellt aber die Entschlüsselung komplexer Stratigraphien, wie sie in besonderer Weise in über Jahrhunderte und Jahrtausende hinweg gewachsenen römischen Städten anzutreffen sind, eine besondere Herausforderung dar. Mit der Eingangsfrage: „How do we date strata?" widmet sich Guido Furlan aus Sicht der italienischsprachigen Klassischen Archäologie in dieser Monographie den Voraussetzungen und Instrumentarien, mit deren Hilfe verschiedene Befunde, Kontexte und Schichten zuverlässig in ein chronologisches Netz gefügt werden können. Furlan liefert somit eine Handreichung zur vor allem relativchronologischen Datierung häufiger Formationsprozesse einzelner Schichten und Kontexte in römischen Städten, um eine besser nachvollziehbare Datengrundlage zu schaffen. Dabei stützt er sich insbesondere auf die Analyse anthropogener Formationsprozesse, mit der archäologische Daten qualitativ ausgewertet werden können.

Die monographisch vorgelegten methodischen Überlegungen gehen aus einer Master- und anschließenden Doktorarbeit hervor, mit der G. Furlan 2015 an der Universität Padua promoviert wurde. Die hier besprochene Monographie umfasst 288 Seiten und ist in fünf Kapitel, einen Anhang und ein Literaturverzeichnis gegliedert. In englischer Sprache wendet sie sich an ein breites Fachpublikum, ist aber mit dem Fokus auf römische Städte in Italien klar an jene adressiert, die sich dezidiert mit der römischen Antike beschäftigen.

Die Einleitung (S. 1–22) definiert den Gegenstand und das Ziel der Untersuchung (S. 1–5) und liefert einen Überblick zur Forschungsgeschichte (S. 6–22). Im zweiten Teil der Arbeit werden die theoretischen Grundlagen (S. 23–42), im dritten Teil die zur Verfügung stehenden Methoden (S. 43–113) erläutert. Im vierten Teil (S. 114–214) legt Furlan eine Auflistung typischer Schichten und Kontexte vor, die häufig in römischen Städten aufzufinden sind, und erläutert an konkreten Fallbeispielen, wie diese zuverlässig datiert werden können. In einem abschließenden Kapitel (S. 215–229) fasst er die Ergebnisse seiner Überlegungen zusammen. Dem Buch ist auch ein Anhang beigegeben, der Dokumente zu einem von Furlan entwickelten ethnoarchäologischen Beispiel enthält (S. 230–245) und knappe Hintergrundinformationen zu den diskutierten Fundstätten liefert: Aquileia im Nordosten Italiens, Nora auf Sardinien und Gortyn auf Kreta (S. 246–262).

Im Verlauf des gesamten Buches behält Furlan die Frage im Blick, wie einzelne Schichten oder Kontexte datiert werden können und welche Rolle dabei Artefakte und Formationsprozesse spielen. Dies spiegelt das erste Kapitel (S. 6–22) exemplarisch wider, in dem das Thema des Buches definiert wird. Furlan geht schlaglichtartig auf einzelne forschungsgeschichtliche Aspekte ein, deren theoretische und methodische Ansätze nach seiner Auffassung besonders vielversprechend für die Frage nach der Datierung von einzelnen Kontexten sind. Für Furlan ist der englischsprachige Diskurs grundlegend, der sich im Rahmen der Stadtarchäologie *(urban archaeology)* im Spannungsfeld der unterschiedlichsten Forderungen verschiedener Akteure entwickelte. Hier betont Furlan vor allem die standardisierten Dokumentationsmethoden und -strategien, die es erlauben, das räumliche, zeitliche und funktionale Informationspotential von Kontexten *(deposits)* und ihren Formationsprozessen *(primary and secondary deposits)* zu bestimmen und sie in eine relativchronologische Beziehung zueinander zu setzen. Für die Erstellung einer relativen Chronologie seien vor allem die in ihnen enthaltenen Artefakte entscheidend. Furlan bezieht sich deshalb stark auf die New Archaeology und insbesondere auf den von Michael B. SCHIFFER in seiner „Behavioral Archaeology" (New York / San Francisco / London 1976) formulierten Gedanken, der archäologische Befund spiegele nicht unmittelbar die Umstände der Vergangenheit wider. Furlan erachtet für die Erstellung eines relativchronologischen Netzes den menschlichen Umgang mit den Artefakten als zentral, da die Nutzungskontexte der Artefakte im Laufe ihres Lebens variieren und somit wichtige Erkenntnisse zum Formationsprozess des Befunds beitragen. Sein Interesse richtet sich besonders auf den Umgang mit residualem Fundmaterial sowie das Potential quantitativer Analysen von Artefakten bezüglich ihrer chronologischen Aussagekraft, die in der italienischsprachigen Forschung vielfach thematisiert wurden. Er bezieht neben der englischsprachigen Debatte vor allem den italienischsprachigen Diskurs zum Thema ein, der häufig disparat in Grabungspublikationen geführt wird und auch natürliche Formationsprozesse miteinschließt. Die Stärke des Buches ist es, den Leser*innen die Diskussion der italienischsprachigen Forschung zugänglich zu machen. Die deutschsprachigen Beiträge zur archäologischen Taphonomie, die vor allem in der Prähistorischen Archäologie diskutiert wurden, bleiben unberücksichtigt. Insgesamt ist die Einführung in das Thema des Buches nicht unmittelbar einsichtig geordnet. Das Kapitel hätte von einer deutlicheren Verzahnung der einzelnen Aspekte miteinander in Hinblick auf das Thema des Buches profitiert. Die Frage, mit welchen Methoden und Theorien eine zuverlässige relativchronologische Datierung archäologischer Stratigraphien gelingen kann, betrifft nicht nur die Stadt- und Siedlungsarchäologie und ist insofern für die gesamte Archäologie relevant.

Im zweiten Kapitel (S. 23–42) diskutiert Furlan die Bedeutung theoretischer Konzepte zur archäologischen Taphonomie für die Datierung archäologischer Stratigraphien. Er strebt vor allem eine Definition der Begriffe *primary* und *secondary deposit* an, die entscheidend für seine weitere Untersuchung sein werden. Beide seien für eine relativchronologische Ordnung der einzelnen Kontexte entscheidend, da *primary deposits* mit einer Datierung ad quem und *secondary deposits* mit einer Datierung post quem versehen werden können. Dazu klärt er zunächst den polyvalenten Begriff des Kontexts und das Problem der Datengewinnung *(sampling)* bis hin zur Definition einzelner Schichten und Kontexte *(deposits)* sowie in ihnen erhaltene Funde, die er als Träger chronologischer Aussagen innerhalb eines Kontexts versteht. Als *primary deposit* definiert Furlan archäologische Kontexte, deren Funde zu demselben systemischen Kontext gehören, in dem auch der Gesamtkontext *(deposit)* entstand. Entsprechend versteht er *secondary deposits* als archäologische Kontexte, deren Funde hauptsächlich einem früheren systemischen Kontext zugeordnet werden können als der Entstehungszeit des archäologischen Kontexts. Um die häufig schwierige Frage zu klären, ob Funde gleichzeitig oder älter sind als der archäologische Kontext, in dem sie gefunden wurden, grenzt er residuales Material *(residuals)* gegenüber lang genutzten Artefakten ab *(false residuals)* und diskutiert die Voraussetzungen dafür, dass jüngeres Material in ältere Schichten eindringen kann *(intrusions)*. Insgesamt bezieht sich Furlan auf grundlegende Konzepte der New Archaeology der englischsprachigen Forschung und bindet Überlegungen der italienischsprachigen Archäologie zu den genannten Problemfeldern mit ein. Furlan stößt auf das Problem, dass Begriffe der englischsprachigen Forschung nicht immer wortgenau übersetzt werden können und häufig in der einen oder anderen Sprache polyvalent sind und somit mehrere Bedeutungsebenen umfassen können. Folgerichtig plädiert er dafür, die Begriffe und Konzepte in der jeweils genutzten Sprache explizit zu machen, um einen internationalen Diskurs zu ermöglichen. Er bezieht sich vorwiegend auf die italienischsprachige Forschung, aber diese Beobachtung wäre auch auf die deutsche zu übertragen, wie allein die hier zahlreich kursiv gesetzten und in Klammern wiedergegeben Begriffe unterstreichen.

Im dritten Kapitel (S. 43–113) evaluiert Furlan Methoden und Verfahren, die zu einem besseren Verständnis von Formationsprozessen und damit auch zu präziseren Datierungen führen können. Dazu gliedert er das Kapitel in drei Abschnitte. Im ersten stellt er naturwissenschaftliche Datierungsmethoden vor, die unabhängige absolute Daten liefern. Er fokussiert sich auf Techniken, die nur wenig in der Klassischen Archäologie genutzt werden: die Thermolumineszenzanalyse einzelner Sedimente, Keramiken oder Lehmziegel sowie die ^{14}C-Datierung von Mörteln. Er sieht in den hier gewonnen Daten absolute Ankerpunkte im chronologischen Netz der archäologischen Stratigraphie und plädiert dafür, sie stärker zur Absicherung und Kontrolle zu nutzen, wenngleich sie bislang nicht eine solch feine Skalierung erreichen, wie dies mit relativen Chronologien der Funde möglich ist. Furlan betrachtet die naturwissenschaftlichen Analysen als Korrektiv für die Datierung einzelner Kontexte, die mithilfe historischer und archäologischer Quellen gewonnen wurden. Es steht völlig außer Frage, dass naturwissenschaftliche Datierungen eine willkommene und wichtige Bereicherung der Datengrundlage bei der Datierung archäologischer Kontexte darstellen. Sie bedürfen aber einer ebenso gründlichen Quellenkritik, wie es auch für archäologische und historische Daten selbstverständlich der Fall sein sollte. Diesen Aspekt vertieft Furlan leider nicht. Auch das Problem, dass naturwissenschaftliche Datierungen in römischen Kontexten meist eine große Standardabweichung besitzen und damit nur allgemein die Datierungen bestätigen können, die durch Keramik oder Münzen vorgegeben werden, lässt Furlan in seiner Betrachtung außen vor. Im zweiten Abschnitt wird die quantitative Analyse der Funde mithilfe unterschiedlicher statistischer Methoden näher besprochen. In ihnen sieht Furlan ein wichtiges Reflexionswerkzeug, um einerseits Vermutungen über Formationsprozesse zu überprüfen und andererseits Datierungen zu präzisieren. Den größten Nutzen sieht er in der Implementierung der Monte-Carlo-Simulation und plädiert für deren Einsatz in der Auswertung großer Fundzusammenhänge. Dies mag aus Sicht anderer archäologischer Disziplinen als der Klassischen Archäologie verwundern, jedoch sind die Potentiale statistischer Analysen und deren Verständnis hier kaum verbreitet. Somit sind die Überlegungen und Beispiele von Furlan besonders wichtig und zeigen wenig genutzte Möglichkeiten der Analyse von Fundmaterial. Der dritte Abschnitt des Kapitels widmet sich der qualitativen Analyse von Funden. Furlan diskutiert hier vor allem den Einfluss der römischen Abfall- und Recyclingwirtschaft auf die Fundzusammensetzung und die daraus folgenden Konsequenzen für die Datierung der einzelnen Fundkontexte. Er widmet sich aber auch der Frage, welche Informationen aufgrund der Zerscherbung und Abnutzung gewonnen werden können, und diskutiert das Potential von geo-, ethno- und experimentalarchäologischen Methoden für das Verständnis von Formationsprozessen im städtischen Raum. Dazu ergänzt er die in der Literatur diskutierten Beispiele durch zwei eigene Versuche. Einerseits prüft er die Zerscherbung antiker Materialen während des Transports mit einer Schubkarre, andererseits erörtert er, wie Räume in einer modernen Wohnung anhand der aktuellen Ausstattung datiert werden können. Die erzielten Ergebnisse sind jedoch wenig überraschend. Keramik zerscherbt geringfügig während des Be- und Entladens und nicht während des Transports. Die Ausstattung von Räumen liegt chronologisch nur selten sehr nahe am *terminus post quem*, sondern wird mehrheitlich von älterem Material bestimmt, das sich im Laufe der Zeit in jeder Wohnung ansammelt. Beiden Untersuchungen fehlt es – wie Furlan selbst auch einräumt – an einer breiten Datenbasis und sie sind wenig mehr als ein Ausgangspunkt für weiterführende Überlegungen. Darüber hinaus ist zu wenig über den Versuchsaufbau und die -bedingungen bekannt. Auch die Übertragbarkeit der Ergebnisse auf antike Realitäten ist durch fehlende Wiederholungen der Versuche, Berücksichtigung antiker Transportmethoden und einer quantitativen Analyse antiker Vergleichsbeispiele nicht gegeben. Durch fehlende Standards erweist Furlan experimentalarchäologischen Versuchen eher einen Bärendienst, wenn er so für deren verstärkten Einsatz werben möchte. Hier wäre eine fundiertere Diskussion notwendig gewesen.

Im vierten Kapitel (S. 114–214) münden die bisherigen Überlegungen im eigentlichen Anliegen der Arbeit. Furlan stellt typische Kontexte zusammen, die in römischen Städten aufzufinden sind *(typology)*, und gibt für jeden Fall ein Beispiel *(analysis)*. Zunächst wird der Formationscharakter der Kontexte *(primary / mixed / secondary / other deposit)* und wie sie datiert werden können *(ad quem / post quem)* bestimmt. In einem zweiten Schritt rekonstruiert er die Dauer des jeweiligen Formationsprozesses und unterscheidet plötzliche, d. h. in kurzer Zeit entstandene Kontexte und kontinuierlich, d. h. über einen längeren Zeitraum entstandene Kontexte. Anhand dieser beiden Vorüberlegungen unterscheidet Furlan nun 28 typische Befundsituationen, die in Stadtgrabungen anzutreffen sind, und erläutert in knappen Fallbeispielen wie sich diese zur Datierung besonders anbieten. Das Repertoire reicht von Abfallgruben über Herdstellen bis zur Verfüllung von Fundamentgräben und Pfostenlöchern.

Furlan macht in seiner Arbeit klar, dass die Datierungen von Befunden und damit die historische Einordnung archäologischer Hinterlassenschaften in vielen Fällen genauer und expliziter begründet und belegt werden müssen als es bei vielen publizierten Grabungsdaten der Fall ist und wegen hohen Kosten- und Zeitdrucks zu oft in den Hintergrund gerät. In der Sache ist ihm unbedingt zuzustimmen und die Arbeit liefert unter den einschlägigen Kapiteln knappe Überblicke, die in das Problem einführen und mit aktuellen Literaturhinweisen zur tieferen Beschäftigung anregen. Allerdings wird die Lektüre der Arbeit durch mehrere Punkte erschwert. Obgleich der Gesamtaufbau der Arbeit klar ist, kann die weitere Unterteilung nicht immer nachvollzogen werden. Häufige Redundanzen in Verbindung mit einer mäandernden Gedankenführung machen es nicht immer leicht, der Argumentation zu folgen und den Sinn und Zweck der Gedankengänge zu erfassen. Da Furlan häufig zu kolloquialen Ausdrücken, rhetorischen Fragen, Passivkonstruktionen und überlangen Sätzen neigt, wird die Lektüre zusätzlich erschwert. Darüber hinaus finden sich im Text mehrfach italienische und lateinische Zitate, die nicht übersetzt oder paraphrasiert werden, aber wesentlich zur Argumentation beitragen. Auch in den Abbildungen wurden italienische Beschriftungen nicht durch englische ersetzt. Ohne Italienischkenntnisse können Abbildungen und Argumentationen daher teilweise nicht vollständig erfasst oder nachvollzogen werden, was angesichts des in englischer Sprache adressierten internationalen Publikums verwundert. Ärgerlich sind auch uneinheitliche Überschriften, Legenden und Aufzählungen. Insbesondere im vierten Kapitel sind die Überschriften der Fallstudien inkonsequent benannt und viele Beispiele beziehen sich auf ein einziges Haus in Aquileia, das aber nur gelegentlich in der Überschrift und im Text *expressis verbis* genannt wird. Die eigentliche Zusammengehörigkeit der Beispiele kann daher nur durch kontinuierliche Lektüre erschlossen werden. Die Abbildungen von Befunden besitzen häufig keinen Nordpfeil und Maßstab, wodurch deren Lesbarkeit beeinträchtigt wird und sie deswegen auch nicht dem Standard des Faches entsprechen. Einige Abbildungen sind illustrativ ohne direkten Bezug zum Text beigefügt oder umgekehrt mit Inhalt gefüllt, der im Text zu knapp dargestellt ist. Diese Schwächen des Buches hätten durch eine sorgfältigere Überarbeitung leicht beseitigt werden können.

Wer sich aber von den genannten Kritikpunkten nicht beirren lässt, findet im rezensierten Buch eine hilfreiche und anregende Lektüre. Sie gibt den aktuellen Stand der methodisch-theoretischen Debatte zu Formationsprozessen und ihrer konkreten Anwendung auf klassisch-archäologische Kontexte wieder. Die angesprochenen Fragen und Probleme bei der Datierung komplexer Stratigraphien sind nicht nur für die Stadtarchäologie interessant, sondern lassen sich auf viele Grabungskontexte in den unterschiedlichen archäologischen Teildisziplinen übertragen. Das Verdienst von Guido Furlan ist es, die englisch- und italienischsprachige Forschung zusammenzuführen und parallele Diskussionsstränge aufzuzeigen, die häufig von der jeweils anderen Seite ignoriert werden. Außerdem zeigt er, wie einfach statistische Methoden gewinnbringend eingesetzt und in die Auswertung einer Grabung miteinbezogen werden können. Gerade in der Klassischen Archäologie sollte die Reflexion der archäologischen Taphonomie stärkeres Gewicht erhalten. Hierzu ist das besprochene Buch ein lesenswerter Beitrag, der auf eine verstärkte Auseinandersetzung mit der Thematik auch im deutschsprachigen Raum hoffen lässt.

DE–14195 Berlin
Fabeckstr. 23–25
E-Mail: thomas.lappi@fu-berlin.de
Orcid: https://orcid.org/0000-0002-2013-8352

Thomas Lappi
Freie Universität Berlin
Institut für Klassische Archäologie

Empfangene Bücher / Books received / Livres reçus

Diese Liste enthält alle seit Erscheinen des vorherigen Bandes der Germania eingegangenen und nicht zur Rezension vergebenen Bücher.

This list contains all books received since the publication of the previous issue of Germania and not allocated for review.

Cette liste contient tous les livres reçus depuis la publication du volume précédent de Germania qui ne ferons plus l'objet d'un compte rendu.

JOBST, WERNER, **Das Heiligtum des Jupiter Optimus Maximus auf dem Pfaffenberg / Carnuntum. 3 Ausgrabungen und Funde im Spannungsfeld der Interessen. Teil 1–2 u. Pläne und Tafeln.** Der römische Limes in Österreich Heft 41.3. Verlag der Österreichischen Akademie der Wissenschaften, Wien 2021. € 249,00. ISBN: 978-3-7001-8399-0. doi: https://doi.org/10.1553/978OEAW83990.

POCHMARSKI, ERWIN, **Die Grabbaureliefs (erster Teil) des Stadtgebietes von Flavia Solva.** Corpus Signorum imperii romani. Corpus der Skulpturen der römischen Welt 4,4. Verlag der Österreichischen Akademie der Wissenschaften, Wien 2021. € 89,00. ISBN: 978-3-7001-8582-6. doi: https://doi.org/10.2307/j.ctv1zqdvgk.

WENZEL, STEFAN / GRÜNEWALD, MARTIN / GILJOHANN, RICARDA, **Römische Landnutzung im antiken Industrierevier der Osteifel.** Monographien des Römisch-Germanischen Zentralmuseums 155 = Vulkanpark-Forschungen. Untersuchungen zur Landschafts- und Kulturgeschichte 13. Verlag des Römisch-Germanischen Zentralmuseums, Mainz 2021. € 99,00. ISBN: 978-3-88467-334-8. doi: https://doi.org/10.11588/propylaeum.768.

DIAZ, JUAN MOROS, **Organización productiva de las ánforas olearias béticas (Dressel 20., ca. 30–270 D. C.). Un modelo de análisis e interpretación de los sellos del instrumentum domesticum.** Union académique internationale corpus international des timbre amphoriques 29. Edicions de la Universitat de Barcelona, Barcelona 2021. € 54,00. ISBN: 978-84-9168-776-4. http://www.edicions.ub.edu/ficha.aspx?cod=13966.

SCHLOTFELDT, SARYN, **Der kaiser- bis völkerwanderungszeitliche Fundplatz Elsfleth-Hogenkamp, Ldkr. Wesermarsch, und sein Umfeld – Ergebnisse neuester Ausgrabungen und Untersuchungen.** Studien zur Landschaft- und Siedlungsgeschichte im südlichen Nordseegebiet 12. Verlag Marie Leidorf GmbH, Rahden / Westf. 2021. € 49,80. ISBN: 978-3-86757-342-9. https://nihk.de/slsn.

MERKEL, STEPHEN WILLIAM, **Archaeometallurgical Investigations at Elsfleth-Hogenkamp. District of Wesermarsch – A Polymetallic Goldsmith Workshop of the Roman Iron Age in Germanic Settled Territory.** Studien zur Landschaft- und Siedlungsgeschichte im südlichen Nordseegebiet 13. Verlag Marie Leidorf GmbH, Rahden / Westf. 2021. € 49,80. ISBN: 978-3-86757-343-6. https://nihk.de/slsn.

Meynen, Henriette (Hrsg.), **Die Kölner Stadtbefestigungen. Einzigartige Zeugnisse aus Römerzeit, Mittelalter und Neuzeit.** Regionalia Verlag, Daun 2021. € 39,95. ISBN: 978-3-95540-370-6. https://regionalia-verlag.de/shop/978-3-95540-370-6/.

Niedersächsisches Institut für historische Küstenforschung (Hrsg.), **Siedlungs- und Küstenforschung im südlichen Nordseegebiet / Settlement and Costal Research in the Southern North Sea Region 44.** Verlag Marie Leidorf GmbH, Rahden / Westf. 2021. € 49,80. ISBN: 978-3-86757-860-8. https://nihk.de/skn.

Krause, Günter, **Archäologische Zeugnisse zur frühen Geschichte Duisburgs.** Quellenschriften zur westdeutschen Vor- und Frühgeschichte 11. Niederrheinische Gesellschaft für Vor- und Frühgeschichtsforschung e. V., Duisburg 2020. € 48,00. ISSN: 0079-9149. https://www.archaeologie-duisburg.de/publikationen/.

Jaksic-Born, Claudia M. / Schwarz, Peter-A., **Ludwig Berger (1933–2017). Kleine Schriften 1957–2017. Bd 1-3.** LIBRUM Publishers & Editors LLC, Basel 2021. € 75,00. ISBN: 978-3-906897-58-5. https://librum-publishers.com/ludwig-berger-1933-2017-kleine-schriften-1957-2017-band-1-3/.

Hinweise für Publikationen der Römisch-Germanischen Kommission

Manuskripte, die zur Veröffentlichung angeboten werden, sind jederzeit an die Erste Direktorin der Römisch-Germanischen Kommission, Palmengartenstraße 10–12, D–60325 Frankfurt a. M. zu richten und können per E-Mail eingereicht werden über redaktion.rgk@dainst.de.

Die Entscheidung über die Annahme zum Druck, die Aufnahme in einen bestimmten Zeitschriftenjahrgang bzw. die Ablehnung wird nach dem Begutachtungsverfahren (doppelblindes Peer-Review) gefällt. Die Autor*innen werden gebeten, Kopien sämtlicher Texte, Daten und Bildvorlagen bis zum Erscheinen des Bandes bei sich aufzubewahren. Beiträge können auf Deutsch, Englisch oder Französisch abgefasst sein. Für die Zitierweise gelten die Richtlinien und Abkürzungen der Römisch-Germanischen Kommission des Deutschen Archäologischen Instituts (abgedruckt in: Bericht der Römisch-Germanischen Kommission 71, 1990, 973–998 und 73, 1992, 477–540). Wir empfehlen die naturwissenschaftliche Zitierweise mit Kurztiteln, bestehend aus Autor*innennamen und Erscheinungsjahr, in den Fußnoten oder in Klammern im Text, mit einem Literaturverzeichnis am Ende des Fließtextes. Elektronische Medien können nur zitiert werden, sofern sie über einen URN *(Uniform Resource Name)* der Deutschen Bibliothek (www.ddb.de) oder einen alternativen *Persistent Identifier* (z. B. *Digital Object Identifier*, doi) verfügen, der die Beständigkeit ihrer URL garantiert.

Satzspiegel (bei Abbildungen einschließlich Unterschrift)

Germania und Bericht RGK:	14,0 : 21,5 cm
Römisch-Germanische Forschungen:	18,7 : 23,7 cm
Kolloquien zur Vor- und Frühgeschichte:	16,0 : 24,5 cm
Confinia et horizontes:	16,5 : 24,5 cm

Manuskript

Bei der Germania ist der Umfang von Aufsätzen auf 30 Druckseiten Text (insgesamt rund 110 000 Zeichen inklusive Leerzeichen) und zehn Druckseiten für Abbildungen beschränkt, der Umfang von Diskussionsbeiträgen auf 15 Manuskriptseiten (ca. 40 000 Zeichen inklusive Leerzeichen) und fünf Abbildungen. Besprechungen umfassen höchstens fünf Manuskriptseiten (rund 16 000 Zeichen inklusive Leerzeichen) und können keine Fußnoten, Tabellen und Abbildungen beinhalten; Literaturzitate kommen in Klammern in den fortlaufenden Text.

Der Umfang für Beiträge im Bericht der RGK ist auf 150 Druckseiten Text (rund 540 000 Zeichen inklusive Leerzeichen) und 30 Druckseiten für Abbildungen beschränkt. Ausnahmen bedürfen der Absprache mit der Direktion.

Bitte achten Sie auf eine gerade auch für Nicht-Muttersprachler*innen möglichst leicht lesbare Sprache und vermeiden Sie insbesondere zu lange Sätze. Die Redaktion ist grundsätzlich berechtigt, kleinere stilistische Korrekturen vorzunehmen.

Neben Text und Anmerkungen muss jeder Beitrag auch die Anschriften aller Autor*innen und ggf. Übersetzer*innen, Bildunterschriften, Abbildungsnachweis, eine Zusammenfassung in der Länge von ca. 100 Wörtern (Germania) bzw. 300–700 Wörtern (Bericht RGK) sowie Vorschläge für Schlagwörter enthalten. Wir bitten alle Autor*innen, auf Vollständigkeit zu achten!

Das Manuskript muss im MS Word-Format (docx) oder als odt- oder rtf-Datei in linksbündigem Flattersatz ohne Silbentrennung und ohne Absatzformatierungen abgefasst sein. Nach Möglichkeit sollen die Dateien über E-Mail an die Adresse redaktion.rgk@dainst.de oder germania.rgk@dainst.de übermittelt werden. In den Texten werden nur fremdsprachige Ausdrücke kursiv gedruckt. In Anmerkungen und Literaturabkürzungen sind die Namen der Autor*innen als Kapitälchen (keinesfalls in Großbuchstaben) zu formatieren.

Abbildungen

Die Abbildungen müssen in publikations- und reproduktionsfähiger (i. d. R. digitaler) Form zusammen mit dem Manuskript eingereicht werden. Die Abbildungen sind wie die Bildunterschriften fortlaufend zu nummerieren.

Diapositive, Negative und Papierabzüge von Fotos müssen in einwandfreiem Zustand sein (keine Kratzer oder Flecken; evtl. Ausnahme: historische Aufnahmen).

Der Nachweis über den Besitz der Bild- bzw. Nutzungsrechte ist schriftlich zu erbringen, Bildunterschriften bzw. Abbildungsnachweis müssen die notwendigen Angaben – wie Name der*des Fotograf*in, ggf. der Bearbeitenden und ggf. von Rechteinhaber*innen (z. B. eines Museums) – hierzu enthalten. Die maximale Größe für analoge Bildvorlagen (auch für Grabungspläne etc.) beträgt DIN A3; im Ausnahmefall müssen die Vorlagen problemlos auf dieses Format teilbar sein. Bei allen Karten, Plänen und Fundabbildungen muss ein Maßstab angegeben sein.

Die Strichstärken aller Abbildungen sollen für die jeweils erforderliche Verkleinerung auf Satzspiegelgröße berechnet sein, damit auch feine Details klar wiedergegeben werden.

Bildlegenden innerhalb von Karten und Plänen (Erklärungen verschiedener Signaturen, Schraffuren, Graustufen) sollten so angeordnet sein, dass sie das Kartenbild nicht störend überschneiden. Karten und Pläne sollen in allen Teilen möglichst schlicht und übersichtlich gehalten sein.

Für die Anordnung mehrteiliger Abbildungen ist ein Layout-Entwurf einzureichen, die Originalzeichnungen sind separat und unmontiert abzugeben. Ausnahmen sind rechtzeitig mit der Redaktion abzusprechen.

Digitale Bilddaten

Mit der Entgegennahme digitaler Bilddaten ist keine Garantie verbunden, dass diese auch tatsächlich für eine Einbindung in die Druckvorstufe geeignet sind. Die Abbildungen (jpg, tif u. ä. per E-Mail oder ggf. per Datenfernübertragung [z. B. WeTransfer] oder Datenträger) bitte auch in einer pdf-Datei mit eingefügten Bildern mitliefern. Die verwendeten Grafik- bzw. Bildverarbeitungsprogramme sind anzugeben.

Modus: Schwarzweiß-Abbildungen sind als Graustufen- (Halbton) bzw. als Strichbilder (Vollton, Bitmap) zu liefern. Es dürfen keine indizierten oder RGB-Farben angewendet werden. Dies gilt auch für Farbvorlagen, die im Druck schwarzweiß wiedergegeben werden.

Größe: Scans von Halb- und Volltonvorlagen sind grundsätzlich so anzulegen, dass sie keinesfalls mehr vergrößert werden müssen.

Auflösung: Graustufenbilder: mindestens 600 dpi, Farbbilder: mindestens 350 dpi, bezogen auf die Reproduktionsgröße (nicht auf das Diaformat); Strichabbildungen: mindestens 1200 dpi.

Dateiformate: Rasterbilder werden ausschließlich als jpg-, tif- oder psd-Dateien akzeptiert. Vektorgrafiken können nur aus gängigen Grafikprogrammen entgegengenommen werden, welche die erforderlichen Informationen zur Weiterverarbeitung in der Druckvorstufe enthalten. Sie müssen als offene Datei, z. B. als Adobe Illustrator- (ai), CorelDraw- (cdr) oder pdf mit entsprechend guter Auflösung, geliefert werden. Nähere Auskünfte erteilt die technische Redaktion. Vektorgrafiken dürfen keinesfalls in Pixel- oder Graustufenbilder umgewandelt sein!

Korrekturen und Druckfreigabe

Die Autor*in erhält eine Korrektur mit Abbildungen nach dem Umbruch regulär als pdf-Datei, bei Bedarf auch als Ausdruck. Bei mehreren Autor*innen bitten wir, eine*n Hauptautor*in zu benennen, der*die für die Korrekturen, auch gegenüber den Koautor*innen, verantwortlich ist. Der Ausdruck dient der Eintragung von Korrekturwünschen, die deutlich lesbar und in roter Farbe auf dem Seitenrand zu vermerken sind; falls unvermeidlich, sind Marginalien oder Erläuterungen mit Bleistift gestattet. Auf dem Deckblatt ist die Druckfreigabe handschriftlich mit Datum einzutragen. Korrekturwünsche können auch elektronisch in die pdf-Datei eingetragen werden. Falls die*der Autor*in keine Korrekturen innerhalb eines vorgegebenen Zeitraums zurücksendet, gilt die Druckfreigabe als erteilt. Wenn die Autor*innen sich nicht anders äußern, geht die Redaktion davon aus, dass sie mit der Veröffentlichung ihrer Adressen (dienstlich oder privat) einverstanden sind. Nach dem Erscheinen des Beitrages erhalten die Autor*innen die Abbildungsvorlagen und sämtliche elektronischen Medien zurück.

Sonderdrucke

Jede*r Autor*in erhält ihren*seinen Beitrag als pdf-Datei. Im Zuge des Korrekturganges, spätestens jedoch vor der Drucklegung, besteht die Möglichkeit zur Bestellung von Sonderdrucken auf Kosten der Autor*innen.

Die Inhaltsverzeichnisse und Zusammenfassungen der Germania und des Berichtes der RGK erscheinen auch im Internet unter der Adresse www.dainst.org (unter Publikationen → Zeitschriften). Digitale Ausgaben beider Zeitschriften sind im *Open Access* verfügbar unter https://publications.dainst.org/journals/.

Guidelines for Publications of the Römisch-Germanische Kommission

Manuscripts submitted for publication at any time should be addressed to the Director of the Römisch-Germanische Kommission, Palmengartenstraße 10–12, D–60325 Frankfurt a. M., Germany and can be sent via e-mail to redaktion.rgk@dainst.de.

The decision to accept a manuscript for publication, to include it in a particular volume, or to reject it (as the case may be) is made on the basis of a double-blind peer review process. Until the volume is published, authors are requested to retain a copy of all texts, data and illustrations. Contributions may be written in German, English, or French. For citation norms, the guidelines and abbreviations of the Römisch-Germanische Kommission of the German Archaeological Institute apply (published in Bericht der Römisch-Germanischen Kommission 71, 1990, 973–998 und 73, 1992, 477–540). We recommend the convention of short citations, consisting of author name and publication year, in footnotes or in brackets in the text with a complete list of references at the end of the manuscript. Electronic media can only be cited if assigned a URN (Uniform Resource Name) by the German Library (www.ddb.de) or an alternative Persistent Identifier (e. g. Digital Object Identifier, doi) that guarantees the permanence of its URL.

Print Space (Illustrations, including captions)

Germania and Bericht RGK:	14.0 : 21.5 cm
Römisch-Germanische Forschungen:	18.7 : 23.7 cm
Kolloquien zur Vor- und Frühgeschichte:	16.0 : 24.5 cm
Confinia et horizontes:	16.5 : 24.5 cm

Manuscript

In Germania, articles are limited to 30 printed pages of text (approximately 110 000 characters including spaces) and ten pages of illustrations, discussions to 15 printed pages (approximately 40 000 characters including spaces) and five figures. Book reviews should not exceed five pages of manuscript (approximately 16 000 characters including spaces) and may not include footnotes, tables of illustration; literature should be referenced within the text, enclosed in parentheses.

Contributions to Bericht der RGK are limited to 150 printed pages of text (approximately 540 000 characters including spaces) and 30 pages of illustrations. To discuss exceptions to these guidelines, please contact the editors.

Please remember that our publications have a wide readership. Authors should therefore write in a clear, straightforward style and avoid overly-long sentences. The editors are authorised to make stylistic changes, when necessary.

In addition to text and footnotes, each manuscript must also include the addresses of all authors as well as translators (if applicable), a list of figures with captions, an abstract of no more than 100 words (Germania), or 300–700 words (Bericht RGK), as well as a list of suggested key words. We request that authors complete all requirements!

The manuscript must be submitted in MS Word format (docx) or as an odt or rtf file; the text should be left-justified, without word-divisions or formatted breaks. If possible, email the file to the following address: redaktion.rgk@dainst.de or germania.rgk@dainst.de.

In text, italic print is only used for terms in foreign languages. In notes and reference abbreviations, authors' names should be formatted in small caps (never in upper case letters).

Artwork

Figures, maps, and diagrams must be submitted in publication- and reproduction-ready (digital) form together with the manuscript. The publication of coloured images must be approved in advance by the editors. Figures as well as captions must be numbered consecutively.

Transparencies, negatives, and photographic prints must be in perfect condition (no scratches or spots; exceptions may be made in the case of historic photos).

Publication permission for all images and graphics has to be provided by the authors. Captions of illustrations must supply the required source information such as the name of the photographer, the originator or the holder of rights, f. ex. a museum. The maximum size for analogue figures (also excavation plans, etc.) is DIN A3; in exceptional cases, the image must be divisible in this format without problems. A scale of measurement must be indicated on all maps, plans, and depictions of finds.

The lineweight of all artwork should be so calculated as to allow the necessary reduction of the image to the dimensions of the print space while still allowing fine details to be reproduced.

Legends within maps and plans (information clarifying various signatures, cross hatching, grey-scales) must be arranged so that they do not obscure or detract from the map. All elements of the maps and plans should be kept as simple and clear as possible.

A layout sketch must be provided in the case of multiple-part illustrations; the original artwork must be provided on separate, un-mounted sheets. Any exceptions must be discussed with the editors well before the publication deadline.

Digital Photos

Our acceptance of digital photographs does not guarantee that they are actually of a quality suited for printing in a publication. Please also provide the illustrations (jpg, tif, etc. by e-mail or digital file transfer [f. ex. WeTransfer] or data medium) in a pdf file with inserted images. The image- or photo-processing programme must be identified.

Modus: Black and white illustration should be submitted as grey-scale (halftone) or as black and white line drawings (fulltone, bitmap) images. No indexed or RGB-colours may be used. This also applies to coloured images that will be reproduced in black and white form.

Size: Scans of half- and full-tone images must be laid out so that it will not be necessary to enlarge them further.

Resolution: Grey-scale images – at least 600 dpi, coloured picture – at least 350 dpi depending on the reproduction size (not the transparency format); line drawings – at least 1200 dpi.

Data format: Halftone images are only accepted as jpg, tif or psd data. Vector graphics can only be accepted if created with common graphic programmes that include the necessary information for further processing during print preparation. They must be delivered as open files, for example as Adobe Illustrator (ai), CorelDraw (cdr), or pdf files in sufficient resolution. Additional information is available from the technical editors. Vector graphics must never be converted into pixel or grey-scale images!

Proofs and Permission to Print

The author will receive a page proof of the article, including illustrations, as a pdf file to correct; if required a printout can be provided. When there are multiple authors, we request that a main author be identified, who is responsible for proof-reading the copy and clarifying issues with the co-authors. Correction-wishes should be written in the margin of the hard-copy, legibly and in red ink; if it is unavoidable, marginal notes or clarifications may be written in pencil. Final permission to print an article following proof reading must be hand-written with the date on the title page of the proofs. Corrections can also be submitted electronically with the pdf file. If the author does not return the corrected copy within a certain period of time, it will be assumed that permission to print has been given. If the authors do not otherwise indicate, the editors will assume that they agree to the publication of their addresses (professional or private). After publication of the article, all artwork and electronic media will be returned to the authors.

Offprints

Every author receives a digital offprint of their item as a pdf file. Additional hardcopies can be ordered with cost during the correction phase until before the printing begins.

The Table of Contents and Abstracts published in Germania and Bericht der RGK also appear in the Internet at www.dainst.org (under Publications → Journals). Digital issues of both journals are available open access at https://publications.dainst.org/journals/.

Recommandations pour les publications de la Römisch-Germanische Kommission

Chaque proposition de manuscrit doit être expédiée à la directrice de la Römisch-Germanische Kommission à l'adresse suivante : Erste Direktorin der Römisch-Germanischen Kommission, Palmengartenstraße 10–12, D–60325 Frankfurt a. M. ou transmise par mail à l'adresse suivante : redaktion.rgk@dainst.de.

La décision concernant la recevabilité d'un manuscrit remis, son intégration dans un volume de revue précis voire son refus est prise par le comité de rédaction suite à un procédé d'évaluation (*peer-review* en double aveugle). Les auteurs sont priés de sauvegarder des copies de tous leurs textes, données et illustrations par leurs propres moyens jusqu'à la parution du volume. Les contributions peuvent être rédigées en allemand, en anglais ou en français. Les normes de citation des références bibliographiques sont indiquées dans les recommandations et abréviations de la Römisch-Germanische Kommission (RGK) de l'Institut Archéologique Allemand (DAI) (publiées dans : Bericht der Römisch-Germanischen Kommission 71, 1990, p. 973–998 et 73, 1992, p. 477–540). Les appels des références bibliographiques dans le texte se feront sous la forme suivante : nom de l'auteur, suivi de la date de la publication dans les notes de bas de pages ou entre parenthèses dans le texte ; une bibliographie sera présentée à la fin du texte. Des références électroniques ne peuvent être acceptées que si elles possèdent un URN (*Uniform Resource Name*) de la *Deutsche Bibliothek* (www.ddb.de) ou alternativement un *Persistent Identifier* (p.ex. *Digital Object Identifier*, doi), garantissant la durabilité de leur URL.

Surface de composition (y compris les légendes des illustrations)

Germania et Bericht RGK :	14,0 : 21,5 cm
Römisch-Germanische Forschungen :	18,7 : 23,7 cm
Kolloquien zur Vor- und Frühgeschichte :	16,0 : 24,5 cm
Confinia et horizontes :	16,5 : 24,5 cm

Manuscrit

La taille des articles destinés à la revue Germania ne devra pas dépasser 30 pages de texte imprimées (max. 110 000 caractères espaces compris) et dix pages imprimées d'illustrations. La taille des tribunes est limitée à 15 pages de texte imprimées (env. 40 000 caractères espaces compris) et cinq illustrations. Les comptes-rendus ne devront pas excéder cinq pages de texte (env. 16 000 caractères espaces compris) et ne doivent comporter ni note de bas de page, ni tableau ni illustration ; les appels bibliographiques se feront entre parenthèses au fil du texte.

La taille des manuscrits destinés au Bericht der Römisch-Germanischen Kommission est limitée à 150 pages de texte imprimées (env. 540 000 caractères espaces compris) et à 30 pages imprimées d'illustrations. Toute exception nécessite un accord préalable de la direction.

Il est recommandé d'utiliser un style de langue facilement compréhensible, notamment pour lecteurs non francophones et plus particulièrement de veiller à éviter plus particulièrement des phrases trop longues. Le comité de rédaction se réserve le droit d'effectuer des corrections minimes d'ordre stylistique.

En plus du texte et des notes, chaque contribution doit être accompagnée des adresses de tous les auteurs et – s'il y a lieu – des traducteurs, des légendes des figures, des crédits des illustrations, d'un résumé d'une taille d'environ cent mots (Germania) voire 300–700 mots (Bericht der RGK) ainsi que des propositions de mots-clés. Les auteurs veilleront à soumettre des dossiers complets !

Les textes seront fournis sous format MS Word (.docx) ou en tant que fichier .odt ou .rtf, justifiés à gauche sans césure des mots et sans style de paragraphe. Si possible, les fichiers devront être transmis par mail à l'adresse suivante : redaktion.rgk@dainst.de ou germania.rgk@dainst.de. Seuls les termes en langue étrangère seront en italique. Les noms des auteurs dans les notes et les appels bibliographiques doivent être écrits en petites capitales (jamais de majuscule).

Illustrations

Les illustrations doivent satisfaire aux exigences de publication et de reproduction (en règle générale sous forme numérique) et être déposées en même temps que le manuscrit. Les figures et légendes seront numérotées en continu.

Les diapositives, négatifs et tirages papiers de photos doivent se trouver dans un état irréprochable (pas de rayure ou de tache ; à l'exception éventuellement de photographies historiques).

Les auteurs doivent attester par écrit qu'ils sont en possession des droits d'images et de publication et reproduction. Les légendes des figures ou les crédits des illustrations doivent contenir les indications nécessaires – nom du photographe ou graphiste et éventuellement des détenteurs de droits (p. ex. un musée). La taille maximale des illustrations analogues, y compris les plans de fouilles, correspond au format A3, le cas échéant les dessins doivent être réductibles à ce format sans problème. L'ensemble des cartes, plans et illustrations d'objets doivent comporter une échelle.

Les épaisseurs des traits de toutes les illustrations doivent être calculées en fonction de la réduction sur la taille de la surface de composition prévue afin de pouvoir reproduire les détails les plus fins.

Les légendes présentes au sein des cartes et plans (explications de différents symboles, hachures, niveaux de gris) ne doivent pas entraver la lecture de l'image. Les cartes et plans doivent rester sobres et synthétiques.

En ce qui concerne l'agencement des illustrations en plusieurs parties, une proposition de mise en page doit être déposée et les dessins originaux doivent être transmis individuellement et non assemblées. Les cas particuliers doivent être discutés en temps et en heure avec le comité de rédaction.

Données graphiques numériques

Lors de la réception des données graphiques numériques il ne peut pas être garanti que celles-ci soient effectivement adaptées pour être intégrées dans le processus de production des épreuves. Les illustrations (transmises par mail ou envoyées par une plate-forme *web-transfer* [p.ex. WeTransfer] ou sur un support de stockage aux formats .jpg, .tif ou d'autres formats semblables) doivent être accompagnées d'un fichier PDF où les images sont insérées directement dans le texte. Les programmes graphiques ou de traitement d'images utilisés doivent être indiqués.

Mode : Les illustrations en noir et blanc doivent être fournies sous forme de nuances de gris (dégradé) ou de dessins au trait (aplat, bitmap). L'usage de couleurs indexées ou de couleurs RVB n'est pas autorisé. Cela vaut également pour des illustrations en couleur reproduites en noir et blanc à l'impression.

Taille : Les scans de dessins en dégradé ou aplat doivent être créés de manière à ce qu'il ne soit plus nécessaire de les agrandir.

Résolution : Images sous forme de nuances de gris : minimum 600 dpi, images en couleur : minimum 350 dpi, en référence à la taille de reproduction (et non au format de la diapositive) ; dessins au trait : minimum 1200 dpi.

Formats des fichiers : Les images tramées seront acceptées exclusivement sous forme de fichiers .jpg, .tif ou .psd. Les graphiques vectoriels doivent être issus de programmes graphiques courants contenant les informations nécessaires à leur traitement ultérieur lors de la préimpression. Elles doivent être fournies sous forme de fichiers ouverts, p.ex. sous format Adobe Illustrator (.ai), CorelDraw (.cdr) ou PDF avec une résolution adéquate. Pour plus d'informations, veuillez contacter la rédaction technique. En aucun cas, les graphiques vectoriels ne doivent être transformés en images bitmap ou de nuances de gris !

Corrections et bon-à-tirer

Après la mise en page, l'auteur reçoit une version corrigée contenant les illustrations sous forme de fichier PDF ou, si nécessaire, sous forme imprimée. S'il y a plusieurs auteurs, un auteur principal doit être nommé qui sera responsable des corrections vis-à-vis de ses co-auteurs. Les demandes de correction doivent être soumises de façon électronique dans les fichiers PDF. Les demandes de correction peuvent également être inscrites sur les épreuves – bien lisibles et en rouge – dans la marge.

L'impression permettra d'annoter des demandes de corrections – bien lisibles et en rouge – sur la marge. Dans les cas où cela est inévitable, des commentaires en marge ou des précisions annotées au crayon de bois seront autorisés. Sur la feuille de couverture, l'imprimatur est à noter manuellement en indiquant la date. Il est également possible d'insérer les demandes de correction de façon électronique dans les fichiers PDF. Si l'auteur ne renvoie aucune correction dans les délais fixés, l'imprimatur prend effet automatiquement. Sauf indication contraire de la part des auteurs, la rédaction considère que ceux-ci acceptent la publication de leurs adresses (professionnelles ou privées). Après la parution du volume, les originaux des illustrations et tous les fichiers seront restitués aux auteurs.

Tirés-à-part

Chaque auteur reçoit sa contribution sous forme de fichier PDF. Lors du procédé de correction et au plus tard avant l'impression, les auteurs ont la possibilité de commander des tirés-à-part à leurs frais.

Les tables des matières et les résumés des volumes de la revue Germania et de Bericht der RGK paraîtront également sur internet à l'adresse suivante : www.dainst.org (sous Publikationen → Zeitschriften). Des éditions numériques des deux revues sont disponibles en *Open Access* sous https://publications.dainst.org/journals/.